FRANCHISING

ROBERT JUSTIS
DIRECTOR OF INTERNATIONAL FRANCHISE CENTER
LOUISIANA STATE UNIVERSITY
BATON ROUGE, LOUISIANA

RICHARD JUDD
DIRECTOR OF ENTREPRENEURSHIP AND
ENTERPRISE DEVELOPMENT CENTER
SANGAMON STATE UNIVERSITY
SPRINGFIELD, ILLINOIS

G32
PUBLISHED BY
SOUTH-WESTERN PUBLISHING CO.
CINCINNATI WEST CHICAGO, IL CARROLLTON, TX LIVERMORE, CA

STAFFORD LIBRARY
COLUMBIA COLLEGE
COLUMBIA, MO 65216

Copyright © 1989

by
SOUTH-WESTERN PUBLISHING CO.
Cincinnati, Ohio

ALL RIGHTS RESERVED

The text of this publication, or any part thereof, may not be reproduced or transmitted in any form or by any means, electronic or mechanical, including photocopying, recording, storage in an information retrieval system, or otherwise, without the prior written permission of the publisher.

ISBN:0-538-07321-7

Library of Congress Catalog Card Number: 87-91243

1 2 3 4 5 6 7 8 M 5 4 3 2 1 0 9 8

Printed in the United States of America

FOREWORD

This text is for the successful entrepreneurs of tomorrow — future franchisors and franchisees. Franchising, by its very nature, creates new businesses. Statistics show that it creates *successful* businesses and, more importantly, *successful* entrepreneurs.

Consider the fact that, according to the U.S. Small Business Administration, one-quarter to one-third of all independently owned, nonfranchised business startups are discontinued in their first year of operation. Almost two-thirds are discontinued in the first five years.

In contrast, the U.S. Department of Commerce estimates that in the past 16 years, less than 5 percent of franchised outlets have been discontinued each year. If we exclude product and trade name franchisors — i.e., automobile dealerships, filling stations, and soft drink bottlers — the Commerce Department estimates that the franchising success rate is even higher. In 1985, the Department calculated that less than 4 percent of franchised outlets were discontinued, many for reasons other than failure.

The overall strength of the franchise system is particularly evident in the high renewal rate of contracts and the low number of contract terminations. Consider the fact that of the 12,543 franchise contracts up for renewal in 1985, more than 90 percent were renewed. In 1985 there were 368,777 franchisee-owned outlets and only 7,450 terminations of franchising agreements (2 percent).

Sales of goods and services through franchise systems reached an estimated $556.2 billion in 1986 and $591 billion in 1987. Retail sales from franchise establishments comprise 33 percent of all U.S. retail sales. Futurist John Naisbitt forecasts that by the year 2010, franchise sales will account for half of all U.S. retail sales. In addition, franchising now employs an estimated 7 million people. A new franchised unit opens its doors for business about every fifteen minutes, every day of the year.

Franchising's popularity reflects a growing realization on the part of many entrepreneurs that there are distinct advantages to affiliation with a national system that allows individual business people to retain their independence — to be in business for themselves but not by themselves. The strength inherent in nationwide marketing, national advertising, and widespread customer recognition has a powerful appeal to entrepreneurs who want and need a greater return on their investment.

In addition to being designed for future practitioners of franchising, this text is also written for those who simply want to learn more about franchising. It defines franchising, discusses how it works, and tells what it takes to succeed.

The International Franchise Association supports and encourages franchising education and the development of courses in franchising at universities and colleges throughout the nation. We are dedicated to developing seminars, programs, and coursework for students and practitioners. We support the development of much-needed source material for use in business classes nationwide.

The International Franchise Association was formed in 1960 by a group of franchise company executives who saw a need for an organization that would: (1) speak on behalf of franchising before government bodies and the general public; (2) provide services to member companies and those interested in franchising and licensed distribution; (3) set standards of franchising business practice; (4) serve as a central point for franchising data and information; (5) provide a forum for the exchange of experiences among member companies; and (6) offer educational programs for top executives and managers.

Today the association is the international voice of franchising. Its membership has grown, and its responsibilities have increased dramatically in the volatile business, legal, and legislative climate that has developed during the 1970s and 1980s.

The International Franchise Association and its members have a keen interest in the education and cultivation of the next generation of franchisors and franchisees. This text is a major contribution toward assurance that the new generation will be well grounded in their chosen field and that there will be broad familiarity with the franchising phenomenon among students of business.

We encourage the use of this text both as a resource guide and as a textbook for college courses and other franchising curricula. This book will help students of franchising better understand its historical development, practices, and regulation, and its tremendous growth opportunities.

William B. Cherkasky, President
International Franchise Association

PREFACE

Buying a piece of a proven idea is the central attraction of franchising. This unique approach to business has spread throughout the world, and its success far overshadows its youth as a method of doing business.

This book is written for students of franchising as well as for those considering going into business as either a franchisor or a franchisee. A three-part perspective is developed throughout the book concerning the franchisor-franchisee relationship: first, a franchisor and franchisee are independent business people who must manage their separate business affairs; second, the franchisor and franchisee are dependent upon each other in order to be successful in business; and third, the franchisor-franchisee relationship brings with it contractual obligations that are legally binding upon both parties.

Many readers have a particularly keen interest in learning about franchising because they see themselves as prospective franchisees. Research, interviews, and observations consistently show that such persons should (1) learn about the nature of franchising and (2) understand the role of the franchisor before (3) determining if they have what it takes to be successful franchisees. This book is intended to help people develop a clear picture of franchising and franchisors and to provide some insights that will assist them in making their own personal decisions about entering the field. The information in the text is presented in a format designed to answer major franchising questions.

The six stages of a franchised business life-cycle formulate the six major sections of the text.

1. *Nature of Franchising.* Prior to starting a franchised business as either a franchisor or a franchisee, it is important for one to under-

stand the nature of the franchising method of business. A franchised business has unique features not typically found in a business run by an independent owner/operator. Also, there are definitely pros and cons of becoming involved in franchising. The first three chapters address these considerations.

2. *Franchising and the Law.* What is a franchise disclosure document (UFOC)? What are the documents that define the franchise? Why are trademarks often considered the heart of the franchise? Why would the franchisee be entrusted with trade secrets? What legal activities help or hinder franchising? The law as it relates to franchising is broad and diverse, covering topics such as contractual requirements, torts, franchisor/franchisee rights, trademarks, registration requirements, antitrust, territorial rights, price fixing, and tying agreements. These areas are covered in Chapters 4 through 6.

3. *Developing the Franchised Business.* Chapters 7 through 11 are devoted to a discussion of what is essential to the development of a franchise system from the franchisor's perspective. Market planning, location, site selection, administrative plans, and policies, as well as financial management considerations are described and explained to illustrate the steps a franchisor goes through in developing a franchised business.

4. *Operating the Franchised Business.* This section is a natural extension of the preceding section about franchised business development. Chapters 12 through 14 describe and explain the necessity and use of a prototype unit or store by the franchisor, administering the franchise package to franchisees, and approaches to supporting and training franchisees so they become competent operators of their businesses.

5. *The Franchisee Arena.* This section, comprising Chapters 15 through 18, focuses on franchisees and what qualifications a franchisor seeks in a prospective franchisee. Franchise opportunities, royalties, advertising, training, and other factors of interest to the franchisee are described and methods of financing are discussed. Management and marketing skills a franchisee may be expected to have or be willing to develop are also discussed. The section also delves into franchisees' legal rights, what is protected under a franchise agreement, and the legal problems a franchisee can expect to encounter in the normal course of operating the business.

6. *Franchisee/Franchisor Relationships.* The concluding section of the book, Chapters 19 through 22, addresses the multifaceted relationships between franchisees and franchisors, examining these relationships from a business perspective as well as from a legal perspective. Fairness and compliance clauses within franchise contracts are highlighted, as well as legal factors associated with franchisee breakaway and noncompliance. The section closes with a discussion of franchising growth and development in an international context.

Throughout the book, success stories and vignettes are included to add practical knowledge and provide special insight into franchising. Biographical sketches show what individuals and franchise organizations are doing in relation to the topic of the chapter and how their activities further the development of this burgeoning field. Case studies are provided at the close of chapters to help the reader analyze franchise situations and develop sound judgment in handling issues and problems that can arise in a franchised business. An Appendix presents a sample disclosure document in order to illustrate in detail a franchisor-franchisee agreement.

Acknowledgments

This book has been a work of love, sweat, and tears. The major push for writing it has come from franchisors and franchisees interested in seeing the field of franchising explored in depth.

Special thanks are extended to writers assisting in the development and presentation of this book, including Douglas D. Smith, James H. Bean, Turid L. Owren, Thomas A. Balmer, James N. Gardner, Robert C. Maple, Richard de Camara, Lewis G. Rudnick, Joseph W. Sheyka, and Charles J. Averbook. Special appreciation is given to Kelly Herzberg for typing and coordinating early development of the book. Assistance has been provided at three institutions — University of Nebraska-Lincoln, Sangamon State University, and Louisiana State University — and the following helped to compile and edit the manuscript: Cheryl Babcock, Jeff Oscar, Al Pawling, Richard Rounsborg, Amy von Scroder, Terry Hendricks, Kay Johanson, Melinda Weinrich, Rosemary Klei, Yvette Poret, Crystal Patterson, Dana Westmoreland, Stephanie Schwandt, Mark Ott, Aaron Pichon, and Laurie Thiel. In addition, Richard Judd acknowledges William T. Greenwood and Kathryn G. Ellis for counsel during this project.

Thanks is also given to the following reviewers: Thomas Paczkowski, Cayuga County Community College; Dr. Peggy Lambing, University of Missouri-St. Louis; Dr. Ed Cerny, Coastal Carolina College; Dr. Robert Kerber, Illinois State University; Daniel J. Schenck, San Joaquin Delta College; Dr. Anthony J. Urbanick, Johnson State College; Dr. Yohannan T. Abraham, Southwest Missouri State University; Fred Kiesner, Loyola Marymount University; Dr. David B. Stephens, Utah State University; Dr. Stephen M. Brown, Eastern Kentucky University; Dr. Dennis J. Elbert, University of North Dakota; Dennis D. Pappas, Columbus State Community College; Dr. Harriet B. Stephenson, Albers School of Management; Dr. George S. Vozikis, Memphis State University; Dr. William J. Engel, Jr., Longview Community College; Dr. Les R. Dlabay, Lake Forest College; Karl C. Rutkowski, Peirce Junior College;

Dr. Susan Vance, Saint Mary's College; Dr. Carolyn Wiley, Texas Woman's University; and Louis G. Hamilton, corporate attorney, U.S. Shoe Corporation.

The authors dedicate this work to their families — Andrea, Laura, Francine, Richard, and Rachel Judd, and Sue, Jeri, and Jill Justis — and thank them for their love and support.

Robert T. Justis

Richard J. Judd

CONTENTS

PART ONE
THE NATURE OF FRANCHISING
---

1 FRANCHISING: HISTORY AND OVERVIEW 3

Incident 3
Introduction 4
History of Franchising 11
Retail Franchising 17
Success Story: Ray Kroc 26
Summary 30
Review Questions 30
Case Study: Hamburger Prince 31
Case Questions 32
References 32

2 FRANCHISING: PROS AND CONS 33

Incident 33
Introduction 34
Franchising: Advantages and Disadvantages 35
Investing in a Franchise 47
Success Story: Stanley Bresler 55

Summary 56
Review Questions 57
Case Study: Rick's Convenience Food Store 58
Case Questions 59
References 60

3 THE FRANCHISE PLAN 61

Incident 61
Introduction 62
The Franchise Feasibility Study 65
The Franchise PERT Chart 82
Success Story: Freida Schreck 88
Summary 90
Review Questions 90
Case Study: Neighborhood Foods, Inc. 91
Case Questions 93
References 93

PART TWO
FRANCHISING AND THE LAW

4 FRANCHISE LEGAL DOCUMENTS 97

Incident 97
Introduction 98
The Disclosure Document 100
Financial Claims 105
Materiality 106
Registration 106
Operations Manuals 107
The Franchising Agreement 108
Success Story: Harris Cooper 115
Summary 116
Review Questions 116
Case Study: Dairy Queen 116
Case Questions 117

5 TRADEMARKS, COPYRIGHTS, PATENTS, AND TRADE SECRETS 119

Incident 119
Introduction 120

Trademarks   121
Copyrights   126
Patents   128
Trade Secrets   131
Franchising Provisions   133
Success Story: Dallen Peterson   136
Review Questions   137
Case Study: The Mechanics Shop   137
Case Questions   138

6   FRANCHISING AND THE ANTITRUST LAWS   139

Incident   139
Introduction   140
Background and Basis of the Antitrust Laws   141
Antitrust Problems Faced by Franchisors   143
Success Story: Lloyd T. Tarbutton   153
Summary   154
Review Questions   154
Case Study: Jo-Ann's Nut House, Inc.   155
Case Questions   156

PART THREE
THE FRANCHISOR ARENA: DEVELOPING THE FRANCHISED BUSINESS

7   MANAGING THE MARKETING PROCESS   159

Incident   159
Introduction   160
Strategic Planning in Franchising   161
Steps in Strategic Planning   164
Determining the Marketing Mix   176
Success Story: Lewis G. Rudnick   195
Summary   196
Review Questions   197
Case Study: Dunkin' Donuts   197
Case Questions   199
References   199

8 LOCATION AND SITE SELECTION 201

Incident 201
Introduction 202
Considerations for Location and Site Selection 203
Geographic Selection 205
Franchise Site Selection 220
Success Story: Robert V. Walker 234
Summary 235
Review Questions 236
References 237

9 MANAGEMENT, ORGANIZATION, AND ADMINISTRATIVE POLICY 238

Incident 238
Introduction 239
Managing the Franchise from the Top 240
Franchise Entrepreneur as Manager 244
Planning Should Be Organized 247
Franchisor Policies 256
Success Story: William Rosenberg 266
Summary 267
Review Questions 267
Case Study: The Medicine Shoppe 268
Case Questions 269
References 269

10 ACCOUNTING AND FINANCIAL STATEMENTS: PRESENTATION AND USES 271

Incident 271
Introduction 272
Financial Statements 273
Success Story: Leo G. Lauzen 290
Summary 292
Review Questions 292
Case Study: The Hair Emporium 293
Case Questions 294
References 294

11 FINANCIAL MANAGEMENT AND FISCAL PLANNING: TOOLS AND TECHNIQUES   295

Incident   295
Introduction   296
Managing Working Capital   296
Financial Planning   306
Pro Forma Statements   306
Success Story: Richard Snell   311
Summary   312
Review Questions   314
Case Study: Your Franchised Business's Cash Flow   314
Case Questions   316
References   316

PART FOUR
THE FRANCHISE ARENA: OPERATING THE FRANCHISED BUSINESS

---

12 DEVELOPING THE OPERATIONAL PROTOTYPE   319

Incident   319
Introduction   320
Areas of Emphasis in Prototype Development   321
Building Successful Franchises   331
Success Story: Samuel Marvin   334
Summary   334
Review Questions   335
Case Study: Michelle's Formal-Wear Business   335
Case Questions   336
References   336

13 ADMINISTRATION AND OPERATION OF THE FRANCHISE PACKAGE   338

Incident   338
Administrative Package   339
Operations Package   345
Success Story: James A. Mather   364
Summary   367

Review Questions 369
Case Study: Certain-teed Rental System 369
Case Questions 370
References 370

14 SUPPORT AND TRAINING FROM THE FRANCHISOR 372

Incident 372
Franchisee Support 373
Communication 377
The Field Representative 382
Franchisee Training 384
Success Story: Alvin C. Copeland 394
Summary 395
Review Questions 396
Case Study: 7-ELEVEN: A Way of Life 397
Case Questions 399
References 399

PART FIVE
THE FRANCHISEE ARENA

15 INVESTIGATING FRANCHISE OPPORTUNITIES 403

Incident 403
Introduction 404
Becoming a Franchisee 404
Success Story: Leon "Pete" W. Harman 427
Summary 427
Case Study: Sue's Southern Kitchen 428
Case Questions 430
References 430

16 FINANCING YOUR FRANCHISED BUSINESS 432

Incident 432
Introduction 433
Financial Obligations of Franchisees 433

Other Franchisee Requirements or Obligations   434
Franchisor Financing Arrangements   435
Financial Resources of Franchisees   439
Preparing a Financial Package   446
Success Story: Craig Cormack   450
Summary   451
Review Questions   451
Case Study: One-Hour Martinizing   451
Case Questions   452
References   453

17   MARKETING AND MANAGING YOUR FRANCHISED BUSINESS   454

Incident   454
Introduction   455
Marketing   456
Management   464
Success Story: E. James Gaylord   470
Summary   471
Review Questions   471
Case Study: Snelling and Snelling   472
Case Questions   473
References   473

18   LEGAL RIGHTS OF FRANCHISEES   475

Incident   475
Introduction   476
Franchisor-Franchisee Relationship   476
The Franchising Agreement   479
The Franchise Defense Manual   481
Laws Regulating Franchising   482
The Most Common Legal Problems of Franchisees   488
Success Story: Herbert Kay   491
Summary   492
Review Questions   492
Case Study: Long John Silver's, Inc. (Jerrico, Inc.)   492
Case Questions   493
References   493

PART SIX
FRANCHISOR-FRANCHISEE RELATIONSHIPS

19 THE FRANCHISING RELATIONSHIP 497

Incident 497
Phases of the Franchising Relationship 498
C.A.R.E. 504
Franchisor-Franchisee Activities: An Opinion
　by Richard de Camara 506
Success Story: James A. Collins 512
Summary 513
Review Questions 514
Case Study: Mr. Steak 515
Case Questions 516
References 516

20 FAIRNESS AND COMPLIANCE 517

Incident 517
Introduction 518
Structuring a Sound Economic Relationship 519
Structuring a Sound Legal Relationship 521
Documenting and Recording the Franchising Relationship 525
Compliance with Disclosure Regulations 526
Success Story: David B. Kenney 529
Summary 530
Review Questions 530
Case Study: The Steak Shoppe 530
Case Questions 531

21 BREAKAWAY FRANCHISEES AND NONCOMPLIANCE 532

Incident 532
Breakaway Franchisees 533
Dispute Resolution 542
Success Story: Irl H. Marshall 545
Summary 545
Review Questions 546
Case Study: Popeyes Famous Fried Chicken and Biscuits 546
Case Questions 547

22 INTERNATIONAL FRANCHISING 549

Incident 549
Introduction 550
The International Marketplace 551
International Marketing Decision 554
Hindrances to International Franchising 562
Franchising in the Future 563
Success Story: John P. Thompson 564
Summary 565
Review Questions 566
Case Study: Tidy Car 566
Case Questions 567
References 567

APPENDIX: SAMPLE FRANCHISE CONTRACT 569

INDEX 655

PART ONE

THE NATURE OF FRANCHISING

CHAPTER 1
FRANCHISING: HISTORY AND OVERVIEW

In studying this chapter, you will:
- Learn about the historical development of franchising.
- Learn an operational definition of franchising.
- Be able to distinguish between the various types of franchises.
- Develop an understanding of how the franchising concept has been applied in various retail businesses.

INCIDENT

Kelly has been working part-time at a unit of a successful franchised restaurant for the past three years while attending college. She was recently promoted to assistant manager, has graduated from college, and wants to begin a career as an independent franchisee within this restaurant system. The firm's success is the foremost reason for Kelly's career decision. Kelly sees franchising as the new direction of American business and wants to be part of it with a first-rate company.

Kelly believes she would be a very successful franchisee. However, she does not yet know enough about how franchises operate, nor does she understand exactly what is expected of a franchisee. Yet Kelly knows she will succeed through her strong desire to learn and commitment to hard work. After several years of owning and operating her own franchise unit, she hopes she will be able to take an extended vacation. But for now, Kelly wants only to learn about how she can become a successful franchisee with this restaurant system.

INTRODUCTION

Franchising, as we know it today, is a unique approach to business which originated in the United States and has spread throughout the world. Approximately 33 percent of all retail sales in the United States are attributed to franchised businesses. Sales of goods and services by all franchise companies reached $591 billion in 1987. (See Figures 1-1 and 1-2.)

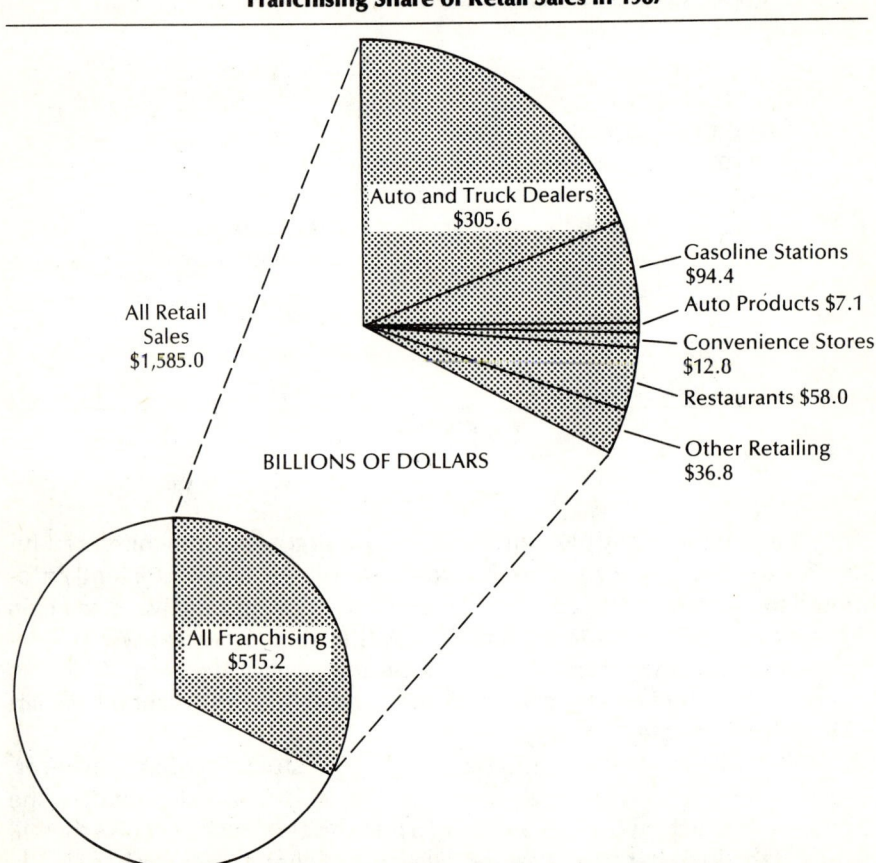

**Figure 1-1
Franchising Share of Retail Sales in 1987**

All Retail Sales $1,585.0

Auto and Truck Dealers $305.6
Gasoline Stations $94.4
Auto Products $7.1
Convenience Stores $12.8
Restaurants $58.0
Other Retailing $36.8

BILLIONS OF DOLLARS

All Franchising $515.2

Source: *Franchising in the Economy 1985-1987.* U.S. Department of Commerce, International Trade Association (Washington, DC: U.S. Government Printing Office, January 1987), p. 15.

**Figure 1-2
Total Franchise Sales and Establishments**

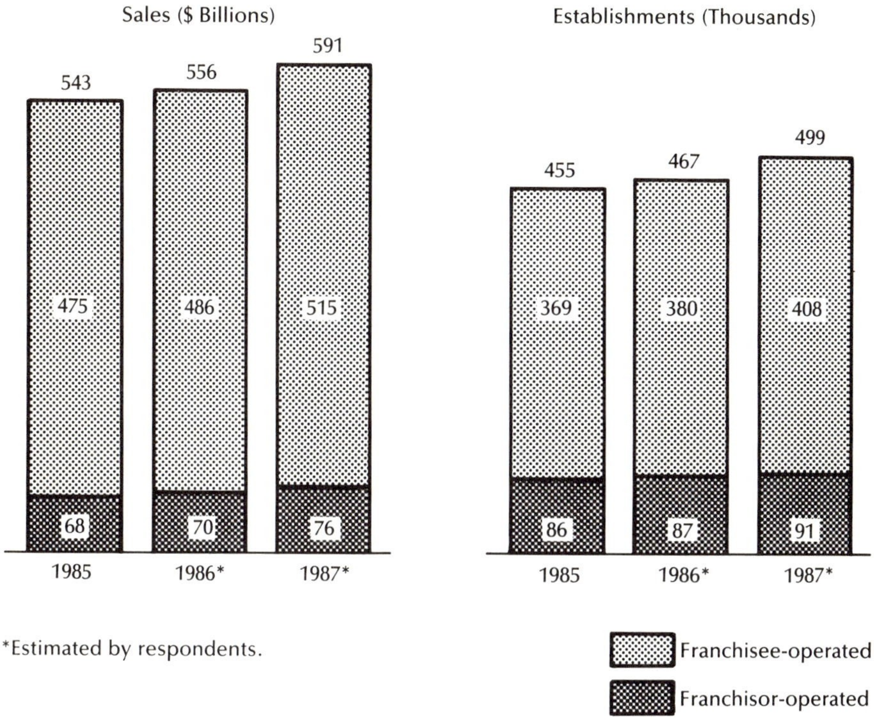

[Bar chart showing Sales ($ Billions): 1985 total 543 (Franchisee-operated 475, Franchisor-operated 68); 1986* total 556 (486, 70); 1987* total 591 (515, 76). Establishments (Thousands): 1985 total 455 (369, 86); 1986* total 467 (380, 87); 1987* total 499 (408, 91).]

*Estimated by respondents.

▫ Franchisee-operated
▪ Franchisor-operated

Source: *Franchising in the Economy 1985-1987*. U.S. Department of Commerce, International Trade Association (Washington, DC: U.S. Government Printing Office, January 1987), p. 2.

There are about 498,000 franchised units in the United States employing more than 6.2 million people full or part-time.[1] Franchising has been such a success for some firms that they have become giants within their respective industries; companies such as McDonald's, Holiday Inns, and Hertz Rent-A-Car have become distinct leaders, comparable in scope of operation and sales volume to some traditional giants of American business and industry such as Union Carbide, General Foods, Alcoa Aluminum, and U.S. Steel.

    A franchisor uses the franchisee's community goodwill, financial equity, business location, and personal drive and motivation to expand the franchised business. The franchisee uses the franchisor's brand or trademark, proven methods of operation, marketing resources, and technical advice to enter, develop, and maintain consumer demand, and ultimately to succeed as a small business owner/operator within the

---

[1] Andy Kostecka, U.S. Department of Commerce, *Franchising in the Economy, 1985-1987* (Washington, DC: U.S. Government Printing Office, January 1987), pp. 1, 2, 47.

community. The franchisee is often given an opportunity to be part of a "turnkey" operation (site, building, architecture, equipment, work-flow and customer-service plans completely determined and installed by the franchisor), with limited capital and prior experience, while having a very good chance of success.

Franchising Defined

Franchising may be defined as a business opportunity by which the owner (producer or distributor) of a service or a trademarked product grants exclusive rights to an individual for the local distribution and/or sale of the service or product, and in return receives a payment or royalty and conformance to quality standards. The individual or business granting the business rights is called the **franchisor**, and the individual or business granted the right to operate in accordance with the chosen method to produce or sell the product or service is called the **franchisee**.

The U.S. Department of Commerce provides a broader definition: "Franchising is a method of doing business by which a franchisee is granted the right to engage in offering, selling, or distributing goods or services under a marketing format which is designed by the franchisor. The franchisor permits the franchisee to use the franchisor's trademark, name, and advertising."[2]

Franchising, then, can be approached from the perspective of both the franchisor and the franchisee. For a franchisor, franchising allows the expansion of a proven concept and method of operation from a single unit to a large operation with multiple locations and multiple product or service offerings. The franchisee has the opportunity to utilize proven methods of operation, large-scale, high-impact advertising, recognized brands or trademarks, and continuing management and technical assistance. These advantages are not typically given to the independent small business owner who may be selling the same product or service.

From either of these two perspectives, franchising can be very appealing. For a franchisor, the franchise approach to business allows growth through an expanding distribution system. Similarly, franchising can be very attractive to an individual desiring to be an independent business owner. The franchising concept provides an opportunity for the franchisee to succeed as a small business owner because of the knowledge, methods, competitive experience, and advertising clout of the franchisor. The franchising method helps franchisor *and* franchisee by providing an agreement that allows both to bring their particular strengths to the business arrangement.

This business arrangement, otherwise called a **franchise opportunity**, has three major components: 1) a trademark and/or logo, 2) the

---

[2] *Franchising in the Economy, 1985-1987*, p. 2.

use of a product or service following a marketing plan, and 3) a payment or royalty fee. These components constitute the essence of what is generally referred to as a **franchise**, whether the arrangement happens to be in auto and truck sales, convenience food stores, restaurants, cleaning services, or gasoline retailing.

Other Descriptions of Franchising

Two other ways of describing franchising should be noted. Franchising can be viewed as a **licensing relationship** within which an owner (the franchisor) of a product, service, or method grants distribution rights to affiliated dealers (the franchisees). The holder of the rights is often given exclusive access to a defined geographic area.[3] Franchising can also be described as "a **continuing relationship** in which the franchisor provides a licensed privilege to do business, plus assistance in organizing, training, merchandising, and management, in return for a consideration from the franchisee."[4] This latter view of franchising comes from the leading trade association in the franchise field, the International Franchise Association.

The ways of describing franchising are summarized in Table 1-1. Each description can serve as an operating definition to allow the reader at least an understanding about the nature of franchising. The authors prefer the first definition: a business opportunity in which the owner (producer or distributor) of a service or trademarked product grants rights to an individual for local distribution and/or sale of the service or products, and in return receives a payment or royalty and conformance to quality standards. This definition encompasses more than the others and also specifies the activities of the primary parties, franchisor and franchisee. It is this definition which we will use throughout the text.

Types of Franchising

In the United States, there are two major types of franchising: product-and-trade-name franchising and business-format franchising. **Product-and-trade-name franchising** has evolved from suppliers making sales contracts with dealers to buy or sell certain products or product lines. In this relationship, the dealer acquires the trade name, trademark, and/or product from the supplier. The dealer (franchisee) identifies with the supplier (franchisor) through the product line. Historically, this approach to franchising has consisted of distribution from a single supplier (or manufacturer) to a large number of dealers either directly or through

---

[3] Andy Kostecka, U.S. Department of Commerce, Bureau of Industrial Economics and Minority Business Development Agency, *Franchise Opportunities Handbook* (Washington, DC: U.S. Government Printing Office, 1983), p. 27.

[4] *Franchise Opportunities Handbook*, p. 27.

Table 1-1
Ways of Describing Franchising

Business Opportunity	An owner (producer or distributor) of a service or trademarked product grants rights to an individual for local distribution and/or sale of goods or services, and in return receives a payment or royalty and conformance to quality standards.
Pattern or Method of Doing Business	A franchisee is granted a right to offer, sell, or distribute goods or services under a marketing format as designated by the franchisor.
Franchise Opportunity	Three components — a trademark and/or logo, the use of a product or service following a marketing plan, and the payment of a royalty fee — constitute the essence of a franchised business.
Licensing Relationship	A franchisor of a product, service, or business method grants distribution rights to affiliated dealers (the franchisees); these rights often include exclusive access to a defined geographic area.
Continuing Relationship	A franchisor provides a licensed privilege to do business and provides management and technical assistance and training in return for a consideration from the franchisee.

regional supply centers. (See Figure 1-3.) An objective of the supplier is to have a dealer (or dealership) in each community or area to provide the product to all potential customers within a geographic area, a region, or the whole country. This franchising approach has been used in the auto and truck, soft drink, tire, and gasoline service industries.

Product-and-trade-name franchising accounted for about 71 percent of all franchised sales in 1987, or approximately $421 billion.[5] (See Table 1-2.) This approach to franchising appears to be in the mature phase of growth. That is, these product categories are characterized by market saturation and intense competition in advertising and price. The number of new franchisees entering this type of franchise relationship has decreased over the past ten years. The total number of gasoline stations, for example, has been in steady decline. The number of automobile and truck dealerships, as well as soft drink bottlers and distributors, has also gradually declined. In 1987 there were approximately 146,000 franchised business units under the product-and-trade-name approach, a decrease of about 31 percent from a decade earlier.[6] However, even though the number of units has declined, total sales volume remains impressive.

Business-format franchising is concerned with the primary ele-

---

[5] *Franchising in the Economy, 1985-1987*, pp. 1-3.
[6] Nancy Suway Church, *Future Opportunities in Franchising: A Realistic Appraisal* (New York: Pilot Industries, Inc., 1979), p. 11.

Figure 1-3
Typical Product-and-Trade-Name Franchising

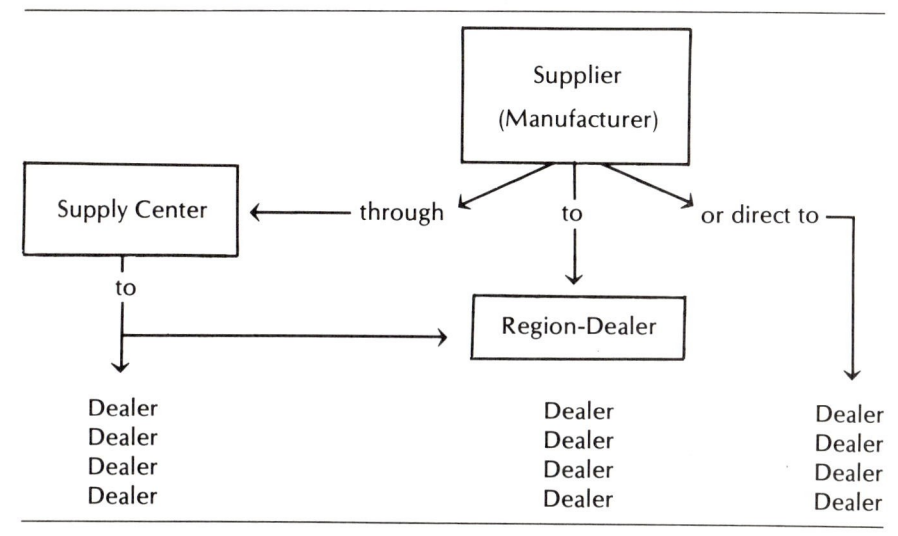

```
                        Supplier
                     (Manufacturer)
                     ↙     ↓     ↘
Supply Center ← through   to    or direct to →
     ↓                     ↓
     to               Region-Dealer
     ↓ ─────────────→
  Dealer              Dealer              Dealer
  Dealer              Dealer              Dealer
  Dealer              Dealer              Dealer
  Dealer              Dealer              Dealer
```

Table 1-2
Product-and-Trade-Name Franchisors:
Number of Establishments and Gross Sales

	Establishments	Sales (Billions of Dollars)
1972	262,100	$115.2
1973	251,395	131.0
1974	230,974	131.3
1975	223,724	144.9
1976	220,946	171.3
1977	211,984	195.9
1978	199,785	241.0
1980	189,823	250.8
1981	181,863	275.7
1982	174,107	277.0
1983	164,986	312.3
1984	160,723	369.8
1985	153,531	401.6
1986	149,050	403.2
1987*	146,000	420.6

*Estimated

Source: *Franchising in the Economy, 1985-1987*, U.S. Department of Commerce, International Trade Association (Washington, DC: U.S. Government Printing Office, January 1987), p. 3.

ments of the **business-opportunity approach** to franchising, described in Table 1-1. This franchising involves the **format** or approach to be used by a franchisee in providing the franchisor's product or service line to the customer. Business-format franchising has been responsible for the tremendous growth in franchising since the 1950s. This approach to franchising has fostered rapid expansion in the restaurant, food service, hotel/motel, printing, retailing, and real estate sectors of our economy.

Most new franchise agreements that are reached today are of the business-format type. The number of franchised units in operation which use this approach to franchising increased to over 352,000 in 1987. As with product-and-trade-name franchising, it is the large franchisors that tend to dominate. Fifty-three franchised companies, using the business-format approach, accounted for 48 percent of the sales and 49 percent of the total number of franchised units in 1985.[7]

Examination of Table 1-3 indicates that, in general, the types of products or services distributed under the business-format approach are in growing industries. The number of new franchisees entering these types of businesses is increasing and sales volumes continue to expand.

Table 1-3
Business-Format Franchisors:
Number of Establishments and Gross Sales

	Establishments	Sales (Billions of Dollars)
1972	189,640	$ 28.7
1973	202,237	32.7
1974	209,727	37.3
1975	210,814	40.9
1976	222,317	46.6
1977	240,524	65.8
1978	245,694	64.3
1979	252,702	72.4
1980	252,548	83.5
1981	260,555	89.1
1982	268,306	99.0
1983	276,195	110.5
1984	283,576	122.3
1985	301,689	141.3
1986	317,751	153.0
1987*	352,495	170.8

*Estimated

Source: *Franchising in the Economy, 1985-1987*, U.S. Department of Commerce, International Trade Association (Washington, DC: U.S. Government Printing Office, January 1987), p. 4.

[7] *Franchising in the Economy, 1984-1986*, pp. 4-5.

HISTORY OF FRANCHISING

The origins of franchising can be traced back through mercantile codes and common law to the Middle Ages. At that time, it was accepted practice for local governments to offer important persons, who might also be high church officials, a license granting them the right to maintain civil order, determine and collect tax revenues, and make other special tax assessments. The licensee (or franchisee) paid the licensor (franchisor) a specified sum from the tax revenues collected or assessments made in order to receive military or other forms of protection. In this way, a monarchy could control the lands within its sphere of influence by providing protection while extracting tax revenues.

In 1562, however, the Council of Trent called for tax reform and ended this system of patronage licensing. But this form of franchising reappeared during the 18th and 19th centuries as similar arrangements were developed by British royalty. These arrangements often called for absolute support of the monarchy in return for the right to develop personal wealth through managerial authority over specific geographic areas.

These relationships also existed in private business and commerce. During the early 19th century in England, tavern and pub owners were experiencing financial hardship, and many did not have enough money to maintain their establishments as required under English law. As a result, many pub and tavern owners turned to the brewing companies for financial assistance. In return for financial assistance, the tavern and pub owners were required to buy all their beer from a particular brewer. However, the owners were not regulated or restricted in any other way by the brewers. They were free to conduct their business as they saw fit. This arrangement assured brewers outlets for distributing their product. Over time, many pubs were bought by brewers who then rented the establishments to tenants who managed the business.

Early Franchising in the United States

Probably the earliest example of franchising in the United States is the McCormick Harvesting Machine Company, which commissioned "exclusive local agents"[8] to sell and service its machinery around 1850. A typical agent for McCormick was an independent businessperson who usually had other interests besides selling McCormick Harvesters. McCormick later instituted company-owned stores to distribute and sell its products.

The first example of a consumer goods firm to use a franchise-

---

[8] Church, p. 11.

oriented system of distribution was the Singer Sewing Machine Company. During the 1850s, Singer experienced difficulty in marketing its new product. Since the sewing machine was an innovative product, Singer first needed to educate the potential consumer about the benefits of using a "machine" for sewing. Since the sewing machine industry was in its infant stage of development, Singer did not have the capital to hire a large sales staff or open a number of company branch offices. Agents working on commission were a natural choice to demonstrate, sell, and repair the Singer line of sewing machines. However, once the sewing machine caught on with the general public, Singer changed its marketing approach to sell and service its machines exclusively through company-owned offices during the 1860s.

The industrial revolution of the late 1800s was a significant event precipitating changes in distribution methods. Certain industries began to concentrate in specific geographic areas — automobile manufacturers in Michigan, tire makers in Ohio, and oil refineries in Pennsylvania, New York, and New Jersey, for example. Companies became larger and fewer in number, thereby having great control over the demand of buyers. Nancy Church describes this process as it took place in the iron industry: "Iron manufacturers were finding it more profitable to deal directly with their customers, and sales agents were being dropped in favor of company-owned sales offices."[9] Direct distribution is quite viable in markets that are concentrated and contain relatively few large buyers, but this approach is not as effective for distributing the wide range of consumer goods available in today's market.

The automobile industry provides the earliest lasting example of franchising in our economy. Around the turn of the century, an auto manufacturer was typically an assembler of component parts produced by other manufacturers. Until 1910, almost all automobiles were sold directly to the customers from assembly plants. Shortly thereafter, many new selling methods were tried: direct mail campaigns were used, agencies were established on a consignment basis, traveling salespeople were sent out through rural America, and large department stores were even used by some manufacturers as outlets. Only one of these approaches seemed to meet with much success — the use of agents on a consignment basis. This success led to the development of franchise networks for the various automobile manufacturers. Thereafter the concept spread to other product and service industries. A brief chronology of these developments is presented below.

Automotive Industry

In 1898, William E. Metzger of Detroit became the first franchisee of the General Motors Corporation. He sold steam automobiles. From that sim-

[9] Church, p. 12.

ple beginning, other franchising relationships were established by manufacturers and enterprising individuals for the distribution of electric and steam automobiles.

Henry Ford envisioned mass production and mass sales of his Model T. Making the assembly-line production profitable required an efficient mechanism for the distribution of the product. However, because Ford lacked the ready capital to establish multiple retail outlets in a short period of time, he focused on establishing dealers in as many communities as possible. The number of dealers was limited only by the anticipated production levels of Ford cars from the assembly plant.

Other auto manufacturers soon followed suit. As a result, the auto industry emerged as the first industry to use the franchise approach to distribution. Even today, the automobile industry accounts for over 50 percent of all franchise sales.

The huge success of the franchise approach in the auto industry was the result of the establishment of exclusive geographic territories. These territories eliminated intrabrand competition. As demand for automobiles grew, the automobile companies became financially stronger and began to franchise with independent dealers on a large scale. By allocating territorial rights and limiting the number of franchisees in specified locales, the manufacturers were able to convince the franchisees to sell only those automobiles manufactured by the parent company.

Other Business Sectors

The methods of franchising that proved so successful in the auto and petroleum industries had application in other business sectors as well. Critical to franchise development was the opportunity for a franchisor to expand by utilizing the capital and motivation of local owner/operators (franchisees). For the franchisee, offering a standardized product or service with brand recognition to the consumer would provide strong appeal to the consumer to purchase the product or service from the local (franchised) business.

Rexall drugstores began with a gathering of about 40 druggists called together by Louis Ligget in 1902. Ligget's idea was to set up a company to manufacture private-label drugs to be distributed and sold exclusively by these druggists. The important goal of the venture was to increase profit as a result of reducing manufacturing and sales costs as well as eliminating middlemen. After some time, Rexall began to open store-owned locations, becoming a corporate chain while still maintaining franchises.

Western Auto, an auto parts company based in Kansas City, began in 1909 by establishing an associate dealership program which enabled persons to open their own stores if they had the money and ambition, even if they had no prior retail experience. Western Auto assists dealers in finding an appropriate site, selecting merchandise, advertising, arranging credit, designing store layout, planning grand openings, and training employees. However, Western Auto has a distinct characteristic that separates it from other franchise systems: it requires no fee or royalty from its franchisees. Instead, it believes it receives sufficient compensation from its markup on Western Auto products sold to its dealers.

In 1925, Howard Johnson offered three flavors of "superior" blend ice cream in his Wollaston, Massachusetts, drugstore. Through franchising, his ice cream business expanded to a group of restaurants on the East Coast. In 1940 the first Howard Johnson Restaurant appeared on a turnpike, and in 1954 the first motor lodge opened. The Howard Johnson franchise system has since grown to over 200 restaurants and about 500 motor lodges.

Another cooperative arrangement among small business owners to enhance their competitive position is illustrated by the Independent Grocers Association (IGA). Independent grocers formed a buying cooperative to make large purchases from food brokers, canneries, or wholesalers in order to get the best purchase prices possible. When a grocer joins IGA, the retail store becomes a franchisee of this national cooperative organization.

The franchise concept was ushered into retail sales when two tailors joined forces and developed a franchise firm called Mode o'Day, which became known as the "biggest little store in the world." The 1930s also saw the advent of the Avon Cosmetics, Fuller Brush, and Culligan franchise systems. Fifty years later the slogan "Hey, Culligan Man" is known far and wide because of the success of this company through its over 1350 franchises across the country.

Franchising from 1950 to 1980

It was not until the early 1950s that the boom in franchising took place. Many companies that today are known to virtually every American household got their start during this period. In 1955, Ray Kroc started McDonald's, stressing "quality, service, cleanliness, and value." That same year, Harlan Sanders found a niche in the food industry with Kentucky Fried Chicken. In 1959, the International House of Pancakes opened its doors and has since sold breakfast to countless millions.

In the 1960s many types of businesses entered the franchising field for the first time. Products and services being offered through franchise relationships now included clothing, business services, groceries, convenience stores, laundries, lawn services, printing, security systems, and vending. In 1968, the franchise industry recorded sales of over $100 billion — more than 10 percent of the gross national product and over 25 percent of the sales of the entire retail industry.[10] With this dramatic

---

[10] *Franchising in the Economy, 1983-1985*, pp. 28-31.

development, fast-buck operators and other unethical businesspeople began using the franchising concept for illegal personal gain. The Small Business Committees of the U.S. Senate and House of Representatives held hearings concerning fraudulent franchising practices. Based on these hearings and with the support of the franchising industry, in the early 1970s several states adopted disclosure/registration requirements for franchised businesses. In 1979, the Federal Trade Commission (FTC) passed Rule 436.1, the Franchise Disclosure Act. This Act identifies the 20 sections that a franchise disclosure document (or prospectus) must have. The disclosure document is prepared by the franchisor and given to a prospective franchisee prior to the establishment of a franchise agreement, or contract, between the parties.

During the 1970s, franchising continued to grow. In 1979, total sales of all franchised businesses was approximately $116 billion through 396,000 business outlets. In 1980, these sales had jumped to over $334 billion generated through over 442,000 establishments. Over the decade, sales had increased over 255 percent, while the number of franchised business units had increased 5 percent.[11]

The 1980s

The 1980s have been a period of continued emphasis on franchising in our economy. Many people have seen the opportunity, through franchising, to invest their funds and energy in the development of business opportunities. Franchising opportunities have been rapidly growing in the service industries such as restaurant, computer, electronics, and convenience food store businesses.

The main reason for the continued interest and the growth in the number of franchised outlets is the success rate of franchises compared with that of independently owned businesses. Approximately 50 percent of new independent business ventures fail within one year, with 65 percent failing by the end of five years. Failures are often due to lack of management skills and/or lack of sufficient capital for the line of business pursued. In contrast, in 1984 only 3.3 percent of the number of franchised outlets were discontinued — for any reason.[12] One reason for the low rate of failure — or discontinuance in franchising — is the franchising agreement itself, which in most franchising relationships has a renewal clause. During fiscal 1985, 12,543 franchising agreements were due for renewal, and only 1,174 (9 percent) were not renewed.[13]

Today, franchising is an integral part of the structural makeup of American and world business. There were roughly 498,000 franchise

---

[11] *Franchising in the Economy, 1985-1987*, pp. 31, 33, 36, 37.
[12] *Franchising in the Economy, 1983-1985*, p. 11.
[13] *Franchising in the Economy, 1985-1987*, p. 52.

outlets in the United States in 1987, about 6 percent more than in 1986.[14] By 1996, it is possible that approximately 50 percent of all retail sales will be made through franchised businesses. This franchising boom is a result of two trends in the American way of life. The first trend is the recent surge in entrepreneurial spirit, the desire "to start a business of my own." Franchising offers an opportunity to budding entrepreneurs to achieve these personal and professional goals more quickly and with less risk than they would incur by going it alone as independent small business owners. The second trend is the change in life styles in the United States and Western Europe which has put growing emphasis on service and convenience.

Each of these trends is particularly conducive to the business-format approach to franchising. For example, the dramatic growth in the number of two-income households has brought with it increased sales of fast food, proliferation of child care centers, and establishment of health care facilities offering no-appointment-needed service and extended hours. Higher incomes have also contributed to the surge in recreation activities, as well as to an increase in the number of motels, hotels, auto rental companies, and other franchised firms catering to travelers.

Currently, there is a rising trend in conversion franchising. In **conversion franchising**, an owner of an existing business becomes a franchisee to acquire some benefit from association with the franchisor, such as a nationally recognized brand or trademark or a customer referral network. Conversion franchising has met with particular success in restaurants and real estate and is becoming apparent in construction, electronics, non-food retailing, home repair, and various types of business services. Century 21 Real Estate is perhaps the best known franchise system that follows a conversion business format approach.

During the 1980s, two changes have occurred in franchising: More women and minorities are entering into franchising agreements, and more budding entrepreneurs are taking the plunge into the franchise type of business as franchisors rather than as franchisees. In each of these circumstances, the numbers are believed to be comparatively small but growing.

Franchising as an approach to business in the 1980s is likely to grow in product/service areas such as general retail merchandise, home furnishings, decorating, home accessories, video and electronic equipment, and automotive care. This growth is anticipated because personal consumption expenditures are expected to grow at approximately a 3 percent annual rate for the rest of the decade. Greater retail expenditures suggest increased spending for goods and services distributed through franchise-formatted businesses. For example, trade sources predict that restaurants will continue to upscale and improve exterior

---

[14] *Franchising in the Economy, 1985-1987*, p. 1.

and interior decor, service, and quality of food. Automotive repair businesses will grow by providing expanded services in transmission repair and muffler, quick lube, tuneup, brake, and painting services, as well as in other specialized car care services.

Franchising is likely to continue to grow in the international marketplace as well. In general, international franchising is beneficial to both importing and exporting countries. For the importing country (where franchised units would be established), new businesses and employment are created, generating more income at the local level. Much of it remains in the local economy with some potential expansion to other areas of the importing country (if supplies or materials are locally purchased). The exporting country (the country of the franchisor) receives income through royalties or other fees and may also export parts or materials for inclusion in the product or service being franchised.

Statistics bear out the acceptance of American franchisors in international markets. In 1971, there were 156 American franchisors with 3,365 franchised outlets in foreign countries. By the close of 1985, there were 342 franchisors with 30,188 franchised outlets in Canada, Asia, Europe, and Latin America,[15] and 192 American companies indicated they were considering extending their operations into foreign countries by the end of 1988.[16] Further, the International Franchise Association (IFA), which is the trade association for franchisors, reports that almost 40 percent of its members are franchising internationally and anticipates that an even greater number will do so in the future.

RETAIL FRANCHISING

Retailing is the prime area of growth for the business-format approach to franchising. Much of this growth has taken place since the 1950s, and we have already mentioned several examples. This section will highlight certain business sectors where franchising has had significant impact on the growth of a business as well as its approach to doing business.

Convenience Stores

The convenience-store concept is built on the premise of a need for local and quick service. Choice of products is limited and the products tend to cost more than the same or similar products found in supermarkets. Many gasoline service stations are being converted into convenience food and gasoline marts. Some convenience stores now offer a wide variety of prepared, ready-to-eat, and deli foods to compete with fast-food restaurants and supermarkets. In 1987, there were over 16,000 convenience

---

[15] *Franchising in the Economy, 1985-1987*, p. 9.
[16] *Franchising in the Economy, 1985-1987*, p. 8.

Table 1-4
Convenience Stores

Item	1986*	1987*	Percent Change 1986-87
Total number of establishments:	15,698	16,576	5.6
Company-owned	9,162	9,654	5.4
Franchisee-owned	6,536	6,922	5.9
Total sales of products and services (in thousands):	$11,706,138	$12,803,131	9.4
Company-owned	7,112,099	7,720,141	8.5
Franchisee-owned	4,594,039	5,082,990	10.6
Total sales of products and services by franchisors to franchisees (in thousands):			
Merchandise (non-food) for resale	2,540	3,249	27.9
Supplies (such as paper goods, etc.)	23,060	26,065	13.0
Food ingredients	222,340	244,229	9.8
Other	3,400	3,700	8.8
Total	$ 251,340	$ 277,243	10.3

*Data estimated by respondents.

Source: *Franchising in the Economy, 1985-1987*, U.S. Department of Commerce, International Trade Association (Washington DC: U.S. Government Printing Office, January 1987), p. 69.

store establishments. (See Table 1-4 above.) About 58 percent were company-owned and 42 percent were franchisee-owned. Total sales were over $12 billion in 1987.[17]

Auto Products and Services

According to the U.S. Department of Commerce, retail tire outlets lead the auto products and service field with approximately 43 percent of total sales volume in this category of franchised business sales.[18] In addition to selling tires, these outlets usually provide a full range of auto services, and may also sell such items as radios and household appliances. Other franchisors, distributing merchandise through franchised units, offer services including car washes, lube and oil changes, auto diagnostic tests, brake and muffler installation and repair, and even parking services. Also, because of higher purchase prices and repair costs, more automobile owners are doing their own maintenance and minor repairs, thus providing considerable opportunity for merchandising of tools and diagnostic equipment needed by the do-it-yourself mechanic. Total sales and

---

[17] *Franchising in the Economy, 1985-1987*, p. 69.
[18] *Franchising in the Economy, 1985-1987*, p. 17.

number of these kinds of establishments continue to grow. (See Table 1-5.)

Restaurants

To many consumers, restaurants typify what constitutes a franchised business. In 1986, sales by franchised restaurants of all types reached over $51 billion, an increase of 8 percent over 1985. The 73,892 franchised restaurants in business in 1985 increased to 78,288 restaurants in 1986, and almost 87,000 were projected for 1987, a 10.4 percent increase. (See Table 1-6.) The greatest concentration of franchised restaurants is in four states, California, Florida, Ohio, and Texas.[19]

It is anticipated that franchising in the restaurant business will continue to expand. Employment in the franchised restaurant sector accounts for about 39 percent of total employment with franchised businesses and should continue to rise in the near future.[20]

Table 1-5
Automotive Products and Services[1]

Item	1986[2]	1987[2]	Percent Change 1986-87
Total number of establishments:	37,407	40,371	7.9
Company-owned	4,830	5,214	8.0
Franchisee-owned	32,577	35,157	7.9
Total sales of products and services (in thousands):[3]	$11,675,777	$12,910,464	10.6
Company-owned[3]	3,964,180	4,503,595	13.6
Franchisee-owned[3]	7,711,597	8,406,869	9.0
Total sales of products and services by franchisors to franchisees (in thousands):			
Merchandise (non-food) for resale	2,070,283	2,239,455	8.2
Supplies (such as paper goods, etc.)	37,828	46,828	23.8
Food ingredients	0	0	0.0
Other	35,120	43,112	22.8
Total	$ 2,143,231	$ 2,329,395	8.7

[1]Includes tire, battery, and accessory stores; auto and truck wash services; brake and muffler repair and other services.
[2]Data estimated by respondents.
[3]Includes sales of non-automotive products (household appliances, garden supplies, etc.).

Source: *Franchising in the Economy, 1985-1987*, U.S. Department of Commerce, International Trade Association (Washington DC: U.S. Government Printing Office, January 1987), p. 55.

[19] *Franchising in the Economy, 1985-1987*, pp. 14, 16, 73, 75.
[20] *Franchising in the Economy, 1985-1987*, p. 16.

Table 1-6
Restaurants (All Types)

Item	1986*	1987*	Percent Change 1986-87
Total number of establishments:	78,288	86,399	10.4
Company-owned	24,372	26,293	7.9
Franchisee-owned	53,916	60,106	11.5
Total sales of products and services (in thousands):	$51,488,142	$57,951,132	12.6
Company-owned	18,332,448	20,376,297	11.1
Franchisee-owned	33,155,694	37,574,835	13.3
Total sales of products and services by franchisors to franchisees (in thousands):			
Merchandise (non-food) for resale	154,797	168,364	8.8
Supplies (such as paper goods, etc.)	237,676	261,154	9.9
Food ingredients	940,539	1,091,975	16.1
Other	64,631	74,155	14.7
Total	$ 1,397,643	$ 1,595,648	14.2

*Data estimated by respondents.

Source: *Franchising in the Economy, 1985-1987*, U.S. Department of Commerce, International Trade Association (Washington DC: U.S. Government Printing Office, January 1987), p. 73.

Increased availability of breakfast menus and late-night drive-thrus, as well as new units in inner-city locations and along superhighways, have lengthened the hours franchised restaurants are open. Longer hours suggest the restaurant business is becoming more and more competitive. To compete with other restaurant chains, many franchised restaurants are offering waiter/waitress service, as well as drive-thru or self-service. Table 1-7 lists the primary services franchised restaurants provide their customers.

In 1984 there were 13 major restaurant franchisors with over 1,000 units each. These 13 franchisors account for 55 percent of all franchised restaurants, and their total sales represent 60 percent of all franchised restaurant sales ($29 billion, of which $20 billion sales were made by franchised units).[21]

In 1985, more existing restaurants were converted to franchisee ownership than were repurchased by the franchisor for company-owned operation. The purpose of many repurchases is to resell the units to prospective franchisees in the future. The trend of repurchasing restaurants for company ownership is shown in Table 1-8. Table 1-9 identifies a

[21] *Franchising in the Economy, 1985-1987*, p. 16.

Table 1-7
Principal Types of Customer Services
Provided by Franchised Chains

	Self-service, drive-in, and drive-thru	Waiter or waitress service
Chicken	28	2
Hamburgers, etc.	99	6
Pizza	73	29
Mexican food	22	14
Seafood	7	7
Pancakes, waffles	0	13
Steak, full menu	20	97
Sandwich and other	49	4
Total	298	172

Source: *Franchising in the Economy, 1985-1987*, U.S. Department of Commerce, International Trade Association (Washington DC: U.S. Government Printing Office, January 1987), p. 17.

Table 1-8
Franchised Restaurant Units Repurchased
and Units Converted to Franchisee Ownership

Year	Units repurchased for company ownership	Units converted to franchisee ownership
1971	783	158
1972	413	145
1973	533	175
1974	477	198
1975	311	184
1976	280	413
1977	305	425
1978	321	312
1979	484	579
1980	394	498
1981	489	426
1982	475	389
1983	279	352
1984	328	339
1985	322	622

Source: *Franchising in the Economy, 1985-1987*, U.S. Department of Commerce, International Trade Association (Washington, DC: U.S. Government Printing Office, January 1987), p. 16.

Table 1-9
Franchised Restaurant Establishments by Type of Ownership
and Type of Major Activity

Major Activity	1987* Firms	1987* Total	1987* Company-owned	1987* Franchisee-owned
Total	470	86,399	26,293	60,106
Chicken	30	9,883	3,545	6,338
Hamburgers, franks, roast beef, etc.	105	34,537	7,848	26,689
Pizza	102	18,113	5,636	12,477
Mexican food (tacos, etc.)	36	4,951	2,236	2,715
Seafood	14	2,826	1,603	1,223
Pancakes, waffles	13	1,981	606	1,375
Steak, full menu	117	9,855	4,481	5,374
Sandwich and other	53	4,253	338	3,915

*Estimated by respondents for 1987.

Source: *Franchising in the Economy, 1985-1987,* U.S. Department of Commerce, International Trade Association (Washington, DC: U.S. Government Printing Office, January 1987), p. 74.

number of franchised restaurant establishments by type of ownership and major activity, and Table 1-10 lists sales volume figures by type of franchise ownership by major activity.

Hotels and Motels

One of the most glamorous areas of franchising is hotel/motel operation. Currently, franchised hotel/motel units maintain approximately 64 percent occupancy rates.[22] Persons traveling on business account for more than 60 percent of occupied rooms, with the remainder split between pleasure travelers and convention-goers. Pleasure travel has been growing steadily for the past several years and is likely to continue growing. The increase in weekend and vacation travel is the result of more single-person households, expanded leisure time, rising disposable personal income, and relatively stable gasoline prices.

There are three types of franchising programs in the hotel industry: traditional hotels, co-owner hotels, and voluntary groups. Traditional hotels, which include Holiday Inns, Howard Johnson's, Ramada Inns, and Quality Court Motels, are involved in the traditional franchising arrangements covering trade name, services, architectural design,

[22] *Franchising in the Economy, 1985-1987,* p. 20.

**Table 1-10
Franchised Restaurant Sales Volume by Type of Ownership
and Major Activity**

Major Activity	Firms	1987* Total	Company-owned	Franchisee-owned
Total	470	$57,951,132	20,376,297	37,574,835
Chicken	30	4,994,913	2,082,946	2,911,967
Hamburgers, franks, roast beef, etc.	105	28,591,880	7,357,159	21,234,721
Pizza	102	8,067,688	2,979,639	5,088,049
Mexican food (tacos, etc.)	36	2,881,165	1,620,012	1,261,153
Seafood	14	1,526,190	874,540	651,650
Pancakes, waffles	13	1,285,229	382,739	902,490
Steak, full menu	117	9,500,179	4,935,440	4,564,739
Sandwich and other	53	1,103,888	143,822	960,066

*Estimated by respondents for 1987.

Source: *Franchising in the Economy, 1985-1987*, U.S. Department of Commerce, International Trade Association (Washington, DC: U.S. Government Printing Office, January 1987), p. 74.

operating procedures, advertising, and franchise royalties. With co-owner hotels, which include TraveLodge and Imperial 400, both the franchisor and the franchisee can have a financial position (ownership equity) in local units. Voluntary groups, including Best Western motels, do not use common architectural styles or operating practices but do use the same trade name and common computer registration.

Table 1-11 shows the total number of franchise establishments, sales, and sales by franchisors to franchisees for 1984 to 1986. Table 1-12 shows the distribution of establishments of franchising companies by size. In 1985, over 93 percent of the sales volume in the franchised hotel/motel and campground category was generated by firms having 151 or more units.[23] The total sales volume of franchisee-owned units is both larger and increasing more rapidly than the sales volume generated by company-owned franchise units.

Auto and Truck Rental Services

Auto and truck rental (and leasing) services are growing in popularity throughout the United States. Rental agencies can be found in almost all airports, providing convenient service to air travelers. Leasing compa-

[23] *Franchising in the Economy, 1985-1987*, p. 78.

Table 1-11
Hotels, Motels, and Campgrounds

Item	1986*	1987*	Percent Change 1986-87
Total number of establishments:	8,033	8,578	6.8
Company-owned	1,121	1,206	7.6
Franchisee-owned	6,912	7,372	6.7
Total sales of products and services (in thousands):	$15,693,894	$16,729,454	6.6
Company-owned	4,664,059	4,945,493	6.0
Franchisee-owned	11,029,835	11,783,961	6.8
Total sales of products and services by franchisors to franchisees (in thousands):			
Merchandise (non-food) for resale	6,516	7,530	15.6
Supplies (such as paper goods, etc.)	23,510	25,369	7.9
Food ingredients	240	240	0.0
Other	0	0	0.0
Total	$30,266	$33,139	9.5

*Estimated by respondents.

Source: *Franchising in the Economy, 1985-1987*, U.S. Department of Commerce, International Trade Association (Washington, DC: U.S. Government Printing Office, January 1987), p.78.

Table 1-12
Hotels, Motels, and Campgrounds:
Distribution by Number of Establishments, 1985

Size Groups	Franchised Companies Number	Establishments Number	Percent	Sales (In thousands)	Percent
Total	43	7,490	100.0	$14,770,576	100.0
501 and greater	5	3,932	52.5	7,303,881	49.5
151-500	8	2,422	32.3	6,434,084	43.6
51-150	9	770	10.3	667,358	4.5
11-50	13	312	4.2	314,053	2.1
0-10	8	54	0.7	51,200	0.3

Source: *Franchising in the Economy, 1985-1987*, U.S. Department of Commerce, International Trade Association (Washington, DC: U.S. Government Printing Office, January 1987), p. 78.

nies are looking more and more to achieve growth through stronger ties with business executives and establishment of corporate accounts.

Many auto and truck rental companies have moved into leasing, and most of these companies are stressing the need for expanded services in order to boost revenues. Some franchised companies are providing express booths at the busier airports. In 1986, gross receipts in the rental industry amounted to $6.1 billion and were expected to rise by 7 percent in 1987.[24] As shown in Table 1-13, the number of outlets continues to increase at about 1 percent per year. Approximately 22 percent of the franchise outlets are owned and operated by the company, while franchisees own and operate the remaining 78 percent. The total number of outlets came to approximately 12,000 in 1987 as a result of increased activity by auto and truck rental companies.[25]

Table 1-13
Auto and Truck Rental and Leasing Services

Item	1986*	1987*	Percent Change 1986-87
Total number of establishments:	11,390	11,520	1.1
Company-owned	2,443	2,479	1.5
Franchisee-owned	8,947	9,041	1.1
Total sales of products and services (in thousands):	$6,101,339	$6,538,135	7.2
Company-owned	3,522,694	3,737,836	6.1
Franchisee-owned	2,578,645	2,800,299	8.6
Total sales of products and services by franchisors to franchisees (in thousands):			
Merchandise (non-food) for resale	0	0	0.0
Supplies (such as paper goods, etc.)	2,392	2,647	10.7
Food ingredients	0	0	0.0
Other	0	0	0.0
Total	$2,392	$2,647	10.7

*Data estimated by respondents.

Source: *Franchising in the Economy, 1985-1987*, U.S. Department of Commerce, International Trade Association (Washington, DC: U.S. Government Printing Office, January 1987), p.82.

---

[24] *Franchising in the Economy, 1985-1987*, p. 22.
[25] *Franchising in the Economy, 1985-1987*, p. 84.

Other Services

Construction companies, house cleaning services, dry cleaning services, equipment rental agencies, educational services, business aids and services, and beauty salons are also becoming successful areas for franchising. The sales volumes and number of units by each of the business categories of service franchising areas are shown in Table 1-14. These figures show the extent of franchising by business category in the United States.

Financial Services

In 1982 the First Interstate Bancorp of California (the seventh largest bank in the United States) announced the creation of a *franchised* banking system to expand its banking and financial services to reach customers in new locations. The typical franchisee of First Interstate Bancorp of California is an existing independent bank that has been converted to a franchised unit of First Interstate. As a franchisee, the bank can use the name and/or trademark of First Interstate Bancorp and provide its depositors access to over 9,000 automatic teller machines located in the western United States and in other world trade centers. The local bank acquires these additional features for a small franchise fee based upon the interest or fees earned by customer use of the expanded services.

A number of banks and other financial institutions can choose franchising to spread their name and seek new markets throughout the United States without a large outlay of capital. Providing financial services through conversion franchising has potential for the future, as many financial institutions want to attract depositors by expanding to provide total financial service packages. Becoming a franchise of an established network would enable rapid introduction of these new services.

SUCCESS STORY
RAY KROC

The story of Ray Kroc is truly a classic tale of American business success. In 1955, at age 52, Ray Kroc opened his first McDonald's restaurant in Des Plaines, Illinois. By 1985, McDonald's sales would grow to more than $8 billion a year from over 8,000 restaurants worldwide. In April of 1988, the ten-thousandth McDonald's restaurant opened. The average restaurant sales exceed $1.1 million annually.

Ray Kroc was born in 1902 in Oak Park, Illinois. He left school following his sophomore year and held various jobs until 1922 when he was hired by Lily to sell paper cups. After 16 years he left Lily to sell a shake mixer called the Multimixer. Selling the Multimixer had its ups and downs, like selling any other product. Sales declined during the war but picked up afterwards, and Kroc found himself a success in a business he thoroughly enjoyed. He even sold a Multimixer to Willard Marriott, who had just opened his first A&W Root Beer drive-in.

In 1954 Kroc discovered a small hamburger stand in San Bernardino, California, that was using not just one but eight Multimixers. The owners of this restaurant were Maurice and Dick McDonald. Kroc was surprised by the tremendous volume of business this walk-up hamburger stand was doing and encouraged the McDonald brothers to expand; no doubt, Kroc wanted to sell Multimixers to each of the stores that the McDonald brothers would open. The brothers did not wish to expand but were willing to listen to Kroc talk about opening several McDonald's restaurants. Kroc volunteered to franchise the McDonald's concept.

In 1960, the company celebrated its fifth anniversary, opened its 200th restaurant, and sold its 400 millionth hamburger. Ray Kroc also promised to fight inflation by holding the price of hamburger to 15¢, which he was able to do. In 1961, he opened Hamburger University in the basement of the Oak Grove Village, Illinois, restaurant and conferred Bachelor of Hamburgerology degrees on the first graduating class.

Other highlights of the McDonald's saga include the following. In 1965, McDonald's celebrated its 10th anniversary with its initial public stock offering at $22.50 per share. The average annual sales for a McDonald's restaurant at that time was $249,000. In 1970, a McDonald's restaurant in Bloomington, Minnesota, was the first to reach $1 million in annual sales. In 1975, the first drive-thru window was opened at a McDonald's in Oklahoma City. By 1982, McDonald's had expanded its menu to include the McChicken and McRib sandwiches and McNuggets. The McRib and McChicken sandwiches were later dropped, while soft ice cream cones were reintroduced.

Today, McDonald's restaurants are found throughout the United States and in 32 other countries and territories. The number of establishments worldwide continues to grow at the rate of about 500 restaurants per year. When Ray Kroc died in January of 1984, he had become an example to the franchised restaurant industry and had established a standard for all to follow. The McDonald's motto is also its promise of Q.S.C. & V. — quality, service, cleanliness, and value.

Information provided courtesy of Joan B. Kroc, August 14, 1985.

Table 1-14
Franchising in the Economy, 1987*

Kinds of Franchised Business	Number of Establishments			Sales (in thousands)			Percent Change 1986-1987		Percent Change 1985-1987	
	Total	Company-owned	Franchisee-owned	Total	Company-owned	Franchisee-owned	No. Estab.	Sales	No. Estab.	Sales
TOTAL — ALL FRANCHISING	498,495	90,952	407,543	$591,331,930	$76,282,106	$515,049,824	6.8	6.3	9.5	8.9
Automobile and Truck Dealers	27,750	0	27,750	305,617,000	0	305,617,000	0.5	4.1	0.8	8.2
Automotive Products and Services	40,371	5,214	35,157	12,910,464	4,503,595	8,406,869	7.9	10.6	10.7	21.1
Business Aids and Services	61,317	6,495	54,822	15,544,556	2,390,135	13,154,421	14.0	15.3	23.0	29.9
Accounting, Credit, Collection Agencies, and General Business Systems	2,595	23	2,572	211,785	4,283	207,502	20.1	23.9	24.7	25.6
Employment Services	5,972	1,865	4,107	3,564,645	1,455,125	2,109,520	14.9	16.2	23.6	30.5
Printing and Copying Services	5,973	142	5,831	1,223,673	35,656	1,188,017	16.3	16.2	32.4	33.0
Tax Preparation	8,260	3,392	4,868	484,801	257,520	227,281	1.7	5.8	1.4	13.5
Real Estate	16,157	335	15,822	5,922,165	89,700	5,832,465	9.4	12.4	16.6	28.2
Miscellaneous Business Services	22,360	738	21,622	4,137,487	547,851	3,589,636	21.3	19.4	36.3	33.3
Construction, Home Improvements, Maintenance and Cleaning Services	22,165	776	21,389	4,937,287	1,443,857	3,493,430	20.5	10.6	26.8	21.4

Table 1-14
Franchising in the Economy, 1987* (continued)

Kinds of Franchised Business	Number of Establishments			Sales (in thousands)			Percent Change 1986-1987			Percent Change 1985-1987		
	Total	Company-owned	Franchisee-owned	Total	Company-owned	Franchisee-owned	No. Estab.	Sales	No. Estab.	Sales	
Convenience Stores	16,576	9,654	6,922	12,803,131	7,720,141	5,082,990	5.6	9.4	9.5	18.1
Educational Products and Services	9,104	537	8,567	851,197	140,560	710,637	10.7	14.0	11.4	10.9
Restaurants (All Types)	86,399	26,293	60,106	57,951,132	20,376,297	37,574,835	10.4	12.6	16.9	21.5
Gasoline Service Stations	117,000	21,060	95,940	94,907,000	17,083,000	77,824,000	-2.6	5.0	-6.1	-5.8
Hotels, Motels, and Campgrounds	8,578	1,206	7,372	16,729,454	4,945,493	11,783,961	6.8	6.6	14.5	13.3
Laundry and Drycleaning Services	3,157	269	2,888	425,046	52,931	372,115	18.2	22.9	34.6	40.2
Recreation, Entertainment, and Travel	8,944	484	8,460	3,191,075	881,605	2,309,470	7.9	20.0	14.4	37.7
Rental Services (Auto-Truck)	11,520	2,479	9,041	6,538,135	3,737,836	2,800,299	1.1	7.2	2.6	15.0
Rental Services (Equipment)	2,903	511	2,392	816,385	292,385	524,000	9.3	13.4	14.0	22.1
Retailing (Non-Food)	50,725	11,617	39,108	25,178,512	7,838,512	17,340,000	10.2	13.9	12.4	22.4
Retailing (Food Other Than Convenience Stores)	23,537	3,742	19,795	11,642,519	3,134,185	8,508,334	13.4	8.3	26.0	15.5
Soft Drink Bottlers	1,250	122	1,128	20,032,000	1,603,000	18,429,000	-3.8	4.1	-10.1	9.3
Miscellaneous	7,199	493	6,706	1,257,037	138,574	1,118,463	18.6	19.7	31.6	33.4

*1987 data estimated by respondents.

Source: Adapted from *Franchising in the Economy 1985-1987*, U.S. Department of Commerce, International Trade Association (Washington, DC: U.S. Government Printing Office, January 1987), p. 27.

SUMMARY

The franchising concept as we know it was not a major factor in American business until automobile, petroleum, and other product-and-trade-name manufacturers and processors sought to expand their markets. Most of the early American manufacturers did not have sufficient capital available to expand as rapidly as they would have liked while still maintaining absolute control over each outlet.

Franchising of commission agents, dealers, and licensees was of great advantage to these industries while they were in their infancy. The manufacturers could focus their attention, knowledge, and capital on product and mass-market advertising, leaving customer relations, point-of-sale practices, and the responsibility for service after the sale with the franchisee. The concept served both the manufacturers (franchisors) and their dealers (franchisees) very well. The industries grew to meet the demands of their customers.

Business-format franchising has been found to be a practical tool for franchisors and franchisees in the areas of service and consumer nondurable retail sales. Stories of phenomenal sales illustrate the durability, practicality, and profitability of business-format franchising in restaurants, hotels/motels, auto services, and other retail sales business sectors. Several of these sectors were briefly described to identify sales volumes, number of establishments, company-owned contrasted with franchisee-owned outlets, and trends to highlight the level of activity. Franchising will continue to make an important contribution to American and world business. Over one-third of all U.S retail sales are made by franchised organizations, and that figure is expected to increase during the 1990s. Franchising, as a method of doing business, enables rapid growth for the franchisor with only minimal capital required to be committed to the expansion effort. The franchisee has a high probability of success, statistically much higher than if he or she were to opt for opening an independently owned business.

Franchising by its very nature tends to create new business. It allows the small or medium-size business to compete with giant corporations through the use of the franchisor's trademark, know-how, and product/service quality standards. Because of the assistance offered by the franchisor, even those with limited experience and capital may become successful in the world of franchising.

REVIEW QUESTIONS

1. The franchising concept was not an important factor in American business until the turn of the century. Today it is a major approach to retailing. What reasons can be given for the dramatic development of franchising in the United States?

2. What is meant by business-format franchising?
3. What is meant by product-and-trade-name franchising?
4. A franchisee has a higher probability of success than a typical owner/operator of a small business. Why?
5. Franchising, by its very nature, tends to create new business. Explain.
6. What steps did Ray Kroc, of McDonald's fame, take to develop his franchised business?

CASE STUDY
HAMBURGER PRINCE

The Hamburger Prince restaurant was developed after thorough investigation of similar restaurants in the United States. The restaurant was designed with the concept of providing high-quality hamburgers at a reasonable price in a very clean, western-style environment. Gale Sullivan believes that his hamburger is the finest tasting and best-quality hamburger around, having worked on his recipe for three years before discovering the "perfect" hamburger.

Gale has been in business for the last five years. He opened his second restaurant at the end of his third year, and his third restaurant at the end of his fourth year of operation. Gale's three restaurants are located in a midwestern community with a population of approximately 200,000. Two of the restaurants are situated along business strips adjacent to the state university located in this community. The third restaurant is inside a small urban shopping center about a 7-minute drive from the university.

The restaurants have two ordering stations and one pickup area for the customers. They also have a highly visible and popular drive-thru window which accounts for approximately 45 to 50 percent of each restaurant's business. Gale is interested in locating restaurants in areas that attract the 15-35 age group. He enjoys the university atmosphere and prefers college student customers, and he has had some success with advertising and promotion through the university's newspaper as well as some local high school newspapers. His most successful promotional efforts came when he emphasized the product quality and speedy service. He started using college students as part-time deliverers and has found this delivery service to be highly successful with sales averaging over $6.00 per order.

Gale Sullivan believes his business could succeed in other cities as well and is investigating the possibility of franchising. He realizes that in franchising there is more than just a market to think about: There are legal and financial concerns, as well as considerations about operational store planning that would need to be explored. Before deciding whether to become a franchisor, Gale Sullivan must answer some preliminary questions about franchising itself.

CASE QUESTIONS

1. If Gale seeks to become a franchisor, what franchise categories would his product and service fit?
2. Does Gale have the basic components within his existing business to initiate a franchise business? If not, what components are missing? Would this be typical for an existing business prior to becoming a franchisor?
3. Consider the demand expressed within the food industry for franchised restaurants. (See Tables 1-9 and 1-10.) Does this data suggest growth, stability, or decline within the segment Gale is considering?
4. Gale Sullivan is pondering becoming a franchisor. Could Gale also consider becoming a franchisee? If so, in what business?

REFERENCES

1. *The Business Failure Record*, New York: Dun & Bradstreet, 1978.
2. Church, Nancy Suway, *Future Opportunities in Franchising: A Realistic Appraisal*, New York: Pilot Industries, Inc., 1979.
3. *Directory of Membership, 1985-1986*, Washington, DC: International Franchise Association, 1985.
4. Kostecka, Andy, U.S. Department of Commerce, Bureau of Industrial Economics, *Franchise Opportunities Handbook*, Washington, DC: U.S. Government Printing Office, 1983.
5. Kostecka, Andy, *Franchising in the Economy, 1982-1984; 1983-1985; 1984-1986; 1985-1987; 1986-1988*, Washington, DC: U.S. Government Printing Office, 1984.
6. Whittemore, Meg. "The Great Franchise Boom," *Nation's Business*, September 1984, pp. 20-24.
7. *Franchise Yearbook 1988*, Los Angeles: Entrepreneur Group, Inc., 1988.

CHAPTER 2
FRANCHISING: PROS AND CONS

In studying this chapter, you will:
- Understand why the franchising concept has become so successful in American and international business.
- Learn the advantages of franchising for both the franchisor and the franchisee.
- Learn the potential disadvantages of franchising to the franchisor and the franchisee.
- Learn the seven steps for franchise protection.
- Understand the financial requirements and administrative responsibilities of a franchised business.

INCIDENT

Jack is considering going into business for himself. He spent six years as a computer operator while putting himself through school, and then after completing a computer science degree at a major university, he began work as a programmer at a large bank in his community. Having been with the bank for five years, Jack is now a systems analyst and manages a small group of programmers.

Jack believes it is time to make a career move. He wants to open a business selling personal computers and other electronic equipment. Jack is confident of his technical skills in electronics, especially computers, but is worried about his lack of actual business knowledge and experience. For this reason, he wants to learn more about franchised electronics business opportunities. He believes a franchising approach would provide for the many basic business operations including accounting, legal, and financial responsibilities, leaving him free to sell computers and train his customers on their new machines. Does Jack have a realistic view of franchising, and is becoming a franchisee the answer for him?

INTRODUCTION

Franchising provides the means for a person to own and operate a small business using a workable business format. Franchising is a joint effort between the franchisor and the franchisee with mutually approved activities including site selection, interior and exterior decoration, product preparation, advertising, selling, buying, and training.

Joint Business Relationship

Franchising is an exciting opportunity for franchisor and franchisee. Both have an opportunity to use their limited capital resources and drive to succeed to turn this type of joint business relationship into a means of generating fair and equitable profits that will reward their individual efforts. When properly developed, the franchising approach helps both the franchisor and franchisee realize the profit potential of the business. As a method of distribution of goods or services, franchising provides opportunities for growth and success for both parties. Before committing to a franchising relationship, however, it is important to evaluate the situation and critical factors of the business opportunity being considered.

In analyzing the factors and conditions of many business opportunities, it is often apparent that the factors critical to success are rooted within the franchisor-franchisee relationship. A franchisor not only operates one business, but also influences other operators (franchisees) as they run their own businesses as parts of an integrated franchise system. The franchisee may resent the influence of the franchisor in the running of his or her local business. The franchisee can argue that the profits and overall success of the franchise system are made at the local level, not at corporate headquarters miles away. Because both franchisor and franchisee have important roles to play in achieving success for the franchise system as well as in reaching their own personal goals, they need to understand the importance of cooperation and mutual trust in developing and maintaining a successful franchised business.

Franchising Basics

Franchising has been a successful means of operating a business for several reasons. Two primary reasons are 1) the tremendous preparation a franchisee undertakes before opening an outlet and 2) the degree of personal involvement brought to the business activities by both the franchisee and the franchisor. The greatest difference between starting a franchised business venture and opening an independent business lies in the extensive training and preparation provided to the franchisee prior to the opening of an outlet. A franchisee is taught how to initiate, run, and control all of the functions of the business.

The franchisor will generally grant the franchisee limited use of the trademark or trade name and the system (business format) in return for a royalty fee. The franchisee receives training, guidance, and preparation to use trade secrets, operational procedures and practices, and system-wide promotions to develop and maintain a profitable franchised business. The initial training of the franchisee and any employees of the franchised unit is essential to the successful continuation of the business.

For example, Orange Julius allows its franchisees to use the name, trademark, and logo and sell the special drink products in return for a royalty fee of 5 percent on gross sales, plus an additional advertising fee of 1 percent of gross sales. In addition, most of the leases or outlet locations are controlled by the franchisor — Orange Julius — and subleased back to the franchisee at a small profit.

Another example is First Interstate Bancorp of California, with franchises that have converted from independent institutions to part of the First Interstate bank network. The local ownership and equity are maintained by the franchised bank, but the name and logo of First Interstate Bancorp, plus the basic services including automatic teller machines and other financial services, are controlled by the franchisor, First Interstate Bancorp. In return for this banking franchise, the local bank pays First Interstate Bancorp a fee based on increased interest income. It is important to note that use of the trade name and use of the financial services system constitute the *value added* which this franchisor allows the franchisee bank to use so that both parties can achieve success as a franchise system.

The use of the franchise system generally includes the product or service sold by the franchise. In the automotive industry, the trademarked automobile is readily seen as the greatest value added which the franchisor provides to the franchisee. Gasoline stations and fast-food restaurants, however, often see advertising as the greatest value added by the franchisor to the franchisee.

FRANCHISING: ADVANTAGES AND DISADVANTAGES

There are many success stories in franchising: McDonald's, Singer Sewing Machine, General Motors, Coca Cola, Kentucky Fried Chicken, Midas, Century 21, Wendy's, and Holiday Inns provide visible examples of large, successful franchised businesses. Also, today, other types of businesses including financial institutions are seeking growth through franchising; as noted earlier, First Interstate Bancorp (Los Angeles, California) is franchising banks throughout the United States to build financial strength and expand market share. Doctors, lawyers, dentists, accountants, and opticians are also developing franchise systems, some of which already have multistate markets. A carefully designed and operated franchise system minimizes risk for the franchisee and the franchisor. In essence, the benefits to be gained from a successful franchising chain are enormous.

Advantages to the Franchisee

The franchisee gains a number of potential advantages from being involved in a franchising relationship.

Established Product or Service. The major advantage was mentioned previously, but bears repeating: the franchisee enters a business which has the benefit of an established product or service name. Consumers are already aware of the name and reputation of the product or service the franchisee will be offering. This advantage is assured to the franchisee by virtue of the fact that every year large franchisors spend millions of advertising dollars to keep the public aware of their gasoline, soft drink, beer, food, or service. Such franchisors will generally spend a large portion of their advertising budget on national campaigns through television commercials and full-page advertisements in popular magazines. If a franchise system deals with a specialty product such as Snap-On Tools, the most effective advertising may be through trade publications targeted at specific markets such as home repair buffs or auto mechanics. In contrast with the national franchise systems, small franchisors tend to use local print, electronic media, and point-of-purchase promotions to attract customers from the immediate area. In either case, the franchisor commonly shares advertising costs with the local franchisee. Typically, the franchisor will charge the franchisee an advertising fee based on the gross revenues of the franchised unit.

Technical and Managerial Assistance. A second major advantage to the franchisee is the technical and managerial assistance provided by the franchisor. The franchisee has the opportunity to benefit from the accumulated experience and knowledge of the franchising organization. One can become a franchisee in almost any type of business without prior experience because the franchisor will provide the instruction necessary to operate a franchised unit, including on-the-job training in a pilot store. Once operating his or her own unit, the franchisee receives assistance in managing day-to-day operations as well as advice for dealing with any crisis situations which arise in the operation of the business. Therefore, to reiterate, a person can enter business — most fields of business — without prior experience in that particular field because the franchisor will supply the pilot training needed to develop precise experience and will provide follow-up assistance once the franchised unit has gotten off the ground.

Most business consultants would warn a potential entrepreneur not to attempt a business venture in an unfamiliar field. Franchising provides the opportunity to do exactly that — and be successful! In fact, some franchisors *prefer* franchisees who have no prior experience in their particular business field. The franchisor can thus train the new franchisee in the methods and procedures of the franchising company, and there will be little or nothing to be unlearned, no bad habits to break. In effect, some franchisors are looking not for people who know the industry but who are motivated and willing to follow instructions.

In addition to managerial guidance, the new franchisee will receive technical assistance from the franchisor. Areas of technical assistance often furnished include location and site selection, store layout and design, store remodeling (if the franchisee is converting an existing site), inventory control and suggested stock purchases, equipment and fixture purchasing, and grand opening of the store. It should be noted that although many franchisors provide these specific services, some provide only selected types of assistance. The types of technical assistance provided are usually what the franchisor has found to be absolutely essential for helping the franchisee to be successful. A franchisee should therefore realize that a full range of technical assistance is not always part of the franchising package.

Quality-Control Standards. A third major advantage to the franchisee concerns the quality-control standards imposed by the franchisor upon the franchisee. Properly administered and controlled, such standards help the franchise to achieve constructive, positive results by ensuring product or service uniformity throughout the franchise system. By setting and maintaining high standards, a franchisor does the franchisee a genuine service. Often franchisees appreciate having standard methods of operation and product or service delivery. Why? If the reason for quality standards being maintained is clearly understood, the franchisee will learn what operations and performance are necessary to be a success. Further, standards of quality are vital in presenting a consistent patronage image, ensuring return business, maintaining employee morale and pride in work, and instilling in employees the value of teamwork.

But, one may ask, why would a franchisee want to continually have to meet standards imposed by someone else? The answer to this is, as long as the quality standards are assessed and maintained in a benevolent authoritative manner, the standards serve both franchisor and franchisee.

For example, in franchised restaurants, if franchisees courteously and efficiently serve an appealing meal in an attractive and comfortable setting, they have a better chance to attract and maintain a large, loyal clientele, which clearly benefits the franchisor as well.

Less Operating Capital. The fourth major advantage is that in many cases an entrepreneur can open a franchised business with less cash than if he or she were to open a business independently. Why? Often, a franchisee can start up with considerably less operating capital because the business may not require as much inventory as a comparable non-franchised business. The knowledge and experience of the franchisor that is available to the franchisee concerning how much stock is needed and when to reorder can dramatically reduce the potential for aging of stock, waste or spoilage of perishables, and unprofitable storage of low-demand items. Also, a new franchisee may be able to receive some financial assistance in the form of credit, as cash or as inventory consigned, from the franchisor or from the franchisor's financial resources. Other specifics associated with a new venture, such as having access to existing architectural drawings for the store and knowing how best to utilize floor space for the product or service, can save the franchisee countless hours and dollars, especially considering the number of seat-of-the-pants judgments that must be made three to six months prior to opening a new business.

Other facets of this advantage can be realized once the business is in operation. A franchisee can expect to share in certain collateral benefits, such as business insurance and health insurance, which because of the group buying power of the parent company are often less expensive than the same coverage sought independently. And, a franchisee can expect to have a higher profit margin than a comparable independent business owner because of group purchasing power, proven operational and quality standards, potentially lower inventory costs, and product or service improvements made through research and development by the franchisor that will become available to the franchisee, thus enabling the franchisee to keep the product or service competitive.

Opportunities for Growth. A fifth potential advantage concerns growth opportunities for operating the territorial franchises. A **territorial franchise** guarantees no competition from the same franchisor within the specified geographic boundaries. A territorial franchisee may later be in a position to subfranchise or license other persons to operate stores belonging to the territorial franchisee. If a new franchised company is enjoying successful growth, its franchisees could have more opportunity for financial gain as territorial franchisees than as operating franchisees. In an **operating franchise,** an owner/operator runs the business usually within an exclusive territory and receives assistance from the franchisor (parent company) or from both a territorial franchisee and the parent company. The main distinction, then, is that the operating franchisee typically does not have the legal right to establish subfranchisees or licensees; the territorial franchisee does. However, there is no real standard within the franchised business field to clearly distinguish a territorial franchise from an operating franchise in the case of all franchised companies. There are even a fair number of operator franchisees who, after careful reinvestment of profits into new locations for the franchised company, have developed their own chain of outlets within the franchise chain. Examples of this can be found in Orange Julius, A&W Root Beer, and Mister Donut. Therefore, opportunity for growth as a franchisee exists whether one has territorial rights or is in business simply as an operating franchisee.

The common thread through these five advantages concerns the *advice and assistance available from the franchisor to help the franchisee become successful*, which the franchisor could not have offered without having gained a thorough understanding of the business by spending considerable time in the specific business field. Therefore, we see this opportunity to benefit from another's experience — to learn from someone else's mistakes — as the primary advantage of entering a franchising relationship.

However, these five advantages have to be tempered with a disclaimer, because what we suggest are distinct advantages to the franchisee may not be so for *every* franchisee. What might be a decided advantage to one could be inconsequential to another. Therefore, the merits and demerits, advantages and disadvantages, for an individual should be considered in relation to the conditions surrounding a particular franchising opportunity.

Disadvantages to the Franchisee

Most franchising agreements work well for both the franchisor and the franchisee. The franchising agreement is meant to develop a strong relationship between these two mutually bound profit seekers. The franchising approach helps both to realize profits and to develop a healthy and prosperous business life. However, there are some disadvantages to the franchisee which can be associated with the franchising relationship.

Failed Expectations. The franchisor's business expertise, experience, selling methods, trademark, and advertising typify what a franchisee implicitly seeks to acquire. Because of such assistance, the franchisee sees value in the franchisee-franchisor relationship. Without such assistance, there would be very little reason for a prospective business owner to enter a franchising agreement. But if a franchisor's sales practices mislead a potential franchisee about what he or she will receive from the franchisor, the franchisee's expectations will of course not be met. Misleading or fraudulent sales practices can actually victimize some potential franchisees.

Franchises are promoted through newspapers, magazines, trade conventions, telegrams, and even phone calls from franchised companies. Some prospective franchisees fail to carefully read the "fine print" or consult an attorney and as a result have little or no understanding of the legal and practical implications of the agreement. What the franchisor will provide is written in the franchising agreement, not necessarily in the sales literature associated with the agreement. Since these agreements can be rather lengthy and are often in small print, some prospective franchisees truly do not understand what they are about to agree to legally. If a prospective franchisee seeks a modification in the contract, the franchisor, who undeniably has the upper hand, will often be unwilling to approve any such modification, especially if it represents a substantial deviation from the standard contract. Franchisors often contend they can serve franchisees best when franchisees conform to quality standards, and so in drafting the franchising agreement particularly focus on the factors believed to be most important to ensure this conformance. It is implicitly important to the franchisor that a prospective franchisee recognize the psychologically superior position the franchisor likes to maintain.

Service Costs. Another consideration that can be an enduring disadvantage to a franchisee is that services provided by a franchisor have costs which must be borne by the franchisee. These services, then, are expense items to the franchisee, and in some instances, they may be of dubious value to the franchisee. In some cases, it may be difficult for the franchisor to maintain the services promised and initially rendered as stipulated in the written franchising agreement. Also, the franchisee could begin to find the franchise fees or royalties excessive, especially after being in business for several months and realizing the effect that the royalties and fees are having on the return on investment. Franchisees may even find it psychologically difficult to share profits earned from their own business by remitting a required percentage back to the franchisor.

Overdependence. The third potential disadvantage to the franchisee concerns the franchisor-franchisee relationship. The relationship may prove to be detrimental if a franchisee develops a problem of **overdependence** on the franchisor. A franchisee can become too dependent on the advice of the franchisor to address operations, crises, changing market conditions, pricing strategy, or promotions and so may fail to apply common sense and knowledge of local customers and market conditions. For example, price discounting can make sense if the local market conditions warrant such moves.

Recent discussion with a franchisor of auto parts illustrated this disadvantage. The franchisor has a policy of no price discounting, *if possible*, to maintain a uniform pricing structure across the franchised organization's outlets. A franchisee in a large city in the Southwest failed to take note of the phrase "if possible" and so lost an opportunity to substantially increase volume by attracting the regular business of an auto repair and service center with 17 locations. The franchisee could have obtained a contract with the repair center if he had been willing to adjust the bid downward only two tenths of one percent. In this case, the franchisor rightfully scolded the franchisee for not using common sense. A fairly knowledgeable businessperson knows that the guarantee of a large volume of business is a solid reason for price discounting.

Restrictions on Freedom of Ownership. Another potential disadvantage to the franchisee is that the franchising contract may contain restrictions or requirements that an independent businessperson would not have to satisfy. For example, territorial restrictions imposed by the franchisor may limit the number of potential customer contacts a franchisee might seek; or, territories may overlap or be inequitably determined by a franchisor. The franchisee might also be required to offer a particular product or service that he or she would not otherwise choose to offer. Further, a franchisee may feel that some of the franchisor's advertising or promotions are impractical given local market conditions, or that a promotion or advertisement is offensive or unwisely encourages the sale of relatively unprofitable product or service lines offered by the franchise.

Termination of Agreement. The next major disadvantage concerns a franchisee's decision to terminate the franchising relationship as a result of perceived or real differences with the franchisor. Lack of cooperation from the franchisor can make it difficult to sell the business to a prospective buyer or to simply dissolve the business entirely. Virtually every franchising agreement contains provisions concerning the franchisee's transfer rights, termination and renewal of the agreement, or a covenant not to compete. Any one or all three of these provisions could be invoked by the franchisor if the franchisee fails to heed all the provisions of the franchising agreement. More will be said about these terms and their meanings and ramifications later in the book.

Performance of Other Franchisees. Perhaps the least-considered potential disadvantage to the franchisee is the effect that lackluster performance by other franchisees can have on one's own business. If the franchisor becomes lax in managing the franchise system or does not enforce the quality standards imposed throughout the network, the poor performance of some in the franchise network can affect the sales of others. Usually, a customer of a multi-unit franchised company will tend to blame the entire franchise and not the single operating unit for poor service or low quality. As the franchising adage goes, a stale cup of coffee at one location will lose customers for the other locations.

The common theme in each of these disadvantages involves the dependence the franchisee has on the franchisor. In effect, the greatest disadvantage is the tendency by franchisees to be overly dependent upon the franchisor and franchise system. Franchisees can depend too much on advice from the parent company, rely too heavily on its advertising and promotional efforts, or follow too closely the operating manual suggestions while neglecting their own common sense and intuitive understanding of the local market and conditions.

In summary, the franchisee must determine whether the advantages of the franchisor's training, operations manuals, blueprints, and products and services outweigh the disadvantages always present in working with a parent company. The franchisee needs to carefully weigh the possible advantages against the disadvantages, while at the same time analyzing the potential profitability of the business, to determine his or her willingness to enter this business activity with the conditions imposed by the franchisor. A franchisee should realize that even though he or she owns the business, certain standards and performance quotas will be established and demanded by the franchisor to ensure that the franchise system will be profitable and successful in the competitive business environment. Ultimately, the decision to enter the franchising field always rests with the prospective franchisee, and typically, the potential advantages tend to outweigh the disadvantages.

Advantages to the Franchisor

Considering possible channels of distribution for General Motors cars, Alfred P. Sloan saw the two primary options to be "manufacturer-owned, manager-operated dealerships, or the selling of cars by anyone and everyone, as cigarettes are sold — with the manufacturer maintaining a system of service agencies. . . ." Sloan concluded that "the franchise system, which has long prevailed in the automobile industry, is the best one for manufacturers, dealers, and consumers."[1] The success of franchising in the auto industry is well documented, but the franchising approach has not worked as well in the selling of furniture, for instance. On the other hand, franchising has become quite successful in appliance sales, oil distribution, restauranting, and many service-oriented business fields.

Expansion. Historically, most businesses have grown through expansion of their distribution system. Yet the average business owner wishing to broaden distribution of a product or service may not have the

---

[1] Alfred P. Sloan, Jr., *My Years with General Motors* (Garden City, NY: Doubleday & Company, 1964), p. 301.

options to consider that Alfred Sloan had. In fact, franchising may be the only viable option for growth, unless that owner would choose to become part of a larger existing company either as a captive producer or as a franchisee, or choose to expand at a slow pace by saving profits earned from the principal business. Whereas a business with sizable funds can choose from several alternatives to expand distribution, a business with limited capital and experience may find franchising to be the only viable method of expansion. Expansion efforts are costly, and franchising provides an opportunity to share this burden on the road to success.

Perhaps the single greatest reason for an entrepreneur to create a franchising chain is to allow a business to expand with limited capital, limited risk, and equity investment. A franchisor does not have to inject large sums of money or incur major debt in order to expand the business into new locations. Franchisors can authorize and then locate franchised operations in selected areas gradually or they can choose to develop business locations throughout a region or country. A franchised company requires few management personnel and therefore has a lower staff payroll and fewer staff problems. This suggests a greater likelihood of effective monitoring and control of company operations. Also, a franchisor may find potential investors willing to buy into the franchised company if the company is seen to promise continuing profitability. Similarly, persons with little or no experience in the franchisor's business field may be willing to buy a franchise as a potentially profitable investment. Thus, franchising can attract capital through direct investment in the parent company or through the sale of franchises to be used for expansion of the franchise system.

A related advantage is that the franchising approach provides an opportunity for the parent company to expand into geographic areas that otherwise might not be likely locations for expansion. When a franchised company acquires a franchisee within a particular community, that franchisee may be able to acquire a commercial site that the parent company would be unable to acquire because of the fear of potential influence patterns and other vagaries that can be associated with zoning ordinances, business regulations, and/or licensing restrictions in the local community.

Another reason for a business owner to expand through franchising is that this type of growth can simplify the management structure and reporting requirements associated with expansion, especially compared with the expansion of a corporate chain. For a corporate chain, a strategy that looks for more rapid growth than the corporation has previously experienced usually requires the formation of a sizable management structure to develop, implement, monitor, and control the enhanced level of operations. Unless a corporation carefully manages its growth phase, growth can be as much a problem as an opportunity. The capacity of central management to control the business activity may not be able to keep pace with the growth of the corporation itself. When this happens, inconsistency in operations, breakdowns in communications, coordination problems, and even cash flow and liquidity problems can virtually negate the advantages of the expansion. In contrast, rapid expansion through a franchising network enables the franchisor to devote more time to operational planning, market analysis and assessment, quality control, and strategies for improving the franchise system itself.

Motivation. Another advantage to the franchisor is that the franchisee is generally more highly motivated than the company-employed manager. When a franchised unit is operated by an owner as opposed to a company-employed manager, that unit will usually benefit from the owner's motivation, self-direction, and personal interest in the success of that operation. In addition, the franchisee is often a respected and influential member of the local community, and so will have community support which will be of assistance in developing a franchised outlet.

Operation of Non-Union Business. In the decision whether to franchise, a business owner should also give consideration to the area of employee and labor relations. There is greater likelihood that company-owned units would be more attractive to union organizers than would franchised units, largely because a single franchised operating unit is less likely to be unionized and to develop labor relations appropriate to the local supply-and-demand conditions of the labor pool. The advantage to the franchisor in this regard is the savings in the amount of wages and benefits to be paid to the employees. Or, to put it in plain terms, it simply costs less to operate a non-union business.

Bulk Purchasing. A further advantage exists for franchisors in businesses that require inventory of parts, completed units for sale, and supplies or packaging associated with the production or sale of the product. Economy of scale in purchasing (that is, purchasing power) can be achieved more rapidly by a company choosing franchising compared with a company that expands through company-owned units.

Other Advantages. There are also some other advantages to being a franchisor. A franchisor is free to use a part of the company's capital for purposes other than expansion, because the franchisee has also invested capital in the new operating unit. Also, cooperative advertising (with franchisor and franchisee sharing costs of advertising) tends to achieve much more than individual advertising. And, since the franchisee is usually a member of the local community where the franchised unit is opened, the franchisor is less likely to stir up hostility than he or she would by opening a "foreign" or non-locally owned corporate chain store. Finally, because the franchisee is a local citizen, not just someone moving into a community to manage a chain store, the franchisee would tend to have a perspective different from that of the corporate manager and would try to ensure community acceptance, sales growth, and profitability over a longer term.

Disadvantages to the Franchisor

Franchising is by no means a miraculous or problem-free solution to a distribution problem. The idea of using money belonging to other individuals to finance the major part of a business expansion is no doubt exciting, but the application of that idea can be fraught with difficulty. The foremost problem or challenge is how to maintain control of the expanding franchise system and oversee the general operations of each business. In addition, a franchisee may in time re-evaluate the franchising relationship and come to the conclusion that he or she would be able to do just as well — or better — without the franchisor. This particular disadvantage of franchising, as well as others, is discussed below. Two perspectives are used to describe potential disadvantages: First, advantages of company-owned units will be discussed alongside disadvantages of franchised units; second, difficulties associated with the franchisor-franchisee relationship will be listed.

Company-Owned versus Franchised Units. Expanding operations by establishing company-owned units has several clear advantages over expanding by franchising. A parent company, or owner, has more control over units the company owns; can institute changes in policy and procedures more readily; can change company mission and market strategy more quickly and perhaps more effectively; and can test out new products or processes with less time and paperwork. Also, since the company controls the outlets by virtue of ownership, the system of reporting — that is, the managerial monitoring and control of the operating units — should be more efficient and effective because the company chain is set up as a hierarchy of managerial authority. The ownership not only establishes company strategies and operating policies but is also assured of the implementation of these strategies by virtue of its maintaining ownership of the company through to the retail distribution outlets. Those responsible for carrying out the operations of a company-owned retail outlet are employees of the company, not independent business owners themselves. And, regardless if the ownership chooses to expand through company-owned outlets or through franchising, it will need to offer basically the same services from the home office — sales promotion, marketing research, accounting and information systems, and a field sales department or unit.

Two other significant points tend to favor the company-owned approach over the franchising approach to expansion. First, a franchisee might typically expect to recover his or her initial investment in perhaps two to three years — that's a 33.3 to 50 percent return on investment to the franchisee. This means that the franchisor has effectively lost out on making this remarkable profit on his or her own, since the franchisor could probably get the money necessary for expansion more cheaply by dealing directly with equity investors or obtaining loans from financial institutions. Second, there can be some legal advantages to a company-owned, fully integrated operation. Integrated chains of stores such as May Company, which owns Famous Barr and Venture Stores, or Wal-Mart Stores, Inc., have become quite successful without franchising. According to Charles Vaughn, "Integrated chains do not so often come under antitrust fire, class action suits, and other legal attacks."[2] Litigation can drag on for so long and become so costly that a business owner considering franchising could be scared off for the legal reason alone. More will be said about franchising and the law in Part Two of this book.

Potential Problems. Within the franchisor-franchisee relationship, there are three categories of potential disadvantage for the franchisor: problems of recruitment, communication, and freedom.

Recruitment. The recruitment problem concerns the difficulty of finding promising franchisees. While there are many who seek franchising as a means to enter business, most lack the experience or motivation and many the proper capital backing they will need to become successful franchisees. Also, prospective franchisees may not fully realize the amount of time, work, and responsibility required to own and operate an ongoing franchised business.

Communication. As in any business relationship, communication problems can arise. In a franchising relationship, a franchisee may develop a sense of independence and thus may no longer feel a need to rely on communication with the franchisor for the successful operation of the business; he or she may conclude that the business would run just as smoothly without the franchisor's advice and seek to discontinue the relationship. This feeling can stem from the franchisee's having to pay fees and royalties established by the franchising agreeement. Most franchisees pay fees to the franchisor on the basis of the franchised unit's gross income. Some franchisees may have a difference of opinion as to what constitutes "gross income," or develop a reluctance to disclose gross income figures to the franchisor. For this reason it is important that the formula for determining any fees or royalties be clearly stated in the written franchising agreement and understood by both franchisor and franchisee. When such understandings exist, the likelihood of resentments based on unclear language or personal intent can be minimized. Also, communication problems can arise between the field office staff and the individual franchisees. The franchisor's staff is available to assist as well as monitor performance of franchisees. Both parties play an im-

---

[2] Charles L. Vaughn, *Franchising*, 2nd edition (Lexington, MA: Lexington Books, D.C. Heath Company, 1979), p. 65.

portant part in the successful delivery of the product or service through the franchised company network. In any organizational arrangement, however, misunderstandings, personality differences, and political maneuverings can blunt the effectiveness of the franchising system to deliver that product or service. Each party to the franchising agreement should operate within the proper boundaries of the agreement, the laws governing business transactions, and professional codes of ethics. When those involved in continuing business transactions deal with one another honestly and professionally, communication problems will not typically occur.

Loss of Freedom. The third potential disadvantage concerns the franchisor's loss of freedom as new franchisees become part of the franchise system. Independent businesspersons can easily make decisions and change policies within their organizations. But once a franchise system is developed, the franchisor or parent company must get permission (often negotiated individually) from franchisees to introduce new products, to add or eliminate services, or to change operating policies. Thus, the franchisor stands to lose a substantial amount of control once a franchise system increases its size to any great degree. It can become extremely difficult for the franchisor to modify product or process in order to meet the ever-changing needs of customers, particularly if the franchise system is spread across a large geographic area containing varied consumer markets.

In summary, potential franchisors and franchisees should carefully examine the advantages and disadvantages of the franchising approach to business. Franchising can be a positive arrangement for both franchisor and franchisee, but each should also understand the drawbacks of being involved in a franchising relationship.

Careful examination of the franchising-only in contrast to the company-owned-only approach to business growth has brought many successful companies to the following conclusion: The use of a combination of company-owned and franchisee-owned operating units appears to be superior to the use of either approach exclusively.[3] Thus, the two approaches do not have to be considered mutually exclusive; they can supplement each other, stimulating growth for the company and strengthening the firm's ability to meet the challenges and opportunities of the marketplace.

INVESTING IN A FRANCHISE

Every business investment involves risk. For a potential franchisee, investing in a franchise is somewhat different from buying stocks or bonds

---

[3] *Franchising*, p. 65.

or investing in bank certificates. Investing in a franchise generally requires both time and money. For most franchisees, time will be the greatest contribution made to the business venture: Sixty-five to eighty hours of work every week is common during the startup of a franchised outlet.

The cost of investing in a franchise also varies according to the success of that particular franchised company. Coca Cola bottlers, General Motors dealerships, and McDonald's restaurants are often known as "blue-chip" franchises because of their successful track records. In other, newer fields such as electronics and computing, franchised companies are newer and so investments in them are perceived as being more risky or speculative, even though these companies may be wildly successful in the future.

When investigating whether to invest in a franchise, one is relying not only on the performance record of the company but also on personal experience, business skills, and aptitude for franchise ownership. It is important that a prospective franchisee have a good understanding of his or her current business strengths and weaknesses in the field being considered, as well as the management skills necessary to run any business.

There are other areas a prospective franchisee should consider before investing in a franchise. The *Franchise Opportunities Handbook*, developed and distributed by the U.S. Department of Commerce, suggests seven areas of protection one should consider before investing in a franchise. (See Table 2-1.)

As we have said, there is risk associated with any form of investment, and some franchises present a greater degree of risk than others. If a person decides to leave a good job to purchase and operate a franchise, he or she will probably have a lot more to lose than if that person were to choose a less risky form of investment. After all, there is always a chance that the franchise will not succeed.

Investigation

It is wise to investigate the franchise being considered by comparison shopping of other franchises in the same line of business, just as it is a good idea to look at more than one car, major appliance, or house before deciding which to buy. A disclosure document (sometimes called an offering circular or prospectus) will help in making the comparison in risks involved, expectations of the franchisor, franchising fees, any continuing payments required after the franchise is open, restrictions on the product or service offered, assistance and training available, statistical information about the franchise, financial statements of the franchisor, and any claims of earnings.

After careful examination of the disclosure document, one should check the accuracy of the information included in the disclosure docu-

Table 2-1
The Seven Steps for Franchise Protection

1. Protect yourself by self-evaluation.
2. Protect yourself by investigating the franchise.
3. Protect yourself by studying the disclosure document.
4. Protect yourself by checking out the disclosures.
5. Protect yourself by questioning earnings claims.
6. Protect yourself by obtaining professional advice.
7. Protect yourself by knowing your legal rights.

Source: U.S. Department of Commerce, *Franchise Opportunities Handbook*, 1984, pp. xxx-xxxii.

ment by talking with more than one franchisee of that company, because no single opinion can accurately paint a composite picture of the company. If the franchise is worth considering, it is a good idea to talk with three or more franchisees who have been in business at least one year, as well as to talk with a new franchisee and a well-established franchisee with a proven track record. Across this range of franchisees, one should be able to get good advice about what to expect in the first year as well as in ensuing years.

It is also important to examine any claims made by the franchisor or the franchised company's representative concerning sales, income, or profits expected from the franchise. Earnings claims are only *estimates*; there is no assurance that every franchisee will do as well. We will address earnings claims in another chapter, as well as discuss the disclosure document in some detail.

Before deciding to "come on board" with a certain franchisor, one should obtain independent professional assistance in reviewing and evaluating the franchise. Such assistance and advice is of particular importance in reviewing the financial statements provided and the franchising agreement to be signed. The assumption should not be made that a disclosure document reveals all that needs to be known about the rights, responsibilities, and consequences of signing a franchising agreement with a company. The disclosure document is not designed to serve that purpose. Prospective franchisees should learn precisely what they will be legally bound to do or restricted from doing, any requirements of state or local laws as they apply in the particular business field, and answers to any personal liability or taxation questions that should be considered before signing a binding contract and entering business. There is no way of stating everything that should be considered before signing, but at least one should be certain that every important promise made by the franchisor or parent company is in writing, clearly stated in the contract.

Financial Requirements

To promote a fuller understanding of the financial requirements placed on a potential franchisee, this section briefly discusses the financial requirements franchisors and franchisees must consider when developing or entering a franchise system.

Franchisor. For the franchisor, there are areas of capital requirement that must be addressed both prior to the development of a franchise system and on a continuing basis as the system is maintained and further developed. These categories are interrelated, and each is distinct and important to the continuation of the franchise system. The four categories are as follows:

1. Capital requirements for industrial research, prototype development, marketing research, and blueprint development.
2. Capital requirements for franchise package including all disclosure statements, franchisee recruitment, promotions, product/service development costs, and operations development costs.
3. Working capital requirements involving the initial advertising and franchisee recruitment expenditures.
4. Reserve and legal capital requirements, including money for registering the firm to do business within a state and for meeting the state's licensing or disclosure requirements. In many states, a certain amount of capital is required to be maintained — as a reserve — in order to do business in that state.

In addition to these considerations, there can be hidden costs which must be borne, including unexpected legal, accounting, and research costs. The franchisor should consider each category of expenditure both from a chronological perspective and in terms of the total financial commitment. A chronological perspective means that capital must be available as each phase of the franchise development plan is entered. (More will be said about the phased development of a franchise system in Chapters 3 and 8.) Also, it is important that capital in all requirement categories be available when payment for these expenditures comes due. This places a formidable burden upon the franchisor in his or her efforts to develop a franchise system.

The capital requirements for a franchise operation can vary according to the particular type of activity and business involved. However, certain key capital requirements seem to be associated with any franchise organization; they are identified in Table 2-2. Typically, a franchisor's initial capital requirements may fall somewhere between $110,000 and $950,000, plus those expenses necessary to build and furnish a company-owned prototype store or outlet. For example, a prototype outlet may be the original restaurant, used as the "design store" for all those that follow. Often a prototype is also used as the showcase or train-

**Table 2-2
Capital Requirements**

	Minimum Requirements	Maximum Requirements
Research blueprint	$5,000	$50,000
Franchise development	25,000	100,000
Working capital	50,000	500,000
Reserve legal capital	30,000	300,000
Total capital required (excluding prototype development)	$110,000	950,000

ing facility for prospective franchisees. The prototype expenditures will involve the costs of land, building, fixtures, and equipment. The fixed costs of the prototype can run anywhere from $5,000 for leasing space, to over $1 million for a restaurant and as much as $7 to $15 million for a hotel or motel.

Franchisee. Like the franchisor, the franchisee will also have financial requirements to consider prior to becoming part of a franchise system. Specifically, the capital requirements or concerns of a franchisee can be enumerated in the following six categories:

1. Franchising fee
2. Real estate or rental costs, including building costs
3. Personal living and travel costs
4. Equipment costs
5. Startup expenses and inventory
6. Working capital

The startup expenses include all legal costs associated with opening any business, such as the review of the franchising agreement plus any leases or contracts to be signed by the franchisee. In addition, an initial inventory would need to be purchased and financial commitments made before the business opens. Inventory selection may be guided by the terms of the franchising contract. For example, a drive-up and walk-in restaurant would likely have napkins, cups, plates, food packaging, place mats, and other items carrying the franchise trademark or logo. Auto parts stores and auto repair shops would perhaps have a specified inventory that comes from the parent company. Each type of franchise may vary considerably as to how much trademarked product or packaging is required for an initial inventory level in a startup franchised business.

Other costs can become substantial and must be carefully planned for. For example, to be considered seriously as a franchisee of Wendy's Old Fashioned Hamburgers, one should have about $700,000 in credit and $150,000 in liquid assets, with which to lease or buy the land, building, and equipment, purchase supplies, and hire employees to operate the restaurant. If, on the other hand, Wendy's arranges for the restaurant site and to have the restaurant built, the additional cost to the franchisee would be $20,000. Added to the franchising fee of $20,000, this means a new Wendy's franchisee would need $40,000.[4] These figures are not out of the ordinary, while at the same time not all franchising fees or startup expenses and required credit lines are in the same range as those required by Wendy's. Some are higher, such as in hotel or motel franchises, and many are lower. For example, a franchisee may be able to open a carpet cleaning franchise with as little as $5,000 total capital commitment.

As observed, initial costs can be substantial, and working capital requirements to maintain adequate cash flow and keep the business afloat can be heavy. A franchisee should not discount personal living costs either. If an owner of a franchised business puts in 60 or more hours per week, he or she should be compensated for that time, not just in business profits but also in salary. A salary is an expense item of the business, whereas the profit made from the business is a residual.

With the financial resources required, personal time and energy committed, and risks associated with entering any business venture, franchising is not really a get-rich-quick opportunity for most franchisors and franchisees. Certainly there are some who have "made it quick," but many franchisors consider their businesses to be long-term investments and will shun prospective franchisees interested only in a fast buck. "If you are going to do that, we don't want you," says R. David Thomas, senior chairman of Wendy's International.[5] Many other respected franchise organizations share Mr. Thomas's view. In effect, franchisees aren't advised to get in the game unless they are planning to remain for the long haul.

The primary consideration for the franchisee is that the capital required will likely be the same or more for starting a franchise business than it will be for starting an independent business in the same field. Almost all basic business expenses (real estate, equipment, inventories, personal expenses, and startup costs) remain the same regardless if the business is independent or a franchise. There are additional costs for a franchise including franchising fees, royalties, travel costs to and from the training facility, and training fees. It is not possible to state absolutely that the costs of becoming a franchisee will be higher than the costs of

---

[4] "Where's the Beef in Franchising?" *Money* (March 1985), p. 149.
[5] Ibid., p. 152.

opening an independent business in the same field, but it is likely they will be higher because many people would not enter business with the amount of new equipment, the same-size building, the amount budgeted for advertising, and the costs incurred for training as they would in many franchised businesses.

Typical elements included in a franchising agreement are listed in Table 2-3. The list is not meant to contain specific elements included in *all* franchise agreements; rather, this list indicates what is *typically* included in a franchise agreement. Each franchise system is unique, having particular requirements or conditions that may not be found in the agreements of other franchise systems. Yet, the listed elements are common, and so should be understood and planned for in considering a franchised business.

Further discussions of financial topics such as cash flow, financial statements, and financial ratios are presented in Chapters 10 and 11. Other elements often associated with a franchising agreement are covered in appropriate chapters in this book, in order to provide information of use to prospective franchisors and franchisees.

Franchisor-Franchisee Relationship

Franchisors and franchisees have a relationship somewhat different from relationships in other cooperating business ventures. Being a franchisee is more than just managing an outlet of a company-run distribution system, or carrying a product for retail sale that has been purchased and inventoried from a variety of wholesalers, distributors, or manufacturers. Being a franchisor requires planning, monitoring, and an involvement with the franchisee that differs from the sort of interaction between the head of a company and the managers of the company-owned outlets or retailers willing to carry the product line.

A Kentucky Fried Chicken franchisee in Lincoln, Nebraska, expressed the relationship rather clearly. Jim Gaylord's description of the franchisor-franchisee relationship follows:

> What is the relationship like? Well, it's like a triangle, or triad. We really have three types of relationships. There is the legal agreement between the franchisor and franchisee — which requires certain activities and responsibilities from each party. Then, there is the business relationship which ties the two firms together in day-to-day activities of providing service to customers. The legal relationship is static, while the business relationship is dynamic — moving and flowing with the changing conditions of being in business. It is this business relationship that really bonds the franchisor and franchisee together — trying to meet consumers' needs through your franchise business. I call this relationship the "marriage." It has its ups and downs, but the basic understanding exists to meet the public's needs while relying on one another to provide the best products and services to the cus-

Table 2-3
Typical Elements Covered in a Franchising Agreement

Franchising fee	Signs
Quality control	Business hours
Advertising	Decor
Products and/or services available	Reporting
Royalties	Bookkeeping
Equipment	Supplies
Location requirements	Personnel (appearance and training)
Facilities	Franchisor-franchisee relationships
Maintenance	Others

tomer as possible. The third relationship is the hardest to describe. There are two independent business people, a franchisor and a franchisee, each acting individually for their own best interest. After all, each is a separate business. They don't have a joint tax return![6]

The authors' discussion with other franchisees and several franchisors operating businesses in auto parts, lodging, carpet cleaning, and phone book covers reaffirms the same concept, even though different words were used and different examples given. In effect, the franchisor-franchisee relationship has three distinct elements or parts: the legal agreement or contract, the business relationship to deliver the agreed-upon product or services to the customer, and the independent stature of each party as franchisor or franchisee. (See Figure 2-1.)

Awareness of this three-part relationship is essential to understanding the franchising approach to business. Whether one is interested in learning about franchising, or in becoming a franchisee or a franchisor, it is very important to understand the relationship and the perspectives and approaches of both parties in the relationship. This triad is also useful for describing the reasons franchising has become so successful as an approach to business in our economy: Because a franchisee is in theory generally more motivated and personally involved than a salaried manager of a business and so would work harder, a franchisor would need fewer employees to maintain the same number of operating stores; also, the quality controls established by the franchisor, when properly developed and reasonably enforced, will help maintain standards of excellence throughout the franchise system and so help to ensure the profitability of the business.

The legal agreement and the operations manual associated with it typically describe the role in the franchise system that franchisor and franchisee play. The supporting descriptions and guidelines in these documents provide direction for the operating policies and procedures contained in the operations manual. Within such an agreement usually a

---

[6] Interview with E. James Gaylord, at Joint Industry/Academic Advisory Council meeting held at the University of Nebraska, Franchise Studies Center, September, 1985.

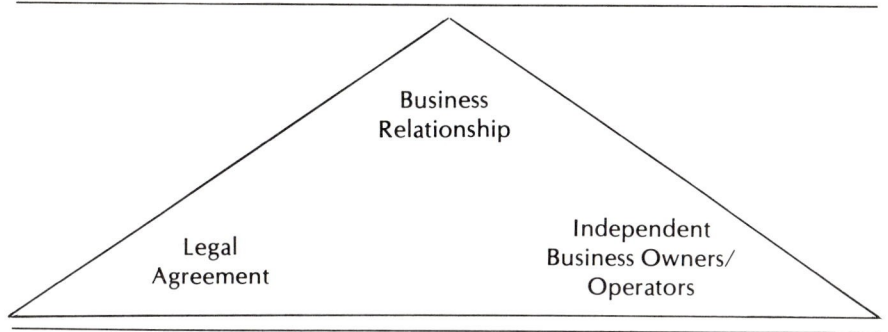

**Figure 2-1
Franchisor-Franchisee Triad Relationship**

```
            Business
           Relationship


   Legal                    Independent
  Agreement               Business Owners/
                             Operators
```

percentage of gross sales is stipulated to be allocated for national and local advertising programs. In addition, franchisees may join together to buy supplies. As we have said, franchisees may buy larger quantities when placing group orders and receive discounts because of the size of their orders.

In considerations of marketing, franchising also allows greater market penetration since the development of several market locations can occur simultaneously, because the franchisees do the development in their particular market areas as independent business owners. In this way, the franchisor serves as the strategist/controller while the franchisee serves as the developer. The franchisee is an independent businessperson, motivated to succeed. Because a franchisee already has his or her own business, with the advantage of help from the franchisor through technical and managerial advice, it is not common for the franchisee to leave the franchising field to start an independent business. After all, the franchisee is not an employee; the franchisee is self-employed while being involved in a joint venture with the franchisor.

SUCCESS STORY
STANLEY BRESLER

Born in 1935, native Chicagoan Stanley Bresler holds a business degree from Roosevelt University and an agricultural degree from Penn State University. He has worked in all phases of ice cream manufacturing and administrative divisions of Bresler Ice Cream Company.

Bresler is now the president of Bresler's 33 Flavor's, Inc., a nationally recognized chain of ice cream shops with approximately 400 franchised and company-owned units in 35 states and Canada. He is also a vice-president and chairman of the board and director of Convenient Food Mart, Inc., a nationwide franchised convenience food store chain with over 1150 outlets operating in 40 states, Canada, and Southeast Asia (Malaysia and Singapore).

Bresler is also the president of Bresler Realty Company, a developer and owner of office and industrial buildings and shopping center strips usually occupied by Convenient Food Mart stores and various other retail businesses. Additionally, he has served and presently serves as a member of the board of numerous other companies. He is the immediate past president of the International Franchise Association and a director of that organization since 1972.

Photo and information provided courtesy of Stanley Bresler, August, 1985.

SUMMARY

Tremendous preparation is needed before a franchisee opens a franchised outlet. There is a strong degree of personal involvement brought to the business activities by both franchisor and franchisee. To a franchisor, franchising means potential for growth at a rate that can far exceed the rate typical of growth through wholly owned outlets. To a franchisee, franchising means the opportunity for extensive training and preparation prior to opening an outlet, plus use of a recognizable name, trademark, or logo associated with the products or services to be offered.

Both franchisor and franchisee have advantages and disadvantages that stem from their involvement in a franchising relationship. The greatest advantage to the franchisee is the help available from the parent organization. Possibly the franchisee's greatest disadvantage lies in the inclination to overdepend on help from the franchisor. The franchisee can rely too much on the franchisor to solve problems or make decisions about running the day-to-day activities of the franchised outlet.

For the franchisor, perhaps the greatest single advantage is the chance to expand the business with limited capital risk and equity investment. Because of the investment by the franchisee, a franchisor doesn't have to inject large sums of money or incur major debt to expand the business into new locations. On the other hand, franchising can be fraught with difficulty for the franchisor. The greatest problem or challenge is whether the franchisor (or parent company) will be able to maintain control over an expanding franchise system while overseeing the general operations of each outlet.

The franchisee-franchisor business relationship is a common mission to ensure that both entities (parent company and franchised unit) succeed. In achieving this goal, there can be problems, particularly in recruiting the right type of franchisees, maintaining accurate and meaningful communication between the two parties, and minimizing the vulnerability of each outlet as new franchisees are brought into the system. An individual franchisee is vulnerable if another franchisee does not maintain the same quality standards. Serving a bad cup of coffee can affect business at all locations of a franchise. Similarly, if the franchisor seeks to modify the product line, eliminate a service, or change an operating policy or other facet of the franchise system, it can be extremely difficult to achieve consensus among all franchisees regarding the proposed change.

Investing in a franchise, like any other business investment, involves risk. Seven steps for protection from the risks of franchising were presented; a potential franchisee will want to consider these steps before signing a franchising agreement.

The capital requirements of franchising were discussed from the perspective of both franchisor and franchisee. A franchisor will have capital requirements that must be addressed prior to development of a franchise system as well as on a continuing basis as the system is maintained or further developed. Capital requirements for a particular franchised operation can vary according to the type of activity involved and business conditions encountered. Typically, a franchisor's initial investment may range from $100,000 to $1,000,000 or more.

Like the franchisor, the prospective franchisee will also have financial requirements to consider. The capital requirements are divided into six categories: franchising fee, real estate or rental costs, personal living and travel costs, equipment costs, startup expenses and inventory, and working capital requirements. Initial costs, as well as working capital requirements, can be substantial. Depending on the franchise an individual seeks, however, one can enter franchising for as little as $5,000. But despite its apparent profitability, franchising is not a get-rich-quick opportunity for most franchisors or franchisees. In fact, many reputable franchisors shun potential franchisees who have notions of becoming "instant millionaires." Entering a franchised business can and probably will be more costly than entering the same field of business as an independent entrepreneur. However, the added financial commitment can pay dividends for those seeking a safer way to enter business.

Typical elements included in a franchising agreement were listed to identify what a prospective franchisee should consider before making the jump into franchising. Topics included in the list are addressed in subsequent chapters of the book.

REVIEW QUESTIONS

1. What are the principal reasons franchising can be a positive experience for both the franchisor and the franchisee?
2. Which of these reasons are common to both franchisor and franchisee?

3. Which of these reasons are different for the franchisor and the franchisee?
4. Who — the franchisor or the franchisee — has a greater potential of advantage through the franchising concept? Explain your reasons.
5. What capital requirements are associated with any franchised business?
6. Can you identify other areas where financial concerns or commitments may have to be addressed if the business considered involves retailing a product? Retailing a service? Wholesaling a product?
7. What are the typical elements covered in a franchising agreement between a franchisor and a franchisee?

CASE STUDY
RICK'S CONVENIENCE FOOD STORE

Rick wants to become a convenience food store franchisee. He has been working in a convenience food store for the four years since he graduated from high school. He has saved approximately $25,000 which could be used for initial investment, startup costs needed in a new business, and short-term living expenses. He believes that he would be successful in owning and managing his own convenience food store.

Rick would like to locate his store in an expanding part of the city where there has been new multiple and single-family housing development. He expects to be open from about 6:00 A.M. to midnight. He wants to offer a complete line of quality merchandise appropriate to a convenience food store, and believes franchising would be the best method for him to enter business. Rick is also thinking that a franchisor would help him find sites and choose a proper location. Rick would like to own the building and the property; however, because of lack of initial investment capital he may have to settle for signing a long-term lease for the location from the franchisor.

Rick really wants to learn the advantages and disadvantages of franchising. He also wants to know whom he should contact to become a franchisee. Also, Rick has heard that some franchisors require their stores to be open 24 hours a day, seven days a week, and often they require that new franchisees get up to two weeks of training in classes, followed by one week of in-store training, before a new store is opened. Some franchisors also have bookkeeping or record keeping assistance available to franchisees. Rick has talked to one franchisee who mentioned that she pays 4 percent of gross sales in franchising royalties. He has also found out that some franchisors keep a computer record of the sales of all merchandise, while other franchisors supply foods based on franchisee orders and requests.

The initial or startup inventory for a convenience food store is estimated at a value of between $37,000 and $57,000. While Rick considers this to be expensive, he knows it is important that he provide quality merchandise to customers. With further inquiries into the food business, Rick has learned that several franchisors will help finance the inventory part of the total investment acquired. The basic equipment costs range from $20,000 to $40,000, with a total startup cost of between $60,000 and $100,000.

Based upon four years' experience in the convenience food store business, Rick has compiled his own gross profit margins as follows:

Inventory	Profit Margin
Baby foods	25%
Beer	40–45%
Beverages	25–35%
Breads/pastries	5–10%
Candies	20–30%
Canned fruits	30%
Meats	25%
Seafoods	35%
Vegetables	30%
Coffee and tea	40%
Dairy products	5–10%
Deli products	35–40%
Dessert toppings	35–40%
Dried foods	30–35%
Frozen foods	20–30%
Housewares	25–35%
Ice cream	25%
Juices	35%
Paper products	25%
Pet foods	35–40%
Snacks	25–30%
Tobacco products	35–40%
Wine	45–50%

Rick believes convenience food store marketing is going to grow, because he feels people want ready access to bread, milk, groceries, beverages, candy, and basic everyday foods. He wants to open his own business, and is excited about the possibility of being able to afford to do so.

CASE QUESTIONS

1. What additional pro-and-con information should Rick seek before franchising?
2. (a) Based on the information Rick has so far, is convenience food marketing growing? Where can Rick get the information needed to determine if it is or is not?
   (b) Why should Rick contact other franchisees or other convenience food store owners before seeking a franchise agreement?

3. Does it appear that Rick has a good understanding of franchising in comparison with operating an independent business?

REFERENCES

1. Justis, Robert T., "Franchisors: Have You Hugged Your Franchisee Today?" *Nation's Business* (February 1985), pp. 46-49.
2. Leroux, Charles, "Franchising America: One Man's Sad View of Our Roadsides," *Chicago Tribune* (March 31, 1985), Section 2, pp. 1, 3.
3. McGuire, E. Patrick, *Franchised Distribution*, A Research Report from the Conference Board.
4. Seltz, David D., *How to Get Started in Your Own Franchised Business*, Rockville Center, NY: Farnsworth Publishing Company, Inc., 1980.
5. Sloan, Alfred P., Jr., *My Years with General Motors*, Garden City, NY: Doubleday & Company, 1964.
6. U.S. Department of Commerce, *The Franchise Opportunities Handbook,* Washington, DC: U.S. Government Printing Office, 1984.
7. Vaughn, Charles L., *Franchising,* 2nd edition, Lexington, MA: Lexington Books, D.C. Heath Company, 1979.
8. "Where's the Beef in Franchising?" *Money* (March 1985), pp. 149-152.

CHAPTER 3
THE FRANCHISE PLAN

In studying this chapter, you will:
- Understand what is meant by a franchisor blueprint for operation.
- Identify and understand the elements of a franchisee recruitment package.
- Learn about the elements essential for a franchisee operations package.
- Learn why it is important to do a feasibility study of the franchise concept, resources to be utilized, and market sought.

INCIDENT

Lyle is excited about an idea he has for starting a new ice cream franchise in town. He wants to go into business for himself, set his own hours, and create his own profit.
    Lyle has talked to several franchisors who have franchised outlets in different towns. Also, he has talked with several ice cream franchisees. They were all helpful in giving him their own personal experiences in the franchise business. Everyone he has talked to shares his enthusiasm. With several estimates of possible startup costs from other franchisees and a brief franchise description pamphlet from a prospective franchisor, Lyle went to see his banker.
    The banker asked him how many other ice cream stores are currently operating in town; Lyle responded that there are two. However, he ne-

glected to include the five soft-serve ice cream stores in town. He also neglected to mention the frozen yogurt store that opened last month.

Lyle is unaware of the specific functions the franchisor performs. He is wondering what would be provided in the way of training, equipment, supplies, and so forth.

Lyle has not considered a location for his store. He also has not evaluated the size and saturation of the ice cream consuming market in his town to date. He does know, however, that he wants to go into business for himself operating an ice cream store.

Is Lyle ready to open an ice cream store? What additional information might he need? How might a franchise feasibility study help him?

INTRODUCTION

If one is thinking about entering a franchised business, has a franchise and wants to expand, or simply wants to know more about franchising, it is of critical importance for that person to understand and implement an appropriate franchise business plan. A carefully developed franchise system can provide phenomenal results for franchisor and franchisees; a franchising system not properly planned or implemented can lead to financial loss and business failure.

A prospective franchisor develops a comprehensive business plan to outline in detail the franchise operations and functions of the organization. As we will soon see, many areas need to be investigated during the process of developing a franchise business plan. A properly developed plan will have three major components or packages: (1) a franchisor's blueprint for business operations, (2) a franchisee recruitment package, and (3) a franchisee operations and success package. These components will be discussed at the beginning of this chapter. Then a detailed outline will be developed identifying the elements essential for determining the feasibility of entering a franchised business. The chapter will conclude with the presentation of a franchise PERT chart illustrating the development steps and functions to be addressed prior to opening a franchised business.

Franchisor Blueprint for Operation

A franchisor's business plan should include a blueprint of operations. Such a blueprint would have the following primary components: marketing strategy and distribution method (Chapter 7); organization structure appropriate to marketing strategy and distribution approaches (Chapter

7); accounting practices and fiscal responsibilities deemed appropriate, along with realistic financial projections (Chapters 10 and 11) based on the strategy to be followed and the market conditions anticipated; and legal documentation for determining the franchisor-franchisee relationship and anticipated activities of each party (Chapters 4, 5, and 6).

Franchisee Recruitment Package

The second component of a franchise business plan is an articulated franchisee recruitment package which would include the following: disclosure documents, franchisee presentation book, recruitment and advertising brochures, franchising agreements and contracts, and recruitment flowcharts. The recruitment package is designed to show to a prospective franchisee what the franchisor has to offer and should contain clear statements about expectations and responsibilities of each party, franchisor and franchisee. This package should describe the business plan concisely through a logical flow of topics that identify (1) the objectives of the franchisor firm, (2) the initial capital and ultimate investment required of a potential franchisee, (3) personal and other qualifications a potential franchisee must have, and (4) the anticipated benefits and responsibilities of becoming a franchisee.

The disclosure document should be given to a prospective franchisee at the first personal meeting between the prospect and the franchisor, or ten days prior to the execution of a contract or a payment dealing with the franchising relationship between the franchisor and the franchisee, whichever occurs first.

The franchising agreement does not have to be presented to a franchisee until due consideration has been given between the franchisor and the franchisee. **Due consideration** is what the franchisor would demand and receive as the price for providing the elements of the franchising agreement. Similarly, the franchisee would demand, receive, or perform certain elements, duties, and responsibilities with respect to the franchisor. In essence, due consideration constitutes the agreed-upon elements of the franchising relationship between the franchisor and franchisee that impose liability or create duties between the two parties.

The franchise brochure (or presentation book) is simply a typewritten or printed booklet provided to a prospective franchisee who has responded to the franchisor's advertisement or seeks information based on a word-of-mouth inquiry. The brochure and recruitment flowchart help explain the product/service format the franchisor is using and identify the steps or processes one should follow to become a franchisee in this particular franchise system. The recruitment flowchart illustrates the steps of the franchisee development process as prescribed by the particular franchisor.

Franchisee Operations and Success Package

The third component of the franchise business plan is the franchisee operations and success package, which should contain the following items: operations manual, financial and bookkeeping systems, advertising and promotional packages, sales manuals, the franchisor or franchisee support package, and the training manual.

The **operations manual** is often identified by the franchisee as the bible of the business. This manual describes in detail each function and subfunction with procedural guidelines and standards for operating the business. For example, an operations manual for a fast-food franchise would cover a wide range of topics, such as planning menus, setting up the required machinery (ovens, broilers, etc.), sanitation standards and procedures, safety procedures, cash register use and procedures, food preparation and cooking procedures, and methods of inventory control, purchasing, and analysis. The purpose of an operations manual is (1) to impart information about the franchisor's system or approach, (2) to modify the values and knowledge of the prospective franchisee toward the franchise approach and procedures, and (3) to develop skills in accordance with the system of operations for the franchised unit. In essence, the franchisee should become knowledgeable about each facet of the business and how they fit together to ensure the successful operation of the franchised unit.

The franchisee also needs to know the **accounting system** for the business. An appropriate record keeping approach must be developed by the franchisor and explained to the franchisee. A franchisee needs to know about each reporting form required by the franchisor, as well as any approaches to financial analysis that will assist the franchisee in becoming an effective financial controller of the franchised unit.

The **advertising, promotion, and sales programs** typically address, among other issues, the amount of advertising and promotional support available prior to and at the time of a grand opening, cooperative advertising arrangements between franchisor and franchisee, under what conditions direct mail is worthwhile, and any "required" participation in national or regional franchisor-sponsored advertising campaigns. It is important that both franchisor and franchisee have a clear understanding of the amount and type of advertising, sales promotion, and public relations themes, including which party is responsible and to what degree each activity is meant to generate sales, heighten visibility, and/or improve the franchise's image within the local community.

The **franchisor support package** is a rather nebulous term that typically refers to the measures franchisors adopt to maintain wholesome relationships between themselves and their franchisee(s). Very often expectations are set forth in writing which indicate the degree to which franchisees are responsible to develop their specific market(s), the level of performance to be maintained in internal operations, a mechanism for measuring the worth of "new ideas" within the franchise system, and what steps would normally be followed to eliminate or at least minimize legal problems in trademark, brand or trade name, or antitrust areas. On all counts, the franchisee needs to understand what is expected prior to acquiring the franchise. A clear understanding is beneficial to both parties, franchisor and franchisee, to avoid potential problems within the franchisor-franchisee relationship. The franchise, once acquired, is the centerpiece of a continuing relationship.

Training manuals need to be prepared so that not only can prospective franchisees be trained, but also future employees within the franchised unit. Training is necessary to fill the gaps between a franchisee's (and employees') existing knowledge and skills and the levels of performance expected by the franchisor. The training manual for employees can be quite different from that of the recruited franchisee. The franchise employee training is often focused heavily toward skill development, clerking, counter behavior, and the specific task to be performed by the employee — donut making, egg preparing, hamburger preparing, or setting and timing an engine. Along with having his or her business skills honed, the franchisee often receives training in facts, attitudes, beliefs, values, opinions, etc., that comprise the "indoctrination" of an auto dealer, fast-food restaurateur, muffler shop owner, or electronics store franchisee.

Thus we can see that the term "franchisor support package" is really a catch-all for the measures a franchisor takes to maintain a constructive relationship with the franchisee. Normally the degree to which franchisees are responsible for developing their specific market(s) and the level of performance to be maintained in internal operations are clearly stated. A means of measuring the worth of "new ideas" within the franchise system is included. Also provided are steps normally followed to eliminate or at least minimize legal problems in trademark, brand or trade name, and antitrust areas. The franchisee needs to understand what will be expected prior to acquiring the franchise. A clear understanding of these expectations will help in avoiding potential problems within the franchisor-franchisee relationship.

THE FRANCHISE FEASIBILITY STUDY

The first step in establishing a comprehensive integrated franchise plan is to determine the feasibility of developing a potential or existing business into a franchise operation. The feasibility study should contain sufficient information to enable either a franchisor or a franchisee to make a "go or no go" decision.

The franchisor's position must be properly analyzed to determine if the franchisor (1) will or will not be able to properly administer the franchising system, (2) will or will not be able to support franchisees through administrative functions appropriate to the type of business being analyzed and do so in a profitable fashion, and (3) will or will not benefit more through franchising than by operating a separate, independent business. If these questions can be answered affirmatively, the prospective franchisor should pursue the next step in making the decision about being a franchisor.

Both the franchisor and the franchisee will deal with the marketplace; the franchisee, however, will do so on more of a day-to-day basis. It is important that the franchise feasibility study show that (1) a prospective franchisee will or will not be profitable given the format proposed in relation to the market forces being confronted, (2) the proposed product/service has or does not have sufficient "utility" or customer demand/preference in light of alternative purchase possibilities, (3) the business operation at the proposed location(s) will attract the consuming public, and (4) the prospective franchisee will be more successful providing this particular product/service through a franchised unit than through an independent business. As with the franchisor decision, if the answers to these questions are in the affirmative, the person should consider further becoming a franchisee within the proposed franchise system.

The franchise feasibility study should show that it is or is not beneficial to both parties to enter the franchising field. If only one party will benefit, then the particular franchise system is not likely to be successful in the long run. When the basic criteria for success of both parties are met, then franchising can be a very rewarding relationship. The franchisor and the franchisee will remain separate and independent business people although they will have an interdependence in their business dealings and objectives. It is important to understand that the failure of one would generally result in the failure of the other.

A well-prepared franchising feasibility study will address critical areas found in most business plans. However, the feasibility study will usually contain some elements not found in plans for other proposed businesses. The franchise feasibility study will contain seven content sections:

1. Executive Summary
2. Introduction or Overview
3. Marketing Segment
4. Management Segment
5. Finance, Accounting, and Taxes
6. Legal Requirements
7. Appendix

Each of the five "substantive" areas (i.e., items three through seven) should spell out the franchising approach to be followed so that an individual would know whether the proposed business could potentially be successful. Each of the seven areas identified above are outlined in Table 3-1 and will be described in the sequence shown.

Executive Summary

An executive summary serves to summarize and capsulize the information contained in the franchise feasibility study. It highlights the major findings in each of the primary content areas, explains the overall feasibility of the franchise as proposed, and recommends actions that can be taken. An executive summary should contain statements directed at both franchisor and franchisee about the critical factors and findings, as well as an opinion concerning the probability of success of the proposed franchise business. The summary is meant to help the franchisor and the franchisee make decisions whether or not to pursue starting the franchise operation.

Introduction

The introduction explains what the study is about. The opening statement should contain the name of the basic product/service and how it is going to be processed, distributed, and/or sold. Simple, clearly stated explanations should be used in showing the ingredients the business intends to utilize in order to be a success.

Following the opening statement, a short history or background of the individuals involved in the proposed business, along with the historical development of the product/service, should be given. It is important to explain who is going to be involved in the business individually by their intended functions or relationship to the business organization.

The introduction should also provide information about local economic conditions (from the perspective of the intended franchisee) as well as the general conditions confronting the industry within which the business will operate. Such information is necessary to make factual decisions about size of unit, anticipated volume of sales by time periods, and more generally, from the industry perspective, anticipated growth rates, market penetration/saturation rates within a region or nation, and anticipated amount of disposable income available for the type of purchase being examined. Economic information can be acquired from local and state departments of economic development, university business research bureaus, local chambers of commerce, various trade surveys, and the U.S. Department of Commerce in Washington, D.C. An in-depth analysis of the industry is important to ascertain the current strength or level of activity in general terms, the size and concentration of various firms within the industry, and the position the proposed business may take both locally and within the industry.

**Table 3-1
The Franchise Feasibility Plan**

I. Executive Summary
    General Overview
    Summary of Findings
    Final Recommendations
II. Introduction or Overview
    Objective of the Feasibility Plan
    History (individual and/or business idea)
    Industry Overview
III. Marketing
    Production Description: Goods and/or Services — detailed report and/or listing
    Target Market
    Site Location
    Pricing Strategy
    Promotion and Advertising: Specific Detailed Plans
    Marketing to the Franchisee
    Advertising Campaign
    Recruitment Brochure
    Recruitment Flowchart
IV. Management
    Organizational Structure (hierarchy chart)
    Personnel Management (wage and salary administration)
    Policies (general and departmental)
    Franchisee Management
        a. Operating Manual
        b. Training Manual
    PERT Chart
V. Finance, Accounting, and Taxes
    Pro Forma Balance Sheet
    Pro Forma Income Statement (profit and loss statement)
    Pro Forma Cash Flow Statement
    Startup or Turnkey Cost
    Other Factors
    Equity, Collateral, and Loans
    Working Capital
    Break-Even Analysis
    Ratio Analysis
    Provision for Taxation
    Financial Records for the Franchisee
VI. Legal Requirements
    Business Structure
    Licenses, Contracts, and Permits
    Insurance: Types and Costs
    Disclosure Documents
    Franchising Agreement
VII. The Appendix
    Training Manual
    Operations Manual
    Advertising, Promotional Package
    Sales Manual
    Franchisee Recruitment Presentation
    Charts, Graphs, Diagrams
    Layout
    Other

Marketing

The marketing process concerns the distribution of goods/services to existing and potential customers to satisfy some want or need. The marketing section of the feasibility study should investigate market potential, competition, site analysis, target market and primary service area, proposed strategies to reach the market, and marketing policies suggested to integrate the various marketing activities into a unified whole. The marketing section is of critical importance to the success of the franchise. Often, six elements are included in the marketing section of a franchise feasibility study. These elements are identified below. Each business organization is unique, however, and so will place more emphasis on certain elements of the marketing section and less on others.

1. Product description
2. Target market analysis
3. Site location and development of proposed primary service area (PSA)
4. Pricing strategies
5. Promotion and advertising (sales manual, advertising campaign)
6. Franchisee marketing (recruitment, brochures, flowchart)

Product Description. The product/service to be distributed through the proposed business needs to be described in detail. Many of us take great pains to develop vacation plans, arranging ahead of time for motels, restaurants, amusement parks, and sporting events in order to make the vacation a success. This same type of thoroughness should be applied in describing each product/service of the proposed franchise. An itemized listing and description of all products/services should be prepared to include brand names, sizes, shapes, numbers, colors, performance specifications, etc. For example, a franchised computer store should have a list of all the computer hardware, accessory equipment, printers, software, and computer programs that will be available at the proposed business, along with the specifications or distinguishing characteristics of the products. In addition, services provided by the franchise should be described and listed. In the computer business example, services such as programming, installation, repairs, and private consulting might be within the list of available services, along with descriptions of what each service constitutes. Knowing precisely and thoroughly each product and service and their specific attributes can provide the competitive edge for the business to be successful in the marketplace.

Target Market Analysis. It is important to properly identify the target market and analyze that market's primary characteristics in order to determine the potential buyer power available through that market. For example, if one is examining a market to determine the potential for a clothing or shoe store, basic demographics and apparel-buying trends must be understood in order to develop an overall profile of the targeted customer group. The type of information one might seek includes the following:

1. Age: 0-4, 5-11, 12-18, 19-25, 26-35, 36-45, 46-65, and over 65
2. Sex: male/female
3. Family income: under $12,000, $12,000-$17,999, $18,000-$24,999, $25,000-$34,999, $35,000 and over
4. Geographical area of the city: northwest, northeast, southeast, southwest
5. Education: high school not completed, high school completed, some college, college graduate, additional education
6. Number of children living at home: 0, 1, 2, 3, 4, 5, or more
7. Marital status: single, married, divorced, widowed

These kinds of information, when considered together, will tend to profile a certain type of customer. Then, it is important to determine the density or concentration of that type of person within the overall market area in which the product or service will be offered. Particular types of demographic data that might be helpful to forecast the market potential for product or service include age ranges, sex, or disposable income. One should be aware, however, that a successful firm develops customer profiles from a variety of sources and uses factors that have tended to be accurate and reflective of the particular market niche and customer tastes associated with that niche. Thus, it is hard to generalize about what information would be reflective of any business.

Site Location. One of the most important factors in the success of a retail business is to have a properly determined location. Location theorists suggest the three most important factors in the success of a business are location, location, and location!

Two, three, or perhaps even five sites need to be initially analyzed and screened to determine the best alternative sites for the proposed business. Before choosing the specific location, it is important to have determined the location of all competitors and the concentrations of potential customers by the "profiling" completed in the step above. One can develop rough approximations concerning the primary service area for each competitor and for the proposed site through drive-time or walking-time analysis.

In urban areas, it is suggested that approximately two-thirds of a store's business is done by people who live or work within a five minute drive or walk of the location, if the product or service offered is in what is considered a convenience goods/service category. (More will be said about categorizing types of goods/services in Chapter 8.) The drive- or walk-time analysis can be used to develop approximate primary service areas (PSAs) for the proposed business site and for each existing competitor. Using this technique to identify zones of probable coverage across the market area, a prospective business can determine areas where the market is basically underserved as well as areas where it is very competitive. The goal is to find a location with convenient access that does not have heavy competition (cross-lapping PSAs) within a market sector with sufficient numbers of people displaying the "profile" the business wishes to attract.

In addition, it is of value to be aware of other types of stores in the area of the proposed location and the attitude of store owners toward customers. It is often suggested that the business owner should know where complementary product/service purchases can be made, which is the underlying philosophy of the shopping center concept. Once the preferred location is found, purchase or lease may be an important factor. Although lease terms should not be the sole determinant in selecting a site, a franchisee may decide to move out of a particular location solely because of increased rent or lease agreements. However, a proposed new location may not have the same accessibility, targeted customer density, or complementary store clustering as the original site. Thus, it is important to consider each of these factors carefully, remembering that location is critical to but not the sole determinant of proper site selection. All factors should be reviewed before a final location is chosen or a change of location is made. (This topic is developed further in Chapter 8.)

Pricing Strategy. The price at which a product/service is offered must cover relevant costs and ensure an adequate profit for the franchisee and the franchisor. Prior to making final determination about a specific price, it is important to determine cost schedules at various levels of anticipated production, promotional costs per unit, and profit desired per unit, and to compare this "ideal" price with the price offered by direct competitors for the same or similar product/service. It is wise to develop a pricing structure, as opposed to ironclad prices, for the items to be sold. A pricing structure provides the franchisee the flexibility to meet competitive shifts and changes in consumer preference and provides latitude for promotions without the need to establish a new price each time a change is necessary. (More will be said about pricing in Chapters 6 and 7.)

An illustration of markup pricing is appropriate since it is a common practice. Markup pricing is one of the easiest forms of price determination, which may explain in part why it is popular. The steps are to determine actual costs of the product (including all overhead) at the anticipated production/sales volume, and to add the profit margin. The final figure is referred to as a "markup" price. Many fast-food restaurants, for example, have 60 percent of the final price allocated to food and wage costs. If the average cost of the elements used to produce a hamburger is $.35, and the wage cost associated with the preparation of the hamburger is $.25, then the total direct cost is $.60. If overhead cost (building, utilities, debt service, etc.) is estimated to be $.12 per hamburger (based on the anticipated number of burgers to be sold in the year divided by the anticipated total overhead cost), then by adding the direct and indirect costs one gets a total of $.72. If the industry standard is a 40-percent markup (i.e., 40% × $.72), then the anticipated cost of the hamburger would be $1.00. If market conditions suggest that the average price for a hamburger in the market is $.80, not $1.00, then it would be advisable for this potential fast-food franchisee not to enter business in this particular market unless the costs could be significantly lowered.

Promotion and Advertising. Sales promotion and advertising are two differing concepts. Sales promotion is associated with specific time-related efforts to improve sales of a specific product, line of products, or services. Advertising, on the other hand, concerns more-general factors of the brand, trademark, or product/service of the business. Advertising is often "institutional" in orientation, promoting the franchise itself as opposed to offering a specific product at a promotional price. Advertising is meant, in many cases, to promote the overall goodwill of the franchise or the attributes of the product line. For example, McDonald's spends millions every year to make certain the consuming public is aware of its product quality, prompt service, and store cleanliness. These types of promotions have their purpose and should be developed with sufficient detail within the proposed franchise plan so that the franchisor and the franchisee have a clear understanding and cooperate appropriately in their use.

Marketing to the Franchisee. To have a successful franchisee recruitment program, a franchisor should develop a recruitment book designed to present to prospective franchisees the benefits a franchisee would gain by joining the particular franchise system. For example, the central features of a three-page recruitment package of West Coast Auto Parts franchise system include having ten dealers that use auto parts obtained for the franchisee (parts distributor) from tire stores, garages, service stations, and new car dealerships; the merchandise needed to service these ten accounts; and a minimum investment of $7,150. The support features of this franchise include no experience needed in the auto parts business, a 60-percent markup, no "dead" stock, free warehousing, and an inventory exchange mechanism. Also, most franchisee brochure packages contain estimates of projected income and gross profit one can expect by amount of sales and number of products carried in the line. Most brochures will indicate that the projected income and profit displayed in the chart or scale used in the brochure are illustrative and not guaranteed.

The recruitment brochure is a vehicle of assistance in working through the initial personal interview between franchisor and prospective franchisee. The brochure informs prospective franchisees about primary attributes of the particular franchise system from a franchisee's perspective and provides points the two parties can discuss to determine level of interest.

The recruitment flowchart outlines the steps a franchisee needs to take in order to be (1) accepted as a prospective franchisee, (2) interviewed, trained, and assigned as a franchisee, and (3) authorized and opened as the operator of a franchised unit. The flowchart provides the overview and steps a franchisee needs to complete in order to operate as an authorized franchised unit operator within the particular franchise system. (Further discussion of these topics is presented in Chapters 13 through 17.)

Management

Management can be simply defined as "getting things done through people." However, management is one of the most critical factors in determining the success or failure of any business. The two main reasons for failure in business are poor management and lack of capital. The management section of the franchise feasibility study is designed to identify and explain the organizational structure and system of operation established by the franchisor to help the franchise system to be successful.

A franchisee, as owner/manager of a franchise unit, should be able to design and operate an efficient organization within the guidelines established by the franchisor and by using the policies and practices developed by the franchisor for dealing effectively with employees and customers. The franchisee needs to be able to respond to changing environmental conditions, making good use of the franchisor's support to manage the resources available in order to ensure that the basic thrust of the organization does not get sidetracked or become dysfunctional. The management section of the franchise feasibility study should include detailed information on the following five elements:

1. Organizational structure
2. Personnel management, policies, and practices
3. Policies and procedures associated with the functional areas of the franchised business
4. Franchisee management, including statements clarifying responsibilities and areas of discretion where complete authority rests with the franchisee
5. PERT charts showing the development of a franchised unit and effective monitoring and evaluation of activities of the unit

Successful development of these topics consistent with the theme of the business format used by the franchisor allows a prospective, then **extant**, franchisee to properly plan, manage, and control a franchised unit. (This general topic area is addressed more fully in Chapter 9.)

Organizational Structure. Every organization, whether it is a family household or a complex, giant corporation, requires commonly understood organizational relationships in order to function effectively. In business, these relationships should not be left to chance, particularly if differing motivations exist for why such organizational relationships exist in the first place. A chart, diagram, or table of organization should be developed to illustrate and clearly identify the position required, authority and responsibility vested in each position, and the placement of each position in regard to the functional and overall thrust of the organization (see Figure 3-1). A president or chief executive officer (CEO) is identified as the head of an operating organization. However, a CEO is unable to perform all the functions of most organizations unless the organization is of the simplest form and has a very limited scope of operations. Therefore, it is important that the various positions, assignments, and functions within an organization be unified toward achieving the objectives sought and that those staffing the positions understand their assignments and have sufficient authority to carry out their responsibilities.

Each franchisor needs to keep the franchise organization structurally consistent with the ever-changing objectives of the franchise system. As the system grows, the product line is modified, and new products/services are added and others deleted. The organization needs to keep structurally current with such changes, or else staffers will begin to ignore the "formal" approach to running the organization, often leading to severe consequences as the organization becomes more and more informally managed (or mismanaged). (Further discussion of the importance and use of organizational factors in franchising is presented in Chapters 6, 9, 13, 14, and 19.)

**Figure 3-1
An Organizational Chart**

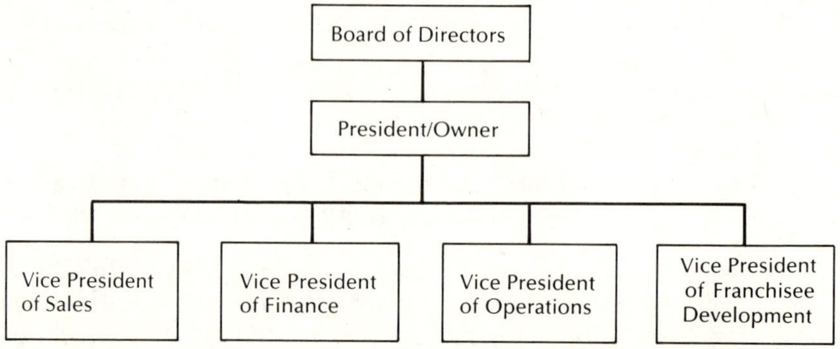

```
                    Board of Directors
                           │
                    President/Owner
         ┌─────────────┬───┴────┬──────────────┐
   Vice President  Vice President  Vice President  Vice President
      of Sales      of Finance     of Operations   of Franchisee
                                                    Development
```

Personnel Management. The franchisor should define and describe the personnel practices of the organization. The franchise organization should have job descriptions and policies relative to the operations and functions of each employee, guidelines for wage and salary administration, and established methods of evaluating performance and determining how raises and/or bonuses are to be administered. In the feasibility study, it is important that personnel needs be addressed and explained. Policies on tipping or gratuities in restaurants, for example, need to be carefully set forth along with their relationship to existing pay schedules, and how such information is to be reported to the IRS and appropriate state departments of revenue must also be explained. In addition, bonuses, commissions, or fringe benefits should be explained by the franchisor for prospective franchisees and their franchised unit operations. (Additional discussion of this topic is presented in Chapters 9, 11, 13, and 14.)

Policies and Procedures. One franchisor noticed that in many of the company-owned units as well as the franchised outlets, overall food costs were rising. Upon investigation, the franchisor realized the policy of allowing employees to take home pizzas not eaten at the end of the day was causing an excessive number of pizzas to be baked during the last hour of business operation. Food costs had risen 4 percent above expected levels. The franchisor changed the policy — no longer allowing employees to take home unused prepared foods — which led to a reduction of 6 percent in food costs, an additional 2 percent below normal expectation.

Policies serve as guidelines for employee actions. As the example above shows, when a policy is not given enough consideration initially, it can be abused to the detriment of the organization. Procedures, on the other hand, identify the steps or elements within a process that are considered appropriate for performing assigned tasks. Of course, procedures can also be abused; as we all know, it can be very difficult working with or managing an employee who does *only* what is required in the manual. Policies exist for the benefit of the organization and its employees. Similarly, procedures should be used to identify how tasks are to be performed, while recognizing that at times variance may need to be allowed for; otherwise, organizations could not accommodate the changing supplier, media, customer, or general community conditions without constantly rewriting the policies and procedures of the franchise system.

There are many policies and procedures to be determined for each franchise. For example, the automotive industry, as a mature industry, has developed many policies over time to deal with varying conditions confronted by parent companies and their respective franchised dealerships. In newer industries, such as the home electronics industry, there are generally fewer policies simply because these industries haven't been around as long. Whereas the automotive industry has clear policies and historic precedent concerning franchisee and employee discounts in purchasing new cars, the computer industry has less information a franchisee can rely upon when trying to determine if employees should be permitted to utilize store computers for their own purposes. However, it is important that employees in any industry receive guidance and training in procedures and are monitored by fair, equitable policies.

Franchisee Management. Sufficient direction should be provided by the franchisor so that each franchisee will know what is expected concerning operations and management of the franchised unit, as well as what elements are essential to the franchisor-franchisee relationship. Included in the operational instructions should be an operations manual and a training manual for the franchisee.

As we noted earlier, the operations manual is known as the "bible," as it describes the functions of the franchisee's business in detail. It provides a step-by-step illustration and/or description for each set of required activities within the store's operation. The training manual may be separate from or part of the operations manual. It provides the information necessary to train unit employees to perform the required functions and operations within the specific business environment of the franchise. For example, the training manual may explain to convenience food store clerks how to operate the cash register, account for cash, account for inventory, and stock food supplies. Training manuals, while often almost too detailed, are needed to help each employee understand the tasks that constitute the responsibilities of the job.

PERT Chart. PERT is an acronym for Project Evaluation Review Technique. A PERT chart is a simple, clearly delineated set of related events presented in sequence. Often, time periods are identified to reflect expectations for completion of each set of activities or events identifed in the sequence. Identifying normative times for each event is beneficial in estimating the length of time through the "critical path" that is necessary to complete the project. A PERT chart can be a useful tool for a franchisor in establishing franchised units. Such charts illustrate the required steps from initiation of the franchise idea to the "grand opening" of the unit by a franchisee. Since each franchise system is unique and can be involved in any of a variety of business activities, such a charting can take anywhere from six months to two years to satisfactorily complete. Seldom does a franchise successfully start up and show a profit in the first 180 days of operation.

PERT charts can be used as a guide (a plan) as well as an implementation tool for both the franchisor and the franchisee. Using the PERT concept, the franchisor can determine those steps absolutely essential (not just desirable) for the development and startup of a franchised unit. The franchisee can see the steps with their requirements and time periods for accomplishment and can thus plan how to best use the time prior to opening the franchised unit.

Finance, Accounting, and Taxes

The priests of Ur in Mesopotamia around 3200 B.C. kept records of the transactions between the priests and the public. Since that time, people have been keeping records to account for financial transactions in their business dealings. These records can and should be valuable tools for assistance in making effective management decisions. In a franchise system, it is important that proper financial records be kept by both franchisor and franchisee. In assessing the feasibility of a franchise, it is essential that financial projections be made for or by the franchisor to estimate income, expenses, cash flow, assets required at various levels of business activity, debt capacity, and equity requirements anticipated for each potential level of business activity.

The major accounting records to be kept by a franchisor and a franchisee would at the very least include:

1. The balance sheet
2. The income statement (profit and loss statement)
3. The cash flow statement

These three financial statements will provide valuable information to make financial decisions concerning initiation, growth or expansion, or even termination of specific franchise operations. We describe each of these accounting records briefly in a context useful to a franchise operation. (These topics are addressed more fully in Chapters 10 and 11.)

Balance Sheet. The balance sheet is a "snapshot" of the financial condition of the franchised business. This financial statement, which used to be called a "statement of financial position," shows how a business utilizes its resources and assets in comparison with the debt and ownership (or equity) of the business. The balance sheet is developed around the following accounting equation:

$$\text{Assets} = \text{Liabilities} + \text{Ownership Equity}$$

The balance sheet differentiates between money used by the franchise business for a short period of time (current assets) and money utilized for longer periods of time (fixed assets). It indicates the difference between the monies received from creditors or loans (liabilities or debts) and the funds injected by the owners of the business (owner's initial equity or investment, plus retained earnings).

Income Statement (Profit and Loss Statement). A business will reap a profit in a given period if revenues exceed expenses. Profit is shown on the income statement through identification of expenses (resources expended or used) to make the sales (which are expressed as total revenue). The expenses are subtracted from the revenue and this figure is considered gross profit. The figure is "gross" because other subtractions from the figure are likely to be made, such as withholding for reserves or taxes.

Usually, the income statement is prepared on a monthly, quarterly, or at least yearly basis in order to indicate the profit/loss relationship resulting from the use of the assets available in that accounting period and the expenses incurred. Revenues into the business are sales made through the franchise's product/service line, plus other forms of revenue such as, for example, rental income from the adjacent building owned by the franchised unit. Expenses are the outflow of resources required to produce and sell the product/service line, including direct cost of production as well as overhead.

Cash Flow Statement. The cash flow statement shows the sources from which the firm obtained its income during an accounting period and how it was spent. The cash flow statement is probably the most important of all financial documents used by a franchisor and a franchisee, because it illustrates the flow of cash through the business across time. It is not like a balance sheet, which captures a picture of the business on a particular day of the year, say December 31, 1990. Rather, the cash flow statement often depicts the business over a period of six months or more, through which the history of revenue income and expenses can be traced and projected into the future. With these comparisons, future cash needs and projected availability of cash can be estimated during different sales highs and lows. Because most business activity is not constant during all twelve months of a year, it is important for an organization to conserve cash shortly after periods of high sales in order to maintain production promotion and normal levels of operation when sales are less than optimal.

The cash flow statement as a projection (or pro forma statement) is meant to anticipate the short falls of the franchise's business during different periods or seasons of the business cycle. The cash flow statement should indicate when funds are expected to be short and when they are expected to be in excess. When excess funds are available, they are often put into a short-term investment vehicle (securities or savings instruments) to generate additional income. In this way, any surplus cash can be working for the firm instead of being idle. In general, the cash flow statement helps the franchisee anticipate cash needs and adjust expenses as well as possible to ensure a smooth outflow of payments, even though income (revenue) tends to come in seasonally or cyclically. Thus, the franchise operator can maximize the use of resources in handling the uncertainties of consumer demand and the certainty of accounts payable.

Startup or Turnkey Costs. One of the most important parts of the franchising feasibility study is the development and presentation of the total costs necessary to open a franchised unit. These startup (or turnkey) costs include all expenses required so that all elements of the business are in place and the operation is ready for the first customer who comes in the door. In many franchised businesses, this would include real property costs, building, advertising, utility hookups, internal fixtures, product inventory, commodities and supplies, and initial salary and wages. These costs should be itemized, providing a complete picture to the franchisee and franchisor of the resource commitment required to start a franchised unit business. While not all expenses may be foreseen, it is important to develop as exhaustive a list as possible. An accurate and current listing will assist the franchisor in planning the startup of future franchised units. Also, these costs can be compared with those of other nonfranchised as well as franchised competitors' new businesses as this information becomes available.

Other Factors. Other factors for consideration in developing an accurate financial picture and proposing appropriate accounting and financial controls include several topics we will briefly discuss. A particular franchise system may find some of these factors less important than others; however, some consideration should be given to each before any of the concepts are rejected.

Equity, collateral, and loans constitute the equipment and capital that can be applied to the business at a given time. Any equipment brought to the new business should be documented and listed along with some measure of value for each piece at the time of the business startup. Any collateral arrangements made to secure loans should be noted not just by one's banker or other source of the loan, but by the franchisee as well. If loans are needed by the franchisee to start up the business, each loan must be documented in the balance sheet, and the appropriate interest rate and approach to be used for its calculation, the length of the loans, and any other conditions that have been stipulated in the loan package should be filed in a secure location.

Working capital is simply an accounting expression that refers to how much cash or capital is available or can easily be made available to pay current debts. Working capital is determined by subtracting current liabilities from current assets.

Break-even analysis refers to a determination of that point in the franchised business activity where revenues (income) exactly equal expenses (costs of doing business). This financial condition can be expressed in mathematical equations or depicted in line graphs, with separate lines representing the costs and the revenues of the firm. At the point of their intersection, the business is neither making nor losing money. Up to the point of intersection the firm is losing money, and after the point of intersection, the firm is making a profit.

Ratio analysis is a method of determining the various financial relationships which would suggest the degree of financial health of a firm. The common marks to determine financial health include liquidity, profitability, and debt/equity position. The ratios are designed to compare the current business activity (1) with that of prior time periods or (2) with that of similar firms in the same industry. The franchisor develops a series of financial ratios on each of the franchisees for purposes of comparison. Such analyses help the franchisor understand the variances in different geographic sectors as well as the differing market/competitive intensities of the various franchisees in the franchise system. (More will be said about ratio analysis and its use in Chapter 11.)

Provision for taxes is a very important consideration. Both franchisor and franchisee must recognize and understand the various tax filings required by federal, state, and local governments. Generally, there are four main areas of taxation in which requirements of reporting about the business's activity and the resulting tax liability must be met:

1. Sales taxes
2. Business taxes
3. Property taxes
4. Employee-related taxes

The franchisor and the franchisee need to understand the filing requirements and obligations of each type of taxation as applied to their line of business and incurred through operation. If taxes are not filed and payments are not made as required, the business can incur civil as well as criminal liability.

Financial Records for the Franchisee. In addition to considering the financial and accounting requirements for a franchisor, it is also appropriate to develop a set of financial figures for a prospective franchisee. Important financial records or position statements for a franchisee would include:

1. Startup or "turnkey" costs per specific franchised unit
2. Financial projections (pro forma)
   a. Balance sheet
   b. Income statement
   c. Cash flow statement
3. Appropriate record keeping journals and headings
4. Financial requirements specified by the franchisor

Before serious consideration is given to "signing on" with a franchisor, a prospective franchisee should have received from the franchisor each of the above types of financial information. It is important that these records and pro forma documents reflect as accurately as possible the business activity of existing franchisees.

Prospective franchisees need to understand what the total startup or turnkey costs of a new franchise will be, as well as the prospective gross sales, typical direct and indirect schedules, prospective profits at various levels of sales/output, the record keeping system required by the franchisor, and the filing requirements, as well as any financial requirements such as franchising fees, royalty payments, advertising cooperative payments, or consultant or service fees expected by the franchisor from an existing franchisee. The more information a prospective franchisee receives before the final decision is made whether to open a franchised unit, the wiser the decision. In the long run, fewer problems, misunderstandings, and potential litigations are likely to take place.

Legal Requirements

There are legal requirements of a franchised operation that must be satisfied. Such requirements usually rest on legal opinion versed in franchising law. Typical factors covered in the legal agreement include:

1. Business structure
2. Licenses, contracts, and permits
3. Types and anticipated costs of insurance
4. Disclosure documents
5. The franchising agreement itself
6. Conditions integral to the franchisor-franchisee relationship

Business Structure. Franchising is a highly competitive and legally controlled business operation. It is important that the franchisor develop a proper business structure which generally would be either (1) a sole proprietorship, (2) a partnership, (3) a corporation, or (4) a holding company.

An anomaly about franchising is that it is generally a highly competitive business activity, but is also a legally "controlled" business relationship. A franchisor has various options to consider for the structure of the business as a sole proprietorship, a partnership, a corporation, or a holding company. In addition, depending on the type of franchise activity, various licenses, contracts, and legal permits may be necessary in order to operate within the boundaries of a particular state. Many states require the listing of the business name, filed through a specific department such as the Office of the Secretary of State or Department of Registration and Licensing. Some franchised firms find it difficult to operate nationally because their name is already in use elsewhere; that is, it has been licensed by another business for use in a particular state. Because of this, it is important that a franchisor register the trade name and any brand names in every state if franchise system development on a national level will be even remotely contemplated.

Insurance is a similarly important factor for the franchisee. The franchisee should have proper coverage in the areas of property insurance, liability insurance, and personal insurance. Insurance is important to cover natural disasters, accidents, emergencies, or other contingencies which can arise and alter the normal course of business activity. Without insurance coverage, the financial health of the firm could be destroyed.

Disclosure Documents. The Federal Trade Commission (FTC) has a requirement called the Franchise Rule, more specifically entitled "Disclosure Requirements and Prohibitions Concerning Franchising and Business Opportunity Ventures" (16 C.F.R. No. 436). This rule requires that all franchisors engaging in franchising practices disclose their business activities through a disclosure document filed with the FTC. Rule 436 has helped reduce the fraudulent or improper use of the franchising concept for personal gain to the detriment of unwitting prospective franchisees. A prospective franchisee should request a copy of the franchisor's disclosure document prior to signing a franchising agreement.

Franchising Agreement/Relationship. The franchising agreement, or contract, between franchisor and franchisee should be drawn up by lawyers, and franchisor and franchisee should have separate legal counsel. This document is the foundation for the franchisor-franchisee relationship and will continue to be central to the relationship between the parties. (Detailed discussion of this document is presented in Chapters 4, 6, 18, and 20.)

Appendix

The appendix is an important visual aid, containing illustrations, diagrams, analyses, and exhibits referenced throughout the franchise feasibility study. An expanded appendix would include the complete training manual, operations manual, advertising and promotion packages, sales manual, site/store layouts, franchisee recruitment presentations, charts, graphs, diagrams, layouts, and other materials which may enhance the franchise activities. A well-prepared appendix can enhance the possibility of successful recruitment of prospective franchisees.

THE FRANCHISE PERT CHART

The franchise PERT chart (Figure 3-2) presents a visual sequence illustrating each developmental step and function to be completed before a franchisor should open a franchised business. A complete franchise PERT chart would include the following phases:

Phase 1. Research and Analysis
Phase 2. Organizational Development (external and internal)
Phase 3. Marketing to Franchisees
Phase 4. Franchisee Selection
Phase 5. Site (Building) and Training
Phase 6. Startup and Feedback

The chart identifies the steps necessary to begin a franchise system. When these steps are followed by a franchisor, some modifications are likely because of the unique characteristics of any particular business organization. However, it is probable that the basic format identified above, if followed faithfully, will have superior results for the franchisor. Each of the phases is briefly described below.

Research and Analysis

The **research and analysis** phase is meant to develop those analyses which are necessary for a wise decision about whether to start a franchise. An obvious area for analysis is the industry, identifying its strengths and weaknesses and charting the industry cycle, if applicable. Also, an in-depth analysis of the intended market would be necessary for measuring current demand and forecasting future demand, as well as for identifying desired market segments, target markets, and market positioning objectives.

The store prototype should be analyzed and the management philosophy critically evaluated. If the store and general management style are not highly successful in existing franchised units, there may be need for change in operational processes, organizational policies, or perhaps management style.

A complete accounting and financial review is in order for the franchisor to understand the overall fiscal limitations or constraints as well as the current financial strengths and weaknesses of the existing organization. In addition, legal analysis should be utilized to determine if the trade name and/or branded items can be registered in each of the states, and to make sure all legal requirements can be met in order to register within the states to qualify for initiating franchisee operations.

Organizational Development (Internal and External)

The second phase of the franchise PERT chart focuses on internal factors necessary in order to develop a franchise system. The legal documents, operating documents, training manual, recruitment brochure, etc., need

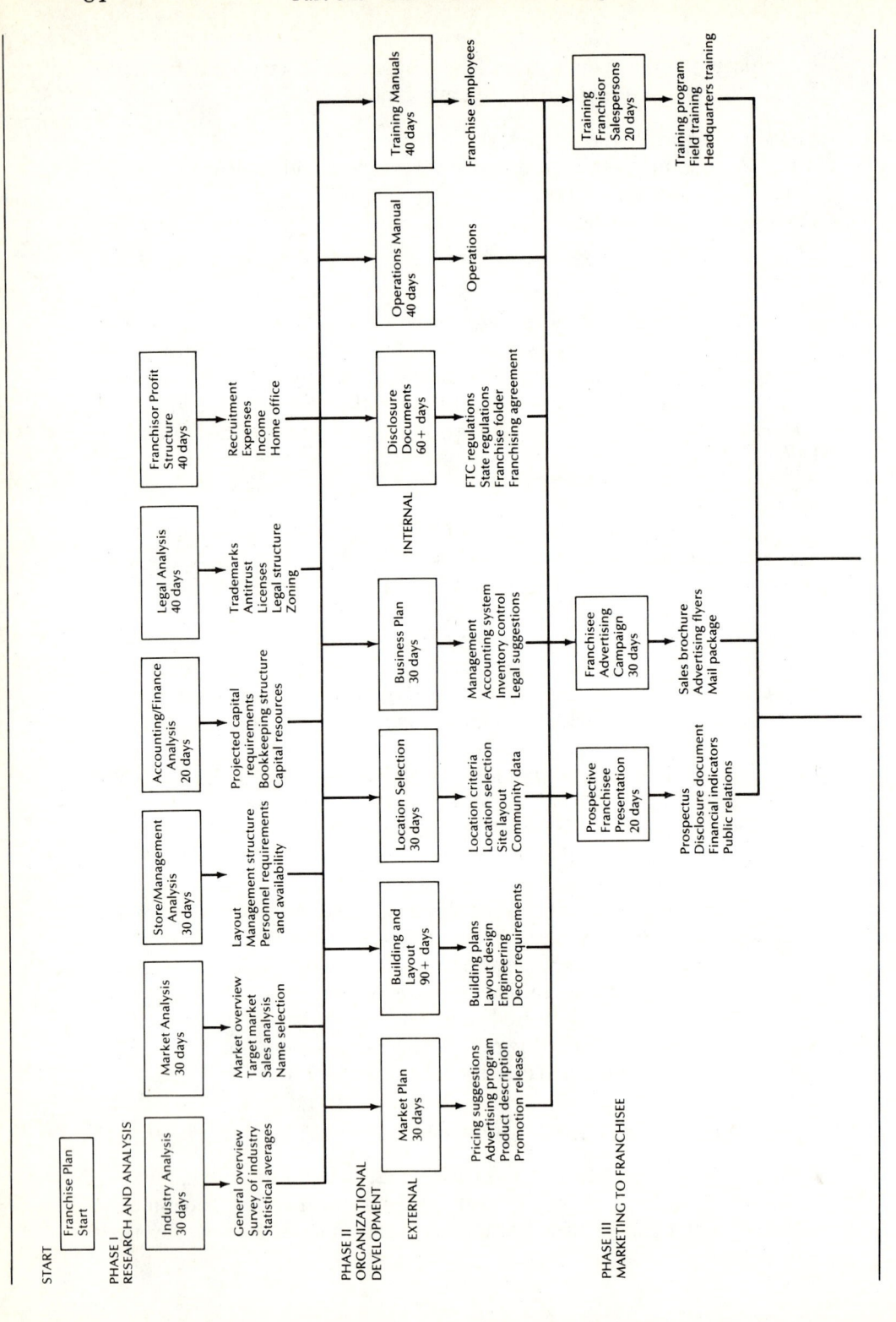

Figure 3-2
The Franchise PERT Chart

START

Franchise Plan
Start

PHASE I
RESEARCH AND ANALYSIS

| Industry Analysis 30 days | Market Analysis 30 days | Store/Management Analysis 30 days | Accounting/Finance Analysis 20 days | Legal Analysis 40 days | Franchisor Profit Structure 40 days |

- General overview / Survey of industry / Statistical averages
- Market overview / Target market / Sales analysis / Name selection
- Layout / Management structure / Personnel requirements and availability
- Projected capital requirements / Bookkeeping structure / Capital resources
- Trademarks / Antitrust / Licenses / Legal structure / Zoning
- Recruitment / Expenses / Income / Home office

PHASE II
ORGANIZATIONAL DEVELOPMENT

EXTERNAL

| Market Plan 30 days | Building and Layout 90+ days | Location Selection 30 days | Business Plan 30 days | Operations Manual 40 days | Training Manuals 40 days |

- Pricing suggestions / Advertising program / Product description / Promotion release
- Building plans / Layout design / Engineering / Decor requirements
- Location criteria / Location selection / Site layout / Community data
- Management / Accounting system / Inventory control / Legal suggestions
- Operations
- Franchise employees

INTERNAL

| Disclosure Documents 60+ days |

- FTC regulations / State regulations / Franchise folder / Franchising agreement

PHASE III
MARKETING TO FRANCHISEE

| Prospective Franchisee Presentation 20 days | Franchisee Advertising Campaign 30 days | Training Franchisor Salespersons 20 days |

- Prospectus / Disclosure document / Financial indicators / Public relations
- Sales brochure / Advertising flyers / Mail package
- Training program / Field training / Headquarters training

84 Part One The Nature of Franchising

Figure 3-2
The Franchise PERT Chart (continued)

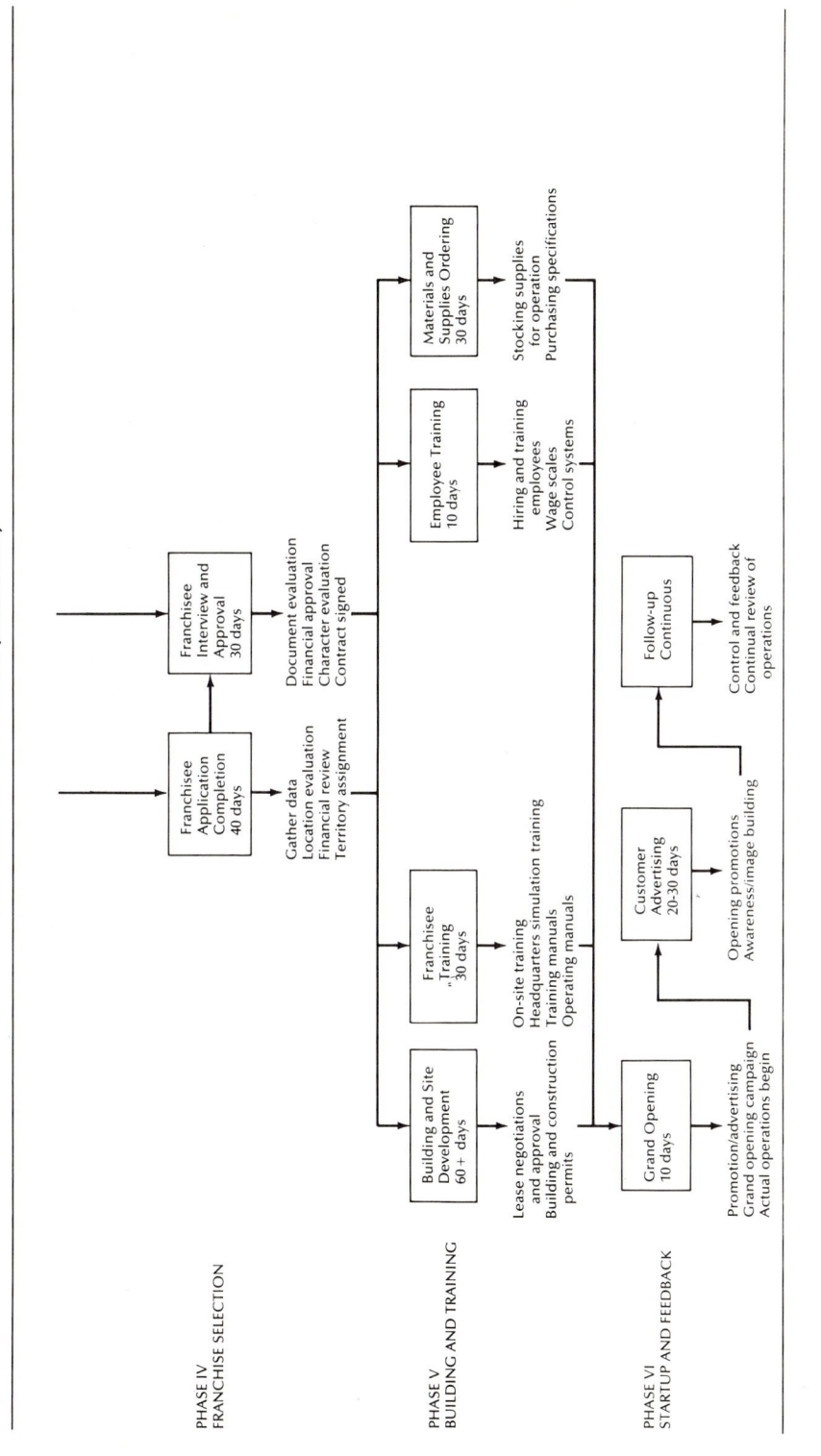

PHASE IV
FRANCHISE SELECTION

- Franchisee Application Completion — 40 days
  - Gather data
  - Location evaluation
  - Financial review
  - Territory assignment
- Franchisee Interview and Approval — 30 days
  - Document evaluation
  - Financial approval
  - Character evaluation
  - Contract signed
- Employee Training — 10 days
  - Hiring and training employees
  - Wage scales
  - Control systems
- Materials and Supplies Ordering — 30 days
  - Stocking supplies for operation
  - Purchasing specifications

PHASE V
BUILDING AND TRAINING

- Building and Site Development — 60+ days
  - Lease negotiations and approval
  - Building and construction permits
- Franchisee Training — 30 days
  - On-site training
  - Headquarters simulation training
  - Training manuals
  - Operating manuals

PHASE VI
STARTUP AND FEEDBACK

- Grand Opening — 10 days
  - Promotion/advertising
  - Grand opening campaign
  - Actual operations begin
- Customer Advertising — 20-30 days
  - Opening promotions
  - Awareness/image building
- Follow-up — Continuous
  - Control and feedback
  - Continual review of operations

to be well developed and approved by the franchisor and by legal counsel when appropriate. Such counsel applies with regard to disclosure documents, contractual relationships, agreements, trademarks, and other components that the franchise system intends to use in the development of the franchise network. The focus is then shifted to such external factors as development of the overall marketing plan, franchisee recruitment strategy, location analysis criteria, and specific elements desired within the franchise feasibility study for a particular location and prospective franchisee.

Marketing to Franchisees

The third phase involves an in-depth analysis and compilation of the marketing package to be used to attract prospective franchisees to the franchise system. A franchisee "profile" can be very helpful — i.e., a profile of the desired attributes of a franchisee of this franchise system. As candidates are recruited, they can be compared to the "ideal franchisee" and judged as to their probability of success in the franchise system. Appropriate mass advertising through audio, video, or print media, as well as word-of-mouth approaches, should be considered in terms of their likelihood of attracting the "ideal franchisee." Seminars advertised in local newspapers, or displays at major trade shows, or strictly word of mouth, or some combination thereof may constitute the right approach. Ultimately it is the judgment of the franchisor and advisers that will determine the specific approach to be taken. Whatever tactic is used, all salespeople and executives of the franchising organization need to be trained to handle franchisee prospects in a similar manner while properly representing the interests of the franchisor.

Franchisee Selection

Obviously, the process of selecting franchisees is of critical importance to the franchisor. As in the draft processes followed in professional sports, proper selection of franchisees can have outstanding results, while poor choices can result in problems for the firm. If the franchising organization has carefully developed its approach, however, requesting appropriate information on the application, conducting a well-designed, informative interview, establishing solid criteria for acceptance or rejection of an application, deliberating and deciding about territorial restrictions as they might apply, and determining any particular legal restrictions or covenants applicable to any particular franchisee prospect, the organization will likely succeed in acquiring people with the talents, capacity, and motivation to be successful in their system.

Site (Building) Selection and Training

Some franchising organizations focus more on site selection and building design than others. McDonald's Corp., Holiday Inns, and Midas International Corporation have been known for exceptionally good site selection methods. In theory, good site selection requires three steps:

1. Determining markets in a geographical area or region that possess the customer demographics closely associated with existing successful businesses in the same field
2. Selecting the market area with the best combination of demographics that exists within the region or area analyzed, and then studying the specific locations in this area that are most likely to produce high-volume sales
3. Examining a number of sites in terms of their "need" for an outlet or store, and forecasting the demand through an appropriate method of trade or primary service area delineation

Once a site is selected and sales volume is estimated, an appropriate building size and layout can be determined. While the site is being prepared and the building is under construction, most franchisees are undergoing training by the franchisor. Such training will be followed by training for employees, delivery of inventory, and promotions to begin announcing the "grand opening."

Startup and Feedback

One of the most exciting moments in any franchise business is the grand opening of a new outlet. Following the grand opening, the franchisor needs to follow up with activities that assist the new franchisee during these early days, as well as to collect information about startup business activity to apply toward the next grand opening. Feedback can be as unwelcome as reminders to make tax payments, but appropriate and regular feedback is essential to a smooth franchisor-franchisee relationship. When the feedback and the franchisor response to such feedback are accurate and helpful, problems rarely become insurmountable.

In summary, the benefits of the PERT chart can be significant to both the franchisor and the franchisee. Proper use of the chart and the associated analyses and judgments to be made require that the franchisor carefully define what information and events are necessary for the initiation and successful operation of a franchised unit. This sequence can be followed over and over again, modified to meet local conditions or particular characteristics of the prospective franchisor-franchisee relationship. The basic ingredients, however, should remain the same.

SUCCESS STORY
FREIDA SCHRECK

In the spring of 1984, Freida Schreck, mother of five young adult children, made one of the biggest decisions of her life. She bought a Norrell Temporary Services franchise that had operated in Springfield, Illinois, for ten years. Freida left a position as officer manager for a construction company and entered business with only an office manager, a part-time clerical person, and herself as owner/operator and "number one" salesperson.

With no previous sales experience and never having owned a business, Freida started virtually from scratch. "Norrell offers some very good support to its franchisees, providing excellent sales courses and sales materials," Freida states. "These helped me immensely."

Freida knew it would take more than learning about ownership requirements and duties to become a success. She knew that the temporary employee service business would be highly competitive and that Springfield is a very competitive market. She has commented that her "first couple of years were a real struggle. With the keen competition, I knew I had to make Norrell different from all the other temporary services."

To accomplish this, Freida concentrated her energies in two primary areas. First, she became active in business and civic affairs of Greater Springfield. She joined the chamber of commerce, became an ambassador for the chamber, and was named Ambassador of the Year for 1986. She worked on the chamber's Secretary Seminar Series, helped initiate a Small Business Resource Group — as a self-help information exchange group for interested small business owners within the community — and chaired the winning team for the 1987 membership drive for the chamber. She serves as president of Women in Management, a group of upper-level management women and business owners. She is a member of the Personnel Association of Central Illinois and has held several offices in recent years. She is also active with the Pilot Club, American Business Women's Association, and Republican Women's Group and often serves as guest lecturer at Sangamon State University and Lincoln Land College. This involvement gives her business and Norrell the visibility she believes is vital to success in the Springfield area.

The second area in which Freida exerts a great deal of energy is in the ownership and operation of her franchised business. Freida designed an approach to help attract new clients. "Times used to be tough," she says. "There were days when our client-hours billed were so low that I had to dip into my savings to keep the business going."

However, with forward vision, Freida moved her offices to a more spacious site that could accommodate the computer equipment she had purchased: "I felt Norrell should stand out from the other temporary employee service companies and developed an in-depth word processing training program for temporaries." Since she discovered it was difficult to find qualified employees with word processing skills, Freida decided to offer such training. She now offers a training program that teaches the use of DOS and a software package. The course lasts four weeks and involves both classwork and hands-on experience. She now has six computers of different brands and 11 software packages for use in training: "This extensive training on different types of equipment makes us very different from the other temporary services." As it turns out, Freida's decision has paid off, for some of the local banks are now hiring Norrell to train personnel who are moved from one department to another.

To further show Freida's keenness to be unique and to provide well-trained temporary employees to Springfield businesses, she leased a proofing machine from a local bank and used it to teach temporaries how to operate this kind of equipment. She went to three of the main banks, learned their systems, and obtained blank forms to make batches of checks and deposits for temporaries to use in developing their skills. This is just one example of what Freida has done to make her business different.

Freida's motto is "Quality and Service." She makes a point of visiting offices in person several times when she has temporaries working on a long assignment. On such assignments, she says that her "office manager or I am there at starting time to check the temporaries in and to orient them to the office. Clients are surprised and grateful for our concern and dedication to provide such good service."

Freida and her office manager, Carol, go even one step further in her quest for quality and service, actually going on assignment themselves in emergencies: "We have taken shorthand minutes at important state board meetings, answered phones, done word processing, and fulfilled secretarial assignments when the client needed someone within an hour and we were unable to find a qualified temporary on that short of a notice. We have stayed the entire length of an assignment or until we have been able to find the right person for the job."

Has her quest of providing quality and service to the business client paid off? "My business has tripled in the last six months and the future looks very promising," says Freida. How does she feel now, three years after entering business as a franchisee of Norrell Temporary Services? "I stand in my office some evenings at 9:30 or 10:00 and think, 'You've come a long way' and start planning a bigger office, more staff, more equipment, ... The sky's the limit!"

Source: Presentation made by Freida Schreck, Norrell Temporary Services franchisee, Springfield, Illinois, to franchising class, December 4, 1987, Sangamon State University.

Photo provided courtesy of Freida Schreck.

SUMMARY

One of the most fascinating experiences is to watch the development of a franchise business from the origin of the product/service idea through to the grand opening of the first franchised unit. The evolution of that idea into a successful franchise system requires time, careful analysis, patience, and extensive planning. The franchisor should develop a franchise feasibility study to enable him or her to understand the various aspects of the proposed franchise business and how each major factor relates to the others. In the first two-thirds of this chapter, where we identified and described the central elements of a franchise feasibility study, we have also made specific reference to other chapters for further development and elaboration of the concepts presented. In essence, much of this text is meant to assist the reader to develop a franchise feasibility study and PERT chart and to understand the sequence of events associated with the inception of the first franchised unit through to its grand opening.

These elements constitute the franchise plan. When the plan is prepared carefully and accurately, it should help the franchisor and franchisees realize their respective dreams. The notion behind the franchise plan is to "plan the work, and then work the plan."

REVIEW QUESTIONS

1. What is meant by a franchisor blueprint for operation?
2. What are the elements of a franchisee recruitment package?
3. What is included in a franchisee operations package?
4. Why is it necessary to complete a feasibility study of the franchise before entering business?
5. What is the most important element of the franchise feasibility study? Why did you choose that element?
6. What is the purpose of the Federal Trade Commission Rule No. 436?

CASE STUDY
NEIGHBORHOOD FOODS, INC.

Jim opened his Neighborhood Foods store three years ago and has been very excited about the growth and prosperity he has found. This past year's sales were over $590,000, with gross profits of $240,000 and realized net profits, after owner's draw, of $35,000. His store area of approximately 2600 square feet with ample parking has been more than adequate for his store's activities. He now wants to franchise the ideas of his store to others.

Jim's store is currently open 365 days a year, 24 hours a day. The store stocks a complete line of top-name, national-brand merchandise commonly used daily in most households. Jim located his store in a relatively new residential area and has found that residents within a one-mile radius provide the greatest pool of patrons for his business. Jim has always been interested in the proper locations of businesses. He believes that location is of utmost importance to the success of his own personal business. He believes that it is a good idea to locate in densely populated residential areas, preferably inhabited by the middle to higher economic groups. Jim prefers a store that can be seen from at least two, if not three, directions and is close to business traffic with convenient parking lot entrances and exits. Jim has also found that it is important for the speed limit on his stretch not to exceed 35 miles per hour, and he prefers being in a location where a large sign may be displayed outside, close to the highway.

Jim discovered after a period of time that the cash registers needed to be located close to the entrance to allow maximum visibility within the store as well as to and from the outside. He also prefers that the entire front be covered with windows to develop a friendly and cordial atmosphere and to allow people from the outside to see all the activities inside. He believes his checkout counter location has reduced theft and shoplifting.

Jim is thinking of establishing an initial franchising fee of $30,000 for the franchise of a Neighborhood Foods store. An additional store opened by the same franchisee would cost $20,000, a third store, $15,000, and every store thereafter, $12,500. He is thinking of a franchising royalty of 4 percent and an advertising fee of 2.5 percent.

Jim realizes he has a long way to go, but he believes he can provide those ingredients which will make the business a success. Jim also feels he will be able to help the franchisees with merchandising, equipment, location, real estate development, training, bookkeeping, and even personal insurance.

NEIGHBORHOOD FOODS, INC.

Income Statement for the Year Ended December 31, 19—

		Percent
Total Sales	$596,320	100.0%
Cost of Goods Sold	418,616	70.2%
Gross Sales	177,704	29.8%
Operating Expenses		
Payroll (not including owner's draw)	55,372	9.3
Advertising	1,056	0.2
Taxes and insurance	4,300	0.7
Maintenance	3,426	0.6
Janitorial	2,000	0.3
Equipment rental	820	0.1
Returned checks	248	0.1
Auto	1,240	0.2
Telephone	430	0.1
Utilities	3,268	0.5
Supplies	2,004	0.3
Totals	$ 74,164	12.4%
Less Owner's Draw	$ 30,000	5.0%
Net Profit	$ 44,164	7.4%

NEIGHBORHOOD FOODS, INC.

Startup Costs

Land	$120,000
Building	185,000
Site Preparation Cost	30,000
Working Capital	18,000
Equipment	56,000
Signs	11,000
Inventory	5,600
	$425,600
Franchising Fee	$ 30,000
Total Estimated Costs	$455,600

Chapter 3 The Franchise Plan   93

NEIGHBORHOOD FOODS, INC.
Inventory

Item	Gross Profit Margin, %
Baby Foods	25–30
Baking Supplies	20–30
Beer	40–46
Beverages	25–35
Breads/Pastries	5–15
Candy/Gum	15–25
Canned Fruits	25–35
Canned Meats	20–30
Canned Seafood	30–40
Canned Vegetables	30–35
Cleaners	25–35
Coffee/Tea	35–40
Dairy Products	5–10
Deli Items	35–40
Dessert Toppings	30–40
Dry Foods	25–35
Frozen Foods	25–35
Housewares	30–35
Ice Cream	25–35
Juices	30–35
Paper Products	20–30
Pet Foods	35–40
Snacks	25–35
Tobacco Products	30–40
Wine	40–50

CASE QUESTIONS

1. Develop a feasibility study for Neighborhood Foods.
2. What are the major problems?
3. Is this a feasible franchise?
4. What are the steps necessary in developing a franchise system?

REFERENCES

1. Broom, H. N., and Longenecker, Justin G., *Small Business Management*, 5th edition, Cincinnati: South-Western Publishing Co., 1979.
2. Church, Nancy Suway, *Future Opportunities in Franchising: A Realistic Appraisal*, New York: Pilot Industries, Inc., 1979.
3. Henward, DeBanks M., and Ginalski, William, *The Franchise Option, Ex-*

panding Your Business Through Franchising, Phoenix: Franchise Group Publisher, 1979.
4. Kotler, Philip, *Principles of Marketing,* 2nd edition, Englewood Cliffs, NJ: Prentice-Hall, Inc., 1983.
5. Seltz, David D., *Franchising: Proven Techniques for Rapid Company Expansion and Market Dominance,* New York: McGraw-Hill Book Co., 1980.
6. Thompson, John S., *Site Selection,* New York: Lebhar-Friedman Books, Chain Store Publishing Corp., 1982.
7. Vaughn, Charles L., *Franchising,* 2nd edition, Lexington, MA: Lexington Books, D. C. Heath and Company, 1979.
8. Whittemore, Meg, "The Great Franchise Boom," *Nation's Business* (September 1984): pp. 20-24.

PART TWO

FRANCHISING AND THE LAW

CHAPTER 4
FRANCHISE LEGAL DOCUMENTS

This chapter was prepared by Douglas D. Smith and James H. Bean of Lindsay, Hart, Neil & Weigler, Portland, Oregon. © Copyrighted by James H. Bean and Douglas D. Smith, April, 1986.

In studying this chapter, you will:
- Learn that a franchising agreement is a contract.
- Understand the importance of the Federal Trade Commission's Rule entitled "Disclosure Requirements and Prohibitions Concerning Franchising and Business Opportunity Ventures."
- Learn about the franchise offering disclosure document and what it contains.
- Understand the requirements for making financial claims in the disclosure document.
- Learn about registration requirements for franchise offerings.
- Know about an operations manual as a legal document.
- Learn what a franchising agreement normally contains.

INCIDENT

Sidney wants to start a fast-food hamburger restaurant franchise system. He started his own hamburger shop approximately three years ago and since that time has developed five other outlets. His shop design is similar to the original McDonald's Corp. restaurant with simple walk-up service and without in-store eating. Sidney has been successful with his six shops, earning profits last year of over $400,000. He now wants to franchise.

Sidney heard that the Federal Trade Commission (FTC) developed a set of rules that require the disclosure of certain information in the process of selling franchise opportunities in the United States. He does not understand what disclosures are required or their purpose. He realizes that he must develop a disclosure document and is interested in learning how to do it. Sidney recently learned that audited financial statements of his business may have to be included in the document.

In addition, Sidney has found out that it may be inappropriate to tell a prospective franchisee how much money might be earned through a franchise. He doesn't understand this. He believes people are interested in becoming franchisees because of the earnings they could receive from operating a franchise. Why, then, should a franchisor be restricted in the way earnings claims are made?

Sidney realizes that he needs to develop a strong franchising contract with the prospective franchisee. This would be a basic statement summarizing how the franchisee would follow the business format prescribed by the franchisor. He is interested in what should be contained in the contract and whether he should try to develop this contract by himself or seek outside counsel.

Sidney is eager to start his franchise system. He is certain that it will be a success. He just wants to understand what legal documents will be required.

INTRODUCTION

Franchising has existed in one form or another for centuries. Notwithstanding this ancient heritage, the development of "franchise law" is relatively recent. The first franchising statute in modern times was introduced in 1971.[1] The courts, however, had been treating conduct arising out of franchising relationships before that time.

It is important to remember that a franchising agreement is subject to the laws of a **contract**. Simply defined, a contract is a legally enforceable business understanding between two parties. All principles of law governing contractual relationships and business practices apply to franchises. Other principles of law also apply to the franchising relationship. For example, the actions of the franchisor and the franchisee may indicate that the franchisee functions as an agent for the franchisor. Le-

---

[1] The California Franchise Investment Law (California Corporations Code, Division 5, Parts 1 through 6, Sections 31000 through 31516) was adopted in 1970 to be effective January 1, 1971.

gal ramifications of agency law cannot be avoided simply by saying in a franchising agreement that the franchisee is not an agent. A franchisee who leaves the franchisor's system and also convinces other franchisees to leave may be wrongfully interfering with the franchisor's rights. This is true even if the franchising agreement is silent on this subject.

There are a number of laws and regulations that specifically deal with franchising. This chapter will deal with state and federal laws and regulations as they relate to the written documents generally used to establish and define a franchising relationship.

The term "franchise" is used to describe many different kinds of business relationships. Specific definitions for the word "franchise" are included in the Federal Trade Commission (FTC) Franchise Rule, formally entitled "Disclosure Requirements and Prohibitions Concerning Franchising and Business Opportunity Ventures"[2] (the FTC Rule). Differing definitions have been devised by several states which have formulated their own franchising laws.

These state laws work in three ways to regulate franchises. First, they specify the required content and delivery of information to prospective franchisees. Second, they may require a franchisor to register with state authorities before offering franchises within the state. Third, they regulate the business relationship between a franchisor and its franchisees, particularly in reference to establishment, termination, renewal, or modification of franchises.[3] There are also state and federal laws that govern the antitrust aspects of the franchising relationship.[4]

The FTC Rule 436 became effective in October, 1979. It does not attempt to regulate the nature or substance of the relationship between a franchisor and its franchisees. It does control a franchisor's conduct by requiring the franchisor to make specified disclosures. It requires detailed and extensive disclosure of information which the FTC deems important or helpful to a prospective franchisee.[5] The FTC Rule is designed to serve two principal functions. First, it prevents the fraudulent misrepresentation of material[6] facts. Second, it requires the presentation of material facts as a franchisor offers franchises to prospective franchisees. The FTC Rule requires the franchisor to deliver the disclosure in-

---

[2] Code of Federal Regulations, Title 16, Chapter I, Subchapter D, Part 436 (16 CFR 436), promulgated December 21, 1978, effective October 21, 1979 (effective date extended from July 21, 1979, 44 Federal Register 31170, May 31, 1979). Cited as "FTC Rule."

[3] There are a number of reporting services that set forth and describe the various state and federal laws that govern franchise disclosure, registration, and relationship requirements. Among them are "The Business Franchise Guide," published by Commerce Clearing House, and "Franchising" by Gladys Glickman, published by Matthew Bender.

[4] Discussed in Chapter 6, below.

[5] " 'A prospective franchisee' is defined as any person who approaches or is approached by a franchisor or franchise broker for the purpose of discussing the possible establishment of a franchise relationship." FTC Rule at 436.2(e).

[6] See a discussion of materiality later in this chapter.

formation to a prospective franchisee in writing. This must be done at the earlier of the first face-to-face meetings[7] between the franchisor's sales representative and the prospective franchisee, or ten business days[8] prior to the time that the franchisee executes any contractual documents associated with the franchise or pays any consideration in connection with it.[9]

The franchisor's franchising contract and all related agreements (i.e., supply contracts, leases, and security agreements) must be delivered to the prospective franchisee in final form, ready for execution, at least five days prior to the date on which they are to be executed.[10]

THE DISCLOSURE DOCUMENT

To make the disclosures required by the FTC Rule, a franchisor must deliver a prospectus document to a prospective franchisee. This document is often called an offering circular.[11] The offering circular must have a cover page bearing language specified by the FTC Rule[12] and a table of contents.[13] It must contain comments that either positively or negatively respond to each disclosure question required to be answered under the FTC Rule. The offering circular may be created in one of two designated formats. The first is prescribed by the FTC Rule itself. The second format is the Uniform Franchise Offering Circular (the "UFOC") as developed by the North American Securities Administrators Association.

A franchisor must use either the FTC Rule format *or* the UFOC format. The formats may not be commingled. A franchisor's choice between the formats might be prescribed by the choice of states in which the franchise is to be offered. The FTC Rule format is often shorter and more easily prepared than one following the UFOC format. However, it is accepted in only 42 states.[14] The UFOC format is accepted in all 50 states and in the province of Alberta.

The substance of the disclosures required by the UFOC is similar to that required by the FTC Rule. The FTC Rule format includes 20 dif-

---

[7] Which is held for the purpose of discussing the sale, or possible sale, of a franchise.
[8] A "business day" does not include Saturdays, Sundays, or holidays.
[9] FTC Rule at 436.1(a)(21). Consideration has been defined as "the cause, motive, price or impelling influence which induces a contracting party to enter into a contract." Black's Law Dictionary (revised 5th edition, 1979).
[10] FTC Rule at 436.1(g).
[11] FTC Rule at 436.1(a)(21).
[12] FTC Rule at 436.1(a)(21).
[13] FTC Rule at 436.1(a)(23).
[14] The eight states in which the FTC format has not been accepted for use each require a franchisor to register a franchise offering before beginning sales efforts in the state. They are California, Indiana, Maryland, Minnesota, Rhode Island, South Dakota, Virginia, and Washington. Eight other states also have registration or specific disclosure requirements. They are Hawaii, Illinois, Michigan, New York, North Dakota, Oregon, Texas, and Wisconsin.

ferent items of information. The UFOC format contains 23 items. To properly prepare an offering circular, a franchisor must analyze the franchise in light of the disclosure information required by each item.

The FTC Rule and UFOC formats include the following items:

1. Information as to the Franchisor and Any Predecessors. This includes the official name, address, principal place of business and parent, affiliated, or holding companies of the franchisor. The length of time the franchisor has conducted a business of the type being franchised and has offered or sold franchises in that business is also included.

Under the FTC Rule, the trademarks, trade names, service marks, advertising, and other commercial symbols used by the franchisor are to be identified in this section. The UFOC discloses whether the franchisor is a corporation, a partnership, or some other form of business entity.[15]

2. The Identity and Business Experience of the Franchisor's Directors, Executive Officers, and Franchise Brokers. The business experience over the past five years must be given for each of the franchisor's directors, the chief executive officer, chief operating officer, financial officers, franchise marketing officers, training officers, and officers who provide services to franchisees. Each person's principal occupations and employers must be included as part of the disclosure. The UFOC also requires a disclosure of the names and business history of any franchise brokers or subfranchisors who are affiliated with the franchisor who will have management responsibility relating to the franchise.[16]

3. Litigation History. Disclosure under this item pertains to three types of litigation (criminal, civil, and administrative) in which the franchisor or any of the persons identified in Item 2 may have been involved. Both the FTC Rule and the UFOC require litigation disclosure for any parent or holding company of the franchisor. The UFOC requires disclosure for related subfranchisors and franchise brokers as well. The FTC Rule requires a disclosure of litigation over the past seven fiscal years. The UFOC requires litigation history for ten fiscal years. The FTC Rule only requires disclosure of litigation in the United States. The UFOC also includes Canadian litigation.[17]

4. Bankruptcy History. This item requires the franchisor to disclose the bankruptcy history of the franchisor, of its affiliated companies, and of its directors and officers. The FTC Rule requires disclosure for bankruptcy information over the past seven fiscal years. The UFOC covers the past 15 fiscal years.[18]

---

[15] FTC Rule at 436.1(a)(1)(3)(6); UFOC Item I.
[16] FTC Rule at 436.1(a)(2); UFOC Item II.
[17] FTC Rule at 436.1(a)(4); UFOC Item III.
[18] FTC Rule at 436.1(a)(5); UFOC Item IV.

5. A Description of the Franchise. The franchisor must give a factual description of the franchise. This includes a general description of the business, a detailed discussion of the business format or product line which is the basis of the franchise system, and an explanation of the market for the franchised goods and services.[19]

6. Initial Funds Required to Be Paid by Franchisee. The franchisor must explain the amount, time for payment, method of payment, and refundability of the franchisee's expenditures to acquire and set up the franchise. In addition to payments to be made to the franchisor, payments to be made to any affiliates of the franchisor and to third parties must be disclosed. These payments may include initial franchise fees, rent, equipment and supply purchases, insurance, and deposits, among other things. The UFOC also requires disclosure of suggested working capital requirements.

The UFOC requires the franchisor to disclose whether identical franchise fees or initial payments are charged for each franchise. In those instances where fees are not identical, a statement of the formula or method for determining the amount of the fee must be disclosed. The UFOC also requires the franchisor to disclose how it will use payments it receives.[20]

7. Recurring Fees Required to Be Paid by a Franchisee. Here the franchisor explains periodic payments to be made to the franchisor or to persons affiliated with the franchisor. These may include royalty, advertising, training, rental, equipment, and lease costs. Both regularly recurring payments and those of a more infrequent nature must be disclosed. The FTC Rule requires a franchisor to disclose possible major expenses such as equipment repair and replacement. The UFOC format requires disclosure of whether any recurring or isolated fees are refundable.[21]

8. Obligations to Purchase from Designated or Approved Sources or Under Certain Specifications. Many franchisors require or advise their franchisees to use specified or approved suppliers. The franchisor should describe the services or goods these suppliers provide. If one of the suppliers is the franchisor or a business affiliated with the franchisor, that fact must be disclosed.

The franchisor must list any products or services the franchisees are required to purchase or lease. These may include inventory materials, signs, equipment, fixtures, business sites, and services. Requirements and specifications established by the franchisor for these things must be disclosed, along with a discussion of how the franchisor issues

---

[19] FTC Rule at 436.1(a)(6); UFOC Cover Sheet.
[20] FTC Rule at 436.1(a)(7); UFOC Items V and VII.
[21] FTC Rule at 436.1(a)(8); UFOC Item VI.

and changes the requirements and specifications. Often required products or services are to be obtained from suppliers specified, approved, or suggested by the franchisor. In this case, the franchisor's method of selecting suppliers should be given.

A franchisor is required to disclose the circumstances under which the franchisor receives commissions, kickbacks, or rebates from suppliers with whom the franchisee is advised or required to deal. The FTC Rule requires a disclosure of whether purchased materials or services are more expensive or more difficult to obtain as a result of the franchisor's specifications. Under the FTC Rule format, a franchisor must justify any supply or purchase restrictions. The UFOC format requires disclosure of the amount of the purchases the franchisor requires the franchisee to make.[22]

9. Financing Arrangements. If the franchisor or a business affiliated with the franchisor offers financing packages to the franchisee, these arrangements are to be disclosed under this item. The UFOC format requires more detailed disclosure than the FTC Rule. The UFOC format also requires examples of the legal documents in which the financing arrangements are set forth.[23]

10. Supervision, Service, and Assistance Obligations of the Franchisor. Under the UFOC format, the franchisor must describe its obligations to the franchisee both prior to opening the business and thereafter. Included are any obligations to provide supervision, services, assistance, site selection, or training. The franchisor must disclose whether it selects or approves franchise locations. The UFOC requires detailed disclosure of the duration, content, and cost of training programs. The training instructors and their relevant training experience are to be identified. The FTC Rule does not mandate comparable disclosures.

Both the UFOC and the FTC Rule require disclosures of the time span from the signing of the franchising agreement to the completion of site selection and the opening of the franchisee's business.[24]

11. Territory and Sales Restrictions. All limitations as to the products or services the franchisee may offer, the customers who may be served, or the geographic area or territory in which the franchisee may operate are to be disclosed. The rationale for such limitations must be given. If the franchisee is given an exclusive territory within which to operate, a description of the territorial restrictions together with the typical boundaries of a territory is to be provided. The UFOC requires a statement whether sales goals must be achieved to preserve territorial

---

[22] FTC Rule at 436.1(a)(10); UFOC Items VIII and IX.
[23] FTC Rule at 436.1(a)(12)(15); UFOC Item X.
[24] FTC Rule at 436.1(a)(17) and (18); UFOC Item XI.

exclusivity. Any circumstances under which territory boundaries may be modified must be revealed.[25]

12. Trademarks, Service Marks, Trade Names, Logo Types, and Other Commercial Symbols. Under both formats, information about registration, litigation, and use of the franchise commercial symbols must be disclosed. The UFOC format requires registration dates, registration numbers, and more detailed information concerning the symbols.[26]

13. Patents and Copyrights. The UFOC format requires detailed disclosure about patents or copyrights that are part of the franchise system. The FTC Rule has no comparable provision.[27]

14. Personal Participation Obligations of the Franchisee. Whether the franchisee must participate personally in the operation should be disclosed. Required participation activities must be described.[28]

15. Modification, Termination, Cancellation, Repurchase, Renewal, and Assignment of the Franchise. This item discloses information about the rights and obligations of the franchisor and franchisee related to modification, termination, cancellation, repurchase, renewal, and assignment of the franchise. Contractual requirements and the franchisor's practices and policies concerning these requirements must be disclosed.[29]

16. Statistical Information Concerning the Number of Franchises and Company-Owned Outlets. The franchisor has to disclose the number of franchises and company-owned outlets in the franchise system. The UFOC format requires disclosure of franchises that have been sold but are not yet in operation. It also asks for an estimate of the number of franchises to be sold during the coming year. Under the FTC Rule, the franchisor discloses how many franchises have been terminated, reacquired, refused renewal, or voluntarily terminated by a franchisee during the preceding fiscal year. This requirement includes the preceding three fiscal years under the UFOC format.[30]

17. Public Figure Involvement in the Franchise System. If a person whose name or identity is known to the general public is involved in the franchise, that involvement must be disclosed. The disclosure includes the nature of the involvement, the benefits the public figure re-

---

[25] FTC Rule at 436.1(a)(13); UFOC Item XII.
[26] FTC Rule at 436.1(a)(1); UFOC Item XIII.
[27] UFOC Item XIV.
[28] FTC Rule at 436.1(a)(14); UFOC Item XV.
[29] FTC Rule at 436.1(a)(15); UFOC Item XVII.
[30] FTC Rule at 436.1(a)(16); UFOC Item XX.

ceives for the involvement, and investment by the celebrity in the franchise system.[31]

18. Financial Information Concerning the Franchisor. Audited financial statements for each of the past three fiscal years must be disclosed. These include balance sheets, income statements, and a statement of changes in financial position. The financial statements must be prepared by an independent accountant using generally accepted accounting principles. Unaudited financial statements may be used in limited circumstances under the FTC Rule.[32]

19. Franchise Contractual Documents. Under the UFOC format, a sample copy of the franchising agreement and all other related contracts must be *attached* to the offering circular. The FTC Rule format requires that proposed agreements *accompany* the offering circular. All contractual documents, in final form ready to be executed by the parties, must be delivered to the prospective franchisee at least five business days prior to execution. This is required regardless of the format used.[33]

20. Acknowledgment of Receipt. Under the UFOC format, the last page of each offering circular is a detachable acknowledgment of receipt. The prospective franchisee signs the receipt and returns it to the franchisor as evidence of the date on which the offering circular was delivered.[34]

FINANCIAL CLAIMS

Perhaps the most sensitive area of franchise sales regulation involves financial claims. Some popular franchises have experienced rapid success. The term "franchising" appears, to some people, to be synonymous with "instant success." Unscrupulous franchise salespersons may use misleading, exaggerated, or fraudulent earnings claims to induce prospective franchisees to invest in a franchise.

A franchisor is not required to make any financial disclosures of franchise sales, revenues, or earnings. If claims are made, they must comply with the FTC Rule or requirements of the UFOC.[35] Oral, written, or visual representations of financial claims must be supported by disclosure information. There must be a reasonable basis to support the accuracy of any claims. Supporting documentation must be in the franchisor's possession.

Under the FTC Rule format, a separate "Earnings Claim Docu-

---

[31] FTC Rule at 436.1(a)(19); UFOC Item XVIII.
[32] FTC Rule at 436.1(a)(20); UFOC Item XXI.
[33] FTC Rule at 436.1(a)(1)(g); UFOC Item XXII.
[34] UFOC Item XXIII. There is no corresponding provision under the FTC Rule.
[35] FTC Rule at 436.1(b) through (e); UFOC Item XIX.

ment" must be furnished to a prospective franchisee. This must contain all claims about actual or projected sales, revenues, or earnings. The UFOC format requires financial claims to be presented in the body of the offering circular. Both formats require a statement of the facts and assumptions upon which any claim is based.

Earnings disclosures and claims must be relevant to the location where the prospective franchisee anticipates operating the franchise. The franchisor should retain complete data to substantiate all claims. This data must be made available to prospective franchisees, the FTC, and relevant state administrators upon demand.[36]

The FTC Rule governs earnings claims in advertising for the promotion of franchise sales.[37] States requiring the registration of franchise offerings may prohibit a franchisor from advertising the franchise until the franchisor has registered. Proposed advertising often must be reviewed by the state administrator. State administrators may prohibit the use of franchise advertising or require the franchisor to modify advertising content to comply with state requirements.

MATERIALITY

The FTC Rule defines as material "any fact, circumstance, or set of conditions which has a substantial likelihood of influencing a reasonable franchisee or a reasonable prospective franchisee in the making of a significant decision relating to a named franchise business or which has any significant financial impact on a franchisee or prospective franchisee."[38] The concept of materiality is relevant to the choice of information to be disclosed. It also determines what changes of information must be made to update an offering circular. Disclosure documents must be revised after a "material" change in the disclosure information. State laws vary on how quickly the revisions must be made.

REGISTRATION

The FTC Rule does not require registration or advance submission of any offering circular or franchising contract documents to the Federal Trade Commission. The franchise laws of 15 states[39] do require advance regis-

---

[36] FTC Rule at 436.1(b) through (e); UFOC Item XIX.
[37] FTC Rule at 436.1(e).
[38] FTC Rule at 436.2(n).
[39] These states include California, Hawaii, Illinois, Indiana, Maryland, Michigan, Minnesota, New York, North Dakota, Rhode Island, South Dakota, Texas, Virginia, Washington, and Wisconsin. Oregon has specific disclosure requirements but does not require registration.

tration. Thirteen of these states[40] require that the offering circular and contractual documents be submitted for review and approval before franchises can be offered in those states. The documents often must be modified to conform with the relevant state franchising laws. State laws describe the disclosures to be made and also may regulate the relationship between the franchisor and its in-state franchisees.

OPERATIONS MANUALS

Every franchise system grows, develops, and matures. As this happens, modifications as to business format, goods and services to be provided, and customer identity are likely to occur. A franchising agreement can be designed to allow for this development. It is important to provide flexibility to make changes while maintaining uniformity and consistency throughout the franchise system.

One difficulty in drafting a franchising agreement is to make it general enough to allow for future modification, but specific enough to guide the parties throughout the life of the contract. This task is most often aided by referring in the agreement to the franchisor's operations manual. An operations manual may be defined as a specified document (apart from the franchising agreement) which contains specifications that may be modified from time to time by the franchisor. The franchising agreement may obligate the franchisee to comply strictly with the operations manual and any modifications made to it.

Operations manuals are commonly used to add new items or services to those required to be sold or performed by a franchisee. The manual may designate new, approved, or required supply sources and revised business location appearance requirements. Often franchisors use their operations manuals to reinforce existing contractual requirements, to institute new sales procedures, and to identify charges the franchisors make for additional assistance and services.

Any changes or modifications made in an operations manual must be reasonable. They must be consistent with the franchising agreement and of the type to have been reasonably anticipated by the franchisee at the time the franchising contract was executed. The reasonableness of a change depends in part upon the following factors:

1. The magnitude of the change in reference to the franchise system and the franchising agreement
2. The financial impact upon the franchisee
3. The need for consistency and uniformity among franchisees

---

[40] Michigan and Texas do not require prior submission and approval of the franchise offering documents.

4. The impact of the change upon the franchisee in competing against competitors outside of the franchise system
5. The impact of the change upon the franchise system as a whole.

It is important to preserve both the franchisor's right to modify the operations manual and the enforceability of the franchising contract. To do so, the franchising agreement should specifically refer to the operations manual and obligate the franchisee to comply with it. The agreement ought to permit the franchisor to modify the manual from time to time, as the franchisor deems appropriate to preserve the goodwill and business advantage of the franchise and the franchise system. The franchisor will want the agreement to state that these unilateral modifications may have a broad scope.

THE FRANCHISING AGREEMENT

The following is a summary of franchising contract terms often used by franchisors. It is beyond the scope of this chapter to explain all the financial, business, and legal ramifications of these terms. Potential antitrust problems must be considered by legal counsel in regard to many of the following points.

1. Introductory Section. The parties to the agreement, the nature of the franchise system, and the identity of the names and symbols associated with the franchise may be listed at the beginning of the contract. Any special materials, patents, copyrights, or other important parts of the system may be discussed in the introductory section.

2. Contract Duration. The starting date and the length of the initial term of the franchising agreement are in this section. Many franchisors give the franchisee some rights to extend or renew the contract. The terms and conditions for extension or renewal may be defined here. Conditions for renewal may include sales quotas or specifications for market penetration. State regulations may significantly affect the parties' rights as to renewal or extension.

3. Franchising Fees and Other Payments. In this section, the initial franchising fee and other payments to be made to the franchisor are discussed. Periodic fees such as royalties and advertising fees are explained. These fees may be specified dollar amounts or percentages of the franchisee's revenues. Also included may be provisions allowing for changes in the periodic fees. Some franchising agreements permit fluctuations in fee amounts based upon cost-of-living adjustments. Late payment penalties and interest charges may also be incorporated into this section.

If fees are based on the franchisee's revenue, the word "revenue" should be defined. Most franchising agreements provide that certain items (e.g., lottery ticket sales or sales tax payments) are excluded from the definition of revenue.

4. Sales of Goods or Services to the Franchisee. As part of the benefits offered franchisees, many franchisors sell equipment, furnishings, signs, inventory, promotional materials, accounting programs, insurance, and management services. Special care should be taken to verify that the provisions of state and federal antitrust and securities laws are met when such goods or services are offered by the franchisor. If the franchisor intends to sell goods or services to the franchisee, provisions regarding those sales can be incorporated here. These may include order and payment requirements, delivery provisions, and warranties.

Provisions for the receipt of commissions, rebates, discounts, and promotional gifts by the franchisee or by the franchisor from third-party suppliers may also be discussed under this section.

5. Financial Reporting and Auditing. The agreement should identify a franchisee's obligation to report business transactions and to account periodically for the franchisee's financial condition. Many franchise systems have uniform accounting methods or systems. The franchising agreement may require a franchisee to use these systems. Franchisors often dictate how franchisees keep their business records and for how long. Most franchising agreements give the franchisor the right to review and audit a franchisee's sales records and income tax returns. This section may describe financial services a franchisor offers to franchisees.

6. Site Selection and Territory Designation. The franchising agreement must be carefully drafted if the franchisee is subject to geographical restrictions on customers, advertising, or locations for the franchise. The franchising agreement may include objective criteria for selection and approval of franchise locations and territories. Territory designations may be described by physical or political boundaries or by the use of maps which mark territory borders. This section may discuss site selection information and assistance the franchisor intends to provide to the franchisee.

7. Business Site Preparation. There are several methods used by franchisors to prepare a site for operation of a franchise. A "turnkey" franchise involves a site being developed by the franchisor and turned over, ready for business, to the franchisee. A franchisor might choose to take substantial responsibility in jointly developing the business site with the franchisee. Or the franchisee may be totally responsible for developing the business site subject to inspection and approval by the franchisor. The franchising agreement should define the extent and nature of each party's responsibilities. Provisions concerning the ownership and leasing of fixtures and equipment may be discussed.

8. Franchise Site Leases. If the franchisor leases the franchise site to the franchisee, the relationship of the lease to the franchising agreement should be stated. The franchisor usually will provide for termination of both the franchising agreement and the lease if either comes to an end. Renewal provisions of the franchising agreement and the lease should be compatible.

9. Trademarks, Service Marks, and Other Commercial Symbols. The commercial symbols associated with the franchised business are an important part of any franchise system. The agreement should state that the franchisor is to remain the owner of all symbols. Most franchising agreements expressly provide that any goodwill associated with the commercial symbols will accrue to the benefit of the franchisor. The goodwill provisions may be subject to state law restrictions.

Standards for the franchisee's use of the commercial symbols and the obligations of the franchisor to protect the commercial symbols should be carefully stated. The franchisee should be required to modify or discontinue the use of certain marks or to adopt additional or replacement marks or symbols.

10. Use of Trade Names and Operating Procedures. The franchising agreement should specify how the commercial symbols are to be used. In addition, the operating manuals, products, services, and methods of doing business that make up the franchise system should be described.

Standards to maintain uniformity of the franchise system must be established. These standards might apply to the franchise location, decor, menus, uniforms, site layout, fixtures, equipment, furnishings, signs, and comparable aspects of the franchise operation. Some franchising agreements include specific construction plans, initial purchase requirements, and startup inventory standards. The nature and use of the operations manual, along with franchisor's right to modify its contents, could be discussed in this part of the franchising agreement.

11. Promotion and Advertising. Franchisors often regulate the content and use of advertising in local, regional, national, and international markets. The franchising agreement may require the franchisee to make periodic payments for advertising efforts managed by the franchisor. Some franchisors establish separate trusts or corporations to oversee the use of advertising funds contributed by the members of the franchise system. These trusts or corporations may be controlled by the franchisor, by the franchisees, or by both.

Franchisees may be required to spend specified amounts for local and regional advertising apart from funds managed by the franchisor. Appropriate standards to maintain the integrity and quality of promotional efforts should be considered.

12. Training Programs. The franchising agreement should outline the nature, content, duration, and location of the franchisor's training programs. Some franchisors have optional as well as mandatory training programs. In some cases, the franchising agreement may be terminated if the franchisee does not successfully complete mandatory training requirements. Provisions for additional training requirements and training costs may be placed in the operations manual to be updated periodically.

13. Franchisor's Right to Inspect the Franchise Business and to Control the Quality of Goods and Services Offered by the Franchisee. One of the primary concerns of a franchisor is to preserve and enhance the goodwill, business value, and public image of the franchise system. Most franchising agreements impose significant control on the franchisee's business operations. The controls include standards of quality for the services and merchandise the franchisee offers. The franchisee's obligations in this regard should be well defined. References to the standards set forth in the operations manual is important. Inspection of the franchise premises and business records provide means to check the franchisee's compliance with these obligations. Penalties for failure to comply with quality-control standards may include monetary claims, the franchisor's stepping in to remedy the problems, or termination of the agreement.

14. Managerial Assistance and Business Guidance to Be Given by the Franchisor. Many franchisors offer follow-up training, on-site assistance, performance evaluations, periodic inspections, and other aids to help the franchisee comply with the franchising agreement. This section of the franchising agreement may contain procedures for these aids.

15. Franchise Business Procedures. This section may include standards, requirements, and limitations on the operation of the franchise. These requirements might refer to fixtures and equipment, uniforms, insurance, warranties made to customers, business hours, and business forms and report documents. Advertising and promotional materials, credit arrangements and use of credit cards, compliance with local and state laws and regulations, maintenance of the franchise location, and comparable subjects could also be covered.

16. Products and Services to Be Purchased by the Franchisee. The franchisor may establish specifications for goods and services obtained by the franchisee. Many franchisors require prior approval of new products, suppliers, distributors, and services. The franchisor's methods for approving new products and services and for designating suppliers and distributors should be stated.

A franchisor may sell goods or services at a profit to franchisees.

However, significant antitrust problems and possible deterioration of the franchising relationship may result. Conflicts are likely if the franchisor attempts to establish unreasonably restrictive standards for products and services which arbitrarily force a franchisee to obtain goods or services from the franchisor. These problems can be avoided by adopting well-reasoned standards for the approval of new products or sources. Competitive bidding and negotiation can be included. Many franchisors establish advisory committees made up of franchisees and other related parties to advise the franchisor on its product and service standards.

17. Confidential Information. Restrictions should be placed on the use and disclosure of trade secrets and confidential information related to the franchise business. Nondisclosure obligations can be imposed on the franchisee's managers, employees, owners, partners, and agents. In order to be legally restricted, persons other than the franchisee may have to execute separate agreements concerning the trade secrets and confidential information. The franchising agreement may require the franchisee to obtain agreements from these persons on behalf of the franchisor.

18. Covenants Not to Compete. Covenants not to compete are restrictions on a franchise operating other businesses that might compete with the franchise system. These covenants are not favored by the laws of most states and must be carefully drafted to be effective. Covenants not to compete afford a different kind of protection from that gained through obligations of nondisclosure of trade secrets and confidential information.

There are two categories of covenants not to compete. Some are in force during the term of the franchising agreement. Others are in force after the agreement terminates. To be enforceable, a covenant not to compete must be reasonable as to its duration, geographic scope, and limits it places upon the future employability of the franchisee.

19. Transfer of Franchising Agreement. Transfer of the franchising agreement by either the franchisor or the franchisee can be restricted. Transfer often is defined to include a sale of controlling interest in a franchisee. Provisions on how to handle divorce, bankruptcy, and death of the franchisee may be included. Transfer might trigger application of the bulk sale provisions of the Uniform Commercial Code. A franchisee should be required to comply with these provisions if they apply.

Many franchisors prohibit transfer of the franchise without the franchisor's prior written approval. Exceptions to this requirement are often allowed for transfers to members of a franchisee's immediate family, a franchisee's partners or shareholders, or to a business wholly controlled by the franchisor. Some states have laws that govern the franchisee's right to transfer the specified circumstances.

A franchisor may establish standards for approval of a prospective transferee of a franchise. These standards may include the character and business background, financial capacity, and management capabilities of the proposed transferee. A prospective transferee may be required to successfully complete franchise training programs before being approved to receive a franchise.

A franchisor may allow the transfer of the existing franchising agreement or may, if the franchising agreement so provides, require the transferee to execute a new franchising agreement in the form then being used by the franchisor. State laws may affect a franchisee's ability to transfer the franchise.

20. Rights of First Refusal. To control the franchise system, some franchisors reserve the right to repurchase the franchise from a franchisee under a right of first refusal. This approach requires a franchisee to notify the franchisor if the franchisee wishes to sell the franchise. Within a defined time period, the franchisor may purchase the franchise upon the same terms that the franchisee would have accepted from another purchaser.

21. Renewal. Many franchisees have the right to renew their franchise for specified periods of time. This right to renew may be absolute or conditional. Among the conditions may be that:

a. The franchisee strictly comply with the franchising agreement prior to renewal;
b. The franchise remain located in the same geographic area originally designated;
c. The franchisee upgrade the franchise premises, fixtures, equipment, and inventory to meet the standards of operation then being required of new franchisees; and
d. The franchisee execute the then current franchising agreement documents.

Some states have specific restrictions and requirements related to the nonrenewal of franchises. Legal counsel should be consulted before the decision whether to renew a franchise is made.

22. Termination. The respective rights of the parties to terminate the franchising agreement may be set forth generally or specifically. Franchising agreements do not generally allow either party to terminate the franchise prior to its expiration without just cause. Some state laws require the parties to exhibit "good faith" or "fair dealing" in connection with termination of franchise rights.

A franchising agreement specifically may list the events which could result in termination. These may include:

a. Failure to follow contract terms (some failures must be followed by written notice from the franchisor and an opportunity to remedy the failure),
b. Failure of the franchisor or franchisee to develop the franchise system or the franchised business location, or to open for business,
c. Failure to provide or pass training programs,
d. Nondelivery of specified items or nonpayment of fees or costs,
e. Abandonment, termination, or expiration of site leases; insolvency (subject to restrictions on termination under the federal bankruptcy laws),
f. Unauthorized transfers,
g. Relevant criminal convictions,
h. Death or disability,
i. The franchisor's decision to withdraw from franchisee's market area, or
j. Noncompliance with the operations manual or standards of franchise procedure.

Some states have franchise laws that regulate or restrict termination rights. Such laws may define specific requirements for notice to be given to the franchisee, opportunities to remedy defaults, and standards requiring repurchase of terminated franchises by the franchisor. Legal counsel should be consulted before termination rights are exercised.

23. Obligations of Franchisee on Termination or Expiration of the Franchising Agreement. Franchisees are typically required to do some or all of the following when a franchising agreement expires or is terminated:

a. Pay all amounts due to franchisor.
b. Return all operating manuals, confidential information, and proprietary materials.
c. Remove, destroy, return, or resell to franchisor all signs and materials bearing the franchisor's commercial symbols.
d. Cancel state trade name registrations.
e. Transfer telephone numbers and directory listings to the franchisor or the franchisor's designee.
f. Modify the appearance of any premises, furnishings, fixtures, or equipment retained by the franchisee to eliminate any suggestion of a continuing affiliation with the franchisor.
g. Sell the franchisee's business assets to the franchisor. The franchisor may then decide to continue operating the franchise in the same location. The price may be established at the fair market value, by appraisal or by a contractually established formula. Purchase issues, such as the time frame for payment and for closing, may be included in the agreement.

24. Miscellaneous Provisions. Among other things, the parties sometimes may specify which state's laws will govern the contract.

There is a difference of opinion concerning the advisability of making a franchising agreement subject to arbitration. Arbitration is favored because of perceived cost and time reductions. The informal nature of the arbitration proceedings may preserve the working relationship of the parties as opposed to alienating them. Arbitration is always an alternative if both parties so elect. It may not be available for federal securities law and antitrust claims. The informal nature of the process makes the discovery of information and the production of documents difficult. Most franchisors will not submit to arbitration issues involving trademarks, operations manuals and system procedures, or claims for payment.

As with other contracts, the franchising agreement often contains provisions allowing the prevailing party to recover its legal fees in any arbitration, trial, or appeal to interpret or enforce the agreement.

SUCCESS STORY
HARRIS COOPER

When Dairy Queen opened its first store in 1940, food franchising was virtually unheard of. With soft-serve an unknown product with tremendous growth potential, Dairy Queen was a natural for such a system. As the decade began to wane, Dairy Queen rapidly expanded from 100 stores in 1947 to 1,466 in 1950 to 2,600 in 1955.

Harris Cooper, then one of the youngest chief executives heading any American corporation, joined the ranks of International Dairy Queen in 1970 as president. He started a legal career in the rental car franchise business and grew up in a family that held major beverage distribution franchises. Cooper's expertise on franchised enterprise systems is unequaled. Under Harris Cooper's guidance, International Dairy Queen has grown to be among the most profitable contenders in today's highly competitive fast-food market.

With 4,850 franchisees in 1984, International Dairy Queen is the leader in noncorporate units. International Dairy Queen is active internationally with 587 stores in 16 foreign countries.

Photo and information provided courtesy of Harris Cooper, August, 1985.

SUMMARY

The development, drafting, and proper presentation of franchise disclosure documents, operations manuals, and franchising agreements should be given careful attention and competent professional analysis. Haphazard or ill-advised franchise terms are potentially perilous and can be costly.

Well thought-out, properly documented offering materials, manuals, and contracts can be the springboard to a well-oiled, profitable, and mutually beneficial franchising relationship.

REVIEW QUESTIONS

1. Why is a franchising agreement a legal document?
2. What are the basic elements of a franchising agreement?
3. Discuss the major components of the FTC Rule.
4. Discuss the advantages and disadvantages of the disclosure document to the franchisor.
5. Discuss the advantages and disadvantages of the disclosure document to the franchisee.
6. What are the requirements for financial claims in a disclosure document?
7. Why is an operations manual a legal document?

CASE STUDY
DAIRY QUEEN*

Juanita is ready to open her own frozen dessert store. She has been working in different jobs during the last six years and has saved enough money to start a franchised business. She currently has $80,000 in savings and plans to spend every cent of it developing her new franchised outlet. She wants to become a "Dairy Queen/Brazier" franchisee.

On investigation of the Dairy Queen franchise offer, she finds that she falls short of the minimum net worth requirement of $150,000. She believes that she can raise the money without having to borrow from commercial banks. The initial franchising fee would be $30,000 with a continuing royalty fee of 4 percent of gross retail sales, plus a sales promotion fee from 3 to 5 percent of gross sales per month.

American Dairy Queen Corporation will provide the plans and specifications for the building. It will help and approve the site location and try to maximize the efficiency of the store in the particular site. An intensive two-week training program for two individuals at the national training center in Minneapolis is also available. Dairy Queen will also provide a minimum of 35 person-days' assistance for the grand opening. It also highly recommends

*Information provided courtesy of International Dairy Queen, Inc., December, 1987.

that the franchisee pay an optional equipment installation fee of $2,000 and an optional construction coordinating fee of $3,000.

The land requirement for a Dairy Queen store generally is approximately 30,000 square feet of land with a minimum of 130 to 150 feet of frontage. Building costs will range from $225,000 to $405,000, depending upon local labor and material, plus the cost of land and site improvements. The average equipment cost ranges from $100,000 to $150,000. The minimum initial cash investment is estimated to be between $80,000 and $100,000. This includes the following:

Initial Cash Investment

Equipment (if purchased)	$25,000 to $45,000
Opening Inventory	8,000 (or more)
Working Capital	26,000 (or more)
Training Expense	6,000
First Half of Franchising Fee	15,000
	$80,000–$100,000

Juanita has sent for and received a confidential information form from American Dairy Queen Corporation. She is to include in this confidential form information about herself as well as her financial resources. Juanita is concerned about the confidentiality of these reports. She wonders if other family members would be contacted once these reports are submitted. Juanita has heard about the Uniform Franchise Offering Circular and is wondering how this would help her. She has received copies of the Dairy Queen operating agreement or franchising contract. In this contract, she has discovered nationally required food items as well as nationally optional food items. She wonders if she would be able to sell additional items in the store, or if she could change some of the existing products.

Juanita wants to know what other contractual or legal obligations she will have. She knows that she will have to do something about a lease. She will be unable to buy the property for the building. She hopes to lease the property from the American Dairy Queen Corporation. She knows about an equipment installation agreement that is available and has heard about the requirement to adhere to certain product standards. Juanita wants to know more about her legal requirements, limitations, and opportunities.

CASE QUESTIONS

1. What legal information should Juanita be aware of before entering into a franchising contract?

2. Is it advisable for Juanita to seek legal counsel before entering into a franchising agreement?
3. What legal document will Juanita need to sign?
4. Why is the disclosure document so important to a franchisee? What does it contain?

CHAPTER 5
TRADEMARKS, COPYRIGHTS, PATENTS, AND TRADE SECRETS

This chapter, with the exception of Objectives, Incident, Success Story, Review Questions, Case Study, and Case Questions, was prepared by Turid L. Owren of Lindsay, Hart, Neil & Weigler, Portland, Oregon.

In studying this chapter, you will:
- Learn about trademarks and trademark protection.
- Learn about copyrights and copyright protection.
- Learn about the various types of patents and their filing requirements.
- Understand the various forms of intellectual property.

INCIDENT

Andrea Herzberg is starting a new health club franchise system. Since opening her first health club and spa two years ago, she has opened a second club within the city and a third club in another city in a neighboring state. Andrea believes her clubs are doing well because they offer a unique variety of services including aerobics, dance, weight training, computer body-composition analysis, diet monitoring and counseling, and exercise programs.

Andrea was planning to name the business Fit for Life, and to distribute advertising using that name as a service mark. She is wondering whether the name would be distinctive as a mark or whether it would conflict with marks currently used by other businesses offering similar services.

Recently Andrea learned that a trademark or service mark could be registered federally at the United States Patent and Trademark Office. She is concerned about the rules, laws, and regulations governing the use of marks associated with her business as she starts to franchise her operation. In addition, she has written and developed an operations manual and training manual and needs to know how to obtain copyright protection for the manuals.

Andrea has also developed a unique stomach exercise machine and is interested in knowing whether she can patent the machine design. The machine is attractive, as well as beneficial, and is used by most of the club members.

Andrea is having a lot of fun with her business, but she recognizes that there are areas where she needs to develop her knowledge. Specifically, she would like to know what she should be doing to protect her intellectual property interests in her service mark, manuals, and machine.

INTRODUCTION

Trademarks, copyrights, patents, and trade secrets are commonly referred to as intellectual property. Such "property" originates from the human intellect, and, if properly developed and used by its owner or author, will be protected by law.

Intellectual property finds a place in this book because it is central to franchising. When a franchisor sells a franchise, it grants to the franchisee a license to use the franchisor's trademarks, copyrighted materials, patented inventions, and trade secrets subject to certain terms and conditions set forth in the franchising agreement.

Trademarks are considered the lifeblood of the franchising concept because they are a tangible symbol of the franchisor's business goodwill. If a franchisor owns a mark which consumers associate with a desirable product or service, a potential consumer will be more likely to purchase the product or service, and, in turn, a potential franchisee will be more likely to purchase a franchise. To protect the goodwill associated with its marks, the franchisor will want to ensure that its franchisees operate the franchised business in conformity with the franchisor's standards. It is in the best interests of both the franchisor and the franchisee to make certain that the marks continue to evoke a favorable association with the franchisor's products, services, and franchises.

This chapter focuses on the basic legal principles of intellectual property: how property rights are created, registered, and enforced. We caution that reading this chapter is not a substitute for obtaining the advice of an attorney specializing in any of these areas. We hope, however, that the chapter will provide the non-legally trained businessperson with some background and insight regarding intellectual property rights so that he or she will be able to determine when legal advice should be sought.

TRADEMARKS

A **trademark** is a word, name, symbol, or device used by a company to identify its goods and to distinguish them from goods manufactured or sold by others.[1] For example, Coca-Cola® is a registered trademark of The Coca-Cola Company, used to identify its cola beverage and to distinguish it from cola beverages manufactured by competitors such as Pepsi Cola Bottling Co.

A **service mark** is essentially the same as a trademark, except that whereas a trademark identifies goods, a service mark identifies a service. Ronald McDonald® is a registered service mark of McDonald's Corporation, used to identify its charitable fund raising and educational and entertainment services.

Trademarks and service marks need not be limited to words or names. The two golden arches and the slogan "You deserve a break today" are also service marks of McDonald's Corporation. The three-tone chime heard on the NBC television network is yet another example of a service mark.

Creation of Trademark Rights

Common law rights may be acquired without registration. In the United States, trademark rights are created by being the first to use a mark in connection with goods or services sold or transported in commerce, as opposed to being the first to register a mark. Trademark rights thus acquired are enforceable in the area in which the mark is used, provided that the owner of the mark does not knowingly permit another to use the same mark for similar goods or services in the same trading area.

Statutory rights provide additional protection. Federal trademark law is embodied in the Trademark Act of 1946,[2] commonly referred to as the Lanham Act. Each state has a trademark statute, which generally follows the provisions of the Lanham Act.

Federal and state registrations provide trademark protection in addition to that created by common law usage. Common law rights generally limit protection to the geographic territory in which the owner has sold goods or services under the mark. Federal or state registrations go further to provide prima facie evidence of the validity of the registration,

---
[1] U.S.C. §1127.
[2] 15 U.S.C. §1051 *et seq.*

the registrant's ownership of the mark, and the registrant's exclusive right to use the mark in interstate or intrastate commerce, respectively.

Selecting the Mark

Not all words, names, symbols, or devices can be used effectively as a trademark or service mark. The primary consideration in selecting a mark is that the mark be distinctive. To avoid the frustration and expense of having to change a mark as the result of a conflict discovered after use, a trademark search should be performed before adopting and using a mark. There are a number of companies that provide search services, which include searching marks throughout the registered and pending files of the United States Patent and Trademark Office. For an additional fee, a search company may conduct an "expanded search" of marks listed in trade directories, telephone directories of many U.S. cities, and state registrations. If the search turns up prior marks that are so close to the chosen mark that the average consumer would likely be confused as to the source of the products or services, the owner of the mark would be well advised to select a different mark and have it searched before using it. Some helpful guidelines in selecting a mark include consideration of the following characteristics:

1. *Coined marks.* A coined mark is a word which has no meaning, and is created solely for the purpose of identifying a product or service. Examples of coined marks include "BIC®" for pens, "Kodak®" for cameras, and "Teflon®" for nonstick coatings. Coined marks provide the greatest trademark protection because anyone attempting to use a similar mark for similar goods or services would have difficulty justifying such usage: coined marks do not suggest or describe the goods or services to which they apply. An infringing user would be viewed as trading on the goodwill of the owner of the mark.

2. *Arbitrary marks.* An arbitrary mark is a word which does have meaning, but which does not suggest or describe the goods or services to which it applies. Examples of arbitrary marks include "Crest®" for toothpaste and "Sprite®" for soda. While not giving quite as strong or broad a trademark protection as coined marks, arbitrary marks are likely to be entitled to relatively strong protection because they are not suggestive of quality or characteristics of the goods or services to which they apply.

3. *Suggestive marks.* As the name indicates, suggestive marks suggest a quality or characteristic of a product or service. Such marks may be valid trademarks if they are not purely descriptive of the product or service. For example, "Wearever®" is a valid trademark for aluminum wares and "General Electric®" is a valid trademark for a variety of electrical appliances.

4. *Descriptive marks.* Descriptive marks are words which describe goods or services, and are not capable of registration as a trademark or service mark unless they have acquired a secondary meaning.[3] Examples include "Beef & Brew" to identify a restaurant, and "Raisin Bran" and "Shredded Wheat" for breakfast cereal. The Lanham Act disallows registration of marks that are merely descriptive of goods or services, unless the applicant can prove that the mark has come to be associated by the public with the applicant's goods or services.[4]

5. *Generic terms.* A generic term is the name for a product or service and cannot function as a trademark or service mark. Sometimes a name that may have originally been registered as a trademark or service mark will lose, or be in danger of losing, its registrability due to common use. Examples include "escalator" as the name for a moving staircase, "aspirin" as the name for acetylsalicylic acid, and "yo-yo" as the name of a toy. The Lanham Act provides that a registered mark will be cancelled if the mark becomes the common descriptive name of an article or substance.[5]

6. *Geographic terms.* Geographic marks are considered weak or nonexclusive marks because they are difficult to protect, and the scope of protection is limited. Extensive and long-term use of a geographic mark can result in trademark protection, however, as demonstrated by such well-known trademarks as "Philadelphia Cream Cheese®" and *The New Yorker*® magazine.

7. *Deceptive terms.* Words that misrepresent a product or service are unlikely to be found registrable by the Patent and Trademark Office due to potential prohibition under the Federal Trade Commission Act, which protects against false and misleading advertising. Examples include "Rejuvenescence" used in connection with the promotion and sale of skin cream, and "Lite Diet" to describe white bread more thinly sliced than other breads.

8. *Secondary meaning.* As noted above, a descriptive or geographic mark may become registrable if the mark becomes distinctive of the applicant's goods or services in commerce. Evidence of distinctiveness may be proved by substantially exclusive and continuous use of the mark by the applicant in commerce for a period of five years immediately preceding the date of filing for registration of the mark.[6] Such evidence may be introduced by filing with the Patent and Trademark Office affidavits disclosing, among other things, the amount and types of advertising, other promotional efforts, and sales of the product or service.

---

[3] Secondary meaning is discussed in footnote 4, below.
[4] 15 U.S.C. §1052(e).
[5] 15 U.S.C. §1052(e) and (f).
[6] 15 U.S.C. §1052 (e) and (f).

Registration

Once a mark has been selected, searched, and used in interstate commerce, an application for a federal registration can be filed with the Patent and Trademark Office. The application requires specification of the following items:[7]

1. The name of the applicant (and whether the applicant is an individual, a partnership, or a corporation);
2. The citizenship of the applicant; if the applicant is a partnership, the names and citizenship of the partners; if the applicant is a corporation, the state or country of incorporation;
3. The address of the applicant;
4. An identification of the goods or services for which the mark was adopted, along with an accompanying drawing of the mark;
5. The date the applicant first used the mark as a trademark on the goods or as a trademark or service mark in connection with the goods or services;
6. The date the applicant first used the mark as a trademark or service mark in interstate, territorial, foreign, or any other type of commerce which may lawfully be regulated by Congress;
7. The manner in which the mark is used on or in connection with the particular goods or services — i.e., "the goods," "the containers for the goods," "displays associated with the goods," "tags or labels affixed to the goods," or other methods, along with five specimens showing the mark as actually used; and
8. The statutory filing fee,[8] made payable to the Commissioner of Patents and Trademarks. The application must be dated, signed, and verified by the individual, partner, or corporate officer.

Upon filing, the Patent and Trademark Office staff will review the application for completeness, and, if complete, will assign the application to an examining attorney for review. The response time for the initial review by the examining attorney is generally three to five months. The examiner will send an action letter to the applicant, approving or rejecting the application for publication in the *Official Gazette*, a weekly publication of the Patent and Trademark Office. The applicant has six months from the date of the action letter to respond. If the applicant does not respond within the six-month period, the application will be presumed abandoned.

Applications are frequently rejected after the initial review. Reasons for rejection include: the drawing of the mark does not conform to the prescribed drawing requirements; the identification of the goods or

---

[7] 15 U.S.C. 1051.
[8] The statutory filing fee is $200 as of October, 1986.

services to which the mark applies is inadequate; the mark is too descriptive; or, commonly, the mark is similar to and likely to cause confusion with an existing registered mark. Written arguments or telephone calls to the examining attorney may be required to obtain a satisfactory resolution of the problem. Once such problems are overcome, the examiner will follow up with a final action letter.

If the Patent and Trademark Office approves the mark, it will be published for opposition in the *Official Gazette.* Any person who believes he or she might be harmed by registration of the mark can oppose registration of the mark on the Principal Register by filing an opposition. If no one opposes registration of the mark within the 30-day period or an extension as may be granted by the Patent and Trademark Office, the Trademark Office will issue a Certificate of Registration.

The Certificate of Registration remains in force for 20 years. However, a registration will be cancelled automatically if the registrant fails to file an affidavit verifying that the mark is still in use between the fifth and sixth years following the date the Certificate of Registration issued. The Certificate of Registration may be renewed for successive 20-year periods as long as the mark is still in use.

Proper Use

Trademark rights can be lost if use of the mark is abandoned or if use of the mark results in the mark acquiring a generic meaning. The Lanham Act defines abandonment as having occurred "when any course of conduct of the registrant, including acts of omission as well as commission, causes the mark to lose its significance as an indication of origin."[9] Here are some tips regarding proper use of a mark to enhance its preservation:

1. Always use the mark as an adjective (never as a noun or verb). For example, "Our office uses only XEROX® copiers," not "The xerox is located in the next room," or "Please xerox this copy for me."
2. Always capitalize the mark.
3. Give notice that the mark is registered by displaying with the mark the letter R enclosed within a circle: ® (or a ™ if the mark is not yet registered).

Enforcement

The owner of a mark may prevent the owner of a later-adopted mark from using the later-adopted mark if the marks are so similar as to cause likelihood of confusion in the mind of the purchasing public regarding the source of the two marked goods or services. Remedies that may be sought by the owner of the infringed mark include: an injunction prohib-

---

[9] 15 U.S.C. 1127.

iting future infringement; a court order that the infringer destroy all material bearing the infringing mark; payment of costs associated with the court action; and, occasionally, payment of attorneys' fees. If the infringer had actual notice of the registration, the owner of the infringed mark may also recover all profits obtained by the infringer as a result of using the infringing mark and damages incurred by the owner of the infringed mark as a result of the infringement.

COPYRIGHTS

A **copyright** is the right of an author or persons deriving their rights through the author to prevent others from making certain uses of original works of authorship. Original works of authorship can include literary, dramatic, musical, artistic, and other forms of intellectual work. The work may be in published or unpublished form.

The source of copyright protection in the United States is federal law.[10] Under the current law, copyright protection is secured automatically upon creation of an original work of authorship. Publication or registration of the work is no longer required to obtain a copyright. Registration may, however, provide additional protections to a copyright owner, as will be discussed in more detail below. The owner of a copyrighted work has the exclusive right to:

1. Reproduce the copyrighted work in copies or phonorecords;
2. Prepare derivative works based upon the copyrighted work;
3. Distribute copies or phonorecords of the copyrighted work to the public by sale;
4. Perform the copyrighted work publicly; and
5. Display the copyrighted work publicly.[11]

Creation of Copyright Rights

The right to claim copyright protection occurs as soon as an original work of authorship is created in a fixed, tangible form for the first time. To be "original" does not mean that the work must be unique — it may be sufficient that the work is original with the author, provided that the work evidences some creativity and is not just a copy of another's work.

Who Can Claim Copyright Protection? Except for works made for hire (see discussion below), only the author or coauthors of an original work, or persons to whom an author transfers by written assignment his or her interest, can claim copyright protection. Assignments of copyright interests should be recorded in the Copyright Office immediately to avoid

---

[10] 17 U.S.C. §101 *et seq.*
[11] 17 U.S.C. §106.

potential later transferees of the same copyright interest from recording an assignment first, thereby prevailing over another's earlier, but unrecorded, interest.

If the work of authorship was created by an employee within the scope of his or her employment, or if the work was specially ordered or commissioned for certain uses, the employer and contractor, respectively, are presumptively considered the authors of the work. If there is any ambiguity regarding whether the work will be considered a work made for hire, the parties should enter into a written agreement clarifying their respective interests in the work.

What Does a Copyright Protect? A copyright protects the fixed, tangible expression of an idea and not the idea itself. Thus, a franchisor who claims a copyright in a menu for a pizza restaurant franchise system, cannot prevent another franchisor from developing a menu for its pizza restaurant franchise system, provided that the latter menu is not just a copy of the former.

Registration of a Copyright

Registration of a copyright with the Copyright Office in Washington, D.C., is a relatively simple, straightforward procedure. There are currently five different application forms available for registering a work, depending upon what type of work is to be registered.

Failure to register a copyright does not mean that the owner of the copyright will not be granted some protection if another infringes the copyrighted work. The advantage of obtaining registration of a copyright in a timely manner (within three months of publication) is that the owner of the copyright will be entitled to claim statutory damages and possibly attorney's fees and court costs in the event of infringement. Note that registration of a copyright is effective as of the date of receipt in the Copyright Office of the properly completed application form.

A copyright generally endures for a term consisting of the life of the author plus 50 years following the author's death. If the copyright is created by two or more authors who did not make the work for hire, the term is 50 years following the last surviving author's death. In the case of works made for hire and anonymous or pseudonymous works, the term is 75 years from the date of publication or 100 years from the date of creation, whichever term is shorter.

Proper Use

When a work is published, all copies should bear a proper copyright notice in such a manner and location as to give reasonable notice of the claim to copyright. Examples of proper forms of copyright notice include: ©1986 John Doe, or Unpublished Work ©1986 John Doe.

Enforcement

The owner of an exclusive right under a copyright may seek an injunction against one who violates his or her copyright interest,[12] and may also recover actual damages and profits of the infringer. If the owner of a copyright registers the copyright within three months of publication of the work or prior to an infringement of the work, statutory damages ranging from $250 to $10,000 may also be awarded. If infringement is found to be willful, a court can award up to $50,000 in statutory damages.

PATENTS

A **patent** gives the owner the exclusive right to exclude others from manufacturing, using, and selling an invention for a limited period of time. There are three types of patents:

1. *Utility patents.* Utility patents are granted for functionally useful inventions, including new and useful processes, machines, manufactured products, and compositions of matter, or any new and useful improvements thereof.[13] The term of a utility patent is 17 years from the date of issue.

2. *Design patents.* Design patents are granted for new, original, and ornamental designs for a manufactured product.[14] The term of a design patent is 14 years from the date of issue.

3. *Plant patents.* Plant patents are granted for the discovery and asexual reproduction of any distinct and new variety of plant.[15] The term of a plant patent is 17 years from the date of issue.

Requirements for Patentability

To be patentable, the invention must be (1) novel — that is, different from what is already known; (2) of a character not obvious to one who has "ordinary skill in the art" to which the invention pertains; and (3) if a utility patent, useful.

Conception of the Invention

Records. Upon conception of an invention, the inventor is advised to prepare a written disclosure which describes the invention in full detail, including accompanying drawings and photographs, to explain how the invention works. Records should be maintained on an ongoing basis to

---

[12] 17 U.S.C. §501(b).
[13] 35 U.S.C. §154.
[14] 35 U.S.C. §173.
[15] 35 U.S.C. §161.

include descriptions of efforts to reduce the invention to practice and later improvements on the invention.

Witnesses. The invention disclosure should be dated and signed by the inventor and by two witnesses who understand the invention. The witnesses preferably should not be directly related to the inventor, to avoid later claims of bias.

Searching the Invention. Prior to filing a patent application with the United States Patent and Trademark Office, the inventor is usually advised to conduct a patentability search of pertinent prior art to determine whether the invention has already been disclosed in prior patents. As with trademark searches, patentability searches can be obtained through professional search companies for a fee. However, an inventor may have such a thorough knowledge of prior art for the invention that conducting a search is unnecessary.

Protecting the Invention Prior to Filing a Patent Application. An inventor should contact a patent attorney before divulging any information about the invention, such as advertising, selling, or publicly using or describing the invention. If an inventor fails to keep an invention secret or delays in applying for a patent, the inventor loses the right to patent the invention.

The Patent Application

A patent application includes: (1) a specification, which is a written description of the invention, including the manner and process of making and using it, in sufficient detail to enable a person of ordinary skill in the art to make and use the invention, and which sets forth the best mode contemplated by the inventor of carrying out the invention;[16] (2) claims, which are numbered paragraphs that define the scope of the invention for which a patent is being requested; (3) drawings, which illustrate the preferred embodiment of the invention; (4) an oath or declaration by the inventor swearing that he or she is the first inventor of the invention for which a patent is being sought and that the application is being made in a timely manner (i.e., no later than one year following the date the invention was offered for sale, sold, or publicly used in the United States); and (5) a statutory filing fee, made payable to the Commissioner of Patents and Trademarks.[17]

After the application has been filed in the Patent and Trademark Office, a patent examiner is assigned to review the application. The examiner's first task is to check the application to establish that it conforms to

---

[16] 35 U.S.C. §112.
[17] The statutory filing fee varies depending upon the type of patent being sought and whether the applicant claims small entity patent owner status.

the filing requirements. The examiner will then search prior patents and publications that are related to the invention sought to be patented. Approximately 12 to 18 months after receiving the application, the examiner will issue an office action to the applicant.

As with trade and service mark applications, a patent application is frequently rejected after the first review. A common reason for rejection is that the claims in the patent application are determined by the examiner to be obvious in view of prior art. The patent attorney then files a written response to the office action, amending claims or further distinguishing the invention from prior patents that have been granted.

After reviewing the written response to the office action, the patent examiner will either concede that the invention is patentable or issue another office action citing deficiencies. Once the Patent and Trademark Office indicates that the application is allowable, an issue fee must be paid. Three to four months after the issue fee is paid, the patent will issue. The patent will be published in the *Official Gazette*, which provides abstracts of recently issued patents.

Patent Notice

After a patent has been granted, the patent number should be placed on the patented invention in the following form: "U.S. Patent No. ——." Failure to place the patent notice on the patented invention could prevent the patent owner from recovering damages incurred as a result of infringement unless it can be shown that the infringer had actual notice of the patent.

Although inventions for which patents are being sought are generally not publicly disclosed prior to issuance of the patent, it could be beneficial to place a "patent pending" notice on an invention while the patent application is being processed to give notice that a patent interest is being claimed.

In order to maintain a grant of a United States patent for the term of 17 years (14 years for design patents), the patent owner must pay maintenance fees (or taxes) to the Patent and Trademark Office. Currently, the maintenance fees are paid three times during the course of the life of the patent: at three and one-half years; at seven and one-half years; and at 11 years.[18]

Enforcement

If a patent owner is concerned about a patent being infringed, the owner should first look at the claims that issue in the patent application to de-

---

[18] 37 C.F.R. §1.20.

termine whether the suspect device in fact infringes. If the patent owner believes that the patent has been infringed, he or she should contact a patent attorney for further action. Such action may merely involve sending a demand letter to the infringer demanding that the infringer cease the infringing activity. If the letter or subsequent negotiations between the parties do not result in a settlement, the patent owner can seek legal action against the infringer for damages of not less than "a reasonable royalty for the use made of the invention by the infringer, together with interest and costs as fixed by the court"[19] and an injunction to stop further infringing activities.

TRADE SECRETS

A **trade secret** is "any formula, pattern, device, or compilation of information which is used in one's business, and which gives (the owner) an opportunity to obtain an advantage over competitors who do not know or use it."[20] Some examples of what can constitute a trade secret include a secret ingredient or a secret combination of ingredients used in a recipe; customer lists; manner of business operation; computer programs; designs; notes; sketches; and so on.

Factors for Identifying a Trade Secret

The most important characteristic of a trade secret is that it must be secret. Secrecy does not have to mean *absolute* secrecy; it may be sufficient that the secret is not generally known to competitor businesses. Following is a list of factors to aid in determining whether certain information will be considered a trade secret:

1. The extent to which the information is known outside of the business claiming the trade secret;
2. The extent to which the information is known by employees and others involved in the business;
3. The extent to which measures have been taken by the business owner to protect the secrecy of the information;
4. The value of the information to the business and to competitors of the business;
5. The amount of effort or money expended by the business in developing the information; and
6. The ease or difficulty with which the information could be properly acquired or duplicated by others.[21]

---

[19] 35 U.S.C. §284.
[20] Restatement of Torts §757, comment b (1939).
[21] Restatement of Torts §757, comment b (1939).

Protection of Trade Secrets

As the above list suggests, in order for a trade secret to be protected by law, the trade secret must be not generally known to others in the business and must be of value to the business. Additionally, the trade secret owner must take reasonable precautions to ensure that the trade secret is kept confidential.

Unlike trademarks, copyrights, and patents, there are no statutory formalities for protecting a trade secret from usurpation by another. The source of trade secret protection is primarily state common law.[22] Litigation involving trade secrets generally focuses on whether a legally protectable trade secret existed, the nature of the relationship between the parties to the litigation (i.e., was there a confidential or contractual relationship), and the circumstances under which the disclosure of information about the trade secret occurred.

Businesses that are concerned with protecting trade secrets should adopt a variety of protective measures, not only to give notice that the company considers such information confidential, but to strengthen any later claim by the company that the information was a company trade secret and entitled to protection. Some suggestions to promote protection of trade secrets include the following:

1. Mark all documents and other materials containing trade secrets "Confidential Proprietary Information of (the Company)," and number each copy sequentially.
2. Keep all trade secret materials in a secure place.
3. Keep an ongoing record of any trade secret disclosures (e.g., what was disclosed, when, and to whom).
4. Limit access to trade secret materials to those persons to whom disclosure is necessary to permit development, design, and engineering work.
5. Discuss the importance of keeping company trade secrets confidential with employees at time of hire.
6. Require employees at time of hire to sign written employment agreements which restrict employee use of trade secret materials while employed by the company.
7. Require key employees to sign non-competition agreements at time of hire.[23]
8. Conduct exit interviews with all employees when they leave, at which

---

[22] Some states have trade secret statutes.
[23] A note of caution: Some states restrict the enforceability of the agreements mentioned in paragraphs 6 and 7. Employers should consult their attorney before attempting to utilize such agreements.

time the employee will be asked to sign a written acknowledgment that all trade secret materials have been returned.

In addition to using employment agreements, consultants and other noncompany persons who require access to trade secret materials in order to perform jobs for which they are consulted should be required to sign "confidentiality agreements" as a prerequisite to allowing them access to the trade secret materials.

A confidentiality agreement provides a broad definition of a company's confidential information and sets forth the parties' agreement that such confidential information is a special, valuable, and unique asset of the company, and that the recipient (a) will keep in confidence and trust all confidential information; (b) will not directly or indirectly use the confidential information for personal purposes; and (c) will not directly or indirectly disclose any confidential information to any person or entity, except with the written consent of the company.

Remedies

As with trademark, copyright, and patent infringements, the most commonly sought remedy by owners of trade secrets that have been misappropriated is injunctive relief. In addition to seeking an injunction, a trade secret owner may also seek damages. Damages are generally assessed to be the profits lost by the trade secret owner as a result of the misappropriation of the trade secret and the profits earned by the wrongdoer as a result of use of the misappropriated materials.

FRANCHISING PROVISIONS

As we have discussed in each of the preceding sections, the owners of trademarks, copyrights, patents, and trade secrets must take precautionary measures to protect ownership interests in such intellectual property.

Franchising Agreement

It is imperative that a franchisor develop a well-drafted franchising agreement that identifies and fully describes the respective rights, interests, and duties of each of the parties with regard to such property. The introductory paragraphs of the franchising agreement should specify that the franchisor has certain rights to trademarks, copyrights, patents, and trade secrets, as applicable, and that the franchisee desires to use the franchisor's intellectual properties in connection with the operation of the franchised business and agrees to do so subject to the terms and conditions set forth in the agreement.

Franchise Standards of Operation

The parties should acknowledge that if the franchisee operates its franchise below the standards required by the franchisor, customers who patronize that franchise will be less likely to patronize other franchises of the franchisor, thereby damaging the business of others. The parties should also acknowledge that it will be difficult for the franchisor to obtain new franchisees for its franchise business if a prospective purchaser observes that the franchisee does not maintain the required standards.

Training. The agreement should require that the franchisee or its manager satisfactorily complete a mandatory training program provided by the franchisor. Failure to complete the training program to the exclusive satisfaction of the franchisor should be grounds for terminating the agreement.

Operations Manual. The franchisee should be required to adhere strictly to any requirements set forth in the franchisor's operations manual. The operations manual generally contains the franchisor's specifications, standards, operating procedures, accounting and bookkeeping methods, marketing ideas, specifications, fixture requirements, and other rules prescribed by the franchisor.

Provisions allowing the franchisor to amend the operations manual from time to time and requiring the franchisee to implement such changes at the franchisee's cost are standard. The franchisee should also agree that the operations manual is and shall remain confidential and the exclusive property of the franchisor and that the franchisee shall not copy or duplicate any portion of the operations manual for any reason.

Ownership. In addition to acknowledging that the operations manual is the exclusive property of the franchisor, the franchisee should expressly agree that the franchisor's trademarks (or any names or marks deceptively similar to them), copyrights, patents, methods of operation, and any other applicable intellectual property owned by the franchisor are the sole and exclusive property of the franchisor. The franchisee should be required to notify the franchisor immediately of any infringement of, or challenge to, the franchisee's use of intellectual property owned by the franchisor.

Confidentiality. The franchisee must agree not to communicate or divulge the contents of the franchisor's offering circulars, franchise agreements, and any attachments, operations manuals or any other information related to the operation of the franchise or the franchise system to any persons except those authorized in writing by the franchisor to receive such information. All security procedures prescribed by the franchisor for maintaining the secrecy of confidential information must be strictly adhered to by the franchisee, and the franchisee must agree that it will disclose confidential information to its employees only as necessary to carry on the franchise business.

To the extent legally enforceable, a franchisee should use its best efforts to obtain written agreements (in a form approved by the franchisor) from all employees, partners, officers, directors, and shareholders of the franchisee and other persons in the franchisee's control to whom any such information is communicated, that they will keep, preserve, and protect all confidential information and that they will not compete with the franchisee or the franchisor during their employment with the franchisee or for a reasonable period after termination of employment.

Termination. In addition to standard language delineating grounds and procedures for terminating the franchising agreement, the franchisor is advised to provide for immediate termination of the agreement if the franchisee breaches any franchise requirements relating to standards of operation (including trademark, copyright, and patent usage, as applicable) or does not keep information and trade secrets related to the franchise confidential.

Franchisee Obligations upon Termination of the Franchising Agreement. Upon expiration or termination of the franchising agreement for any reason, express provisions regarding the franchisee's obligations upon termination should be set forth. Some examples of post-termination obligations of a franchisee include that the franchisee:

1. Immediately cease using the trademarks (or any names or marks deceptively similar to them), the operations manual, and any other applicable intellectual property owned by the franchisor.
2. Return to the franchisor all copies of the operations manual in the franchisee's possession or control.
3. Notify all telephone, directory, and listing companies of the termination of the franchisee's right to use the franchise names and trademarks and authorize the transfer of all telephone numbers and directory listings to the franchisor.
4. Cease doing business under the franchisor's names, trademarks, styles, and dressings and refrain from identifying itself as a franchisee of the franchisor.
5. Abide by all provisions of any post-termination covenants not to compete.

SUCCESS STORY
DALLEN PETERSON

In 1980, Dallen Peterson and his wife, Glennis, recognized a void in the field of professional home cleaning services and opened the first Merry Maids in Omaha, Nebraska. Since that time, Merry Maids has grown to become the nation's largest home cleaning company with over 250 franchised offices across the United States and in Australia.

Each new Merry Maids franchise owner participates in a week-long training program at the company headquarters in Omaha. Here they learn about the latest advances in customized home cleaning as well as the procedures to be followed in hiring and training personnel, marketing and advertising their services, and managing and scheduling their business via the company's exclusive Data Management software system. And, in order to graduate, franchisees visit and actually clean several homes following Merry Maids professional home cleaning procedures and using the cleaning products manufactured and distributed by the company.

Dallen Peterson foresees continued and significant growth in the professional home cleaning industry. Today more than 60 percent of the working population is made up of families in which both the husband and wife work. Yet the traditional housekeeper, who performed such services as cleaning, doing laundry, and ironing, is a rarity.

Peterson believes that Merry Maids has only begun to fill this gap between the growing demand for home cleaning and the declining availability of reliable house cleaning help. "We haven't even scratched the surface," he says. "Our best estimates are that we are serving less than one-half of one percent of the potential market today."

Dallen Peterson is one of the original members of the University of Nebraska–Lincoln's Franchise Studies Advisory Council, and his company was one of the first to afford UNL students the opportunity to participate in a Franchise Studies summer internship program.

Photo and information provided courtesy of Dallen Peterson, August, 1985.

REVIEW QUESTIONS

1. Discuss the importance of trademark laws.
2. What are the registration requirements of trademarks?
3. Discuss patent laws and how they protect patents.
4. Why is it important for a franchisor to safeguard and police all trademarks?
5. Discuss laws pertaining to trade secrets and their applicability to franchising.

CASE STUDY
THE MECHANICS SHOP

Chad and Heather understand that in order to succeed, they must expand their business in the right place and at the right time. They believe it is very important to take some time to identify the market that has the greatest potential and then place their next business there. They are also thinking about franchising their business.

Chad and Heather have been working together for the last three years. They started by opening their own mechanics repair shop, specializing in muffler and transmissions. Their service now includes complete automotive repair and has been very successful. Their first stores, opened within the last year, have sales averaging $8,000 and $7,000 per week, respectively.

Both Chad and Heather have worked in the automotive repair shop. Heather used to have primary responsibility for sales and customer service, but has gradually taken over the administrative operations of the three shops, which she supervises and visits on a daily basis. Chad has resumed responsibility for all the financial and training portions of their business and has developed a very efficient record keeping system which is utilized at all three stores.

Chad and Heather have recently worked out some preliminary investment figures for prospective franchisees. These figures include the initial startup costs except for the purchase of the property and building.

Initial Investment Costs

Equipment and Supplies	$40,000
Leasehold Improvement and Installation	15,000
Inventory (Parts)	8,000
Utilities	1,000
Rent	1,500

Working Capital	6,000
Recruitment and Opening	2,000
Fixtures and Furniture	2,000
Franchising Fee	20,000

Chad and Heather are now wondering how they should identify their business. They want to pick a name and logo that franchisees and consumers would find attractive and which would be associated with outstanding automotive repair service. They have considered using a name and logo that would be either suggestive or descriptive of high-quality mechanic (muffler and transmission) services.

Heather has developed a new tool that removes old mufflers easily and also provides a better method of installing new mufflers. She wants to know how to patent this new tool and how long it will take before the patent issues.

Chad and Heather have also decided to videotape training sessions for all new franchisees and their employees. They want to know if they can copyright or otherwise protect these tapes. Some of their employees will also be given access to customer lists that Chad and Heather consider to be a trade secret. They need to know what steps they should take to protect the customer lists.

Chad and Heather want to base their business upon quality, friendliness, and outstanding service. They know the auto repair business and have been very successful. They are worried about the legal requirements of starting their own business — especially concerning trademarks, patents, copyrights and trade secrets.

CASE QUESTIONS

1. What steps do Chad and Heather need to take to develop their service mark?
2. What legal advice should they seek?
3. How should Heather develop her patent?
4. What should Chad and Heather know about copyrighting their videotape training films?
5. What steps can Chad and Heather take to protect their customer lists?

CHAPTER 6
FRANCHISING AND THE ANTITRUST LAWS

This chapter, with the exception of Objectives, Incident, Review Questions, Success Story, Case Study, and Case Questions, was prepared by Thomas A. Balmer and James N. Gardner of Lindsay, Hart, Neil & Weigler, Portland, Oregon.

In studying this chapter, you will:
- Understand the basics and importance of antitrust laws.
- Learn about the antitrust problems faced by franchisors.
- Understand tying agreements.
- Learn about price discrimination and price fixing.
- Learn about territorial allocations and their problems.

INCIDENT

Mike Babcock is the founder, president, and CEO of the Chocolate Yogurt franchise. It has been in operation for approximately three years and has grown to over 120 stores throughout the northwestern and western United States. Mike is very concerned about some difficulties arising within his franchise system. These are primarily problems with prices as well as exclusive territory (location) rights for franchises within his organization.

Almost a year ago, Mike made a suggestion to his franchisees that they sell the plain, non-fruit frozen yogurts at a fixed price of 85¢ for a small cone, $1.25 for a medium cone, and $1.65 for a large cone. Several of his franchisees have been very upset at this pricing suggestion, believing it is an effort by the franchisor to fix prices for the franchisees. Several lawsuits have been brought against him by his franchisees claiming that his actions constitute price fixing.

Another problem which has recently come up is that a prospective franchisee is in the process of suing Mike because he would not grant that person a franchise. The prospective franchisee is claiming that Mike talked to other local franchisees who do not like the prospective franchisee and it is because of this that Mike is refusing to grant the franchise. Mike claims that he never talked to other franchisees about the prospective franchisee. He simply believes that it is better for the existing franchisees that there not be an additional franchise within that given geographic territory.

It is difficult for Mike to run the Chocolate Yogurt franchise company when he always has to be concerned with legal constraints. He simply wants to know how to properly conduct and organize his business so that he will not have to worry about antitrust or other legal rules or regulations regarding his business.

INTRODUCTION

For many business people, the term "antitrust" conjures up visions of multibillion dollar mergers, jail sentences imposed on price fixers, and lawsuits that drag on for years. Antitrust laws often seem complex and mysterious, presenting insidious traps for the unwary.

While antitrust law can be complicated, the basic concepts are relatively straightforward. Businesses involved in franchising can avoid most serious antitrust problems with common sense and an understanding of some basic rules. In this chapter, we will begin with a brief review of the major antitrust laws. These laws set the competitive rules of the game for American business. Although some of them rarely arise in franchising, the rules are important to understand because they are an integral part of the legal context in which franchisors, franchisees, and suppliers operate. We will then turn to the antitrust rules that directly affect franchising. The kinds of arrangements and actions by franchisors that may violate the antitrust laws will be examined. We will also focus on identifying the antitrust problem areas and avoiding difficulties before they arise.

BACKGROUND AND BASIS OF THE ANTITRUST LAWS

The same independent, entrepreneurial spirit that motivates many people involved in franchising has been a driving force in the American economy since the early days of the Republic. The development of new, competing enterprises has played an important political and social, as well as economic, role. The industrial revolution during the late 1800s made many Americans feel that industry was becoming dominated by a handful of giant "trusts." Politicians and others believed — sometimes correctly, sometimes not — that the trusts had successfully eliminated competition within particular industries, driving up prices, discouraging innovation, and stifling new business entrants.

In response to these concerns, Congress in 1890 passed what is still the major antitrust law, the Sherman Act. The broad terms of the Sherman Act prohibit two separate kinds of conduct: agreements or conspiracies which restrain trade, and "monopolization" or attempts to monopolize trade or commerce.

Over the past century, the courts have faced the task of applying these very general restrictions to particular situations. For example, it quickly became clear that virtually any contract is in some sense a "restraint of trade." It means that a buyer will purchase a product from a particular seller, and not purchase that item from other sellers. Yet binding contracts are, of course, essential to business transactions. The courts therefore interpreted the Sherman Act to prohibit only *unreasonable* restraints of trade. Later court decisions further divided restraints of trade into (1) restraints that are illegal *per se* (that is, illegal in and of themselves), removing the requirement that anticompetitive effects be shown in particular circumstances; and (2) those restraints that are judged under the "rule of reason" and are illegal only if it can be shown that they adversely affect competition. The most important of the *per se* offenses include agreements among competitors to fix prices, divide geographic territories, or rig bids. For example, an agreement between two gasoline stations at a busy intersection to fix the price at which they sell gasoline is *per se* illegal, and the stations have violated the antitrust laws even if competition is not harmed because consumers can still choose a lower-priced station.

Under the "rule of reason," however, courts look to the effect of the restraint on the particular market involved, the purpose of the restraint, and other factors peculiar to the area and product involved. The restraint will be condemned as illegal only when it appears, based on all the facts, to suppress or destroy competition.

Most of the restraints which have been dubbed *per se* illegal involve agreements among competitors, often called "horizontal" agreements, rather than agreements between buyers and sellers of products, including franchisors and franchisees, which are characterized as "vertical" restraints. In addition, the law is often more lenient towards restrictions related to the products that may be sold, location, and other non-price restraints than it is to agreements which directly affect prices. Thus, potential antitrust problems range from *horizontal price* restraints, which are most likely to violate the antitrust laws, to *vertical non-price* restraints, subject to the rule of reason, which are least likely to be illegal.

The other major provision of the Sherman Act prohibits monopolization. It is important to remember that "big is not necessarily bad" — the law forbids *monopolization*, not simply monopoly. Illegal monopolization will be found only when a firm has acquired a very large share of a particular market through some unfair or predatory means and not simply by producing a better product or expanding in response to demand. In recent years, there have been few successful monopolization cases, and the government's 1982 decision to drop its decade-long antitrust suit against IBM signaled less-vigorous enforcement efforts in this area.

While the basic terms of the Sherman Act have not been changed substantially since 1890, the penalties for violation have been sharply increased. The Sherman Act is a criminal statute; violation can subject individual defendants to jail sentences of up to three years. In addition, convicted individuals may be fined up to $100,000 and corporations up to $1,000,000. More daunting to most businesses than criminal charges is the prospect of civil antitrust cases brought by competitors or customers. A party that brings a successful suit can recover three times the actual damages caused by the defendant's actions, as well as court costs and attorney's fees. The severity of these penalties leads most businesses to carefully review practices and policies to avoid potential antitrust claims.

The basic policy of the Sherman Act in favor of free competition is supplemented by the Clayton Act, passed in 1914, which restricts particular business practices. Its most notable provision is that which prohibits corporate mergers that may substantially affect competition. For many years, the government used this law to bar virtually all mergers between competitors or potential competitors, even when the probable impact in the marketplace was unclear. Recent enforcement policies and court decisions, however, have allowed most mergers. Still prohibited are those mergers between major competitors in industries which have only a few other companies.

More relevant to franchising, however, is the provision of the Clayton Act which prohibits certain kinds of agreements between buyers and sellers of goods. Two types of provisions are illegal if they will substantially reduce competition. Sellers may not sell one product on the condition that the buyer buy some other product from the seller. Second, it is illegal for sellers to sell their products on the condition that the buyer stop dealing with the seller's competitors. Because the rules involving such "tying" and "exclusive dealing" contracts are so important to franchising, we discuss them in detail later in this chapter.

The third major antitrust statute, the Robinson-Patman Act, passed in 1936, prohibits price discrimination. This law makes it illegal for a seller of a product to charge different prices to two different buyers, if that difference in price may substantially reduce competition. Finally, the Federal Trade Commission Act covers some of the same ground as the antitrust laws and broadly prohibits "unfair methods of competition." The Federal Trade Commission also polices unfair advertising and deceptive practices, including any which might be used in the sale of franchises; but that topic is beyond the scope of this chapter.

In addition to being aware of these federal antitrust statutes, businesses must be concerned with the laws of each state which are designed to protect competition and to prevent restraints of trade. These laws may be enforced by state officials, and private parties may bring suit under them. While there is variation among the states, the provisions often parallel the federal laws.

ANTITRUST PROBLEMS FACED BY FRANCHISORS

We can now consider in greater detail the law as it relates to franchising. Monopolization and merger issues will ordinarily not be of particular concern to any but the very largest franchisors. However, the sale of products to franchisees and the restrictions and requirements often imposed on franchisees are fertile ground for problems of vertical price fixing, tying, and exclusive dealing. Identifying and coping with these antitrust hot spots are the goals of the next part of this chapter.

Price Fixing

The most serious antitrust offense is, fortunately, also the easiest to recognize. Price fixing is simply an agreement among two or more persons or firms to sell a product or service at a particular price or to take actions that will directly affect price.

Price fixing problems faced by franchisors come in both horizontal and vertical varieties. When independent competitors agree to fix prices, the result is horizontal price fixing, a clear violation of the antitrust laws. This law applies to franchising just as it does to other forms of business. For example, if two fast-food hamburger franchisors agree on the prices that will be charged in their franchisees' stores, they are violating the Sherman Act. It would also be a violation for the two franchisors to agree on the prices they would charge for their franchises — the initial prices, royalties, and so on.

Franchisors may also unwittingly become involved in price fixing through the actions of their franchisees. Suppose a photo-finishing franchisor has suggested that its franchisees charge $4.95 for developing a 24-exposure roll of color film. Later, several franchisees meet to discuss prices, agree to charge $5.50, as they believe that would be a more reasonable price, and urge the franchisor to adopt that as the suggested price. In this case, the franchisees have clearly violated the antitrust laws by agreeing among themselves to fix the price. More importantly, if the franchisor in response to their urging agrees later to adopt $5.50 as its suggested price, it may be found to be part of a conspiracy it had no part in starting.

Although all businesses must exercise caution to avoid horizontal price fixing, as the preceding example demonstrates, franchisors will not encounter serious horizontal problems very often. On the other hand, *vertical* restraints — agreements between franchisors and franchisees or between any manufacturer or distributor and retailer — come up on a daily basis. Because these issues arise so frequently, let us consider in finer detail the activities that may present vertical price fixing problems.

Suppose you are a franchisor of Gourmet Ice Cream. Your marketing studies indicate that an important part of the upscale image you hope to promote is a relatively high price, so you decide that the basic, single-dip ice cream cone should sell for $1.50. Knowing that the Sherman Act prohibits agreements to fix prices, how do you encourage franchisees to sell the ice cream cones at what you believe to be the appropriate price? Let us consider the possibilities:

1. You set a price and insist it be followed. This is illegal. You may not lawfully agree with existing franchisees that they will charge a particular price for the ice cream cones. That would be an agreement to fix prices, and even though it is vertical rather than horizontal, it is still a *per se* violation of the law. This kind of vertical price fixing is also known as "resale price maintenance."

2. You tell your franchisees that $1.50 is your "suggested" price. One franchisee begins selling the ice cream cones for 99¢, and the other franchisees complain to you. You agree with them that you will protect those charging the full price by terminating the discounter. Again, this is a violation of the Sherman Act because there is an agreement (this time between you and the franchisees who are urging that the discounter be terminated) and because that agreement is a means of enforcing adherence to a resale price.

3. You announce the price at which you expect franchisees to sell and that franchisees who depart from that price will be terminated. As

long as your action is *unilateral* and not part of an agreement with any franchisee, there is no antitrust violation because there is no contract or conspiracy. The protection for such unilateral action is known as the "Colgate Doctrine" because of the important Supreme Court case in 1919 upon which it is based.

4. You announce the suggested price and simply urge your franchisees to adopt it, giving them the reasons you believe such a pricing strategy is appropriate. This may not always be as persuasive as the threat of termination, but it avoids any suggestion of an agreement and may be more conducive to stable relationships with franchisees. Again, since your action is unilateral, it is legal.

5. You decide to acquire one or more of your franchises and run them as franchisor-owned stores. Following such an acquisition, you could set whatever price you believe to be appropriate. There would be no agreement because there are no longer two different entities to agree.

The prohibitions against vertical price fixing should rarely interfere with a franchisor's successful operation. If suggested prices are carefully thought out, franchisees will be inclined to charge those prices because they contribute to the uniformity of the franchised outlets and are, presumably, set at a level that will be beneficial to both the franchisor and the franchisees.

The Law of "Refusals to Deal"

A motel franchisor offers its franchises for sale on a nationwide basis and receives inquiries from many prospective franchisees. Must the franchisor sell to each interested buyer who can pay the necessary initial fee? What are the permissible reasons for rejecting a proposed buyer? The antitrust rules regulating such "refusals to deal" help provide the answers to these questions.

As we have already seen, when a franchisor takes action solely on its own, there can be no agreement and therefore no antitrust violation (unless the franchisor has a monopoly over a particular product or service). Thus, our motel franchisor, if acting completely independently and not in consultation with existing franchisees, may refuse to sell a franchise to a particular buyer for a good reason, a bad reason, or no reason at all. This is known as a **unilateral refusal to deal** and is related to the well-established principle that the antitrust laws do not require a seller to sell to every buyer that comes along.

The more common, and more difficult, situation exists when the franchisor does in fact consult with existing franchisees or has, by agreement with existing franchisees, limited its discretion to grant new franchises. Suppose, for example, that the motel franchisor has an agreement which gives an existing franchisee the exclusive franchise in a particular town. If the franchisor rejects a prospective franchisee in the same town, the prospective franchisee may claim that the action violates the antitrust laws because it is based on an *agreement* (the franchising contract with the existing franchisee) which restrains trade by allowing only one franchise in the town. Non-price restraints, such as the territorial allocation adopted by our franchisor, are judged under the "rule of reason." They violate the antitrust laws only if they unreasonably restrain competition in light of all the circumstances. The inquiry then turns to whether the franchisor's decision was intended to reduce competition or had that effect. If the motel franchisor can show that it turned down the prospective franchisee not because of the exclusive territorial agreement with the existing franchisee, but because the prospective buyer had a criminal record or was insolvent, there is no antitrust violation. These are, of course, legitimate business reasons for not wanting to sell a franchise to a particular person, reasons which demonstrate that the rejection was not based on an intent to reduce competition.

Suppose the motel franchisor turns down the prospective franchisee because the franchisor has determined that its franchisees will operate most effectively if they have exclusive territories. The franchisor provides for such territorial exclusivity in the franchising agreements. In considering whether the restriction is generally procompetitive or anticompetitive, courts will look at several factors: What choices regarding price and quality do the other motels and hotels in town offer consumers? What difficulties (if any) are faced by potential competitors seeking to open hotels or motels in that geographic area? Does the franchisor dominate the motel market in the particular town? Often, a careful review will indicate that while competition between franchisees of the same franchisor is restricted by territorial exclusivity, such protection makes each franchisee a stronger competitor with other hotels and motels. In such circumstances, the restriction does not violate the antitrust laws. However, when a number of restrictive practices — prohibitions on franchisee ownership of other hotels, the reservation of certain towns for development by the franchisor itself — are imposed in addition to exclusive territorial arrangements, courts have occasionally found antitrust violations.

The law pertaining to refusals to deal is also relevant when the franchisor terminates the franchising relationship with a particular franchisee. Suppose one of the motel franchisees, in violation of the franchising agreement, opens an additional motel using the franchise name and concept at a new location. May the franchisor terminate the franchisee for breach of the agreement, or is the franchisor likely to face an antitrust suit if it does so? Whether the franchisor has an antitrust problem depends upon the reasonableness of the territorial restraint. If the territorial exclusivity can be reasonably justified, the franchisor's "refusal to deal" is not illegal.

The antitrust aspects of refusals to deal are sometimes spoken of as if they were great mysteries. However, the simple fact is that the legality of a refusal to deal depends entirely upon the answers to two questions: (1) Was the refusal a *unilateral* action or one arising from an agreement, and (2) what was the reason for the action? Unilateral action is generally permissible. If the termination of an existing franchise is used to enforce an agreement to fix resale prices, it is *per se* illegal because price fixing is *per se* illegal. If it is used to enforce an allocation of territories among franchisees, legality will depend upon the effect on competition. Finally, a termination or refusal to deal that does not violate the antitrust laws may nevertheless run afoul of other restrictions. The terms of the franchising agreement often set forth detailed standards for the conduct of both the franchisor and the franchisee and these must be carefully followed.

Selling to Franchisees

Perhaps the most common antitrust questions facing franchisors are those which relate to the products, services, and trademarks that the franchisor allows or requires its franchisees to use. These questions go to the very heart of the franchising relationship: What is it, exactly, that the franchisee obtains as part of the franchise? What distinguishes the Gourmet Ice Cream franchise from other sellers of ice cream?

Tying Agreements. In our overview of the antitrust laws, we noted that the Sherman Act prohibits agreements that unreasonably restrain trade. The Clayton Act makes it illegal to condition the purchase of one product on the purchase of a second, separate product, if the effect may be to substantially lessen competition. Both of these statutes may apply to tying arrangements, which take their name from the fact that the purchase of one item is "tied" to the purchase of another.

The whole concept of a franchise involves a "bundle" of products, services, and/or trade names. The Gourmet Ice Cream franchisor may sell franchisees the right to use its logo, trademark, and operating plan. The franchisor may also sell franchisees the ice cream mix itself, disposable bowls and utensils, or employee uniforms. The franchise package for an accounting franchisor might consist of trademark, logo, computer software, and training manuals. Often, the franchisor considers everything it sells to the franchisee to be essential parts of a "package" that is the franchise. The franchisor may want franchisees to purchase each element of the package because it believes that each is critical to the success of the operation. Or the franchisor may attempt to increase its revenues by selling franchisees additional products.

Franchisees, however, may not see things the same way. They may believe the franchisor is imposing unreasonable requirements on them, forcing them to buy particular items from the franchisor at inflated prices. They may think some items are frills that their struggling franchise can do without or that can be replaced with lower-cost substitutes.

Before turning to particular questions of tying that arise in franchising, it may be helpful to understand the rules against tying as recently laid down by the U.S. Supreme Court. The Supreme Court has identified three elements that must be shown in order to prove that a tying arrangement is automatically or *per se* unlawful:

1. The existence of two separate products, the purchase of one (the "tying" product) being conditioned on the purchase of the other (the "tied" product);
2. Sufficient economic power (on the part of the seller) with respect to the *tying* product to restrain competition in the *tied* product;
3. An effect upon a substantial amount of commerce in the tied product.[1]

In addition, even if the market power described in item 2 is absent, the tying arrangement may nevertheless be unlawful if it *unreasonably* restrains competition.

The thrust of these elements demonstrates the basis for the prohibition against tying. A sufficiently unique tying product may give a franchisor (or manufacturer) such leverage over a franchisee (or distributor) that the franchisee could be forced to buy products it would not otherwise buy or, at least, would not buy from the franchisor. When a seller uses one product to obtain dominance in sales of other products, there may be harm to competition in the market for the second, tied product because the buyer is not allowed to make its own choices in the market.

For the franchisor, many questions regarding tying can be resolved by determining that what is being sold is really a single product, not two separate products. If the items are commonly sold as a package, and are not separately available in the marketplace, there can be no tying violation. For example, one must generally buy a shoe for the right foot as a condition for buying a shoe for the left foot (and vice versa). However, this is not an illegal tie-in because there is no independent market for right shoes; they are normally sold in pairs with left shoes.

Franchisors often claim that the franchise is a comprehensive package and each particular item is an integral part. For example, courts have ruled that a trademark and the prefabricated housing components to which the trademark applies are a single product. Another recent case decided that a franchise for a weight-loss program and the diet supplement sold through the franchise constituted a single product.

---

[1] *Jefferson Parish Hospital District No. 2 v. Hyde*, 466 U.S. 2 (1984).

Another case concluded that an ice cream store trademark and the mix used in making the ice cream constituted a single product.

However, other franchise product packages have encountered antitrust problems because there was not a close connection between the two items being sold to the franchisee. A federal appeals court recently decided that a franchise to operate a beauty salon was a separate product from a bookkeeping service that the franchisor wanted to sell to franchisees. In other cases, franchise trademarks and standardized store operations have been found to be products separate from supplies sold to the franchisees. The law in this area is particularly confusing, and legal counsel should be consulted when franchisors consider the bundle of goods and services they require franchisees to buy.

Even if the products or services being sold are considered two separate products, the tying arrangement violates the antitrust laws only if the seller has enough market power with respect to the tying product to restrain competition in the market for the tied product. Two indicators are important. First, does the seller so dominate the market for the product that buyers will purchase that product even though it means they must also buy a less desirable product from the seller — a product they might not want at all or might prefer to buy from another seller? Second, does the seller's leverage therefore harm competition in the market for the second product?

In one recent case, a hospital required all of its surgical patients to use particular anesthesiologists. But the court found that the hospital did not have sufficient leverage in the hospital services market to restrain trade in the market for anesthesiology services because the hospital accounted for only 30 percent of the hospital beds in its geographic area. The court reasoned that patients (buyers) who wanted anesthesiology services other than those required by the hospital could easily go to another hospital. In many such situations, sellers of a particular product or service will not have enough power in the market for that product or service to adversely affect competition in the market for the tied product.

Franchisors must approach potential tying claims very carefully. The usual tying claim is made by a disgruntled franchisee who asserts that the franchisor has unlawfully tied the sale of particular products or services to the franchise trademark or operating plan. A number of cases have held that where the tying product is patented or copyrighted, or is a well-known trademark, it automatically gives the seller sufficient leverage over buyers to force them to buy the less desirable tied product. Some other courts have questioned these decisions on the ground that the mere fact that an item is patented, copyrighted, or trademarked does not mean that it does not face vigorous competition in the market.

It is virtually impossible to develop a set of clear guidelines for avoiding tying problems from past court cases. Certainly, the safer course for a franchisor is to limit the products the franchisee is required to purchase from it to those that are intimately related to the franchise and its trademark. The further the tied product deviates from what the public perceives as an inherent part of the franchise, the greater the likelihood that it will be treated as a separate product for purposes of the tying analysis. Moreover, particular care must be taken when the purchase of another product or service is required in order to purchase a patented or copyrighted product or the right to use a well-known trademark.

Given the uncertainties of the rules regarding tying, how can the franchisor satisfy its legitimate concern that products offered by the franchisee are of high quality and consistent with the franchise concept? As with most business problems, solutions exist that are both practical and legal. One common approach is to sell products to franchisees at relatively low prices. For example, a video-rental franchisor may require its franchisees to sell blank videotapes, preferably those which carry the franchisor's trademark. Rather than requiring the franchisees to purchase the tapes from the franchisor, the franchisor may achieve the same result through attractive pricing; since the franchisor can buy in bulk, it may be able to resell the tapes to its franchisees at a lower price than the franchisee can get from competing sellers. While the franchisor may make less profit on the sale of the tapes, it will make some profit, increase recognition of its trademark, and be able to exercise quality control.

Another common means for a franchisor to maintain quality control and standardization among franchisees, while avoiding illegal tie-ins, is to specify particular sources from which products may be purchased. A good example of an arrangement that does not violate the antitrust laws is described in the 1977 case of *Kentucky Fried Chicken Corp. v. Diversified Packaging Corp.* Kentucky Fried Chicken had a reasonable business concern that the packaging used for its products, including the cardboard boxes used for takeout orders, meet certain standards of strength and appearance. Franchisees could buy the packaging from Kentucky Fried Chicken Corp. or from a number of other suppliers that had been examined and approved by Kentucky Fried Chicken as meeting its standards. In addition, the franchisor had detailed specifications, and packaging companies that met those specifications could be placed on the approved list. The federal appeals court concluded that this method of quality control did not constitute illegal tying.

Full-Line Forcing. Sometimes franchisors require franchisees to carry the "full line" of a franchisor's products. In some ways, this is like a tie-in because as part of purchasing the right to use the franchisor's trademark and concept, the franchisee is required to purchase products or services from the franchisor. As long as the franchisee is allowed to purchase other, competing products as well, such requirements generally do not violate the antitrust laws. For example, if the video-rental franchisor requires that franchisees stock a number of the franchisor's products, including its trademarked blank tapes, but also allows the franchisee to stock competing blank tapes, there is probably no adverse effect on competition in the market for blank tapes and therefore no antitrust violation.

Exclusive Dealing. Another variation of the restrictions imposed on franchisees is an "exclusive dealing" requirement. Suppose the video-rental franchising agreement does not require franchisees to sell blank videotapes, but provides that, if they do, the cassettes must be purchased from the franchisor. This is not a tying problem because there is no requirement that the tapes be purchased at all. The courts have generally allowed such exclusive dealing provisions unless there has been a showing that the agreement unreasonably restricted competition. Questions regarding exclusive dealing also come up in the context of the initial purchase of a franchise, if a franchisor decides that it will not sell franchises to buyers who own franchises sold by competing franchisors. Again, these restrictions violate the antitrust laws only if competition in the market for buying and selling franchises can be shown to have been adversely affected.

Price Discrimination. The Robinson-Patman Act makes it unlawful for a seller to discriminate in the prices it charges different buyers, if that discrimination adversely affects competition. This federal statute applies to franchisors that sell goods to franchisees, just as it does to all other sellers. An example will show, however, that franchisors should have little difficulty determining when the law applies and avoiding serious problems.

A franchisor begins selling franchises for weight-reducing clinics with an initial franchise fee of $20,000. Several are sold, but the price appears to be somewhat high, and is cut for succeeding franchisees to $17,500. This does not violate the federal price discrimination law because that statute applies only to the sale of "commodities," which does not include franchising rights. (However, the franchisor and its attorney would have to carefully review state franchise and price discrimination statutes which might apply to such discrimination between franchisees.) The same analysis would apply to the franchisor's sale of accounting services to different franchisees at different prices; again, these are not commodities and any discrimination in price is thus not illegal under the Robinson-Patman Act.

Suppose, however, that the weight-loss clinic franchisor sells scales to two franchisees at different prices. Most of the elements of illegal price discrimination exist: two *sales* of *commodities* of like grade and quality to *different purchasers at different prices*. But, for those sales to be unlawful, it must also be shown that the effect of the price discrimination may be to substantially lessen competition. If the weight-loss clinics, like many franchises, operate in different geographic areas which the franchisor has selected precisely so that two franchisees will not be in competition with each other, the franchisor might successfully argue that the price discrimination does not have any adverse effect on competition because the two franchisees operate in different market areas.

Questions of price discrimination also arise when a franchisor sells products to franchisees at one price and to non-franchisee purchasers at a higher price. The key question is whether competition between the franchisees and the non-franchisee buyers is harmed by the price discrimination. If the non-franchisee buyers are in different geographic areas or if they operate in different functional markets (i.e., they sell to different categories of buyers) than the franchisees, there will be no violation. Franchisors must also be cautious when granting discounts, favorable credit terms, or promotional allowances or services to some purchasers (whether franchisees or not) but not to others. Some franchisors choose to bypass most of the potential problems under the Robinson-Patman Act by simply refusing to sell to non-franchisees at all.

Franchisor-Owned Stores

Up to this point, we have been considering the impact of the antitrust laws on the relationship between a franchisor and an independent franchisee. Many franchisors, however, in addition to selling to independent franchisees, own a number of franchises themselves. This practice, known as *dual distribution*, may affect the impact of the antitrust laws, sometimes allowing the franchisor wider latitude in conduct and sometimes raising additional antitrust concerns.

Applying the antitrust law to the dual distribution situation draws on concepts that we have already discussed. For example, although a franchisor may not agree with its franchisees on the prices at which particular products will be resold, it may set the prices for products to be sold through franchisor-owned stores. Because the franchisor and the franchise it operates are considered to be one entity (even if one is a corporate subsidiary of the other), there can be no "agreement" on price and thus no antitrust violation.

On the other hand, certain franchisor practices that are unlawful only if they have an adverse effect on competition, such as territorial allocation, must be more closely examined when there are franchisor-owned stores. As we have seen, *vertical* agreements between a franchisor and independent franchisees are much less likely to present antitrust problems than *horizontal* agreements between competitors, whether at the franchisor or franchisee level. In dual distribution, one person or company is both the franchisor and a franchisee, and there are aspects of both vertical and horizontal arrangements. The existence of dual distribution does not automatically mean that, for example, exclusive territories are illegal. Rather, the courts usually ask whether the vertical or horizontal aspects of the system predominate and whether there is actually an adverse impact on competition.

The treatment of dual distribution systems can be illustrated by considering a hypothetical photocopying franchise. If the independent owners of a number of small photocopying stores organize an umbrella entity to standardize their operations and, perhaps, act as a franchisor for new stores, the arrangement is predominantly horizontal. If part of the agreement is that each member will remain within its exclusive geographical territory, the courts would probably consider this to be a horizontal allocation of territories and *per se* illegal. In the more common situation, however, the photocopying franchisor may have a number of independent franchises and be the owner of several franchises. Here, the existence of exclusive territories is probably the decision of the franchisor: it is imposed *vertically* on franchises (including those owned by the franchisor), rather than being the result of a *horizontal* agreement among formerly independent sellers, as in the prior example.

As courts have grown more familiar with dual distribution, the trend appears to be towards finding antitrust violations only when the arrangement is between competitors and has a clearly adverse impact on competition.

SUCCESS STORY
LLOYD T. TARBUTTON

Lloyd Tarbutton was born in the rural community of Easton, Maryland. He left home when he was 15 years old, worked his way through high school, and at 17 came to the Norfolk–Virginia Beach area to live. Shortly after that, he served in the U.S. Navy during the Korean War and afterward returned to the Virginia Beach area.

For five years, he worked with the world's largest advertising agency and attained the position of District Sales Manager. In 1962, he founded Tarbutton Associates, a company which he heads today as chairman of the board. This company has three main divisions: franchise consulting, real estate, and hotel/motel management. Under the franchise consulting division, he assists companies desiring to use the franchising method of marketing in starting up their operation or expanding an existing franchise operation.

> Tarbutton is also co-founder of Econo Lodges of America, Inc. (formerly known as Econo-Travel Motor Hotel Corporation), which introduced to the world an entirely new industry, the budget motel business. He began using the franchise concept of marketing in starting his company and has continued to be a success.
>
> In addition, Tarbutton has served in various executive positions of the International Franchise Association, including that of president. He served on the board of directors, as a member of the executive committee, and as chairman of the past presidents' advisory council. He was chairman of the first Far East International Symposium on Franchising held in Tokyo, Japan. Likewise, the first European International Symposium on Franchising, to be held in Amsterdam, by the IFA, was also chaired by Tarbutton.
>
> Tarbutton is an internationally known business consultant, specializing in the areas of franchising, self-motivating management, and creative sales and marketing techniques. He is a founder and served as vice-chairman of the board of the Franchising Political Action Committee, Inc., which is headquartered in Washington, D.C., for many years. He is active as a trustee of the Old Dominion University Educational Foundation and is chairman of the Center for Economic Education at the university.
>
> Photo and information provided courtesy of Lloyd T. Tarbutton, August, 1985.

SUMMARY

State and federal antitrust laws are designed to ensure competition in the marketplace, and they apply to franchises as well as to most other businesses. The most serious antitrust offenses — horizontal price fixing and territorial allocation — can be avoided by most franchisors without much difficulty. Franchisors are more likely to confront issues such as vertical price fixing, the tying of one product or service to another, and exclusive dealing. Vertical price fixing is *per se* illegal — that is, it is prohibited even if there is no demonstrable effect on competition. But, there are lawful ways to encourage franchisees to sell at suggested retail prices. Similarly, while tying and exclusive dealing may be unlawful in certain circumstances, franchisors have a variety of means to achieve their legitimate business goals without violating the antitrust laws. With common sense and a little advance planning, franchisors can successfully avoid most serious antitrust problems.

REVIEW QUESTIONS

1. Discuss the importance of antitrust laws related to franchising.
2. What are the advantages and disadvantages of antitrust laws to the franchisor?

3. What are the advantages and disadvantages of antitrust laws to the franchisee?
4. Discuss price discrimination and its effect on franchisors.
5. What are tying agreements, and how do they affect franchising today?

CASE STUDY
JO-ANN'S NUT HOUSE, INC.*

Jill and Jeri want to start their own candy store. They think it would be fun to own a candy store in a shopping center not far from their homes. One of the favorite candy stores that Jill has visited often while on the East Coast visiting her daughter and son-in-law is Jo-Ann's Nut House. Jill and Jeri have written to Jo-Ann's and received some informative literature about franchising and the prospects for opening a candy store in their midwestern town. Jo-Ann's Nut House is a candy and nut retail store with locations in regional mall shopping centers. The size of the average store is 500 square feet, and the lease on the location is purchased by Jo-Ann's Nut House, Inc.

Jo-Ann's has five regional warehouses from which candy is shipped biweekly in company trucks to the stores. The shops are designed and merchandised to promote sales of candies, nuts, chocolates, and selected holiday gift items. The franchisee of Jo-Ann's receives all the benefits of being an independent operator, along with the advantages of being an integral part of a very professional organization. Jo-Ann's company headquarters provides help with selecting a site, setting up the store, buying, distributing, marketing, advertising, training, supervising, and controlling the budget. Jo-Ann's has also set up a franchisee council and a product review committee with the help of the franchisees and the company headquarters.

The franchising fee is determined by the length of the lease with the shopping center. A lease is computed at a rate of $1,500 per year or is set at $15,000 for a ten-year lease. In addition, a 6 percent royalty on sales is paid weekly. The initial startup costs follow:

Startup Costs

	Low	High
Franchising Fee	$ 7,500	$ 15,000
Construction and Improvement of Business Premises	20,000	80,000
Installation of Fixtures and Equipment	8,000	18,000

* Information furnished courtesy of Specialty Retail Concepts, Inc., September, 1987.

Small Equipment Package	2,500	4,500
Initial Inventory	6,000	12,000
Initial Working Capital	3,000	6,000
Total	$47,000	$135,000

These figures do not include working with the franchisee's lease or rent payments, which may increase the startup costs of the franchise.

Jill and Jeri believe they now have the time to be very successful operators of a candy store. They believe that with adequate training they can be successful managers as well as operators. They have the opportunity of picking their products from over 300 items on the approved products list — many more items than their unit would reasonably be able to display. They have also learned that if the proposed franchised unit is successful, they may qualify for additional franchises in their local community.

CASE QUESTIONS

1. What legal activities should Jill and Jeri expect from their franchisor?
2. Generally, what legal activities are franchisors expected to perform?
3. Why should Jill and Jeri seek legal counsel and advice?
4. What legal parameters do franchisees have to protect themselves when becoming new franchisees? What protection will they have five years down the road?

PART THREE

THE FRANCHISOR ARENA: DEVELOPING THE FRANCHISED BUSINESS

CHAPTER 7
MANAGING THE MARKETING PROCESS

In studying this chapter, you will:
- Learn the steps involved in strategic market planning.
- Learn about strategic planning in franchising through examining the market function and activities.
- Understand how a hierarchy of objectives and strategies can be developed within a franchise organization.
- Learn how to develop a marketing mix for the franchise.
- Understand the role and use of channels of distribution.

INCIDENT

Six years ago, after finishing college with a degree in exercise physiology, Amy opened her own exercise studio. While in school Amy worked as an assistant trainer on the men's and the women's basketball teams. With this background Amy has a good understanding of the human body and what types of exercises might do more harm than good.

In those six years, the exercise studio has become so busy that Amy is considering expanding. One of her options is to franchise. The market possibilities are endless, especially since the national interest in good health has become a way of life for many people. Amy believes her exercise studio can capitalize on that interest because it offers a "fun" way to get, and stay, in shape.

Several of Amy's instructors have expressed interest in participating in her plans to expand. With help from Amy they could select and decorate a studio. Most importantly, Amy could train prospective franchisees in appropriate and correct exercise techniques as well as provide concise information about health issues.

Amy believes she has a good chance for success through growth as a franchised business. She has a valuable service to offer prospective exercise studio owners, who in turn have a valuable service to offer customers. She senses that once her chain of studios becomes established, the franchise name will be associated with quality exercise programs and conscientious instructors.

Amy's next step is to determine exactly how to market the business. What considerations are essential as she begins to develop a marketing plan? What strategies might she consider? Can she accomplish her business objectives through the marketing function and activities involved in a franchise system?

INTRODUCTION

The most notable characteristic of franchising is deeply embedded in the overall concept of franchising — the intent to increase revenues by creating new business units. In a practical sense, though, the most fundamental element of franchising involves marketing. Franchising is an approach to business ownership and operation that requires bringing the product or service to the customer at the right time, at the right place, and at the right price. The concepts of product, place, price, and promotion within an appropriate time frame for the purchaser constitute the classic principles of marketing for any business venture.

As a prospective franchisor, Amy needs to be aware of the characteristics of the market for her studio's service. What is the estimated size of the market? What is a reasonable estimate of her share of the market? Conditions in the market can determine the success or failure of Amy's or anyone's business. Thus it is essential to develop an overall marketing strategy that focuses the efforts of the business on satisfying the customers' needs, at a profit.

Amy should know what her customers like and dislike. She should also ask such questions as, is the buyer the user of her exercise classes? Is the person who makes the decision to buy a membership in her studio the same person who actually pays for the membership? Who else influences the purchase? Within a household, because the decision to purchase or use (and perhaps to continue purchasing or using) can be made by different persons, the roles played are not always easy to identify. For example, when a family goes to a fast-food restaurant for lunch, does the driver choose the particular restaurant? Who else influences this decision? Is the decision linked to other factors such as how close the restaurant is to the workplace or to major shopping areas? What is ordered and by whom? What effect do location, convenience, price, service, product quality, and restaurant atmosphere have on the decision?

Using a marketing concept, a prospective franchisor can develop an orientation to focus on consumer needs and put together an effective marketing strategy that uses the basic components of a marketing mix. A **marketing strategy** consists of identifying one or more target markets and creating a marketing mix. In our example, Amy must determine the customers most likely to purchase memberships and use her exercise club.

Once a target market has clearly been established, the next step is to develop an appropriate marketing mix. The **marketing mix** consists of controllable factors to be considered in combination to satisfy the needs or wants of customers in the target market. These factors include product, promotion, price, and place.

Two general concepts — marketing strategy and marketing mix — are essential components of this chapter. Initially, we will discuss strategy from an overall business perspective to identify how the market orientation fits into a general strategy for the business itself. The four components of the marketing mix will be described in order to explain how to determine a marketing mix for a franchising approach to expansion.

STRATEGIC PLANNING IN FRANCHISING

Strategic planning is the process of formulating and maintaining organizational objectives and operational capacities to allow the franchise organization to function effectively within its ever-changing environment. The steps of this process are shown in Figure 7-1. The resulting plan is a comprehensive and integrated approach to the production and distribution of goods or services which recognizes existing environmental pressures and opportunities. Planning becomes "strategic" when the business owner realizes that most of the planning activity involves examining his or her business and deciding what should be maintained, what should be dropped, and what should be added in order to ensure the continuing success of the firm.

The Changing Marketplace

The late 1980s and 1990s promise to be full of surprises. A franchisor today must design a company with products or services that can withstand shocks. Economic forces, both long and short term, have produced

**Figure 7-1
Steps in Strategic Market Planning**

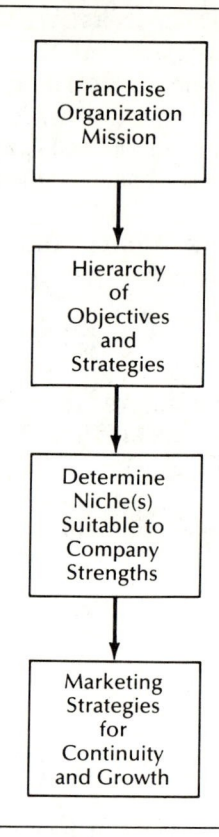

```
┌─────────────┐
│  Franchise  │
│Organization │
│   Mission   │
└──────┬──────┘
       ▼
┌─────────────┐
│  Hierarchy  │
│      of     │
│  Objectives │
│     and     │
│  Strategies │
└──────┬──────┘
       ▼
┌─────────────┐
│  Determine  │
│   Niche(s)  │
│ Suitable to │
│   Company   │
│  Strengths  │
└──────┬──────┘
       ▼
┌─────────────┐
│  Marketing  │
│  Strategies │
│     for     │
│  Continuity │
│ and Growth  │
└─────────────┘
```

an unstable marketplace and unpredictable competition. The influx of women into the labor force, the economic maturation of the baby-boom generation, revolutionary technological innovations, increased foreign competition — all these realities have changed traditional American business practices. In a dynamic marketplace, independence, adaptability to sudden changes, and acceptance of risks can provide the edge a business will need to stay competitive.

The franchisor and the franchisee will need to be sensitive to the changing habits, tastes, desires, and spending patterns of their customers to ensure the profitable continuance of the business. Strategic planning is a tool a franchise firm can use in a dynamic marketplace to keep the firm adaptable, to face new opportunities, to avoid or minimize effects of negative pressures or threats, and to build upon the firm's strengths. In simpler terms, strategic planning allows a franchised business to attain and then maintain competitiveness in its target markets.

Because franchisor and franchisee desire both short-term and long-term profitability, they of course intend the business to have continuity, to survive over time. Strategic planning makes it more likely that they will succeed in this goal, because it involves making decisions in the present that will help to ensure the success of the business in the future.

Problems in Applying Strategic Planning to Smaller Businesses

Strategic planning is used by many major corporations and is generally recognized as a valuable tool to determine the best strategies to increase market share or profit margin on a firm's products or services. But there are some problems in applying strategic planning in smaller businesses. Since the vast majority of franchised firms are not large corporations, we should first clarify what we mean by smaller businesses. Characteristics to consider typically include size of work force, amount of assets, and total profits. However, the primary characteristics of a business are often not immediately discernible. A number of these qualities are shown in Table 7-1. Typically, the owner of a small business, like Amy in our earlier example, has limited resources and as a result operates on a rather small scale. Small business performance (profits and costs) can be highly susceptible to changes in consumer buying patterns. Government regulations and compliance requirements can have a significant impact on operating costs. Also, the small firm usually doesn't have specialized staff personnel readily available to address legal questions, personnel issues, or tax questions. And, perhaps most important of all, the small business

Table 7-1
Typical Characteristics of Smaller Firms

- Limited resources are available to achieve business objectives.
- Scale of operation is smaller, which can mean a higher cost structure because firm lacks size to be able to purchase in large, discounted quantities.
- Governmental regulations and compliance requirements can significantly increase operating expenses.
- Business performance is highly susceptible to changes in customer buying behavior.
- Minor changes in operating efficiency can affect availability of resources and business profitability.
- Firms are often without specialized staff to address legal, accounting, and other needs of the business.
- Owner often lacks objectivity needed to evaluate and plan activities efficiently, or lacks ability to delegate responsibility effectively.
- Business often fails to have sufficient working capital, financial controls, or materials or inventory on hand, or has not adequately analyzed the impact of fixed overhead on the cost of products or services.

owner often lacks the time to step back and evaluate, plan, and objectively determine what should be the next step to achieve the market, profit, and operational goals of the business.

There are some other reasons why strategic planning may be inappropriate or difficult for a smaller business to implement. Typically, strategic planning has been used by companies that have several or many product lines. Some larger firms keep the situation manageable by forming a holding company that has separate business entities under it which are held accountable for their performance by the holding company, each entity controlling its particular product or service lines. For example, Mobil Corporation is not only a major oil company (with a large number of franchisees), but it is also a holding company with retailing, real estate, and restaurant businesses. This is a situation not normally found in smaller firms. Therefore, developing the overall business mission, objectives, and strategies from a multi-business perspective is obviously not realistic for most small businesses.

Several tools are appropriate for use by smaller firms and can be effectively utilized in franchising: analysis of market share, competitive analysis, competitive advantage/disadvantage analysis, and analysis of direct and indirect costs of production or operations. Thus, the process of strategic planning and some tools are appropriate and will be helpful to the great majority of existing franchised businesses as well as to budding franchisors.

STEPS IN STRATEGIC PLANNING

There are several steps a successful franchisor takes in the strategic planning of a franchised business.

Franchise Organization Mission

Establishing the franchise mission is the first step in strategic planning. The franchised business exists with the aim of accomplishing something within and through its economic environment. The methods to be used to accomplish the overall mission should be clearly set forth by the franchisor before any franchisees are recruited; otherwise, the mission may become blurred as growth takes place and goods or services become varied, or if marketplace conditions change sufficiently to make the original mission inappropriate. The simple-sounding questions to be addressed are perhaps the most difficult for the franchisor to answer: What is my business? Who is my customer? What are the needs of my customer? What do I want my business to be in the long run?

A successful franchisor asks and answers these questions in order to formulate a carefully prepared mission statement. The mission statement must provide a shared sense of opportunity, challenge, and motivation for the owners, franchisees, and employees of the organization. It should define the target markets or business areas in which the franchisor intends to operate; a target market can be described in terms of products or services offered, customer groups targeted, customer needs or wants to be fulfilled, or some combination of these.

In the past, a firm's mission statement was expressed in concrete and rather narrow terms, such as "we are in the typewriter business" or "we are in the steel-making business." More recently, as a result of more-dynamic, less-stable economic conditions, mission statements have been expressed in terms that address the customer, not the product. For example, "meeting the information processing needs of our customer" might be the mission statement today that once was "we are in the typewriter business," the main difference being that the old statement does not allow for market and technological change. The typewriter company could quickly go out of business if the firm failed to offer electronic calculators, word processing, and other forms of information processing desired by customers.

Hierarchy of Objectives and Strategies

The second step in strategic planning is for the franchisor to use the mission statement to formulate a detailed set of **supporting objectives** for the major functions of the business and the distribution network being established, maintained, or further developed. Objectives should be determined for functions such as marketing, finance, human resources, and operations, and then arranged in a hierarchy according to importance; the marketing objectives provide the overall direction for the franchised business in clear, understandable terms (see Figure 7-2). From this hierarchy, specific plans to implement the marketing strategy need to be spelled out so as to provide as many quantifiable targets or "hoped-for" results as possible. In so doing, the entrepreneur gains a stronger sense of what should take place in terms of planning, organizing, and controlling the management activities of the franchise organization.

Determining Niche(s) Suitable to Company Strengths

This third step in strategic planning is useful to all franchised businesses, whether they provide just one or more than one product or service. The step involves choosing a propitious niche within which the franchise can target its operations in its industry. The niche may be a segment of the total line of products and services offered by competitors within the industry, or it may be a predetermined group of customers targeted according to characteristics such as size of group, income level, and location. In either case, the reason for seeking a niche is to identify the target group to whom the product or service is to be offered. If the franchised

Figure 7-2
Hierarchy of Objectives and Strategies for a Franchised Exercise Studio (Hypothetical)

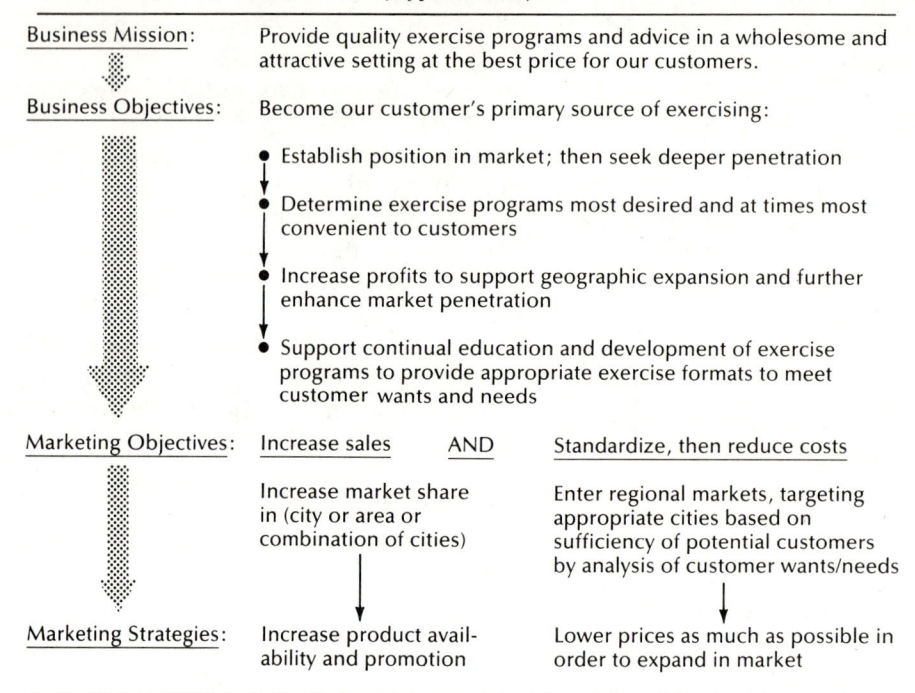

Business Mission: Provide quality exercise programs and advice in a wholesome and attractive setting at the best price for our customers.

Business Objectives: Become our customer's primary source of exercising:

- Establish position in market; then seek deeper penetration
- Determine exercise programs most desired and at times most convenient to customers
- Increase profits to support geographic expansion and further enhance market penetration
- Support continual education and development of exercise programs to provide appropriate exercise formats to meet customer wants and needs

Marketing Objectives: Increase sales AND Standardize, then reduce costs

| Increase market share in (city or area or combination of cities) | Enter regional markets, targeting appropriate cities based on sufficiency of potential customers by analysis of customer wants/needs |

Marketing Strategies: Increase product availability and promotion | Lower prices as much as possible in order to expand in market

---

firm chooses wisely, its niche will be unserved or underserved by competitors, in which case the niche can provide profitability as well as growth. The firm should choose a market niche in which it can favorably strive in the daily competition to serve its customers.

Of course, the strategic advantage of carefully choosing a niche does not preclude the franchised company from seeking to develop more than one market niche. As a firm grows and gains experience within its industry and markets, it may choose to make additions to its product or service line that can be offered efficiently and effectively to its customers. For example, an accounting and business services firm specializing in payroll, accounts payable/receivable, and inventory accounting systems may decide to add other services, such as auditing, tax preparation, or consulting on management information systems. Likewise, a fast-food restaurant franchise may expand its scope of operation to include serving breakfast, while a domestic cleaning franchise may provide broader options for cleaning homes, including lawn care or minor household repairs.

The decision by a franchisor to try to boost profits typically involves some form of expansion. The question becomes whether to expand along customer lines or along product or service lines, or both. Figure 7-3 presents an expansion matrix for a franchised firm seeking to grow. The franchisor may seek to expand by providing the same product or service in new locations to attract a greater number of currently targeted customers, or it may seek new types of customers to whom to offer the current product or service. Or, the franchisor may choose to expand the product or service line. Such expansion typically includes providing products or services to complement the line already being offered to the customers.

A franchised business often opts to expand in order to achieve **synergistic** results for the business. Synergy occurs when two separate actions performed together produce a greater effect than either can separately. This is sometimes called the "1 + 1 = 3" effect. For example, having a restaurant inside a franchised motel makes the motel a more convenient place for travelers to stop. The intention is clearly to increase sales over what they would be if the restaurant and motel were independently owned and operated or located one or two miles apart. Another, somewhat different example is franchised restaurants that expand their business to include serving breakfast. With this approach, the aim is to get the lunch or dinner customer to patronize the restaurant more than just once a day.

Because synergy is often part of the expansion goal of the franchisor, the approaches considered should be carefully thought through.

Figure 7-3
Franchise Expansion Matrix

	Present	Associated in Use	Similar Production Technology
Present			
Geographical Expansion			
New Types			▓

(Rows: CUSTOMERS; Columns: PRODUCTS)

Source: Adapted from: Wm. H. Newman, James P. Logan, and W. Harvey Hegarty, *Strategy, Policy & Central Management*, 9th edition (Cincinnati: South-Western Publishing Co., 1985), p. 94.

Figure 7-3 also presents the "cells" within which the intended expansion options can fall. As the franchised business moves further away from its present customers or its current product or service, the benefits of synergy diminish. At the extreme (lower right corner of the matrix in the figure), new customers are needed and a new product or service must be provided; here the benefits of synergy to the franchise can virtually disappear. A franchisor considering this type of expansion (that is, involving both a new customer group and a new product or service) is effectively seeking expansion through conglomeration. Typically, a franchised firm looking to expand will consider combinations of niches that supplement or reinforce one another in a synergistic way. Before expanding, the franchisor should plan carefully in order to avoid losing benefits the firm has accrued by concentrating on its present product or service and customer group.

Once the market niche is determined and related to the firm's primary strengths (the unique characteristics or methods of the business), the mode of expansion — along product/service or customer lines — can be examined whenever the franchisor considers expansion. An expansion decision should always bring the franchisor to re-examine the next and final step in strategic market planning.

Marketing Strategies for Continuity and Growth

Several basic options are available to a business trying to enter a market and grow, whether the business is large or small. We want to consider these basic options in terms of how a franchised firm would "fit" or interact with its market. Table 7-2 proposes four generic or natural marketing strategies with factors typical to the ownership decision orientation as well as descriptive characteristics associated with the market strategy. Some franchisors, particularly those with highly innovative businesses, would tend to choose the initiator strategy. This strategy is expensive, however, and since many new franchised businesses do not have large amounts of capital available to them, it is more commonly used by large, established franchising firms with already strong or even dominant positions within a particular industry or market, as is evident in restauranting and in the automotive aftermarkets (that is, firms offering products or services to keep the car running and in good repair). For example, Honda re-entered an almost forgotten motorcycle market very aggressively, capturing the interest of youth as well as other potential customers who would not ordinarily make this sort of purchase.

The second strategy, early imitator, is usually not used by a franchised business for an extended period of time. Trying to expand the number of franchised units and enter additional markets usually requires that the franchisor reduce flexibility, thus stabilizing product or services offered and developing operational consistency, effective adver-

Table 7-2
Four Market-Focused Business Strategies

Strategy Type	Business Profile	Characteristics
Initiator	Entrepreneurial; growth-oriented; high-risk-taking (comfortable gambling in all-or-nothing situation).	Knowledge of current customer needs/wants in order to stimulate demand for product/service; access to capital; good timing.
Early Imitator	Has good market sense; introspective; intuitive; risk-taking; willing to commit to change without full knowledge of costs/benefits of product development or modification of manufacturing facilities.	Flexibility in relation to current product and/or production; speed and efficiency in making necessary product/service modifications; ability to differentiate product/service from that of competition in such a way as to ensure uniqueness of product/service to customer (i.e., high sensitivity to customer).
Follower	Externally dedicated (to market), yet internally focused (on production); seeks to produce high-volume or high-value product/service; carefully examines new opportunities for costs/benefits in relation to known strengths of firm; looks for market trends to be established before committing resources.	Knowledge of market pricing and demand levels; desire to maximize market share based on known strengths of firm; entry into market when strong opportunity exists for providing product/service at attainable level: i.e., low product/service cost, low overhead, and efficiency of operation.
Market Segmenter	Seeks niche or opportunity for market skimming; market-dedicated, but lacking capacity for high volume at present; willing to take only minimal risk; avoids head-to-head competition.	Goal of discrete segments with promise of strong demand; flexibility; concentration of firm's resources.

tising, better field service to existing franchisees, and high-quality training to recently signed franchisees.

The third strategy, follower, is perhaps the most accommodating strategy for a budding franchise firm. The characteristics of this strategy can be very positive in the short term: market demand is strong; existing firms in the market appear to be growing as consumer demand increases; methods of operation are tested to enable the firm to determine the most effective and efficient ways to deliver product or service; and new competitors are entering the marketplace almost daily. The long-term scenario is not so accommodating. As more and more competitors enter the market seeking to be profitable while demand is strong, price competition begins to take place and the market becomes "mature" — that is, the number of suppliers is sufficient to meet demand. As one or more firms try to deepen their penetration in the market, price competition inevitably increases. This ultimately forces out of business producers that are inefficient or that do not have sufficient capital resources to survive a period of heavy price competition.

Some budding franchised firms might choose the fourth option, to be a market segmenter, as their initial strategy for market entry and growth. Market segmentation is actually an excellent choice, but it requires the franchisor to be particularly aware of customer needs and target market dynamics. Many new franchised businesses fail because they do not have sufficient experience and market knowledge to successfully follow this strategy. The market segmentation approach has been used very effectively in the automotive aftermarket industry. There are franchises to service virtually every part of an automobile, including radiators, seat covers, mufflers and transmissions, or to do such work as rustproofing, bodywork, diagnostic tests, and lube and oil changes. The restauranting business has also become a segmented industry, with franchises offering full menu or specialty menu, with full or limited service, in ornate or merely functional surroundings.

Before choosing a market strategy, a franchisor must consider the following points about the franchisor-franchisee relationship. Franchisees deserve professionalism and expect the franchisor to develop marketing strategies with the highest degree of competence. Franchisees also want to participate in planning for their own future. A franchisee has the market expertise; it is up to the franchisor to tap this expertise. When their advice is sought and their ideas, problems, and market information considered in the planning of the business, franchisees are likely to feel more a part of the business and thus be better motivated and more loyal to the franchise system.

The franchisor should consider a six-step approach to marketing strategy. First, objectives are formulated. Second, the threats and opportunities of the marketplace need to be identified and assessed. Third, the target market(s) are determined. Fourth, the product mix is determined.

Fifth, the marketing plans of action are developed. Sixth, market research is conducted to provide market intelligence. Figure 7-4 illustrates these six steps, which we will now discuss more fully.

Objectives. The franchisor should develop a set of objectives based on the mission of the franchise organization that are consistent with the scope of the business. Figure 7-2, earlier in this chapter, identifies the mission and specific objectives our example franchisor, Amy, intends to pursue for her exercise studio. The objectives of a franchised business should be specific and quantifiable, or closed-ended, in order to be clearly conveyed and understood.

Threats and Opportunities. The franchisor should monitor the external environment to identify factors which may pose major threats to or provide significant opportunities for the franchised business and its products. The purpose of this external monitoring and evaluation is to counterbalance the human tendency to become so engrossed in day-to-day activities that one fails to recognize developments in the marketplace that can have significant impact on the firm. The franchisor should regularly examine the external environment, listing then updating threats and opportunities in order to keep current with market trends. This assessment can be invaluable when developing action plans to capitalize on opportunities or prepare for impending threats to the business. Figure 7-5 lists some external factors that can have immediate or long-term impact on a franchised business.

Examining the questions in Figure 7-5 and supplying the information pertinent to each question, if it applies to the particular business, can

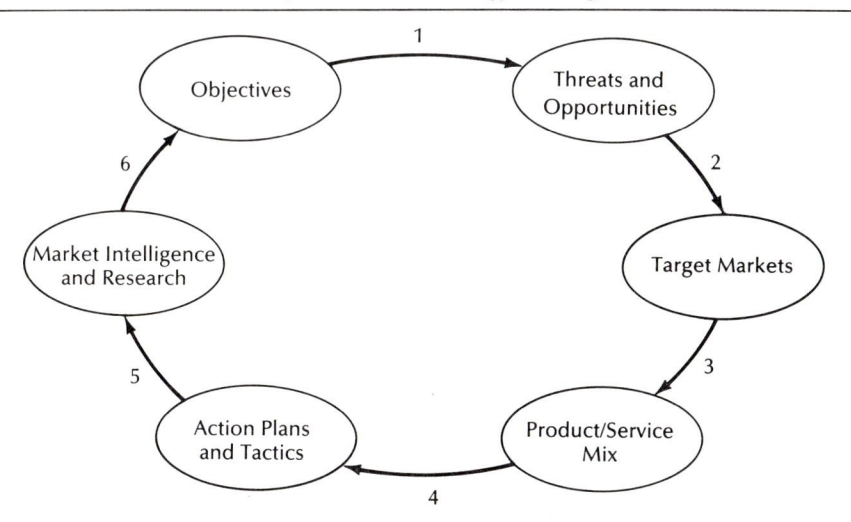

**Figure 7-4
Steps in Market Strategy Making**

**Figure 7-5
Environmental Factors to Monitor and Assess**

Competition

To what extent is competition increasing/decreasing? In what ways?
Are there any new developments in the market? product substitutes? costs? prices?
Is there change in strategy by a competitor? What type is it? What does it mean?

Target Market(s)

Are there any demographic trends taking place that will affect market size?
Are there any changes in submarkets?
What demographic trends can mean opportunity? threat?
Are there any new developments in the distribution channel? reliability? cost?
Are changes in advertising or promotion necessary? what? how effective?
Is there any change in market potential? market strength? market share?
Is there further need for product differentiation? From where is it likely to come?

Government

Are any changes in regulation possible? probable? What will the impact be?
Is there any change in tax law or other incentives that might affect strategy?
Are there any political risks in existing franchise territories? next expansion?

Technology

Are existing technologies for my business stable? maturing?
What technologies are being considered? Is there a likelihood of breakthrough?
How fast is the impact of a change in technology for my business? industry?

Suppliers

Is availability of substitutes on the horizon? When are they available? Are there potential cost savings/increases?
Are supplies to franchisees timely? cost-effective? profitable? increasing or decreasing?

Sociocultural

Are there any emerging trends in fashion, life style, preferences?
What are the possible implications and their immediacy?

Overall Economy and My Industry

What are the prospects of change in the current situation of relative economic health?
What is the economic health of my industry? submarkets of the industry?
Does rate of inflation, deficit, balance of payments, trade barriers, or recession affect my business? how? what is status now? in the future?
What changes in the overall economy and my industry would affect strategy?

help the franchisor stay "on the pulse" of events or conditions that can affect the business. In reviewing the questions, one could respond that a particular item would have a great impact but a low probability of occurring and so would not be worth the firm's time or resources to collect or analyze information about it. Or the response could be that even though an event is likely, it would occur so far off into the future that there is probably little need for immediate concern. The purpose of examining these factors and making such assessments is to provide the franchised business time to react and to develop contingency plans to accommodate major changes that will affect the firm's market, customers, or suppliers.

Target Markets. Based on the objectives and the knowledge of environmental factors and market threats and opportunities, the franchisor develops the broad marketing strategy for achieving those objectives. The overall strategy includes clear descriptions of target markets or market segments on which the franchisor intends to focus. Each specific market or market segment will have unique characteristics, usually couched in terms of consumer preferences and spending patterns. A franchisor should determine the attributes of each segment and develop strategies that can best serve the franchise from a competitive standpoint. These attributes can be categorized in accordance with common buying factors such as price, and consumer sensitivity to it; product quality, standardization, and features; product or service delivery — modes, cost, speed; and marketing support/service required with and after the sale. The franchisor wants to find the product- or service-specific factors that address customer requirements and response to the firm's marketing approach.

Product Mix. The marketing strategy should include considerations of the product line to be offered to the customer, and it should consider this set of products in light of all products that compete for customers in the target markets. For example, in the fast-food restaurant industry, major franchising firms pay special attention to their product line, raising questions of whether a particular food item should be featured, whether the product line should be expanded by adding similar items, or whether the line needs a more extensive overhaul, replacing one or more items or modifying others. For example, given the increased demand for white meat products during the 1980s, many franchised restaurants have added chicken and/or fish items to their product lines. Several franchised restaurants have added breakfast menu products, modified store hours, and added to and deleted from the product line based on season of the year. In conjunction with the product mix offered by the franchised business, the type of advertising and any sales promotion, pricing, packaging, and distribution methods should be incorporated into the marketing strategy. Once a firm becomes large and has locations widely dispersed throughout a geographical area, there may be some necessary modifications due to differences in life style, climate, or other geographic or sociocultural characteristics.

Plans of Action. In developing the franchised business plan, the franchisor should turn the marketing strategies into specific plans of action or tactical programs that provide answers to the following questions: What exactly is to be done in each market segment offering the product? When will the activities be started and completed? Who is responsible for these activities and their outcomes? And how much will it cost to implement this plan of action?

For example, efforts to promote a new product in a market where the franchise firm has a foothold would differ from those directed at a market segment in which the franchise's products have not yet appeared. (The differences are discussed in the section titled "Promotion" later in this chapter.) The approach to be taken varies depending on the target audience, the objective of the promotion, and the amount of money available to promote the product. The tactical elements of the promotional campaign for use by the franchisee would include such elements as point-of-purchase displays; national or regional advertising by the franchisor, including advertising copy and the times, days, and dates when the advertisements will appear or air; and any available information about what the competition might be doing in their promotional campaigns during the same period.

The various plans of action for each product, location, type of promotion, and running dates can be organized on a monthly, quarterly, semiannual, or annual basis through use of a table with weeks or months identified in columns and market action plans or tactics identified in rows. Figure 7-6 illustrates a media schedule for a franchised auto body repair firm. The schedule shows that the "evening news" will be used each weekday from February through May and September through November. From June through August, one advertisement will be aired between the fifth and seventh innings of the "game of the week" on one network. A nationally distributed daily newspaper will carry an advertisement in the sports section on the first three working days of the month. And an advertisement will appear four times, once per quarter, in a nationally distributed weekly news magazine.

Typically, the market objectives (anticipated sales results) and budgets are developed on a monthly or quarterly basis. This allows the franchisor to monitor the progress of each product by location and type of promotional effort once the cooperative advertising method has been selected. This approach helps the franchisor and franchisee plan advertising costs, and over time, learn the benefits of such expenditures by evaluating type of advertisement in terms of sales performance at the time of the advertisement.

Figure 7-6
Media Schedule of a Franchised Auto Body Repair Firm

Medium	Jan.	Feb.	Mar.	Apr.	May	June	July	Aug.	Sept.	Oct.	Nov.	Dec.
Television:												
"evening news"		//////	//////	//////	//////				//////	//////	//////	
"game of the week"						/ / /	/ / /	/ / / /				
Newspaper: (national distribution)												
sports section	/	/	/	/	/	/	/	/	/	/	/	
Magazine:												
weekly news magazine	/					/		/				/
Cooperative:*												
Radio—jingle with message	(Franchisee develops schedule, breadth, and depth of coverage using local media mix with some franchisor cooperative cost sharing and assistance in development or presentation of advertisements.)											
Newspaper—mats available												

*Franchisor agrees to pay a portion of the franchisee's advertising costs and may supply materials, audio or video tapes.

Market Research and Intelligence. To properly guide a franchise network, the franchisor needs a great deal of information. Much of the information can be hard to acquire, is not available at all, or comes too late for the franchisor to act on an opportunity. Market research and intelligence can be viewed from both an internal and an external perspective.

Internal market information is data from controllable activities of the franchise system. A well-designed internal market information system tracks the primary elements of the franchise distribution mechanism and the important facts about product sales. Such a system could include: (1) a list of equipment by type and age at each franchise location, (2) supply and inventory levels by location, (3) sales performance by type of service performed or goods sold, (4) relevant profit and loss data by location and/or product categories, (5) promotional costs per unit sold by type of promotion utilized, and (6) daily accounts receivable and accounts payable data. These types of information are critically important in evaluating performance in light of market objectives, determining strong or weak points in the marketing plans of action, and proposing future marketing strategies or tactics including estimated budget requirements.

External market information needs are outside the realm of activities controlled by the franchise system. These information needs are usually associated with market issues, problems, and threats or opportunities. Researching problems of the market involves several steps. First, the problem, issue, threat, or opportunity must be carefully defined. Once it is defined, it must be determined what information about the problem is necessary so that a judgment or decision can be made. Second, a data collection plan is determined. The plan identifies the types of information needed from primary and secondary sources. Primary data collection (direct observation, field experiment, customer survey) requires developing instruments, determining sample size, and choosing a contact method to retrieve the desired information. Secondary data collection (through trade publications, government publications, periodicals, books, or commercial surveys) usually provides the starting point of data collection and offers the advantage of low cost and quick availability. It will often happen that the precise information needed is not available from secondary sources, or if it is, the information is incomplete, unreliable, or obsolete. When this is the case, the franchise firm must use primary data collection methods, which typically cost more and require more time to complete. However, primary data collection is often more relevant and reliable because it enables the franchisor to obtain the precise information needed to address the problem at hand. The third step is the actual collection and analysis of the information to determine the relationships within the data as they apply to the problem. Finally, judgments must be made about the information analyzed to assist the franchised firm in making decisions about the market problem or issue.

Often, a franchisor will seek outside help from a university or private market research firm to perform studies when primary research is required. However, some larger franchisors operate their own market research departments in order to build statistical data banks to improve their analytical capabilities as well as increase their knowledge of their particular markets and the industry on the whole.

DETERMINING THE MARKETING MIX

As we have already demonstrated, marketing strategy is important to an entrepreneur. Finding opportunities and developing marketable products or services for those opportunities are the primary functions of all budding business ventures. In order to achieve success, the franchisor will need to understand the marketing mix. The **marketing mix** is that set of controllable elements the franchisor and franchisee put together (or integrate) in order to reach the target market. To be successful, the franchise organization must have a product that addresses a want or need of a group of people, is available where these people want it, and is priced within an acceptable range. Also, the product must have qualities or characteristics that can be communicated or promoted to the targeted group of people. The elements that constitute the marketing mix are otherwise known as the "four P's" of marketing — product, promotion, price, and place (see Figure 7-7).

The franchising concept is not often cited or compared to other types of firms in a marketing distribution system. Often, a holding com-

**Figure 7-7
The Marketing Mix**

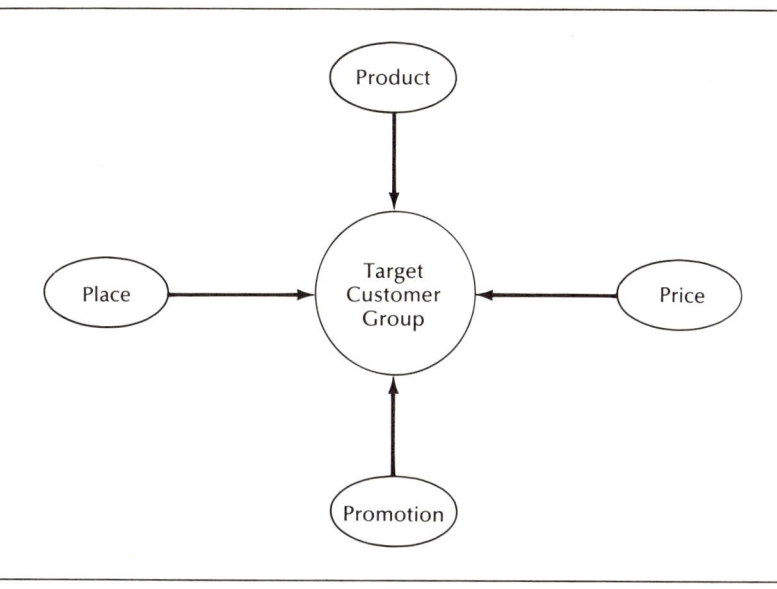

[Diagram: Product, Place, Price, and Promotion each with arrows pointing to a central "Target Customer Group"]

pany or parent firm may seek to achieve the "place" objective through several alternatives to franchising. It could develop company-owned retailers or distributors, or establish units that are jointly owned by the parent and a local entrepreneur in a stock or partnership arrangement. Or perhaps it could establish a free-standing relationship between independent distributors or retailers, in which the retailer or distributor would handle several lines with a diversity of brands from a wide variety of companies. In any event, the parent firm or holding company considering these alternatives must face the same reality as the budding franchisor: If the qualities or unique characteristics of the product do not meet customer needs, the franchising attempts of distributors or retailers to meet the "place" objective will be for naught. The other marketing mix factors — price, promotion, and product — must be put in proper balance by the franchising organization; otherwise the whole endeavor may fail.

Product

The first "P" to be considered in the marketing mix is **product**. Product is not just the item or service itself. Rather, it carries with it a unique set of physical and "psychological" characteristics or attributes designed to satisfy the wants or needs of a group of people. For example, a "Big Mac" is not just a McDonald's hamburger; it is designed to carry with it the attributes that the company name suggests — clean environment, prompt service, and competitive price. Likewise, "Corvette" has a host of attributes connected with it, apart from the warranty, sales approach, and road performance estimates.

Psychological and social factors are so important, in fact, that a franchisor requires its franchisees to follow certain prescribed practices consistent with the product's purpose, characteristics or attributes, and image in the targeted market. For each product, a franchisor must answer the following: How should the product be designed? What unique characteristics should be included and what options allowed? How should the product be named, labeled, and packaged? And what type of warranty or service guarantee should be offered? The franchisor must determine the importance of each product characteristic and then establish specifications to ensure homogeneity for marketing and distribution through the franchise network.

Consistent quality in product is an identifiable characteristic of successful franchise systems. Customers like to feel they are getting their money's worth, and they like to know what to expect, whether they are having a transmission repaired, staying in a hotel, or having their photos finished. The success of such firms as Aamco Transmissions Inc., Holiday Inns, Inc., and Moto Photo suggests in part that some customers will bypass competent independents to deal with a franchise chain because they believe they will receive a consistent, quality product.

By failing to recognize the importance of product consistency to the consumer, one franchisee can immeasurably hurt the business of other franchisees in the same distribution system. As we have said, a bad cup of coffee served by one donut shop affects other franchisees and thus sheds an unfavorable light on the franchise system itself. The underlying principle is to establish guidelines for maintaining product consistency and then to make sure these guidelines are followed throughout the franchise system.

Life Cycle. Every product has a life cycle. Even though different products have different cycles, life cycles always have four stages: introduction, growth, maturity, and decline. A product life cycle is illustrated in Figure 7-8.

The first stage, the **introduction**, is a period of slow, gradual sales growth. During this stage, the product does not have much name recognition or customer loyalty. The product itself may be completely new, or it may be an old product with new features. Sales and profits tend to be low. If the product is targeted properly and meets consumer acceptance, the **growth** stage begins. In the growth stage, the life-cycle curve takes a dramatic upward surge. This sharp increase reflects the product's recognition and acceptance as it is sought by growing numbers of consumers in the target market. As more consumers seek more of the product, market demand increases, and sales and profits may seem to soar. The

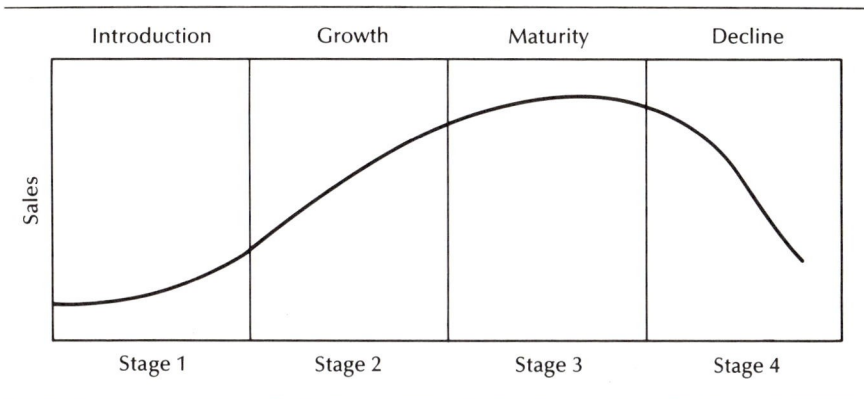

**Figure 7-8
Product Life Cycle**

Introduction	Growth	Maturity	Decline
Stage 1	Stage 2	Stage 3	Stage 4

income to the franchisor is typically enough to cover research, market development, and promotional costs as well as yield substantial profits. The **maturity** stage occurs when the rate of sales growth slows and, ultimately, sales level off. For some products in highly competitive franchise industries, such as fast-food restauranting, sales may actually decline as competition intensifies for the customers in the target group. But sales of the product are still usually at a relatively high level with reasonably predictable production and inventory schedules. The franchise organization reaps the benefits of operational efficiency through high-volume processing. Franchisors may also try to create increased sales by penetrating deeper into existing markets, expanding into new locations, entering new markets in various ways, or broadening the scope of business activity within the target market through the addition of new products or services. Some examples follow:

1. Expanding into complementary segments of the market (as some fast-food franchises have by serving breakfast);
2. Changing the packaging or image (such as using two-liter plastic bottles for soda, or claiming "orange juice isn't just for breakfast anymore");
3. Finding new uses for the product (such as by informing households that baking soda can be used to keep the refrigerator odor-free); or
4. Finding new ways to deliver the product to deepen market penetration (such as the Burger King mobile units that can park at university campuses, along a beach, or on the fairway of a state fairground).

During the **decline** stage of the product life cycle, it is typical for sales volume to drop as demand shifts to other products. Inevitably, new products become available and gain the favor of consumers. Under decline conditions, maintaining the franchise network and seeking to meet ever-shifting market demand are critical to the survival of the franchised firm.

The franchisor must determine if the decline is due to a temporary fluctuation in the market, or if it is the result of a permanent change in the target market population. Typical courses of action for a franchisor are (1) to cease to produce the product; (2) to change or improve the product and offer it to the market segment that is shifting (as with the McDonald's conversion from chicken sandwich to Chicken McNuggets); or (3) to phase out the product gradually, replacing it with a new one that will appeal to the shifted market. This last option suggests that the franchised firm should maintain the product within the line for perhaps six months or longer, waiting until the shift in customer preferences has been completed before entering the market with a new product. The reason for a stalling tactic is obvious: A franchised firm will probably not want to risk having another product "failure" that the consuming public might remember and associate with the franchise.

The decline stage can create a difficult set of circumstances for a franchised firm. Because a franchisor will want to change the product to keep pace with the changing preferences of the target market, conflicts can arise with some franchisees. Signs will need to be replaced with newer logos, menus changed, pictures or models of products or services updated, or costly interior renovations completed. Often a franchisee may not see the need to spend money to make the changes called for by the franchisor. In some cases, franchisees feel strongly that such changes should be paid for by the franchisor, or at least that the franchisor should share the costs of the changes through some sort of cooperative plan. Some franchisees refrain from making any changes until absolutely essential, agreeing to change only when sales fall or when it is apparent that other franchised units have clearly benefited from the change. Some franchisees are content with a gradual decline in sales, as long as it eventually settles at a satisfactory level and can be maintained there. Others may even try to sell their franchised business, while still others are content just to close up shop! Some franchisors faced with sustained decline in demand and reluctant franchisees may withdraw from franchising altogether, choosing instead to operate only company-owned establishments.

New Product Development. A franchised firm cannot rely in the long run on its initial products. Consumers want and *expect* new or improved products, so the firm must introduce new products to replace those with limited or declining consumer interest. For this reason, a franchised firm needs to have objectives and plans of action to develop new ideas and assess, test, and distribute new products through the franchise system.

A franchised firm can either acquire or develop new products. Products can be acquired through licensing arrangements with a manufacturer or producer. It is also possible to license a clearly identifiable product design and have the franchisor execute the design. On the other hand, the franchised firm can develop its own new products, although innovation and product development can be very costly and risky. Ford Motor's ill-fated Edsel is a famous example of a new product that failed. The Coca-Cola company took a considerable risk in changing its formula and introducing "New" Coke. Within weeks, however, responding to reaction from consumers, it introduced the old formula as Classic Coke.

New products or services fail for various reasons. Perhaps the idea is good but the market is not ready to accept it. Or the idea is good and is acceptable in the market, but the market is not large enough. Or product design may not be complete or executed as well as it should have been. Or the product or service just wasn't "positioned" appropriately to meet the needs of the market.

New Product Testing. Some franchisors and franchisees must experience failure before they determine that trial testing a new product is clearly necessary. Making financial and legal commitments to a new product before actually testing the product is not exclusive to franchise organizations. Many large, fully integrated firms have done the same. For example, in the mid-1950s Procter & Gamble Co. began research and development to create a better potato chip. The typical potato chip soon becomes stale, is easily broken, may be burnt or already stale when bought, can taste greasy, and is packaged in bags that are hard to reseal and store. P & G spent over ten years developing a way to dehydrate potatoes into a tissue and slice this tissue into a uniform chip that could be stacked. Pringle's New-Fangled Potato Chips were test marketed in 1968 and were distributed nationally by 1975. That year, total sales were approximately $100 million, representing about 10 percent of the potato chip market. However, sales and market share soon declined. Diet consciousness, notions about "junk" food, and concern about preservatives and additives began to plague Pringle's and other competitive products. P & G changed its advertising approach several times and its method of making the chip so that it could claim it contained no preservatives or artificial ingredients. It has successfully used the slogan "I've got the fever for the flavor of new Pringle's." Its sales and market share have correspondingly increased.

Analyzing the product helps the franchisor to determine the attractiveness of the idea. Do the sales, cost, and profit projections satisfy the firm's objectives? What are sales histories of similar products? What are consumer opinions about these products? What are the estimated costs — including research and development, production, inventory, and financing — to produce or provide the product?

If the product idea makes it through such an analysis, physical versions of the product should be developed. Testing the prototypes provides valuable information. Does the product actually have the attributes sought? Can it be produced at the budgeted cost? Does the product meet the safety or quality standards for this product category? If the product idea is a service, can the performance of the service be adequately monitored to ensure a high level of quality?

Testing the product in trial markets should provide good estimates of first-time purchase, first repeat purchase, and frequency of purchase to help in developing a realistic sales forecast. This information is important because many consumers will try a product or service once, but not rebuy it. Or, market tests may show high first-repeat sales but little sustained repeat purchase. Tests might also show a high rate of first-time purchase but low frequency of repurchase, which suggests buyers use the product infrequently, perhaps only on special occasions.

The franchisor with a new product profits from being able to distribute financial risk over an expanding number of franchised outlets or units, and is able to add new units speedily at relatively low cost. On the other hand, the franchisee in a successful franchise network profits by being part of an organization that has capability to develop new products. A franchise organization does not have to have a richly financed franchisor or parent company to introduce a new product. Although this condition would be welcome, many new products have entered the market without it. Costs and risks can be shared by the franchisor and the franchisee, thus allowing product testing and market introduction to take place more quickly and cheaply than if the franchisor had to do it alone.

Promotion

Promotion is a central element of the marketing program of a franchising firm. It can be defined as the marketing activity that communicates to the target customer group the product available, its qualities or characteristics, its price, and where and when it is available. A franchisor must first design a promotional strategy, then develop an effective message and gather feedback for that message. He or she must also determine how much will be spent on promotions by devising a promotional budget.

Promotional Strategy. Having the target audience clearly in mind is the beginning point of a promotional strategy. The audience could be current buyers, potential buyers, or even persons who could influence buyers. The audience may be individuals, specific groups, or the general public. Once the target audience is known, the franchisor must determine what response is being sought. Obviously, the ultimate response is purchase of the product. However, purchase decisions often result only after a long process of decision making. The franchisor therefore needs to know where the target audience now stands in relation to a purchase decision and what information is needed to move them toward purchase.

A target audience may be in any of six stages of buyer readiness: awareness, knowledge, liking, preference, conviction, or purchase.[1] The target audience may be totally unaware of the franchised firm or know only the name or one or two attributes of the product offered. If so, the franchisor must build awareness, perhaps simply by creating name recognition through repetition of the franchise name. Culligan International Co.'s theme, "Hey, Culligan Man," has been used for years, and Goodyear has made its name recognizable in part by effective use of its blimps at sporting or other major media events. On the other hand, if the franchisor discovers that the target audience has company or product awareness but knows little more, the firm should build product knowledge, such as through promotions that show the product in the context of its delivery. Mr. Goodwrench, Midas International Corporation, Curtis Mathes Corporation, and 7-ELEVEN Convenience Stores are several examples of franchise systems effectively using this approach.

If the target audience knows the product and has an unfavorable attitude toward it, the franchisor has the difficult task of determining the reasons for the attitude and presenting a promotional campaign to change these attitudes. If the unfavorable feelings are rooted in poor product quality or service, the franchisor needs to improve the product and then communicate its improved quality.

Often a target customer group might like the product but not prefer it to the available alternatives. The franchisor should try to build consumer preference in this customer group. The promotional message to accomplish this could address quality, performance characteristics, durability, value, or other attributes which show product superiority. For example, in areas where high water tables produce wet basements several times a year, a franchisor of a basement waterproofing system tries to convince homeowners that its system is the best for maintaining a dry basement. And, with the expanding demand for chicken in fast-food markets and various competitors adding chicken to their menus, Kentucky Fried Chicken Corp. reminds the consuming public that chicken is the only thing it serves, and "they do it right!"

Some part of the targeted customer group may be convinced the product will meet its needs, but just may not get around to making the purchase. Promotional campaigns such as limited-time offers, weekend sales, premiums with purchase, or 10-day trial purchases are approaches a franchisor can use to convince customers to take the final step.

Before selecting a promotional theme, a franchisor should consid-

---

[1] Philip Kotler, *Principles of Marketing*, 2nd edition (Englewood Cliffs, NJ: Prentice-Hall, Inc., 1983), pp. 430–431.

er at what point in the decision-making process the targeted customer group is. In this way, promotional messages can be more effectively developed to meet the specific information needs of the target customers.

Developing an Effective Message. The franchisor must figure out what kind of appeal will produce the desired result. Typically, such appeals address the targeted customer's self-interest, showing how the product will provide the claimed benefits. Focus is on quality, value, performance, or cost/benefit. Negative emotional appeals address basic emotions such as fear or guilt to elicit response to do things a customer "should do," such as quit smoking by using product X, or prevent skids on icy roads by buying tire Y. Positive emotional appeals are also effective. Such appeals address emotions including love, joy, or pride. Apparel, fragrance, and some food franchise firms have successfully used positive emotional appeals.

The message structure of the promotion must also be considered. Should the message draw a conclusion or should that be left to the targeted group? Should the argument or appeal be placed first, in the middle, or last in the message? Structure will be discussed further in the sections on advertising and mass appeals.

Gathering Feedback. After developing and disseminating a message, the franchised firm should measure the effect of the message on the targeted group. This requires collection of information that answers the following questions: Did consumers recognize or recall the message? What was recalled — name, price, location, product features? How did they "feel" about the message? What is their attitude about the franchise *now* compared with *before* the message? This information enables the firm to reinforce or modify the content or format of the message, or even the media chosen to advertise, in order to achieve the desired result of enhanced sales within the target market area. Data can be collected by telephone survey or by short questionnaires to be completed and returned to the company. Completion of questionnaires can be handled in a variety of ways, such as by requesting customers to fill them out while still at the counter, by providing them to be filled out when the product is delivered, or by leaving them where customers will notice them, such as in the motel room or in the rental car. Often a price discount or some other tactic is used to encourage completion of the questionnaire.

Promotional Budget. Determining the amount of money to be used for promoting the firm and its product is a difficult marketing decision. Promotion can get expensive. It is not uncommon to find 30 to 50 percent of sales revenue spent on promotion in the cosmetics business, or 3 to 7 percent in the fast-food business. Although it is difficult even for franchisees to obtain explicit information from franchisors concerning their promotional budget and marketing strategies, they should be aware of what the franchisor is spending for promotion. Even smaller franchisors should have a budget for promoting the product. Down to the most basic level, the promotional budget should:

1. Set objectives in terms of target audience awareness of the product, where and when it is available, and at what price; and
2. Identify product sales gains by targeted geographic area, by population density, or to achieve a certain share of market.

The advertising dollar should then be budgeted to achieve these measurable targets.

There are four common methods of determining the promotional budget. First, using what is referred to as the **affordable method**, franchisors can determine the budget based on what they think the company can afford to spend. Though often used, this method ignores the impact of promotion on sales volume and makes long-range market planning and franchise expansion difficult.

A second method, the **comparative-parity** approach, is based on the firm's objective to match the promotional efforts of the competition. This approach is often used when competition is apparent but not particularly aggressive; it seeks to increase market share at the expense of the direct competition. Comparative parity has been found useful and cost-effective in markets where the product life cycle is in the growth phase, thus allowing each primary competitor to grow along with the market. Clearly, this approach is not used by the major competitors in the fast-food industry today. In recent years this industry's promotions have become increasingly aggressive, particularly since Burger King developed advertisements making direct comparisons with McDonald's.

The **objective-task** approach to promotional budgeting requires the franchised firm to define its objectives, determine what performance is needed to achieve the objectives, and estimate the costs of completing these performance tasks. The sum of the performance-task costs is the proposed promotional budget. If we reflect back to the beginning of this chapter and consider the recommended steps for strategic marketing of the product, we can see that the objective-task approach is the one recommended in most cases for a franchised firm.

The **percentage-of-sales method** sets promotional expenditures at a certain percentage of current or anticipated sales. Traditionally, automobile franchisors such as General Motors Corp., Ford Motor Co., and Chrysler Corp. have used this approach, budgeting a fixed percentage for promotion based on the planned car price. Domestic oil companies have also used this popular method, appropriating a set fraction of a cent for each gallon of gas sold under their brand label. Promotional expenditures vary directly with what the company can afford based on sales volume.

In general, how much weight the promotion receives in the overall marketing mix depends on the stage of the life cycle the franchise's product is in, the intensity of competition within the industry, and how much product awareness must be developed and sustained in order for consumers to purchase the product in the market.

Four Tools of Promotional Strategy. Franchised firms differ considerably in how they divide a promotional budget. For example, Avon Products, Inc. and Mary Kay Cosmetics, Inc. concentrate promotional efforts on personal selling, while Chevrolet Motor Division, McDonalds Corp., Pepsi Cola Bottling Co., and Miller Brewing Company focus on mass advertising to heighten awareness of the product in the minds of the consumers. Whatever approach is taken, promotion is a key element in the marketing program of a franchised firm. Most franchisors require their franchisees to contribute to the parent firm to mass advertise the franchise name and/or products, and some pressure franchisees to participate in sales promotion campaigns as well.[2] Being a member within a franchise system enables the franchisee to obtain the assistance through the franchisor of advertising agencies to which a typical independent entrepreneur would not have access.[3] Each promotional tool has its unique characteristics. Effective use of each tool, alone or in concert with the other tools for promotion, requires that a franchisor understand these tools and determine how each tool should be used in the franchised business. The four promotional tools — mass advertising, sales promotion, personal selling and publicity — are discussed below.

Mass Advertising. Communicating to the target customer group what is sold, where, when, and at what price is the principal function of mass advertising. Obviously, when a franchisee puts up a sign with a familiar name such as Burger King, Midas, Ford, or Days Inn, the franchise is immediately recognized and the product attributes are recalled by those who see the sign. However, many potential customers may never see the sign simply because they do not pass by the location of the franchised unit. Or, in the case of such specialty businesses as carpet cleaning, temporary-help agencies, clean water systems or emergency plumbing repair, there may not even be a sign for the customer to see.

In order to achieve brand recognition, franchised organizations often use mass advertising. It is in mass advertising that the franchisor can be of greatest assistance in the promotion of the franchised product or service. Advertising on national or regional levels with a carefully selected mix of radio, telephone directory, newspaper, television, billboard, and magazine media can be of great benefit to a local franchisee. The franchisor may delegate responsibility for local promotional efforts to

---

[2] Charles Vaughn, *Franchising*, 2nd edition (Lexington, MA: D. C. Heath & Company, 1979), p. 45.
[3] Vaughn, p. 45.

the franchisee, while still fulfilling the important function of providing guidance with respect to media mix, budgets, types of appeals, and frequency of advertising, in order to achieve effective results from each promotion dollar spent. Much of the franchisor's guidance concerns what the advertising themes are going to be over the next quarter or year, the general content and method of the appeal to be used, and how a franchisee might "tie in" a local sales promotion with the mass advertising theme.

In the past 20 years, the newer franchise firms, particularly the fast-food franchisors, have been very successful in creating consumer awareness. To achieve a high level of brand or franchise awareness requires expenditure of tremendous amounts of money. For example, the McDonald's franchise system spent approximately $423 million on advertising in 1983. This represents 4.9% of its sales of $8.6 billion (from over 7,700 units, 5,300 of which were franchisee-owned) and almost quadruples the $125 million it spent on advertising in 1978.[4]

Large franchise systems usually adopt an advertising theme and often a character or symbol of the institution, brand, or product. Examples include slogans such as Burger King's "Have it your way," McDonald's "You deserve a break today," and Wendy's "Where's the beef?" or recognizable characters such as Ronald McDonald, the Colonel, Big Boy, and Dutch Boy, which are designed to appeal to particular customer groups. Other symbols, such as the Goodyear blimp or the Budweiser Clydesdales, are intended to have a more universal appeal.

Mass advertising is an effective way to reach geographically dispersed target customers at a relatively low cost per customer, even though the total dollar commitment can be quite large. Mass advertising is just what the phrase implies — "mass," meaning that it is aimed at large numbers of people over a broad area. The essence of mass advertising is to build up an institutional or specific brand image for a product that can also be useful in conjunction with other types of promotional efforts without inhibiting those specific approaches. For example, mass advertising can be used for triggering quick sales, for running a special deal, and so on. It can also be used successfully with personal selling.

Sales Promotion. Sales promotion is another ingredient in the promotional mix. It requires a communication to take place that includes an incentive, along with an invitation to complete the purchase decision. Coupons, contests, premiums, and buy-one-get-one-free offers are sales promotions used by franchised firms to create a strong and quick consumer response to bolster sagging sales. Sales promotions are typically short-term, and so they have not brought much success for franchised firms attempting to develop long-term brand loyalty. As a well-known illustration of sales promotions, in 1975 McDonald's Corp. celebrated its

---

[4] McDonald's Corp., *Annual Report, 1983.*

twentieth anniversary by selling the single hamburger at its original price (15¢). This sales promotion was strongly backed up by other types of promotions, including mass advertising and national and local publicity. A potential problem with sales promotions lies in the friction that may arise between franchisor and franchisee. The franchisor may strongly urge local franchisee participation in a sales promotion designed to improve sales for a brief period of time. On the other hand, franchisees may resent such promotions since premiums or price discounts cost them money and affect their profit margin. The franchisees who object the most and are the least willing to actively participate in the sales promotion are often those whose profits are marginal and whose sales need a general boost.

Another perspective on sales promotions concerns what the franchisee can do, perhaps independent of other promotional efforts that may need to be linked with the franchisor. A "catalog corner" concept has been used successfully by a gardening service franchisee. The franchisee's catalog is attached to a table or display in other, non-competing stores within the local market. Along with the catalog there is an attractive stand-up sign with pictures highlighting the types of gardening services available. The franchisee pays the participating merchant a commission for every referral. The benefits to this franchisee have been increased sales, valuable advertising, and exposure to new potential customers. A cosmetics distributor and a wig franchisee have also used this notion through displays in barbershops, boutiques, and hotel lobbies.

Can sales promotions be used by service-oriented franchised businesses? A company that steam cleans or sprays siding, cleans chimneys, or repairs roofs can seek participation with department stores or national chain stores such as Sears or Macy's to promote these types of services to their customers. The store receives a commission on any sales.

Franchisees of tangible products such as candy, popcorn, light bulbs, and frozen pizza can seek clubs, churches, or other community-based organizations to sell their product as a funding program to finance the organization's own projects. Also, franchisees trying to get established within a community can have their product or service included in coupon booklets sold by local organizations, such as the Lions, Kiwanis, or Jaycees. In the booklet, a service station might offer a free car wash with a coupon, a pizzeria might offer a 20 percent discount with a coupon, or a drugstore might offer $2.00 off the regular price of a prescription. Such fund drives to sell coupon booklets or products depend on the membership of the sponsoring organization for a large number of people to sell the franchisee's product or service to increase sales, without adding to overhead or having to modify the product or its image. It is a good practice for a franchisee to check with the franchisor prior to initiating autonomous sales promotion efforts. The franchisor can often provide solid information on which sales promotion efforts have worked well in the past and may provide additional support or arrangements for additional inventory or media advertising in conjunction with the promotion.

Personal Selling. Personal selling is considered the most effective means of influencing buyers' preferences, convictions, and actions. Many franchisors take the position that the franchisee should be the salesperson. If this is the case, it is important that franchisors select franchisees with capabilities to perform the personal selling function when it is a necessary element of that particular business. Personal selling is immediate and interactive between the seller and the buyer, enabling each to observe the other's needs and characteristics and make adjustments as necessary. It permits a wide range of conditions and circumstances to be used to assist the buyer in making the purchase decision — from impersonal order-taking to personal friendship. Since franchising covers so many different product and service lines, all degrees and types of selling may be necessary in one franchised firm or another.

In the field of automotive sales, personal selling is certainly very important, in contrast to its importance in selling mouthwash or aspirin at a drugstore, even though a pleasant smile or friendly comment in any selling situation might encourage the customer to return. Effective personal selling keeps the customer's interests at the center of the business relationship, with the hope of developing a long-term relationship. Also, personal selling tends to put the potential buyer under a social pressure to respond, even if with a "no, thank you."

According to the U.S. Department of Commerce's *Franchising in the Economy, 1985-1987*,[5] the number of business and personnel franchised services is expected to rise significantly in the next decade. This includes businesses in tax preparation, record keeping, automated bookkeeping and billing, collection systems, tax advising, and computer schooling. Other areas expected to experience significant growth include employment agencies; home improvement businesses such as floor care, burglar and fire alarm, water conditioning, and cleaning services; travel; equipment rental; car washes; parking services; interior decorating, carpeting, and upholstery of homes and commercial establishments; educational services; lawn care; dietary and exercise training; and day care centers. Moving across this sampling of franchising opportunities with high growth potential, we can see that each provides a service to the customer that would not be initially accomplished by an automated or mechanized approach. Rather, the types of products and services illustrated suggest the need for personal selling in order to show how the product or service can meet the needs of the customer. Since much of the personal selling in a franchised business is done by the franchisee, it is

---

[5] Kostecka, Andrew, *Franchising in the Economy, 1985-1987*, U.S. Department of Commerce, International Trade Administration (Washington, DC: U.S. Government Printing Office, January, 1987), pp. 1-16.

incumbent upon the franchisor to select franchisees with capabilities in personal selling and, insofar as possible, to train franchisees in these techniques as they apply to the particular franchised business.

Publicity. Publicity includes those efforts by the franchised firm to communicate to the general public and targeted groups information about the firm or its products without the firm's having to pay for such dissemination as it would with an advertisement. Certain circumstances are "prime" uses of publicity within a local community, or perhaps even regionally or nationally. Opening a new store, pilot testing a new product within a community, changing the graphics or colors on established signs (like the change in the Holiday Inns signs in the mid-1980s), celebrating an anniversary (like McDonald's thirtieth year), or suddenly lowering prices can be legitimate news items within a community.

An advantage of publicity for the franchised firm is the potential credibility associated with the news story. Consumers tend to accept news stories as being more authentic and credible than paid advertisements. Also, publicity can reach people who otherwise tend to filter out advertising messages. A well-thought-out publicity campaign, coordinated with mass advertising, personal selling, and sales promotions, can be extremely effective for the franchised firm, whether the firm is large or small.

Price

Determining price is not an easy process. As we have said, rarely should a franchisor establish a specific price; rather, a pricing structure should be developed that is flexible enough to accommodate fluctuations in demand and costs. Pricing is a delicate factor and may involve legal problems due to antitrust laws. All franchisees of the firm are independent business owner/operators; as such, it is illegal for them to conspire with one another or with the franchisor to set prices (see Chapter 6).

The automobile industry franchisor-franchisee relationship illustrates the pricing situation. The auto company (franchisor) is required by law to post a sticker price on each new car. The sticker serves as a basic guide for the customer as to what is the stated retail value of the automobile. The local dealer (franchisee) is not required to sell the car at the sticker price. The franchisee has latitude to arrive at a price for the car by negotiating with the customer. Such elements as trade-in allowances, costs of optional equipment and dealer-installed accessories, and financing arrangements shape the actual price paid by the customer. If an auto manufacturer were to force the franchisees to sell the cars at a certain price, the practice, termed "resale price maintenance," would be illegal.

In developing a price for an item within a product line, the overall notion is to determine the price based on the costs to produce and sell the item, plus a reasonable profit. However, this notion does not take into account the dynamics of market demand. What if the price, as so determined, is higher than what customers are willing to pay? Pricing a product based solely on cost of product and profit margin doesn't consider factors such as the amount or intensity of competition, price cutting or discounting by the competition, or the cost of replacing a poor seller with a different product. Changing price every few days, weeks, or months is not very plausible from a market perspective, nor is it consistent with sound business practice in general.

Basically, the price of product items within a particular franchised unit will be set by the franchisee. The franchisor can assist the franchisee in identifying and scheduling the franchised unit's costs and even furnish cost or operational data from company-owned units to guide franchisees in setting price.

Using Franchisor-Provided Information. A franchisee should be careful in establishing prices based on "suggested" or "normal" costs provided by the franchisor. The company-run units should be sure to have salary figures included for the management personnel in the operating expense statement or cost schedules provided. A franchisee, like a manager of a company-owned unit, should be able to take home a salary from the operation of the business, especially after putting in 50 to 60 hours a week. An operating expense statement that fails to provide for the franchisee's time is misleading as to the actual costs involved in the operation of the business and the return on investment. Some franchise owner/operators use the "anticipated" or "normal" cost schedules provided by the franchisor as information to compete against. Franchisees can use these costs and prices from the company-owned units as guides in establishing their own unit's cost objectives and profit margins.

The bottom line of pricing, however, is not determined in the very short run. If a franchised unit does not operate at a profit for some period of time, say one year, the unit will need to become more efficient (reducing costs) or raise prices in order to realize a profit. As noted before, raising prices is not always a unilateral matter. The effectiveness of raising prices as a way to make a profit depends on whether consumers will accept the new price level. This is why pricing is such an important ingredient in the initial marketing mix.

Strategic Pricing. It is likely that both the franchisor and the franchisees will at some point give serious consideration to promotional pricing, market-skimming pricing, market-penetration pricing, and discriminatory pricing. We will briefly discuss each of these as specific strategies for modifying standard pricing practices.

Promotional pricing is always short-term. A franchisee may temporarily sell a product below the normal price, and sometimes even below cost. Reasons for promotional pricing could be (1) to attract new customers into the store to try the product, in order to temporarily expand the franchised unit's penetration into the established market segment; (2) to act as a loss-leader to attract both new and regular customers to the firm for the promoted product (some customers will buy other items at regular prices while they are there); and (3) to encourage purchase of the product in the off-season at the promotional price, thus leveling out production workloads and perhaps resulting in increased sales during the regular season.

Pricing of a product can change as the product moves through the stages of the product life cycle. At the entry or introduction stage of a patented innovative product (such as Pringle's), the franchisee could choose to set a **market-skimming price.** This is the highest price one would estimate the potential customers would be willing to pay, considering the particular benefits of this new product in comparison to those of known alternatives. As the customer base moves from early buyers through majority to late majority groupings, the price is lowered. In this way, the franchised firm can seek a maximum price level from each group of customers.

Using another approach to pricing, **market-penetration pricing**, a franchisee would set the price of a new item relatively low in order to attract a large number of buyers and gain a large share of the market. Because the product is distinctive at the time of market entry, if sales volume increases rapidly (as hoped), production or inventory costs per unit decline. Following a market-penetration pricing strategy, the franchised firm would seek to lower the price further, based on the declining cost of the product per unit. If the target market demand is price-sensitive, the further reduction in price should stimulate further sales, achieving for the franchisee a deeper market penetration. Another facet of this pricing approach is that low price tends to discourage competitors from entering the market segment.

Discriminatory pricing occurs when a franchisee modifies the basic price structure to differentiate types of customers, geographic location, or time. For example, senior citizens or children under age 12 might receive a discount. A franchised unit may choose to charge higher prices for products offered inside a theme park, compared with prices for the same products at another location. Time discrimination can be illustrated by the practice of charging different prices for the same product based on the season of the year, weekday compared to weekend, or time of day. For price discrimination to work effectively, the market must be divisible into discrete segments with the segments having different demand intensities. Before seriously considering price discrimination, the franchisee should be certain that the form of price discrimination is not illegal and that it will not build customer resentment or ill will.

Marketing Mix and Pricing. The pricing of the franchisee's products should not be made in isolation from the other market mix factors. The franchisee should try to establish a set of prices which achieve the maximum profits that can be realized on the total line of products or services offered. Each product is likely to have certain unique demand characteristics. Also, each product is likely to have some particular production costs and be subject to different amounts of competition. If a franchised operation has a product line of low-, medium-, and high-quality items and the customer group is price-sensitive, then customers will tend to upgrade along the product line if the price difference between two styles or models within the line is small. For example, if a hamburger costs $1.05 and a cheeseburger $1.12, it is likely customers will move up to cheeseburgers. However, if the price difference is large, the customer will probably continue to buy the lower-priced style or model. The task of the franchisor, through mass advertising and promotional efforts, and the franchisee, through direct selling, is to establish perceived quality differences that are consistent with the price differences within the product line.

Ultimately, the approach to pricing of the product will be a reflection of the objectives sought through pricing. Does the franchisor and/or franchisee seek maximum profit, market leadership, product quality leadership, or simply survival in the long run? Most products are price-elastic; that is, as prices increase, lesser quantities are demanded by consumers in the marketplace. For most products, a sure way to decrease number of sales is to increase the price on each unit for sale. Conversely, for most products, decreasing price will tend to increase the number of sales. However, price sensitivity by customers is not the only variable associated with the pricing decision. Costs can also vary at different levels of production and with degree of operations experience. An "old hand" can often achieve lower costs than a novice in running a franchised outlet because of the years of experience and the intuitive feel associated with the business and its customer groups. Between the two points, price and cost, the franchise operator seeks to make profit.

Place

Providing the product when and where customers want it constitutes the **place** element of the marketing mix. The particular advantages of the franchising concept are most apparent in this marketing element — getting the product to the customer using a minimal amount of time and money.

Traditional channels of distribution are identified in Figure 7-9. The first channel provides complete control to the producer, which is advantageous in marketing a product with high sales volume potential, but it also incurs the highest distribution costs because all the distribution functions (and their costs) are borne by the producer. The third channel option is most often used by small manufacturers or assemblers because

Figure 7-9
Traditional Channels of Distribution

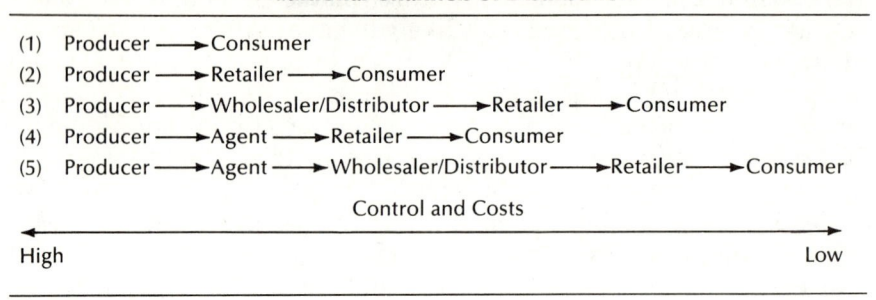

(1) Producer ⟶ Consumer
(2) Producer ⟶ Retailer ⟶ Consumer
(3) Producer ⟶ Wholesaler/Distributor ⟶ Retailer ⟶ Consumer
(4) Producer ⟶ Agent ⟶ Retailer ⟶ Consumer
(5) Producer ⟶ Agent ⟶ Wholesaler/Distributor ⟶ Retailer ⟶ Consumer

⟵—————————— Control and Costs ——————————⟶
High   Low

of the need to use the promotional, financial, and sales capabilities of wholesalers. In examining the five options illustrated, notice the tradeoff made between cost of distribution and control of the channel.

Franchise Distribution Channels. A franchisor must ask the basic question, What channel will best suit my business philosophy and reach the target market? The options include (1) distributing directly from the franchisor through franchised retail outlets, (2) distributing directly from the franchisor through both company-owned and franchisee-owned retail outlets, and (3) distributing from the franchisor through franchised wholesalers to the retail level. A franchisor can link several successive stages in the production/distribution system together or be located at only one place or stage within the channel.

These three approaches to distribution can be illustrated as follows. The *producer/manufacturer as franchisor* sponsors a retail franchise system; this approach is commonly used in the automobile industry. General Motors Corp., for example, licenses dealerships to sell cars and trucks. The dealers agree to meet certain conditions and standards of selling and servicing GM vehicles. The *product firm as franchisor* sponsors a retail system that may contain independent franchisees as well as company-owned retail locations. Service is a prime component within the franchising arrangement. The franchisor organizes a whole network or system for bringing the product to the targeted customer group. Well-known examples of this approach to franchise distribution can be seen in restaurants (Wendy's, Burger King, Kentucky Fried Chicken), auto rental (Hertz, Avis, Budget), and in the motel business (Holiday Inns, Ramada Inn, Howard Johnson's). The *producer/manufacturer-sponsored wholesale franchise* approach is illustrated in the soft drink industry. For example, Pepsi and Coca-Cola license bottlers (wholesalers/distributors) in various geographic markets. The wholesalers/distributors buy syrup concentrate, carbonate, and bottles (or cans), and distribute the soft drinks to various retailers within local markets.

Distribution and Promotion. After the distribution channel has been determined, the next question is, Who promotes the product? The franchisor usually promotes the product regardless of the approach to distribution chosen. Manufacturer/producer-sponsored franchise systems typically use a blend of "push" and "pull" approaches. Automobile franchise networks often use a "push" approach to move products by offering discounts and sales promotional awards to dealers and salespersons to serve as incentives for them to push product through the channel. Soft drink and beer franchisors often attempt to balance their franchisor-sponsored promotion between "push" and "pull" approaches, providing incentives to the wholesalers and distributors as well as coupons to the targeted customers and mass advertising appeals to "pull" the customers toward the purchase of their particular product. A "pull" approach is meant to pull the product through the channel by ensuring that target customer groups are aware of the product and are making requests for it. In effect, consumer requests to retailers cause retailers to request the product from their wholesalers/distributors, who in turn ask the producer/manufacturer for the product. Fast-food franchise systems often use a "pull" promotional strategy to assist in the introduction of a new product/service to their line. For example, the massive, multimedia advertising by McDonald's Corp. of the McDLT sandwich was designed to create demand "pull" from consumers, as compared to relying on sales promotional efforts by the independent franchisees to stimulate demand for the new sandwich offering.

SUCCESS STORY
LEWIS G. RUDNICK

Lewis Rudnick is a partner in the law firm of Rudnick and Wolfe, Chicago, Illinois, and a graduate of the University of Illinois, Columbia University Graduate School of Business, and Northwestern University School of Law. Rudnick specializes in franchising and business law.

Rudnick served as assistant general counsel of the International Franchise Association from 1965 to 1973, general counsel from 1973 to 1981, and special counsel from 1981 to the present. He was a member of the governing committee of the American Bar Association Forum Committee from 1981 to 1983, and a member of the Illinois Franchise Advisory Board from 1974 to 1983. Rudnick has been a member of the Industry Advisory Council Committee to the Franchising Regulation Committee of the North American Securities Administrators Association since 1979, and is currently a member of the Franchise Industry Advisory Council of the International Center for Franchise Studies at the College of Business Administration, University of Nebraska–Lincoln.

Rudnick is a contributing editor of the *Franchise Legal Digest*, published by the International Franchise Association, has authored numerous papers and articles on franchising law for the *Franchise Legal Digest*, the *Journal of the Forum Committee on Franchising*, law reviews, and other publications, and is a frequent speaker on topics in franchising law.

Photo and information provided courtesy of Lewis Rudnick, August, 1985.

SUMMARY

Marketing must be considered in the context of other functions of the franchise firm. The potential for conflicts can be reduced if the franchisor and the franchisee seek a customer orientation and resolve problems of resource allocation.

Strategic planning provides the approach to unify the organization through determination and implementation of the franchise mission, objectives, business portfolio, and marketing strategies. To achieve growth, the franchisor needs to identify market opportunities and move toward target market groups in which advantages over competitors can be realized. Once strategic plans have been developed, the franchisor should prepare plans for the firm's products, its institutional name or brand(s), and the intended target markets. The major planning elements include objectives of the franchise, marketplace threats and opportunities, target markets, product mix, marketing strategies to be deployed, and plans of action to implement the strategies. Plans of action should include budgets and evaluative feedback and controls.

The marketing of product/service requires utilization of a market mix comprising four elements known as the "four P's": product, promotion, price, and place. Combined, these elements form the basis for an effective franchise marketing program.

Product refers to both goods and services, as well as the "psychological" attributes associated with goods or services. It can also extend as far as the brand name, packaging, and even the architecture of the retail outlet.

Promotion covers mass advertising, sales promotion, personal selling, and publicity. Both franchisors and franchisees often deplore the costs associated with promotion, yet most see it as essential for survival and growth of the franchise organization. Mass advertising is the area in which the franchisor can probably be most helpful to the franchisee, using mass media to "pull" products through the channel of distribution. The franchisor can also guide franchisees in their advertising at the local level through advice and cooperative cost-sharing for local promotions tied to regional or national themes.

Marketing the product requires that a price be determined. It is illegal for domestic franchisors to set the price at which the franchisee will sell the product (see Chapter 6). However, the franchisor can assist the franchisee in developing a pricing structure by helping to determine costs. Franchisors can also assist franchisees by collecting market intelligence and conducting market research studies of customer attitudes and habits, including price sensitivity.

The place element of the marketing mix concerns providing the products where and when the consumers want them. A franchisor may franchise at the wholesale/distributor level or at the retail level. Practice varies from industry to industry as to the most preferred approach. A dual system is often found; that is, one in which a franchisor has independent franchisees as well as company-owned outlets at the retail level.

REVIEW QUESTIONS

1. Why must marketing fit in with other functions of a franchised business?
2. What is strategic planning in marketing? How is it used?
3. What are the "four P's" of marketing? Provide an example of how each can be applied in franchised merchandise retailing; in franchised service retailing.
4. Explain the legal consideration associated with product pricing in the franchisor-franchisee relationship.
5. What is meant by a dual system in franchised product distribution?
6. Distinguish between sales promotion and mass advertising. How might the distinction be made in franchise retailing compared with franchise wholesaling?
7. It is said that products have "psychological" attributes. Explain.
8. Explain the potential conflicts between the franchise's decisions about customer orientation and resource allocation.

CASE STUDY
DUNKIN' DONUTS*

Ramone walked out of a downtown Dunkin' Donuts store and knew that this was the kind of franchise he wanted to open. Ramone had been looking for a franchise for the last year and a half. He had raised approximately $38,000 to help start a food service business. He had looked at many different kinds of stores and had finally found the one he would like to operate.

*Information provided courtesy of Dunkin' Donuts of America, August, 1987.

Dunkin' Donuts has over 1,400 stores worldwide, more than any donut shop competitor. Dunkin' Donuts has a national advertising and promotional budget currently over $18 million annually. In addition to being the largest franchise chain of donut shops in the world, it also has the highest average sales per shop — approximately $400,000.

Dunkin' Donuts attributes its success to certain factors. First is the concept itself: Superior products at the right price with prompt, courteous service in clean, well-designed, conveniently located shops. Second, and just as important, is the franchising system. Hundreds of dedicated franchise owners diligently maintain standards and upgrade work records to earn very handsome financial rewards.

Estimated Costs and Cash Requirements

Minimum Cash Required	Region I	Region II
Franchising fee	$40,000	$30,000
Working capital	$19,000	$19,000
Total minimum cash required	$59,000	$49,000

Estimated Cost Ranges	Region I		Region II	
Minimum cash required[1]	$ 59,000	$ 59,000	$ 49,000	$ 49,000
Equipment[2]	$ 65,000	$ 85,000	$ 65,000	$ 85,000
Signs[2]	$ 7,000	$ 14,000	$ 7,000	$ 17,000
Total estimated costs	$131,000	$158,000	$121,000	$151,000

[1] Minimum cash required refers to the amount of cash needed to acquire franchise rights. These funds must be unencumbered.
[2] Equipment and sign costs will vary for each shop.

In addition to being able to meet the basic financial requirements, which excluded land or building, Ramone was excited about the required six-week training program at Dunkin' Donuts University in Braintree, Massachusetts. The training program is to teach product methods and also to ensure product quality and freshness, proper training, employee motivation, merchandising techniques, accounting, budgeting, and record keeping. A great deal of this training time is spent in learning the operations necessary to ensure cleanliness and a good image.

Ramone was still uneasy about the marketing needs of the franchise. He didn't know for sure who was the target market of a franchised donut shop. He didn't know what kind of research was necessary to understand the marketing process or if Dunkin' Donuts would help with the marketing program. He read in the brochure that Dunkin' Donuts "concentrates on a single sales theme and directs the message to consumers who are likely to become regular customers." Ramone was hoping that Dunkin' Donuts might help him with advertising. He would also need help in finding a good location. Ramone was also wondering about new products and if there was a continuous effort to improve the product line.

Ramone knew he could be a success, because Dunkin' Donuts is a corporation committed to the future and profitability of its franchisees. He wanted the opportunity to prove himself. If the franchisor would buy the land and put up the building, Ramone felt that he could finance a new Dunkin' Donuts operation.

CASE QUESTIONS

1. What does Ramone need to know before becoming a Dunkin' Donuts franchisee?
2. What marketing information should Ramone seek?
3. What marketing mix should Ramone look for with his business?

REFERENCES

1. Curry, J. A. H., et al., *Partners for Profit: A Study of Franchising*, New York: American Management Association, Inc., 1966.
2. Curtis, David A., *Strategic Planning for Smaller Businesses*, Lexington, MA: D. C. Heath & Company, 1983.
3. Dixon, Edward L., Jr., ed., *The 1980 Franchise Annual Handbook and Directory*, Lewiston, NY: International Franchise Opportunities Press, Inc., 1980.
4. Henward, DeBanks M., and William Ginalski, *The Franchise Option: Expanding Your Business Through Franchising*, Phoenix, AZ: Franchise Group Publishers, 1979.
5. Izraeli, Dov, *Franchising and the Total Distribution System*, London: Longman Group Limited, 1972.
6. Justis, Robert T., Richard J. Judd, and David B. Stephens, *Strategic Management and Policy: Concepts and Cases*, Englewood Cliffs, NJ: Prentice-Hall, Inc., 1985.
7. Kotler, Philip, *Principles of Marketing*, 2nd edition, Englewood Cliffs, NJ: Prentice-Hall, Inc., 1983.
8. McCarthy, E. Jerome, *Basic Marketing*, 7th edition, Homewood, IL: Richard D. Irwin, Inc., 1981.
9. McDonald's Corporation, *Annual Report, 1983*.
10. McGuire, E. Patrick, *Franchised Distribution*, Report Number 523, New York: The Conference Board, Inc., 1971.
11. Rosenbloom, Bert, *Marketing Channels: A Management View*, 2nd edition, New York: Dryden Press, 1983.

12. Tate, Curtis E., Jr., et al., *Successful Small Business Management*, 3rd edition, Plano, TX: Business Publications, Inc., 1982.
13. U.S. Department of Commerce, *Franchising in the Economy, 1983–1985*, Washington, DC: U.S. Government Printing Office, 1985.
14. Vaughn, Charles L., *Franchising*, 2nd edition, Lexington, MA: D. C. Heath & Company, 1979.

CHAPTER 8
LOCATION AND SITE SELECTION

In studying this chapter, you will:
- Learn how site selection can mean the difference between success and failure for a franchised business.
- Understand how the site selection process fits into an overall growth plan for a multi-unit franchised business.
- Learn an approach to allocating franchises within a geographic area and for selecting specific sites within those areas.
- Understand how the difference in type of business can influence location and site selection decisions.
- Recognize the importance of market share to site selection.

INCIDENT

Eva and Carlos have made the decision to franchise their record store chain. Currently they jointly own and manage four record stores in two state university towns. They credit their tremendous volume of business to the college student market. Eva and Carlos center their marketing strategy on the college community, and they time their major promotions to coincide with the university calendar of events.

To adequately serve the college student market, a store manager needs to be aware of student tastes and trends. Because of this, Eva and Carlos believe they could not successfully operate a new business in other university towns outside their state. They have determined the logical alternative is to franchise.

First they want to find prospective franchisees in other state university towns. Once Eva and Carlos find the type of franchisee they feel would be capable of handling a business, that person will go through a six-week training period. Each potential franchisee will work in one of the existing stores and learn the ins and outs of the retail record business. Then the new franchisees will begin operating their own stores in their towns. All record ordering will be channeled through Eva and Carlos. However, the franchisee will have the freedom to determine the quantities and selections in demand in their local communities. The franchisee will also receive weekly window layouts and a page of promotional ideas. The franchisee will have the option to use these ideas when and if desired.

Eva and Carlos are convinced that franchising is the best plan for expansion of their record business. Franchisees will have the benefit of Eva and Carlos's experience but will be encouraged to make many of their own business decisions to profitably serve their community. The only problem is that Eva and Carlos are not sure which college town and which site within a town would be the best place to open a record store franchise.

INTRODUCTION

Selection of the right location for a proposed franchise outlet can mean the difference between success and failure and can be the crucial factor in whether a franchise will be a moderate or a big success. Location theorists often claim that the three most important criteria for success of any business are location, location, and location! This concept applies to franchised businesses as well. If a business person lacks the knowledge and skill appropriate to the particular business field and is also a poor manager, the franchise is most assuredly on the road to failure. But if the franchise has a good location, there is a chance the business might succeed even in spite of the owner's shortcomings.

Selection of a suitable location is of extreme importance to both franchisor and franchisee. Factors associated with a specific site can affect the initial cost of many franchises and profitability forecasts of a proposed franchised outlet, and can also project the rate of growth of the business at the proposed site. A franchisor has the responsibility for planning the growth and development of the franchise system within a particular area, across areas, cities, states, and regions. Both franchisor and franchisee want the best possible site within a locale that displays the demographic characteristics and traffic patterns that will increase the chance for success in the organization's line of business. Further, some franchisees will want to expand at a particular site once they become established, or they'll want to add sites by opening a second or third location. Therefore, the growth plan of the franchise organization is of critical importance to the franchisor and the franchisee as well.

CONSIDERATIONS FOR LOCATION AND SITE SELECTION

The potential location and site selection considerations are endless. Does a franchisor wish to expand through single-unit franchisees and small geographic areas within cities, or is the franchisor looking for large geographical areas and multi-unit franchisees? Will the franchisor have the financial capacity to purchase outright or acquire over time through a lease arrangement the sites that the franchisees will operate? If not, will the franchisee be required to purchase land or building? Will there be any shared equity arrangements between franchisor and franchisee? If the franchise is to be located within a shopping center or mall, will the franchisor be responsible for the lease contract?

Many franchise organizations have established specific retail site qualifications. Such franchises require certain population densities, income levels, and traffic patterns. Other franchises, such as Manpower and Snelling and Snelling, may simply require that a franchisee locate in a downtown or business area. Still other franchise systems, such as those offering business services, may simply require space in the franchisee's home or other noncommercial location.

Whole books have been devoted to the topics discussed in this chapter. Although it is not the purpose of this book to exhaust the subject, we intend to provide some understanding about location, site selection, and layout considerations from a franchising perspective. First, the general considerations made by a franchisor prior to developing a franchise system are discussed, followed by a discussion of concepts and techniques useful for determining target trade areas, development map and market share, site selection considerations, and factors associated with types of real estate programs of franchised businesses. Franchisees' considerations about general location and specific site factors are presented. These considerations are combined into a checklist that can be used by a prospective franchisee to evaluate a proposed site. For the last topic, layout, we present material about layout characteristics for a manufacturing operation, warehousing or distribution center, and retail outlets with perspective on franchised businesses in each of these types of business activities and locations.

Franchise Expansion

Frankly, site selection and other location considerations are looked upon by the franchisor and the franchisee quite differently. The primary topic addressed in this chapter is a location model for a franchisor specifically interested in the concept of developing territories with multiple-unit operations. A franchisor's plans for expansion would range from this concept, as used by some of the well-known companies including Ford Motor Co., General Motors Corp., Wendy's International Inc., McDonald's Corp., Midas International Corporation, Kentucky Fried Chicken Corp., down to a single-unit expansion stemming from the franchisor's base of operations and likely to be within the same geographic locale.

Overhead and Distribution

Regardless if the intended expansion plans of a prospective franchisor are international or simply local, two points must be considered in developing the expansion plans: overhead and distribution. The plans begin with a determination of what level of operational support will be provided to a given zone, districts, territory, location, or specific site. Consideration should be given by the prospective franchisor to the types of operational characteristics of a functioning franchisor within a franchise distribution system. (See Table 8-1).

A prospective franchisor has numerous details to work out prior to initiating the first plans for expansion. Sources of supply, distribution and inventory scheduling, warehousing (if required within the line of business activity), and costs and profit margins by type of product or service, as well as the cost of acquiring and maintaining the name, design, copyrights, and registration necessary to prepare franchisor-franchisee contracts, need to be worked out. Once determined, such services and their costs should be identified as overhead of the corporation

Table 8-1
Overhead and Distribution Considerations for a Prospective Franchisor

1. Determine the steps involved and costs of incorporation.
2. Determine the steps involved and costs of registering to do business in two or more states.
3. Determine the franchisor's corporate capital structure, including projected cash flow and profit/loss figures over the next two or three years.
4. Determine any short-term financing arrangements for selected franchisees to provide funding for building, land, equipment, or inventory.
5. Develop policies for site selection and franchisee involvement, if any, in selecting or approving a particular site.
6. Determine sources for raw or finished goods, inventory requirements, costs and projected profit margins, warehousing needed, or other factors associated with the franchisor's distribution system in order to identify the components and their costs.
7. Determine proprietary status of name, trade, and service brands or marks, corporate logo, and designs or other registrations necessary for the franchisor to operate legally within a particular state or states.

(fixed costs of doing business) or as costs associated with distribution (services expected by a franchisee from a franchisor) to provide inventory, supplies, or products through the franchise distribution system.

Determining these factors — and their associated costs — is of extreme importance to the development of a franchise program. One of the keys to success in franchising is to have a package that does not require large-scale financing by the franchisor or the franchisee. Another key is to set up the distribution system to the degree that franchisees have faith in the franchisor's and the franchise system's ability to deliver. Therefore, a predictable distribution system that is efficient and responsive to a franchisee's needs, and the legal propriety of franchised names, marks, or brands that are not too costly for the franchisee to support, are considerations the franchising organization should address prior to actually expanding the franchise.

The particular topics listed in Table 8-1 are addressed in more detail in other sections of the book, under legal considerations, franchisor and franchisee financing, and administration and operation of the franchise package. The purpose of addressing these topics here has been to highlight the importance of overhead costs and distribution factors and costs as primary considerations that underlie any proposed expansion by a franchisor. These costs can vary considerably, and the philosophy of expansion can also vary from franchisor to franchisor. For example, some franchisors use a shotgun approach, developing as many franchised units within a state or trade area as they can, as quickly, practically, and profitably as possible. Other franchisors use more of a rifle-shot approach, identifying and establishing a master franchisee within a fairly large territory or district and relying on that franchisee to do the further development within the specified territory. Some franchisors have used the concept of a company store "seeding" as the method to enter a new trade area or state, as establishing a franchisor-owned (or company) store as the first in a trade area lifts the burden of operational support and distribution from the newly forming franchisees within a trade area, placing it in the more controlled environment of the company operations of the franchisor.

Once overhead and distribution factors have been determined and their costs have been identified in relation to any proposed expansion, a franchisor can turn attention to the geographic questions of expansion.

GEOGRAPHIC SELECTION

For successful expansion, a franchisor needs to know what characteristics about the franchised product or service are measurable. The franchisor needs to learn what type of people patronize the franchisor's own operating unit as well as any franchised units. A franchisor would want to know about the people who are primarily from the immediate area around the store — Are they residents or do they work in the nearby office buildings? Are they male or female, young, old, or middle-aged? Do they come in alone, as couples, or with children? Where are they on the socioeconomic scale? Identifying patron characteristics can be very useful in estimating market potential and type of clientele for a proposed site as well as for prospective areas considered for expansion. In addition to profiling the franchised firm's customer, the franchisor should also analyze the competition, and the cost of real estate if the franchisor has a real estate program, and from these analyses carefully develop estimates of the costs of serving any new franchised units in the proposed expansion area.

The overall objective of analyzing locations and determining particular sites for expansion is to forecast the sales volume (and therefore profit) that can be generated at a certain location. Certain areas and regions thus might be considered more attractive than others. The general business expansion taking place across the southern United States is a normal outcome of the population increases of recent years. As people have moved south, cities and even areas of a state have had increased activity such as road building, improvement/expansion of sewage facilities, expansion of power-generating capabilities, and various types of construction including commercial, governmental, and residential. Such activity naturally leads to expansion of businesses offering consumer products and services to meet the increased demand. Other areas of the country have also experienced population increases, but not on the same scale as the southern regions. Surely, every region of the country has interest in enhancing economic development and seeking the increased employment, tax revenues, and business sales volume associated with such development. Some very successful franchise systems have developed in northeastern, midwestern, and northwestern states. Franchise development should not be exclusive to southern states or to any single region. For development, a franchisor needs a logical method to establish what geographic areas could be considered for expansion. If a franchisor intends to become a nationwide distribution system and perhaps international franchise system, geographic market areas need to be examined and those that offer optimal opportunity for franchise system development need to be identified.

The Location Model

There is basically a three-step approach (Figure 8-1) to identification of areas for system expansion and determination of specific sites within a chosen area. These steps are as follows:

1. Selection of geographic areas for franchise system development;

Figure 8-1
Three-Step Approach to Identifying Areas for System Expansion

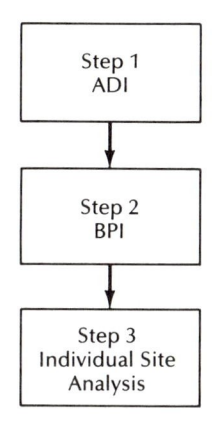

```
┌─────────────┐
│   Step 1    │
│    ADI      │
└──────┬──────┘
       │
       ▼
┌─────────────┐
│   Step 2    │
│    BPI      │
└──────┬──────┘
       │
       ▼
┌─────────────┐
│   Step 3    │
│Individual Site│
│   Analysis  │
└─────────────┘
```

2. Determination of the number of franchises to be established within a specific geographic area; and
3. Individual site selection based on criteria used to distinguish between specific site alternatives.

Location models can help franchisors take steps appropriate for developing expansion plans for their franchise system. Each step should be fully considered before any further step is taken. Accomplishment of these steps will generally yield a successful and profitable franchise system for the franchisor.

Distribution of Franchises

The first step in geographic selection is to determine the proper distribution of franchises within the total geographic area covered by the franchise organization. By example, if the United States is to be the total area, then it should be divided into geographic sections, and then into manageable subsections or franchise areas, depending on how extensive a distribution system the franchisor can set up. A franchise area could be an entire metropolitan area or portion thereof, a multicounty district, or perhaps a multistate region.

ADIs. One way of dividing the United States into franchise market/geographic areas is to use the Arbitron ratings map. The Arbitron Company, a research division of Control Data Corp., initiated a ratings map in its 1966–1967 Arbitron television market report. The units of the map are determined by **areas of dominant influence** (ADIs). Since that time, the ADI system has gained general acceptance as a basic approach to structuring advertising and promotion as well as determining extent of distribution systems. We suggest this approach to geographic area selection because a potential franchisor in any part of the country can get information on the particular ADI area in which the franchised firm operates or information about other areas of the United States under consideration for franchise development.

The ADI approach divides the United States into dominant television market areas. Each county is assigned to an ADI, with no overlap, according to the market influence a local television media beams to its viewers. A particular ADI may be made up of counties in one, two, or more contiguous states. Criteria identifying the level of market influence as shown on an ADI map are based on viewership rather than political boundaries. The television viewing ratings provide a franchisor the opportunity to determine how the franchised firm's advertising budget might be spent most effectively, through concentrated advertising, dispersed advertising, or on-site promotions within a particular ADI area.

Some franchisors may use the ADI as the criterion for allotting new franchises within specific areas targeted for growth. However, most franchisors use multiple criteria for choosing desirable geographic areas for franchise development. The size of a franchise area, and perhaps even the proposed franchising fee, may be determined by the size, scope, or perceived importance of a particular geographic area or territory. Within the ADI, Arbitron ranks the different counties across the U.S. according to population and location. The four major ADI classifications include:

A: Those counties within the 25 largest metropolitan rating areas
B: Those counties not included in A, but with population greater than 150,000
C: Those counties not included in A or B, but with populations over 35,000
D: Those counties not part of A, B, or C

To illustrate, the state of New York has eleven ADIs: Buffalo, Elmira, Binghamton, Rochester, Syracuse, Utica, Albany-Schenectady, Troy, Watertown, Carthage, and New York (Poughkeepsie). Elmira and Binghamton ADIs include counties from Pennsylvania, while Albany-Schenectady and Troy include portions of states of Vermont and Massachusetts. The New York (Poughkeepsie) ADI includes counties in New Jersey, Connecticut, and Pennsylvania. The largest ADI is the New York (Poughkeepsie) ADI, with 7.72 percent of the television households in the United States. The number of ADIs in New York, counties by Arbitron size classifications, and rank by percent of total television households in the United States are shown in Table 8-2.

The ADI concept originated within the advertising industry and was designed to offer potential advertisers maximum dollar efficiency

Table 8-2
Example of County/ADI Size Classification for the State of New York

ADI	Number of Counties [Classification:] A B C D	Rank in Total TV Market	Percentage of Total Households
Albany-Schenectady-Troy	— 5 6 3	52	0.56
Binghamton	— 2 3 —	133	0.18
Buffalo	— 2 8 1	35	0.72
Elmira	— — 3 —	166	0.10
New York (Poughkeepsie)	18 6 3 1	1	7.72
Rochester	4 — — —	71	0.41
Syracuse	— 3 4 3	67	0.43
Utica	— 1 2 —	159	0.12
Watertown-Carthage	— — 2 1	172	0.09

Source: Courtesy Arbitron Ratings Company.

for customer/market penetration in a specific area. Advertisers were interested in knowing how much advertising expenditure would be needed to ensure a certain level of customer exposure for an advertised product. A certain percentage of people exposed to an advertisement would be influenced to buy, which would yield a particular level of sales revenue for the company paying for the advertisement.

Using the ADI as the sole criterion for allocating franchises might be more suitable for multi-unit franchised distribution firms, where a master franchisee or area-wide franchisee would be established, than it would be for allocating single-unit franchises. The ADI concept is used to determine the overall number of individual franchisees considering forming franchise clusters to pool their advertising dollars in order to launch promotional campaigns. For example, franchises of a well-known pizza restaurant have been allocated in many instances based on ADI areas. This means that if a franchisee wished to establish five pizza restaurants in the state of Texas, the franchisee would be urged to cluster these restaurants within a specific ADI area rather than locate restaurants across ADI areas such as El Paso, Houston, Austin, Dallas-Fort Worth, and Lubbock. These five areas are in different ADI media markets. The cost of advertising for the five would be substantially higher than if the five stores were located in a single ADI market such as Dallas-Fort Worth, where the five stores could share the marketing media costs uniformly.

Population. Another approach often used in allocating franchises is simply identifying the number of people within a particular geographic territory. The U.S. Bureau of the Census tabulates population figures at the state, county, and census tract levels. A franchisor could attempt to maintain "parity" for franchisees by assigning territories based on population contained within a specific area. For example, NAMCO Systems, Inc. franchises territories for the sale and distribution of telephone book covers based on population within a specified territory. Other franchisors, such as Meineke Discount Muffler Shops, determine a specified service area or zone such as a two-mile radius around a particular muffler shop as that franchisee's territory. Other franchisors, such as Southland Corp., which franchises 7-ELEVEN convenience stores, and Midas International Corporation, do not grant exclusive areas or territories. Instead, a right to operate is granted for a specific location only and the franchisor has the right to establish other shops or stores at any other locations whatsoever.

As one can see, there are various approaches that can be used to determine territory for a franchise. The best approach is the approach that works best for the franchisor. The Arbitron ADI concept is one criterion that may be useful to a franchisor considering area, state, or regional growth within the range of possibility. Such ratings and media audience concentrations can be very helpful in developing advertising budgets and proposing cost-effective approaches to increasing visibility of the franchise's product or service.

Number of Franchised Units

The second step in geographic selection is to determine the number of potential franchised units the franchisor would like to have within a specified geographic area.

BPI. A useful tool to assist in this determination is *Sales and Marketing Management* magazine's "Survey of Buying Power," in which a **buying power index (BPI)** is found for each of the geographic subunits of a particular ADI. The buying power index statistics suggest the consumer buying power available in a particular area, which can be compared to the buying power judged necessary for a single unit to operate profitably within a proposed geographic area. Once sales, income, and profitability standards have been established, the number of franchised units viable for a geographic area can be determined. The "Survey of Buying Power," published annually in July, provides a variety of statistical data useful for a franchise location decision, such as population totals, age-group distribution, and retail sales analysis by county or standard metropolitan statistical area (SMSA). The BPI is a powerful tool for determining market potential and can be defined as

> a weighted index that converts three basic elements — population, effective buying income, and retail sales — into a measurement of a market's ability to buy, and expresses it as a percentage of the U.S./Canada poten-

tial. It is calculated by giving weight of five to the market's percent of U.S./Canada effective buying income, three to its percent of retail sales, and two to its percent of population. The total of the weighted percents is divided by ten to produce the BPI.[1]

The buying power index offers a franchisor the opportunity to identify an area's potential buying power. Similar to the ADI, the BPI uses county boundaries for categorizing the market-based information. To use the BPI as an aid in decision making, an ADI is chosen wherein franchises have already been established and have proven profitable. The proportion of profitable units to all similar units within the specific ADI can be used to develop a normative ratio to suggest the number of franchised units that a similar ADI area could sustain. If an ADI geographic area is considered fully developed (saturated) according to the franchisor for the particular industry in question, then BPI information may be useful for maintaining, expanding, or possibly retrenching the number of franchised units within a particular market area.

As an example, a hypothetical franchisor, Anything Fast Food Company, located in Cincinnati, Ohio, conducts an analysis of its outlets in the metropolitan area. This franchisor believes that 30 franchised outlets is the extent to which this area can be developed for Anything Fast Foods. The population of the Cincinnati area of 1,403,500 is sufficient for this franchisor, with 30 units, and the other fast-food firms and their outlets to satisfy the demand for fast-food restauranting by consumers. The buying power index for the greater Cincinnati area is 0.6007.[2] Dividing the BPI (0.6007) by the number of existing stores (30 is the number beyond which the franchisor will not expand because the market is believed to be saturated) will yield a figure of 0.0200 BPI. This figure (0.0200) suggests the lowest buying power index this franchised firm believes necessary to meet the costs and market demands associated with a single Anything Fast Food outlet. In general, when a marketplace for a particular product or service is considered saturated, the addition of more outlets by any particular supplier will tend to hurt other existing suppliers, causing some to leave the market. An oversupply will exist, given the level of demand for the product or service. Therefore, Anything Fast Foods, with its 30 units in Cincinnati, which it considers a maximum penetration level for itself considering the remaining competition, can then apply this minimum amount of buying power (0.0200) it deems necessary to other metropolitan market areas in which it develops franchised outlets.

---

[1] 1983 Survey of Buying Power, *Sales and Marketing Management*, Vol. 131, No. 2 (July 25, 1983).
[2] 1985 Survey of Buying Power, *Sales and Marketing Management*, Vol. 135, No. 2 (July 22, 1985).

A franchisor would use the BPI information, provided on a county-by-county basis, in examining new areas for possible entry. While a county-by-county or statewide analysis can be quite useful, it often does not adequately reflect the promotional and advertising needs that a franchisor involved in consumer durable and nondurable sales and distribution would have. That is where the ADI information becomes helpful. By combining the BPI and ADI information, one can develop a broad scope of fairly concrete information about an overall market area as well as specific segments within that overall market. A franchisee, considering a selection of a second or third outlet to be owned and operated under the franchising agreement, could also use the ADI and BPI information, rather than just site selection factors. For example, an Anything Fast Food franchisee considering additional units within the Santa Barbara, California, area (which has a BPI of 0.1602)[3] could seek approval from the franchisor for a total possible of eight franchise site approvals (0.1602/0.0200 = 8). The franchisee used the minimum BPI figure considered appropriate by the Anything Fast Food franchisor and divided that minimum figure (0.0200) into the BPI figure for the market area within which he or she resides, in this illustration Santa Barbara, with a BPI of 0.1602. Therefore, both franchisor and franchisee can utilize the same information and cooperate in the franchise development program of the firm.

The franchisor would have market-oriented information to guide decisions such as whether promotional expenses should be reduced or increased for a unit to be located in a particular area. New York, Buffalo, and Rochester would require advertising expense payments in three different media markets. However, using the ADI, the franchisee may seek economies of scale by choosing sites within the same media viewing area. Let's assume that the Anything Fast Food Company is considering development of a system of outlets in upper New York state. Using the ADI and BPI tools, the franchisor could concentrate activity and resources in a specific area of the state in order to enhance competitive position and profitability.

For example, through examination of ADI maps, a franchisor may choose the Rochester area as a possibility for expansion (see Table 8-3). Review of the ADI information shows there is one major city, Rochester, and identifies suburban Monroe county with three additional counties, Livingston, Ontario, and Wayne, within the Rochester ADI. On first consideration, Orleans County also appears to be part of this area, but closer examination reveals that it is part of the Buffalo ADI. The BPI for each county and major city within this ADI is also identifiable within the "Survey of Buying Power" data sheets or displays. The BPI for each area

[3] 1985 Survey of Buying Power.

Table 8-3
Location Model for Franchise System Development of Anything Fast Food Company[1]

ADI[2]	TV Population	Households	BPI	BPI/Standard[3]	Maximum Number of Outlets Feasible
Rochester, NY	943,000	337,500	0.4430	22.150	22
Major City:					
Rochester	234,700		0.0931	4.655	5
Counties:					
Suburban Monroe	470,500	257,300	0.2479	12.395	12
Livingston	58,200	18,800	0.0229	1.145	1
Ontario	92,400	31,500	0.0400	2.000	2
Wayne	87,200	29,900	0.0391	1.955	2

[1] Use Location Analyses Evaluation Checklist for specific sites under consideration.
[2] Although Orleans and Livingston counties are geographically considered a suburb of Rochester, Orleans is a part of the Buffalo ADI. If the suburban market is the target and outlets are opened in both counties, the franchise may find that promotion costs are substantially greater than if a comparable unit were to be opened in one of the ADI contiguous counties.
[3] For our purposes, 0.0200 is used as the standard in each case.

within the selected ADI is divided by the BPI minimum or "standard" chosen by the franchisor. In our illustration, 0.0200 is being used for the Anything Fast Food Company. This standard or minimum is used to propose the maximum potential number of outlets that could be opened and operated profitably for each county and major city within the ADI under consideration. In Table 8-3, note that there are approximately 22 outlets feasible for the ADI area of Rochester: five in the city of Rochester, twelve in suburban Monroe, and five in Livingston, Ontario, and Wayne counties.

Targeted Trade Area. Through the use of the Arbitron ratings and the buying power index, a general trade area can be targeted for consideration. Some franchisors use this method exclusively, expanding only through the sale of multi-unit franchises. For example, Rocky Rococo Pan Style Pizza expands by franchising to one company to develop one of the 211 ADI television markets as determined by the Arbitron Ratings Company. Rocky Rococo puts its franchising document together as a territorial development agreement, serving as an umbrella for the individual franchising agreements for each restaurant. Each franchisee has:

1. A nonrefundable territorial fee to provide to the franchisor
2. A development schedule designed to put enough restaurants into the ADI in a 24 to 36-month period to be able to advertise consistently on

television throughout the year with an advertising budget based on percentage of sales; and
3. An exclusive area to develop (which can be all or part of an ADI, or encompass several ADIs).[4]

This approach to expansion was pioneered in the franchised restaurant business by Wendy's International Inc. It has pursued this strategy nationally and has achieved significant success.

Development of Target Trade Areas

The third step in geographic selection is development of target trade areas for consideration, which might include specific cities, counties, or sections within cities. Normally a franchisor will do a market analysis of a specific city or county to determine likely areas in which to open new franchised outlets. Some franchisors, especially large companies, such as franchising motel companies, automotive manufacturers, oil companies, and franchisors in the automobile aftermarkets, take extensive pains to examine transportation networks, industrial development patterns, and financial capabilities of the communities in question, and assess the overall economic condition of the community from a historical perspective in order to make judgments about the future economic and business health of the communities. The overall economic perspective relates to how well the local community being examined reacts to higher or lower interest rates, higher or lower unemployment, inflation, recession, and aggressive growth or decline. From this economic and market data, trade areas are judged worthwhile or not for entry. The definition of a targeted trade area may differ from franchised company to franchised company, as may the specific items used by franchising firms to develop their sales projections and particular cost schedules.

There are two basic approaches for delineating a target trade area. If it is the first site for a new franchisor locating what will be the pilot operation or facility, the target trade area is often determined through a "best guess" approach, particularly if the business deals with a unique line of product or new type of service not available elsewhere. On the other hand, the more common approach for proposing sites is to estimate, based on logic, experience, and available information, the site or sites where competitive advantage is most favorable. Stated another way, when one moves outward from a proposed site, at some point competitive advantage is lost to alternative shopping choices. It is within this delineated "ring" around the proposed site that competitive advantage exists. Therefore, a trade area can be considered as a circle from which a signifi-

---

[4] From text of letter received form Wayne Mosley, President, Rocky Rococo Corporation, Madison, Wisconsin, February, 1986.

cant portion of the business will be derived. Obviously, trade areas are not precise circles; they often appear as amoeba-like forms, or are rectangular or triangular when natural boundaries or barriers elongate or dramatically shorten the area.

Primary Service Area. Whatever the particular shape of the target trade area, the objective is to determine a geographic space within which a **primary service area (PSA)** for the proposed business would be large enough to sustain the business activity and to help it to be profitable. A primary service area is an area from which a retail goods or service provider can expect to attract two-thirds or more of its business activity. The size of a PSA depends on factors such as traffic systems, traffic patterns and conditions, and physical barriers or boundaries such as rivers, undeveloped lands, railroad tracks, or limited-access superhighways. Also, the PSA for a particular franchised business depends upon site, overall economic health of the trade area, size of the facility to be opened, and location of existing competition. Therefore, defining the PSA is basic to determining whether a specific area "needs" a particular franchised outlet, whether the area can support such an outlet (or the addition of one more outlet), and whether existing competitive conditions would allow another competitor to exist within the trade area.

A PSA should be selected only after careful consideration of the factors that reflect what the present buying habits of residents of the area are, and how the buying habits might change if the franchisor opened a business within the trade area in question. The techniques which follow are directly related to retail products considered as convenience or shopping goods or services, which constitute a great part of the goods and services offered by franchises today. The factors important in determining size and shape of a primary service area (PSA) include:

1. *Alternative Shopping Choices* — that the drawing power of a shopping facility or convenience goods site is a function of the size of population around the facility and the distance to the nearest alternative shopping or convenience facility;
2. *Barriers and Pockets* — that the potential market is measured in terms of the total market less that share of the total market now absorbed by existing outlets, and that natural physical barriers separating the target trade area from alternative trade areas will determine the market potential;
3. *Drive-Time Analysis* — that the number of customers a store can expect to attract depends on convenience factors such as the amount of time and trouble a customer must exert to reach the store, based on the accessibility of the location to people living nearby, using driving time as a basis for measurement; and,
4. *Intuition* — that the use of a given shopping facility is largely a matter

of habit and traditions within a community, which means relying heavily on judgments of people knowledgeable about the economic and market characteristics of the targeted trade area and of people knowledgeable about the particular business activity.

Population. Through use of Arbitron ratings and the buying power index or other appropriate methods, a general trade area can be targeted for consideration. Once this broad delineation of a proposed target trade area is determined, the next step is to estimate and forecast the population for the trade area. Why? Because population is a fundamental source of information about a target trade area upon which site selection decisions are made. The primary data source is the U.S. Bureau of the Census, which conducts a census every ten years. But ten years is a long time, and census data can become obsolete quickly. Sometimes special censuses are made by counties or cities, and usually this information can be acquired at little or no cost from the appropriate governmental office. However, the information is not always uniform with the U.S. Census data and may only involve fundamental counts associated with housing units and population. The more-extensive data from the Bureau of the Census divides the United States into a number of subdivisions: states, regions, SMSAs (Standard Metropolitan Statistical Areas), and counties. Information is collected and is available to provide the detailed information about population, housing, and income within the uniformly defined geographic area called a *census tract*.

Other sources that can provide population estimates during the ten-year span from one census to the next include local planning departments of a county or city, local chambers of commerce, and even the U.S. Post Office. When population estimates are obtained from sources other than the U.S. Census Bureau, it is wise to ask about the method used in arriving at the estimates. One should try to learn if estimates are predicted on number of possible postal deliveries, building permits, and building demolitions, or the basis used if a regression model was developed to make the estimates.

Competition. The second consideration is the amount of competition in the proposed site. In evaluating competition in the proposed site, one should first locate all the competition by type or category of competitiveness on a map. For example, fast-food competition might include fried chicken outlets, ice cream parlors, traditional restaurants, snack bars, pizzerias, baked potato shops, and coffee shops. Therefore, when undertaking a study of locating a hamburger-oriented restaurant with drive-thru capability, it can be important to look at all of these types of fast-food retailers as potential competitors. However, restaurants similar to the type being proposed clearly provide the most direct and strongest competition. As a result, one would not give as much weight to ice cream parlors, baked potato shops, or coffee shops, or perhaps even pizzerias, snack bars, traditional restaurants, and fried chicken outlets, as one would to other hamburger-oriented fast-food outlets in the same trade area. When there is wide variation in considering one competitor to another, other factors should be considered such as the square footage of competitors' outlets or the level of sales each competitor might be generating, to reflect how strong the competition is in relation to the outlet location being considered. Further, the image of each competitor should be considered, in terms of how it relates to the market it is serving. For example, in franchised businesses such as auto parts/repair/replacement, some franchises project a high-quality image, stressing service and dependability, while others emphasize price discounting. Therefore, giving the same weight to all existing competitors in the target trade area, even though they may be trying to appeal to different segments of the market, would tend to distort the market analysis.

Three other points should be mentioned in our discussion about location and competition. First, a competitor's square footage is not as important a factor when there is little variance in what the consuming public expects from a certain type of retail business as it is when there is wide variance in customer attitude about company logo, trademark, and level of product selection. For example, when a franchised convenience store is competing with other convenience stores, franchised or not, simply the existence or absence of competition within a certain geographic section of the trade area will enable one to evaluate the strength of the competitive environment.

Second, locating competitive stores or outlets within one area, such as "clustering" of franchised auto dealerships, furniture stores, or fast-food outlets along a business strip or inside a shopping mall, tends to improve potential sales for all competitors because of the added attraction for the consuming public of variance in choice. However, retail outlets that offer very similar product choices (such as convenience stores) tend to dilute the market, dividing up the retail pie into thinner slices as additional business enters the trade area or cluster of stores.

Third, the specific location of the competition in relation to the proposed business site can be extremely important. A site should be chosen that gives one a competitive advantage. For example, being two blocks away from a major intersection when the competitor is at or near the intersection can be a disadvantage. On the other hand, if the store is located more conveniently than that of the primary competitor, and closer to the specific neighborhood or other population concentration from which the customers are to be drawn, the site is likely to be viewed more favorably than the competitor's. The reason is simple: The site is closer to the customer, and in business activity where convenience is a factor, this may provide the advantage over the competitor.

Demographic Map of Trade and Primary Service Area

The determination of a primary service area (PSA) is based on careful consideration of factors which reflect the present purchasing habits of consumers within the trade area. A map of the general area under consideration should be used to determine (1) the alternative shopping choices for the proposed product/service; (2) the barriers or pockets of the trade area, as natural or man-made physical barriers that identify the target trade area from alternative trade areas; (3) the extent to which the "convenience" factor (the amount of time and trouble a customer must exert to reach the location) affects the purchase decision, using drive time as a basis for measurement; and (4) the habits and traditions within a community that suggest which trade areas within a community would be preferable to other trade areas within the same community.

Figure 8-2 illustrates a primary service area with a proposed site and the existing competition for a franchised auto center. The primary service area for the proposed service center includes all of the area west of the heavy line in the figure, which corresponds with 96th Street, between Blondo on the north and Shirley Street on the south. The service area for the proposed location extends westward in a cone shape to about 168th Street and in a northwesterly direction to about 168th Street and Maple Road. The geographic area covers about six square miles. The western boundary is a natural one. The area west of 168th Street, about a five-minute drive from the proposed site, limits the primary service area since it is relatively undeveloped land. The same is true of the area north of the primary service area. The southern and eastern boundaries of the primary service area are estimated lines which reflect points where driving time to alternative auto service centers would be about the same as the time to drive to the proposed site.

Drive-Time Analysis. Drive-time analysis is a study of driving time that uses a proposed location and alternative or competitive locations as the points of reference. A drive-time analysis helps answer questions about the need for and convenience of a retail outlet offering a product or service that has convenience as one of its primary attractions. There is no absolute criterion by which to judge one location as being better or worse than another. However, a generally accepted drive-time limit can be determined by examining the nature of the shopping facility proposed and the nature of the product or service offered to the public. Drive-time analysis helps suggest convenience of one location over that of alternative locations. Convenience is a function of a consumer's discretionary purchasing power and leisure time. More specifically, the amount of trouble a consumer will go through to get to a given location or to make a given purchase depends on how familiar the customer is with the product, how much money is available for purchase, and how much

Figure 8-2
Primary Service Area with a Proposed Site and Existing Competition for a Franchised Auto Center

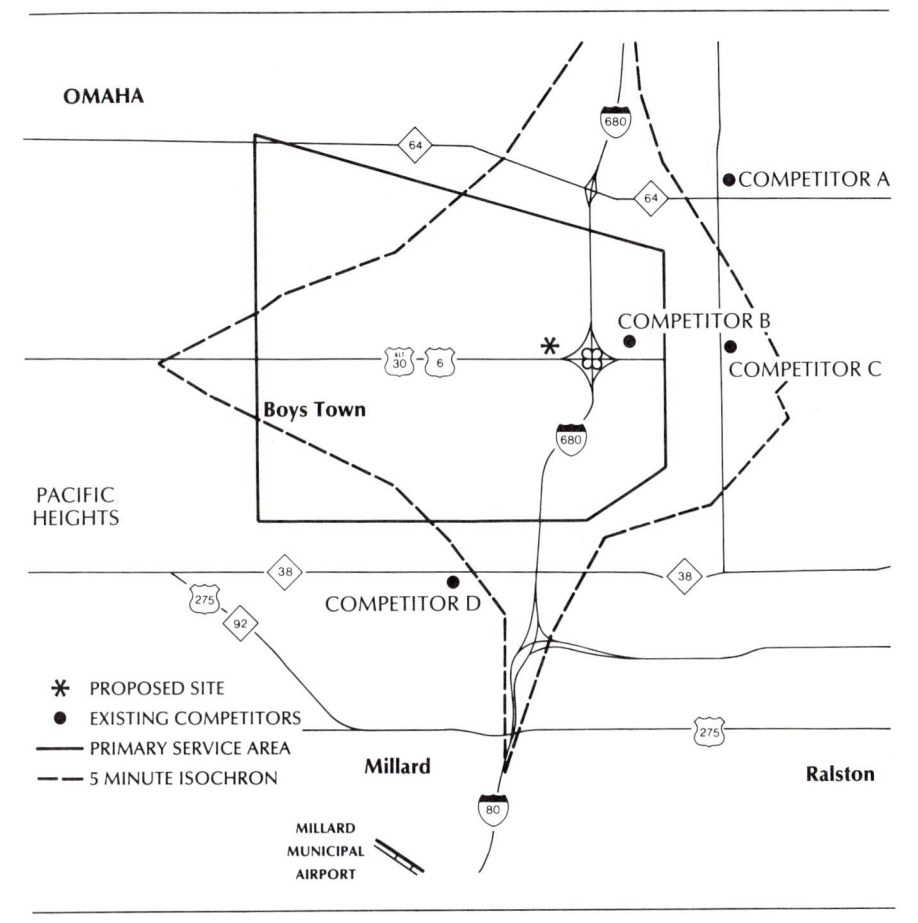

time the customer has to travel to alternative locations offering the product or service. Further, the more important leisure time is to customers, the less effort they will exert to patronize a particular location for the product or service.

As suggested, convenience can be as important a factor associated with a proposed facility as the attributes of the product or service offered for sale. Therefore, traffic conditions, parking, ease of entry and exit, business operating hours, and the mix of products and services available all affect the relative convenience of a particular site. A five-minute drive time suggests trade area for convenience goods such as food and personal services. In contrast, shopping goods such as clothing or specialty services such as jewelry repair, health services, and mechanical replacement or repair can have a trade area that extends to between 15 and 30 minutes in drive time.

Demographic Data. The habits, patterns, and traditions of a community represent the more subjective information about a proposed site and its trade area. In order to solidify judgments about the worth or quality of a proposed site and its primary service area, a franchised company will often want demographic data about the primary service area or trade area and contrast that information with the overall community data. Such information typically collected includes population, age characteristics, housing, distribution of families by income classification, distribution of heads of households in the PSA by occupational category, retail sales by the county/city/trade area, industrial activity, and perhaps other data comparisons. Some franchised companies, particularly in restauranting, motels, and auto dealerships and service centers, will do extensive research beyond the items listed above, considering other factors such as transportation networks, financial capabilities of the communities, and a historical economic reaction rating. A historical economic reaction rating is an indication of how well the business community reacts to recession, inflation, interest rates for short-term and long-term financing, volatility of local interest rates in relation to national trends, unemployment level, and overall rate of economic growth of the community in relation to other communities the firm is considering. Tables 8-4, 8-5, 8-6, 8-7, 8-8, and 8-9 illustrate several types of demographic information franchisors often collect about proposed sites and the community under consideration.

FRANCHISE SITE SELECTION

Often it is the responsibility of the prospective franchisee to develop the market information. For franchised retail locations, a franchisor nor-

Table 8-4
Comparative Population Data:
Primary Service Area (PSA) and City SMSA, 1970 and 1980

	1970	1980	Total Percentage Increase	Average Annual Percentage Increase
PSA*	9,651	24,925	160.7%	16.1%
City SMSA	540,290	637,754	18.0%	1.8%

*PSA includes U.S. Census Tracts: 67.02; half of 68.02; half of 74.01, 74.03, 74.04, and 74.05; half of 74.06; and half of 74.07.

Source: U.S. Bureau of the Census, 1980.

Table 8-5
Comparison of Age Characteristics:
Primary Service Area (PSA) and City SMSA, 1980

Age Group	Percent Distribution	
	PSA	City SMSA
Under 24	44.6	48.9
25–34	15.3	12.9
35–44	17.8	11.5
45–54	12.8	10.1
55–64	6.9	7.7
Over 65	2.6	8.9

Source: U.S. Bureau of the Census, 1980.

Table 8-6
Distribution of Heads of Households in PSA
by Occupational Group, 1980

Occupational Group	Percent in Occupational Group
Professional	25.6
Managerial	25.0
Skilled	11.8
Service	14.1
Self-employed	7.4
Delivery	5.2
Laborer	0.6
Clerical and Clerk	2.2
Salesperson	1.0
Government	6.5
Other	0.6
TOTAL:	100.0

Source: U.S. Bureau of the Census, 1980.

mally tells a new franchisee that the company will assist in site selection and must have approval of the final site. Wendy's International Inc. has a single person responsible for the approval of locations; Burger King Corporation has an extensive board-of-review procedure.

Whatever the number of steps and degree of control by the franchisor in the site selection process, a franchisor will typically address approval of a site from three distinct viewpoints: (1) real estate, (2) operations characteristics and sales forecast, and (3) marketing. The real estate view considers the specifics of appropriate zoning, local ordinance clearances, land purchase or lease, property development and facility building, site ingress and egress, and flow of traffic. Operations charac-

Table 8-7
Distribution of Families in PSA by Income Group, 1979

| | Percent | |
Income Group	PSA	City SMSA
Under $4,999	1.8	7.5
$5,000–$7,999	1.5	8.6
$8,000–$9,999	4.3	15.6
$10,000–$14,999	7.8	15.5
$15,000–$24,999	31.5	30.5
$25,000–$34,999	35.3	17.2
$35,000 and over	17.8	5.1
TOTAL:	100.0	100.0

Source: U.S. Bureau of the Census, 1980.

Table 8-8
Retail Sales:
County to Be Examined and City SMSA for 1983-1986

	1983	1984	1985	1986	Percent Change, 1983-1986
County	$ 860,934	$1,004,124	$1,087,255	$1,182,433	37.3%
City SMSA	$1,405,113	$1,684,875	$1,814,316	$2,586,982	84.1%

Source: Based on figures in *Sales and Marketing Management*, Survey of Buying Power (July 25, 1983), for years considered. Figures included in table are illustrative only.

teristics include size of unit proposed, break-even point of sales in relation to cost of operation, and calculations of one-year, three-year, and five-year financial return on investment (ROI). It is of extreme importance that marketing considerations also be addressed in a site selection process to determine who the customers will be (based on demographic profiles) and what their tastes and preferences are. Such preferences or specific desires indicate the "hot points" between the franchisee and the customer.

Often a prospective franchisee is much like the typical person considering entry into business as an independent business owner/operator. In many cases the franchisee has little understanding about what is required to develop location or to assess existing properties as potential business locations. As a result, the franchisee usually seeks advice from different people, some professional, in addition to seeking the advice of the franchisor. It is important that both the franchisor and the franchisee understand who are the professionals the franchisee is likely to deal with

Table 8-9
Employment Characteristics:
County to Be Examined for Recent Years

Industry*	Number of Employees in County — Recent Year	Most Current Year	Percent Change
Agricultural Services	372	306	−17.2
Mining	192	215	−10.9
Contract Construction	9,048	8,840	− 2.3
Manufacturing	34,952	35,737	+ 2.2
Transportation/Public Utilities	11,215	10,994	− 1.9
Wholesale Trade	15,538	15,207	− 1.5
Retail Trade	27,852	30,530	+ 9.6
Finance, Insurance, and Real Estate	14,005	15,582	+11.2
Services	28,846	34,241	+18.7
Unclassified	331	428	+29.3
TOTAL:	142,351	152,080	+ 6.8

*Excludes government employees, railroad employees, self-employed persons, etc.

Source: Based on figures in *County Business Patterns* for recent years.

in examining alternative sites and selecting the site appropriate for the business location. These professional parties typically will be:

1. The franchisee's banker, who will usually lend from 65 to 80 percent of the cost of site development;
2. An attorney, who will provide consultation on tax matters, leases, contracts, zoning restrictions, and any other general business developments particular to the community and site being selected;
3. A real estate broker, who usually provides advice concerning prime or "hot" commercial areas as well as the relative costs within these areas of the community; and,
4. An accountant, who will determine the amount of cash available to the franchisee that can be used for development of the property, as well as advising about the tax considerations (important for all investors or business owners).

In the site selection process, the franchisee is much like a student in the real-world classroom. The quality of information available, the accuracy of the analyses made, and the wisdom of ultimate decisions made by the franchisor and the local professionals may well determine the success or failure of a particular site. However, in most franchise location decisions, the franchisee has the ultimate responsibility for the decisions. Therefore, the franchisee should actively *make* the final decision and not just be held responsible for the decision.

Franchisors vary in their involvement with franchisee site decisions. As we indicated earlier, franchisors seek different levels of involvement. Two examples are provided. (See Tables 8-10 and 8-11.) Rocky Rococo Corporation expands only through the sale of multi-unit franchises based upon ADI television markets, which is patterned after the approach developed by Wendy's. For Rocky Rococo, specific site selection for the next franchised unit is at the discretion of the multi-unit franchisee. However, Rocky Rococo seeks to ensure that prospects possess certain characteristics before they are permitted to become franchisees.

As another example, Taco John's International has a general outline for a franchisee to use. Each franchisee has a sequence of steps to follow and develops the information the franchisor considers essential to ensure proper site development. (See Table 8-11.) Site selection is one of the most important jobs a franchisee will do in setting up the business. Well-chosen sites, consistent with market demands, are of utmost importance to the franchisor in ensuring the franchise system will develop profitably. Finding an appropriate location for the business is the first hurdle within the newly minted relationship between franchisee and franchisor.

Table 8-10
Four Key Points for Franchisees of Rocky Rococo Pan Style Pizza

1. *Adequate Capitalization.* A prospective franchisee must have sufficient capital to bring the multi-unit franchisee restaurant company to the advertising threshold number of restaurants (in accordance with the ADI territorial market and the territorial agreement established). Not acceptable would be a franchisee trying to build a multi-unit chain parlaying each restaurant into the next with thin capital.
2. *Development Experience.* Key in the multi-unit restaurant business is finding and procuring appropriate locations at the best price. There is the need to deal successfully with the local community for everything from zoning and building permits to liquor licenses, all of which takes experience. There is also the need to oversee a construction project (not necessarily as a general contractor, but at least to ride herd) to bring each restaurant in on time and within budget.
3. *Successful Experience in Multi-Unit Operations.* Since each franchisee is new to the Rocky Rococo business, it is critical that a person successful in developing multi-unit operations take the lead in the day-to-day operations of the restaurants. This means recruiting, training, supervising, and leading the values of the operating group.
4. *Tie-In with Company's Food-Service and Business Values.* Rocky Rococo is in the hospitality industry and its customers must be invited back with consistently high-quality food and service, cleanliness, and courtesy. It looks aggressively into the background of each prospect relative to this set of food-service values. The company believes, and seeks to instill in franchisees, the belief that Rocky's is a permanent business and one that must be invested in. No one should expect to get rich quick. Franchisees must respect and "buy into" this point of view.

Source: Adapted from material provided by Wayne Mosley, President, Rocky Rococo Corporation, Madison, Wisconsin, February, 1986.

Table 8-11
Site Selection Guidelines for Franchisees of Taco John's

1. Contact a local CPA, determining the type of program which best suits one's financial capabilities in terms of:
   a. Purchasing land
   b. Building to suit
   c. Leasing
   d. Establishing a partnership
2. Discuss at length tax consequences of the investment and the appropriate type of business entity that will best serve the overall tax plan, considering factors such as:
   a. Purchasing the land with one corporation and leasing to another corporation
   b. Holding the ground within the same corporation as the restaurant entity to build balance sheet asset value
   c. Leasing equipment to cut down overall initial cost
   d. Establishing separate entities such as limited partnerships or Subchapter S corporation groupings
3. Contact a local banker.
   a. Determine the viability of loans by type, for
      i. Land
      ii. Building
      iii. Equipment
   b. Establish what the approval process will be.
   c. Try to ascertain the amount of collateralization to be required, the acceptable debt-to-debt ratio, and the maximum amount of funds that can be lent by type of need. (Note: At least three financial institutions should be contacted.)
4. Contact franchisor.
   a. Establish market analysis.
   b. Establish priority areas for consideration.
   c. Request demographic information.
   d. Establish the type of building parameters for the given area considered.
   e. Request assistance.
5. Contact a real estate broker (commercial)
   a. Indicate the type of business involved.
   b. Indicate acceptable parameters to the franchisor.
   c. Indicate the amount to be invested and the tax considerations that are applicable. Request a list of viable, properly zoned locations. (Be specific by trade area being considered.)
6. Contact the franchisor.
   a. Review location under consideration.
   b. Receive pertinent advice/approvals.
7. Contact a CPA and a lawyer.
   a. Determine information for development of a *pro forma* break-even analysis for the business.
   b. Establish the tax consequences for each business entity involved in the franchised business being formed.
   c. Review all leases and/or sales agreements.
   d. Prepare to submit option on the business site/building.

Source: Adapted from correspondence/site selection and sales from Rex L. Washburn, General Manager, Taco John's, Cheyenne, Wyoming, December, 1984.

Site Profile

Finding the appropriate location involves careful analysis of more than just one site. As the franchisee is collecting information from the CPA and lawyer and is visiting sites, the analysis of consumer demographics for each site being compared and the costs of each site should be considered. A detailed examination of a site should be based on specific factors that address both the sites' characteristics and the nature of the business to be located at the sites. When a high volume of traffic is important, a good arterial street, preferably without a median strip, or a marked highway with a substantial traffic count is superior to a side street, divided highway, or interstate highway. Traffic speed limits of 15 to 25 miles per hour are preferable to lower or higher limits. Location within a particular block or shopping strip can also be important. Generally, a far corner or a mid-block location that has good visibility is preferable to other locations within a given block. Adequate frontage is a necessity for most retail businesses. Store and driveway frontage of less than 100 feet should be avoided if possible. Typically 100 to 200 feet of frontage is considered sufficient. A width of 35 to 45 feet is adequate for most retail locations. The homeward side of the street is often considered superior to the side of the street on which the majority of people drive to work. Demographic factors that are given significant weight typically include concentration of young families with children, proximity to schools, high schools, junior colleges or universities, 24-hour institutions such as hospitals or industrial plants, and median-family-income households within the primary service area. For some types of businesses, proximity to shopping centers or being located within a shopping center can be of extreme importance to provide sufficient walking traffic in front of the store.

A checklist can be developed by the franchisee that identifies pertinent information about the type of customer sought, the physical site characteristics, and the desires, preferences, and habits of the target customer group. Table 8-12 illustrates such a checklist. Obviously, a checklist for an auto service center would likely differ from a checklist for a franchised coffee shop or home decorating business.

Types of Franchised Businesses

The type of business and how the product or service is presented to the customer can make all the difference in the world in shaping the decision about site selection. There are three types of businesses, and their general characteristics should be considered before a checklist is developed by the franchisee.

Unique Business. The **unique business** typically has a craft or high-quality image associated with the product or delivery of the service.

Table 8-12
Location Analysis Evaluation

Personality Profile Characteristics	Potential Impact
Population size	5 4 3 2 1 × 5 4 3 2 1 =
Age group	5 4 3 2 1 × 5 4 3 2 1 =
Household income	5 4 3 2 1 × 5 4 3 2 1 =
Number of children at home	5 4 3 2 1 × 5 4 3 2 1 =
Sex	5 4 3 2 1 × 5 4 3 2 1 =
Employment	5 4 3 2 1 × 5 4 3 2 1 =
Children	5 4 3 2 1 × 5 4 3 2 1 =
Number of families	5 4 3 2 1 × 5 4 3 2 1 =
Number of single adults	5 4 3 2 1 × 5 4 3 2 1 =
	Subtotal =

Physical Site Characteristics	
Area image	5 4 3 2 1 × 5 4 3 2 1 =
Visibility	5 4 3 2 1 × 5 4 3 2 1 =
Access	5 4 3 2 1 × 5 4 3 2 1 =
Parking	5 4 3 2 1 × 5 4 3 2 1 =
Traffic count	5 4 3 2 1 × 5 4 3 2 1 =
Trade barriers	5 4 3 2 1 × 5 4 3 2 1 =
Site value	5 4 3 2 1 × 5 4 3 2 1 =
Rent value	5 4 3 2 1 × 5 4 3 2 1 =
Population	
1 mile	5 4 3 2 1 × 5 4 3 2 1 =
2 miles	5 4 3 2 1 × 5 4 3 2 1 =
3 miles	5 4 3 2 1 × 5 4 3 2 1 =
Distance from office	5 4 3 2 1 × 5 4 3 2 1 =
Distance from home	5 4 3 2 1 × 5 4 3 2 1 =
Construction	5 4 3 2 1 × 5 4 3 2 1 =
Evaluation	5 4 3 2 1 × 5 4 3 2 1 =
Sign/light acceptability	5 4 3 2 1 × 5 4 3 2 1 =
Nearby competition	5 4 3 2 1 × 5 4 3 2 1 =
Nearby shopping center	5 4 3 2 1 × 5 4 3 2 1 =
Nearby offices	5 4 3 2 1 × 5 4 3 2 1 =
Nearby college	5 4 3 2 1 × 5 4 3 2 1 =
Building code	5 4 3 2 1 × 5 4 3 2 1 =
Frontage street	5 4 3 2 1 × 5 4 3 2 1 =
Secondary street	5 4 3 2 1 × 5 4 3 2 1 =
Utilities	5 4 3 2 1 × 5 4 3 2 1 =
	Subtotal =

Frequency Pattern	
Breakfast	
Daily	5 4 3 2 1 × 5 4 3 2 1 =
Weekly	5 4 3 2 1 × 5 4 3 2 1 =
Group size	5 4 3 2 1 × 5 4 3 2 1 =
Lunch	
Daily	5 4 3 2 1 × 5 4 3 2 1 =
Weekly	5 4 3 2 1 × 5 4 3 2 1 =
Group size	5 4 3 2 1 × 5 4 3 2 1 =
Dinner	
Daily	5 4 3 2 1 × 5 4 3 2 1 =
Weekly	5 4 3 2 1 × 5 4 3 2 1 =
Group size	5 4 3 2 1 × 5 4 3 2 1 =
Coming/going home	5 4 3 2 1 × 5 4 3 2 1 =
Coming/going work	5 4 3 2 1 × 5 4 3 2 1 =
	Subtotal =
	Total =

Customers are "drawn" to the location from a community as compared to living in the immediate geographic area of the business location. The reason for the wider draw is the uniqueness of the product or service and the limited number of competitors. Examples of unique or specialty franchised businesses include franchised garden centers, picture framing shops, automobile undercoating businesses, or upscale franchised restaurants. There are usually limited choices available within a community for such services or products. Also, there is often a craft or high-quality connotation associated with the product or service in this category. These types of businesses can usually do very well in many locations within the community, even on the outskirts of town, as long as the customers continue to feel that the product or service is worth the inconvenience of going to a business that is "off the beaten path."

Competitive Business. A **competitive franchised business** offers the same or similar kinds of products or services that other franchised or independent businesses provide within the community. Convenience is a major factor in determining site for the business. Convenience food stores, ice cream shops, fast-food restaurants, donut shops, and pharmacy/variety stores typify the competitive franchised business category. They are often located throughout a community with particular concentration in high-traffic and high-consumer-density locations such as established business strips, shopping centers, downtown areas, or near offices or plant locations. It is desirable to have heavy walking as well as driving traffic in the vicinity since the business activity is usually price-competitive and convenience-oriented. A business trade area is usually limited geographically as determined by convenience factors and amount of direct competition and its location in relation to the business's location. Nearness to direct competition is usually seen as undesirable.

Comparative Business. With **comparative franchised businesses**, such as catalog stores, and businesses selling cosmetics, home furnishings, shoes, sporting goods, hardware and paints, consumer electronics, computers, as well as auto repair shops, lube-and-oil-change centers, printing centers, diet centers, and travel, recreation, and leisure businesses, location should normally be near competitors so that potential customers can compare products. As a result, the franchisee and any employees must be able to explain or demonstrate the advantages of the product or service over competing products or services. Comparative-type businesses often locate along business strips, within shopping centers or malls, or on neighboring street corners. High-rent locations are not essential but can encourage sales growth by virtue of the usually higher traffic and consumer density at such locations. Thus the two keys for these types of business are location near competition for customers to comparatively shop, and effective assistance to the customer in explaining advantages and determining value of the product or service.

Obviously, any of the product or service examples cited in the previous three illustrations can conceivably be within any of the three business categories. For example, a convenience store can be classified as a unique business when only one exists within a community. The same can be said for the examples identified in the comparative business category. In essence, the availability of like products or services, the relative nearness to direct competition, and the degree to which customer assistance is of importance tend to suggest the business category in which a particular franchised business activity would be classified.

Market Share

Before the final determination is made on a specific site, it is important to ascertain the appropriate market share forecast for the proposed franchised business. **Market share** refers to the portion of total market volume a business would likely have under normal operating conditions. If a market area has expressed demand of $7 million for women's clothing, and there are 20 women's clothing stores competing in the area, the "normative" gross sales for a single store would be approximately $350,000. This would be an average or normal market share for each women's clothing store in that market area and would not reflect consumer preferences, share of market of a particular store, competitive practices of the stores, or their size or attractiveness.

There are different ways to ascertain market share. Whatever the approach, three major variables will likely be considered: population, average amount of money spent by consumers, and buying power of the community.

Number of Facilities and Total Population. An easy (and common) method of estimating market share is to determine the number of facilities and total population within a specific trading area from the census tracts or local chamber of commerce data. Once the population figure is known, and the franchisor determines the average amount of money spent on the proposed product category, mutiplying these figures together will yield the area's annual sales. For example, if Sally were interested in starting a fast-food restaurant franchise, she could determine a basic trade area within the community. If this trade area contained 30,000 people and the average person spent $750 per year at fast-food restaurants (as determined from the "Survey of Buying Power" or the "Economic Census of Retail Trade"), then the area's total estimated sales would be $22.5 million. The formula can be stated as: Individual purchases of fast food × population = area's estimated annual sales, or $750 × 30,000 = $22,500,000.

Because the business is new, Sally would probably not have sales as strong as existing local competitors. She may subjectively determine that her annual sales level would be roughly $700,000 (one-third of the average in the first year of operation). Subsequent sales projections and estimates of market share will have actual sales data on which to base the projections.

Dollar Amounts. A second method of determining market share is to find the exact dollar amounts spent per year on the specific products or services that Sally intends to offer in the trade area. Sources of this information include the *Economic Census*, published by the U.S. Department of Commerce, and the "Survey of Buying Power," published by *Sales and Marketing Management*, or trade publications that deal with the particular products or services. In the example of Sally's fast-food restaurant, the trade association for food restaurateurs in the state identified the average individual expediture on fast food as $771 per year. With a population of 30,000 in the trade area, the total sales for that area would amount to $23,130,000. However, the estimated sales (or market share) would be approximately $925,000. Therefore, population (30,000) × individual annual purchase ($771) ÷ number of competitors (25) = estimated sales ($925,000) per store in the trade area. This figure suggests the average or typical market share for one unit (restaurant) in the trade area. Because Sally's business is new, she may not be able to expect a full market share for perhaps the first several years. As in the first example, Sally should estimate her sales at a figure somewhat less than average, perhaps somewhere between 40 and 60 percent of the average for a restaurant in the trade area in her first year of operation. This estimate would suggest Sally would have a sales estimate somewhere between $370,000 and $555,000. Actually, tighter estimates should be made, and would be based on the strength of competition, the nearness of the restaurant to other restaurants of similar type, pricing structure, and ambience, as well as the overall strength of the competition within the restauranting activity in the trade area.

A method that includes the three critical sales estimating variables — population, number of competitors, and either individual purchases made or overall purchases made within a community — can provide a reasonable estimate of a typical market share for the average competitor of a particular product or service within a trade area. Unless a franchisor has national-brand recognition, coupled with significant amounts of advertising, and good location, a franchised unit in a new market area is not likely to achieve the average sales level for the existing competitors within the marketplace. The checklist suggested in Table 8-12, knowledgeable judgments of local professionals, and prior history of the franchising company upon entry into similar markets will suggest the sales that can be achieved within the first, second, and third years of business. Before a final site selection is made, a map can be used to pinpoint each competitor in the market area. The map is useful in determining where conditions would appear to be most competitive and may identify areas that have been underdeveloped or overlooked by the existing competition. A new, developing, or redeveloping area within the community may be favorable for a new franchise.

Layout

Considerable time and effort will be spent in selecting a proper location or site for development. Similarly, a franchised business should give serious consideration to effective exterior and interior design. With existing buildings, exterior factors can severely limit the normal decisions to be made about structural shape, exterior composition, atmosphere, or image, as well as parking and walking traffic entrances and exits. Typically, the sign identifying the business, the window treatments, and the lighting of the exterior of the business comprise the major decisions a franchise owner would confront in the identification of the business within the immediate trade area. Obviously, each of these factors may be constrained by the landholder or by local ordinance. Determining what is allowable for creating sufficient identification of the proposed business can be of critical importance in the site selection process.

Inside the building, the critical questions concern sufficiency of space and the franchised business's ability to use that space efficiently. Some businesses, typically those that rely on heavy walk-in traffic, seek to construct their own buildings to ensure that the franchisor's preset internal design or layout can be accommodated.

Generally, retailers, service firms, and distributors or manufacturers should carefully design and develop effective interior designs. Appropriate layout can be a major undertaking. A layout needs to be neat, clean, and attractive enough to draw people into the business. Many hours can be spent in analyzing space and in changing and assessing alternative use of interior space before a proper layout is determined. A proper layout will provide for ease of customer movement in the store as well as allow for efficient work flow. Interior layout should facilitate sales, be attractive, and provide an appropriate atmosphere that makes customers feel comfortable while making a purchase.

Warehouses and Manufacturers. A franchisee can be a distributor between a manufacturer, or bottler, and the retail marketer. Proper layout and work flow is important for such franchised businesses. Franchised soda and beer bottlers are prime examples. Warehousers, bottlers, furniture assemblers, and other distributors generally require easy access for deliveries, storage, pickup, and shipping of the final goods. The most common layout design is a square or rectangular building with "receiving" at one end, "storage" (or display) or "assembling" in the middle, and "delivery" (or shipping) at the other end of the building. This design facilitates customer pickup and delivery at one end, while at the same time allowing materials or components to be received from trucks or boxcars at the other end of the building. Beer distributors usually do not have an assemblage area since their products are usually received in barrels, bottles, or cans already packaged for further breakdown and distribution to retailers.

Another concept used by many franchised discount merchandisers and/or warehouses is a U-shaped design, in which both receiving and shipping of goods occurs along the same side of the building. Customers (retail or wholesale) enter one end of the building, walk through the U-shape of the interior, and exit at or near the same point at which they entered. Other franchised and non-franchised businesses such as convenience food and grocery stores also use this concept. Typically, office activity is located in the middle of the U-shape, on a second level, or close to the check-out counters near the exit.

Retail Stores. Retail store layout should be very attractive and have a positive influence on customers. Some of the characteristics necessary for an effective retail outlet for consumer durable or non-durable goods would include:

1. Adequate entrance and exit space and doors for normal customer traffic at near-peak times.
2. Appropriate service available to the customer, based on the type of decision required in making a purchase, such as assistance in identifying or determining a need, assessing available alternatives, making the decision to buy, or perhaps simply order-taking.
3. Appropriate displays, counters, or racks that assist traffic flow and encourage browsing where desired.
4. Sufficient aisle space.
5. Attractive decor.
6. Effective lighting for the atmosphere sought.
7. Control of cash registers, goods, and exits.
8. Overall attractive atmosphere or ambience.

When determining the store layout, it is important that two concepts receive primary consideration: customer traffic and employee traffic.

Customer Traffic. The customer should be able to move freely through shopping areas without feeling hindered or constrained. It may also be important for customers to be able to "feel" the merchandise prior to selection, choose the items they want unassisted, and pay for the items at a cash register prior to departing the store. This enables customers to choose a variety of goods at their own pace, requiring only one stop for actual purchases to be recorded at a cash register or check-out counter.

Another factor important to interior layout is customer traffic flow. The franchised business should determine how a customer's space should be provided to primarily meet the needs of destination traffic or shopping traffic. A customer who has already decided on what to purchase and simply needs to place the order or present the goods at a checkout station goes directly to the area where the purchase can be made. In retail stores this customer typically moves against the normal customer traffic flow. This person is a *destination* traffic customer with the purpose of making a particular purchase. In contrast, *shopping* traffic customers seek to "shop" the store, moving from aisle to aisle, counter to counter, or department to department to scan the merchandise available for sale. Most shopping-traffic-oriented stores develop an interior design to move customers from right to left, or left to right, following a pattern of aisles through the store. The shopping-oriented customer will usually follow the main flow of traffic through a store, usually in a right-to-left pattern. This pattern runs counter to the left-to-right movement of a destination-oriented shopper. Point-of-purchase displays, consistency in merchandise display location, and grouping of similar product categories can help reduce problems of traffic flow. Thus, the destination-oriented shopper, who wants to minimize time in the store, as well as the shopping-oriented customer, who wants to use time to examine merchandise and scan the product available, can both be served well by a carefully designed store layout.

Employee Traffic. The second concept addresses the difficulty employees can encounter carrying out their assignments to assist customers. Work flows vary considerably, from sales representatives being with the customer constantly to assist in making purchases, to unassisted customers selecting merchandise from inventory on open shelves for presentation at a check-out counter. Some of the most difficult work flow patterns occur in the restaurant industry. A flow pattern that causes one employee to cross another employee's path while both try to serve customers can be nerve-racking, counterproductive, and potentially dangerous. An employee should not have to interfere with another employee while serving a customer. This important factor is sometimes overlooked in planning work stations, work processing, and delivery routes to the customer. A common problem is that one employee has to wait to receive the remainder of an order before completing the transaction or otherwise serving the customer. While it may not be possible to eliminate all employee "crossovers" or "waiting lines," it is important to try to reduce or eliminate as many of these flow problems as possible through careful design of the product/service work processes and work flow. Table 8-13 lists some points about work activity and production plans a franchisor and franchisee should consider in designing store layout.

Table 8-13
Work Activity and Production Planning Considerations

Work Activity Questions

1. Why is the activity being performed? Is it essential, or can it be eliminated?
2. Who is performing the activity and where is it performed in the overall work space available for use?
3. Can the activity be performed in another way? Is another location in the work space available?
4. Can the activity be combined with another operation or set of work tasks?
5. Can the work sequence be changed in such a way that the overall volume of work activity is reduced?
6. Can the work sequence be simplified to reduce or eliminate unnecessary delays?

Production Planning Alternatives

1. Produce goods at a constant level in order to equal the average monthly demand of the product for the year. (Inventory would increase when demand is lower than average and would decrease when demand is higher.)
2. Produce goods only after order is taken. (Produce to meet demand as it occurs; no inventory of finished goods.)
3. Produce goods to a certain level to meet expected consumer demand. Subcontract any production beyond that level.
4. Produce complementary products that fit the work-area design and skills of employees to balance out the fluctuations in demand. Attempt to achieve a constant product level.
5. Use sales estimates and prior experience to initiate special sales inducements (e.g., lower prices) when sales volume is expected to be low.
6. Do not expand production beyond a certain level, regardless of demand. Expansion of production capacity should be carefully considered before commitment to expand is made.

SUCCESS STORY
ROBERT V. WALKER

As chairman of the board of Kahler Corporation, Robert Walker oversees all aspects of the company. He ensures the continuation of long-range planning and achievement of goals spelled out in each annual business plan; he outlines and approves expansion activity, improvement of results for shareholders, employee recognition, and industry recognition for the company. Walker serves as Kahler's spokesman in communities served by the company and in the hospitality industry, and he provides leadership in all areas of hotel management and operations.

A graduate of the University of West Virginia, Walker began his career in 1952 as a traveling auditor for the American Hotels Corporation of New York. In 1954, he was promoted to assistant regional vice-president, and was named midwest regional vice-president two years later. From 1960 to 1963, he was general manager of the Townhouse Motor Hotel in Mobile, Alabama. During that period he founded and served as president of the Mobile Innkeepers Association. In 1963, he joined Holiday Inns, Inc., and managed properties in Oakland and Fresno, California, and Cocoa Beach, Florida, before leaving to become regional operations manager for the Sheraton Corporation in 1966. Between 1968 and 1975, Walker served first as director and then vice-president of Sheraton franchise development.

Walker has been designated a Certified Hotel Administrator by the Educational Institute of the American Hotel and Motel Association. He is a member of several AH&MA committees, including chairman of the Industry Advisory Council, a member of the board of trustees of the Educational Institute, a member of the executive committee of the Educational Institute, and a past chairman of the association's franchise operations committee. He is on the executive committee of the board of directors of the AH&MA and is a member of the board itself. He is also a member of the Minnesota Hotel & Motel Association.

Photo and information provided courtesy of Robert V. Walker, August, 1985.

SUMMARY

Site selection and location considerations are usually critical to the successful expansion of a franchise system. Selecting the right location can mean the difference between success and failure not only for a particular franchisee's business but also for the franchise system. This chapter has been written primarily from the perspective of the franchisor, specifically one interested in developing multiple territories with multiple-unit operations.

Regardless of the intended expansion plan, two points are usually considered when developing the expansion plan: (1) overhead and (2) distribution. Overhead considerations include steps within and cost of incorporation, costs of registration in two or more states, determination of the capital structure, determination of short-term financial arrangements to be made for franchisees, and establishment of policies about site selection and involvement within the selection process, if any. Distribution considerations address source of supplies, inventory requirements, warehousing, or other factors associated with distributing and the costs of distributing a product.

The location model we have developed utilizes a three-step process. The first step is selection of a geographic area appropriate to the development of the particular franchise system. The ADI (area of dominant influence) is a helpful tool for structuring marketing advertising and promotion as well as distribution systems. Second, once a general market has been determined, the BPI (buying power index), a tool utilizing information from *Sales and Marketing Management's* "Survey of Buying Power Index," can suggest the consumer buying power available in the area under examination. The franchisor would use this information on a county-to-county basis, examining the proposed areas for possible entry and using the buying power information for comparison against the market characteristics and sales levels required for the franchisor to enter a specific market area.

Specific site consideration is the third step in the location process. Specific sites are proposed and examined in a variety of ways. The approach proposed recommends examination of alternative shopping choices, barriers and pockets that tend to separate the targeted trade area from alternative trade areas, and drive-time analysis.

Site selection guidelines and criteria were illustrated in the information provided by the Rocky Rococo and Taco John's franchise organizations. Ultimately, two or more desirable sites should be profiled for a comparison and contrast of the strengths and weaknesses of the specific sites under review. The site that meets the criteria better than the others would probably make the best choice for the franchised business location.

Once a site is selected, building and layout considerations become important. Effective exterior and interior design can considerable affect the overall growth and success of the franchise system. Ready identification, easy ingress and egress, and appealing atmosphere can help the franchised business on its road to success. Also, an interior layout ensuring customer convenience, traffic flow, and efficient utilization of production space is essential. Clearly, location and site selection decisions can make or break the franchise.

REVIEW QUESTIONS

1. What are the major reasons why site selection is such an important decision for both the franchisor and the franchisee?
2. Briefly describe the three-step approach to the allocation of franchises within a geographic area.
3. What is an area of dominant influence (ADI)? How is the ADI concept used in geographic area selection?
4. What is the buying power index (BPI) as developed by *Sales and Marketing Management*? How is it used by franchisors in area selection?
5. Describe the use of a demographic profile for a specific area by a prospective franchisor. How are the demographics related to marketing the

product or service? How does the demographic profile assist a franchisor in choosing a site?
6. Explain the concept of market share. How would a franchisor use this concept to assist in choosing specific sites?
7. Describe basic approaches used to determine market share.
8. Describe how "layout" factors can vary among different types of businesses such as manufacturers, warehouses, and retail stores.

REFERENCES

1. Arbitron Ratings: Television, 1984-85 University Estimates Summary.
2. Boyd, Harper W., Ralph Westfall, and Stanley F. Stasch, *Marketing Research*, 5th edition, Homewood, IL: Richard D. Irwin, Inc., 1981.
3. Certo, Samuel C., *Principles of Modern Management*, Dubuque, IA: W. C. Brown Company, Publishers, 1980.
4. Green, Charles N., Everett E. Adam, and Ronald Ebert, *Management for Effective Performance*, Englewood Cliffs, NJ: Prentice-Hall, Inc., 1985.
5. Luck, David J., Hugh G. Wales, and Donald A. Taylor, *Marketing Research*, 4th edition, Englewood Cliffs, NJ: Prentice-Hall, Inc., 1974.
6. Mandell, Maurice I., *Marketing*, 3rd edition, Englewood Cliffs, NJ: Prentice-Hall, Inc., 1985.
7. Schwartz, George, *Development of Marketing Theory*, Cincinnati: South-Western Publishing Co., 1963.
8. 1983 Survey of Buying Power, *Sales and Marketing Management*, Vol. 131, No. 2 (July 25, 1983).
9. Selz, David D., *Franchising*, New York: McGraw-Hill Book Company, 1980.
10. Thompson, John S., *Site Selection*, New York: Lebhar-Friedman Books, 1982.
11. Vaughn, Charles L., *Franchising*, 2nd edition, Lexington, MA: Lexington Books, 1979.
12. Vesper, Karl H., *New Venture Strategies*, Englewood Cliffs, NJ: Prentice-Hall, Inc., 1980.

CHAPTER 9
MANAGEMENT, ORGANIZATION, AND ADMINISTRATIVE POLICY

In studying this chapter, you will:
- Learn about the functions of management in a franchise system.
- Understand franchise management practices and their importance to a franchisor.
- Learn the ten commandments of a successful franchise organization.
- Investigate leadership principles important to franchising.
- Understand the importance of quality and quality controls in franchises.
- Learn about franchisee advisory councils and how they operate.

INCIDENT

Dick has been franchising a burger-and-fries drive-up restaurant for the past four years. He presently has a chain of 14 franchised restaurants in three states. Six of these restaurants have been added in the last six months. Dick's franchising fee to the franchisees is relatively high compared with fees for other drive-up restaurant franchises, but Dick believes the higher fee is justified because of the well-known name, recognition, and management he provides the franchisees.

He helps a new franchisee begin operation by supplying financial, location-selection, promotion, and operations guidelines, to which a new franchisee is required to adhere very closely. Dick established strict policies and guidelines to ensure that each franchise is operating efficiently and effectively.

Once franchisees begin operations, they must follow Dick's guidelines for managing the business, as well as his financial and administrative controls. Dick contends that the less flexibility a franchisee has in operating the franchise, the greater the chance the franchised unit will be profitable.

Dick has received only a few complaints over the years on the policies by which he requires his franchisees to operate. However, several prospective franchisees have decided to go with another drive-up franchisor to enjoy more flexibility in managing, and to avoid being subject to the strict controls imposed by Dick.

Is Dick correct in his assumption that a franchisee should be given as little flexibility as possible? Should he continue his stringent control strategy or allow for more flexibility?

INTRODUCTION

A franchisor, like any other business owner, must determine objectives and achieve results in order for the franchise system to survive. A franchise system will not last long unless the franchisor plays the central role in guiding the organization and evaluating performance. Gone are the days when the franchisor could "rule from the top," or when the franchisor-franchisee relationship was a vertical relationship. Today, franchisors face substantial market uncertainties into which they "command" the franchise network and control the actions of franchisees.

To guide a franchise network, the franchisor must have more than just legal authority.[1] The franchisor will not be able to control franchisees merely by pointing to a line in the franchising agreement and demanding rigid compliance. Carefully developed programs to motivate franchisees and gain their cooperation in achieving the franchise system's objectives need to be established and implemented.[2] The newer "look" between franchisor and franchisees is something like that shown in Figure 9-1.

With franchisors and franchisees operating on a relatively equal level, and with the franchisor pre-superimposed in the center, the real authority held by a franchisor in the franchised network rests in the managerial assistance that can be provided to the franchisees. To the extent this assistance and organizational guidance is effective, the franchise network, as well as the independent franchised businesses, becomes profitable and payment of residual fees to the franchisor is justifiable.[3]

---

[1] Joseph P. Guiltinan, Usmail B. Rejob, and William C. Rodgers, "Factors Influencing Coordination in a Franchise Channel," *Journal of Retailing* (Fall 1980), pp. 41-58.
[2] Shelby D. Hunt and John R. Nevin, "Power in a Channel of Distribution: Sources and Consequences," *Journal of Marketing Research* (May 11, 1974), pp. 186-193.
[3] David D. Seltz, *How to Get Started in Your Own Franchised Business* (Rockville Centre, NY: Farnsworth Publishing Company, Inc., 1980), p. 1.

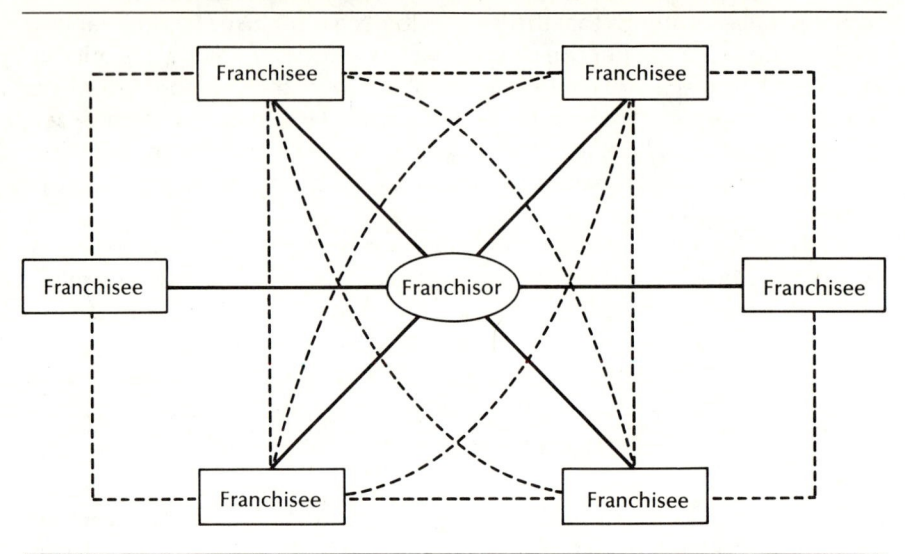

**Figure 9-1
The Newer Look of the Franchisor-Franchisee Relationship**

This chapter will address two primary themes. First, good management is a prerequisite to long-term profitability, growth, and survival. It can mean the difference between success and failure. Major topics and a perspective on effective management by the franchisor are presented in an overall view. Second, primary services provided by the franchisor to franchisees are discussed, as well as points for a franchisor to consider when attempting to motivate franchisees.

MANAGING THE FRANCHISE FROM THE TOP

The top manager in an organization typically has the title of chairman of the board, president, or chief executive officer. In a franchise system, this person is the chief policy-making officer in the firm. What does it take to be a successful head of a franchise system? No tangible or quantitative measurement or formula is known. Some simply attribute success to luck. However, success in the long run generally has growth and profitability as derivatives of the goals and objectives of the franchised business over time.

What does it take to be a successful franchisor or franchisee? Perhaps the starting point should be to ask the question a little differently. What does it take to be a successful entrepreneur? The first requirement is managerial ability. Dun & Bradstreet suggests that over 90 percent of business failures are attributable to lack of managerial ability.[4] Clearly, a franchise entrepreneur needs the ability to conceptualize, organize, and manage a business. (See Figure 9-2.)

Entrepreneurs typically tend to work harder and take greater risks than the person working as an employee in someone else's company. They tend to have high motivation to achieve, versatility, self-confidence, and adventurousness.[5] However, the entrepreneur needs even more than that. Opportunity within the environment is essential. A business needs money to succeed — to pay rent, buy materials, hire employees, pay marketing expenses, and so on. And the entrepreneur must have a "genuine" business opportunity. A business opportunity is genuine when new businesses open up or when existing providers are ineffective in providing a product or service. In any event, a genuine opportunity requires that people (potential customers) express economic or market need for the proposed product or service. With hard work, and perhaps some luck, an entrepreneur can be successful.

Franchising Is a Two-Way Street

The most important ingredient for success of a franchise system is the interdependence between the franchisor and the franchisee. Each provides for the other. The franchisor, who comes up with a profitable way to produce, sell, or distribute a product, must monitor or oversee every unit within the franchise system. On the other hand, the franchisee, looking for a limited-risk entrepreneurial opportunity, desires a business venture that can be managed effectively and profitably. The franchisee ex-

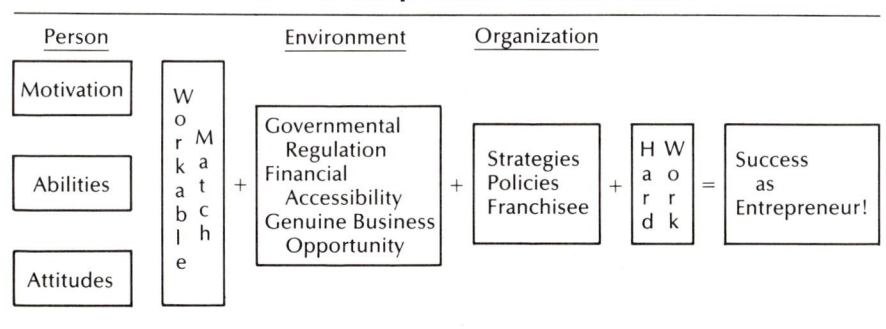

**Figure 9-2
Success in an Entrepreneurial Business Venture**

Person (Motivation, Abilities, Attitudes) + Workable Match + Environment (Governmental Regulation, Financial Accessibility, Genuine Business Opportunity) + Organization (Strategies, Policies, Franchisee) + Hard Work = Success as Entrepreneur!

---

[4] *The Dun & Bradstreet Failure Record* (New York: Dun & Bradstreet, Inc., 1981), pp. 12-13.
[5] David McClelland, "Achievement Motivation Can Be Developed," *Harvard Business Review* (November-December 1965), pp. 6-8.

pects to receive an accepted business name, a product to sell or distribute that has a positive image, training, and other assistance from the franchisor while putting up a limited amount of capital to be part of the franchise system.

The franchisor is not in the position that many administrators or managers in government or private corporations are in. Nor is the role of the franchisor similar to the position of an independent business owner. The franchisor is responsible to and for each unit in the franchise system. The system itself is no stronger than its weakest link. To achieve effective and profitable results requires controls at many levels, and the controls must be balanced by incentives to and support from the franchisees. Characteristics of a successful franchisor would typically include a high degree of managerial ability, extensive knowledge of competition and market conditions, keen sensitivity to operating costs and quality control, and ability to motivate people.[6]

Making the transition from an entrepreneurial single-unit firm to a multi-unit, professionally managed franchise system requires the franchisor to make several transitions in the development of the organization. An overview of a successful organizational development plan is illustrated in Figure 9-3.

The franchisor or senior manager of a rapidly growing franchise system has to cope with the day-to-day problems of being in business while keeping a constant eye on new developments and the intended growth plan of the organization. It is likely that the franchisor is going through this process for the first time. He or she has probably not built a company before. This growth requires thinking about the franchise organization as a whole and the planned-for changes in the key areas as a progressive set of events or activities to achieve successful growth. The six major organizational developmental tasks identified in Figure 9-3 show how to convert from an entrepreneurial to a professionally managed firm.

Identifying and defining the market niche is the fundamental step where the franchisor can develop a competitive advantage in providing the product or service to customers. The second task is designing the product or service to actually meet the wants, needs, or expectations of the targeted customer group. This requires analyzing the needs of present as well as potential customers in order to design the product or service that will meet the customer need. This also means the franchise firm must be able to "produce" the product through the franchise delivery system with internal processes that ensure the product does in fact meet customer needs.

The third task involves problems and challenges associated with growth — seeking franchisees, opening franchised units, increasing

---

[6] E. Patrick McGuire, *Franchised Distribution*, A Research Report from the Conference Board, p. 17.

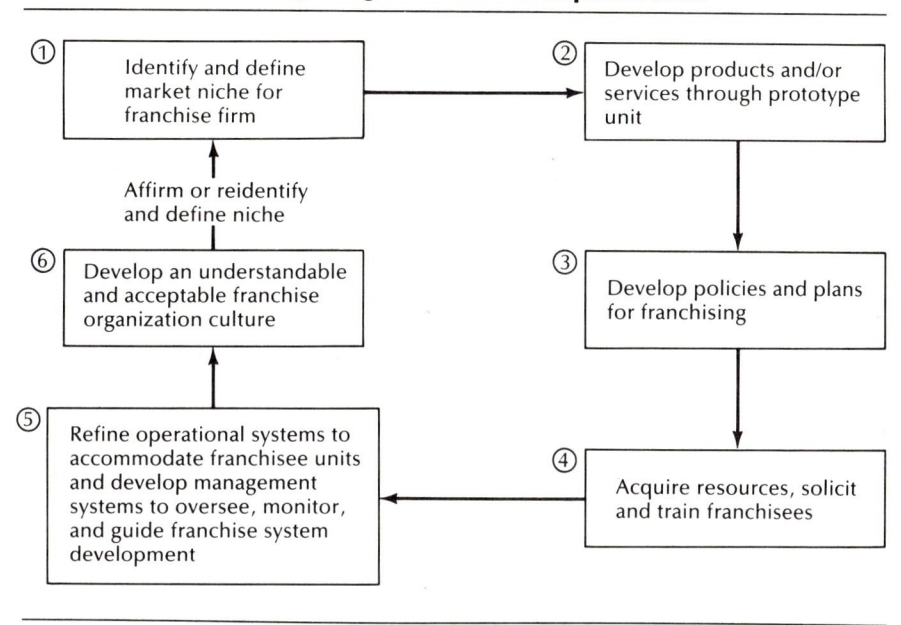

Chapter 9 Management, Organization, and Administrative Policy 243

**Figure 9-3
Six Major Organizational Development Tasks**

① Identify and define market niche for franchise firm
② Develop products and/or services through prototype unit
③ Develop policies and plans for franchising
④ Acquire resources, solicit and train franchisees
⑤ Refine operational systems to accommodate franchisee units and develop management systems to oversee, monitor, and guide franchise system development
⑥ Develop an understandable and acceptable franchise organization culture

Affirm or reidentify and define niche

sales, and facing seemingly endless operational problems associated with product, purchasing, collections, payables, and delivery. Developing the policies and plans for controlling the anticipated growth can keep the problems manageable while allowing the firm to continue development toward meeting its growth objectives.

The fourth step is the implementation phase of step three: acquiring the financial and human resources necessary to implement the planned course of development of the franchise system, including recruitment, selection, training, and supervising the grand openings of the first franchised units.

Fifth, the operational systems of the prototype unit and warehousing and distribution systems must be carefully examined to ensure that the policies and procedures followed can, in fact, provide sufficient support to the new franchisees. Such examination will also include establishing appropriate monitoring and control procedures so the franchisor can guide further franchised unit development as well as ensure consistency in product/service offerings to the public. As the franchise system grows, a set of shared values, beliefs, and norms that govern the way the franchise system operates on a day-to-day basis will either emerge or be formally determined.

Sixth, the organizational culture can be a critical factor in developing an aura of success and can have profound impact on the behavior of franchisees and employees within the franchise system. Major franchise systems in the automobile, restaurant, and electronic product industries often remind the customer through media advertisements about their corporate images, such as "quality is job one" and other similar statements about the corporate culture of the franchise system.

FRANCHISE ENTREPRENEUR AS MANAGER

Each franchisor is in some way an entrepreneur, and each entrepreneur is to some degree an innovator. A franchisor, as entrepreneur, is seeking to identify newer or better things to provide for a customer or find newer or better ways of doing things for the customer. In any event, the innovative process implies providing useful goods or services, soundly conceived to meet customer needs. The ultimate test of the franchisor's innovative efforts is the satisfaction of the customer. If the customer isn't satisfied, the business will ultimately fail.

The franchisor must do more than provide the idea and overall approach for meeting the customer needs. The franchisor must also develop an efficient method of identifying and assembling necessary supplies and materials, provide an operational method for efficiently producing or assembling the product/service, and determine and implement effective methods of selling or delivering the product/service to the customer. Ultimately, the success of the franchise system, large or small, will rely heavily on the capabilities and ingenuity of the system's management — franchisor and franchisees. The management responsibilities can be generalized through discussion of the management process. However, the particular focus and extent of activity required in each area by the management will be conditioned by the size and unique operating characteristics of the franchised firm. It is for this reason that what works best in a large firm doesn't necessarily work best in a smaller firm, nor does what works best within restaurants work best in auto service or home cleaning services.

The franchisor should consider developing an approach consistent with the conditions confronted by the developing firm, as well as the strengths and weaknesses of its ownership/management, in order to determine what needs to be done and by whom in order to accomplish the objectives of the franchise organization. This requires planning. Figure 9-4 depicts an analytic approach a franchisor can use to systematically and comprehensively plan the development of the organization.

A new, small-sized franchising firm should start with an uncomplicated approach. The approach suggested in Figure 9-4 provides flexibility for the franchisor and management team of employees and franchisees to start out simply and increase sophistication as their planning

Figure 9-4
A Strategic Planning Process Useful to Franchisors

Steps in the Strategic Process	Factors/Variables Under Consideration	Outcomes/Results of Assessment
Scanning/Assessing the Environment		
External	Influence of major groups: customers, lenders, stockholders, employees, the community, competitors, suppliers, government	Competitive issues in industry
		Stress points in relationships
	Changes in national and international economic conditions, in technology, in social conditions, in the business climate	Trends affecting industry/firm
		Discovery of untapped markets
Outcome:	An understanding of opportunities and threats facing the firm	
Internal	The firm's capabilities in functional areas of business, its facilities, location(s), and business image	The firm's ability to compete as is or to change
	The firm's management, structure, and culture	Management's core values and how the firm operates
Outcome:	An understanding of the firm's strengths and weaknesses	
Developing Strategic Plans	Outcomes from above	
	The firm's mission and analysis of past strategic results	Definition of business and its strategic mission
	Firm's objectives	Updated objectives
Outcome:	Appropriate strategies with long-, medium-, and short-range plans	
Implementing Strategic Plans	Resource attraction and allocation	Funds to operate
	Operating system (policies, methods, procedures)	Innovation
	Control system (standards, monitoring, comparison)	Control of costs
	Management Information Systems	Market response
Outcome:	Operating results with objectives achieved	
Continuing Review	Review results and fine-tune plans	
Outcome:	Strategic plans responsive to changing markets	

Source: Figure developed by Jerry Geisler, Dean, School of Business and Management, Sangamon State University, 1988. Used with permission.

skills develop. The first step is *scanning/assessing the environment* from each of two perspectives: external and internal. (See Figure 9-4.) External influences on the firm, such as customers, lenders, stockholders, competitors, suppliers, and government regulatory agencies, can help the firm clearly identify the competitive issues it confronts. Being alert to changes in national and international economic conditions, change and advances in technology, and changes in social conditions or in the business "climate" enables the franchising firm to understand the trends affecting the industry as well as the firm, and can help the management team discover untapped market opportunities. An examination of the franchised business from an internal perspective provides understanding of opportunities and threats, as identified in the external analysis, that face the business. Factors for consideration include the firm's capabilities in each function area of the business, its facilities, locations, image, as well as the firm's management, organization structure, and culture. This internal and external analysis provides objective information for the management of the franchised business to examine and with which to make appropriate choices and develop tactics to reach the firm's goals. This two-part analysis is what many would call a **situation audit**. A situation audit is the attempt to determine the franchised business's current operating situation in the context of the environmental factors (external and internal) that affect operations. Practically, the small franchisor would identify the objectives and analyze the importance of each to the firm in the short and long run, ranked in priority; analyze current sales performance and sales trends by product or service and by unit or location; analyze current available resources; and identify strengths and weaknesses within the firm. The general purpose of this analysis is to stimulate a consciousness within the franchised business to identify problems and opportunities in order to determine future courses of action.

The second step is *development of the strategic plans* for the franchised business. Once the external and internal analysis has been completed, the firm's mission and analysis of past results can be carefully examined and refined if necessary. The firm's objectives can then be updated and a particular course of action determined to exploit potential opportunities while remedying existing or anticipated problems. The course of action becomes a plan of action for the franchised business, addressing such related areas as what must be accomplished by the marketing group, the training and development group, the research and development group, or the purchasing group.

The third step, *implementation of strategic plans*, can be categorized as long range, medium range, or short range, depending on the time frame in which it is to take place. The overall purpose of this step is to allocate the firm's resources so as to achieve the best possible market response given the conditions the firm confronts. Reallocation of resources among existing functional areas may be necessary in order to complete this step.

The fourth step is *continuing review* of the operating results and market results of the strategic plans. Careful use of the data provided by the information retrieval system as well as feedback from internal operations will help in fine tuning the plans and modifying policies and procedures to help the business become as efficient as it can. The goal of this fourth step is to ensure that the strategic planning process, as developed and utilized within the franchised firm, keeps the business responsive to the ever-changing needs of the market and alert to the social, cultural, political, and economic factors influencing the firm's environment.

PLANNING SHOULD BE ORGANIZED

To avoid the pitfalls of random action, the franchising firm should formalize its planning effort as soon as possible. As noted before, the approach does not have to be sophisticated. It should simply be precise and objective. Planning helps the franchisor keep a proper perspective on individual whims and personal aspirations. Consistent growth and development usually requires an approach other than "shooting from the hip." A new, small-sized franchised firm should not expect that formal, systematic planning will immediately bring dramatically favorable benefits. Rather, formal planning can provide the basis for knowing the strengths of the firm and utilizing these strengths in an ever-changing marketplace. Also, it can be used as the basis for developing management talent within the firm, as well as for a control tool. Formal planning is the initial process, the completion of which enables the remaining elements of the process of management to be utilized.

The Process of Management

The franchisor must provide direction that can be described through the management functions. Good management is needed in small and large firms alike. Thus, the small franchisor must perform the same general management functions as the chief executive officer of a large franchise system. The management process described here primarily involves day-to-day business operations, although a franchisor or franchisee, as owners of their respective businesses, are also concerned with strategic planning as discussed in the preceding section.

Planning

Planning is the primary responsibility of the owner/manager. Planning concerns the following:

- Determining the overall goal, mission, and objectives of the franchise.
- Formulating policies, plans of action, and procedures (when appropriate) for attaining the objectives of the franchise organization.
- Developing standards for costs, sales targets, and performance for incorporation into a budget and sales forecast, which can be used as an operating control.
- Developing the franchise's line of products, services, and processes in the long run to ensure continuity for the organization as well as adaptability to the ever-changing needs of the marketplace.

Organizing

Organizing is the coordination of human, financial, and physical resources deemed necessary to reach the objectives set forth in the planning phase. Activities in the organizing function include identifying the jobs required to be performed, staffing each job with people qualified to do the required tasks, determining how much authority and responsibility each person should have as an employee of the business, and clearly defining the authority-responsibility relationships to avoid confusion and overlap of authority. Job descriptions and an organization chart describe and graphically represent these relationships.

Organization Chart. An organization chart is particularly useful for showing these relationships as well as indicating the formal decision-making and communications channels. Usually, the organization chart is simple because of the small size of many franchised businesses. However, business growth implies change to reflect new franchisees, territories, and required staff assistance. These relationships should be reflected in the formal organizational chart. Figure 9-5 illustrates the franchisor organization prior to the sale of the first franchise. Figure 9-6 shows a franchise organization at full development. Table 9-1 identifies a job title with some of the duties and responsibilities that could apply to a franchise sales position.

Multi-Unit Franchising. A major movement in the franchising field is the utilization of multi-unit franchises. A **multi-unit franchisee** is one who owns and operates more than one franchise. Often this occurs in an urban area. Most generally, multi-unit franchisees are granted geographical areas, primarily ADIs (areas of dominant influence). As we discussed in Chapter 8, the ADI is a television market coverage area designated by the Arbitron rating system, and is a very common method of allocating geographical territories based on a market's media for advertising and promotion. The ADI is simply a map that outlines television viewing markets exclusive of one another based on measurable viewing patterns.

**Figure 9-5
Franchise Organization Chart Prior to Sale of First Franchise**

```
                    Board of Directors
                           |
                       Franchisor
                           |
         _____
         |                                    |
     Director                          Director of
        of                             Operations
    Franchisee                         (Training)
      Sales                            (Marketing)
                                       (Financial)
                                       (Company-
                                       Owned Stores)
```

Other franchisors may allocate geographical areas to prospective franchisees through designated market areas (DMAs) as developed by The A. C. Nielsen station index. This index also divides the country up into television markets and is easily used, although not as often, by the franchisor to designate franchise geographic areas.

The multi-unit franchisee generally will begin with one unit and utilize the proceeds and profits to expand into the second, third, and fourth units. Many franchisors wish to limit a franchisee to one, two, or three units. However, some franchisors seeking rapid development and expansion may encourage a franchisee to expand to as many as five, ten, or even 20 franchised units.

Area Developer. One of the most popular ways to create multi-unit franchises is to simply draw up an area development agreement. With this development agreement, the franchisee (developer) is given the right to develop and operate multiple units in a given area. This right generally is accompanied by obligations to establish a specific number of franchises in the designated territory over a given amount of time.

The franchisee will develop the territory as rapidly as possible, utilizing separate independent franchising agreements for each new franchised outlet. An area development agreement would usually cover the number of units to be developed in a given time, site selection, approval methods, any restrictions on transferring developmental rights, and any specific conditions which may cause the franchisee/developer to be in default. For example, if the franchisee fails to meet the schedule of development, then the franchisor would have the right to reduce the area or revoke the exclusivity granted under the original development

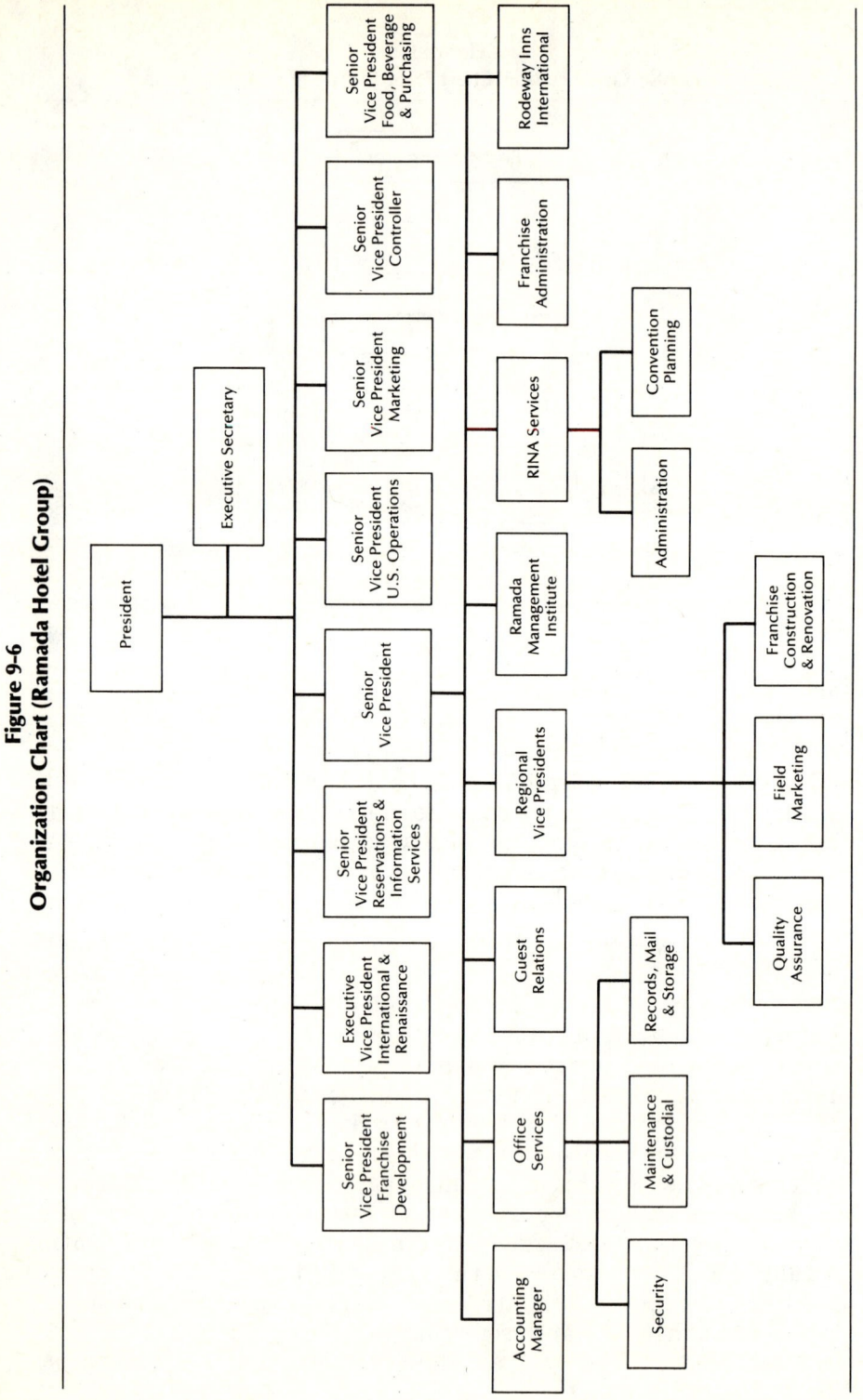

Figure 9-6
Organization Chart (Ramada Hotel Group)

- President
  - Executive Secretary
  - Senior Vice President Franchise Development
  - Executive Vice President International & Renaissance
  - Senior Vice President Reservations & Information Services
  - Senior Vice President
    - Ramada Management Institute
    - RINA Services
      - Convention Planning
      - Administration
    - Regional Vice Presidents
      - Franchise Construction & Renovation
      - Field Marketing
      - Quality Assurance
  - Senior Vice President U.S. Operations
  - Senior Vice President Marketing
  - Senior Vice President Controller
    - Franchise Administration
    - Rodeway Inns International
  - Senior Vice President Food, Beverage & Purchasing

Under Senior Vice President Franchise Development / Executive VP International & Renaissance:
- Accounting Manager
- Office Services
  - Maintenance & Custodial
  - Security
- Guest Relations
  - Records, Mail & Storage

Source: Courtesy of Robert N. Wilson, Director, Ramada Inc., December, 1987.

**Table 9-1
Director of Franchise Sales**

Responsible to: Direct responsibility to the Franchisor Board of Directors

Authority: Functional authority for all phases of franchisor sales activities as overseen by the franchisor's directives and policy statements of the franchisor organization.

Responsibility: Line of responsibility to include, but not be limited to:
- Advertising and promoting the franchise.
- Performing the franchisor representations to prospective franchisees.
- Setting forth and administering franchisee qualification procedures.
- Performing as the sole, or when with others the primary, negotiator of franchisor-franchisee contracts.
- Submitting reports on advertising and promotion, as well as prospective franchisee recruitment and contract negotiations.
- Participation, as desired, in franchisee training.
- Submitting all executed documents and down-payment monies to Franchisor Board of Directors.

agreement. However, in any case all existing franchising agreements would remain in effect.

The developer may have to pay initial development fees to retain the geographic area for the reserved geographic area. In addition, the franchisee will often need to meet unit quotas and abide by the predetermined developmental schedule.

Master Franchisee. Another major method of developing multi-unit franchises is through a **master franchisee** or subfranchisor. This individual has the right to offer and sell franchised units, collect fees, and provide services within a given territory. Often this individual is not a franchisee, but rather an agent who is directly responsible for selling franchises in a given geographic area.

The master franchisee makes a subfranchising agreement with the franchisor. This agreement allows the franchisee to act as an intermediary who will collect royalty fees, advertising fees, and even initial franchising fees. Only a portion of these fees, according to the subfranchising agreement, are paid back to the franchisor. The subfranchisor is generally responsible for enforcing the terms of the franchising agreement and the operations manual, collecting all franchising fees, and providing initial and continuing training, evaluation, and reports on each franchised unit.

The franchisee will sign a franchising agreement with the subfranchisor which obligates the subfranchisor to fulfill most functions and obligations of the franchisor. The subfranchisor may often retain a majority of the fees, providing only a limited portion back to the headquarters organization.

Area Representative. Another method of developing multi-unit franchising is through development of an **area representative**. This "area rep" is generally an employee of the franchisor who has the right to solicit for prospective franchisees but does not have the right to contract with franchisees. All contracts are made directly between the franchisees and the franchisors. The area representative acts in essence as a sales representative for the franchising company, but also often has responsibilities for training franchisees, providing periodic inspections, controlling standards, setting up marketing and advertising schedules, and sometimes consulting.

Franchise Broker. The **franchise broker** is generally an independent third party who simply solicits prospective franchisees for the franchisor. Franchise brokers generally work for several franchisors at the same time and provide information to prospective franchisees concerning many franchising opportunities. Once a contact has been developed, the franchise broker will contact the franchisor for a disclosure meeting and possible signing of the prospective franchisee.

Directing

Direction is used to achieve the franchise organization's objectives while building an organizational climate conducive to encouraging superior performance. There are five major activities associated with the directing function: giving directives, supervising, leading, motivating, and communicating.

Giving Directives. Directives can be given in either written or oral form. Written directives, or orders, may be in the form of memos sent directly from the franchisor to those in the next hierarchical level of the franchise organization, notices placed on bulletin boards for all employees to read, or instructions included prominently within the narrative of the operating manual for use in the pilot, or perhaps, franchisee unit. Oral directives involve face-to-face contact and are specifically designed for the two or more persons involved in the communication.

Supervising. Supervising concerns the training and disciplining, if required, of personnel employed in the franchise organization. Supervision includes activities to ensure prompt and proper execution of orders or directives. Supervising duties are required of every employee who is also a manager in the firm. The pilot unit manager, for example, supervises the unit's personnel in accordance with the franchisor's directives and the franchise organization's policy statements, consistent with what would be solid business practice for the operation of the unit.

Leading. Leadership behavior is meant to influence others to willingly provide effort and cooperation in order to achieve the objectives of the organization. The franchisor, and each manager in the organization, should be aware of techniques helpful for influencing others to do their work well.

Motivating and Communicating. A natural by-product of effective leadership is a good work environment. Within a work environment, the most important resource is the people. Understanding people and how and why they behave as they do is a very important part of a franchisor's or franchisee's job. It is easy to oversimplify or stereotype employees' attitudes and behaviors. It is a wise franchisor or franchisee who recognizes individual differences in people and communicates effectively with employees in light of these differences.

Like the employee, the franchisor and subsequently the franchisees within the franchise chain should be examined in a motivational context. Is there a set of entrepreneurial motives as compared to managerial motives to which a person can address his or her particular interests as a potential franchisor or franchisee? Table 9-2 lists the essential elements of two famous motivational theorists and suggests differences between entrepreneurs and managers in terms of the respective theories.

Choosing to become a franchisor or franchisee involves consideration of both types of career options — entrepreneur or manager. As Table 9-2 indicates, there are some clear distinctions between entrepreneurs and managers. The primary difference is the degree to which specific needs are to be satisfied. Comparison of the McClelland and Maslow theories suggests that entrepreneurs have opportunity for more self-expression, more income, more job security, and greater freedom in choosing what to do and when to do it. On the other hand, managers have greater security by having a regular income, less risk, and less worry when away from the job.

Controlling

Controlling involves the determination of standards and methods of evaluating performance against those standards to appraise operating results. Evaluation should be followed by prompt praise, concurrence, or punitive action when the results significantly deviate from the standard. Evaluations are required in each functional area of the franchise organization, whether formally or informally determined. A franchisor would likely have an interest in making the following types of appraisals:

- Appraisal of performance of subordinate manager, e.g., Directors of Training, Purchasing, Franchise Sales, and Pilot Unit Manager.
- Appraisal of policies associated with franchisee recruitment, franchisee screening and selection, franchising contracts, franchisee training,

Table 9-2
Comparison of Needs: Entrepreneurs vs. Managers

McClelland's Theory	Maslow's Theory	Needs	Entrepreneurs vs. Managers
	Physiological	Minimum income needs/base salary; basic working conditions, e.g., heat, facilities	Initially, entrepreneurs might have higher tolerance for adverse conditions; with seniority, or longevity, managers are more tolerant of adverse conditions.
	Safety and Security	Job security; safe working conditions; stable demand for employable skills; pension.	Entrepreneurs have high risk propensity; managers have higher needs for job security, being more willing to "stay put," hoping to become more secure and to have more economic value in the organization in time.
Need for Affiliation	Social	Compatible work group members; teamwork; professional friendships.	Entrepreneurs often "go it alone"; managers often have higher needs for, and place higher value upon, affiliation and work-related friendships.
Need for Achievement	Self-Esteem	Overall responsibility and authority held/exercised; job title/position in firm; importance of promotion.	Entrepreneurs might fulfill need from seeing their names on business marque; managers might fulfill need from job title and/or status factors available in the organization.
Need for Power	Self-Actualization	Autonomy; challenges of the job/task; creativity.	Entrepreneurs create their own success, often with their firms being a reflection of their personalities and values; managers create autonomy and challenge within the constraints of the employing firms.

Source: Figure developed by Daniel J. Gallagher, Associate Professor of Business Administration, Sangamon State University, 1988. Figure used with permission.

franchisee operations, minority group franchising opportunities, site selection practices, etc.
- Appraisal and analysis of financial transactions.

To be effective in the long run, the franchisor will need controls and methods of determining appropriate performance in such areas as costs, output, sales, profits, quality, employee morale, and labor turnover. In essence, the control process helps the franchisor stay abreast of what is currently happening in the business by providing continual feedback in important areas so the firm can stay on a course to achieve its objectives. The three basic steps in the controlling process are determining standards, comparing performance to standards, and taking corrective action.

Determining Performance Standards. Standards for each person in the organization identify what performance levels are expected to achieve the franchise's goals. Not only should overall firm goals and objectives be set, but also realistic standards for individual performance. Otherwise, objectives may not be achieved. A form of management by objectives (MBO) can be effectively utilized here.

Comparing Performance to Standards. By comparing actual performance to standards, franchisors can determine if employees are operating at acceptable levels. Performance standards can be checked at various times and in various ways. The key is that the control standard must be measurable and comparable to actual performance. Performance can be checked hourly, daily, weekly, or monthly. It can be checked against activity (phone calls made, customers visited, slide presentations made, etc.) or by outcome (sales quota expected, or sales by product/service category by territory or by franchised unit).

Taking Corrective Action. Franchisors should take corrective action when performance reveals significant deviation from the control standard. Deviation can be either positive or negative. Reward, at least in the form of praise, should be provided to persons achieving more than the standard. Performance significantly below the standard should be noted and corrective steps taken to improve future performance.

Thus, by having predetermined standards, the franchisor can monitor activities without continually having to personally oversee the specific activities of each employee. Most employees do not like "close" supervision if they have standards and goals to shoot for. Employees need a relative degree of freedom to do what is requested by the leader (franchisor or franchisee); the franchisors and franchisees need to bear responsibility for activities such as planning, monitoring economic and technological changes, and competitive positioning.

To summarize, the essentials of management — planning, organizing, directing, and controlling — apply to the franchise organization as much as to any business enterprise. The planning function concerns formulation of the franchise's goals and objectives and overall policies for internal operation. The organizing function addresses the structural requirements of the firm, identifying jobs by functional or divisional arrangement with associated authority and responsibility for each position. Directing involves an overlap of processes and activities such as supervising, issuing orders, leading, and motivating subordinates to achieve individual and franchise objectives. The controlling function includes determination of performance standards, appraising performance with standards, and providing rewards or taking corrective action.

FRANCHISOR POLICIES

A franchise often starts out small, and because of its size is usually a highly centralized operation. In time, emphasis shifts from seeking and acquiring franchisees to maintenance of the ongoing franchise distribution network. To assist the franchisor and other major officers of the firm in making this transition is the set of organizational and operational policies. Policies guide operational work activity, assist in coordination of effort across functional lines and areas of the business, and help reduce conflict between individuals and units by providing statements about certain areas of the business and how these areas should be addressed in order to achieve the overall franchise objectives. Examples of such policies are product features, promotional strategy or approach, franchising fees, license fees, rental lease fees, sale of materials or semi-finished product/goods, royalty fees, and policies associated directly with services to be provided by the franchisor to the franchisees.

Enhanced communication between central offices and franchisees in the field can have merit. For example, if the president or director of sales were to make two to three telephone calls per week to the franchisees of the chain, it is likely that within a manageable period of time all franchisees would receive a personal call from the central office. This helps the morale of franchisees and provides an open channel to identify and resolve grievances early before they become major points of contention between the franchisor and the franchisee. For example, franchisees surveyed by *The Conference Board* believed their respective companies should be spending more money on advertising the franchised products/services and less on efforts to recruit new franchisees.[7] In the early stages of developing a franchise network or chain, this is a difficult line for a franchisor to walk, trying to build the franchise network through re-

---

[7] E. Patrick McGuire, *Franchised Distribution*, A Research Report from the Conference Board, p. 29.

cruitment while needing an ever-larger portion of the budget to generate brand recognition and patronage.

Franchisor advertising, if exaggerated or deceptive, can result in criticism and complaint by franchisees, as well as by the general public. It can also draw criticism from other franchisors who are reasonably meeting the needs of their respective franchisees and the consuming public.

Franchisors or directors of franchise sales can feel pressure from the board of directors to generate new franchised outlets. When this is the case, they may be hasty in selecting new franchisees or simply lower the screening standards. These practices often lead to increased franchisee terminations, poor market representation, and depending how the arrangements were handled, increased litigation for the franchisor. The common error or omission seems to be in not thoroughly checking applicants' references and personal data. Past business experience, experience in the line of business of the franchise, reference checks on each named person to be identified as owning the franchise, financial condition, and educational background should be carefully examined.

Ten Commandments of a Successful Business

Jim Peterson, chairman, CEO, and president of Whataburger, Inc., has developed the ten commandments of running a successful business. These ten points include:[8]

1. Leadership
2. Staying with the business one understands
3. Developing and maintaining a unique niche
4. Keeping first-hand touch with the customer
5. Relentless pursuit of management principles and fundamentals
6. Organization
7. Freedom from government intervention
8. Strong fiscal responsibility
9. Strategic development
10. Picking winners

Leadership. Peterson lists leadership as the first commandment and states that it is absolutely necessary in order to ensure the success of any franchising organization. Four factors are required for a successful leader. These include that the person (1) must have a sense of vision, (2) must be able to articulate vision, (3) must be able to develop agenda to accomplish strategic vision, and (4) must have the self-confidence to make it happen.

---

[8] Jim Peterson, President, Whataburger, Inc. Material presented in Visiting Executive lecture at the University of Nebraska–Lincoln, April 16, 1987.

The leader must have flexibility to learn and change. All leaders make mistakes and mistakes can be corrected. However, it is a serious blunder for a person to do something and continue to do it wrong even when advised otherwise. Leaders need to be able to accept advice and to correct their blunders.

A leader must have a good sense of vision, so that he or she is able to see where the business will be ten years later. A leader must be able to understand the problems of growth and how to overcome difficulties when developing, creating, and building the business.

A good leader must also be able to articulate the vision. The leader must be able to describe to the employees the roles which they will fill in building and developing the business. The leader must be able to articulate self, personality, and vision to employees so that they will be able to understand the objectives, goals, and desires of management.

There is a need for the leader to be able to develop the agenda to accomplish the strategic vision. The leader must be able to stipulate the eight to ten major priorities which would accomplish the mission of the organization. The ten to 15 primary objectives of an organization need to be broken down to different departmental objectives, and these departmental objectives must be broken down to individual priorities to highly motivate and direct the employees so they will feel involved and part of a growing company.

Two items exist within the agenda that are very important. These include (1) the necessity to know something about the company so that it can become better and (2) the need to measure performance and to reward good performance. Additionally, training should be provided for all employees. Every three months the employees should be reviewed and personal questions should be asked such as "Do you like your job? How do you like your job? Are you satisfied with what you are being paid?" The franchisee needs to listen to what is being said. "How can we improve operations around here?" The performance of each individual needs to be measured. Marketing research is very important to make sure that the training and performance of employees meets the standards and expectations of the consumers. It is always important to remember that people cause success.

A leader needs to have self-confidence to be able to function effectively. In addition, the leader should help train the employees so that they will also develop self-confidence. Self-confidence comes from developing self-esteem and having a good feeling about oneself. First, self-confidence comes out of the knowledge which may be gained from asking questions, learning, continued reading, and questioning the entire operation and business processes. Employees should think of their job opportunity as a beginning and should endeavor to communicate and gain information about the organization. The franchisee should set up networks of information, convert the information to knowledge, and then convert the knowledge to action.

$$\text{Information} \rightarrow \text{Knowledge} \rightarrow \text{Action}$$

Second, an individual needs to be honest. It is important for the franchisee and the employees to be open and to help customers get what they desire. If honesty is compromised, there will be trouble. If there is a question about the weight requirements of a product, a business should always exceed the requirements rather than fall short.

Third, the franchisee and employees should operate by the Golden Rule: Do unto others as you would have them do unto you. It is important to understand and abide by the Golden Rule. The franchisor should go into the restaurant as a customer and think as a customer. The franchisor should also, from time to time, act as an employee and think as an employee.

Fourth, perseverance is very important to developing self-confidence and to ensuring the success of an organization. And fifth, physical stamina is important — an individual must be in good physical condition and health to endure the rigors of a growing business experience.

Stay in Business You Understand. It is important that franchisors stay with the business they understand. Almost all successful business people have followed this principle. They have created and expanded the business opportunities within their spectrum of knowledge and experience.

Develop and Maintain Unique Market Niche. There is a need for the franchisor to develop and maintain a unique marketing niche. It is important that the franchisor develop a high-quality product. The primary advertising and promotional activity of the franchisor will always be to promote quality. In the food-service business it is important to provide consistently fresh, made-to-order, quality products.

Keep in Touch with Customers. The franchisor must keep in first-hand touch with the customer by going into the franchised outlet and talking with customers. Jim Peterson talked to customers for two days and discovered that in one particular location there were no senior citizen discounts for early dining hours. Once he found this out, it was an easy step to provide the discounts and improve the organization's image within the community. Further questions revealed that diners felt the highchairs were not safe and so were fearful of putting their children in them. Additionally, one customer complained about finding gum underneath the booth. These were all matters which were quickly corrected and changed.[9]

---

[9] Peterson.

Maintain Management Principles and Fundamentals. The franchisor needs to maintain a relentless pursuit of management principles and fundamentals. It is important to establish the principles and fundamentals upon which the organization will operate. Jim Peterson will write to or visit with an unsatisfied customer within 30 days of the complaint. He will also pick up litter around the outside of a store before going into the store, thereby setting an example for employees, franchisees, and staff members. People follow examples, so if an owner does something, others will follow suit.[10]

Develop and Maintain Strong Organization. It is important that the franchisor develop and maintain a strong organization. The organization must exist so that people will know what their responsibilities are and how to respond to management directives. The organization should allow for adjustments and innovations. Management should also allow people to know how they will be evaluated and rewarded. The organizational structure is very important to allow for a smooth flow and operation of a business. The organization should improve business opportunities rather than hinder profitability.

Remain Free from Government Intervention. The franchised business should remain free from government intervention. Jim Peterson often spends up to one week per month in Washington, D.C., working to ensure freedom of business opportunities from government intervention.[11] Regulations to ensure health, property, and personal safety are essential. However, it is important to Peterson that government intervention and regulations be limited to those areas of utmost necessity. The greater the freedom of operation, the greater the chances for success and development.

Develop Fiscal Responsibility. The franchisor should develop strong fiscal responsibility within the organization. Franchisors often need to develop financial ratios which are important to their industry and specifically to their business. Most fast-food, non-meat franchises will operate with a cost of goods sold plus labor cost of 50 percent to total sales volume. This ratio of foods costs plus labor costs to gross sales may be increased to 60 percent in meat-service businesses.[12] Other ratios are important for different industries and operations. Deviations from correct ratios often illustrate problem areas. Franchisors need to understand their financial picture and understand the financial responsibilities they have.

---

[10] Peterson.
[11] Peterson.
[12] Winn Sanderson, President, Piece of the Pie, Inc. Material presented in Visiting Executive lecture at the University of Nebraska-Lincoln, December 11, 1986.

Develop Strategic Program. The franchisor is responsible for developing a strong strategic development program. The franchisor needs to explain the vision of the operation to the other individuals within the organization. This vision needs to be developed through strategic planning and development. Organizations need to establish their objectives and from these objectives develop departmental plans which can accomplish the strategies proposed. These programs need to be reviewed at least yearly to update and develop the proper strategy. Environmental and social changes may often require more immediate changes, but the strategic plans of an organization should be reviewed at least once a year.

Pick Winners. It is important that franchisors and franchisees pick winners. One of the greatest needs of a successful franchise is good, honest, hard-working people. There is no need for individual stars; there is a tremendous need for good people who are willing to work hard to develop the right franchising concepts and develop and encourage an image of integrity and honesty within the organization. The greatest resource an organization has is the people within that organization. People build success.

Motivation

Jim Peterson also reports five basic steps on motivating and developing employees. These include:[13]

1. Improvement-oriented attitude
2. Measuring everyone's performance
3. Evaluation
4. Feedback
5. Recognition

It is important that all employees have an attitude of improvement, growth, and development. Employees' attitudes are very important to customer satisfaction and the perceived quality of the business. Employees need to have an attitude that demonstrates their willing acceptance of job responsibility. This generally makes them happier and provides for a better working environment.

Everyone's performance should be measured on a regular basis. In most cases, this should be broken down to a minimum of three and a maximum of four different performance areas. It is difficult to measure only one or two areas and it is hard to measure more than four.

Employees should be evaluated at least three times a year on their basic performance. This evaluation should be face to face between the immediate supervisor and the employee.

[13] Peterson.

Additionally, feedback needs to flow between the franchisor and all employees. When an employee is dissatisfied, the reasons for that dissatisfaction should be brought out into the open. Additional information should be provided to all employees about their performance on a regular and continual basis. If mistakes do occur, then they should be properly pointed out and corrected.

Recognition is very important in motivating employees. Many times this recognition provides status and a feeling of self-achievement for the individual. Recognition also increases self-esteem. Individuals have a tendency to work harder and better when they have been recognized for their accomplishments and suitably rewarded for their good performance. It is important that everyone in the organization be able to grow and develop. Recognition provides the opportunity for employers to properly reward and aid the development of employees.

Quality

It is very important for the management of an organization to know how customers honestly perceive the quality of the product or service. Quality is the customer's perception of the product, and the customer's perception is greatly influenced by the employee or server. Jim Peterson points out that the attitude of the customer is made up of three key factors:

1. "70 percent — the way the customer is looked at;
2. 20 percent — based on the tone of the server's voice; and
3. 10 percent — exactly what the employee (server) says."[14]

The employee is there to make the customer feel comfortable, not to win an argument. If there is a problem, the employee may simply say, "This is our fault; let us correct it for you."

The quality of the product will also be influenced by the condition of the premises. If the office or store is clean and bright, then quite often a positive feeling will prevail. Additionally, a feeling of security is often important to customers. If the airplane is dirty, will the engine be clean and operative? People are interested in whether they will be robbed if they enter or eat at your store. Businesses should be free of bars on windows and should provide well-lighted areas, including parking lots. Friendly employees often provide a feeling of security and warmth to the customer.

The availability and convenience of a product also reflects on the quality of that product. Another key quality factor is the completeness of the service. It is estimated that 35 percent of customers are never thanked before leaving the store. The business has not been completed until a "thank you" is offered the customer. Also, packaging needs to be

---

[14] Peterson.

properly identified. And there is no need to ask, "Is that all?"; a more complete question would be "Would you like something else?"

Timeliness is also important to ensure the quality of the product or service. It may be acceptable to take 15 minutes for the purchase of an airline ticket, but if it takes more than 3 minutes to receive a fast-food order, then the quality or service may be deemed poor or inferior. Food service for a restaurant with table service may take up to 12 minutes for appropriate delivery of the order, but if more than 5 minutes is taken to deliver a car rental agreement, then the service may be deemed inadequate. Finally, the degree of personalization or name recognition is also important to ensure the quality and reputation of the store.

Franchisors need to collect information from their franchisees in a timely report (see Table 9-3). Many franchisors collect information from their franchisees regarding gross sales, cost of goods sold, and labor costs on a weekly basis. Long John Silver's collects such information from its company-owned stores on a daily basis via a computer system.[15]

Franchisee Advisory Council (Joint Council)

There is a great need for strong communication lines between franchisor and franchisee. Coupled with the franchisor-franchisee relationship is the need for the development of a franchisee advisory council or joint council between franchisor and franchisee. The franchisee advisory

Table 9-3
Frequency with Which Franchisees Report Sales to Their Franchisors*

Frequency of Franchisee's Sales Reports	Total, All Companies	Fast-food & Beverage	Nonfood Retailing	Personal Services	Business Products/ Services
Weekly	29.5%	26.3%	31.1%	32.1%	28.0%
Monthly	48.7	56.1	28.9	59.0	44.0
Yearly	8.0	7.0	17.8	1.8	8.0
Not required to report	13.6	10.5	22.2	7.2	20.0
TOTAL	~100.0%	~100.0%	100.0%	~100.0%	100.0%

*Note: Based on information reported by 183 franchised companies. Includes 57 franchisors of fast foods and beverages, 45 of nonfood consumer products, 56 of personal services, and 25 of business (or industrial) products and services. Column totals may not add to exactly 100.0% due to rounding.

Source: E. Patrick McGuire, *Franchised Distribution* (New York: The Conference Board).

[15] Eugene Getchell, Vice President of Franchising for Long John Silver's, Inc. Material presented in Visiting Executive lecture at the University of Nebraska-Lincoln, February 19, 1987.

council is not the only, and may not be even the appropriate, means for improving franchisee relations. Yet the advisory council is often advantageous for both franchisor and franchisee. It provides the opportunity for franchisees to work with and provide counsel to franchisors. It may also help develop advertising and marketing campaigns in conjunction with the franchisor. This council may also hear the grievances of the franchisee and may suggest managerial actions for the franchisor. It is designed to help and promote a strong relationship between the franchisor and the franchisees.

Franchisors have often found franchisee advisory councils to be effective in helping develop mutual trust, improved communications, policy changes, product introduction, program development, feedback, improved sales, improved motivation, and opportunity to work together to improve the entire franchise system. Many councils have proved effective and have strengthened the franchisor-franchisee relationship while increasing sales throughout the system.

Franchisee councils have usually developed along one of three paths:

1. The franchisor has called together a group of appointed or select members and has conducted the council according to the franchisor format and dictates.
2. The franchisees of a specific franchisor have met with other franchisees to form a council to provide advice and suggestions for the franchisor. The franchisor is often later invited to join under the terms and conditions the franchisees have established.
3. The advisory councils are initiated and formed jointly by both the franchisor and the franchisees. They have both worked together to establish the bylaws for the councils and have mutually agreed upon the operations and structure of the council.

The bylaws or "ground rules" of the franchisee councils are generally established to allow for the free interchange of ideas between franchisor and franchisees, and they are developed to protect both sides. The bylaws of the organization generally discuss council membership and officers, frequency of meetings, dues, quorum size, and responsibilities. They may be periodically changed to reflect the conditions of the council and the interaction between the franchisor and the franchisees. The council executives representing the franchisees and the franchisor generally will determine the council's exact purposes and limitations. Members of the council should be satisfied that the goals and purposes of the council can be achieved.

Council Membership and Officers. Membership in franchisee councils generally occurs in one of two ways:

1. Members are elected by franchisee peers.
2. Members are appointed by the franchisor.

Some franchisee advisory councils may even include all franchisees of the franchise system and even managers of company-owned stores, each owner/manager having one vote in determining council positions.

In addition to the franchisees who are represented on the council, it is important that the board chairman, company president, or other top management personnel from the franchisor's office be invited to participate. This allows for the proper interaction between franchisor and franchisee organizations.

Officers for councils may be elected by the council or appointed by the franchisor. Many franchisors name an executive vice-president as the president of the council or franchisee system. Other organizations allow the franchisee to elect or appoint the president (or chair), one or two vice-presidents, and a secretary/treasurer. These officers are responsible for organizing and convening meetings, appointing committees, developing agendas, and working with the franchisee and franchisor organizations.

Council Functions. Many councils, when organized, create five basic standing committees including:

1. Operations
2. Marketing
3. Products/services
4. Finance
5. Grievances

These committees play an important role in handling the proper functions and interactions between the franchisees and the franchisor. Most of the problems associated with the franchisor-franchisee relationship may be presented and worked out by these specific standing committees. The use of advisory council committees often places the responsibility for harmonious and strong working relations on the franchisees. At times, the franchisor may ask the council members to help resolve problems with a particular franchisee. After hearing the situation, the committee may choose to work with both the franchisee and the franchisor to resolve the conflict or dispute.

Most councils hold national council meetings once a year. A council may invite all franchisees to participate in such meetings. This practice allows the opportunity for all franchisees to assemble and meet other franchisees and to work with the franchisor.

In addition to the national council, regional councils may be established throughout the country. A regional council generally comprises three to seven states and meets once a year approximately six months after the national council meeting. Regional council agendas often include reviews of the marketing, management, operations, finance, and legal aspects of operating a franchised unit within the respective franchise system. In addition, all products and services are reviewed. Any new products to be offered by the franchisor are presented and demonstrated to the franchisees. The expenses for the franchisee council are generally shared by the franchisor and the franchisees.

Advisory councils are important for the strength and unity of the franchise system. The council provides a vital input mechanism for the franchisees to the franchisor management staff at the control office. The franchisor needs input to ensure the proper function and operation of the franchise system. A properly operating franchisee advisory council can provide the suggestions and advice necessary to ensure the continuation and development of the entire franchise system.

SUCCESS STORY
WILLIAM ROSENBERG

Born in Boston, Massachusetts, and educated in its public schools, William Rosenberg had to leave school after the eighth grade to work full-time for the Western Union to help support his family. At 17, he joined a company that distributed ice cream from refrigerated trucks. There his hard work and skills paid off. At age 20, he was promoted to assistant manager, at twenty-one to branch manager, and finally to national sales manager.

At the start of World War II, Rosenberg joined Bethlehem Steel Company at the Hingham, Massachusetts, shipyard. He was elected union delegate and then appointed by management as contract coordinator.

When the war ended, Rosenberg borrowed $1,000 to add to his $1,500 in war bonds and began an industrial catering business conducted from trucks. Within a short time, he had 140 catering trucks plus 25 in-house cafeterias and a vending division. When he discovered that 40 percent of his business was coffee and donuts, he established a shop that specialized in those products, and Dunkin' Donuts was born.

After opening six shops, he decided on franchising as the method of expansion, and the rest is history. Dunkin' Donuts is now an international company with over 1,500 shops in 42 states, plus Canada, Puerto Rico, and the Orient.

In 1959, while attending a "Start Your Own Business" show, it occurred to Rosenberg that he and other industries needed a united group to educate legislators and the general public — a clearinghouse organization for the industry. To meet that need, he and a group of exhibitors founded the International Franchise Association. Over the years the association has become the voice of franchising and has set the standards for the industry. Rosenberg served one term as president and several terms as director. He was honored as the first recipient of the International Franchise Association's Hall of Fame Award in recognition for his many contributions to the success of the franchise system of distribution.

Photo and information provided courtesy of William Rosenberg, August, 1985.

SUMMARY

A prospective franchisor will need more than a legal agreement and a "hot idea" to be successful in franchising. The franchisor, like most other entrepreneurs, must be self-motivated, willing to work long hours, and eager to provide the product/service in a market niche that can be considered a genuine business opportunity.

The franchisor should be well versed in the art of managing — planning, organizing, directing, and controlling — the franchise operation, as this is of critical importance in the relationship between the franchisor and the franchisee. Policies should reflect the strengths of the franchising concept and organizational approach to effectively deliver product or service to the target market. In applying the management concepts, problems can take place. Jim Peterson has developed the ten commandments of a successful business; these include leadership, staying with the business one understands, developing and maintaining a unique niche, keeping first-hand touch with the customer, pursuing management principles and fundamentals, organization, freedom from government intervention, strong fiscal responsibility, strategic development, and picking winners for employees. Motivation and quality control are important management functions. Franchisee advisory councils are a valuable mechanism to assist in the effective operations of a franchise system.

REVIEW QUESTIONS

1. Explain the functions of management in a franchising context. How might your explanation differ from the functions of management when considering a typical, large bureaucratic business organization? A large, company-owned chain-store organization?

2. Illustrate a franchise management practice for each of these functions of management: planning, organizing, staffing, and controlling.
3. Why are quality and quantity controls of such importance in franchised firms?
4. What is a franchisee advisory council? How do franchisee councils operate? How do such councils relate to the formal hierarchy of a franchise parent firm?

CASE STUDY
THE MEDICINE SHOPPE

Kara is a professional, having recently graduated from pharmacy school and registered as a pharmacist in her state. She recognizes the need for professional business guidance to allow her to successfully operate her own pharmacy. She realizes that her consumers would rely upon her professional skills and seek her help because she works in the health care profession. She wants to be her own boss, to own her own store and not be part of a large chain.

Kara's dream has always been to open her own pharmacy, yet in today's fast economy, it is difficult for anyone to start a business and make it profitable. For her, it is even more difficult to buy an existing pharmacy because of the high sale price and the low return on investment. One of her best options is to become a franchisee of Medicine Shoppe International, Inc.

The Medicine Shoppe franchise offers her a way of maintaining a sound balance between professionalism and profit. It would help her find a prime location with approximately 800 to 1,000 square feet in a high-traffic area. In addition, she would receive help with interior decor, external signs, and internal fixtures, in an attempt to maximize the image exposure and efficiency of the location.

The Medicine Shoppe program enables the franchisee to purchase in volume and develop specific inventory-control guidelines. The parent company is involved in daily marketing needs, pharmacy supplies, generic and other ethical drugs, promotional materials, fixtures and equipment, store insurance, and promotional articles. The Medicine Shoppe also has its own private label with over 100 items currently available.

An intensive one-week training seminar at the Medicine Shoppe's corporate headquarters helps train the franchisee in all aspects of business. Additionally, a six-week grand-opening program generates tremendous exposure of the business to consumers in the marketing area. Substantial assistance is given in site selection, lease negotiation, store layout, personnel selection and training, opening procedures, purchasing, inventory control, record keeping, budgeting, and management.

The initial capital required is approximately $60,000, which includes the original franchising fee of $16,000 plus fixtures, supplies and inventory, and opening promotions. In addition, a 5 percent royalty fee on all gross receipts is to be paid to the company.

Kara has little if any managerial background. She is very well aware that many pharmacists have failed because of poor managerial ability, and she knows that most businesses in general fail because the owners lack management experience and expertise. Because of her lack of knowledge in management, Kara is gravely concerned about opening a Medicine Shoppe franchise.

CASE QUESTIONS

1. How should the franchisor help Kara with her management problems?
2. What primary management problems should Kara be addressing?
3. How important is the management function to a franchisee?
4. What additional information does Kara need to open the store?

REFERENCES

1. Lewis, Mack O., *How to Franchise Your Business*, A Quick Step-by-Step Guide, New York: Pilot Industries, Inc., 1974.
2. Vaughn, Charles L., *Franchising*, 2nd and revised edition, Lexington, MA: Lexington Books, 1979.
3. Broom, H. N., and Justin G. Longenecker, *Small Business Management*, 6th edition, Cincinnati: South-Western Publishing Co., 1983.
4. Vesper, Karl, *New Venture Strategies*, Englewood Cliffs, NJ: Prentice-Hall, Inc., 1980.
5. Lovelock, Christopher H., *Services Marketing*, Englewood Cliffs, NJ: Prentice-Hall, Inc., 1984.
6. Day, George S., *Strategic Market Planning*, St. Paul, MN: West Publishing Co., 1984.
7. Porter, Michael E., *Competitive Advantage*: Creating and Sustaining Superior Performance, New York: The Free Press, A Division of Macmillan, Inc., 1985.
8. Mendelsohn, Martin, *The Guide To Franchising*, 4th edition, New York: Pergamon Press, 1985.
9. Justis, Robert T., and Richard Judd, "Master Franchising," in *Journal of Small Business Management*, Vol. 24, No. 3, July 1986, pp. 16-21.
10. Justis, Robert T., and Richard Judd, "Strategies for Multi-Level Franchising," unpublished working paper presented at Society of Franchising annual meeting, San Francisco, CA, January 1988, 12 pp.
11. Weinrauch, J. Donald, "Franchising an Established Business," *Journal of Small Business Management*, Vol. 24, No. 3, July 1986, pp. 1-7.

12. McGuire, E. Patrick, Conference Board: *Franchised Distribution.*
13. Glueck, William F., *Management Essentials,* New York: The Dryden Press, Holt, Rinehart and Winston, 1979.
14. "Franchising Fever," *Time,* New York: Time, Inc., August 31, 1987, pp. 36-38.
15. Pride, William M., and O. C. Ferrell, *Marketing: Basic Concepts and Decisions,* Boston: Houghton Mifflin Company, 1987.
16. Stoner, Charles L., and Fred L. Fry, *Strategic Planning in the Small Business,* Cincinnati: South-Western Publishing Co., 1987.
17. Justis, Robert T., Richard J. Judd, and David B. Stephens, *Strategic Management,* Englewood Cliffs, NJ: Prentice-Hall, Inc., 1985.

CHAPTER 10
ACCOUNTING AND FINANCIAL STATEMENTS: PRESENTATION AND USES*

In studying this chapter, you will:
- Learn about the usefulness of financial records within a franchised business.
- Learn about the measuring and reporting of the financial information of the franchise.
- Develop an understanding of the purpose, components, and use of the four key financial statements: income statement, balance sheet, funds flow statement, and statement of retained earnings.
- Learn about the five primary types of financial ratios and what they measure.
- Develop an understanding of the importance of financial statement analysis for planning and control within a franchised business.

INCIDENT

Bonnie operates Bonnie's Hot Tubs Inc., a successful hot tub sales and rental franchise system. After only a year as a franchisor, she has eight successful franchised units. Different accounting procedures are being used by a number of her franchisees, as a result of their unfamiliarity with financial

---

*Prepared in collaboration with Robert C. Maple, Assistant Professor of Business Administration-Finance, Sangamon State University; National Association of Securities Dealers, Registered Principal; and Branch Manager for National Securities Corporation in Springfield, Illinois.

statements and accounting procedures. Bonnie is worried. As the number of her franchisees increases, this problem could compound itself. More specifically, Bonnie is considering whether or not to obtain additional bank financing, and this accounting/financial statement problem could jeopardize the loan process.

Bonnie believes the solution is to develop a standardized accounting system with software for use on a personal computer. She could then require her franchisees to attend a training session to learn how to use the package, after which they would purchase the software and hardware and run the accounting system at their own stores.

Bonnie knows the accounting procedures she would like her franchisees to follow, but she knows relatively little about financial analysis and financial planning. She believes computer software or models could greatly assist the standardization effort. Should she attempt to develop new accounting software or adapt an available software package to her needs? What type of hardware would best suit Bonnie and her franchisees? What can Bonnie do to find answers to these and similar questions?

INTRODUCTION

Every franchise must keep a set of financial records. Too often the franchisee is a beginner, opening a business for the first time, and is not fully aware of what it takes to run a business, particularly from the point of view of managing the finances. Like many other business people, a franchisor (or franchisee) may see financial statements as complicated, technical documents prepared by professional accountants and understood only by loan officers. The prevailing attitude may be that financial records are useful only for filing taxes, borrowing money, and reporting to regulatory agencies.

Accounting and financial records are basic to any business, franchised or otherwise. Simply put, accounting is a process of measuring and reporting the financial information of the franchise. It is the process by which money, assets, and resources are measured and their flow through the company is recorded. Financial accounting is very important because it provides owners and managers with the information often necessary for making appropriate business decisions. This information should be reviewed by management each fiscal quarter.

The financial flow is the heartbeat of a franchised business. It is a written documentation or recording of business transactions shown through financial statements. The financial statements provide a franchisor and franchisees the basic format to report the financial activities of a franchise network or franchised unit. A business owner is ultimately responsible for the functions and operations of the business. Therefore, the owner must keep financial records in accordance with commonly held principles of accounting. Such rules are referred to as generally accepted accounting principles (GAAP). They include widely agreed-upon definitions, procedures, conventions, and forms, and are used to develop financial statements which may be used by anyone. Because the statements are written to follow standard procedures, anyone familiar with basic accounting principles should be able to read and undestand them. Often the format of these statements is specifically mandated by federal or state regulatory agencies, such as the Federal Trade Commission, the Internal Revenue Service, or the Securities and Exchange Commission.

FINANCIAL STATEMENTS

Financial statements are informational pictures of the financial status of a particular business firm for a certain period of time. Private corporations usually will not be required to publicly disclose these informational pictures. However, the franchisor may be obliged to publicly disclose selected financial statements to obtain outside financing, such as bank loans or lines of credit, or to offer private stock placements (Regulation D stock) such as intrastate offerings (Rule 147), Regulation A offerings, and Rule 144 sales. Generally, any investor or creditor willing to assume capital risk for the franchisor will want to analyze the financial statements. These statements should be audited each year, but must be reviewed by the firm's manager each month.

Franchisors capitalizing or financing their business by public stock placements must always publicly disclose four key financial statements:

1. Statement of Earnings — the income statement.
2. Statement of Financial Position — the balance sheet.
3. Statement of Change in Financial Position — the funds flow statement.
4. Statement of Changes in Share Owners' Equity — the statement of retained earnings.

All of these key financial statements are used by a financial decision maker. We will now discuss each of these statements, with special emphasis on the income statement, the balance sheet, and the funds flow statement.

Income Statement

The income statement (profit and loss, or statement of earnings) is a record of revenues versus expenses for a stated period of time, such as a day, week, month, quarter, or year. (See Figure 10-1.) The income statement shows the accounting profits or losses of a business through accounting of receipts or revenues minus the expenses (costs of business, goods sold, or related expenses). Once expenses are deducted from business revenue, the result is profit (or loss) for that particular period of time.

An annual statement (often used for tax reporting or for disclosure to stockholders) illustrates the financial activities of the franchise for the fiscal year of operation. A fiscal year may or may not coincide with the

Figure 10-1
Hypothetical Consolidated Income Statement
Bonnie's Hot Tubs Inc.
Income Statement
Year Ending December 31, 1986

Income		
Net sales	$900,000	
Other	100,000	
Gross Operating Income		$1,000,000
Deductions from Income		
Cost of goods sold	620,000	
General/administrative expenses		
Office equipment rental	8,000	
Rent, leases	40,000	
Insurance	15,000	
Selling/operating expenses		
Selling expenses	55,000	
Wages, salary	74,500	
Other	13,500	
		826,000
Net Operating Income		174,000
Depreciation		25,000
Income Before Interest and Taxes		149,000
Deductions for Interest Charges		
Interest on bank notes	$3,000	
Interest on notes payable	2,000	
Interest on private loan	2,500	
Interest on long-term debt	4,500	
		12,000
Net Income Before Taxes		143,000
Taxes (45% tax rate)*		64,350
Net Income After Taxes		$ 78,650

*1986 federal corporate tax rates

calendar year. For example, a fiscal year may be April 1 through March 31, or July 1 through June 30, rather than January 1 through December 31. The income statement can be easily compiled when the appropriate financial data has been collected and recorded.

Usually, income and expense figures are initially entered in an accounting book referred to as the journal. The invoices (bills) are entered into a journal as an "original book of entry." Items not normally entered on a daily basis, such as depreciation, are entered into the journal as adjustments at the end of the month or reporting period. After all entries have been journalized, each transaction is posted (transferred) to the general ledger, which may be a bound book, a computer printout, or even a set of file cards. The general ledger keeps track of all financial transactions by category (i.e., wages, telephone, rent, supplies, etc.). Once amounts have been posted or ledgered, they are balanced, credits versus debits. These balanced amounts are then used to prepare the financial statements. This process, while not necessarily difficult, does require time and skill to accurately report the financial activities and the resulting financial condition for the period.

The income statement generally identifies the revenues first, followed by all expenses. The expenses are deducted from revenues in order to show the profit (or loss). Therefore, the income statement summarizes the revenues and expenses of the franchise during the specific fiscal year and reveals a net profit or loss.

A brief explanation of the items included in the income statement is helpful to understand the critical elements and value of such a financial statement. The income statement presented in Figure 10-1 is somewhat abbreviated for purposes of analysis. A large franchised company will have many more items presented on its income statement, whereas a small firm is likely to have fewer items to record and analyze.

Income. Sales, fees, or revenues flowing into the franchised business are recorded as income to the franchise. Revenues generated from normal, day-to-day business (sales) are considered "operating income." Revenues such as dividends or interest from investments are considered "other income." It may happen that certain products become damaged. The business would use the heading "allowance for sales returns" to account for such occurrences. The price associated with sales returns is subtracted from the gross sales. After adjustment, the result is the "net sales" of the franchise.

Cost of Goods Sold. The "cost of goods sold" equals the amount of "goods available," less "ending inventory," at the close of an accounting period. This is calculated by adding the value of beginning inventory to the cost of goods purchased (or manufactured) during the accounting period, then subtracting the value of ending inventory at the close of the period. In other words, the market value of the goods available at the beginning of an accounting period is added to the cost of all goods purchased, and this new figure is subtracted from the market value of the inventory remaining at the end of the period. This final figure is the total cost of goods sold. Remember, however, that franchised businesses providing a service, rather than a tangible product, also have inventory bought and sold and must replace this inventory for future sales.

Gross Profit. The gross profit, also referred to as the "gross margin," is the difference between cost of goods sold and net sales. This is the business profit before expenses, interest, and taxes. Gross profit comparisons are important for identifying financial performance over time, or for comparing the financial performances of different franchised units for the same period of time.

Operating Expenses. Franchisors can divide their operating expenses into two major classifications:

1. General/administrative
2. Selling/operations

General/administrative expenses are expenses of the franchisor and of operating the main headquarters. This category may include such items as rent, salaries, wages, employee benefits, insurance, taxes, and other general expenses. Selling/operations expenses are those costs directly associated with the "selling" of the product. Often these costs fluctuate; that is, as production (or service) activities increase, costs usually rise. Conversely, as production activities decrease, these costs should fall. Items often included here are costs of sales, wages, salaries, commissions, advertising, supplies, car or delivery expenses, insurance, and other selling expenses.

Net Income Before Interest and Taxes. To derive this figure, we subtract the operating expense figure from the gross margin. This will show what each franchised unit or franchise system (when figures are available for all units) earned during a given time period.

Taxes and Interest. Almost all businesses will have to pay some type of tax. Generally, taxes are subtracted from the pre-tax earnings if the business is a corporation. Corporate taxes are not paid on proprietorships or partnerships; rather, the income is reported on the owner's personal tax return. The taxes paid are based on federal and applicable state taxation levels and regulations. Interest paid on a principal to produce a business revenue is tax deductible. Interest payments are usually considered the highest form of debt in the firm and must be paid when due. This is why debt service reduction is very important to the income statement analysis.

Net Profit (Income). The final, or "net," profit represents the sum of all revenues minus the sum of all expenses and is the profit figure which a franchise reports. This sum is commonly called the "bottom line." Net profit is the amount of earnings available which may be used to reinvest in the business, pay dividends to shareholders, provide bonuses, or provide additional product/service research and development for the franchise system. Overall, net profit is a measurement of the performance of the franchise over a period of time. Usually, an income statement is developed to reflect a month's, quarter's, or year's performance. It identifies and accounts for income, expenses, and profit. The income statement, when compiled on a monthly basis, will show how much was "cleared" or "over-spent" for that month.

Reinvested Earnings. Often the franchisor will plow growth funds or reserve funds back into the business, and these are usually considered reinvested (retained) earnings. However, reinvested earnings, unlike other income statement items, are often subject to significant IRS regulations.

Balance Sheet

A balance sheet is an accounting statement which illustrates the value of the assets, liabilities, and equity (net worth) of a franchise at a specific time. (See Figure 10-2.) The balance sheet (also referred to as a statement of financial position or condition) is simply a "snapshot" of the fiscal condition of the franchise at a given instant in time. This statement is divided into two counterbalancing sections: (1) assets (what the business owns) and (2) liabilities (what the business owes) and owner's equity (owner investment capital). These sections are generally divided into a two-column "T" account format with the assets on the left equaling the liabilities and owner's equity on the right. A one-column statement form would list the assets at the top and the liabilities and equity at the bottom. The assets of the business can be divided into two major categories, current assets and fixed assets. These assets represent the properties of the business which are used to provide for future benefits or sales for the franchise.

Balance. The concept of balance can be illustrated simply. If a franchise owner purchases $1,000 worth of new merchandise (or supplies) by using credit, the franchise's assets are increased by the value of the new inventory of merchandise or product. At the same time, liabilities are increased $1,000 by virtue of the franchised business incurring an account payable by buying the merchandise on credit. On the other hand, if the franchise owner spends $1,000 cash to buy the new merchandise, assets would be increased by the $1,000 increase in merchandise inventory, but the "cash" account would be decreased by the

Figure 10-2
Hypothetical Consolidated Balance Sheet
Bonnie's Hot Tubs Inc.
Balance Sheet
as of December 31, 1986

ASSETS		
Current Assets		
Cash	$180,000	
Temporary investments	20,000	
Receivables	200,000	
Inventory	200,000	
Total current assets		$ 600,000
Fixed Assets		
Land	$ 95,000	
Building	280,000	
Equipment	125,000	
Accumulated depreciation	(150,000)	
Net fixed assets		350,000
Franchisor goodwill		50,000
Total assets		$1,000,000
LIABILITIES AND STOCKHOLDERS' EQUITY		
Current Liabilities		
Notes payable	$ 50,000	
Accounts payable	100,000	
Accrued expenses	25,000	
Interest payable	25,000	
Total current liabilities		$ 200,000
Long-term Debt (8.5% bonds)		200,000
Total Liabilities		$ 400,000
Equity		
Proprietorship equity	$ 50,000	
Partnership equity	200,000	
Paid in excess capital	100,000	
Retained earnings	250,000	
Total Equity		600,000
Total Liabilities and Equity		$1,000,000

cash outlay. Therefore, total assets would be unchanged. Liabilities and equity would also remain the same since this transaction would not involve either an equity or a liability account.

Current Assets. Cash and resources that can be changed into cash within a brief period of time (usually 12 months from the date of the balance sheet, or one cycle of the business's operations) are considered current assets.

- Cash — money in hand and on demand, as available in checking or savings accounts.
- Short-term or temporary investments, including interest or dividends that can be expected to be converted into cash within one year, marketable securities, stocks, bonds, certificates of deposit, and time-deposit savings that are valued on the balance sheet at either original cost or market value, whichever is less.
- Accounts Receivable — amounts due from customers or clients in payment for merchandise or services received.
- Inventory — raw materials on hand, finished goods available for sale, and any work in process, which usually has a value determined on a "unit" basis.
- Prepaid Expenses — includes goods or services bought or rented in advance of their actual use, such as office supplies, office space, insurance protection, or taxes.

Long-term Investments. Long-term investments, often called long-term assets, are holdings the franchised firm intends to keep for at least one year. Such investments typically yield an interest accrued or dividend paid back to the firm. Examples of such long-term investments are bonds, stocks, other marketable securities, or special savings accounts set aside for specific purposes such as to build a cash reserve, to purchase a new building or remodel an existing business location, or to reduce debt.

Fixed Assets. Fixed assets, often called "Plant and Equipment," include the resources the firm owns or acquires for use in running the business. Such assets are generally not intended for resale. Land would be listed at its original purchase price, while other fixed assets would be listed at cost, less any depreciation. Also, fixed assets can be leased. When fixed assets are leased, it may be necessary to list both the value of the assets and the liability of a leased property item.

Other Assets. Resources of the business not otherwise identifiable in a preceding category are listed here. These assets are created from superior entrepreneurial capacity (know-how) or granted as exclusive privileges by governmental authorities. Usually, such assets are intangibles such as trademarks, labels, and copyrights often associated with franchised businesses. The trademark "Big Mac" is a good example.

Liabilities. Liabilities of the franchised business include all monetary obligations the firm has created and any claims creditors may have on the firm's assets. They are usually categorized as current or long-term liabilities. Current liabilities are debts or obligations payable by the franchised firm within a normal cycle of the business, or 12 months. Usually the following types of liabilities are found in a franchised business:

- Accounts Payable — amounts owed to the franchisor or other suppliers for goods or services purchased by the franchisee for use by the business.
- Short-term Notes — short-term, borrowed funds, often necessary to purchase inventory. The amount shown in the account is the balance of the principal due to such creditors. This is often contractual debt incurred to ensure that essential supplies or functions of the business continue uninterrupted.
- Current Portion of Long-term Notes — current amount due on notes owed to creditors when the terms of the notes exceed 12 months. Mortgage payments on the business building illustrate the amount owed and payable this year and the amount owed in total for the extended-year note.
- Interest Payable — accrued fees or interest charges due for use of both the short-term and long-term borrowed funds and credit that has been extended to the franchised business.
- Taxes Payable — amounts estimated to have been incurred during the accounting period, as well as taxes mandated to be collected, such as gasoline, retail sales, and worker's compensation taxes.
- Accrued Payroll — salaries of the owners and non-owners who are employed in the franchised business, as well as any hourly wages currently owed.

Long-term Liabilities. These are debts usually used to finance capital assets such as buildings, machinery, or fixed assets. Long-term liabilities are then balance sheet items entered as mortgage payments, bonds, or long-term notes. These liabilities are "fixed cost" to finance "fixed assets" and are contractual obligations which must be paid when they are due. Generally, long-term liabilities are obligations owed over a period that exceeds 12 months or one cycle of business.

Equity. Equity is often called the net worth of the business. It is the owner's claim on the assets of the business. In a corporation, the owners are shareholders — that is, persons who have invested capital (as cash or other assets) into the business in return for shares of stock. A franchised corporation's equity would be the sum of the contributions made by the shareholders, plus earnings of the business retained within the firm after paying dividends. On the other hand, a proprietorship or partnership arrangement would have as its equity the sole owner's original investment (or the partner's original investment), plus any earnings after ownership withdraws.

Total Liability and Equity. The sum of the total liabilities plus equity must always equal the sum (or total) of the assets.

Funds Flow Statement

The two basic types of change in financial position are inflows (sources of capital) and outflows (application of the capital acquired). The funds flow statement contains four major classifications: (1) cash on hand, (2) cash receipts, (3) total cash disbursed, and (4) net cash flow. This is why the funds flow statement is often referred to as the cash flow statement. (See Figure 10-3 for a typical chart of accounts used in a funds flow statement.)

"Cash on hand" refers to that cash brought forward from the previous accounting period (generally a month, quarter, or year). "Cash receipts" refer to all income which actually occurs in the form of cash. Cash sales would be listed here but credit sales would not; credit sales are listed on a cash flow statement only when they have been collected. Total cash available is simply the sum of the cash on hand and the total cash receipts for that period. The major ways to increase a cash position are by (1) sales from operations, (2) cash flow from depreciation and depletion, (3) any sale through owner's equity or debt, and (4) sale of noncurrent assets.

Figure 10-3
Hypothetical Cash Flow Statement
Bonnie's Hot Tubs Inc.
Change in Financial Position
Years Ending December 31

	1986	1985
Sources of Funds		
Net income from income statement	$ 900,000	$735,000
Expenses not requiring a current outlay of funds:		
depreciation and deferred taxes	45,000	38,000
Total from Operations	$ 945,000	$773,000
Other sources: disposition of property and equipment	100,000	82,000
Total	$1,045,000	$855,000
Application of Funds:		
Expenditures for properties and goodwill	$ 595,000	$327,000
Short-term investments	67,000	52,000
Payment of cash dividends	22,000	8,000
Total	$ 684,000	$387,000
Increase (Decrease) in Working Capital	$ 361,000	$468,000

The cash disbursement section is a very important tool for controlling expenses of the business. Expenses need to be closely monitored and compared with those of other similar franchised businesses or with previous financial data from the same business. There are also four major applications of working capital (decreasing cash flow position) in a franchise: (1) operating expenses, (2) buying back ownership by retiring stock or some form of cash dividend payment, (3) purchasing additional assets, and (4) decreasing the debts or liabilities of the franchise. Subtracting the total cash disbursed from the total cash available yields a new net cash flow position. This end-of-the-month figure allows the franchised business owner to see the cash position of the business.

During months of peak sales, generally November and December in retail business, the cash flow position should be quite high. However, during months of slow sales, January and February, the cash flow position for the month may be very low. Also, during months of heavy inventory purchasing, such as September and October, the cash flow position may be low. Cash "flows" through a franchise as a result of customer purchases and operating expenses required of the franchised business to make the sales. Additional capital may be received through new equity financing or equity injections. On the other hand, assets may be decreased when inventory equipment, land, buildings, or even accounts receivable are sold, resulting in a cash increase. This would simply reduce the asset account and increase the cash flow profile. Additionally, most increases in liabilities result in an increase of cash to the business account.

A cash flow statement provides a picture of the cash balance for the business over a period of a month, quarter, or year. A franchisor should know that the use of cash to purchase inventory or to create an increase in accounts receivable is similar to the decision to purchase equipment, land, or building. If a franchisor allows an expenditure of $166,000 to increase the hot tub inventory, but the new inventory has a poor design or poor styling, then the resulting low sales will mean a loss of cash or an increase in short-term debt. Such a cash loss may have additional consequences because of the inability to sell this "dead" inventory, and the result may be a decrease in working capital.

Importance of the Cash Flow Statement. The cash flow statement and the cash budget (to be discussed in Chapter 11) may be the most important financial tools available to both franchisor and franchisee. Both statements allow the separate business owners to understand the cash position and to know when each may need to borrow money to meet obligations or invest money because of excessive cash flow. By using a cash flow statement, an owner is alerted to the financial strengths and weaknesses of the franchise and may react accordingly. In addition, seasonal periods and broader cyclic trends can be identifiable. A franchisor or franchisee should always be concerned about the relationship between sources of funds and application of funds. This relationship constitutes the working capital of the business. The cash budget (presented and discussed in Chapter 11) illustrates this relationship on a month-to-month basis.

Changes in Working Capital. The following types of uses summarize changes in the levels of working capital:

- Increases
    1. Net income from operations
    2. Cash flow from depreciation or in land/minerals depletion
    3. Sale of securities for cash, such as bonds, common stock, preferred stock, or stock rights
    4. Sale of noncurrent assets
- Decreases
    1. Purchases of noncurrent assets
    2. Payment of cash dividends, not a stock dividend or a stock split
    3. Repayment of long-term debt

Statement of Retained Earnings

The retained earnings statement shows the additions and subtractions from the retained earnings for a given period of time. It specifically shows the franchisor's current profits and adds these earnings to previously recorded retained earnings. Basically, the statement indicates how the earnings are divided between (1) the stockholders and (2) the continuing financial needs of the business. It does not represent cash. For example, if Bonnie's Hot Tubs Inc. records $83,150 in retained earnings, Bonnie did not necessarily make $83,150 in profits for 1986. However, the business has retained profits of $83,150 for 1987. (See Figure 10-4.)

Figure 10-4
Hypothetical Statement of Retained Earnings
Bonnie's Hot Tubs Inc.
Statement of Retained Earnings
Years Ending December 31

	1986	1985
Retained earnings, January 1	$ 27,000	$ 13,850
Additions: Net income for the year	78,650	95,850
	$105,650	$109,700
Deductions: Common stock dividends	22,500	82,000
Retained earnings, December 31	$ 83,150	$ 27,700

The franchisor or franchisee, as well as the banker, the creditor, the tax preparer, and the prospective investor, will find data in the financial statement to help them make decisions. Financial decision makers have a variety of financial tools available to analyze business financial statements. Perhaps the most useful of these tools is the financial statement or ratio analysis. The franchisor's comparisons of various items on the business's financial statements provide a clearer informational picture. Specifically, the general purpose of ratio analyses of financial statements is to determine the success of the franchise in meeting its overall business objectives. These objectives are to meet current obligations and to meet interest costs and repayment of long-term obligations while earning a specific return on invested funds.

Financial Ratios

There are five major categories of financial ratios: liquidity, profitability, activity, coverage or leverage, and market. Several of the most commonly used ratios are discussed below. Table 10-1 presents a general description of these ratios.

Liquidity ratios indicate how well the franchise meets its short-term debts or financial obligations. Two measures are commonly used: the current ratio and the acid test. The **current ratio** is current assets divided by current liabilities, with both figures coming from the balance sheet.

$$\text{Current Ratio} = \frac{\text{Total Current Assets}}{\text{Total Current Liabilities}}$$

This relationship illustrates the ability of the franchisor to pay current debts using only current assets (cash, inventory, accounts receivable). The higher this ratio, the better the franchisor's ability to pay off

Table 10-1
Primary Ratios and What They Measure

Liquidity	Ability of the franchised business to pay its short-term debts.
Profitability	Overall effectiveness of the franchise leadership and management team to generate a profit.
Activity	How effective the franchised business is in using the available resources; focus is on the generation of sales in relation to an asset base.
Leverage (or Coverage)	The amount of long-term debt the franchised business carries and its ability to meet these debt obligations.
Market	The performance of the common stock of the franchised business if the stock is not significantly owned by insiders.

these short-term liabilities or debts. A general rule is that the current ratio should be 2 to 1 ($2 to every $1, or 200 percent). However, many businesses operate with a current ratio of 1.5 or even 1.2 to 1, and are very successful. For any business venture being considered, it would be wise to find out the industry averages, and more particularly, the averages for the franchised businesses within the particular industry before making judgments about what ratio is "good" or "insufficient."

The current ratio of Bonnie's Hot Tubs is calculated as $600,000 to $200,000 or 3 to 1 and the working capital is $400,000 ($600,000 current assets —$200,000 current liabilities).

The **acid test** or quick ratio is developed by subtracting current inventory from total current assets and dividing that figure by current liabilities:

$$\text{Acid Test} = \frac{\text{Current Assets} - \text{Inventory}}{\text{Current Liabilities}}$$

Each of these figures is found on the balance sheet. This ratio indicates the extent to which a franchisor can pay current debts without relying on future sales of inventory. A general rule of thumb is to maintain a ratio of 1 to 1, or $1 of current assets minus inventory to $1 of current liabilities. When the acid test ratio dips below a ratio of 1 to 1, there is a developing "dependency" on inventory, rather than other current assets such as cash and accounts receivables, to help pay debts. The acid test or quick ratio for Bonnie's franchise is:

$$\frac{\$600,000 - \$200,000}{\$200,000} = 2:1$$

Profitability ratios are generally developed from the income statement and measure the ability of the franchise organization to turn sales into profits and to generate profit from assets. The two most common profitability ratios concentrate on operating income and the effects of taxes and fixed expenses on operating income.

The net profit margin is found by dividing net income after taxes by the total sales for the period:

$$\text{Net Profit Margin} = \frac{\text{Net Income After Taxes}}{\text{Total Sales}}$$

This ratio describes the net or "real" profitability of the business. It is of interest to note that the average net profit margin of most businesses is between three and seven percent. When a net profit margin rises above twelve percent, more and more competitors are attracted to the arena to share in the market demand because of the high net profits available. As more competitors enter the market, profits tend to decline because of the increasing competition for the customer.

Therefore, the net profit margin for Bonnie's Hot Tubs may be calculated as $174,000 ÷ $1,000,000 = 17.4 percent. This indicates that Bonnie's franchise was able to generate more than 17 cents of operating profit on each dollar of sales.

A second important profitability ratio is the net return on assets calculation. This ratio measures the firm's ability to generate an after-tax return on assets:

$$\text{Net Return on Assets} = \frac{\text{Net Profit After Tax}}{\text{Total Assets}}$$

Specifically, Bonnie's net return on assets is $174,000 ÷ $1,000,000 = 17.4 percent. The net return on assets and the net profit margin should be a similar percentage, since assets are always used to produce sales.

Activity or efficiency ratios measure the franchise's ability to use capital and assets to maximum efficiency. Generally, three ratios are calculated to measure business efficiency — inventory turnover, collection period ratio, and the fixed asset turnover.

$$\text{Inventory Turnover} = \frac{\text{Net Sales}}{\text{Inventory}}$$

More specifically, this ratio indicates the number of times the average inventory expenditure of the franchise is turned into dollars. The basic objective is to increase this ratio overall. The inventory turnover for Bonnie's firm is $900,000 ÷ $200,000 = 4.5 times.

Determining the average collection period for accounts receivable tells the franchisor the average length of time it takes from the point of purchase to the point of payment for a particular sale. To determine this figure requires using net sales figures from the income statement and accounts receivable figures from the balance sheet; it is illustrated as follows:

$$\text{Average Collection Period} = \frac{\text{Accounts Receivable}}{\text{Net Sales}} \times 360 \, (\text{days})$$

Generally, a favorable decline in this ratio indicates increased efficiency in the collection of accounts receivable. The average collection period of Bonnie's Hot Tubs is calculated as follows:

$$\frac{\$200,000}{\$900,000} \times 360 \, \text{days} = 80 \, \text{days}$$

Therefore, Bonnie's average age of receivables is 80 days.

As indicated above, the correct way to view financial ratio analysis is by an industry approach. In our example, a review of the average collection period of 72 days may indicate Bonnie's Hot Tubs is taking too long to collect its accounts receivable. Businesses usually pay their receivables within 35 to 65 days, while customers often take 30 to 45 days to make payment. This set of days-for-payment by business and by customer will, of course, vary from industry to industry.

Other operating ratios also require information from both balance sheet and income statement. The fixed asset turnover ratio indicates the extent to which the business's fixed assets are used in generating sales, while the total asset turnover ratio shows how efficiently the franchised firm is utilizing its assets to generate sales. The ratios are indicated below:

$$\text{Fixed Asset Turnover} = \frac{\text{Total Sales}}{\text{Fixed Assets}}$$

$$\text{Total Asset Turnover} = \frac{\text{Total Sales}}{\text{Total Assets}}$$

The fixed asset turnover of Bonnie's Hot Tubs is $1,000,000 ÷ $500,000 = 2 times, or for each dollar invested in fixed assets Bonnie's firm earns two dollars. The total asset turnover is $1,000,000 ÷ $1,000,000 = 1 time.

Leverage ratios measure long-term debt and the franchisor's ability to take care of the obligations associated with this type of debt. Various ratios using balance sheet information can be computed, such as the debt ratio, debt/equity ratio, debt-to-capital ratio, and the short-term-liabilities-to-total-debt ratio. One leverage ratio, the times-interest-earned ratio, is generated from the income statement as follows:

$$\text{Times-Interest-Earned Ratio} = \frac{\text{Net Income Before Taxes} + \text{Interest Expense}}{\text{Interest Expense}}$$

This ratio indicates the proportion that interest expense constitutes in relation to the net income of the firm. This proportion gives a quick indication of what income obligation is associated with long-term debt. The banker is very much interested in the times-interest-earned ratio in that it measures solvency, the ability to pay back interest. Here is the times-interest-earned ratio for Bonnie's Hot Tubs:

$$\frac{\$137,000 + \$12,000}{\$12,000} = 12.4 \text{ times}$$

Bonnie's franchise thus earns more than 12 dollars for every dollar the firm must pay in interest.

The debt/equity ratio can be used to estimate the amount of debt a franchisor can carry based on the equity invested in the business. This is estimated as follows:

$$\text{Debt/Equity Ratio} = \frac{\text{Total Current Liabilities} + \text{Long-term Debt}}{\text{Total Stockholders' Equity}}$$

Specifically, Bonnie's debt/equity ratio would be 0.66 to 1:

$$\frac{\$200,000 + \$200,000}{\$600,000} = 0.66$$

The debt-to-asset ratio, another leverage or debt ratio, is found by dividing total debt by total assets. This would indicate that Bonnie's business assets are financed by 66 percent debt and 34 percent stockholder equity.

Market ratios are useful in assessing the performance of the common stock of the franchised firm, if it is a corporation. A franchised corporation may be closely held with limited or no stock being traded by virtue of being an actively traded public corporation. The ratios often used to assess the performance of this stock of such firms are shown below:

$$\text{Dividend Yield} = \frac{\text{Dividend Per Share of Common Stock}}{\text{Price Per Share}}$$

$$\text{Earnings/Share} = \frac{\text{Net Income After Taxes} - \text{Preferred Dividends Paid}}{\text{Number of Shares of Common Stock Outstanding}}$$

$$\text{Price Earnings Ratio} = \frac{\text{Current Market Price Per Share}}{\text{After-Tax Earnings Per Share}}$$

$$\text{Dividend Payout} = \frac{\text{Dividend Per Share of Common Stock}}{\text{After-Tax Earnings Per Share}}$$

Generally speaking, these market ratios are evaluation ratios. The supply and demand relationships upon the security or "market value" of the security have significant effects on that security market ratio.

Uses of Financial Statement Analysis

As indicated above, many outsiders, such as the banker, the creditor, and the investor, may be interested in the financial picture of a franchise. Our discussion of the various financial statements has indicated that the key financial ratios of liquidity, profitability, activity or efficiency, leverage, and market are very useful in analyzing this picture. Generally, these ratios may be viewed as analyzing the "bottom line," which is the return to the franchised business owner. Figure 10-5 below presents a linear relation of these ratios to the "bottom line."

How Important Are Financial Ratios?

Financial ratios do not have much significance unless they can be compared with other financial ratios. First, within the franchised business, comparisons with ratios from previous years provide an indication of the current state of the firm's financial affairs. Second, comparisons of the business with like businesses within the industry help provide an understanding of how well this firm serves its customers in contrast to the average firm. For example, it would be of little use to examine the financial ratios of a single Midas Muffler franchise without looking at Midas's position in the industry and the average performance ratios in the muffler industry in general. Table 10-2 presents an overview of the meaning of financial ratios.

Ratio analysis involves interpreting a relationship between two financial figures. This relationship is commonly expressed as a ratio, percentage, or fraction. For example, the current ratio is developed by dividing total current assets by the total current liabilities. If the current assets are $200,000 divided by $100,000, the relationship (current ratio) is $200,000 divided by $100,000, which yields a ratio (2:1), a percentage (200%), or a fraction (2/1). Current ratios often encompass the entire corporation's or firm's product line. Therefore, we should understand that ratios may not be mutually exclusive to "our" product line. For example, if we were to analyze, say, Mobil Oil's financial ratios and compare these ratios to Exxon's, we should be familiar with the "nonconsolidated" statements. These statements include a breakdown of individual product lines. Mobil Oil's product lines include Montgomery Ward's, which is a

Figure 10-5
Financial Ratios

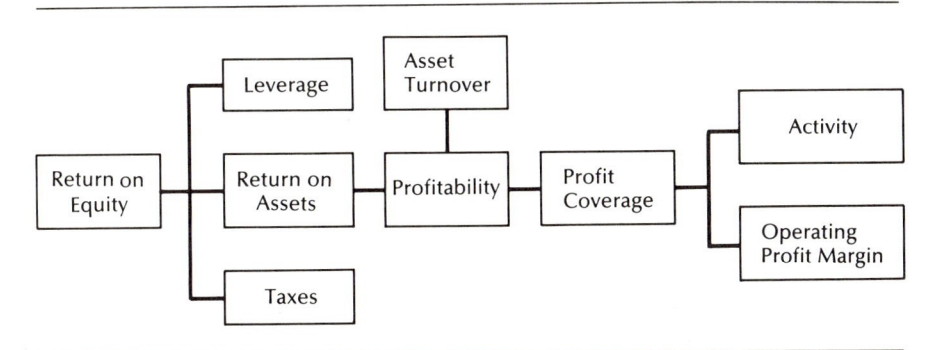

Source: Figure developed by Sally Jo Wright, Associate Professor of Finance, Sangamon State University, 1988. Used with permission.

**Table 10-2
Financial Ratios Useful for Analyzing a Business
with Interpretations and Normative Expectations**

Ratio	Interpretation	Norms
Return on investment	The rate of return on total assets employed; a measure of management's overall performance in generating a profit.	Should at least be equal to the market rate of return on Treasury bills during the time period in question.
Return on equity	The rate of return on stockholder's investment in the company; a measure of management's performance in generating a profit for the owners of the company.	Same as above.
Net profit margin	The amount of after-tax profits per dollar of sales.	None exists.
Gross margin	The amount of gross profit generated per dollar of sales.	None exists.

Source: Adapted from Manab N. Thakur, Memphis State University, "How to Conduct Financial Analysis for Policy Casework," in R. T. Justis, R. J. Judd, and D. B. Stephens, *Strategic Management and Policy* (Englewood Cliffs, NJ: Prentice-Hall, Inc., 1985), pp. 620-621.

retail merchandising operation. And Exxon includes office machines and home/office computers in its product lines, not just petroleum products. Therefore, the reader must be aware of appropriate use of financial statement and ratio analysis. After all, the purpose of financial statement and ratio analysis is to "red flag" key fiscal areas for further analysis and review.

SUCCESS STORY
LEO G. LAUZEN

Comprehensive Accounting Corporation, Aurora, Illinois, is the country's largest franchised accounting service company. In 1948, the company's founder, Leo G. Lauzen, was inspired with the idea of providing professional accounting services to all types of small businesses.

While attending the University of Illinois, Lauzen asked one of his accounting professors why all the examples cited in class were multimillion-dollar companies. He wanted to know who took care of the small business owner's accounting needs. The professor responded that taking care of small business was not the purpose of the accounting profession. Only four months and four credits short of earning his degree, Lauzen dropped out of school to concentrate on the development of reasonably priced accounting services for small and medium-sized businesses.

During his first year of operation Lauzen earned an average of two cents an hour. Seventeen years later, by 1965, his operation was servicing 825 accounts and he was earning $250,000 in profits per year. His was the largest monthly double-entry accounting service in the country.

At this point he was no longer personally handling all the accounts himself, and he felt the quality of the service was declining. Without even realizing that the action he took was "franchising," in an effort to maintain the quality standards he had established and to expand the company, Lauzen sold these accounts to several of his employees, and the first Comprehensive Accounting franchises came into existence. This action motivated these franchisees to carry on the high standards that had originally been established and to increase their client base.

An extensive survey conducted by Comprehensive determined that the single greatest reason for business failure was that many business people know their trade but do not know how to run a business. The average business owner is not sufficiently versed in sales and marketing, advertising promotion and public relations, business management, business law, accounting, insurance, financing, or personnel and human resources. To make a business successful, one needs to gain knowledge in these areas. Taking a positive step in the education of the business owner, Comprehensive Accounting developed computer software to give the owner a pictorial view of business trends. Using three-color graphs, the owner can compare sales results of the current year with those of the previous year; see where the major expenses are; and compare sales, expenses, and profit margin on a monthly basis for the past 12 months. Comprehensive invested more than half a million dollars in research and development to create this new management tool. The company's franchisees can thus provide this valuable service as a method of assisting their clients in the operation of their businesses.

Because Lauzen's company has more than 425 franchisees and over 22,000 clients, it was economically feasible to pursue this development. An individual accountant without this type of support would not be able to accomplish an undertaking of this magnitude. Now in the works at Comprehensive is the establishment of "How to Succeed

> in Business" seminars which will provide the business owner with information to help the business become a success.
>
> In 1985 Lauzen's company entered the realm of master franchising, offering master franchises to those individuals in the top one-third of the franchise system. These franchisees, who have the most successful trade records, now have the opportunity to expand and develop their futures to an even greater level.
>
> By taking an idea and turning it into reality, Leo Lauzen has surpassed even his own dreams. Today Comprehensive Accounting has a net worth of over $6 million with a pre-tax profit for the year ending June 30, 1985 of $1,600,000.
>
> Photo and information provided courtesy of Leo G. Lauzen, October, 1985.

SUMMARY

Calculating key financial ratios is not difficult. However, the analysis and managerial interpretations may be significantly difficult, especially for a franchise, because most financial ratio data is collected for larger firms (i.e., corporations). Yet for many industries, including various wholesaling, retailing, manufacturing, and service categories, ratios are compiled and published on an annual basis. These reference figures are available through sources such as the Robert Morris Associates *Annual Statement Studies, Moody's,* Standard & Poor's *Corporation Records, Value Line Investment Survey,* and *Industry Surveys.* Such sources provide fact sheets on companies, editorial comments on corporations, and information about industry averages and ratios for comparative purposes. Using available published compiled ratios and industry data, a franchisor can compare a franchise's financial data to national averages for that industry. In addition, a franchisor can compare company-owned competitors to franchisee-owned stores, or any single franchise to the industry average or to the average of all franchises combined.

REVIEW QUESTIONS

1. Explain the importance of developing and maintaining financial records in a franchised business.
2. Describe the importance and use of a balance sheet. What are its primary components?
3. Describe the importance and use of an income statement. What are its primary components?

4. Explain the funds flow (cash flow) statement. What are the types of "flows" in such a statement?
5. Describe the major ways a franchised business can increase the cash position of the firm.
6. Identify and describe the five major types of financial ratios.

CASE STUDY
THE HAIR EMPORIUM

Rolando and Rosa have been operating their own hair salon for the past six years. They have been very successful and now are interested in franchising their particular hair system throughout the United States. They are aware that the hair care industry is an $11 billion activity in this country. Rolando and Rosa specialize in women's, men's, and children's hair care and believe they can provide their services on a profitable basis for other franchisees.

Rolando and Rosa have estimated that the total cost for a new location would be between $65,000 and $136,000. This includes:

Franchise Fee	$20,000
Leased Deposit	$ 5,000
Leased Improvements	$15,000–$65,000
Real Estate Rental Costs	$ 2,000–$ 5,000
Equipment and Trade Fixtures	$17,000–$30,000
Opening Supplies	$ 1,000
Working Capital	$ 5,000–$10,000

They would expect that a new franchisee should have one-fourth to one-half of the total investment in cash and should be able to finance the balance through some lending source.

Franchisees would have the opportunity to open multiple stores after successfully operating the first Hair Emporium salon for a sufficient length of time and generating sufficient profits. It is anticipated also that the franchisee would be in operation approximately six months after the initial signing of the franchising agreement. Additionally, they plan to offer a one-week course in hair care, cutting, hair forming techniques, settings, hair sculpturing, and management.

Rolando and Rosa have a major concern about the accounting methods and record keeping. They have hired a local bookkeeper to keep track of their own records, but find it more and more difficult each year in dealing with the local accounting firms and taxes.

They are concerned about what kind of accounting service they should provide for the franchisees and whether they should also utilize a computer system. They have kept a basic journal but have never developed an itemized general ledger.

CASE QUESTIONS

1. What type of accounting records and/or financial statements should Rolando and Rosa keep themselves and also offer their franchisees?
2. Are balance sheets and operating statements important or necessary on a monthly or yearly basis?
3. Should they recommend a common accounting procedure for all franchisees?
4. Discuss the following financial/accounting records for the Hair Emporium: journal entry, detailed general ledger, bank account reconciliation, monthly payroll register, accounts receivable, comparative operating statements, taxes, and monthly business/accounting consultation.

REFERENCES

1. Broom, H. N., Justin G. Longenecker, and Carlos W. Moore, *Small Business Management*, Cincinnati: South-Western Publishing Co., 1983.
2. Fess, Philip E., and Carl Warren, *Accounting Principles*, 14th edition, Cincinnati: South-Western Publishing Co., 1984.
3. *Financial Ratios*, New York: Robert Morris Associates, 1978.
4. "Financing Small Business," *Small Business Reporter*, Bank of America, 1980.
5. Henward, DeBanks M., and William Ginalski, *The Franchise Option*, Phoenix, AZ: Franchise Group Publishers, 1979.
6. Seitz, Neil, *Financial Analysis: A Program Approach*, 3rd edition, Reston, VA: Reston Publishing Company, Inc., 1984.
7. Small Business Administration, "The Profit Plan," *Business Basics*, Washington, DC: U.S. Government Printing Office, 1980.
8. Vesper, Karl H., *New Venture Strategies*, Englewood Cliffs, NJ: Prentice-Hall, Inc., 1980.
9. Wilcox, Kirkland A., and Joseph G. San Miguel, *Introduction to Financial Accounting*, 2nd edition, New York: Harper & Row Publishers, 1984.

CHAPTER 11
FINANCIAL MANAGEMENT AND FISCAL PLANNING: TOOLS AND TECHNIQUES*

In studying this chapter, you will:
- Develop an understanding of the financial function within a franchised business.
- Learn about objectives and evaluating factors for making choices about sources of capital for the franchised business.
- Be able to identify the capital requirements confronting any franchised business.
- Learn about financial ratios useful in analyzing the financial condition of a franchise operation.

INCIDENT

Bonnie's Hot Tubs has been very successful after just two years of operation, so she has decided to expand. Yet many of her franchisees are having difficulty planning and managing financial resources, especially cash. For example, financing in the short run — from whom, when, and at what cost — has been difficult to plan. From the normal course of running the business, current cash assets and net working capital are being managed. At month's end, however, the cash available is just not sufficient. The timing differences, or

---

*Prepared in collaboration with Robert C. Maple, Assistant Professor of Business Administration-Finance, Sangamon State University; National Association of Securities Dealers, Registered Principal; and Branch Manager for National Securities Corporation in Springfield, Illinois.

synchronization, between cash outflow due to the costs of franchise and the sales of products and services usually do not require short-term financing. However, there are times when outflow exceeds inflow.

One particular franchisee of Bonnie's Hot Tubs is meeting with the bank Monday morning to try to arrange a short-term loan to cover the temporary cash shortage. Three types of interest rates are available to the franchisee: "add-on," "simple," or "discount" rates. Which type of interest is most advantageous to the franchisee? Also, what unneeded assets or liabilities may be eliminated in the future so that the franchisee can better manage the working capital?

INTRODUCTION

In this chapter we continue our discussion about the financial matters of a franchised business. In Chapter 10 we addressed financial statements, what accounts and categories are needed, how to analyze financial statements, and introduced ratio planning. This chapter is concerned with the ability of a franchised business to manage working capital, develop a cash budget, evaluate financial performance, and forecast future financial needs.

Financial planning and management are essential to any business. Both franchisor and franchisee need to understand the tools of financial planning. Working capital management and cash budget management are keys to the continuing success of the business, as is the ongoing and timely review of all financial statements.

MANAGING WORKING CAPITAL

Successfully managing the **working capital** in the franchised business may be the key to maintaining the profitability of the franchise. Working capital refers to all the current assets of the firm; more specifically, net working capital equals current assets minus current liabilities:

Current Assets — Current Liabilities = Net Working Capital

Working capital for Bonnie's Hot Tubs is $600,000 — $200,000 = $400,000. These funds are generated from the operation of the franchised business. Sales of goods and services bring into the business new working capital (current assets), and expenses incurred in order to create sales (current liabilities) reduce working capital.

Generally, responsibility for "managing" working capital means one must keep track and understand the position of cash, marketable securities (investments), and inventory, as well as accounts receivable as current assets, accounts payable, and other current liabilities. Understanding these concepts and keeping an appropriate balance between cash inflow and outflow are essential to effective net working capital management. Managing net working capital is critical to enhancing business profits. An owner should keep in mind that working capital is generally 50 percent of total assets and liabilities.

Timing is essential to effective capital management. The key is to maximize cash inflow while minimizing cash outflow. In practice, this means one should try to buy resources at the lowest possible cost, while selling the products at the highest possible price (given competitive conditions), and at the same time collecting as early as possible from accounts receivable. In other words, working capital management is an attempt to achieve a balance by maintaining as low a level of cash on any given day (minimizing idle funds) in relation to current liabilities (claims against cash that are to be paid) in order to have sufficient funds available to avoid nonpayment of these obligations.

Often, timing of cash income and outflow is predictable. For example, Bonnie's Hot Tubs franchisees can forecast a 37-day working capital cycle based on past business practice. Figure 11-1 illustrates a Bonnie's Hot Tubs franchisee with a cash flow period (capital cycle) of 37 days. This period of time is a normative (or average) period for the franchisee to (1) order the parts from Bonnie, (2) receive the parts, (3) assemble the parts into a complete hot tub, (4) display the hot tub in the showroom, (5) generate a customer order, and (6) install the hot tub with final payment made by customer. Working capital management is the attempt to minimize the cash "gap" between ordering the parts and receiving payment for the hot tub installed at the customer's location. This cash gap is narrowed through the management of inventory to the management of cash to pay for the inventory. The balance sought here is the risk tradeoff between anticipated level of sales (customer demand) and amount of inventory to be purchased.

To reiterate, working capital management is managing the flow of funds into and out of the franchised business. More specifically, it is managing the "gap" between purchasing the product materials and selling the product or supplying credit to the customer. Businesses by nature are cash deficient and must manage working capital — especially cash. Managing cash is perhaps the most dynamic element of running a business.

Cash Management

Cash may be the most critical financial component of working capital, and as a result it is the item watched most carefully. Operational policies and managerial actions of the franchised firm should be aimed toward effective accumulation, expenditure, and control of cash. The franchisee

Figure 11-1
Working Capital Cycle for Bonnie's Hot Tubs Inc.

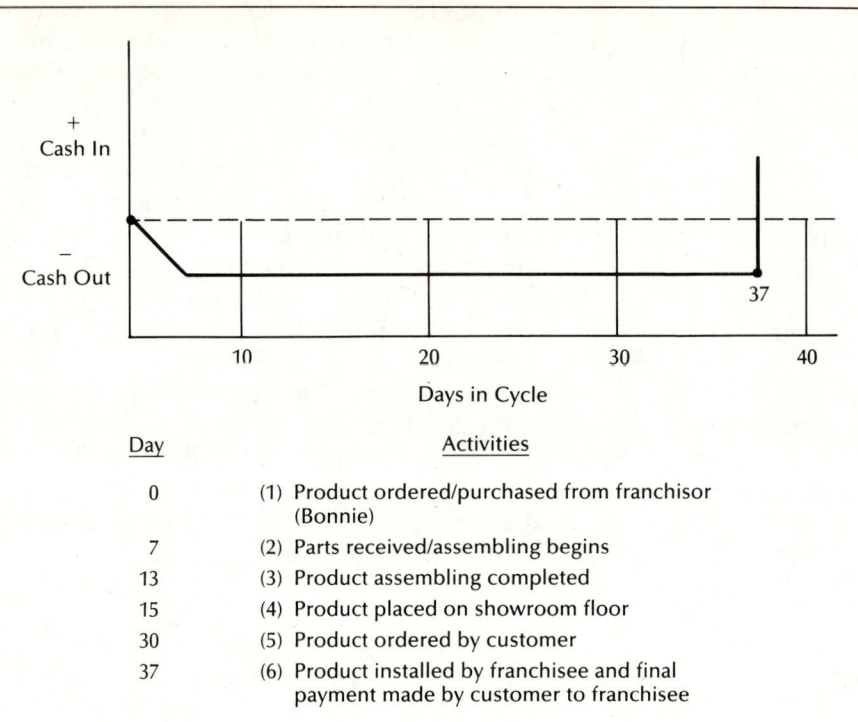

Day	Activities
0	(1) Product ordered/purchased from franchisor (Bonnie)
7	(2) Parts received/assembling begins
13	(3) Product assembling completed
15	(4) Product placed on showroom floor
30	(5) Product ordered by customer
37	(6) Product installed by franchisee and final payment made by customer to franchisee

should seek to minimize the risk of running out of cash. Sales are the main source of cash inflow. Cash in low levels must be balanced against the outflows due to purchases of inventory in order to make the sales, and other expenses of the business. Yet, if the franchisee simply allows cash to remain idle, then no opportunity gain (earned interest) can be made.

There is another way to achieve the balance or synchronization associated with managing cash. The franchised business must ensure that bills due (accounts receivable) are collected in a timely manner. The franchise owner may develop policies and practices to expedite payments from customers for purchases made. The well-worn reason of "the check is in the mail" can cost the franchise an opportunity to earn interest on marketable securities, or it can cause a loss of sales as a result of unpurchased inventory or insufficient stock to make sales. Methods to help synchronize cash inflow with outflow are cash discounts and lockbox systems to assist in the inflow of cash, and the timely investing of idle cash through marketable securities or time-deposit accounts that earn interest. The goal of the franchised firm should be to keep its available cash working at all times. The following examples are part of a viable cash management program.

Cash Discounts. Cash discounting means reducing the price of the product or service if payment is made earlier than what is typical business practice for making payment. For example, the policy of 2/10 net 30 is a common cash discounting practice. This means the seller will allow a 2 percent discount off the purchase price if the customer pays for the product or service in full within ten days instead of the 30 days normally taken to make payment in full. If Bonnie's Hot Tubs had such a policy, a customer who would buy a $800 hot tub could settle the debt owed to Bonnie by paying $784 within 10 days of making the purchase, or by paying the full $800 within 30 days. The **lockbox** concept means the business has a post-office box for receiving payments that is managed by a commercial bank. Customers who are accounts payable of the franchised business send their payment to the post-office box instead of to the place of business. This practice facilitates the collection of cash because the commercial bank is directly collecting payment and making the deposit to the account of the franchised business. Lockboxes are practical and are used by a number of large, high-volume businesses. Smaller chains and franchises may find the costs of maintaining a lockbox system prohibitive, and so may rely primarily or solely on offering cash discounts to encourage early payment. Franchise systems in areas such as auto parts, auto service or repair, tires, home cleaning, lawn service, and business services may wish to have a policy known to their customers which rewards early payment. Other franchises, such as those which have a high volume and a low unit price per product or service (fast-food restaurants, beverage or snack shops, etc.), typically collect cash at the point of purchase, so they will have little need for cash discounting or other early-remittance policies.

Marketable Securities. Marketable securities or other liquid investments can also be significant components of the cash assets or net working capital of the franchised business. Typically, marketable securities are very liquid, interest-bearing, low-risk financial assets. Examples of marketable securities are bank certificates of deposit (CDs), government securities (T-bills), and commercial paper held by the franchised business as short-term investments.

Sound financial planning for the franchised business owner is to hold only enough cash to ensure the availability of sufficient working capital, while investing all excess cash. These excess funds, invested at "market" (i.e., competitive) rates, can be used by the business during times when working capital has become unexpectedly short. For example, if a sales promotion planned between the franchisor and the franchisee necessitates purchasing more inventory than normal, the franchisee could sell marketable securities to have the cash to spend for the additional inventory. Financing the inventory by selling the marketable securities may be significantly "cheaper" than extending the line of credit with the franchisor or other supplier or by seeking a short-term loan from a bank.

Idle cash resulting from excess working capital does not earn a return. Idle cash will not have a compounding effect for the franchisor (or the franchisee); that is, it does not work to increase the amount of cash available to the business. Investing the idle cash in marketable securities is an effective way to manage the cash account to the best advantage of the business. The following equation illustrates this concept and indicates how a franchisor or a franchisee can calculate earned interest on marketable securities:

$$\text{Annual Interest Rate} \times \frac{\text{Number of Days Invested}}{365} \times \text{Amount Invested} = \text{Earned Income}$$

For example, if a Bonnie's Hot Tubs franchisee has idle cash of $15,000 available for two months or 61 days, the cash may be invested at the market rate, say 8.5 percent, to earn interest for the franchisee:

$$0.085 \times \frac{61}{365} \times \$15,000 = \$213.08$$

The *opportunity cost* of cash in this illustration is $213.08. It is the amount the franchisee would forgo — or not earn — by having the $15,000 remain idle for those 61 days. The $213.08 should not be used to supplement the regular cash account. Rather, it should be used to create a reservoir of cash for unscheduled or unanticipated cash outflows.

Accounts-Receivable Management

Accounts-receivable management addresses the firm's policies and activities associated with the selling of product or service on credit. Credit in this situation means the cash the franchisee is using to finance the sale. If the franchisee has a credit policy of "40 days same as cash," the customer has 40 days to make the payment for the purchase. This policy also means the franchisee must be willing to finance the customer for 40 days. To effectively manage working capital, the franchisee should attempt to make sure the customer will pay in full within these 40 days.

A franchisee should realize that there is a direct relationship between sales volume and credit. The more generous (or liberal) the franchisee's credit policy, the more the sales volume increases. Yet, the more purchases made because of generous or lenient credit terms, the greater the risk of "bad debts" as a result of these credit sales. As credit terms are relaxed or lowered, more and more people find they can purchase products or services by scheduling out the payments. Unfortunately, some of these people become too extended in their credit purchases and find themselves unable to pay. Thus, the seller can increase sales volume through liberal credit policies, but a certain portion of those sales will be made to people who will be unable to pay. This results in the creation of bad debt for the franchisee as the seller, because product/service has been provided or sold, but payment has not been received. This condition can destroy the balance sought through management of working capital.

Managing working capital isn't easy, but experience with customer credit and planning sales volume will greatly increase effective management of accounts receivable. It is important to remember that the ultimate goal for the franchisee is to reduce cash commitment (or financing investment) in accounts receivable, which in turn increases the effectiveness of working capital.

Inventory Management

Inventory management is another way to significantly reduce working capital requirements. Every franchisee should know that when inventory is low, the possibility of lost sales increases. If the franchisee doesn't have the materials to assemble, combine, etc., to make a sale, then a sale can't be made. The franchisee can take a number of actions to enhance inventory control to minimize the risk of losing sales, but in general a franchised business should try to keep inventory investment costs at a minimum, while being certain not to run out of product. Other factors to manage are costs of making orders, carrying costs (financing of inventory), and related costs attributable to inventory such as insurance, storage, taxes, and, of course, obsolescence. The franchisor will often develop an approach to inventory management, test it, and then recommend it to franchisees to help them minimize their inventory costs. There are models such as the economic order quantity (EOQ) approach that can help the franchisor and the franchisees manage inventory more effectively.

Current Liability Management

Accounts payable are short-term obligations created by the franchisee in buying supplies, materials, or services associated with running the business. The franchisee does not pay cash for the supplies, but rather purchases the products or services on credit extended by the seller. Accounts payable are liabilities of the business. Liabilities must be managed as effectively as the assets (cash, marketable securities, inventory) in working capital. Generally, current liability management involves the financing of current assets. Figure 11-2 illustrates the difference be-

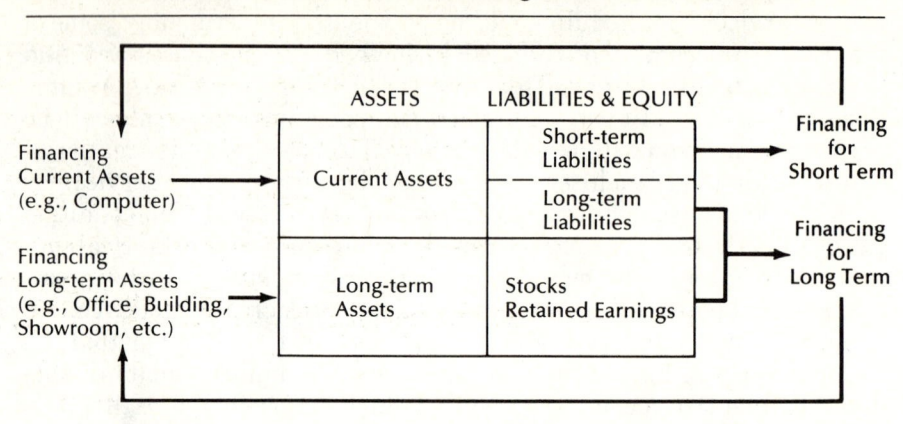

Figure 11-2
Role of Current Liabilities for Financing the Franchisee's Assets

	ASSETS	LIABILITIES & EQUITY	
Financing Current Assets (e.g., Computer)	Current Assets	Short-term Liabilities	Financing for Short Term
		Long-term Liabilities	
Financing Long-term Assets (e.g., Office, Building, Showroom, etc.)	Long-term Assets	Stocks Retained Earnings	Financing for Long Term

tween current liability management and the capitalization of the business.

Let's say that Bonnie's franchisee purchases a $9,000 computer system for use by the business to develop and maintain the franchisee's records as well as to assist in financial planning and control. The purchase will be financed by a three-year bank note, which is a short-term liability for the business. On the other hand, if the franchisee were to build a new office or add a new showroom, it is likely the financing would be either through a mortgage (as a long-term liability) or through issuance of bonds or stocks in the company (from the equity portion of the franchisee's balance sheet). The rule of thumb for accounts payable management is to finance the current assets in such a way as to ensure that the asset is bought and paid for before the asset is fully depreciated.

Accounts-payable management is an important consideration when the franchised business is seeking to obtain a short-term loan. If net working capital is not properly managed, or seasonal sales dictate, the business owner may find it necessary to borrow for the short term in order to have sufficient cash to purchase inventory or pay salaries. The cost of borrowing can be significant and can cause a drain on working capital. The franchised business owner not only forgoes the opportunity to receive interest earned from invested funds (that otherwise would be idle cash), but also has to pay interest — out of working capital — for the funds borrowed.

Borrowing funds is a normal and appropriate activity for a business. From time to time funds will be borrowed for a number of reasons such as meeting short-term obligations of running the business, purchasing equipment, constructing a building, or purchasing vehicles for delivery. These actions are part of the typical capital requirements of being in business. It is the unexpected, unplanned borrowing of funds that runs counter to effective management of working capital.

Methods for borrowing funds in the short term can vary significantly. The most common methods involve borrowing at (a) simple, (b) add-on, or (c) discount interest rates. Table 11-1 illustrates the differences between these methods of computing interest. For instance, if a franchisee borrows $4,200 to pay for a shipment of inventory needed for the next season of merchandise, the stated annual percentage rate (APR) in each example is the same, but the annual interest rate differs depending upon the approach taken by the lender. The annual interest rate is 22.32 percent for the "add-on" approach, 25.4 percent using the "discount" method, and 12.5 percent using the "simple interest" approach.

In the "add-on" approach, the interest charged is "added on" to the amount borrowed, meaning the balance of the loan is $4,725 for the year. Monthly payments are $393.75, and the franchised business receives the $4,200 to pay for the inventory. Using the simple-interest method, the interest charge is $289.80, which is added to the $4,200 borrowed, for a balance of $4,489.80. Monthly payments of $374.15 will clear the loan in one year. The discount method has interest of $525, which instead of being added to the amount of the loan is deducted from the proceeds of the loan. The franchised business receives $3,675, has a balance of $4,200, and will pay $350 per month to clear the loan in one year.

So we can see that getting the best rate of interest is not the critical question; rather, it is what method is being used to finance the funds to be borrowed. Within a local marketplace, the rates of interest for short-term loans are likely to be the same or similar. The method used to calculate the interest for the loans makes the primary difference. Therefore, it is to the advantage of the franchise owner to seek simple-interest borrowing if

Table 11-1
Interest Comparisons by Methods

	Add-on	Discount	Simple
Amount Financed	$4200	$4200	$4200
Stated APR*	12.5%	12.5%	12.5%
Loan Maturity	1 year	1 year	1 year
Repayment Terms	monthly	monthly	monthly
Interest Charges	$525	$525	$289.80
Loan Proceeds	$4200	$3675	$4200
Balance Due	$4725	$4200	$4489.80
Monthly Payments	$393.75	$350	$374.15
Annual Simple Interest Rate	22.32%	25.4%	12.5%

*According to the Fair Credit in Reporting Act, nominal interest rates are stated in annual percentage rates.

at all possible, and to avoid the discount method, as it is usually the most costly for the borrower.

As shown in Table 11-1, the franchised business can minimize the number of times it confronts opportunity costs of cash. If the franchised business owner does not effectively manage the cash, the firm will either quickly or gradually deplete its cash, and its costs of doing business will increase. The costs may increase because of the interest payments that must be made to acquire cash to cover the short-term obligations incurred. If the market conditions confronting the franchised business are highly competitive, the firm may only survive in the short run.

To summarize this section on working capital, franchisees should keep two objectives in mind regarding cash management. First, the franchise owner should maintain a keen interest in the level of cash available in the business, in order to determine and maintain the level of cash that could be invested to maximize the time value (opportunity gain) of funds. Second, the franchise owner must understand working capital and its components in relation to the business in which the franchise is engaged and the competitive conditions confronted. This is important in order to forecast accurately the minimum cash balances needed at a given time within the firm. By keeping minimum cash balances available, the short-term as well as long-term obligations can be met in a timely manner. Any excess cash can be invested and can reap a return on the investment prior to the time when that sum of cash is needed by the business.

To achieve these two objectives, the franchised business owner must be able to forecast cash needs or balances. This is usually accomplished by development and use of the *cash budget*. Figure 11-3 illustrates a cash budget set up on a monthly basis for the first quarter of 1987. This figure reveals the monthly cash receipts (cash in) and cash disbursements (cash out) for Bonnie's Hot Tubs.

The cash budget, as illustrated for Bonnie's Hot Tubs Inc., is a significant financial planning document. The various types of sales and other income are estimated for the period, in this example a quarter of a year. Cash disbursements such as salary or wages, rent or lease payments, insurance premiums, royalties to be paid to the franchisor, and utilities are usually more predictable than income, because these expense items are relatively fixed. Variable expenses typically are accounts payable, inventory purchases, taxes (based on sales made as well as income or withholding taxes), and other costs attributable to the specific activities of the business venture. These costs will fluctuate with the level of sales experienced by the firm.

In a franchised business, there may be a cooperative advertising fee, a percentage of sales that a franchisee remits to the franchisor to assist in developing and paying for mass media advertisements. The cash changes for Bonnie's Hot Tubs are noted at the bottom of Figure 11-3. The

Chapter 11 Financial Management and Fiscal Planning: Tools/Techniques 305

Figure 11-3
Hypothetical Monthly Cash Budget

Bonnie's Hot Tubs Inc.
Monthly Cash Budget
First Quarter, 1987

	January	February	March
Cash Receipts (In) +			
Beginning accounts receivable	$24,000	$26,700	$21,000
Credit sales	29,500	32,500	18,000
Cash sales	17,500	19,400	9,200
Interest income	4,000	4,000	4,000
Total Receipts	$75,000	$82,600	$52,200
Cash Disbursements (Out) −			
Fixed:			
Salary/wages	$ 9,200	$ 9,720	$ 8,500
Rent-lease	13,500	13,000	13,000
Utilities	2,800	2,800	2,800
Insurance	1,700	1,700	1,700
Royalties	1,000	1,000	1,000
Other	2,700	3,600	4,800
Variable:			
Accounts payable	18,000	24,000	36,000
Inventory	6,500	7,800	12,400
Taxes	3,200	4,100	3,600
Other	—	—	—
Total Cash Disbursements	$58,600	$67,720	$83,800
Cash Changes			
Beginning cash	$27,400	$43,800	$58,680
Change in cash	+16,400	+14,880	−31,600
Ending cash	$43,800	$58,680	$27,080

decline in the cash position by the end of March is not just due to a decline in sales (see Cash Receipts). Notice how the inventory accounts payable figure has increased. This change reflects the purchases made in December and January to maintain the sales levels of January and February. In March the inventory had to be paid for, and at the same time, sales declined. Even though there was a high level of sales in two of the three months of the quarter, the third month did not have the same or similar level of sales and the inventory and taxes for those sales had to be paid. It is not surprising when a franchisee says, "On average my sales have been fair to good; I just can't understand why I don't have any money in the business!" This is precisely why a cash budget is needed: to help the franchised business owner understand the cash flow within the business and forecast the cash needs associated with the level of sales the business seeks to achieve.

FINANCIAL PLANNING

Financial planning is a logical next step from the development and use of a cash budget and other financial tools mentioned in the preceding section. Generally, the term **financial planning** refers to the business owner's ability to plan and forecast the appropriate use of funds for the business. Financial planning helps the franchisor and the franchisee make independent judgments for their own businesses concerning cash surpluses, cash shortages, levels of sales to be sought, and those fixed and variable costs essential to produce the sales. Financial tools combined with financial ratio analysis can be used to assess the franchised business's performance.

Financial planning takes into account the long-range and short-range goals of the franchised firm, as well as the economic factors associated with the competitive conditions in the industry and the overall state of the economy. Our immediate task here is to review techniques or tools used to make financial forecasts, particularly in franchised businesses.

PRO FORMA STATEMENTS

Once again, the starting point of any financial planning system is the cash budget. The cash budget identifies the activities of the business in terms of cash receipts and cash disbursements and identifies the trends or changes occurring month to month and quarter to quarter. Usually, after two or three quarters (six or nine months) the franchised business owner may be able to accurately predict or project cash changes. But more important than predicting changes in cash, the owner must understand the relationships peculiar to the type of business and the level of marketplace competition and must learn to predict sales and costs with some degree of accuracy. After eight or 12 quarters (two or three years), the history of the business's activity as depicted through the cash budget and its changes allows for more accuracy in forecasting. After specific trends are revealed within the cash budget, the franchised firm can estimate financial statements for periods into the future. These financial statements are called **pro forma statements**. Technically, pro forma means "in form only." Practically, pro forma financial statements are financial planning documents for the business to use as it tries to expand into new products or markets and/or deepen its market penetration.

Pro forma statements are planning tools which are always adjusted for accuracy after the facts (business activities/sales performance) are known. Therefore, these statements are never formally evaluated by an independent auditor or certified public accountant to attest to the accuracy of the business's activities. The two pro forma statements usually developed are the income statement and the balance sheet forecasts.

Up to this point only the "cash" perspective of the pro forma statements has been reviewed. Once the cash budget is developed, it can be used by the franchised business to project a more comprehensive view of the financial future of the business. The pro forma income statement and balance sheet can be prepared. Each is a separate budget plan which helps the franchisor or the franchisee see where expected revenues will come from and in what amounts on a month-to-month basis. A budget plan can be extended into the future to indicate one, two, three, or more years of planned sales revenue and operating expenses. The primary value of such a plan is to help the business keep on target with its intended rate of growth and evaluate this growth on a regular basis. The pro forma income statement and balance sheet can also be very helpful to a franchisor who intends to phase down or out of a particular district or area. The budget plan would show how the franchise system plans to retrench and in what stages that retrenchment will take place over a period of time.

Pro Forma Income Statement

The first step in setting up a pro forma (or operating plan) income statement is to develop sales projections. The initial sales projections are taken from the cash budget (Figure 11-3). The cash receipts section of the cash budget reveals the sales on a month-to-month basis. Although a pro forma income statement can be prepared monthly, it is most commonly prepared as a quarterly statement; that is, activities over three months are recorded together. Four quarterly periods equal one year's income and expense activity for the business.

In order to bridge from the cash budget to the pro forma income statement, some basic questions must be asked about the data in the cash budget. For example, will trends (sales, costs, etc.) identified in the cash budget on a month-to-month basis continue? Will other noncontrollable economic factors (the nation's money supply, rate of inflation, interest costs, etc.) create deviating trends? More specifically, the overall economy could be entering or coming out of a recession, which is a noncyclical trend. Or other noncyclical factors could affect the economy, such as insurrection in a foreign country, forming or dissolving of cartels of critical resources, assassination of a world leader, or major changes in a business regulation or tax law.

After the basic assumptions about the overall economy, as well as the local economy where the franchised business operations are, have been made, then the historical trends presented in the cash budget may be used for developing future projections. Let's use Bonnie's Hot Tubs to illustrate. One can project sales for the second quarter of 1987 (the months of April through June) by using a percentage of sales to "plug" sales into the pro forma income statement. Specifically, we will assume that sales will continue at the current pace with no major increases or decreases. Next, we will select the major items (or fiscal variables) from the company's Year-End Income Statement (see Chapter 10, Figure 10-1). Each variable should be presented as a percentage of sales. Total sales will equal 100 percent. The associated costs to make the sales, the administrative expenses, and gross profit should be represented in percentages that total to 100 percent which equals total sales. (See Figure 11-4 for an illustration.)

Economic Assumptions in Financial Planning

Making valid, logical assumptions concerning the economies of the United States and the particular local community is significant to the franchised firm's financial planning. For example, let's assume that the local economy of a given town is not growing. In fact, conditions are sluggish and the local economy is actually slumping. Young people are moving out of the area and disposable income is generally decreasing. In this type of economy, the local Bonnie's Hot Tubs store should reduce projected sales. A franchised unit's sales reflect the effort of the franchisee to produce sales and make a profit within a particular market area. However, overall economic conditions can also shape the sales that will be made. Boosting sales efforts will not always result in dramatic sales increases if there are fewer and fewer people willing or able to buy. Therefore, factors such as effective buying income, construction starts, utility usage rates, and general retail sales levels can be used and compared with the same statistics for earlier years to determine overall rate of growth, stability, or decline within a local economy.

The basic, and most essential, variable of the financial planning tools is the **sales forecast**. The percentage-sales method (used in Figure 11-4) is a common device to project sales in the next period or year. It is simply an extrapolation of past sales set in terms of the general economic conditions confronting the local economy. However, there are three other sales forecasting techniques a franchisor or franchisee can use: (1) extrapolation or trend analysis, including "grass roots" input; (2) executive decision making — setting sales goals by the management team; and (3) the more sophisticated econometrics or statistical modeling methods. The percentage-sales method used in Figure 11-4 is an extrapolation technique that requires the executive or management team to make key as-

Figure 11-4
Hypothetical Pro Forma Income Statement

Bonnie's Hot Tubs Inc.
Pro Forma Income Statement
for Year Ending December 31, 1986
and First Quarter Ending March 31, 1987

	Year Ended 12-31-86	Quarter Ended 3-31-87
Sales 100%	$1,000,000	$250,000
Cost of Goods Sold		
Labor	106,000	26,500
Materials	384,000	96,000
Overhead	78,000	19,500
Delivery	52,000	13,000
Subtotals	620,000	155,000
Gross Margin	380,000	95,000
Expenses		
Selling expense	137,000	34,250
General	57,000	14,250
Other	31,000	7,750
Subtotals	225,000	56,250
Operating Profit	155,000	38,750
Interest	12,000	3,000
Profit Before Taxes	143,000	35,750
Income taxes	64,350	16,100
Net Income	$ 78,650	$19,650

sumptions about the overall and local economies. Large franchised systems, such as large fast-food restaurants, auto parts/services, or major rental companies, often use all three techniques. The most commonly used technique is extrapolation or trend analysis, including "grass roots" input, in which the franchisor calls local franchisees or requests written estimates to evaluate future sales potential.

Pro Forma Balance Sheet

The cash budget is used to plan liquidity. The income statement is used to plan profitability for the franchise business. The **pro forma balance sheet** is a budget or plan of the assets and liabilities of the business. It is a natural extension of the cash budget and the income statement. Figure 11-5 presents a hypothetical pro forma balance sheet for Bonnie's Hot Tubs.

Figure 11-5
Hypothetical Pro Forma Balance Sheet

Bonnie's Hot Tubs Inc.
Pro Forma Balance Sheet
as of December 31, 1986 and March 31, 1987

	Year Ended 12-31-86	Quarter Ended 3-31-87
ASSETS		
Current Assets		
Cash	$ 180,000	$15,000
Investment	20,000	1,700
Accounts receivable	200,000	16,700
Raw materials	80,000	6,700
Finished goods	120,000	10,000
Total Current Assets	600,000	50,100
Fixed Assets	550,000	54,200
Less Depreciation	(−150,000)	(−29,200)
Total Assets	$1,000,000	75,100
LIABILITIES AND EQUITY		
Current Liabilities		
Notes payable	100,000	8,300
Accounts payable	50,000	4,200
Due franchisor	25,000	2,100
Interest payable	25,000	2,100
Total Current Liabilities	200,000	16,700
Long-term Liabilities	200,000	16,700
Stockholders' Equity	350,000	24,400
Retained earnings	250,000	17,300
Total Liabilities and Equity	$1,000,000	$75,100

The data contained within the pro forma balance sheet comes from the cash budget, any changes in taxes or retained earnings (the pro forma income statement), and the *actual* balance sheet variables contained in the last quarter's balance sheet. The pro forma balance sheet is not an audited financial statement, but rather is a *planning tool* which provides an analysis of what funds are needed to operate and effectively manage the franchised business. For example, to determine the first quarter's ending inventory for Bonnie's Hot Tubs, we would use the following equation:

Chapter 11   Financial Management and Fiscal Planning: Tools/Techniques   311

Beginning Inventory + Purchases
  = Costs of Goods Sold + Ending Inventory

Table 11-2
Determining Ending Inventory

Year-end inventory	xxx
Plus: Purchases during the current quarter	+ xxx
Equals: Total inventory available	xxx
Less: Cost of goods sold for current quarter	− xxx
Equals: Ending inventory, first quarter	xxx

Therefore, the various assumptions used in the cash budget and pro forma income statement affect the pro forma balance sheet. The inverse of this is true also. That is, the pro forma balance sheet affects the pro forma income statement and cash budget. Therefore, planned sales revenue, operating costs, asset development/depreciation, and liabilities are linked through these statements about future efforts planned within the franchised business.

SUCCESS STORY
RICHARD SNELL

Ramada Inns, Inc., headed by Richard Snell, chairman, president, and chief executive officer, is one of the world's largest hotel chains with 59 company-operated and 512 franchised properties worldwide at the end of 1984. The company began in 1954 when a group of investors purchased an inn in Flagstaff, Arizona. The group adopted the name "Ramada" and in 1959 sold its first franchise. In 1963, with 25 company-operated and 15 licensed Ramada Inns, Ramada went public and named one of its founding partners, Marion Isbell, as its president, chairman, and chief executive officer.

However, while most of the country continued to think of Ramada as merely a "roadside inn," the company was undergoing major changes. In the late 1970s, Ramada began repositioning its hospitality product. By 1981, it had spent approximately $70 million in redesign and refurbishment to upgrade its properties, and it introduced a new hotel concept, the Ramada Renaissance Hotel, to provide customers with a more elegant hotel in the moderate price range. Ramada also entered the gaming industry with its purchase of the Tropicana Hotel and Country Club in Las Vegas in 1979, and the completion of the Tropicana Hotel and Casino in Atlantic City, New Jersey, in 1981.

Yet the rapid growth and expansion into new and challenging markets had strained the company's financial resources. Ramada needed leadership that could carry it through difficult financial times, so in 1981, Ramada appointed board member Richard Snell chairman and chief executive officer of the then $415 million corporation.

As a result of Snell's pragmatic, no-nonsense approach to business, Ramada returned to financial stability and made great strides toward repositioning its hospitality product. In 1983, with 593 properties under the Ramada banner, the company reported a profit for the first time in three years. The Tropicana Hotels in Las Vegas and Atlantic City reported a nearly five-fold increase in operating income from 1982 to 1983. And by 1984, the Ramada system had opened 15 Renaissance Hotels worldwide and had invested approximately $625 million since 1981 in refurbishing existing hotels and inns. In 1985, Ramada introduced a new inn featuring a residential ambience.

Snell expresses his approach to management as one of "letting the people who know the business run it." But he still spends approximately 20 percent of his time visiting properties to get a feel for the cleanliness of the hotel and the friendliness of the people, or "lending dimension to what you see on paper."

Snell summarizes his thoughts about the Ramada franchise system as follows: "Ramada has gone through the pains of growing up and we've learned some valuable lessons. One of the primary lessons is that in our business, success is making people feel good, cared about, and confident in their environment, whether they are your customers, employees, or whomever. They are the ones who will make it or break it, and it's up to us to give them the encouragement they need to make it."

Photo and information provided courtesy of Richard Snell, August, 1985.

SUMMARY

Financial planning allows the franchisor and the franchisee as independent business owners to develop solid accounting systems and budgeting systems which are synchronized (or linked) with the sales goals of the franchised business. Financial planning enables the franchisor and franchisee to evaluate performance of the franchise system for the franchisor, and the franchised unit for the franchisee.

Figure 11-6 provides an overall view of the financial process, illustrat-

Chapter 11 Financial Management and Fiscal Planning: Tools/Techniques 313

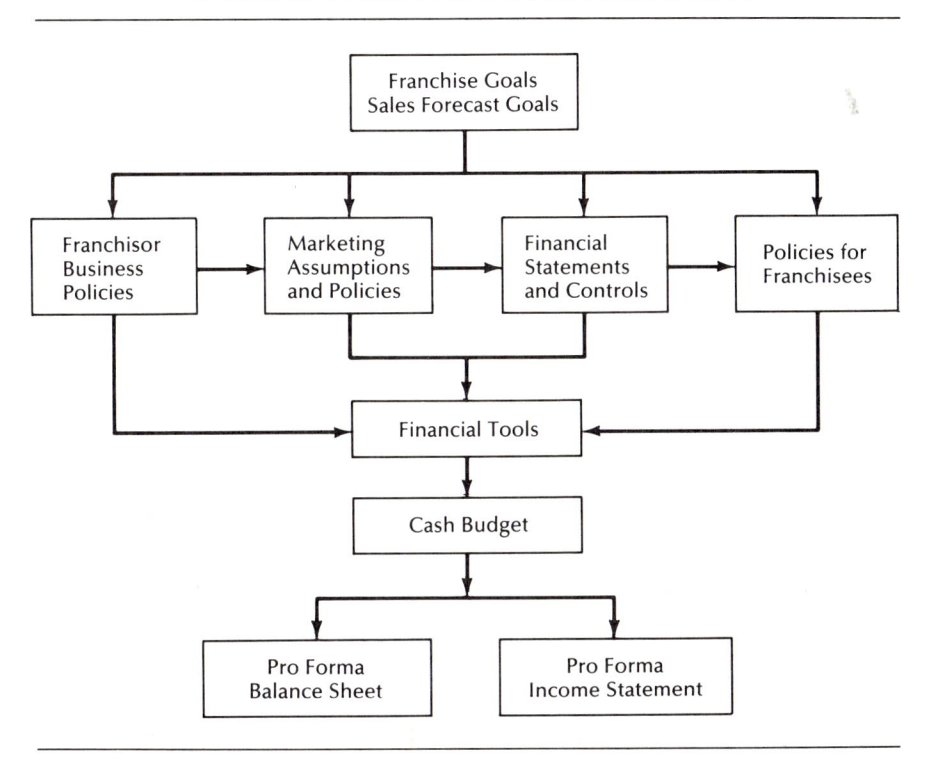

**Figure 11-6
Overview of Financial Process in a Franchised Business**

```
                    Franchise Goals
                    Sales Forecast Goals

  Franchisor      Marketing         Financial         Policies for
  Business   →    Assumptions  →    Statements   →    Franchisees
  Policies        and Policies      and Controls

                    Financial Tools

                    Cash Budget

           Pro Forma              Pro Forma
           Balance Sheet          Income Statement
```

ing the financial planning and budgeting process through the various financial tools necessary to complete this essential type of planning.

The financial planning process illustrated in Figure 11-2 begins with the franchise owner's goals and assumptions about how well the business can do given the economic and competitive conditions it confronts. The marketing, financial, and operating objectives of the franchise should be integrative and comprehensive for the franchise to be truly effective in following a strategy for success in the marketplace. The financial policies and objectives help establish the financial controls. The financial controls and financial statements help management understand what the past period's performance means in relation to what is planned for the future. This requires the franchisor or the franchisee to understand the use of financial tools. It is through the financial tools described in this chapter and the essentials of business finance presented in Chapter 10 that a cash budget, pro forma balance sheet, and pro forma income statement can be developed.

Appropriate use of these financial statements allows the franchised business to pursue effective working capital management, accounts-receivable management, inventory management, marketable securities and liquidity mangement, and short-term and long-term debt management. Figure 11-7 illustrates the balancing act a franchised business owner must perform. The owner seeks to achieve a balance between the inflow and outflow of cash through the accounts described in this chapter.

The financial planning process involves the development of a cash budget, followed by essential pro forma statements. These pro forma financial statements are useful to plan, coordinate, evaluate, and control the franchised business's operations. The overall planning documents are essential for financial forecasting and effective management of the franchised business.

Figure 11-7
"Balancing Act" Involved in Achieving Positive Cash Flow

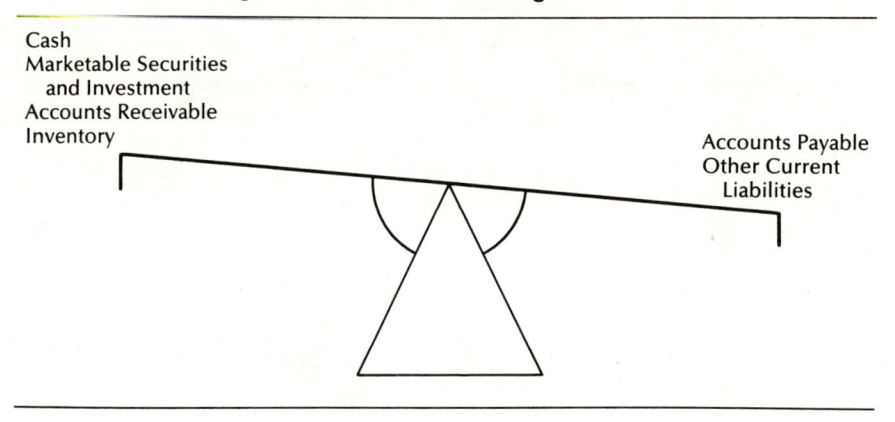

Cash
Marketable Securities
  and Investment
Accounts Receivable
Inventory

Accounts Payable
Other Current
Liabilities

REVIEW QUESTIONS

1. What is a cash budget?
2. What is a pro forma balance sheet?
3. What is a pro forma income statement?
4. How are each of these statements used in a franchised business?
5. What interrelationships exist between these statements?
6. Why should a franchised business be interested in financial planning?

CASE STUDY
YOUR FRANCHISED BUSINESS'S CASH FLOW

The figure provided identifies a projected cash flow for "Your Franchised Business." Sources of cash and anticipated disbursements for the next twelve months have been projected. Net profit amounts, loan payments, withdrawals, depreciation, and income tax payments have been carefully determined. The result is that a net cash flow as well as a cumulative cash

Your Franchised Business
Projected Cash Flow

	Preoper-ating	Oct	Nov	Dec	Jan	Feb	Mar	Apr	May	June	July	Aug	Sept	Total
Cash Sources														
Equity	$20,000	—	—	—	—	—	—	—	—	—	—	—	—	$ 20,000
Loan	$65,000	—	—	—	—	—	—	—	—	—	—	—	—	$ 65,000
Net Profit	0	478	1,001	2,234	1,738	1,491	1,745	1,749	1,752	2,008	2,010	2,264	2,267	$ 20,737
Depreciation	0	300	300	300	300	300	300	300	300	300	300	300	300	$ 3,600
Total	$85,000	778	1,301	2,534	2,038	1,791	2,045	2,049	2,052	2,308	2,310	2,564	2,567	$109,337
Disbursements														
Purchase of Business	$50,000	—	—	—	—	—	—	—	—	—	—	—	—	$ 50,000
Franchise Royalty Fee	$ 9,200	—	—	—	—	—	—	—	—	—	—	—	—	$ 9,200
Improvements and Equipment	$17,000	—	—	—	—	—	—	—	—	—	—	—	—	$ 17,000
Deposits	$ 1,400	—	—	—	—	—	—	—	—	—	—	—	—	$ 1,400
Loan Payments (Principal)	0	400	405	410	415	420	425	430	435	440	445	450	455	$ 5,130
Owner's Draw	0	1,000	1,000	1,000	1,200	1,200	1,200	1,200	1,200	1,200	1,200	1,200	1,200	$ 13,800
Income Taxes	0	—	—	—	—	—	—	1,047	—	—	—	—	—	$ 1,047
Total	$77,600	1,400	1,405	1,410	1,615	1,620	1,625	2,677	1,635	1,640	1,645	1,650	1,655	$ 97,577
Net Cash Flow	$ 7,400	(622)	(104)	1,124	423	171	420	(628)	417	668	665	914	912	$ 11,760
Cumulative Cash Flow	$ 7,400	6,778	6,674	7,798	8,221	8,392	8,812	8,184	8,601	9,269	9,934	10,848	11,760	

flow is available as a planning/control tool as well as a projection of cash sources and disbursements that can help others identify anticipated results of your business in its first year. After carefully examining the projected cash flow figures, answer the following questions.

CASE QUESTIONS

1. Why is a cash flow projection considered an important tool to both the franchisor and the franchisee?
2. Explain why the net cash flow figure is negative in October, November, and April of the projected year.
3. Given the total amount of cash available, does the anticipated disbursement of cash appear to be realistic?
4. Explain how this franchised business can have a total net profit in excess of $20,000, while the net cash flow is less than $11,760.

REFERENCES

1. Bank of America, "Buying a Franchise," *Small Business Reporter*, 1981.
2. _____, "Financing Small Business," *Small Business Reporter*, 1980.
3. Ernst & Whinney, *Deciding to Go Public — Understanding the Process and the Alternatives*, Ernst & Whinney No. 42323, 1984.
4. Henward, DeBanks M., and William Ginalski, *The Franchise Option*, Phoenix, AZ: Franchise Group Publishers, 1979.
5. Justis, Robert T., Richard J. Judd, and David B. Stephens, *Strategic Management and Policy: Concepts & Cases*, Englewood Cliffs, NJ: Prentice-Hall, Inc., 1985.
6. Thakur, Manab N., "How to Conduct Financial Analysis for Policy Casework," in Robert T. Justis, Richard J. Judd, and David B. Stephens, *Strategic Management and Policy: Concepts & Cases*, Englewood Cliffs, NJ: Prentice-Hall, Inc., 1985, pp. 617–639.
7. *The State of Small Business: A Report of the President*, Washington, DC: U.S. Government Printing Office, 1984.
8. Vaughn, Charles L., *Franchising*, 2nd edition, Lexington, MA: Lexington Books, 1979.

PART FOUR

THE FRANCHISE ARENA: OPERATING THE FRANCHISED BUSINESS

CHAPTER 12
DEVELOPING THE OPERATIONAL PROTOTYPE

In studying this chapter, you will:
- Learn the importance of an operational prototype to a franchised business.
- Understand major areas of emphasis in developing a prototype facility.
- Learn about uses a franchisor has for a prototype facility.
- Learn why a well-functioning prototype can have importance to persons other than the franchisor.

INCIDENT

Seven years ago, Joe and Mary Body began a lawn and landscaping business which they operated from their home part-time and on weekends. Joe worked for their state's Department of Conservation as a horticulturist. Mary is talented in art, sculpture, and abstract design. By pooling their abilities, Mary and Joe realized they had the capability to design unique and very attractive lawns, gardens, and landscapes for residential as well as commercial properties.

Three years ago, Joe left his job to devote full-time effort to the rapidly growing business. Mary also began to work full-time. Operating out of their home had become impractical, so they moved the business into a commercial location along the highway near the edge of town that had five acres of ground available for use by the business. No structural modification of the building was needed. Joe used three acres to assemble an interesting array of plants, trees, and displays which showed various textures, shapes, and overlapping natural forms that can be used in landscape design. Mary developed illustrations of lawns, gardens, and landscapes for homes as well as commercial buildings with limited or spacious, flat or sloping grounds. Customers could use these displays to develop the type of design most suitable to their location and structure.

The equipment used by Joe and Mary is standard for their type of business. The difference is in their unique compositions, use of space, and designs available to make the "perfect" landscape.

Today their business is booming. They have nine employees and are considering opening another location in a town of similar size 60 miles away. Their first idea was that Joe would run one store and Mary the other, but they realize an expansion would not work. *Both* Mary's and Joe's talents are needed for their business to be successful. So they started thinking about franchising.

Joe and Mary found they had a number of questions about franchising. Could they put together a training manual and develop a training program of the fundamental elements they found so successful in their business? If they were to seek franchisees, should they train them in their existing location? What are the truly essential components of their operation that every franchisee should be required to utilize? What type of store design or layout should they have, and what type and amount of equipment? Should they have a grand opening for a franchisee-operated store?

As each question comes up, Joe and Mary are not discouraged. Rather, they are becoming more interested and excited about the possibility of operating a franchised business.

INTRODUCTION

Before a business has a meaningful chance for successful expansion, one or more pilot operations should be opened and operating successfully. Successful expansion is based on tested and proven ideas which have been found desirable by customers and which have proven profitable to the entrepreneur.

Before starting a franchise, one must first determine which business arena to enter. After putting together the necessary resources, the franchisor opens one or perhaps two or three pilot operations in different marketing or geographic areas. The first operation should be well planned, with careful consideration given to location, building design, interior design, fixtures, equipment, store layout, and ambience, as well as the product or service to be offered. Effective advertising, record keeping, marketing, production controls, financial planning and controls, and employee and franchisee training approaches need to be developed. The startup of a franchised pilot operation is identical to the startup of a typical retail business, with the following exception: Plans for growth of the firm to become a multi-unit operation should be part of the initial business plan. The store prototype is essential to the growth plan of the franchisor. It is part of the overall plan development which we discussed in Chapter 3. The major components of prototype development are identified in Table 12-1.

AREAS OF EMPHASIS IN PROTOTYPE DEVELOPMENT

The seven areas of prototype development to be considered and planned by a franchisor include product/markets, site selection, facility construction, opening-day considerations, management/training, purchasing/finance development, and quality control. These areas are the ABC's of developing a prototype operation. A prototype serves various purposes. It is a pilot operation within which much of the testing of new product, modification of operations work schedules and work routines, physical placement of equipment, interior design and ambiences, and other factors are considered in order to achieve efficiency in operation, appropriate product/service presentation to the consumer, fair pricing, efficient customer service, and effective advertising and on-site promotions, as well as effective administrative policies and procedures for management of employees. The prototype facility is the model from which the franchisor tests market acceptance of products and services and develops administrative approaches to efficiently and effectively plan, organize, and control the franchised business. We will discuss each of the major areas of emphasis in the order in which they appear in Table 12-1.

Products/Marketing

A prototype store is where customer reactions to products or services are first tested. Because product development is integral to surviving in to-

Table 12-1
Areas of Emphasis in Prototype Development

- Products/Marketing
- Site Selection for Prototype Unit
- Construction of a Prototype Unit
- Opening-Day Considerations
- Prototype Unit as a Training Center
- Purchasing of Supplies and Materials
- Quality Control

day's sophisticated, segmented markets, the prototype must properly display and effectively market the products that will be offered to the public. New products should be tested for quality, consistency, and customer appeal in this operation. The prototype is thus used as the test-market location and as a center for product development for the franchise system.

Marketing, advertising, and promotion are important to the success of a franchised business. Through the prototype operation, marketing tactics and strategies can be tested and evaluated. The likelihood of consumers to buy the product or service, consumption patterns, and the controllable marketing variables used to satisfy the target market are all measured by the franchisor. Market research and analyses identify types of customer groupings, sales potential for a particular franchised unit by geographic site, potential sales in the industry, appropriate channels of distribution between franchisor and franchised units, and effectiveness of advertising and promotion. However, much of the value of market research at this stage of the franchise system's development is that it provides preliminary information to assist in shaping the overall marketing and distribution scheme. Market research will not guarantee customer purchases or satisfied customers. But the prototype facility provides an opportunity for the franchisor to test and evaluate customers' preferences in order to provide at least some general information about decisions to purchase.

The prototype facility provides an opportunity for the franchisor to determine if the product or service will have enduring customer appeal and if the products are effectively packaged, presented, or displayed. The prototype also enables the franchisor to try out different merchandise displays, which can be easily changed in order to make them more appealing to customers. The product/market information gathered at the prototype facility can be examined in light of other factors about the franchise system which are also monitored at the prototype facility, such as approaches to administrative control, scale of operation to profitability, and other factors including rate of employee turnover, training costs, and labor costs per unit of output.

Site Selection

One of the biggest concerns of both franchisors and franchisees is choosing appropriate sites for offering the product or service. Unless the franchisor is a seasoned veteran in location analysis, site selection is a risky business. Because it is important to determine the best possible site for a proposed franchised unit, the franchisor and franchisees must carefully analyze demographics and such specific factors of a location as physical characteristics of the property and routes of access.

The primary reason to have two or more prototype operating units is that it enables the franchisor to compare how products or services are received by customers in different markets. Regional tastes, customs, and employment patterns can suggest the reason for differences in buyer preferences for some types of franchised businesses. For example, franchises utilizing temporary employment tend to flourish in urban settings experiencing economic growth. In affluent suburbs of major cities on the East and West Coasts, pastel colors, mirrors, brass, marble, and rich woods are being used instead of Formica and metal in the interiors of fast-food restaurants to add individual style and sophistication. Also, certain products may sell better in one region than in another. Soup may be a big seller in New England, while chili may be preferred in the Midwest and South. Also, location within a community can affect the level of sales for a particular franchised operation. Certain locations of a city may attract some types of customers while other locations may attract other types. For example, a seafood-restaurant franchise may try to establish a location convenient for middle to upper-income families. A franchisor needs to understand the variances in buyer tastes and preferences that exist across regions as well as within communities, in order to offer the best mix of products or services to the customers in a particular locale.

Another reason a franchisor may wish to have two or more prototype units is to determine the various strengths and weaknesses of each prototype, provided, of course, that the operational, location, or design characteristics differ. Comparisons can be made between differing prototypes to determine if the unique characteristics affect operational efficiency, volume of sales, or customer attitudes about location, convenience, interior/exterior design, or ambience. The franchisor can thus obtain information that can be applied to future site selection, design, and operational layout. This type of information can help both franchisors and franchisees realize greater market acceptance and penetration, as well as enhanced potential for profitability in the long run.

Site selection is typically not a quick process. It may take from two months to a year to choose the site for the initial prototype, and the same amount of time to find a site for each additional prototype. For example, a franchisor must make certain that materials and supplies can be readily shipped to the location, determine the relative costs of promotion per target customer, and estimate the relative strength of existing competition before making the final decision about where to locate a prototype.

Construction of a Prototype

One of the most interesting experiences for a budding franchisor is the development of the first prototype unit. Usually, detailed plans are developed and the details for the building and interior layout are specified. Modifications are often made, however, as the building is constructed.

The visual appearance of the store exterior or interior, and even the operations layout, may be changed from the original blueprints. Additional construction materials may be necessary, and even an entire floor plan for the unit could be changed. The reasons for such changes vary widely. The operational space available, based on the blueprints, may not be sufficient or may be too great in relation to the space available for customers. Entrance and exit doors may be more convenient to customers when placed to one end of an exterior wall rather than in the center of the wall. Table or aisle space can be too much or too little. The number of windows and their location may need to change as the site is developed, based on amount of afternoon sun, direction of winds, nearness of other buildings constructed since the site was chosen, or existence of trees, fences, or other obstructions not accounted for in the blueprints.

It is important for the franchisor to choose a licensed, experienced contractor. The contractor should see that all subcontracts are cost-competitive, provide advice or directly assist in blueprint preparation, and make certain that all licensing requirements and local ordinances or codes are met. Regular visits to the site by the franchisor will help ensure that plans are being followed correctly and any misunderstandings based on blueprint modifications or other problems are minimized.

Construction of the facility takes time. It can take from three months to over a year to build a prototype, depending on the business activity and the type of building required. Construction of hotel/motel facilities will almost certainly take much longer than construction of a 1,000-square-foot store, and certainly much longer than a 100-square-foot drive-up photoprocessing pickup/delivery station. Although actual construction time may be greater than originally anticipated, it is important that the building and fixed facilities meet the needs of the franchised business. The knowledge and experience gained from going through a facility development — from blueprint design to turning the key on opening day — are invaluable to the franchisor in future design and construction. The original franchised unit may cost the franchisor time, energy, and anguish, but subsequent site constructions may run much more smoothly because of the lessons learned in building the first prototype. Figure 12-1 illustrates the interior layout of a pharmacy store. Note the placement of displays, the location of the prescription drug counter, the organization of the merchandise departments, and the space allotted for efficient customer movement that helps establish and maintain security.

Opening-Day Considerations

A thrill to many business owners is the grand opening of their new store. Even franchisors with hundreds of locations get excited about the opening of an additional unit. However, no matter how well a franchisor has

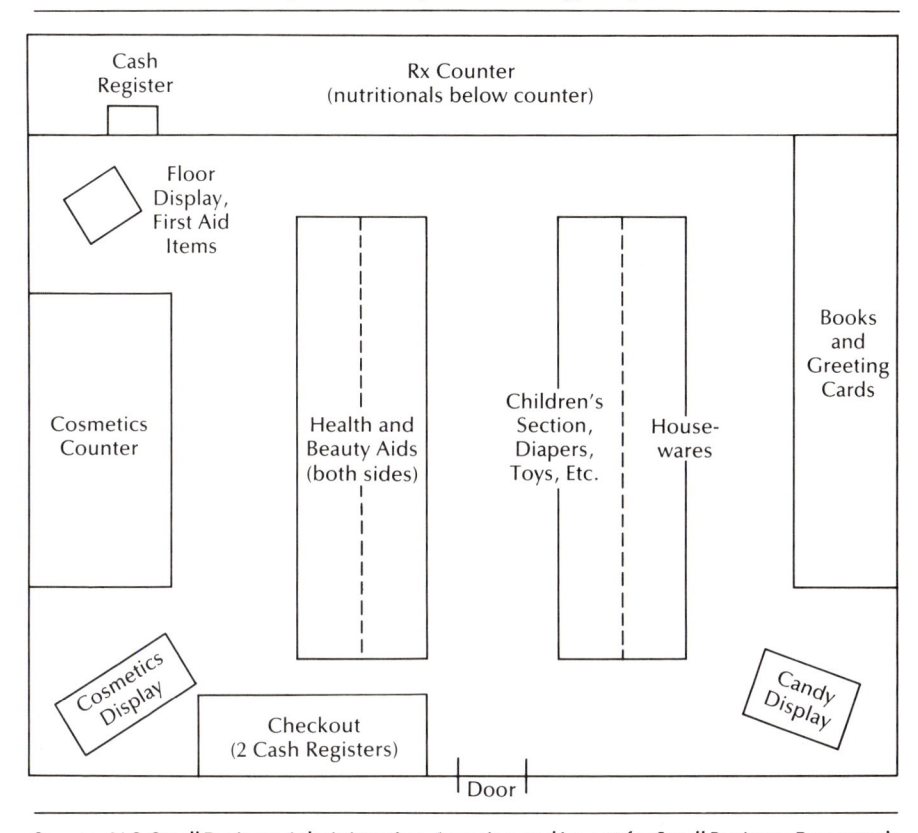

**Figure 12-1
Sample Pharmacy Store Prototype Layout**

```
┌─────────────────────────────────────────────────────────────┐
│   Cash              Rx Counter                              │
│ Register      (nutritionals below counter)                  │
│   ┌─┐                                                       │
├───┴─┴───────────────────────────────────────────────────────┤
│                                                             │
│        ◇  Floor                                   ┌──────┐  │
│           Display,                                │      │  │
│           First Aid                               │      │  │
│           Items                                   │      │  │
│  ┌──────┐         ┌──────┐   ┌──────┐             │Books │  │
│  │      │         │      │   │      │             │ and  │  │
│  │      │         │      │   │      │             │Greet.│  │
│  │Cosm. │         │Health│   │Child.│  ┌──────┐   │Cards │  │
│  │Cntr. │         │ and  │   │Sect. │  │House-│   │      │  │
│  │      │         │Beauty│   │Diaper│  │wares │   │      │  │
│  │      │         │ Aids │   │Toys, │  │      │   │      │  │
│  │      │         │(both │   │ Etc. │  │      │   │      │  │
│  │      │         │sides)│   │      │  │      │   │      │  │
│  │      │         │      │   │      │  │      │   │      │  │
│  └──────┘         └──────┘   └──────┘  └──────┘   └──────┘  │
│     ◇ Cosmetics                                     ◇ Candy│
│       Display         Checkout                       Display│
│                   (2 Cash Registers)                        │
├────────────────────────┬─────┬──────────────────────────────┤
                         │Door │
```

Source: U.S. Small Business Administration, *Location and Layout for Small Business*, Presentor's Guide Series (Washington, DC: U.S. Government Printing Office), p. 41.

prepared, there are still going to be questions that simply can't be answered until opening day or the period just prior to opening. Will there be sufficient people available to hire who have the necessary skills to staff the business? Will the location attract enough customers for the unit to be profitable? Will customers come back once they have tried the product? Will they be pleased with the appearance and the operation of the new store? Will it be possible to effectively hire and train the staff within the time allotted? The answers to such questions will come, sometimes pleasantly and sometimes not. In any event, the franchisor will spend a great deal of time at that first prototype unit. Work days of 12 or 16 hours are not uncommon for the franchisor during the first several weeks after the opening of the prototype unit.

The franchisor has a key role to play in opening the first franchised unit: to instruct the staff about proper sales techniques, work flow, inventory ordering, storage of supplies, sales displays, and methods of attracting as well as increasing sales. The franchisor is the primary source of information for the staff concerning the products, work processes, and techniques for ensuring that proper bookkeeping and accounting procedures are being followed and that materials or food, labor, and supplies are being used within the anticipated guidelines of cost and quality. Also, by being present at closing time, the franchisor has the opportunity to discuss operational problems that might have arisen during the day, customer complaints, or ways to improve sales.

The time of the grand opening is when new advertising and sales promotion efforts are heaviest. Local celebrities, or even the mayor or the governor, may be invited to participate in the ribbon-cutting ceremony that marks the opening of the prototype. In an attempt to reach as wide an audience as possible, the franchisor will often invite other local business people, community leaders, and the news media, and will have a written history and description of the business available to interested persons attending the event. Copies of this literature are often provided to the various news media several days before the grand opening, so that media representatives can present their coverage of the opening as part of that day's news.

The franchisor will spend the first several weeks and possibly months developing, implementing, and monitoring each facet of the business in accordance with the standards of operation established for the prototype. Inventory will be reviewed for turnover, sales will be examined in terms of unit cost and profitability by product, and overall sales level of the facility will be studied in light of drawing power in the market. Management style, employee incentives or commissions, and wage levels by job type should be evaluated to ensure internal wage consistency among jobs within the prototype unit as well as among similar jobs within the community. Through such careful examination of the actual operation of the prototype facility, the franchisor can determine if the objectives, work plans, operational procedures, and levels of sales are appropriate to a continuing and profitable franchised facility.

Prototype Unit as a Training Center

Almost all franchisors develop training manuals for use by beginning franchisees. In some franchised businesses, the only training new franchisees receive is on the job and in their spare time by reading the operations manual provided by the franchisor. Many franchisors try to provide training for their franchisees in the controlled environment of the prototype facility, which is a good place to break in new franchisees, as well as to train existing franchisees in new reporting procedures, use of new equipment, changes in technology, or managerial skills in employee and customer relations.

A franchisor can require franchisees to attend a training program. Typically, a prototype facility provides the greatest learning opportunity for new franchisees, since there they can get from one to three weeks or more of actual experience in running a franchised unit (see Table 12-2). As a franchise system grows, it may be beneficial to establish additional training centers throughout the entire market region. Multiple prototype facilities can reduce travel expenses for franchisees attending training programs and enable the franchisor to have facilities that differ in size, layout, and method of operation for comparative testing of ways to better serve customers. A few large franchisors have established separate facilities to train hundreds, even thousands, involved in becoming franchisees of their system. For example, McDonald's has its Hamburger University near Chicago, Illinois, Holiday Inns of America has a training center in Olive Branch, Mississippi, and Midas's Institute of Technology is located in Chicago, Illinois. Other franchise systems, including Wendy's and Kentucky Fried Chicken, have multiple training centers or prototype units.

At the prototype facility, new franchisees (and sometimes members of their staffs) are introduced to the major facets of operating the franchised business. A new franchisee who will be running a restaurant will learn approved, effective methods of cleaning frying pans, ovens, stoves, grills, and grease pits. The franchisee will also learn about each piece of equipment — size, function, durability, and cost — and the specifications of the furniture to be used in the unit. The trainee will be given the opportunity to actually use meat and bread slicers, electric mixers, and peelers, as well as be taught the correct temperature settings for refrigerators and freezers and appropriate placement of worktables, dishwashers, and sinks. Any word processing equipment recommended by the franchisor will ordinarily be used in the training program too. If a

Table 12-2
Length of Training Program for Franchisees

Length of Total Training Program for Franchisees	Total, All Companies	Fast Food and Beverage	Nonfood Retailing	Personal Services	Business Products/ Services
5 days or less	13.5%	3.5%	9.8%	23.0%	21.5%
6 to 10 days	16.3	19.3	14.6	13.5	17.8
More than 10 days	70.2	77.2	75.6	63.5	60.7
	100.0%	100.0%	100.0%	100.0%	100.0%

Note: Based on information reported by 189 franchise companies. Includes 57 franchisors of fast foods and beverages, 45 of nonfood consumer products, 58 of personal services, and 29 of business (or industrial) products and services.

Source: E. Patrick McGuire, *Franchised Distribution* (New York: The Conference Board).

computer is to be used by the franchisee, the trainee will receive instruction in its use for cash management and accounting of receivables and payables. Not surprisingly, because there is much for the franchisee to learn, the training sessions required by the successful franchise systems are rigorous. In fact, as one franchisor has put it, "When a prospective franchisee compares living at the prototype with training received at boot camp, then the prototype training is a success!"

One method of training new franchisees is for the franchisor or other headquarters staff to role-play different "types" the franchisee may encounter. The average customer, the cheating employee, the dictatorial manager, and the panhandler looking for a free meal — all are roles typically enacted. By not knowing just what will come next, the franchisee-in-training learns how to deal with the uncertainties of operating a business and the changing demands on his or her managerial skills before being faced with these kinds of situations in reality. Development of managerial skills is very important. It is generally held by franchisors in the computer software business, for example, that computer expertise is not required to operate a franchise. The tendency is that computer experts can answer the technical questions but are not necessarily capable of running a store. The winning formula has been found to include a combination of solid management and training.

Purchasing Supplies and Materials

Purchasing the right products in the right quantities at the right price is a very difficult task for most franchise owners. Initially, many products are bought from suppliers who visit the store. However, it may be more profitable and sensible for the franchisor to seek competitive bids from alternative suppliers of the services or products. One franchised restaurateur in the Pacific Northwest, for example, prepays for the firm's total fish supply from a seafood warehouse during the early fall to ensure sufficient supplies during winter months.

The prototype facility is the unit at which the franchisor can develop product, supply, and material specifications, and determine the appropriate price/quantity standards for cost-effective purchasing throughout the system. These standards, developed through the franchisor's experiences at the prototype, will be the guideposts used by new franchisees in purchasing supplies and materials for their franchised units.

Franchisees are generally free to purchase supplies at whatever prices and in whatever quantities they desire, as long as the supplies meet the standards of the franchise system. Franchisees can develop virtually their own approach to purchasing for the business. However, because many franchisors can purchase supplies in much greater quantities than a single franchisee can, the franchisee can often reduce costs by buying from the franchisor.

The prototype unit provides the franchisor with the opportunity to study costs. For many franchised businesses operating in retail and service sectors, competition from chains, independent businesses, and other franchise systems can be keen. Control of stock by type of item and minimum quantity needed is based on analysis of past sales and which items have sold profitably. Also, services offered to the customer by the franchise, such as delivery, gift wrapping, clothing alterations, and weekend or evening hours, will affect costs and so should be analyzed to determine which services are important to attract repeat business. At some franchised outlets, such as auto rental agencies and beauty salons, franchisees will often provide magazines and newspapers or even television, so that customers won't mind the wait quite so much and will thus be more likely to return. But each additional service has a cost that must ultimately be included in the price paid by the customer. By not providing a service, the franchise may be able to pass the cost savings on to the customer through lower prices; however, some segments of a market may demand that particular service. The franchisor must therefore learn what services are important to the market segment and determine the costs associated with those services in developing the pricing strategy.

In franchised service businesses, service is the primary product sold, with parts or warranties typically secondary. These businesses prosper when customers are satisfied and keep coming back. In service businesses, increased productivity is usually achieved through better utilization and performance of personnel.

A franchisor should determine standard costs for a product or service, including the fixed and variable costs associated with each unit sold. Because advancements in productivity in labor-intensive service fields have not kept up with those in manufacturing fields, skillful planning and tight controls are needed to ensure continuing improvements in efficiency of operation of franchised service businesses. The prototype unit is often the laboratory for testing methods of operation, identifying standards for supplies, establishing performance levels, trying out new machinery or work processes, and developing job descriptions appropriate to the work activities within the operation.

Careful planning and control are important in order to keep a lid on costs of food, materials, equipment, supplies, and labor. As these costs become excessive, profits are inevitably lowered. Since most financial problems that can arise in the franchisee's unit will occur in the prototype store, this store can be a valuable facility for the franchisor and franchisees to help identify general strengths and weaknesses of the system's operations.

Quality Control

The success of a multi-unit franchised business typically depends on standardization of product or service, work processes, and extra services offered to the customer. Customers expect the same quality of products and services throughout the entire franchise system. A customer of a franchised computer store in Tampa, Florida, would expect the same product, warranties, and services after sale at a Portland, Oregon, outlet. The purpose of quality control is to check the products or services offered within the franchise system to make sure they consistently meet certain standards. Quality control in a franchised business can apply to the operations of the business, from selection of appropriate materials and supplies down to the performance of the last task that provides the finished product or service to the customer. Ideally, quality control will reduce waste of materials (input side) and minimize rejects and customer dissatisfaction (output side).

Standards of quality should be kept at a level that will attract and maintain customers. In a competitive market, this means standards should be relatively high. While advertising may attract customers for their initial visit or purchase, it is the quality of operations and product or service that satisfies customers and brings them back for more purchases.

The quality-control program is developed in the prototype facility. A good quality-control program helps reduce waste while increasing potential for profitability. The franchisor should cover quality control in the appropriate manuals, discussing how to test for defective products and identifying the upper and lower quality-control limits of the business. For example, a franchised restaurant system may provide latitude for franchisees to assemble their hamburgers but place limits on the fat content, diameter, and thickness of the patty. As a franchise system grows, field representatives often work with franchisees to check for product defects and try to help franchisees prevent defects in the first place.

Some quality-control problems may be intrinsic to the production/operation process itself. If the problem is associated with the employee performing a task unsatisfactorily, the employee should be made aware of the problem, retrained in order to eliminate the problem, or, if necessary, replaced. If the problem is due to faulty machinery, the machine should be adjusted or replaced. But if the quality-control problem lies in the operational system itself, the system should be analyzed and constructively changed. It does no good for the franchisee to blame employees, as this will not solve the problem and will probably strain working relations. The franchisor representative, the franchisee, and the employees should share in discussion of ways to improve quality of products or services; this will help build commitment to and responsibility for achieving and maintaining the standards of the system. The successful franchise systems are very aware of this need to maintain high quality-control standards. Ford Motor, for example, has demonstrated its awareness by stressing in some of its advertisements that "quality is job one."

BUILDING SUCCESSFUL FRANCHISES

An important key to developing a successful franchise system is to use the operational prototype effectively. The time, money, and management skill required to develop this pilot unit can be the most important factors in ensuring a profitable franchise system. Regardless of the nature of the franchised business, franchisors are realizing the importance of proper prototype development. The prototype serves as the model unit where techniques and procedures factors for system expansion are developed for implementation.

National Video, Inc., a renter of video cassettes based in Portland, Oregon, started out with no prototype and had no corporate-owned operation of any kind until there were several hundred units in place. Then in the fourth year of business and with a great deal of time and money, it developed a prototype. Since then the prototype has helped the franchisor to sell hundreds of additional franchises.[1]

Developmental Stage

The prototype outlet is the hands-on, experimental facility for the franchisor where new products are tested and some merchandised, and in which operational processes are examined to develop the best work flow possible for the business. Developing an effective prototype facility may take months or even years. Remember, the prototype is the model unit upon which the entire franchise system is to be built. Unless the prototype can meet consumer demands and can change with consumer preferences over time, there will be no need to expand beyond the initial unit. Likewise, unless the operating system, processes, policies, and controls are effectively managed such that a reasonable profit can be made, there also will be no need to consider expansion.

A smoothly running prototype unit has more importance to the franchisor than just its profitability. The franchisor also uses the prototype to sell prospective franchisees on the franchise system, as well as to attract interest in the system from other financial sources. Commercial loan officers are far more impressed with a smoothly operating store than with a feasibility study when they are determining loan worthiness and lending limits. Some may even want to pay a visit to the prototype unit prior to making a loan decision.

As one can see, the prototype unit can serve a variety of purposes. However, there are five principal reasons a franchisor should develop an operational prototype: (1) to design interior work and customer-service layouts; (2) to develop and test training procedures; (3) to establish appropriate financial planning and control systems and procedures; (4) to

---

[1] Ron Berger, President, National Video, Inc., letter to author, April 1, 1988.

develop, test, and fine-tune advertising and other marketing techniques; and (5) to provide a proving ground for examination of business concepts, strategies, and procedures.

A franchisor should test different layouts to determine the most appropriate use of space, the most efficient work flow, and the best customer traffic patterns. New training methods as well as new materials to be used in training franchisees are typically tried out at the prototype before being implemented by field staff or included in training programs offered to new franchisees. The financial goals, cost standards, and reporting mechanisms should be tested and evaluated in the prototype before being implemented throughout a franchise system. Also, questions about advertising displays, sales promotions, and media mix can be answered before major resources are committed. Perhaps most important to the franchisor is to answer the question, Is my entrepreneurial idea and approach to business amenable to being franchised? For the business to effectively grow, it must be set up in such a way that someone else can be taught to run the business, while being profitable enough to provide for a sharing of those profits between the franchisee and the franchisor and still provide sufficient motivation for both parties to seek efficiency in operations and high volumes of sales.

Prototype as a Misleading Sales Tool

Unfortunately, a prototype facility can be improperly used as a misleading sales tool to sell franchise opportunities to people and then provide little or no value after the new franchisee has already invested in the business. Several franchisors have had lawsuits brought against them charging fraud and misrepresentation for the purpose of the sale of franchises based on the prototype operation.

In the late 1970s, a franchise system built a prototype store in a major California shopping center. It spent large sums of money to advertise and promote that particular unit. Potential franchisees were brought in to see the unit and examine its impressive sales records. Once franchisees bought into the franchise system, however, they could not seem to match the prototype's sales figures, and they complained about this to the franchisor. These franchisees had built their new units exactly according to the franchisor's specifications and designs, and they had followed the recommended procedures for operating the units, but none of them could duplicate the success of the franchisor's prototype unit. In time, disgruntled franchisees left the system, and ultimately the franchise system went out of business.

Prototype as a Special Place

The prototype facility is used by the franchisor as proof that the franchise system can operate successfully, as a facility to train prospective franchisees, and as the experimental unit in the chain. As a result, it is often pampered and closely directed by the franchisor.

Some franchisors have learned that it may not be appropriate or even possible to have a standard operation or standard facility (in appearance, amount of space, or even interior layout). Some find it necessary to tailor the essential components of their franchised business to the various demographic, cultural, or geographic features of their locations. For instance, many computer businesses, day-care centers, realtors, and banks have found it inappropriate to "clone" prototype appearances or specify recommended work flow. However, while the prototype may differ from the actual franchised units in the specifics of decor, work process, or even size, it still plays an important role in establishing standards for the franchise system, evaluating types of services to be offered, developing product specifications, and even recommending effective advertising tactics and sales approaches. First Interstate Bancorp of California has franchised banks throughout the world, none of which look precisely alike. Yet these franchises offer many of the same or similar services in their respective financial markets.

Financial Credibility

As we have suggested, the prototype is a model from which potential franchisees and other interested persons can develop an understanding of the franchised business, including what performance level is expected of a single unit involved in the sales and distribution of the franchisor's product. One group potentially interested in learning more about the franchised business is members of the financial community. Financial investors examining investment opportunities seek limited partnerships in ventures that demonstrate solid potential to succeed. Also, after visiting the prototype, banks or other lenders can form firmer opinions about the amount of money they would be willing to lend and the interest rate on that amount. For example, Ron Berger of National Video found that because he had no track record, banks were not interested in his venture and growth plans. But after he developed the prototype and had hundreds of units in operation, numerous banks believed the franchise would be a good investment and offered financing for the various franchisees.[2]

Having a prototype in operation helps the franchisor's expansion plans. Many regional shopping malls, for example, are hard to enter without a profitable track record. A smooth-running and profitable prototype can provide the evidence of success for a franchised business intent on expansion. And, expansion into prime locations inside shopping malls,

[2] Berger.

as well as well-chosen independent locations, is of vital importance to the success of many retail and service franchised businesses.

Although the costs and amount of work required in the creation of the prototype can be extensive, the rewards can also be great. A prototype that runs as smoothly as the franchisor intends will provide satisfaction to the franchisor. The payoff for the time and energy will come through franchising fees, royalty payments, and other money paid to the franchisor by the franchisees.

SUCCESS STORY
SAMUEL MARVIN

The concept for Barn'rds International was developed by Samuel Marvin. An owner of 15 Arby's Roast Beef restaurants, Marvin wanted to develop a higher-quality and better-focused operation that would capitalize on trends toward more healthful eating and certain styles of dining.

Barn'rds primary concept is to take the basic foods in demand by the majority of Americans and develop a series of systems to serve a fresher and tastier menu to the consumer than that offered by anyone else in the market.

In 1980, Marvin used a mock-up of a store built in a warehouse to work out the production flows of the food items that would ultimately become the staples of the Barn'rds menu.

After that, Marvin entered into partnership with Philip James, who had spent the previous 15 years building a large, successful company. James sold that company so that he could devote his time to Barn'rds.

Subsequently, Barn'rds franchises have opened in Iowa, Kansas, Nebraska, Colorado, and Texas. Franchisees must strictly follow the Barn'rds system, especially in food preparation. It is this commitment to the tested Barn'rds system that ensures the high level of quality that will attract customers and keep them coming back.

Photo and information provided courtesy of Samuel Marvin, August, 1985.

SUMMARY

In this chapter we have focused on elements a franchisor should **consider** before establishing the first franchised unit. We have presented **seven areas** of emphasis in the development of the franchisor's pilot or prototype facility. Each area was discussed to show why such a facility is important to the franchisor and why it may be of importance to others with potential interest in the franchisor's business, such as potential franchisees, investors, and commercial lenders.

A franchisor should take great care in developing a prototype facility. It is here that the product is tested for customer reaction, new products are screened, advertising displays are evaluated, franchisees are trained, interior design and work flow approaches are analyzed, and standards of operation and accounting are developed, questioned, and modified. The prototype will be unique within the franchise system by virtue of the various purposes it serves. It is from this facility that many of the system's improvements in product and procedure are initiated, evaluated, and instituted.

REVIEW QUESTIONS

1. Why is it important that one or more prototype facilities be developed prior to site selection for franchised units?
2. What are the basic areas of emphasis a franchisor should consider in developing a prototype?
3. What is the prototype's importance in training franchisees in the operations involved in running a franchise?
4. Why is a franchisor's prototype facility important to people other than the franchisor? Who are those other interested parties and why would they be interested in the prototype?
5. A prototype can be a tool used by a franchisor to mislead the public, potential franchisees, and investors or creditors. How does this occur? What can a franchisor do to ensure that the prototype does not mislead the public?

CASE STUDY
MICHELLE'S FORMAL-WEAR BUSINESS

Michelle has owned her own formal-wear business for the last three years. Her annual sales are close to $160,000, with average rental fees between $35 and $50. Dressing up is becoming more and more fashionable, with occasions such as weddings, black-tie dinners, proms, debutante balls, and formal business affairs.

Michelle is determined to branch out and franchise her business. She wants to use her current location as the main or prototype store, but is wondering if she should redecorate or remodel, since new and prospective franchisees will be using this shop as the showcase. She knows her location needs to be fashionable as well as readily accessible.

Michelle believes she must provide a complete turnkey operation to prospective franchisees. She must design and construct the interior layout and decor of each store, stock it, hire and train personnel, and develop a grand opening program. Each shop must be established in a very competitive and choice location. Michelle must also develop sales strategies that will appeal to the bride, because the vast majority of the time the bride determines the tuxedo style and color to coordinate with the rest of the bridal party.

Estimated Startup Costs

Franchising Fee	$12,500
Equipment and Furnishings	$ 8,000 - $10,000
Inventory	$50,000 - $60,000
Leasehold Improvements	$15,000 - $40,000
TOTAL	$85,500 - $122,500

The formal-wear business has an unusually high gross profit margin because of the low ratio of cost of goods to price for rental.

Michelle is also thinking of changing the store name and image before franchising. Some names that she feels might be successful include "The Formal Boutique," "Formal Wear International," or even something using her own name. What should she do to get started in franchising?

CASE QUESTIONS

1. What kind of prototype store is necessary for a formal-wear business?
2. Is the prototype store important? Why?
3. What should be done at the prototype or display store?
4. Is Michelle ready to franchise? Why or why not?

REFERENCES

1. Curry, J. A., et al., *Partners for Profit*, New York: American Management Association, 1966.
2. McDonald's Corporation, *Annual Report for 1981*.
3. McGuire, E. Patrick, *Franchised Distribution*, New York: The Conference Board, Inc.
4. "Franchising: The Strings Attached to Being Your Own Boss," *Changing Times* (September 1984), pp. 69–74.

5. "Small Is Beautiful — A New Survey of Hot Growth Companies," *Business Week* (May 27, 1985), pp. 88–98.
6. "Franchise Facts: Softening Up Software Customers," *Venture* (June 1985), p. 144.
7. Vaughn, Charles L., *Franchising*, 2nd edition, Lexington, MA: Lexington Books, 1979.
8. "Where's the Beef in Franchising?" *Money* (March 1985), pp. 149–152.

CHAPTER 13
ADMINISTRATION AND OPERATION OF THE FRANCHISE PACKAGE

In studying this chapter, you will:
- Learn why a franchisor has an administrative and an operations package.
- Learn about the components of the administrative and operations packages.
- Understand the purpose of the franchisor's brochure and what information is included in the brochure.
- Learn why franchisors develop informational manuals for franchisee trainees and for prospective franchisees.

INCIDENT

Betty would like to open a franchised donut business. She has sought information from large franchisors with well-known names and solid reputations and has narrowed the field to two franchise systems. She received disclosure documents, sample franchising contracts, and fee schedules, along with information showing sample franchisee financial statements from several of the franchisors she contacted. Next, Betty intends to contact several donut franchisees to get their opinions about the franchising arrangements they have with their respective franchisors.

What other type of information should Betty seek? Would a franchisor normally be willing to supply Betty with the type of specific information she is requesting? Are there sources of information Betty can use other than what is provided by franchisors in the donut industry?

ADMINISTRATIVE PACKAGE

The written information provided in the franchise package represents the types of support a franchisor provides a franchisee. A franchise package is generally divided into two parts, the administrative portion and the operations portion. The administrative portion (often called the administrative package) consists of those materials developed and given by the franchisor to prospective franchisees in order to (1) solicit franchisee applicants to the business, (2) provide basic information about the franchise, and (3) illustrate the follow-up forms used to sign franchisees. An administrative package should explain the basic purpose and substantial requirements of the franchise program, specifying intrinsic values and services provided to a franchisee, suggesting probability for franchisee success in the franchise system, and identifying a typical offer the franchisor makes to a franchisee.

The purpose of an administrative package is to solicit and sign franchisees. The administrative package should explain the overall operations and format (basic approach) of the franchise system. It will typically include items relative to disclosure documents required by law, essentials of the franchising agreement, and even explanations of the recommended bookkeeping system and certain advertising practices used by the franchisor.

This package is designed by the franchisor to help a franchisee understand the responsibilities of both parties in running the franchised unit. Some administrative packages, through the information provided on advertising, purchasing, and bookkeeping, recommend methods of reporting to the franchisor and of maintaining an internal reporting system inside the franchisee's business. For the franchisor, this package is very important. It covers at least six major areas associated with costs of doing business and controls utilized by both franchisor and franchisee:

1. Administrative Expenses
2. Recruitment Costs
    a. Advertising
    b. Sales
3. Promotional Costs
4. Training and Schooling Costs
5. Supplementary Services and Related Expenses

6. Administrative Cost Forms
   a. Personal contact (see Figure 13-1)
   b. Follow-up (see Figure 13-2)
   c. Personal data sheet
   d. Financial data sheet

When properly prepared, this package will enable the franchisor to have a controllable, tactical approach to franchisee recruitment, as well as to further understanding of the total costs associated with starting a franchised business. The franchisee is likely to view the administrative package somewhat differently. The franchisee is primarily interested in learning about the franchise system, including how it operates and what requirements or conditions a franchisee with this company must meet. The franchisee would be interested in learning about the items identified in the following list:

1. A description of the business, its product and/or services.
2. Background information about the franchisor and franchised company.
3. Historical information concerning development and operation of a franchised unit.
4. Amount of money required for acquisition of a franchise.
5. Assistance offered by the franchisor (financial, training, and service) to a franchisee.
6. Site, equipment, and building information.
7. Marketing factors associated with promotion and sale of the franchise system's products or services.
8. Information about termination, cancellation, and renewal of franchising agreement and any restrictions that may apply.
9. Financial information about franchisees and the franchise system.

Notice how the needs of the two parties, franchisor and franchisee, differ when the information in the previous two lists is compared. Although both parties address virtually the same information, each has a separate perspective on that information. The franchisor needs to organize the information in a logical sequence that describes the franchising organization, its administrative reporting approach, its approach to recruitment and training of potential franchisees, and its support services to the new franchisee. The franchisee is seeking information from a different perspective, often for purposes of comparison. By examining the differences between franchising organizations, their training, approach to advertising, financial health, promotional and marketing approaches, and reporting requirements, the potential franchisee can determine the advantages of one franchise system over another.

Figure 13-1 illustrates a typical personal-contact information sheet. Usually the name of the franchise system is at or near the top.

Chapter 13 Administration and Operation of the Franchise Package 341

Figure 13-1
Sample Personal-Contact Information Form

NAME OF BUSINESS

Directions for Distribution:

   1st sheet to prospective franchisee master file
   2nd sheet to headquarters
   3rd sheet retained by salesperson

PERSONAL CONTACT

Date_____ Time_____ Prospect's Number_____
Prospect's Name _____
Address_____ Phone Number _____
City_____ State_____ Zip _____
How contacted: ____Phone   ____Letter
                    ____Office   ____Field
                    ____Trade Show   ____Other
Results: _____
_____
_____
_____
_____

Signature _____ (Salesperson)
Signature _____ (Region or District)
Signature _____ (Headquarters)

When someone makes a franchising inquiry to a field representative, an existing franchisee of a franchised business system, or a district or headquarters office, preliminary information about the nature of the contact should be recorded. The prospect's name, address, and phone number should be taken down, as well as how the contact was made — by phone, letter of inquiry, personal visit to the office, stopping at a trade show booth, or some other means. Also, the impressions of that initial contact are recorded by the person contacted. For example: "Mr. Jones appears to be seeking comparative information. I provided a disclosure document and discussed possible expansions for the Southwestern District. I will follow up in two weeks to assess if sufficient interest exists to make any further contact"; or, "Sal Walters of Roanoke, Virginia, appears to have strong interest in our hot tub franchise. Roanoke could use a franchisee. I will follow up with a personal visit." Typically, the bottom of the form is reserved for signatures, usually including that of the franchising representative first contacted by the interested party. There may also be other signatures or marks to identify where the inquiry contact sheet has been passed. Usually a copy of each contact sheet goes to the district or regional office, if the administration of franchisee development takes place at that level. If not, the inquiries are sent to the home office of the franchisor. It is these initial contact sheets that provide the basic information utilized by those involved in franchisee recruitment.

Figure 13-2 provides an illustration of a typical follow-up contact. The first part of the follow-up sheet provides basic information about the first contact. If the franchisor expresses an interest in the prospect, further processing takes place. Typically, the phone conversations and letter to set up an appointment, and every other step of the recruitment process, need to be recorded so that the interaction between the franchisor and the prospect can be efficiently and effectively managed. The next third of the form identifies the type of information provided and activities completed that comprise a step-by-step sequence leading to an agreement between the prospect and the franchisor. The last lines of the

Figure 13-2
Sample Follow-up Contact Information Form

NAME OF FRANCHISED BUSINESS

Prospective Franchisee's Name _____

Address _____ Phone Number _____

City _____ State _____ Zip _____

Prospect's Number _____

Original Contact Date _____

Original Contact By _____

HOME OFFICE USE

____ Yes, Needs Further Processing   ____ No, Reject

By _____

Reason: _____
_____

Initial inquiry received, date: _____

First response package mailed, date: _____

Date assigned: _____

Name of sales representative: _____

Master file started, date: _____

Initial phone contact, date: _____

Initial sales letter mailed, date: _____

**Figure 13-2
Continued**

Additional phone date: _____ Results: _____

Additional phone date: _____ Results: _____

Additional phone date: _____ Results: _____

Additional phone date: _____ Results: _____

Additional follow-up date: _____

Appointment letter mailed, date: _____

Appointment made for, date: _____

Accommodation _____ yes___ no___

Reservation _____ yes___ no___

Prospect _____ yes___ no___

Date of presentation made: _____ Those attending: _____

Personnel data sheet evaluated, date: _____ By whom: _____

Financial sheet evaluated, date: _____ By whom: _____

Following recommendation: _____ Positive____ Negative____

Closing agreements signed ____ Check received ____

Credit form completed ____ Site report developed ____

Successful franchise sales: Check when completed

Franchise agreements _____   Check received _____

Site report _____   Credit form _____

Corporate resolutions _____

Receipt of disclosure document _____

HOME OFFICE USE

Staff Recommendation   ____ Accepted   ____ Rejected

By Whom: _____   Date: _____

Board of Directors   ____ Accepted   ____ Rejected

Agreement, By Whom: _____   Date: _____

Notices mailed, Date: _____

Acceptance ____ Rejection ____ Licensee ____ Sale representative ____

Remarks: _____

Source: Adapted from Pizza Inn Personal Data Sheet

form indicate home office action on the application, noting when the agreement was signed and when notices were mailed, and containing any summary remarks about the application. The form thus provides a sequence of steps useful for a franchisor to develop a prospective franchisee from the point of serious inquiry to the signing and formalization of the franchising agreement.

Administrative Expenses

The franchisor must develop a method of determining the expenses of administering a franchise program. The primary administrative costs are typically those of hiring and training salespeople to recruit or solicit prospective franchisees. In addition, the non-personnel costs of franchisee recruitment, such as costs of publishing brochures, advertising, or promoting the business through trade shows, should also be considered. Further expenses may be incurred in running background checks on prospective franchisees, performing analyses of their current or former businesses, and inquiring into their credit ratings. By estimating the number of franchisees expected to be signed in the next planning period — month, quarter, or year — and by estimating the costs of franchisee recruitment and selection, including the personnel and non-personnel costs directly associated with such recruitment, the franchisor can develop an administrative expense schedule that can be used in the future for both planning and control. In addition, most franchisee recruitment costs are ultimately assignable back to the franchisees through the income and expense accounting of the franchisor.

The administrative package concerns not only recruitment and selection of franchisees, but also development of disclosure documents and franchising agreements, bookkeeping, and writing of manuals necessary to develop and support the franchise system.

Recruitment Package

The franchisee recruitment package usually consists of a recruitment brochure, a disclosure document, and other information about the benefits and opportunities of becoming a franchisee with the franchise system. This package is used as part of the franchisor's response to initial inquiries by a prospective franchisee. The annual report of the franchised business (corporation) may also be provided by the franchising firm; a number of franchising businesses have superb annual reports and are happy to make them available to prospective franchisees. The franchising brochure briefly discusses the major points about the franchise and the principal people involved in running the franchise system. Most brochures will include the types of information found in the following list:

1. Description of the business
2. The principal people in the franchise system (primary ownership)
3. The franchise system
    a. Territory covered
    b. Operating assistance
    c. What is needed for a franchisee to get started
    d. Ongoing assistance available through the franchisor
    e. Franchise system's regional or national advertising program
    f. Marketing programs utilized
    g. Credit card systems (if applicable)
4. Operating a franchise
    a. Location
    b. Training
    c. Insurance
    d. Assistance
    e. Management and planning
    f. Standards of performance
    g. Trademarks and trade names
    h. Duration of the franchising agreement
    i. Franchising and other fees
    j. Franchisee right to assign and/or transfer
    k. Business forms recommended/required and supplies
5. Investments
6. Franchise application (attached, or information on how to receive one)

The franchise brochure is meant to address initial questions or concerns of prospective franchisees. Usually it is a well-developed color brochure describing the franchise concept, organization, and operation, franchisor assistance, and nominal sales figures and projections. The brochure should also contain the initial application form for a prospective franchisee, as inclusion of an application encourages a prospect to make contact.

OPERATIONS PACKAGE

The second part of a franchise package is the operations package. The operations package is fairly extensive, and the materials are often put in the form of manuals. The information contained in the manuals is meant to assist the franchisee in properly conducting the operations of the franchise. Eliminating any one of the manuals or information packages may cause a breakdown in the financial flow, operational work activities, or required reporting procedures on which the success of the franchise system depends. There are at least ten major manuals or information packages which make up the operations package:

- Operating Manual
- Training Manual
- Location Selection Criteria (and procedures, franchisor involvement in the choice and type of assistance provided, if any)
- Marketing Manual
- Advertising Manual (sometimes included in Marketing Manual)
- Field Support Manual
- Quality-Control Forms
- Pre-Opening Manual
- Site Inspection Manual
- Reporting Manual (including financial forms and approved procedures)

Explicit statements in the manuals concerning each area of running the franchised business help franchisees understand the nature of the business they are entering, the reporting requirements, and proven procedures for efficient operation of a franchise. The manuals should be written clearly and concisely, so that a person without experience in the particular business can learn the requirements and operating processes of the franchise system. Many prospective franchisees have experience in many types of employment or businesses; but entering a franchising relationship is different, as there are separate and distinct activities and responsibilities for a franchisor and a franchisee as well as areas in which the two must work together. These factors, plus the franchisor's method of operation, must be understood by the franchisee if the franchise is to be a success.

Development of the operations package, including the manuals and information package, is the responsibility of the franchisor. The operations package is meant to help ensure the success of the entire franchise system. We discuss the manuals or information packages in the remainder of the chapter.

Operating Manual

The operating manual is often referred to as the "bible" of the franchise system. It should be thoroughly developed, so that a franchisee can rely on it for ready and regular reference to address the vagaries and uncertainties of day-to-day operations of the franchised business. It should describe each major function and operating procedure of the business. Not only should the manual present a step-by-step explanation of operations, but it should also provide an overview of the major thrusts of the franchise system. The manual typically illustrates in graphs, charts, and/or pictures how the franchisor and franchisee conduct business together, as well as identifies each essential facet of the daily operations of a franchised business. The operating manual is also an instructional tool useful

Chapter 13 Administration and Operation of the Franchise Package

in the programs run by the franchisor for training new franchisees. Often, the operating manual covers the essential administrative, legal, and functional aspects of the franchise system. Because the system's procedures and policies may change with the changing business climate, the operating manual is probably best kept in a looseleaf binder. Thus as administrative policies, operating procedures, and personnel practices are changed, the franchisee and franchisor can update the particular section by removing the old pages and inserting the new. Topics often included in an operating manual are identified in Table 13-1.

**Table 13-1
Sample Outline of Topics Included in the Operating Manual**

SECTION ONE: INTRODUCTION

    Company History
    Franchisor and Administrative Staff
    Franchisor/Franchisee Obligations

SECTION TWO: GENERAL RULES OF OPERATION

    Important Success Factors
    Quality Standards
    Warranties and Replacement Practices
    Customer Relations
    Inventory Systems
    Quality and Variety of Product

SECTION THREE: UNIT OPERATIONS

    Pricing
    Quality
    Franchise Image
    Customer Service, Courtesy
    Credit Policies
    Maintenance Requirements
    Store Hours
    Employee Discounts
    Community Relations
    Brand Policies

SECTION FOUR: MANAGEMENT

    Wages and Salaries
    Purchasing, Receiving
    Quality Control
    Advertising
    Legal Documents and Practices
    Accounting/Financial Reports
    Insurance Reports
    Customer or Employee Accidents
    Inventory

**Table 13-1
Continued**

Supervision
Personnel Practices
Planning, Organizing, Control
Franchisor-Franchisee Relationships

SECTION FIVE: STORE OPERATION

Position Descriptions
Individual Responsibilities
Store Opening Procedure/Checklist
Store Closing/Checklist
Maintenance and Housekeeping
Opening and Closing Out Registers
Equipment Maintenance
Inspections

SECTION SIX: SALES OPERATIONS (may be separate manual)

Selling Methods
Exchanges, Adjustments, Refunds
Order Taking
Check Cashing
Credit Accounts
Sales Tax
Supplies/Purchasing
The Customer Is Always Right, Except . . .
Promotional Activities: Display, Grand Opening, Mail, Sales and/or Seasonal Promotions, Weekly, Monthly Promotions: TV, Radio, Newsprint, Direct Mail

SECTION SEVEN: INVENTORY

Purchasing
Receiving
Inventory Control
Loss Prevention, Shoplifting, Pilferage
Pricing Policies, Procedures
Order Forms

SECTION EIGHT: MAINTENANCE CONTROL

Restrooms
Parking
Utility Cost Control
Fire Protection
Repairs
Plumbing, Electrical, Mechanical, Construction
Pest Control
Fire Prevention/Control
Preventive Maintenance
Alarms, Locks, Keys, Entrances/Exits
Background Music

The sections and items included in Table 13-1 are intended to present a comprehensive view of what might appear in a franchisor's operating manual. Obviously, each franchise system has its own unique set of operating procedures. Some items in this table might not be included in a manual for a carpet-cleaning franchise, for example, but that franchise system might include more detail for other items.

Procedures incorporated in the operating manual should be carefully developed and then tested "under fire" in the franchisor's prototype unit to ensure that they are understandable and that by reading the manual, employees and franchisees can learn precisely what constitutes the operating procedures of that franchised business. This manual is one of the greatest means of assistance provided by the franchisor to the franchisee. By having clear, understandable operating procedures available to them, both franchisor and franchisee will know exactly what is expected in the operations of the franchised business.

Existing franchisees are an important source of information when the franchisor seeks to improve the operating manual, because franchisees have gained practical experience in applying the concepts and procedures within the operating manual on a daily basis in their own businesses. Illustrations are often incorporated in the operating manual to display techniques or provide a picture of some facet of the operations, showing the best way to wash a dish, set up a display, stock a shelf, and so on. In addition to illustrations, definitions and descriptions provide instruction or sequencing of work activities necessary to ensure quality and consistency in preparation and delivery of products or services.

Training Manual

A franchisor works closely with the franchise system's franchisees. The interaction with new franchisees is primarily directed to teaching operating procedures and personnel management. Franchise training programs can be classified into two categories: (1) formal training programs and (2) ongoing training programs.

Formal Training Programs provide opportunity for the franchisor to help new franchisees develop specific knowledge about the franchise system and the business factors important to running a successful franchised unit. Administrative and operating functions are stressed. The training is typically given in a central location of the business, such as the prototype for the franchise system or a district or regional franchised unit operated by the franchised company or a franchisee. A well-known example of a formal training site, and one we've discussed in earlier chapters, is Hamburger University, founded in 1961 by McDonald's Corporation. Hamburger University has become an international management training center for McDonald's licensees, managers, and corporate personnel. It is accredited by the American Council on Education and offers a number of courses for college credit. More than 2,000 students graduate annually from this suburban Chicago, Illinois, facility. Many large franchise systems have such a facility, or two or three, in order to accommodate their franchisees. Having several regional training centers is of great advantage to a franchise system that is national in scope.

Many smaller franchisors find it convenient to use their first unit, the prototype, as the training facility. Often it is located near the franchise system headquarters and may even be housed within the same building. Close proximity provides the opportunity for a franchisor to closely scrutinize training content and methods and be involved in evaluating performance of new franchisees as they learn to become authorized representatives of the franchise system. A prospective franchisee should successfully complete all training offered by the franchisor prior to being granted the franchise. In this way all franchisees are certain to have the same training, and therefore, the same opportunity for understanding the policies and practices of the franchise system. With this common set of norms for operating a franchised unit, mutual expectations between franchisor and franchisee can be upheld. Almost all franchisees agree that formal training is important and should be a prerequisite service provided by a franchisor. Formal training helps both franchisor and franchisee achieve success in their franchise system.

Ongoing Training is usually provided by field staff of the franchisor after the franchisee has entered business. Traveling field representatives provide on-site training for franchisees as well as for the franchisee's staff, when appropriate. Typically, the first ongoing type of training is provided just prior to the opening of the franchised outlet. This means training a complement of perhaps 20 to 30 people in restaurants, 50 or more in motels, or perhaps only one or two in smaller, service-oriented franchised outlets. The franchisor's field representative also provides the continuous training to the franchisee and staff depending on the franchisee's needs and/or the administrative and operative changes suggested by the franchisor. Many franchise systems also provide training manuals for use by the franchisee to train employees. This type of training is often encouraged by the franchisor, as it tends to bring the franchisee and staff closer together, providing them with the same information at the same time. Of particular benefit is training provided by the franchisee to staff of the same type provided by the franchisor to the franchisee. Thus, employees will be able to understand not only the operational facets of the franchised business, but also the overall perspective, the general goals of the franchise system, and the objectives and policies of the franchise system for profitability and growth.

Training Program Development. Training programs are generally developed based on the notion that new franchisees have little or no specific business knowledge about the franchise system. It is important for the franchisor to recognize that educating the franchisee is not based only on what the franchisor feels needs to be taught, but also on what the franchisee needs to *learn* in order to be a successful operator. Training franchisees in the business of the franchise system should be a blend of development of concepts and practical application of those concepts. Franchisees need to become familiar with all aspects of the business, including advertising, promotion, bookkeeping, management, reporting, inventory control, marketing, and the other activities essential to the day-to-day operations of the franchised outlet. Also, franchisees should be instilled with pride of ownership in their business, loyalty to the franchise system, and a sense of confidence in the future.

A training program should develop basic management and business skills. Basic economics, profit motives and incentives, cost controls, management and leadership practices, financial tools, and marketing principles, as they apply to the franchised business, should be included in the training. The formal training program provided at the prototype or other designated facility should be as thorough but as concise as possible. Such programs can last from five days to two months, depending upon the amount of classroom (conceptual) and on-site (practical) training provided. While the classroom is vitally important, the majority of what franchisees take back to their own units is usually the practical information acquired in on-site training. Franchisors have also found that group training is more effective than individual training. Three to five new franchisees are preferable for a training program, for in these small groups franchisees can interact more closely with one another to discuss common experiences and personal insights gained through the training program. This opportunity to exchange ideas is important to the attitude development and knowledge formation of each franchisee.

After formal training at the franchisor's facility, the franchisee will typically receive from three days to two weeks of additional training at the franchisee's own location, providing an opportunity to apply the conceptual and practical training. This second stage of training focuses on actual operations at the particular franchised unit, and utilizes the skills learned at the training facility. This unit training is usually handled by the franchisor's field representatives; it takes place just before and continues through the grand opening of the outlet. An outline of a formal training program is presented in Table 13-2.

Proper training is important. It can have a dramatic effect on the success or failure of a franchise system. The franchisor has the responsibility to train new franchisees so they are familiar with all aspects of the franchised business operations and the management functions asso-

Table 13-2
A Typical Formal Training Program for New Franchisees

SECTION ONE: INTRODUCTION

    Executive Summary of Business Facts
    Information About Business Industry
    Information About Franchisor
    Required Activities with Franchisor
    Contracts, Licenses, Permits, and Any Other Legal Requirements

SECTION TWO: FINANCE

    Balance Sheet — how to develop, read, and use
    Income Statement — how to develop, read, and use
    Cash Budget — how to develop, read, and use
    Pro Forma Income and Balance Sheets — how to use
    Record Keeping Procedures — a system and its procedures
    Cash Register — how to use
    Reading Cash Register Tapes
    Procedures for Opening Register
    Procedures for Closing Register
    Inventory Control
    Credit Sales
    Check Sales
    Petty Cash
    Reconciliation
    Cash Register
    Bank Statements
    Sales Slips vs. Cash
    Night Deposits
    Payroll
    Social Security Requirements
    Federal, State (and County or City) Withholding Taxes
    Lease
    Insurance

SECTION THREE: MARKETING

    Target Market
    Advertising/Promotion
    Pre-Opening Activities
    Grand Opening
    Post-Opening Activities
    Merchandising
    Customer Relations
    Products — Definition and Description

SECTION FOUR: OPERATIONS

    Personnel and Store Operations
    Housekeeping and Maintenance
    Management
    Sales Operations
    Inventory
    Unit Operations (also, see Operating Manual)

**Table 13-2
Continued**

SECTION FIVE: SERVICE/PRODUCTION

  Equipment Ordering
  Inventory Control
  Ordering Control
  • From franchisor
  • From other suppliers
  Cost Factors
  Serving
  Service/Product Preparation Methods
  Warehousing Storage Methods
  Sanitary Control
  Kitchen Operation (or Production Floor Operation)
  Portion (or Specific Weight, Color, Size, Thickness) Control

SECTION SIX: MANAGEMENT OF PERSONNEL

  Job Specifications
  Recruitment, Selection, and Training of Employees
  Weekly Work Log/Monthly Schedules
  Motivation
  Personnel Development
  Labor Laws and Regulations
  Franchisor Assistance

ciated with making the operation profitable. A good training program will allow sufficient time for questions to be asked and answered accurately and concretely, and will allow for interactions between new franchisees. Trainees will likely learn the most useful information from hands-on exercises and operations rather than classroom instruction at the training facility. But each component is important in the development of a firm grounding in the concepts of the franchise system as well as the tools and skills necessary to run a franchised unit.

Location Selection Criteria

One of the most crucial decisions confronting the franchisee (and the franchisor as well) is selection of the site for the new franchised business. Many franchised businesses depend heavily on walk-in traffic; others depend on drive-in/drive-thru traffic. Some need extensive advertising; others need merely to have their business name in the phone book. Franchised businesses also differ in how important the choice of location is to the success of the business. Based on the type of business the franchise system is engaged in, the franchisor will prepare a list of factors to be investigated prior to making the location decision.

As we discussed in Chapters 3 and 8, location for a new franchised business is usually based on a variety of factors including economic strength and potential of a particular region; economic strength and potential of metropolitan area or market area; availability of transportation for supplies; employment trends and employment mix; demographic characteristics within the community or particular market segment in terms of usage or purchase of the product or service; traffic ingress and egress at sites being considered; land development and construction costs; and location of primary competitors within the primary service area.

Although a location selection manual may be developed to assist franchisees in determining optimal sites, the final determination often rests with the franchisor. A site must meet the criteria of the franchisor prior to any final decisions for purchase, development, and construction by the franchisee. Many franchisors will actually purchase the land, then lease it back to the franchisee on an intermediate- to long-term basis, for 5, 10, 20, or even 30 years. Obviously, by owning the land, the franchisor gains enormous leverage on the franchisee. In many mall and shopping-center locations, the franchisor will obtain the lease and then sublease to the franchisee. For some franchising systems in which location is not as important for customer traffic, site selection is of little importance, but access to the intended target market may be of critical importance. In such instances, the selection criteria include availability of transportation and immediate access to the territory to be covered.

Marketing Manual

The marketing manual describes the franchisor's marketing philosophy and discusses in detail the features and characteristics used to market the franchised business's offering, which may be consumer or industrial goods, durable or nondurable goods, or a service. The brand name is described, and the franchisor's quality concept is articulated as being higher, the same as, or lower than that of the competition. If there is a family of brands or if other products are to be given the same brand name, this is also covered in the marketing manual. Sometimes the brand name is used horizontally to cover product differences, or else there may be individual brands in franchised businesses, such as the different sandwiches available at some franchised restaurants. Also, several products may be marketed under a family branding approach, such as with auto parts from major auto manufacturers. All these variances should be stated in the marketing manual.

Other factors discussed in the marketing manual include information about packaging, labeling, and consumer services that franchisees should make available. The manual might also contain information about appropriate ways to feature a product within a line, how to promote a featured product, or the right amount and quality of service to offer in order to minimize complaints and maximize customer satisfaction.

Along with product classification, product features, and customer services, the marketing manual should state the franchisor's pricing policies, including new-product strategies, product-mix strategies, price-adjustment strategies, and how to initiate price changes and respond to price changes of the competition. (See Chapter 7 for a more detailed discussion.) In addition, the marketing manual should state policies concerning physical distribution of the product as well as the conditions under which the product can be sold at wholesale, if the franchisee's business is retail.

The marketing manual should also describe the market position the franchise system seeks, in terms of the market segment and customer groups targeted and the competitive position the franchise system wants to reach and/or maintain. Information about customers is provided in the form of a customer profile, identifying the typical sex, age, and income characteristics, what the customer seeks to derive by purchasing the product, and the price range most appropriate for triggering purchase decisions, as well as what services customers will want to accompany the purchase of the product. Sometimes a marketing manual will explain how to gather the appropriate information to develop a reasonable market share for the products offered, how to penetrate new market segments, and how to deepen penetration in established market segments. Some marketing manuals also contain basic information about how to perform market research within the franchisee's local trading area, from measuring general economic conditions of a community to testing consumer attitudes about products or services offered by the franchisee.

The marketing manual contains a wealth of information about how the franchise system attracts and maintains customers through the basic product, pricing, place, and distribution policies, as well as information about current customers and collecting market intelligence. It clearly identifies the marketing philosophy of the franchise system. However, one major factor concerning the marketing of the franchised product or service — advertising and promotion — may not be included in this manual. Some franchise systems prefer to include advertising policies and promotional strategies in a separate manual. Advertising for many franchised systems involves regular if not daily participation by the franchisee. Separating the advertising policies and strategies from the rest of the marketing information allows for such information to be contained in one smaller manual and easily updated as market conditions dictate and as the franchise system modifies its approach to the market.

Advertising Manual

From a broad perspective, advertising means effective communication and promotion of the franchised product to the targeted audience. This means the franchisor must know who is the audience targeted and what response is sought, and so choose the appropriate messages, as well as be able to determine whether an advertisement or promotion is effective. The advertising and promotional strategies are then budgeted and appropriate cost-sharing arrangements are made between the franchisor and the franchisees.

An effective advertising manual covers at least four topics: advertising, promotion, graphics and signage, and public relations. As noted in the previous paragraph, the major decisions in advertising are to determine the objectives of the particular advertisement, what message is to be conveyed, the media most appropriate for conveying the message, the impact of the advertisement, and its anticipated cost. Plans to advertise by means of radio, television, and print media should describe to the franchisee what sales tool is appropriate for what market condition, suggesting which mix is most effective in attracting customers. An advertisement should express at the appropriate level of detail the usefulness and advantages of the product being offered. Recommended advertisements should be tested by the franchisor to ensure that advertisements to be used by the franchise system and by its franchisees have been found successful.

The advertising manual will also contain illustrations of direct mail pieces and newspaper display mats (with space for the franchisee to plug in the location or other necessary information), as well as audiovisual disk sampler presentations, brochures, and presentation booklets when personal selling is the primary means of making sales.

Promotional materials are designed to attract market response or enhance existing customer demand. Contests, cents-off coupons, rebate or refund offers, and product samples or demonstrations are sales tools used by many retail franchise systems. Sales promotions through the sales force of a franchisee would also be included when personal selling is the principal method of generating sales. Bonuses based on sales volume, or sales contests for trips, merchandise, or cash would be described in the manual.

The graphics program of a franchise system provides the franchisee with information about how, where, and when to use the trademarks, logos, and service marks. Both franchisor and franchisee need to be keenly aware of the signs of the franchise system, and must guard and protect all trademarks and logos. The franchisor is required to show the franchisee what is permitted in the use of registered trademarks. All trademarks, logos, and service marks must receive consistent use. The franchisor should take immediate action to stop any unauthorized modification or inappropriate use by franchisees or other parties. Franchisees are often requested to help the franchisor identify any copying or modifications of the franchise system's works. The franchisee should never be permitted to use the trademark of the franchisor without written consent.

Most franchisors insist on one unchangeable sign for the entire franchise system. Although different sizes and types of signs are usually permitted, the particular signage is unmodifiable and consistent regardless of location. Usually, this means all colors must be identical with the illustrations provided in the manual, using the same style of type, word order, and word authorization. Any changes or personalization of such signs may result in loss of trademark protection for the franchise system, which would also result in loss of "added value" or goodwill to the franchise system.

The last major topic usually covered in an advertising manual is public relations. The purpose of a public relations program is to generate favorable publicity for the franchise system as well as for the individual franchise locations. In this broad context, public relations is usually aimed toward building an image of good corporate citizenship for the franchise system. The tools discussed in the advertising manual should include the franchise system's approaches to product publicity, press relations, internal and external corporate communications, and lobbying if the franchise system has an interest in promoting or defeating government regulations or legislation. Franchisees are often encouraged to become involved in community activities such as community service projects, scout troops, sports team sponsorships, and other activities that tend to enhance the name of the franchise system as well as the local franchise as an active participant in promoting the community.

Field Support Manual

Successful franchise systems have developed extensive field support systems for their franchisees. Franchisors have learned such support is necessary to help ensure their success, for when the franchisees are successful, the franchise system prospers. Instead of the vertical or top-down approach traditional in business relationships, the franchisor-franchisee relationship in many franchise systems has become horizontal. A sense of equity, fairness, and mutual respect is sought in the relationship. After all, the franchisor and franchisee are independent, yet interdependent, in their business agreements and practices.

The field support manual should identify and outline the services provided by the franchisor to each franchisee. This manual would likely include such services as training, inspection, record keeping, financial planning, and quality-control standards and procedures, as well as recommend forms and procedures for use in evaluating the performance of the franchised business.

Most of the personal interactions between the franchisor and the franchisee occur through the franchisor's field representatives, who periodically (often monthly) visit the franchisee to discuss overall operations, sales performance, problems in production, sales promotions that were or were not effective, training needs, upcoming promotional campaigns, or any problems with the building, work process, or equipment. An inspection of the facility might also be included, or a review of records kept by the franchisee. Because the field representative is the mouthpiece of the franchisor, he or she must thoroughly understand operations procedures, comprehend the details of the franchising agreement, and have good human-relations skills. Also, the field representative must serve as the promoter and motivation builder for the franchisor, lifting sagging spirits wherever they are evident in the franchised unit.

Quality-Control Forms

Proper quality control helps the franchisee maintain desired standards of product quality, service performance, and presentation. Standards appropriate to the market niche targeted by the franchise system must be strictly adhered to by both franchisor and franchisee. Franchisors generally want the highest-possible standards for their product and its delivery in the marketplace, because they realize that consumers are becoming increasingly interested in product quality. A franchise system's reputation can be permanently tarnished by a greasy donut, a bad cup of coffee, a surly sales representative, or an indifferent counter clerk. The franchisor must address each point of contact between the franchised business and the customer and develop standards for product quality as well as for interaction with the customer. Policies and standards should exist for the following types of customer interactions: credit on product or service sold; technical services available; maintenance services available (if applicable); customer inquiries about the company, products, product features, delivery schedules, or order backlog policies; and how complaints or adjustments to purchases are to be made.

New franchisees might find the franchise system's field representative visiting the business weekly or perhaps even daily during the first weeks or months of operation, with the dual purpose of helping the franchisee and grading the performance of the new franchised business. General areas of quality control will include at least the physical appearance of the business location, adherence to operating procedures and conformance to quality-control standards, and personal appearance of employees. Once the new franchised business is running smoothly, the frequency of visits tends to diminish, with visits made on a biweekly, monthly, or bimonthly basis.

The evaluation forms used by field representatives should be included in the field support manual, with an explanation of what is being evaluated and how the evaluated data will be used. Inclusion of such forms and their explanations is important to ensure an atmosphere of trust and openness between the franchisor and the franchisee.

Chapter 13 Administration and Operation of the Franchise Package

Pre-Opening Manual

Most franchisors prepare a pre-opening manual. Usually the manual is not lengthy or overly descriptive. The manual almost always includes checklists of activities and steps that must be completed before a grand opening can take place. There are four time periods considered important prior to the grand opening of a franchised business:

1. Six months prior to grand opening
2. Three to six months prior to grand opening
3. One to three months prior to grand opening
4. 30 days prior to grand opening

These checklists help the franchisee follow a logical plan to complete essential activities before opening the business. A time-balanced approach helps ensure that the franchisee has not forgotten to complete these activities or is not trying to accomplish too much before the grand opening. Table 13-3 presents checklists of activities to be completed six months prior to the grand opening and three to six months prior to the grand opening.

Table 13-3
Typical Checklists for Franchisees Three to Six Months Prior to Opening

Six Months Prior to Grand Opening

____ Yes	____ No	Franchise feasibility study completed
____ Yes	____ No	Franchising agreement completed
____ Yes	____ No	Financing available
____ Yes	____ No	Site selection announced
____ Yes	____ No	Building blueprints approved
____ Yes	____ No	Franchisor-franchisee relationship developed

Three to Six Months Prior to Grand Opening

____ Yes	____ No	Instructions begun
____ Yes	____ No	Formal franchisee training completed
____ Yes	____ No	Fixtures and equipment ordered
____ Yes	____ No	Name registered
____ Yes	____ No	Bank account opened
____ Yes	____ No	Licenses applied for

From examination of the items included in Table 13-3, we see that the franchise feasibility study must be approved, and the necessary legal, financial, site, and building requirements must be fulfilled and approved. Also, the first "publicity" for the new business can take place with the announcement of the new site for the franchised business. These activities are followed by the less visible but essential activities of training new franchisees, ordering fixtures and equipment, registering the name of the business with the state, county, and city if necessary, opening a bank account, and applying for appropriate licenses.

Table 13-4 identifies typical activities during the three months prior to opening. Notice how the checklist items become more external and public-oriented as we near the opening date. Also, the basic activities essential to opening a business are shown, such as installing fixtures, ordering inventory, arranging for utilities, initiating the bonding and training of persons selected as employees, training franchisees in the store, developing displays, and inspecting any construction that has been required as well as the fixtures or equipment to be used in the business.

Table 13-4
Typical Checklist for Franchisees Three Months to 30 Days Prior to Opening

One to Three Months Prior to Opening

___ Yes ___ No		Basic instruction completed
___ Yes ___ No		Fixtures received and installed
___ Yes ___ No		Early publicity developed
___ Yes ___ No		"Coming Soon" sign displayed
___ Yes ___ No		IRS forms and schedules, withholding schedules, and employment wage and hour regulations obtained
___ Yes ___ No		Inventory ordered
___ Yes ___ No		All utilities and services arranged
___ Yes ___ No		Hiring, bonding, and training of personnel begun

30 Days Prior to Opening

___ Yes ___ No		Staff training by field representative received
___ Yes ___ No		In-store franchisee training received
___ Yes ___ No		All construction and installation of fixtures and equipment completed and inspected
___ Yes ___ No		Merchandise displayed
___ Yes ___ No		Grand opening publicized/advertised
___ Yes ___ No		Grand opening program followed

Site Inspection Manual

Part of the motivation for a franchisor to develop a franchise system is to ensure consistency throughout the business units in the system. A franchisor should develop an approach to site inspection that helps the franchise system achieve consistency in the external attributes of a business site, as well as the internal features of the outlet. A site inspection manual for a franchise system that must attract customers to the business location is typically more detailed than a manual for a system that takes the service to the customer. Rather elaborate site inspection criteria are used for franchised businesses such as hotels or motels, auto repair shops, nursing homes and health care facilities, general merchandise stores, automobile dealers, furniture and home furnishing stores, and restaurants.

The items included in a site inspection will vary depending on the business being examined. Typically, an inspection will look at certain physical attributes as well as less-tangible factors such as store ambience, attractiveness of decor, cleanliness of restrooms and operating equipment, neatness of customer service and work production areas, and personal appearance of employees. Figure 13-3 presents an example of a form that might be included in a franchisor's site inspection manual.

**Figure 13-3
Sample Site Selection Form**

APPEARANCE	Good	Satis-factory	Unsatis-factory	Comments
External:				
Building	X			New
Grounds			X	Sod to be placed
Access	X			Near major intersection
Parking			X	Lines to be painted
Overall		X		Deficiencies to be completely rectified within one week according to franchisee
Internal:				
Equipment	X			New
Walls	X			Freshly painted
Ceiling and Lights		X		Too dim in A.M.
Floors	X			Clean, bright
Counters and Fixtures	X			Clean, dust-free
Furniture	X			New
Signage	X			New
Overall	X			Request additional lighting around soffit of serving counter

**Figure 13-3
Continued**

MAINTENANCE	Good	Satis-factory	Unsatis-factory	Comments
Customer Areas:				
Entry		X		Sales display too close
Order/Purchase			X	Promo in disarray
Seating			X	Too tight
Exit	X			Good egress
Restrooms	X			Clean/neat
Overall		X		Promo displays to be put in front and side windows away from door; recommended modification in seating arrangement for better traffic flow
Work Area:				
Production	X			Clean
Storage	X			According to manual
Office	X			Orderly
Trafficways	X			Clear, uncluttered
Overall	X			Daily maintenance of work areas is evident. Well organized and clean.
Preventive:				
Adherence to schedule on equipment	X			Records approved
External/Internal:				
Signage	X			O.K.
Insect/Rodent	X			Records approved
Overall	X			First month of operation records are in order for each area.

Location: Cincinnati   Date: 10-17-90   Field Supervisor: Al Belz

The sample site inspection form identifies two major categories, appearance and maintenance. The appearance category lists items for inspection that are internal and external to the business facility. The maintenance category contains items by which to rate neatness and cleanliness of customer and employee work areas, as well as adherence by the franchisee to the recommended preventive maintenance program. From the completed form, one can readily see that the location being inspected is a newly constructed site at which some work on the grounds and parking area needs to be completed. The equipment and interior features receive high marks, as would be expected of a newly constructed building provided it has been built in accordance with the franchisor's specifications. Note the item "ceiling and lights." The field supervisor has recommended that the franchisee add more lighting under the soffit above the service counter in the hot tub showroom. With the business facing northwest, the lighting in the showroom could be improved during the morning hours by addition of a fluorescent lamp above the service counter whose fixture is hidden within the soffit. Such "differences" between one franchised business location and another are understandable. Not all businesses can face east or south in order to enjoy daylight in the customer service areas. The field supervisor has found the promotional items on the service counter in disarray and a life-size display promotion sign placed too close to the entrance, preventing customers from entering the business comfortably. Recommendations are indicated on the form. The work area of the franchisee passed inspection with flying colors. Each item for inspection was rated highly in accordance with the specifications set. Also, the preventive maintenance program implemented by the franchisee was shown to be in accordance with the recommended time intervals, and internal records indicate that the maintenance has been performed.

A franchisor's site inspection manual will describe each item that is included in an inspection, along with the criteria used and procedures to be followed by the franchisee. Each maintenance item may have a daily or weekly log for the franchisee to complete. The appearance features are to be checked every day. The value of a site inspection for the franchisee is to help that person make changes that will enhance the image of the business to its customers and in the community in general. To the franchisor, the completed site inspection checklist provides regular, written information gathered by the field representative about important quality-control features of the franchise system. Another major category for inspection and evaluation is personnel. Information regarding appearance and behavior of employees, attitude of the franchisee, turnover rates, absenteeism, and sick days used can be requested by the franchisor. The purpose of collecting information about personnel at a franchised location is to provide a vehicle for discussion between the field representative and the franchisee about any problems or issues involving employees and to help the franchisee encourage and maintain high-quality customer service.

Reporting Manual

The franchisor, working with an accountant, needs to develop a standardized accounting and record keeping system. A well-planned system will provide a means of obtaining accurate financial information with a minimum of time and effort. The record keeping parts of the financial system should allow for weekly, biweekly, or monthly income statements reflecting sales and expenses, a cash budget which helps the business plan its financial activities, and a balance sheet on a monthly, quarterly, semiannual, or annual basis. (We discussed these financial reports in Chapters 10 and 11.) Other financial record keeping forms are illustrated in Figures 13-4, 13-5, 13-6, and 13-7. These forms were developed by Comprehensive Accounting Corporation, a franchisor of monthly accounting, bookkeeping, and tax service practices. The figures illustrate the types of records a franchisor and franchisee should maintain in order to control costs, report earnings and taxes, and determine profit.

SUCCESS STORY
JAMES A. MATHER

A veteran of World War II and a former student at the Detroit Arts and Crafts School, James Mather was employed by Alexander Film Company for nine and a half years. Mather and two friends then started their own business, Leadership Training Institute, Inc., which promoted and taught three Dale Carnegie courses. Mather's two friends left the business after six and a half years, so he decided to liquidate the business and start another.

In 1961 he became a franchising consultant, which led to the development of his own franchise in 1963. With three friends, Mather started the first Mr. Steak in Colorado Springs. The Mr. Steak restaurant system developed quickly, and included waitress service of USDA-graded, aged beef, with each meal cooked to order.

Today Mather serves as chairman of the board of Mr. Steak, Inc., which now operates 255 restaurants in 36 states and Canada. He teaches and speaks on the subject of franchising, as he was twice a franchisee, worked as a franchising consultant, and developed the franchised restaurant concept of Mr. Steak.

Photo and information provided courtesy of James A. Mather, August, 1985.

Chapter 13 Administration and Operation of the Franchise Package 365

Figure 13-4
Operating Statement Performance Graphs

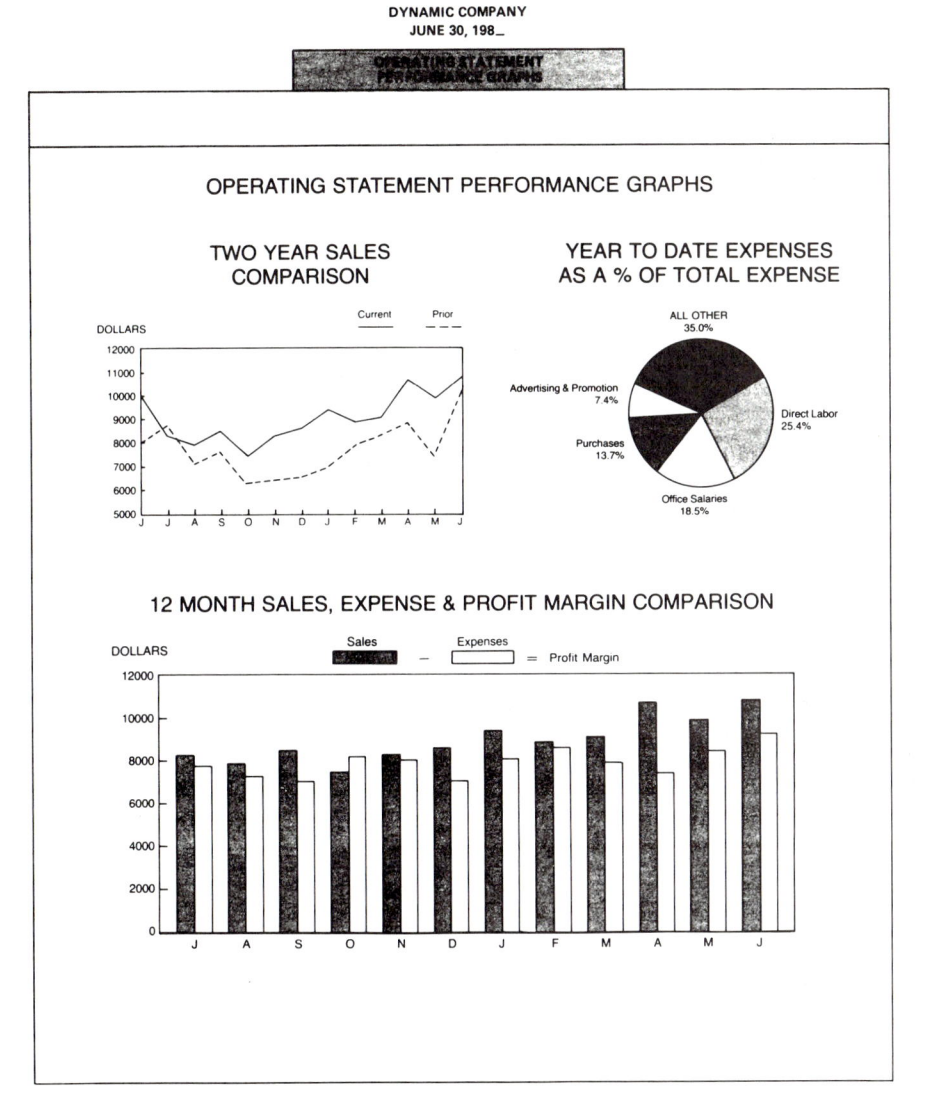

Source: © 1984 Copyright Comprehensive Accounting Corporation. ® COMPREHENSIVE is a service name and mark of Comprehensive Accounting Corporation. Reprinted with permission from Comprehensive Accounting Corporation.

**Figure 13-5
Detail General Ledger**

DYNAMIC COMPANY
JUNE 30, 198_

DETAIL GENERAL LEDGER   Page 3

DATE	INDEX	DESCRIPTION	CURRENT MONTH	YEAR TO DATE
5-31	510	OPERATING SUPPLIES		
		Beginning Balance		1,700.55 Dr
6-09	510	01015 Lubrication Oil	45.08 Dr	
6-19	510	01031 Camore Container	276.32 Dr	
6-19	510	01032 Paper Company	257.06 Dr	
		Current Total	578.46 Dr	
		Ending Balance		2,279.01 Dr
5-31	530	REPAIRS & MAINTENANCE		
		Beginning Balance		397.91 Dr
6-09	530	01011 Valley Hardware	9.13 Dr	
6-09	530	01013 Midway Lumber Co	22.93 Dr	
6-09	530	01014 Stein Brothers	2.36 Dr	
6-17	530	01025 W C Electrical	78.98 Dr	
6-30	530	01058 Fire Equipment	114.46 Dr	
		Current Total	227.86 Dr	
		Ending Balance		625.77 Dr
5-31	534	ADVERTISING & PROMOTION		
		Beginning Balance		2,671.70 Dr
6-19	534	01034 Lumbermen Inc	239.60 Dr	
6-22	534	01036 Crane Studios	127.00 Dr	
6-29	534	01049 EOM Services	332.16 Dr	
6-29	534	01054 The Artist Shop	364.00 Dr	
6-30	534	00010 Reverse Payables	218.70 Cr	
6-30	534	00011 Accrued Payables	107.59 Dr	
		Current Total	951.65 Dr	
		Ending Balance		3,623.35 Dr

PROCESSED BY COMPREHENSIVE
"PREPARED WITHOUT AUDIT, FROM INFORMATION SUBMITTED BY CLIENT"

Source: © 1984 Copyright Comprehensive Accounting Corporation. ® COMPREHENSIVE is a service name and mark of Comprehensive Accounting Corporation. Reprinted with permission from Comprehensive Accounting Corporation.

Figure 13-6
Check Register

JUNE 30, 198_
CHECK REGISTER*
Page 4

DATE	LINE OR CHECK NO.	DESCRIPTION OR PAYEE	ACCOUNT CODE	NET AMOUNT	DATE	LINE OR CHECK NO.	DESCRIPTION OR PAYEE	ACCOUNT CODE	NET AMOUNT
6-03	1001	CARLTON CO	595	18.64	6-19	1031	CAMORE CONTAINER	510	276.32
6-05	1002	ANDERSON D	517	267.75	6-19	1032	PAPER COMPANY	510	257.06
6-05	1003	BARRETT E	403	148.00	6-19	1033	STEEL COMPANY	402	580.42
6-05	1004	CHAPMAN C	403	199.57	6-19	1034	LUMBERMEN INC	534	239.60
6-05	1005	FREEMAN N	403	52.18	6-19	1035	POSTMASTER	512	100.00
6-05	1006	STANDARD INS CO	535	203.62	6-22	1036	CRANE STUDIOS	534	127.00
6-08	1007	POSTMASTER	512	100.00	6-22	1037	HARDWARE ASS'N	556	5.44
6-08	1008	C W RUSSELL	539	142.20	6-22	1038	LUMBERMENS ASSOC	556	5.48
6-08	1009	DAVID ANDERSON	539	114.85	6-22	1039	HARDWARE DEALERS	556	5.40
6-09	1010	DELIVERY SERVICE	512	54.26	6-22	1040	MATERIAL DEALERS	556	17.17
6-09	1011	VALLEY HARDWARE	530	9.13	6-22	1041	IMPLEMENT ASSOC	556	4.90
6-09	1012	VILLAGE WATER CO	526	11.50	6-22	1042	ANDERSON D	517	267.75
6-09	1013	MIDWAY LUMBER CO	530	22.93	6-26	1043	BARRETT E	403	148.00
6-09	1014	STEIN BROTHERS	530	2.36	6-26	1044	CHAPMAN C	403	199.57
6-09	1015	LUBRICATION OIL	510	45.08	6-26	1045	FREEMAN N	403	52.18
6-09	1016	COMPREHENSIVE	564	155.00	6-29	1046	TRAVEL SERVICE	539	100.00
6-09	1017	MOBIL OIL CORP	552	107.34	6-29	1047	EDISON COMPANY	526	99.12
6-12	1018	ANDERSON D	517	267.75	6-29	1048	UNITED PARCEL	512	76.56
6-12	1019	BARRETT E	403	148.00	6-29	1049	EOM SERVICES	534	332.16
6-12	1020	CHAPMAN C	403	199.57	6-29	1050	TRAVELERS INS	535	139.64
6-12	1021	FREEMAN N	403	52.18	6-29	1051	TEXACO INC	552	77.02
6-15	1022	PULLMAN	232	1,000.53	6-29	1052	C W RUSSELL	595	45.00
6-17	1023	UNITED PARCEL	512	121.72	6-29	1053	UNITED PARCEL	512	5.17
6-17	1024	BELL TELEPHONE	529	143.93	6-29	1054	THE ARTIST SHOP	534	364.00
6-17	1025	W C ELECTRICAL	530	78.98	6-30	1055	REALTY CORP	141	5,000.00
6-19	1026	ANDERSON D	517	267.75	6-30	1056	UNITED PARCEL	512	115.11
6-19	1027	BARRETT E	403	148.00	6-30	1057	WATER SERVICE	566	5.21
6-19	1028	CHAPMAN C	403	199.57	6-30	1058	FIRE EQUIPMENT	530	114.46
6-19	1029	FREEMAN N	403	52.18	6-30	1059	DEPT OF REVENUE	233	103.75
6-19	1030	STEEL DIVISION	402	642.43					
		****TOTAL****				59 ENTRIES			13,840.49

PAYROLL RECAP
	GROSS PAYROLL		517	1,400.00
	GROSS PAYROLL		403	1,920.00
	FEDERAL TAXES WITHHELD		232	579.64-
	STATE TAX WITHHELD		233	70.36-
	NET PAYROLL			2,670.00

*Journal Entry, Employee Number and Gross Amount also included on actual statement.

PROCESSED BY COMPREHENSIVE
"PREPARED WITHOUT AUDIT, FROM INFORMATION SUBMITTED BY CLIENT"

Source: © 1984 Copyright Comprehensive Accounting Corporation. ® COMPREHENSIVE is a service name and mark of Comprehensive Accounting Corporation. Reprinted with permission from Comprehensive Accounting Corporation.

SUMMARY

The administrative and operations package represents the support a franchisor provides a franchisee. Often these two forms of support are divided into two separate packages, the administrative package and the operations package. The administrative package contains the materials used by the franchisor to solicit prospective franchisees to the franchise system, the basic information concerning the franchise, and the follow-up forms used to trace to conclusion the actions and decision made on each prospective franchisee.

The administrative package contains the recruitment, promotional training and schooling, and supplementary services offered by the franchi-

Figure 13-7
Monthly Payroll Register

MONTHLY PAYROLL REGISTER												DATE 6-30-8_		Page 6
NAME DYNAMIC COMPANY					FED ID 36-2666765		STATE ID			SUC ID		LOCAL ID		
MO	DAY	ACC NO	CHECK NO	REG HRS	HRS OVER	TIPS	MEALS	GROSS AMT	COMBINED TAX	STATE TAX	LOCAL TAX		DEDUCTION MISC	NET AMOUNT
NAME DAVID R. ANDERSON					ADDR 4321 MAIN				SSN 329-32-2663		517		EMPL NO 0201	
CITY HOMETOWN					STATE AN	ZIP 99999								
6	05	517	1002	40, 0				350 00	74 24	8 01				267 75
6	12	517	1018	40 0				350 00	74 24	8 01				267 75
6	19	517	1026	40 0				350 00	74 24	8 01				267 75
6	22	517	1042	40, 0				350 00	74 24	8 01				267 75
TOT. MO.		SUC	.00	160 0				1400 00	296 96	32 04				1071 00
TOT. QTR.		SUC	1950.00	520 0				4550 00	965 12	104 13				
TOT. YR.		RATE	8.75	1040, 0				9100 00	1930 24	208 26				
NAME ELMER O. BARRETT					ADDR 1234 MAIN				SSN 333-09-8278		403		EMPL NO 0202	
CITY HOMETOWN					STATE AN	ZIP 99999								
6	05	403	1003	40, 0				180 00	28 23	3 77				148 00
6	12	403	1019	40 0				180 00	28 23	3 77				148 00
6	19	403	1027	40 0				180 00	28 23	3 77				148 00
6	26	403	1043	40 0				180 00	28 23	3 77				148 00
TOT. MO.		SUC	720.00	160 0				720 00	112 92	15 08				592 00
TOT. QTR.		SUC	2340.00	620 0				2340 00	366 99	49 01				
TOT. YR.		RATE	4.50	1040, 0				4680 00	733 98	98 02				
NAME CARL V. CHAPMAN					ADDR 5678 MAIN				SSN 708-03-7642		403		EMPL NO 0203	
CITY HOMETOWN					STATE AN	ZIP 99999								
6	05	403	1004	40, 0				240 00	36 12	4 31				199 57
6	12	403	1020	40 0				240 00	36 12	4 31				199 57
6	19	403	1028	40 0				240 00	36 12	4 31				199 57
6	26	403	1044	40 0				240 00	36 12	4 31				199 57
TOT. MO.		SUC	960.00	160 0				960 00	144 48	17 24				798 28
TOT. QTR.		SUC	3120.00	520 0				3120 00	469 56	56 03				
TOT. YR.		RATE	6.00	1040, 0				6240 00	939 12	112 06				
NAME NORMAN D. FREEMAN					ADDR 9100 MAIN				SSN 312-05-8609		403		EMPL NO 0206	
CITY HOMETOWN					STATE AN	ZIP 99999								
6	05	403	1005	15, 0				60 00	6 32	1 50				52 18
6	12	403	1021	15 0				60 00	6 32	1 50				52 18
6	19	403	1029	15 0				60 00	6 32	1 50				52 18
6	26	403	1045	15 0				60 00	6 32	1 50				52 18
TOT. MO.		SUC	240.00	60 0				240 00	25 28	6 00				208 72
TOT. QTR.		SUC	780.00	195 0				780 00	82 16	19 50				
TOT. YR.		RATE	4.00	390, 0				1560 00	164 32	39 00				
MONTH			540 0					3320 00	579 64	70 36				2670 00
QUARTER			1755 0					10790 00	1883 83	228 67				MO SUC X .027 00
YEAR			3510 0					21580 00	3767 66	457 34				1920 00 51 84
**TAXABLE FICA WAGES 3320.00 x .06650						220.78 FICA**								
													PREPARED BY COMPREHENSIVE	

Source: © 1984 Copyright Comprehensive Accounting Corporation. ® COMPREHENSIVE is a service name and mark of Comprehensive Accounting Corporation. Reprinted with permission from Comprehensive Accounting Corporation.

sor, as well as the approach taken to developing administrative control over the recruitment, selection, and training process of franchisees. When carefully prepared, this package provides a franchisor with clear purposes, policies, and procedures for the recruitment, promotion, selection, and training of franchisees. Also, by incurring and documenting the actual costs in development of this package, the franchisor has a basis for forecasting the costs associated with franchisee recruitment in the future growth periods of the franchise system.

The prospective franchisee's perspective on the administrative package is different from the franchisor's. The prospective franchisee is interested primarily in learning the requirements associated with owning a franchise, how it operates, and what services the franchisor provides, often for the sake of comparison. Specific information is often sought, including the financial requirements of purchasing the franchise, site, and equipment; building information; marketing factors and assistance from the franchisor; termination, cancellation, renewal, and restrictions that can be placed on a franchisee; and the financial solidity of the franchising system itself.

The operations package contains materials often separated into different manuals that address specific parts of the operations of the franchisor's approach to business, including operations, training, location selection criteria, marketing, advertising, field support, quality control, pre-opening, site inspection, and reporting/accounting forms and requirements. The material contained in the manuals is vitally important to a franchisee, helping reduce the risk of business failure because the errors and uncertainties have been worked out. The franchisee is guided and supported by the franchisor's proven methods of doing business in the particular industry.

REVIEW QUESTIONS

1. What are the typical components of a franchisor's administrative package?
2. How does the information of interest to a prospective franchisee differ from what the franchisor puts into the administrative package?
3. What information is typically included in a franchisor's brochure?
4. Briefly describe each of the major manuals a franchisor may develop. What is the purpose of each? What are the primary elements contained in each?
5. Why should a franchisor develop manuals or information booklets for prospective franchisees and franchisees-in-training?

CASE STUDY
CERTAIN-TEED RENTAL SYSTEM

In a midwestern city with a population of about 160,000, John Certain believes he has developed a wonderful idea for a franchising business. John has been the owner and operator of a late-model used car sales business for over ten years. The business has been successful, even though John has experienced several lean years.

Considering various ways to increase cash flow, John began thinking that renting used cars might be profitable. As a result, John has begun a rental business as a sideline to his used car sales business. The rental business has been quite successful during the first five months of operation and has led John to thinking about franchising. He is considering franchising his rent-a-car concept based on two primary factors: (1) the business would rent used rather than new cars; and (2) the lower rental fees would appeal to budget-conscious travelers and to government and business clientele. John wants to develop the franchise trademark and logo around his name, so he came up with "Certain-teed Rental System."

John obtained a list of used car dealers from his state's Used Car Dealer Association and is working on a franchise brochure to mail to this group of dealers. He sees the attraction to used car dealers to become franchisees as being their ability to increase utilization of current facilities by having a profitable secondary business with minimal additional expenses. Also, rental of used cars should increase floor traffic in the sales section, as well as be a good outlet for some hard-to-sell trade-in vehicles.

Considering today's budget consciousness, rental car users would be more concerned with daily cost of a car than with the car's vintage. John believes he could undercut the average price of new-car rentals by about 50 percent. And, the market is wide open, since literally thousands of cities are without a major new or used rental car company.

John knows he must create some administrative policies and develop operational procedures for prospective franchisees. Based on his experiences and recent conversations with friends in the used car business, he plans to address the following areas: an insurance liability pool for franchisees to join if they so desire; logos and trademark design and appropriate usage; design of the customer contact; tax benefit possibilities for a franchisee; maintenance/safety guidelines for rental cars; a computerized bookkeeping system; promotional kits for advertising; and a proposed schedule of gross income based on level of rental business activity.

CASE QUESTIONS

1. What else should John Certain consider?
2. Has he missed any major areas of administrative or operational policy?

REFERENCES

1. Curry, J. A. H., et al., *Partners for Profit: A Study of Franchising,* New York: American Management Association, Inc., 1966.
2. Day, George S., *Strategic Market Planning: The Pursuit of Competitive Advantage,* St. Paul, MN: West Publishing Company, 1984.
3. Justis, Robert T., and Richard J. Judd, "Master Franchising," *Journal of Small Business Management,* Vol. 24, No. 3 (July 1986): pp. 16-21.
4. Lovelock, Christopher H., *Services Marketing,* Englewood Cliffs, NJ: Prentice-Hall, Inc., 1984.
5. Mendelsohn, Martin, *The Guide to Franchising,* 4th edition, New York: Pergamon Press, 1985.

6. "The Franchise 100: The Most Profitable Franchises in America for the Franchisee," *Venture* (September 1985): pp. 40-46.
7. Bekey, Michelle, "How a Little Company Got Big," *Venture* (September 1985): pp. 52-53.
8. Vaughn, Charles L., *Franchising*, 2nd edition, Lexington, MA: Lexington Books, 1979.

CHAPTER 14
SUPPORT AND TRAINING FROM THE FRANCHISOR

In studying this chapter, you will:
- Understand the services provided by a franchisor to a franchisee.
- Be able to recognize success programs provided by franchisors.
- Realize the importance of an effective communication system to the franchisor-franchisee relationship.
- Understand the importance of the field representatives or middlemen.
- Recognize the value of franchisor training and what it generally entails.
- Understand the contents of a training manual or training program necessary for the development of the franchisee.

INCIDENT

Sally has an idea she thinks can be franchised. For the past several years she has been working for a large company designing software packages with application to microcomputers. From this position and through conversations with sales staff of the company, Sally has become aware of the general public's fear and lack of understanding of computers. She knows the underlying cause of much of the fear and misunderstanding is lack of familiarity with equipment and software, which often leads to inefficient or incorrect utilization of computers.

Sally's idea is to develop a training program for first-time computer users. Once the program has been designed, she would allow others to use it. She believes the best audience for her program would be independent computer and software dealers and some service companies. She hopes to franchise to the independent dealer network. Her fee would be a portion of the income received from dealers who would offer training sessions. Sally would continually update the program and add other, more advanced courses as needed.

Sally's main service to the franchisee would be to train the dealers in the use of the package. Aside from the training package and the software program, she would not need to provide anything tangible to the franchisee, so startup costs would be minimal.

Does Sally appear to have a good idea for development of a franchise organization? Is she correct about the minimal startup costs? What else should Sally be considering?

FRANCHISEE SUPPORT

Constructive support of franchisees is essential for efficient operation and ultimate success of a franchise system. The franchisor is responsible for developing and maintaining a support organization which satisfies the needs of each franchisee. Through training, the franchisor attempts to instill confidence in franchisees so they can be more productive and profitable in their implementation of the franchisor's methods. Also, the franchisee should leave the training program with a thorough knowledge of the operational requirements and processes of the franchise system. Franchisees-in-training should be made to feel that, if they adhere to the franchisor's proven approach, success will follow.

The franchisor's support organization and training are presented together in this chapter because these are the primary methods of support a franchisee receives. (See also Chapters 12 and 13 for discussions of training relative to the major topics of those chapters.) The major responsibility of the support organization or office of the franchisor is to develop and maintain sufficient and accurate communication between the franchisee and the parent organization. A prospective franchisor should be aware of the primary motivations one generally has in seeking a franchise opportunity: profitability, chance for self-employment, ability to run one's own business and be very successful at it, and opportunity to enjoy growth through the franchising arrangement. The franchisor's support structure should be designed to help franchisees realize these goals.

Profitability

The most compelling reason for a person to enter business of any type is the opportunity to make a profit. Capitalism is founded on the notions of free markets and profitability. A franchisor, through the framework available, must assist the franchisee in making a healthy profit, for if the franchisee is successful, the franchisor will also succeed. Franchisees are usually happiest when sales are strong and there is a good margin of profit over costs. They become discouraged when sales slide or profits shrink. The franchisor's support staff serves as the intermediary between the franchisor and the franchisee, providing training, insights, and helpful suggestions to maintain strong sales and improve profitability for the franchisee.

Self-Employment

One of the most exciting features of being in business is the opportunity of being one's own boss. Many new entrepreneurs have left their jobs because of conflicts with superiors or subordinates, reluctance to follow someone else's policies and procedures, or the feeling of not being able to make a positive contribution to the organization. Franchising provides such people the opportunity to be self-employed without having to learn on their own how to be successful through trial and error. The franchisee has the advantage of being able to look to the franchisor's proven approach and methods, which can be seen as a form of trust by the franchisee in the franchisor. Maintaining the bond of trust is not easy, as it must be nurtured and proven over and over again. It is the franchisor's support staff that provides the methods, programs, and suggestions for improvement and assists in solving problems, if necessary, to help the independent business owner, as a franchisee, to achieve success in business. The support staff needs to realize that, while franchisees continually rely on the franchisor to assist in the development of the business, they value their independence as well. Support staff should not demean or take away from the franchisee's independence as a business owner but should offer assistance and elicit cooperation along the lines beneficial to the franchisee and the franchising organization.

Striving to Be Successful

All of us desire to be successful. In our personal lives we seek affiliation, acceptance, recognition, and status within our peer groups. In business, we want to lead or be part of a successful organization. Franchisees are like most other business people. They want their businesses to succeed and grow in size and profitability.

Franchisors need to recognize that the franchisee's strong motivation to succeed is probably similar to their own motivation to become successful. A franchisor should provide whatever services, supplies, products, or support will enable the franchisee to improve the business. Success breeds success, and the greatest support for a franchisee is the opportunity for success. A franchisor's support staff should offer instruction, praise, encouragement, and other positive communication to the franchisee. A franchisee will not be successful if negative attitudes develop about the business, its future, the relationship with the franchisor, or the franchisee's abilities as a capable business owner.

Opportunity for Growth

Countless franchisees, facing the drudgery and daily trials of running a business, lose hope about expanding the business. Their energies are consumed with day-to-day operational concerns and the desire to keep up with the routines of business. Many franchisees would love to expand, but they feel they don't have the energy, or they would be taking too great a financial risk, or they feel they don't get enough support from the franchisor.

At some point in the development and operation of a business, the owner will want the business to grow. The success of a franchise system depends on growth, and for this reason the franchisor should be aware of the growth intentions of its franchisees. Being provided those services, new products or applications, marketing techniques, and carefully planned and franchisor-supported promotional campaigns will help franchisees keep a positive outlook on the business and continue to look for ways to expand the business and increase its profitability.

A Success Story

A field representative for a large franchised restaurant system entered one of the system's units. To her delight, the restaurant was busy and had a friendly ambience. The franchisees of this particular restaurant, Tom and Alice, are husband and wife who have been franchisees for four years. They are pleased with their franchise and with their franchisor. Tom and Alice are a hard-working couple, and during the first eighteen months of operation, they often spent 10 to 14 hours every day working at the store. Their two children, ages 16 and 14, help out after school and on weekends. Tom handles all food operations, including preparation and sales, and he is responsible for maintaining the general appearance of the building and grounds. Alice supervises the staff, oversees customer relations, and maintains the record keeping system.

The restaurant is bright, clean, and nicely decorated. The counter clerks wear neatly pressed uniforms and hats that display the logo of the franchise. Work and service counters are kept spotless, food-storage areas are clean, and food processing is performed according to the standards of the franchise system.

The clientele is primarily families and downtown workers. The restaurant is often used for business lunches, and in the evening is frequently filled with students from a local university as well as with families coming into the downtown area.

The owners appear to be contented. They follow the directions of the franchisor and use the operations manual as their "bible." They abide by the sales manual and serve the full range of menu items provided by the franchisor. Tom and Alice realize that extra effort is needed to keep the restaurant clean and tidy, but they know the profits and success that result from the quality service they provide and are committed to doing whatever is necessary to maintain the high standards of the franchise system.

A Failure Story

In the southwestern section of the same city, the field representative enters another franchisee's restaurant, located along a major trafficway leading to the city's shopping mall three blocks away. At this location, she notices a number of problems right away. The rest rooms appear neglected, perhaps not cleaned for the past several days. In the dining area, papers, straws, and plates litter three of the nine tables. Only two of seven employees are wearing a uniform; one wears a cap with the franchise logo, and the rest are wearing blue jeans and t-shirts. The storefront could use a coat of paint. A small plot of grass in front of the restaurant is overrun with weeds. Windows look filmy and dirty. The kitchen and food processing areas are cluttered with spilled food and empty cups and storage containers.

The franchisee doesn't seem interested in taking time to mingle with the customers or serve them a second cup of coffee. A waitress approaches the field representative, asking her how to handle a customer complaining about cold food. Discussion with the franchisee leaves the field representative feeling that he is sour and full of complaints. He blames many of his problems on inferior equipment and lack of proper training. And although he has not followed suggested pricing guidelines, nor did he purchase the recommended equipment for the restaurant when he opened for business, he complains that sales are unsteady and the equipment is insufficient to handle the orders during peak periods. He complains about sunlight coming through the windows and creating uncomfortable temperatures in the restaurant; however, he did not follow the recommended architectural design supplied by the franchisor. This franchisee has stated that he wants to get out of the business, having had four profitable months, three break-even months, and five "loss" months in the past year. He believes that the major problems are insufficient sales, poor communication with employees, and a lack of understanding and the "right kind" of support from the franchisor. Yet his location is in a strong business area, and the field representative has devoted more of her time and energy and more company resources to helping this franchisee over the past two years than she has provided to Tom and Alice in the past four years.

COMMUNICATION

Constructive, positive communication is one of the requirements of a successful business. Areas of accountability need to be delineated between franchisor and franchisee, as well as between franchisee and employees. This means that objectives, performance standards, and duties must be clearly understood and accepted. Information systems used in the franchise system, which form the links between performance, managerial accounting, and decision making, must also be understood. Information usage — who gets what information, from whom, and how often — forms the basis of an effective feedback system. The feedback system of the franchise organization should make everyone aware of the importance of two-way communication — of listening, offering constructive criticism, motivating employees, and using incentives and rewards.

The support and the training provided by the franchisor to the franchisee will foster the development and maintenance of a communication system for the franchise. The effectiveness (or ineffectiveness) of the communication system will dramatically affect the success of the system. It is important for the franchisor to be accurately informed about the various activities and changes taking place within the franchise system as the company seeks to improve performance and profitability. Effective communication through carefully planned systems of information, recognition, and reporting is critical for continued growth and development of the franchised business. Communication is also integral to the superior-subordinate relationships within the franchisor's and the franchisee's organizations. The more effective the communication, the more effective will be the supervision. Of the various approaches to developing effective communications between franchisor and franchisee, the following methods have been most successfully used by franchise systems: telephone contacts, mail contacts, personal visits by the franchisor's field representative to the franchisee, franchisee sub-group meetings, and corporate meetings.

Telephone Contacts

One-to-one verbal communication is one of the most effective modes of communication. Frequent contact helps to ensure closeness and continuity within a relationship. As contact tapers off, the closeness diminishes, and questions can even arise about the reasons for developing and continuing the relationship. In a franchise system, telephone contacts are important to keep the franchisee informed about plans or current activities of the parent company, to evaluate franchisee performance or records, and to let the franchisee know what assistance to expect from the franchisor. Phone contacts can be set up in many different ways. Strongly service-oriented franchisors encourage their field representatives to make contact not only on a planned, routine basis, but also spontaneously, or even by using a different approach such as a conference call involving several franchisees.

Planned telephone calls to the franchisee on a particular day each week or month are very useful. Such calls are typically franchisor-initiated and are meant to discuss sales levels, product/service support, and advertising and promotional plans, as well as to respond to questions or issues raised by the franchisee during the previous call. These calls help develop the interrelationship between franchisor and franchisee and can be one of the mainstays of support between them. The calls should be friendly, helpful, and positive. They are not intended for faultfinding or for enhancing the power of the franchisor over the franchisee.

Spontaneous telephone calls tend to boost the morale and feelings of interdependence of the franchisee and the franchisor. It can be exciting for a franchisee to receive a call from the home office "just to find out how things are going." Such calls help the franchisor understand the immediate concerns of the franchisee, get a feel for the franchisee's general attitude over time, and determine if there is anything the parent company could or should be doing over and above the regular services it is providing. These calls are often cordial, designed to help improve communication between franchisor and franchisee. However, the spontaneous call can instill fear. The franchisee may wonder, "Why am I getting a call from the home office? What have I done now?" The franchisor should try to dispel any feelings of fear, keeping the tone of the conversation amicable and showing genuine interest in the franchisee's progress.

Conference calls provide an effective means of contacting several franchisees at the same time. These calls are generally prearranged by letter or earlier phone contact to help ensure "attendance" of franchisees within a district, area, or region. Such calls are generally used to inform franchisees of new product/service activities by the franchisor, new advertisements or upcoming promotions, or new contests or customer relations projects. The conference call is an effective way to instill in franchisees their importance both as individuals and as members of the franchise team. Franchisors generally consider the expenses of conference calls to be low when they consider the goodwill fostered and the results often obtained with these calls.

Mail Contacts

Use of the mail is the primary method of providing and explaining instructions, supplying advertising and promotional materials, and discussing any legal matters that come up. Also, mail contact is the principal means of reporting district sales levels and personnel changes within the company, distributing newsletters, and providing evaluative reports to franchisees. Mail is often used to provide follow-up information after spontaneous or conference calls, giving suggestions for advertising, promotions, or general marketing, or perhaps responding to a question or issue raised by a franchisee.

Letters are often sent on a regular basis from the sales manager and/or the president of the franchise system to franchisees, to assure them of continued support and service from the home office. Personal letters from the franchisor to a franchisee suggest the acceptance and importance of the individual franchisee in the franchise system.

House organs or newsletters can be very effective in explaining various activities within the franchised company, recognizing top salespeople or locations, expressing the opinions of the president, announcing new territories or new franchisees, and presenting other information of a positive and helpful nature. Franchisor Arthur Sells of NAMCO provides a weekly newsletter to franchisees to help maintain friendly and positive lines of communication between the home office and the field company. (See Figure 14-1.) He includes information such as weekly, quarterly, and yearly sales activities; new markets opened; editorials; topics of interest, such as tips on coping with stress; selling techniques; and various words of wisdom that relate directly with personal selling, the primary method of making sales for NAMCO.

Activity reports are required by almost all franchised firms on a weekly or biweekly basis. These reports typically address such information as sales volume, number of sales, expenses, call-backs, and sales to individuals, community groups, and institutions. The central thrust is to provide a picture of the type of sale made, by client category (if important in that business) and by expenses incurred for each category of sales. Each week the home office should send out the report forms for the franchisee to complete, detailing the sales activities, expenses, personnel costs and/or changes, and other activities important for tracking performance. Each month the franchisee manager at the home office may develop a franchisee profile which illustrates the strengths and weaknesses of each unit within a district, area, or region. Activity reports are very helpful for the franchisor to make constructive suggestions to individual franchisees for improving operations and/or congratulating franchisees for work well done.

Visits

Personal visits by a representative of the franchise home office are very important to the franchisee. These visits are usually made by field representatives of the franchisor, but are occasionally made by the franchising company's president, vice-president, franchising director, sales manager, or regional or district supervisor. The personal visit is a good public relations tool the franchising company can use to encourage and uplift the spirits of the franchisees and their employees. Personal visits are also

**Figure 14-1
Sample NAMCO Newsletter (Page 1)**

The Eagle

Since 1953 — The Weekly Newsletter for Successful Selling — Nov. 13, 1987

**Honor Paid to Alden Sells for Meritorious Week, Quarter & YTD
Veteran Salesman, Bob Paulhus Has a #2 Week
MORE "CLEAN-UP" WINNERS**

EDITORIAL

LETTERS TO THE EDITOR:

Thanks to Joe Gredesky, President of NAMCO Marketing of Greater Akron for his letter to the Editor (included in this week's newsletter). We encourage people to contribute to our Newsletter, even when those contributions are critical of our performance. Most importance is, the thrust of Joe's letter is exactly on the point raised by Ken Cherry in Buffalo a few weeks ago. By now, most should have received and reviewed the tape made at the meeting. If you remember, Ken stated: "The best way to grow your franchise is to grow the people necessary to help accomplish the task." Ken also pointed out that the new NAMCO was going to work in a variety of directions to help you double; even triple your current income: Joe calls it "a double eagle incentive program."

Even though I do not entirely agree with Joe, when he states: "we

**Sales Week Ending Nov. 7
1st Week in November**

**WEEK
TOP FIVE**

A. Sells	Hudson Valley	$2,575
B. Paulhus	Rhode Island	2,540
M. Douyard	S/W Conn	2,360
D. Jonmaire	Buffalo South	1,995
R. Reitenga	Ann Arbor	1,628

**QUARTER
TOP FIVE**

A. Sells	Hudson Valley	13,225
M. Douyard	S/W Conn	12,878
D. Jonmaire	Buffalo South	11,610
D. James	Burlington	9,520
B. Paulhus	Rhode Island	8,890

HONORABLE MENTION

P. Pliskow	Oakland County	7,520

**YEAR TO DATE
TOP FIVE**

A. Sells	Hudson Valley	164,508
P. Pliskow	Oakland County	98,485
E. Cavallaro	New Hampshire	92,958
P. Nolin	Oneonta	89,190
R. Reitenga	Ann Arbor	75,727

HONORABLE MENTION

M. Drellos	Albany	70,875
D. Jonmaire	Buffalo South	68,021

CONSISTENT PRODUCERS

C. Storch	Dayton	10 weeks
D. Jonmaire	Buffalo South	10 weeks
A. Sells	Hudson Valley	4 weeks
D. James	Burlington	4 weeks
R. Reitenga	Ann Arbor	2 weeks
B. Paulhus	Rhode Island	2 weeks

INSIDE NEWS

**To the Editor
(Joe Gredesky)**

Task Force

Pulling Out All the Stops

"I'll Give You Seven Minutes..."

All This and More in This Week's Newsletter

PEOPLE IN THE NEWS

ALDEN SELLS (Hudson Valley) starts the first week in November off #1. Alden made five sales this week for $2,575. All five sales were on Middletown West/Mount Hope Area; CORNELIUS, DODD, & CONNELL, INC. (funeral home), HORTON MEMORIAL HOSPITAL, BARMANN'S REALTY, SCOTTIE'S QUALITY (auto body), and SKIP'S AUTO REPAIR. Alden had to shorten his week last week. On the way to see a customer that had been recommended to him, Alden was involved in a car accident. His almost-

---

Source: Reprinted by permission. *The Eagle* is a publication of National Merchandising Corp. & Namco Systems, Inc.

very effective for addressing problems raised by the franchisee or the franchising company, showing genuine commitment to resolve any such problems.

Initially, the most important reason for field visits is to get to know franchisees on their own turf. By the time the business is open and operating, the franchisee has probably met the president and support staff from the home office. However, personal meetings on the turf of the franchisee are different from meetings at the home office. Usually, "get-acquainted" visits to the new unit in the early months of operation are brief and supportive, and are beneficial to both franchisor and franchisee.

Support-service visits to the franchisee should not be confused with "get-acquainted" visits. The primary purpose of the franchisor's support staff is to provide service to the franchisee. Their visits should aim toward helping resolve problems that arise in the franchisee's operations and providing advice and assistance in meeting reporting requirements of the franchisor, as well as giving helpful hints in dealing with changing competitive conditions. Support service is of little value when advice consists of knee-jerk or off-the-cuff opinions. Careful consideration of the specific problems raised by the franchisee should be made by the home office *prior* to the support-service visit. In this way, advice, assistance, and specific recommendations will carry the weight of thorough consideration before they are presented. A franchisee will readily see the difference between blue-sky suggestions and thoughtful counsel.

Training visits are usually made by members of the home office staff. Often the staff who make these visits are those involved in the preopening and grand opening training of the respective franchisees. The franchisee must be able to see the value of the royalty fees being returned to the business, and one important way of accomplishing this is to provide service through training visits. These visits usually address either (1) problems in business operation that can be overcome by additional on-site training of the franchisee and staff, or (2) changes in operating procedures or personnel, financial, or marketing approaches recommended by the franchisor. Training is perhaps the greatest intangible benefit or service provided by the franchisor to the franchisees.

Franchisee Sub-Group Meetings

Meetings between franchisees can be very beneficial to the franchisees as well as to the parent company. Many franchisors have learned through experience that one of the greatest forms of support for weaker franchised units is the sharing of experience, techniques, and advice by stronger, more successful franchisees. Some franchisees tend to reject recommendations or suggestions from the home office, yet readily accept criticism and suggestions from their franchisee peers. Because peer-group influence is always a strong determinant of people's attitudes and behavior, it can serve to benefit the franchisees as well as the franchisor through franchisee meetings.

One approach used to encourage franchisee meetings is for the franchisor to assist in the development of area, district, or regional franchisee organizations. These groups may meet on a quarterly, semiannual, or yearly basis to discuss problems and strengths of their respective businesses. In these meetings, one or more franchisees may come forth to assist other, typically newer, franchisees with training and support. The meetings usually follow a seminar format, with workshops, training sessions, or panel discussions devoted to topics of specific interest to attending franchisees. Sometimes franchisee councils call meetings to draw franchisees from adjoining territories for training and sharing of information. These regional meetings are usually under the direction of the more successful franchisees of the district or region and have franchisor representation available to assist in training and participate in informal interchanges about common problems, conditions, or approaches used within the franchise system.

Corporate Meetings

Corporate meetings are often utilized by franchisors to bring together franchisees on an annual or other regular basis to share information and provide training. At these meetings, an informal atmosphere is encouraged through dinners or social gatherings. The training sessions or seminars are designed to refresh and improve managerial skills and provide a forum for presentations about company performance, new products/services or marketing techniques, and any changes in operational procedures or reporting requirements. Often, open dialogue is encouraged through formal discussions, question-and-answer periods, and informal gatherings.

THE FIELD REPRESENTATIVE

One of the most effective means of communication between franchisor and franchisee is the franchisor's field representative. The field representative helps ensure a smooth, continuing relationship between franchisee and franchisor. Small franchise organizations without a staff of field representatives often depend upon the legal, contractual agreement to maintain the franchisor-franchisee relationship, which can lead to the relationship being "controlled" through use of the written contract. Large, successful franchise systems have found the field representative almost indispensable to developing and maintaining a positive, cooperative relationship with the franchisees.

"Middleman" or field representative titles are numerous (see Table 14-1), but the functions and operations generally remain the same. Field representatives are under the direction of the franchisor to be the eyes, ears, and mouth of the company. They are assigned territories or a group of franchisees, and they have the task of overseeing, supervising, evaluating, servicing, and motivating their franchisees.

Typically, the larger the franchise chain, the more complex the field representation network. For example, several large national chains use regional managers to coordinate and provide franchisor services to franchisees. Each regional manager might supervise three or four area managers, each of whom supervises perhaps five to seven district managers. Each district manager in turn would be responsible for and supervise approximately ten individual franchised units. Such an authority structure seems complex, but it can provide for steady contact downward and upward through the reporting and service lines of communication. A structured, responsible approach to reporting and servicing units in the field suggests that a franchisee should be visited at least every two weeks by the representative.

The middleman function is to help support the franchisee's business. The field representative may wear a variety of hats — that of handholder, tyrant, wise parent-figure, or sympathizer. The effective field representative learns to be sensitive to the needs of the franchisee, demonstrating an interest in helping the franchisee to increase profits. The field representative, as a middleman, can be said to perform five distinct functions for the franchising firm: (1) to represent the franchisor in the franchisor-franchisee relationship; (2) to act as a consultant to the franchisee, providing problem-solving skills and professional advice that will help the franchisee become even more successful; (3) to provide training at the franchisee's site for employees as well as for the franchisees themselves; (4) to serve essentially as a management guide for the franchisee, helping the franchisee/entrepreneur develop managerial competence in decision making, delegation, record keeping, and operations control; and (5) to be a motivator for the franchisee. The overall goal of the field representative is to help the franchisee reach his or her potential and to nurture a positive attitude and maintain high morale among franchisees and among the franchisees' employees.

Table 14-1
Typical "Middleman" Titles Used in Franchising

Field Representative	Business Management Representative
Field Consultant	Regional (Area) Marketing Manager
Area Manager	Services Representative
Field Coordinator	Sales Representative

FRANCHISEE TRAINING

Training is a very important part of a franchisor's program for growth and development. In one sense, the franchising process can be viewed as an attempt to reproduce in other locations the successful model or prototype operation. This depends heavily on effective transfer of knowledge and skills from one location to another. A recent International Franchise Association survey ranked training as a highly important communication mechanism between franchisor and franchisees.[1]

Many persons interested in becoming franchisees lack specific experience in the business they seek to enter. A formal training process is often the primary, if not the only, approach used to teach the necessary business operations that will enable one to succeed in the business. Various studies indicate that franchisors in fast foods, accounting and business services, computer sales and service, and financial and insurance services feel that the training provided to their franchisees accounts for a significant measure of their success as franchise systems.[2]

Developing a Training Operation

The training component of a franchise system involves three major actions by a franchisor: designing and implementing a training unit or function, establishing a training location, and developing the training program, including the philosophy, learning, and skills to be achieved and the methods to be used in providing the training.

Almost every franchisor has a training unit or training function formally established within the franchise organization. The person in charge of training typically has experience in each major function of the franchisor's business. This person may have originally been a trainee, an assistant manager, a franchisee, an original partner, a manager at a competitive company, or even someone from outside the industry; there appears to be no specific career development pattern for one performing this important function. However, there are two critical requirements that must be met by anyone put in charge of a franchisee training program: The person must be knowledgeable about effective training processes, and must have both depth and breadth of understanding of the

---

[1] *Franchisor/Franchisee Communications Survey Report* (Washington, DC: International Franchise Association, 1985), p. 9.
[2] See for example: Helen LaVan, Joseph Latona, and Ray Coye, "Training and Development in the Franchisor-Franchisee Relationship," *Society of Franchising Proceedings*, First Annual Conference (Omaha, Nebraska, September 1986), pp. 175-185; Doris Fenske, "Franchising: Is the Time Ripe?" *Best's Review* 85, No. 7 (November 1984), pp. 16-24; Peter Franklin, "Where's the Beef in Franchising? The Founder of Wendy's Tells What It Takes to Succeed," *Money* 14, No. 3 (March 1985), pp. 149-154; Leo Lauzen, "Franchising: Another Strategy to Start Your Own Business," *Management Accounting* 66, No. 1 (July 1984), pp. 50-53.

operational needs and characteristics that will ensure success in the particular franchised business. The reason such depth and breadth is necessary is that this person needs to be able to incorporate into the training program (1) production/operations methods of the franchised business, (2) accounting, marketing, and personnel practices, and (3) effective methods of developing and maintaining constructive franchisor-franchisee relationships. Usually, because the training function is critically important to the continuity and growth of the franchise system, the head of training is part of the upper-management of the organization.

The training center for a franchisor can be located almost anywhere. Typically, the center is the original location of the franchisor, or the prototype (if the original location is not used as the prototype). Training centers may also be located regionally. Some franchisors, such as McDonald's (Chicago, Illinois) or Dunkin' Donuts of America (Braintree, Massachusetts), choose to centralize training to enhance their control of the training process and ensure continuity of subject matter to be presented. Holiday Inns, Inc., offers coursework for new franchisees at its Holiday Inn University in Memphis, Tennessee, and Long John Silver's provides training at the Jerrico Center in Lexington, Kentucky.

Training programs vary considerably from one franchise system to another. Most franchisee training programs are at least five days long and may last for up to two months. Alternative training programs are often provided that vary in length, complexity, and subject matter. Training enables the franchisor to teach the franchisees and other employees the skills necessary for them to be successful within the franchise system.

Development of the training program is usually grounded in a philosophy of learning, by which the training objectives, the skills to be learned, and the training methods to be utilized are carefully put together. The franchisee needs to learn the business rather than be taught or simply given training about the franchise through books or manuals. The business is best learned through a blend of lectures, group discussions, situational problem analysis, and independent, hands-on performance under the guidance of experienced trainers. The focus is often on self-application through actual performance of operations required within the franchise system, whether the training takes place in a training center or on the job at the franchisee's own franchised business.

Franchisee training is generally divided into three major components: (1) pre-opening training, (2) grand opening training, and (3) continuing (post-opening) training.

Pre-Opening Training

Probably the most intensive training occurs during the pre-opening period. Most franchise systems require at least two weeks, with some systems offering as much as 300 hours of pre-opening training. This training typically consists of classroom as well as hands-on experience. Subjects often addressed include planning the franchised business, hiring, purchasing, merchandising, advertising, business management, cash and inventory control, and production/operational methods.

Many franchisors have found that working with a limited number of franchisees, say between three and 12, works best, providing sufficient peer interaction while allowing sufficient individuality to enable participants to get the most out of the learning experiences. Franchisees have the opportunity to meet and discuss their expectations, desires, strengths, and worries with other franchisees as they individually and collectively anticipate running their own operation. When franchisees meet for training, their interaction is very helpful in developing loyalty to the franchise system, creating individual identity within the franchise organization, and learning or improving skills of operation for the franchise.

A franchisee training program usually includes a training manual (see Table 14-2) that covers topics pertinent to the franchised business. These topics include the system utilized by the franchisor, finance, marketing, operations, service/production, and management/personnel. The training manual, which may also include audio or video tapes, typically provides descriptions of all franchise operations and usually includes operating procedures suggested or required by the franchisor. As such, the manual is very important to both franchisor and franchisee. For the franchisor, the manual not only offers a training approach, but also affords protection in case any dispute or question arises regarding appropriateness of methods used in training franchisees. For franchisees, the manual provides an organized approach to the information they need to know in order to function effectively within the business environment of the franchisor. Thus, the manual provides a ready reference to refresh the memory or to solve a specific problem that arises during a workday.

Grand Opening Training

Most franchisors send either the training manager or a member of the training unit to work with the new franchisee for the grand opening of a franchised business. Such service may or may not be available for smaller, service-oriented franchised businesses. Grand opening training consists of one to two weeks of in-depth work experience in which the trainer assists the franchisee with the grand opening of the business. The trainer, alone or with the new franchisee (which is preferable), trains the staff in operating procedures associated with service/production, finance, marketing, and operations. The franchisor's representative often stays with the franchisee until the newly opened unit is running smoothly, which may take from several days to several weeks. The length of time can vary considerably as a result of the normal difficulties of any

Table 14-2
Sample Contents of a Franchisee Training Manual

INTRODUCTION

Executive Summary
Industry Information
Franchisor Information
Required Activities with Franchisor
Contracts, Licenses, Permits

FINANCE

Balance Sheet
Income Statement
Source and Use of Funds Statement
Cash Budget
Record Keeping Procedures
Cash Register Procedures
Credit Sales Procedures
Check Sales Procedures
Petty Cash
Reconciliations: Bank, Cash, Sales
Night Deposits
Payroll
Social Security
Withholding Taxes
Leases
Insurance

MARKETING

Target Market
Customer Groups
Advertising
Promotion
Pre-Opening Activities
Grand Opening
Post-Opening Activities
Merchandising
Customer Relations
Product/Service Definitions and
  Descriptions

OPERATIONS

(See Operating Manual)
Personnel
Store Operations
Housekeeping
Maintenance
Management
Sales Operations
Inventory
Unit Operations

SERVICE/PRODUCTION

Equipment Ordering and Specifications
Inventory Control
Ordering Control from Suppliers and
  Franchisors, and Cost Schedule
Serving
Service/Product Preparation Methods
Warehouse Store Methods
Sanitary Control
Kitchen Operation
Portion Operation and Control

MANAGEMENT/PERSONNEL

Job Specifications
Recruitment
Selection
Training
Developing and Maintaining Work Logs
Motivation of Employees
Personnel Development
Labor Laws and Regulations

---

grand opening or because of unexpected problems or complexities. Some service-oriented franchisors provide between two and seven weeks from the time the training begins to the actual grand opening of the franchised business. This period includes one to three weeks of intensive training at headquarters as well as one to three weeks of on-site training to prepare for the forthcoming grand opening. At the time of the grand opening the franchisor representative stays with the new franchisee for the first full week of operation. Most franchisors are convinced that the same trainer should follow through with the franchisee from headquarters training through the grand opening of the business. This closeness helps build the business relationship between the franchisor and the franchisee, giving evidence of the franchisor's commitment to serving the franchisee and hopefully earning loyalty, enthusiasm, and team spirit from the franchisee in return.

Continuing Training Programs

As a group, franchisors do not follow a consistent approach to continuing education or training of their franchisees. Some franchisors provide no training beyond the formal pre-opening training. Some franchisors provide training at quarterly, semiannual, or annual meetings between the franchisor and the franchisees. Others hold seminars on specific topics of current interest to franchisees as the need arises. Some of the large, national or international franchise systems provide a regular schedule of training at their headquarters or at the site of the franchisee requesting the training. Considered in its broadest context, most franchisor-provided training is more or less informal and takes place through a one-to-one relationship, addressing specific problems or needs of the franchisee. The training is given during the regular weekly or monthly visit by the field representative to the franchise site and addresses such areas as quality control, financial or accounting methods, advertising or marketing developments, or new methods, equipment, or products/services being introduced by the franchisor. In addition, some franchisors provide specialized training and advice to some franchisees but not to others. For example, a franchisee who has a territory that appears ripe for expansion may receive training or assistance in location analysis, market analysis, lease negotiations, or building design and construction services. Also, specific marketing plans may be developed area by area within a franchise system to help franchisees capitalize on differing demographics and consumer attitudes toward the system's product or service. Such marketing programs are usually developed at franchisee-funded marketing departments located at the system headquarters.

Many franchising firms provide ongoing training to their franchisees and the employees of the franchisees. Ongoing training varies widely from franchisor to franchisor and from industry to industry. Regional and national meetings for franchisees are often loaded with training opportunities such as marketing updates, industry trends, new product/

service developments, franchisor policy/procedure changes, or informal exchanges of ideas among franchisees themselves or between franchisors and franchisees. Many franchised companies utilize their home office training facility for these conference-type training programs as well as for focused, hands-on training of franchisees or their employees in new operations or financial/accounting procedures.

Field representatives play an important role in the delivery of continuing training. They often work directly with the franchisee at the business site, providing expert counsel, giving on-the-spot management and operational suggestions, providing instructional video or audio materials for the franchisee and employees, and serving as a conduit for sharing new ideas that are developing across the franchise system.

Ongoing training is the primary method for most franchisors to initiate new products/services into the franchise system. The franchisor has responsibility to provide continuing improvement in operational procedures that reflect the latest and best techniques for providing product/service to the customer. Also, the franchisor is usually responsible for developing any new products/services or modifying existing products to meet the changing needs of the customer. The ongoing training format is the ideal vehicle for transferring the knowledge and skills required to keep the franchise system lean, up-to-date, and efficient.

Illustration of an Approach to Franchised Business Training

Training is one of the cornerstones of successful development of a franchise system. Gene Getchell, Vice President for Franchising of Long John Silver's, Inc., summarizes the value of a franchise training program in the overall scheme of franchising as follows:

> A successful franchise is one in which the franchisor provides the franchisee with a support system for every major facet of the business. Among these support systems, a strong training program is the keystone to overall success. Show me a franchisee who believes in ongoing training and makes the investment of time, people and money involved with training, and I'll show you a strong, profitable franchisee.[3]

Long John Silver's, Inc., is a subsidiary of Jerrico, Inc., which operates the Jerrico Center for Training and Development in Lexington, Kentucky, for its food service concept. The basic philosophy of the Center is to develop Jerrico's "people resource." The mission of the Center is stated as follows:

---

[3] Eugene Getchell, Vice President for Franchising, Long John Silver's, Inc., a division of Jerrico, Inc. Material quoted from letter submitted to authors, July, 1987.

... [to be] an equal partner with Operations in pursuing the corporate mission of 'Exceeding Our Guest's Expectations' of superior quality product, friendly, efficient service in a clean, attractive environment. To succeed in this mission we must put forth our best efforts to train each member of the Long John Silver's team in every aspect of their job.[4]

Jerrico is a leader in food-service training, providing both centralized training at the headquarters facility and courses throughout the country. Over 11,000 management personnel have been trained at the Jerrico Center since it opened in 1974. Courses are offered throughout the year for all levels of management as well as for hourly employees.

The training programs for hourly employees are structured to provide each employee with standards for specific performance tasks, in order to ensure consistent performance for the company. The training is also designed to provide employees with the opportunity for advancement through cross-training in several areas of job responsibility. This type of training is offered on site for the franchisees.

Jerrico offers eight separate training programs for franchisees and managers within the business. Each course description provides information about who might benefit from the course, how long the course will last, the training site, any prerequisite courses, the objectives of the course, what materials are required, and a brief overview of the course identifying what subjects are included and what the format will be. (See Figure 14-2 for illustration of Jerrico's Phase I and II training programs.) The Jerrico Center also offers courses in supervisory development and instructor training; the latter prepares franchisees for conducting certain courses in their restaurants, which helps them cope with the dual role of developing management trainees and managing a restaurant. Figure 14-3 identifies the objectives of four specific training modules included within the Phase III/Basic Management course.

The Jerrico Center is a self-contained training environment, with its own equipment and computer laboratories, classrooms, recreation facilities, and staff offices. Trainees can utilize the libraries, basketball courts, swimming pool, cafeteria, and other university facilities during their time at the Center. Jerrico also provides in-house audiovisual services to facilitate the design and development of presentations for major meetings within the corporation.

---

[4] Getchell.

Figure 14-2
Phase I and II of Jerrico Management Course

Phase I and II

PHASE I

Developed for:
Management-trainees

Length of Program:
Jerry's Restaurants: Four (4) Weeks
Long John Silver's: Three (3) Weeks

- Beginning within one week of hire date.

Training Location:
Accredited Phase I Training Restaurants designated within each region.

Class Size:
Maximum three (3) Trainees

Pre-requisites:
(None)

Objective of Program:
The Phase I training program provides new management trainees with an extensive introduction to the basic aspects of restaurant operations.

Overview of Program:
The trainees work closely with an accredited training manager to observe, practice, and develop expertise in the basics of food service operations. The emphasis of training in Phase I is on Guest awareness, product preparation, food/plate preparation, administrative activities, opening/closing procedures, food ordering and other aspects of restaurant operations.

Each trainee is evaluated daily and weekly. These evaluations provide feedback to the trainee and performance information to the superior.

Upon successful completion of Phase I, the trainee is immediately assigned to an accredited Phase II restaurant.

Program Materials:
Materials and support available through Regional Training Coordinator.

- Instructor's Manual
- Trainee's Guide
- Support materials available in the restaurant

(For further information contact Training Coordinator.)

PHASE II

Developed for:
Management Trainees

Length of Program:
Three (3) Weeks

Training Location:
Accredited Phase II Training Restaurants established within each region.

Class Size:
Maximum two (2) Trainees

Pre-requisites:
Phase I

Objective of Program:
The Phase II training program provides management trainees, who have successfully completed the Phase I program, with advanced management skills under less supervision.

Each trainee is evaluated daily and weekly. These evaluations provide feedback to the trainee and performance information to the superior.

Upon successful completion of Phase II training, the management trainee is immediately assigned to their assigned (home) restaurant where the knowledge will be routinely practiced from an assistant manager's perspective.

Program Materials:
Materials and support available through Regional Training Coordinator.

- Instructor's Manual
- Trainee's Guide
- Support materials available in the restaurant

(For further information contact Regional Training Coordinator)

Source: Reprinted with permission from Long John Silver's, Inc.

Figure 14-3
Phase III of Jerrico Management Course

PHASE III/BASIC MANAGEMENT PREP: SUPPLEMENTAL INFORMATION

A FEW WORDS ABOUT PHASE III/BASIC MANAGEMENT:

All Phase III/Basic Management course modules have specific objectives and purposes. Below is a list of current modules and a brief description.

A-LINE: Students practice proper operations on the A-Line Cash Register system. (*Testing)

ACCOUNTING: Students learn and demonstrate an in-depth knowledge of the Profit and Loss Statement, as well as resolve discrepancies between projected and actual monthly statements during a P & L review. (*Testing)

ALL-STAR (Jerry's Restaurants Only):   Students become familiar with the All-Star Training Program for hourly employees and how to establish/conduct this program within their restaurants.

COACHING: Students practice coaching skills discussed in class in order to analyze and correct specific employee performance problems.

COMMUNICATIONS PRINCIPLES: Students become aware of the skills a manager must have in communicating with all kinds of people. Special emphasis is placed on applying these basic principles of effective communications to assertiveness and listening.

COST CONTROL: Students discuss procedures for analyzing specific cost control problems and outlining plans for dealing with these.

EFFECTIVE COMMUNICATIONS: Students practice effective speaking in formal and informal situations to develop both platform and extemporaneous speaking skills.

ENERGY CONSERVATION: Students learn of the critical need for energy conservation and how it affects our personal and professional lives, as well as bottom line.

EQUIPMENT LAB: Students learn about all equipment of a unit in order to build a working knowledge of maintenance and minor repairs. (*Testing)

FIRE FIGHTING: Students identify various types of fires and demonstrate ability in the operation of a manual fire extinguisher.

FIRST AID: Students discuss knowledge and skills to meet the needs of most minor situations when emergency first aid care is needed and medical assistance is not immediately available.

FLAGSHIP TRAINING PROGRAM (Long John Silver's Only):   Students become familiar with the Flagship Training Program for hourly employees and how to establish/conduct this program within their restaurants.

GUEST EXPECTATIONS: Students discuss and practice ways of meeting and exceeding Guest Expectations.

**Figure 14-3
Continued**

INTERVIEWING TECHNIQUES: Students discuss the process of selecting individuals through a well-planned interview and careful decision making.

LEARNING OLYMPICS (Team Competition): Students reinforce their knowledge of operations and management skills by participating as a team in an "end of course" skills competition.

LOCAL SHOPPE MARKETING: Students identify and plan for local marketing opportunities.

MOTIVATIONAL TECHNIQUES: Students become aware of their own responsibilities to use techniques designed to motivate their employees as they brainstorm the characteristics and "movers" of a motivated person, motivational approaches and perceptions.

P & L ANALYSIS (Franchise): Students study and discuss the basic elements of a P & L statement and apply that knowledge in analyzing an actual P & L. (*Testing)

PERFORMANCE APPRAISAL: Students will discuss and practice specific techniques for conducting an effective performance appraisal.

PLATE COST/SALES MIX (Franchise): Students complete practice exercises to gain skills in basic concepts and formulas involved in the development of plate costs and preparation of a sales mix sheet. (*Testing)

PROFESSIONAL DEVELOPMENT PLAN (PDP): Students discuss and develop a personal development plan necessary to handle the complexities of day-to-day management in a timely manner.

QUALITY ASSURANCE: Students identify and discuss the principal factors and processes in achieving and maintaining high standards of product quality. (*Testing)

SANITATION: Students discuss the principles, objectives and responsibilities of a food service worker and manager in the areas of cleanliness and sanitation.

SCHEDULING: Students perform an analysis of techniques required to complete an employee schedule and organize a shift.

SITUATIONAL LEADERSHIP: Students discuss the need for leadership styles that vary with each individual they manage by analyzing and evaluating the effectiveness of their personal leadership styles, as well as identifying situational leadership techniques which apply to their subordinates.

TEAM COORDINATOR MEETINGS: Students gain experience in leadership and communication requirements for working with peers and superiors by taking on the leadership role for one team project during the course.

TEAM PROJECT PRESENTATIONS: Students practice group dynamics and decision making in a teamwork-oriented assignment that is compiled after class and presented as a team at the end of the course.

**Figure 14-3
Continued**

TIME MANAGEMENT: Students discuss various helps and hindrances to effective time management and address areas for increasing their personal time management skills.

TRAINING TECHNIQUES: Students discuss principles of effective training and conduct and analyze a training session using the "Four-Step" training method.

REV: 05/87

Source: Reprinted with permission from Long John Silver's, Inc.

SUCCESS STORY
ALVIN C. COPELAND

It wasn't until 1972 that Alvin Copeland, New Orleanian by birth, Cajun by demeanor, and entrepreneur by inclination, harnessed his love of Cajun-spiced food and launched a revolutionary fried chicken chain that intended to show the world what it had been missing.

At the start, Copeland had little more than the rags to make his own rags-to-riches story come true. Living with his grandmother in a housing project, the man who would revolutionize the fast-food industry with Popeyes Famous Fried Chicken and Biscuits first delivered papers for a few pennies, then divided his time between bagging groceries in a supermarket and making donuts at a shop owned by his brother.

"All you have to do is believe in yourself," says Copeland, who found inspiration in the success stories of his day. The values he read about in Horatio Alger tales — hard work, imagination, ability to survive disappointment — became the principles by which he lived. His formula for success is simple: "I owe it to 16-hour days, working two and even three jobs at a time, self-confidence, taking calculated risks, setting goals and pursuing them, and learning something new every day about the business I'm in."

While owning and operating a couple of donut shops for his brother, Copeland spent what little spare time he had experimenting with fried chicken recipes. He felt that the fried chicken served at fast-food restaurants around the country varied from good to horrible, but he was never quite satisfied with it, raised as he was on the piquant Cajun foods of southern Louisiana.

The first Popeyes Famous Fried Chicken and Biscuits restaurant opened in 1972, with one location in the New Orleans area. Over the next 14 years it grew to over 650 outlets around the world and produced $400 million in annual sales as of 1986. The chain continues to grow every year.

The success of this innovative chicken-and-biscuit chain has made Copeland a wealthy man. Yet far from giving him an excuse to slow down, it has given him the capital to speed up, to pursue his dreams with even greater enthusiasm.

In 1983, Copeland pushed the concept perfected with Popeyes Famous Fried Chicken into a whole new arena, starting a restaurant that bears his family name. Copeland's of New Orleans has grown in that short time to ten restaurants — five in the New Orleans area, and others in Dallas, Houston, Washington, D.C., and other major markets nationwide. At the same time, Popeyes itself continues to evolve, and Copeland personally directs the research and development of each new Cajun-style fast-food idea.

Photo and information provided courtesy of Alvin C. Copeland, August, 1987.

SUMMARY

Constructive support of franchisees is essential for effective operation and overall success of a franchise system. A franchisor is responsible for developing a support organization that ensures sufficient and accurate communication between the franchisor and the franchisee. The support organization should address the needs of both parties, ensuring that their expectations concerning profitability and adequate planning and control are met, and that any problems are handled promptly and with a shared concern for their resolution. Obviously, appropriate and accurate communication is of critical importance. Phone and mail contacts, as well as personal visits, are made by most franchising organizations to their franchisees. The purpose of these visits may be to address a local problem, to provide training, to fulfill the requirements of a field review, or simply to maintain a personal, one-to-one contact.

Franchisees may call meetings among themselves as well. Many of them have learned that one of the best forms of support is the sharing of experiences and techniques among fellow franchisees, the result of which often is to help weaker franchisees become stronger. Most franchisees are aware that a weak link affects all others in the system, so they are usually interested in strengthening that weak link.

From one perspective, the franchising process can be viewed as an attempt to reproduce in other locations the successful model or prototype operation of the franchisor. Reproducing the model heavily depends on effective transfer of knowledge and skills from one location to the other. This is evidence of the critical importance of an effective training program for franchising.

The development of a training function of a franchisor has three major components: design and implementation of the training unit, establishment of a training location or locations, and development of the precise content of the training to be imparted. The actual training typically includes instruction emphasizing the philosophy of the franchising organization and the required information and critical skills that will enable one to operate effectively as a franchisee, through the use of effective formal and informal training techniques that ensure the franchisee-in-training is adequately exposed and provided the realistic opportunity to learn everything necessary to begin operation as a licensed franchisee of the franchising system. Usually the production or service methods are carefully reviewed, the accounting, marketing, and personnel practices are worked out, and the ways to maintain the franchisor-franchisee relationship on both a personal and a professional level are discussed. Franchisee training is often divided into three areas — pre-opening (formal), grand opening (on-site), and continuing (post-opening) training. Many franchisors have found that pre-opening training tends to be more effective when a limited number of franchisees are involved, say between three and 12 persons. The smaller group provides sufficient peer interaction while allowing sufficient individuality, in order to maximize the learning experience necessary before one is ready to operate a franchised unit.

REVIEW QUESTIONS

1. Why should a franchisor have a support organization? What function does it serve for the franchisor? For the franchisee?
2. Identify the different types of "visits" that a franchising organization makes to a franchisee's business. Explain the purpose of each type.
3. Effective support is ensured by effective communication between the franchisor and the franchisee. Explain what is meant by this statement.
4. Why do many franchisors consider training of franchisees to be critical to the development and growth of a franchise system?
5. Identify and briefly describe the three major types of training a franchisee might expect from the franchisor.

CASE STUDY
7-ELEVEN: A Way of Life*

Southland Corporation of Dallas, Texas, operates the 7-ELEVEN convenience-store chain through 34 divisions spread across 41 states, the District of Columbia, and five provinces of Canada. Southland is the largest operator and franchisor of convenience stores in the world and is America's seventh largest retailer. There are over 7,000 7-ELEVEN stores in operation throughout the United States, serving approximately eight million customers every day. A typical 7-ELEVEN store carries approximately 3,000 items, including soft drinks, groceries, beer, tobacco, magazines, housewares, and health and beauty aids. Other items, particularly fast foods, are regularly being added to the product offerings.

Southland pioneered the convenience store concept in 1927, when it opened as an ice company that also sold milk, bread, and eggs as a convenience to its customers. The name "7-ELEVEN" originated in 1946, when the stores operated between the hours of 7 A.M. and 11 P.M. Today the vast majority of 7-ELEVEN stores are open 24 hours.

There are basically two operational types of 7-ELEVEN stores. The neighborhood type is operated as an updated version of the Mom-and-Pop store. Forty percent of the stores are operated by franchisees, with the remainder being managed by the corporation. Of the franchised locations, many are owned and operated by couples whose families also work in the store. The typical 7-ELEVEN store is in a suburban location with easy access. However, 7-ELEVEN also operates "city stores" in some densely populated urban areas. The store's competition is broad-based, including fast-food restaurants, other convenience stores, supermarkets, and "g-stores" (gasoline stations with a small convenience store on the premises).

On the marketing side, the 7-ELEVEN management team works to develop programs to attract additional customers and bring in existing customers more often. Recently, two segments of the population were being targeted: older people, who historically have not been convenience-store customers, and working women.

Franchisees have played a significant role in the success of 7-ELEVEN stores. In fact, many franchisees have been with Southland for more than 20 years. Not only do they understand the business, but they also do an excellent job of tailoring their stores to the needs of the neighborhoods they serve. Many of the successful market programs provided by 7-ELEVEN stores were first introduced by various franchisees and are now an integral part of the entire 7-ELEVEN system. Approximately 40 percent of the 7,000-plus stores in the United States are franchised. As the company has grown, this percentage has remained stable.

*Information provided courtesy of The Southland Corporation, November, 1987.

The 7-ELEVEN real estate representatives research and select potential sites based on population, traffic flow, convenience to homes, and competition. The company buys or leases a site, builds the unit, and leases to the franchisee. Typically, all equipment in the store, including heating and air conditioning units, shelving, cash registers, refrigerators, and vaults, is leased to the franchisee. Once control has been taken, the franchisee is responsible for maintaining the equipment. The company arranges for the initial inventory, and the franchisee is responsible thereafter for ordering and stocking merchandise. 7-ELEVEN provides lists of recommended merchandise and retail prices, as well as names of vendors that offer high-quality merchandise at a competitive price; some recommended vendors may be affiliated with 7-ELEVEN, and some merchandise may be produced by divisions of Southland. However, franchisees are free to purchase merchandise from any vendor and establish their store's retail prices.

Before being accepted by 7-ELEVEN as a franchisee, the applicant is required to complete the Store Operations Training Program, which includes (1) actual, two-week, in-store experience at a 7-ELEVEN Training Store in order to learn the basic operations; and (2) a one-week formal training program at the regional training center in either San Diego, California, or Bethlehem, Pennsylvania. The prospective franchisee learns a variety of management skills, techniques, and procedures essential to the successful operation of a 7-ELEVEN store. The cost of the training is included in the initial franchising fee paid by the applicant. After completion of these two training periods, the applicant has about one week prior to opening the store. The purpose of this is to allow the new franchisee time to clear up any personal business, hire staff for the new store, and prepare for the grand opening. During this time, as well as during the grand opening period, 7-ELEVEN provides support staff to assist and advise the new franchisee.

About 250 to 300 prospective franchisees enter the 7-ELEVEN training cycle each year. Applicants entering the training programs are evaluated at each stage, from the initial meeting to the actual changeovers just prior to the grand opening of the store. According to Wayne Beeder, Manager of Franchise Affairs for Southland, there is no single set of criteria used to evaluate a franchise applicant. However, personality traits, entrepreneurial interests, and financial capacity, as well as the evaluation of the field representatives, are significant in selection of applicants for entry into the training program. The training staff also makes recommendations concerning each applicant/trainee. Training staff can also recommend that trainees be disqualified, a form of quality control so that 7-ELEVEN can avoid having poorly prepared and unmotivated franchisees representing the franchise system.

The new franchisee has 120 days after becoming a franchisee to terminate and not continue as a franchisee. If the franchisee chooses to leave during this period, the company will refund the franchising fee, less any training expenses, a practice not common to many other franchising companies in this field. What this policy does is to allow some breathing and thinking room for the new franchisee to determine if the arrangement is satisfactory.

CASE QUESTIONS

1. Why would 7-ELEVEN want to maintain a policy allowing the franchisee to completely back out after being selected, trained, and assisted into operation as a full-fledged franchisee?
2. Do you think the policy of refunding the franchising fee should be more common in franchising? Why or why not?
3. What costs and benefits accrue to 7-ELEVEN by having such a refund policy?
4. How might this policy affect the selection of representatives and training staffs of 7-ELEVEN stores?

REFERENCES

1. Atkinson, John W., "Motivational Determinants of Risk Taking Behavior," *Psychology Review*, Vol. 64, No. 6 (1957), pp. 359-372.
2. Dunnigan, J. A., "Keeping It Altogether — Franchisors Reveal How They Maintain 'Family Ties'," *Entrepreneurs Franchise Yearbook*, Vol. 2, 1987/88, pp. 294-304.
3. Frazier, Gary L., "On the Measurement of Interfirm Power in Channels of Distribution," *Journal of Marketing Research*, Vol. 20, May 1983, pp. 58-66.
4. Hotsh, Ripley, "Dear Diary: I'm Now a Franchisee," *Nation's Business* (November 1985), pp. 53-60.
5. Justis, Robert, "Franchisors: Have You Hugged Your Franchisee Today?" *Nation's Business* (February 1985), pp. 46-49.
6. Justis, Robert T., *Managing Your Small Business*, Englewood Cliffs, NJ: Prentice-Hall, Inc., 1981.
7. Kushell, Robert, "Is Being Z for Thee?" *Entrepreneurs Franchise Yearbook*, Vol. 1, 1987, pp. 27-31.
8. Lambert, Douglas M., and Christine Lewis, "The Methodology for Assessing Franchisee Expectations and Perceptions of Franchisor Role Performance," Proceedings of the Society of Franchising, University of Nebraska-Lincoln, September, 1986.
9. Luxenberg, Stan, "The Ideal Operator," *Roadside Empires*, New York: Penguin Books, 1986.
10. Mayo, Ken, "Retailer, Train Thyself," *Business Computer Systems*, Vol. 3, No. 9 (September 1984), pp. 66-74.

11. Ruekert, Robert, and Gilbert Churchill, Jr., "Reliability and Validity of Alternative Measures of Channel Members Satisfaction," *Journal of Marketing Research*, Vol. 21 (May 1984), pp. 226-233.
12. Sato, Gayle, "Who Is the Ideal Franchisee?," *Entrepreneurs Franchise Yearbook*, Vol. 2, 1987/1988, pp. 14-21.
13. Stanworth, John, and James Curran, "How Franchising Brings a New Perspective to Us and Them," *Personnel Management*, Vol. 15, No. 9 (September 1983), pp. 34-37.

PART FIVE

THE FRANCHISEE ARENA

CHAPTER 15
INVESTIGATING FRANCHISE OPPORTUNITIES

In studying this chapter, you will:
- Learn what is involved in choosing a franchise.
- Evaluate yourself as a prospective franchisee.
- Learn how to investigate and compare franchisors.
- Be able to develop questions about franchise opportunities.
- Understand what should be included in the disclosure document.
- Learn where to find information about franchisors and franchises.

INCIDENT

Ramona has just finished college and wants to start her own business. Having heard about the 95 percent success rate of franchises, she has decided to investigate the possibility of opening her own franchised business. She is very interested in a donut, yogurt, or popcorn business.

Ramona has taken the time to drive around and talk to several local franchisees. The result of her research was discouraging. She found that startup costs were high, some profits were not as high as she had expected, and the workdays were very long.

Ramona learned that the average franchising fee was $32,000, with total startup costs averaging $120,000. Estimated sales approached $365,000, with profits ranging between 8 and 16 percent of annual revenues. Some of the franchisors mentioned that they spend more time training franchisees in how to keep the store clean than in how to make a better product.

INTRODUCTION

Selecting the right type of franchised business may be the most important step taken by a prospective franchisee. A poor selection may create terrible problems for both the franchisee and the franchisor. Currently, because there are no laws requiring a franchisor to grant a franchise, the franchisor has the freedom to choose whoever would appear to be best for the franchised company. Therefore, it is up to the prospective franchisee to carefully investigate all possibilities and determine where the best opportunity lies before signing on with a franchise.

BECOMING A FRANCHISEE

Franchising is a risk, but very different from the risk of investing money in the stock market. One invests money in a particular company by buying shares of stock in the company, and after a period of time, that company either will provide a good return or will not provide a good return on the investment. In a franchised business, however, more than just money is invested. Time, energy, effort, and one's lifeblood are poured into the business. Also, some franchises are less risky than others; some are "blue-chip" franchises and have a tremendously successful track record. But they are also fairly expensive in terms of franchising fees and startup costs. Other, newer franchises, without a proven record, are often less costly but are riskier.

    Before committing to a particular franchise system, the prospective franchisee needs to investigate the opportunities the franchise has to offer. He or she needs to take the steps which will ensure the best possible return on the investment. The franchisee needs to investigate not only the business skills of the franchisor, but also his or her own business aptitude, experience, and managerial abilities.

    The franchisee must go through a rigorous investigation process before finally deciding to start a franchised business. The ten basic steps of choosing and starting a franchise can be listed as follows:

1. Self-evaluation
2. The business arena
3. The franchise (the four "P's" of franchising)
4. Disclosure documents
5. Profit/earnings claims

6. Professional advice
7. Legal rights
8. Disclosure meeting
9. The signing
10. Training/grand opening/operations

By following these steps, franchisees will assure themselves of being selective and hopefully wise in choosing their new line of business. In this way all risks may be identified, and the franchisee can move forward with the greatest understanding of the limitations and potential of each franchise option.

A franchisor is not obligated to grant a franchise to every applicant. However, the refusal to grant a franchise to a qualified prospect, if such refusal is part of a conspiracy or a group boycott, is a violation of the Sherman Antitrust Act and is therefore against federal law. A prospective franchisee does not need to obtain permission from existing franchisees to open a new outlet in a specific area. If such permission is sought and refused, and the franchisor does not grant a franchise, then a group boycott may have been formed, which would be in violation of the Sherman Act.

In addition, if the franchisor decides to open a company-owned store close to existing franchisees, the franchisees may claim the franchisor is desirous of forcing them out of business, and again the franchisor would be in violation of the Sherman Act. If company-owned outlets are set up to be in direct competition with existing franchises, this is also a violation of the Sherman Act.

The franchisor must make these kinds of decisions alone, without including existing franchisees in territorial agreements and limitations. The law also requires that franchised outlets receive the same pricing schedules and any other cost advantages made available to company-owned stores. Anytime a franchisor holds a competitive advantage over its franchisees, the franchisor is likely to run afoul of the law.

It is not always necessary for the franchisor to "sell" the franchise to the franchisee; rather, it is frequently the case that the franchisee must be able to meet certain qualifications in order to be granted a franchise. Often, at the beginning of the sales or disclosure meeting between the franchisor and the prospective franchisee, the franchisor will indicate that the prospect needs to prove that he or she is worthy of and eligible for a franchise. The disclosure or sales meeting is primarily a chance for the franchisor to explain the operations and opportunities of the franchise. It is during this meeting that the franchisee needs to demonstrate his or her qualifications to the franchisor.

Franchising still remains the least risky method of business ownership. It provides entrepreneurs a relatively safe opportunity to be their own boss and develop their talents. Franchising is not for everyone, however. It is for individuals who are willing to take some risk in becoming an entrepreneur and feel they can work within the confines of a complex business system.

Self-Evaluation

The first step in the process of becoming a franchisee is to take a good hard look at oneself. It is necessary to ask whether one is willing to make a personal and business sacrifice to spend long, hard hours developing and starting a franchise. Individuals must know if they have sufficient energy, maturity, and managerial experience, the right leadership characteristics, and the ability to work with others — prerequisites of becoming a good franchisee (see Figure 15-1).

The prospective franchisee should determine the time that will be required to operate the franchise. Work weeks of 60 to 100 hours may be necessary, which obviously will have some effect on the franchisee's family or social life. The franchisee should find out if the family is also willing to sacrifice, or if it will be able to get by with the franchisee out of the house so much.

Some franchisors will help prospective franchisees take a good look at the franchise opportunity and their individual potential. Other franchisors will simply find out if sufficient money is available, without looking at the capabilities and personality of the prospective franchisee. The prudent franchisor — who is often the most successful franchisor — will determine whether the franchisee possesses those managerial and leadership characteristics which will help ensure the success of the business. If the business involves personal contacts with customers, then the franchisor should select franchisees with a friendly and congenial personality and a demonstrated ability to work closely with customers and employees.

Prospective franchisees also need to examine their physical, social, emotional, and learning capacities. Will the franchisee be able to work under the controls and guidelines of an authoritarian franchisor? Does the franchisee have the ability to work closely with the franchisor as well as with potential customers?

Qualification. When a prospective franchisee applies for a franchise, he or she generally needs to fill out an application form, which becomes a confidential qualification report, in which the prospect agrees that any information provided may be verified by the franchisor. Franchisors should check this information thoroughly, because the responsibility of granting franchises affects not only the franchisors themselves, but also the consuming public, the prospective franchisee, the franchised company, and those franchisees already in business. These personal qualification forms may request the following:

Figure 15-1
Franchise Self-Evaluation Form

DATE OF EVALUATION   SCORE

		RATING
		5=Excellent
		4=High
		3=Average
		2=Low
		1=Poor

Directions: Mark the square which most accurately represents own characteristics.

	5	4	3	2	1
ACTIVITY LEVEL					
Drive					
Energy					
Endurance					
MATURITY LEVEL					
Self-Motivated					
Self-Confident					
Common Sense					
Stability, Composure					
MANAGERIAL EXPERIENCE					
Motivation					
Problem Solving					
Skills					
Use of Resources					
OWNER CHARACTERISTICS					
Goal Setting					
Long-Term Involvement					
Taking Initiative					
Seeking Responsibility					
DEALING WITH OTHERS					
Use of Feedback					
Communications					
Adaptability					
Sense of Ethics					
WORKING WITH SELF					
Dealing with Failure					
Tolerance of Ambiguity					
Internal Focus of Control					
SELF AS FRANCHISEE					
Desire					
Accept Heavy Workload					
Motivate Others					

OVERALL RATING (TOTAL SCORE) _____
GENERAL COMMENTS _____
_____

SHALL I BECOME A FRANCHISEE? _____
WHY? _____

Score: 105-125 Do It Now; 95-104 Go For It; 85-94 Think Twice; 75-84 Be Very Careful;
         Below 75 Try Something Else

- Personal information
- Education
- Reason for becoming a franchisee
- Personal references
- Specific information about site location
- Personal characteristics
- Employment history

In addition to the personal qualification forms, a confidential financial report is also required. Most franchisors have found that the prospective franchisees need sufficient nondebt capital to ensure the success of the franchise and to see that the debt burden of the franchise is not too great. Franchising fee payments almost always must be of a nondebt nature.

So that the franchisor can determine the financial position of the franchisee, a complete financial report is required of every potential franchisee. Any misrepresentations are grounds for nullification of subsequently signed agreements or contracts. The financial report generally requires a listing of personal assets, liabilities, and net worth. In addition, these reports often require information about current sources of income, contingent liabilities, supplementary schedules, banking relations, loans, life insurance, stocks and bonds, real estate, credit accounts, and bank and finance company statements. The confidential financial report and the personal information form give the franchisor some information by which to properly evaluate the personal and financial status of the prospective franchisee. While this information is very important, the final decision to grant or not grant a franchise is often based on the character of the franchisee (see Figure 15-2).

The Business Arena

The prospective franchisee needs to decide which type of business and which type of franchise distribution system are most desirable. A franchisee should look at different industries to determine what type of business or franchise is most attractive. Additionally, the franchisee should determine if the product or service is seasonal or cyclical, what type of competition is present, and if governmental standards and regulations reduce the probability for success and profitability in that business.

The U.S. Department of Commerce annually publishes a book entitled *Franchise Opportunities Handbook*, by Andy Kostecka, which lists different categories of franchises available to interested prospects. The categories include the following:

Automotive Products/Service
Auto/Trailer Rentals
Beauty Salons/Supplies

Figure 15-2
XYZ Franchise
Franchisor Interview Form

Applicant's Name _____ Date _____

Address _____

    Interview with   Date   Score

1. _____ _____ _____

2. _____ _____ _____

3. _____ _____ _____

4. _____ _____ _____

RATING
5=Excellent
4=High
3=Average
2=Low
1=Poor

Directions: Mark the square which most accurately represents applicant's characteristics. A total score of 90-100 is outstanding.

                                                            5   4   3   2   1

EDUCATIONAL BACKGROUND
    Appropriate/Sufficient
    Intelligent
    Ability to Reason

MANAGERIAL EXPERIENCE
    Skills
    Motivation
    Past Accomplishments

INDIVIDUAL IMPRESSIONS
    Appearance
    Positive Attitude
    Expression, Diction

POTENTIAL ABILITY
    Organized, Self-Managed
    Financially Strong
    Responsible
    Realistically Ambitious
    Works Well with Others

MATURITY
    Self-Confident
    Self-Motivated
    Common Sense

ABILITY TO WORK WITH FRANCHISOR
    Communicate
    Adaptable
    Sense of Ethics

OVERALL RATING (TOTAL SCORE) _____

GENERAL COMMENTS _____

_____

DO YOU RECOMMEND THIS PERSON TO BECOME A FRANCHISEE? _____

WHY? _____

_____

_____

Business Aids/Services
Campgrounds
Children's Stores/Furniture/Products
Clothing/Shoes
Construction/Remodeling — Materials/Services
Cosmetics/Toiletries
Dental Centers
Drug Stores
Educational Products/Services
Employment Services
Equipment/Rentals
Foods — Donuts
Foods — Grocery/Specialty Stores
Foods — Ice Cream/Yogurt/Candy/Popcorn/Beverages
Foods — Pancakes/Waffles/Pretzels
Foods — Restaurants/Drive-Ins/Carry-Outs
General Merchandising Stores
Health Aids/Services
Hearing Aids
Home Furnishings/Furniture — Retail, Repairs, Services
Insurance
Laundries, Dry Cleaning Services
Lawn and Garden Supplies/Services
Maintenance/Cleaning/Sanitation — Services/Supplies
Motels, Hotels
Optical Products/Services
Paint and Decorating Supplies
Printing
Real Estate
Recreation/Entertainment/Travel — Services/Supplies
Retailing Not Elsewhere Classified
Security Systems
Swimming Pools
Tools, Hardware
Vending
Water Conditioning
Wholesale/Service Business — Miscellaneous

Entrepreneur magazine publishes once each year in its January issue the "Franchise 500," which provides valuable information and insights into many franchising organizations. *Entrepreneur* also publishes an annual yearbook which includes a listing of nearly all franchised companies, and also discusses franchising opportunities and how to select franchises. Also, the *Franchise Handbook* provides an alphabetical list of franchisors according to industry and is published semiannually by

CESA Publications, Inc. These publications provide information of value to prospective franchisees in their investigation of the different business arenas involved in franchising.

After having looked at the various opportunities available and having decided on a particular industry, the prospective franchisee must contact the appropriate franchisors in that industry. A franchisee should probably choose the top two or three franchise systems and investigate each of them before making any final determination. Remember, before actually signing the franchising contract, a prospect may always choose another business opportunity which better suits his or her personality. It is always a good idea to investigate before investing.

The Franchise

Choosing the best possible franchise involves investigating and analyzing the four "P's" of franchising:

1. Product
2. Process
3. Profitability
4. People

Product. One of the first steps in choosing a franchise is for the prospect to analyze the product or service which he or she wishes to sell. The quality, value, and demand for the product are very important. Continuing availability of the product is critical and needs to be assured. Consumer awareness of the product should be high, although with start-up franchises, there may be a lack of awareness or acceptance that may be a severe limitation to the success of the franchise. The prospective franchisee should also understand the requirements of maintenance, upkeep, and handling of the product. If the product is technical in nature, this may exclude some technically unsophisticated franchisees.

Rating: 5=Excellent, 4=High, 3=Average, 2=Low, 1=Poor

	5	4	3	2	1
Product or Service:					
Positive reputation	___	___	___	___	___
Customer need	___	___	___	___	___
Growing market	___	___	___	___	___
Safe	___	___	___	___	___
Patented/guaranteed	___	___	___	___	___

	Continued				
Self-interest	___	___	___	___	___
Identified with known personality	___	___	___	___	___
Future need	___	___	___	___	___
Strongly desirable	___	___	___	___	___

Process. Before choosing a business, prospective franchisees need to understand the process or business format of operations which they should employ to achieve success. In addition to knowing sales methods and service and repair procedures, the prospect should understand the accounting, financial, marketing, and management systems to be employed by the franchisor, and should understand how the products will be distributed and specifically what kind of selling is involved. Additionally, the franchisee should be aware of the training and continuing services available from the franchisor. Some franchisors offer extensive continuing services, while others offer little support once the franchise process has begun. The prospective franchisee should determine the number of franchises and company-owned outlets, as well as the length of time the franchisor has been in business. The prospect should also find out if the franchised company belongs to the International Franchise Association, whose members must meet high standards and follow a stiff code of conduct.

Rating: 5=Excellent, 4=High, 3=Average, 2=Low, 1=Poor

	5	4	3	2	1
Business Format Process:					
Marketing	___	___	___	___	___
Promotion	___	___	___	___	___
Brand recognition	___	___	___	___	___
Management	___	___	___	___	___
Training	___	___	___	___	___
Accounting	___	___	___	___	___
Financial	___	___	___	___	___

Site selection   _____ _____ _____ _____ _____

Headquarters held   _____ _____ _____ _____ _____

Service/repairs   _____ _____ _____ _____ _____

Financial support   _____ _____ _____ _____ _____

Number of franchisees   _____ _____ _____ _____ _____

Advertising   _____ _____ _____ _____ _____

Profitability. Prospective franchisees should evaluate the profitability of any franchise opportunity. Some franchisors provide earnings claims or profitability statements for their businesses. (See Figure 15-3.) These statements, in accordance with Federal Trade Commission requirements, must stipulate the franchise system's sales or earnings, plus the percentage of franchises that earn above and/or below the stated sales or earnings. Indications of potential earnings plus working capital requirements are often found in the basic disclosure documents. In addition, the prospective franchisee may calculate a rough estimate of earnings by obtaining, from the corporate consolidated financial statements in the disclosure document, the total revenue from franchisees and dividing that by the number of franchised units in the system. This would reveal the franchisor's average revenue per franchised unit. Knowing the franchising royalty fee percentage (e.g., 5 percent royalty fee) enables one to make a guesstimate of the total sales for that particular business. For example, if the royalty fee is 5 percent of annual gross sales and the average royalty payment per franchise is $17,500, then the annual sales average per unit would be $350,000. If the average revenue per unit to the franchisor is $40,000, then dividing $40,000 by 5 percent (0.05) gives average sales per unit of $800,000. But probably the best method of determining sales profitability and operating expenses is to call existing franchisees and ask them for information and advice. However the information is obtained, the current financial condition and situation of the franchisor should be analyzed.

Rating: 5=Excellent, 4=High, 3=Average, 2=Low, 1=Poor

                         5   4   3   2   1

Profitability:

  Profits   _____ _____ _____ _____ _____

  Revenues   _____ _____ _____ _____ _____

Figure 15-3
Postal Instant Press (PIP)
Number and Percentage of Franchised Stores Achieving Gross Sales at Levels Indicated During Calendar Year 1983

	Total No. of Reporting Locations	Gross Sales Less Than $75,000	\$75,000	\$100,000	\$120,000	\$150,000	\$200,000
			\multicolumn{5}{c}{Number of Reporting Stores — Percentage With Gross Sales Exceeding:}
All Reporting Franchise Stores	729	63- 8.6%	666-91.4%	602-82.9%	538-73.8%	413-56.7%	242-33.2%
			\multicolumn{5}{c}{Gross Sales Achieved Measured by Years in Operation}
1 to 2 Years	147	34-23.1%	113-76.9%	82-55.8%	62-42.2%	32-21.8%	10- 6.8%
2 to 4 Years	139	9- 6.5%	130-93.5%	116-83.5%	100-71.9%	75-53.9%	31-22.3%
4 to 6 Years	121	7- 5.8%	114-94.2%	106-87.6%	94-77.7%	73-53.9%	40-33.0%
6 to 8 Years	88	2- 2.3%	86-97.7%	82-93.2%	78-85.2%	58-65.9%	38-43.2%
8 to 10 Years	61	4- 6.6%	57-93.4%	54-88.5%	54-88.5%	45-73.8%	26-42.6%
10 to 14 Years	173	7- 4.0%	166-96.0%	164-94.8%	153-88.4%	130-75.1%	97-56.1%

Schedule of Gross Sales for Calendar Year 1983

Reporting Full Year Gross Sales	Number of Stores Reporting	Percentage of Stores Reporting
Under $75,000	63	8.6%
$ 75,000 – $100,000	62	8.5%
$100,000 – $120,000	66	9.0%
$120,000 – $150,000	125	17.2%
$150,000 – $200,000	171	23.5%
Over $200,000	242	33.2%
ALL STORES REPORTING	729	100.0%

The above schedule reflects the gross sales achieved, within the range indicated, by franchised stores that reported sales volumes for the full calendar year 1983 and the percentage of the total stores reporting.

Source: Reprinted by permission of Postal Instant Press.

Chapter 15 Investigating Franchise Opportunities

Continued

Cost of goods sold	___	___	___	___	___
Labor costs	___	___	___	___	___
Expenses	___	___	___	___	___
Return on investment	___	___	___	___	___
Earnings claim	___	___	___	___	___
Forecasted revenues	___	___	___	___	___
Startup costs	___	___	___	___	___
Franchising fee	___	___	___	___	___
Royalty fee	___	___	___	___	___
Advertising fee	___	___	___	___	___
Other fees	___	___	___	___	___

People. Perhaps the most important aspect of choosing a franchise is understanding the people with whom the prospective franchisee will be working. Any prospect should meet, interview, and discuss the franchising process with each executive of the franchise system. Franchising, because of its contractual nature, is similar to a marriage in that it demands a great deal of interaction and cooperation between the two main parties, franchisor and franchisee. The strength of the franchise, and its most important resource, is the people involved in the franchise. The prospective franchisee should investigate everyone connected with the business, including the franchisor, officers, and directors, and should find out if the franchisor has a reputation for making a rush sale to obtain a quick franchising fee and commission.

Rating: 5=Excellent, 4=High, 3=Average, 2=Low, 1=Poor

	5	4	3	2	1
People:					
Franchisor chairman	___	___	___	___	___
Franchisor president	___	___	___	___	___
Franchisor operations executive	___	___	___	___	___

Continued

Franchisor sales executive	___	___	___	___	___
Other principals or directors	___	___	___	___	___
Service departments	___	___	___	___	___
Advertising and promotions	___	___	___	___	___
Finance and accounting	___	___	___	___	___
Sales and marketing	___	___	___	___	___
Site selection	___	___	___	___	___
Personnel and training	___	___	___	___	___
Research and development	___	___	___	___	___
Purchasing	___	___	___	___	___
Manufacturing and operations	___	___	___	___	___
Field support	___	___	___	___	___

It is important to study each franchisor and each operation as thoroughly as possible. One of the best ways to accomplish this is through comparative shopping. A prospect should look at several franchises at the same time, just as one would look at several cars or houses before making the decision to purchase.

The prospective franchisee should formally inquire of the franchisor about the franchise. This contact is very important. The franchisor will generally send a "kit" in response to the inquiry, which includes promotional material for all prospective franchisees. This kit may also contain the franchisor disclosure documents, confidential qualification forms, and confidential financial report forms. If the franchisee is serious about discussing further details with the franchisor, then he or she should fill out the personal application and financial information forms, and send them to the franchisor. Upon receipt of these confidential records, the franchisor or sales representative will generally make a personal appointment with the interested prospect.

In addition, the franchisee should seek out other information about the franchise through various sources generally found in libraries, such as Dun & Bradstreet's credit ratings, *Value Line*, *Entrepreneur*, and other business publications that include information about franchised businesses. Also, area franchisees may be contacted, as well as chambers of commerce and the local Better Business Bureau. These resources often provide valuable information about a prospective franchisor.

Disclosure Documents

Most earnest inquiries to a franchisor will result in the prospective franchisee being sent information about the franchised business as well as a disclosure document (or Uniform Franchise Offering Circular). If a disclosure document is not provided initially by the franchisor, the franchisee should be sure to ask for one. The disclosure document was developed as the result of Congress enacting FTC Rule 436 in 1979. This Franchise Rule is formally titled "Disclosure Requirements and Prohibitions Concerning Franchising and Business Opportunity Ventures." It was created in an attempt to curtail widespread abuse, deception, and unfair practices by certain unscrupulous franchisors. The Franchise Rule has enabled prospective franchisees to properly analyze and investigate the business and activities of all reliable franchisors. Any franchise operating in the United States has to provide information in the disclosure document outlining the affairs and practices of the franchise.

This disclosure document is of great assistance to a prospective franchisee in comparing one franchise with another, enabling the prospect to learn what to expect from different franchisors before making a decision to invest. The disclosure document contains detailed information on 20 different subjects which are vital to an understanding of the operations of the franchised business. These subjects include identification, litigation, bankruptcy, fees, business description, and basic operations.

After having read three or four disclosure documents from different companies in the same industry, the prospective franchisee should check the accuracy of the information. One of the best ways to begin this investigation is to contact different franchisees listed in the disclosure document and ask them about their experiences in the business. These franchisees are generally very willing to talk to prospective franchisees and provide verification of the information given in the disclosure document.

It is important for a prospect to talk to several franchisees from different locations throughout the country. It is also valuable to talk to new as well as veteran franchisees to discuss the training programs, potential earnings, franchisor-franchisee relationship, and personal satisfaction with the franchise (see Figure 15-4). Newer franchisees will be able to explain the problems associated with training, grand opening, and first year of operations. They will also be able to help the prospective franchisee understand the support system that the franchisor will provide during the initial training and startup period. If the franchisor has recommended certain franchisees for the prospective franchisee to con-

Figure 15-4
Franchise Checklist Evaluation

NAME OF FRANCHISOR _____ DATE _____

ADDRESS _____

Directions: Mark the square which most accurately represents the franchise position.

RATING: 5=Excellent; 4=High; 3=Average; 2=Low; 1=Poor

EXISTING FRANCHISEE
    Average Profitability (5 units) $ _____
    Investment Startup $ _____
    Favorable Relations with Franchisor
    Strength of Operations
    Reliability of Franchisor's Promises
    Required Sales Quotas
    Training Programs
    Favorable Contract
    Favorable Territory
    Promotion/Advertising

Subtotal = _____

FRANCHISOR
    Fees
        Initial Franchise Fee $ _____
        Royalty Fees   _____ %
        Advertising Fees   _____ %
        Other Fees   _____ %
    Values
        Value of Product or Service
        Value of Training
        Value of Trademark
    Activities
        Franchisor's Experience
        Franchisor's Litigation
        Exclusive Territory
        Renewal/Termination Rights
        Contract Length
        Disclosure Document (U.F.O.C.)
        Restrictions
        Market Potential and Acceptance

Subtotal = _____
TOTAL = _____

Score: 110-125 Superior; 100-109 Excellent; 90-99 Very Good; 80-89 Good; 70-79 Average; Below 70 Substandard sult, it is best that the prospect contact additional franchisees not recommended by the franchisor.

Litigation. The Franchise Rule requires that any litigation involving the franchise system be reported in the disclosure document. A description of any and all lawsuits in which the franchisor, officers, directors, or management personnel have been or are involved should be included. This becomes important because some state laws prohibit selling certain items such as firearms, tobacco, and ammunition to convicted felons. The prospective franchisee may also be interested to know if any actions have been taken against the franchise's officers for fraud, embezzlement, restraint of trade, or unfair or deceptive business practices.

Franchise Costs. The prospective franchisee should investigate all costs associated with the franchise. This would include, but would not be limited to, the initial franchising or licensing fee; periodic royalties; advertising fees; service fees; bookkeeping, accounting, and data processing fees; and any additional management assistance fees to be paid to the franchisor. The franchisee should be able to determine these initial costs and be able to understand when and how fees are to be paid to the franchisor. The franchisee should realize too that these initial costs do not generally include the startup costs of actually building and opening the franchise. Estimates of these costs may or may not be provided by the franchisor to the prospective franchisee. If they are provided, they are only close approximations or guesstimates of what franchisees have paid to start their franchises. The prospective franchisee should contact other franchisees to determine what their actual startup costs were and what help they received from the franchisor in starting the business.

One additional cost that may be associated with the franchise is the cost of the land and/or building. Many long-established franchise systems require that new franchisees lease the land from the franchisor. This means that the franchisor has either purchased and built the property (if free-standing) or signed the lease with the property owner and is subleasing the space to the new franchisee. These costs should be determined and discussed with the franchisor and with other franchisees.

Training/Startup Assistance. Most franchisors regard the training of franchisees as vital to their success. Training programs will last from three days to eight weeks to ensure that franchisees are sufficiently knowledgeable about every aspect of the business operation.

If the franchised business requires some sort of technical expertise such as that needed to prepare food items or use cleaning equipment, then the franchisor should provide training to develop the technical skills required. The franchisor should also provide training in correct selling techniques and proper ways of handling customers, if applicable to the business.

The franchisee should determine how much training and support will be available in the actual startup of the business. Quite often the franchisor will send a number of experienced staff employees to help with the grand opening. The franchisee must be careful to anticipate the costs of this assistance. Sometimes the franchisee must bear not only the cost of the training, travel, and meals at the franchisor's training facility, but also the payment of the salaries or wages of all franchisor staff members helping with the grand opening. This can get to be very expensive. The franchisee should make sure that all training obligations and continuing support programs — and who pays for them — are specified in the franchising agreement.

Territory/Location. Most franchisors will not guarantee an "exclusive franchise territory," though they may establish geographical territories within which they agree not to operate a company-owned facility, or a radius around one franchise within which they will not offer another franchise. The prospective franchisee should remember, however, that franchisors generally reserve all rights to establish additional franchises wherever they wish.

The franchisor often reserves the right of refusal for a specific site selection. The franchisor may often help by providing location suggestions and analysis for choosing specific sites, and often will have location standards and profiles of other successful site selections. Frequently the final site determination is made by the franchisee with approval from the franchisor. The prospective franchisee should remember that it is unlawful for franchisees and a franchisor to agree upon or enforce a territorial division policy. Generally, however, if additional franchises are to be granted within an area, the franchisor often provides the established local franchisee the first option to purchase and build the new franchise.

Term and Renewal. Almost all franchising agreements are set up for a specified term, generally from five to 20 years. Some franchisors have found that the agreement may be renewed for perpetuity without any objections on the part of either the franchisor or the franchisee.

At the expiration of the term, most franchisors provide a one-time right of renewal to the franchisee. The franchisee should understand the terms and conditions of the franchisee renewal, and such fine points as whether a "good cause" must be given for nonrenewal or termination by the franchisor, or if the franchisor has the option to purchase all equipment if the agreement is terminated or not renewed. The prospective franchisee should thoroughly review and understand the terms and renewal options and have them recorded in the franchising agreement.

Profit/Earnings Claims

Any claims made by the franchisor regarding sales, income, or profits which can be expected from the franchise should be closely examined and analyzed. Earnings claims are simply estimates and cannot be guaranteed by the franchisor. (Refer to Figure 15-3.)

Most franchisors will not (in disclosure documents or in disclosure meetings with interested prospects) provide earnings claims to prospective franchisees. If earnings claims are provided, then they must be backed by audited statements and by information regarding the percentage of existing franchises that have actually achieved the results that are claimed.

When reviewing any earnings claims regarding sales, profits, or income, a prospective franchisee must be certain to ascertain how many franchisees showed those figures during the first year of operation, when operating results are normally not as good. First-year results of franchises throughout a system are generally similar. Such information is usually attainable only from franchisees who have recently completed their first year.

Professional Advice

All prospective franchisees should seek the advice of a competent accountant, attorney, banker, or other professional before signing any agreements. It is wise for a prospect to review especially the financial statements with an expert in the field. A professional accountant, banker, or other experienced business adviser may be able to give counsel as to whether the franchisor's financial condition is sound and whether the franchisor will be able to fulfill its commitments to the franchisees.

The prospective franchisee should also contact an attorney before signing any franchising agreement. The disclosure document does not include everything the franchisee needs to know about the consequences of signing a franchising agreement and the related contracts. An attorney will be able to advise the prospect about the legal rights granted by the franchising agreement and the obligations assumed by franchisees. Although most franchising agreements are fairly rigid, an attorney may be able to suggest important changes in the contract which might provide better protection of the franchisee's interests. Legal advice at the outset generally saves on the cost of legal advice should problems later arise.

Any promise or representation made by the franchisor to the franchisee should be put in writing and incorporated into the franchising agreement. If such promises do not clearly appear in the contracts, then they are not legally binding upon the franchisor or the franchisee.

Legal Rights of Franchisees

The Franchise Rule (Rule 436) issued by the Federal Trade Commission provides franchisees and prospective franchisees with certain legal rights under federal law. These rights include the following:

1. The right to receive a disclosure document at the first personal meeting with a representative of the franchisor to discuss the purchase of a franchise; but in no event less than ten business days before signing a franchising or related agreement, or paying any money in connection with purchase of a franchise.
2. The right to receive documentation stating the basis and assumptions for any earnings claims that are made at the time the claims are made; but in no event less than ten business days before signing a franchising or related agreement, or paying any money in connection with the purchase of a franchise. If an earnings claim is made in advertising, the prospect has the right to receive the required documentation at the first personal meeting with a representative of the franchisor.
3. The right to receive sample copies of the franchisor's standard franchising and related agreements at the same time the disclosure document is received, and the right to receive the final agreements to be signed at least five business days before they are signed.
4. The right to any refunds promised by the franchisor, subject to any conditions or limitations on that right which have been disclosed by the franchisor.
5. The right not to be misled by oral or written representations made by the franchisor or its representatives that are inconsistent with the disclosures made in the disclosure document.

No federal agency will have reviewed the disclosure documents and other franchisor legal instruments before the franchisee obtains them. If they appear to be inaccurate, or if the franchisee thinks he or she has been denied any rights under federal law, the franchisee should send a letter describing the violation to Program Advisor, Franchise and Business Opportunities Program, Federal Trade Commission, Washington, DC 20580. For additional information, see the *Franchise Opportunities Handbook*, U.S. Department of Commerce, 1988.

Franchising is an increasingly popular method of doing business, and with increased popularity comes the increased chance of unscrupulous participants. The best protection for the prospective franchisee is to know the legal rights afforded both the franchisee and the franchisor. Before signing any documents or making any final commitments, the prospective franchisee should obtain whatever legal counsel is needed to clarify which rights are protected — and which are not protected — by the franchising agreement and the federal laws pertaining to franchising.

Disclosure Meeting

One of the most exciting times for a franchisor and a franchisee is when they first get together to discuss the operations of the business, in what is generally referred to as a disclosure meeting. At the disclosure meeting the franchisor will "disclose" the general business practices and obligations of owning a franchise.

The franchisor may often include a franchise sales presentation or flip chart (or even a movie or slide presentation) which discusses the operations of the franchise system. This sales kit generally explains the history, organization, and operations of the franchise system. Usually included in the sales prospectus are the following:

1. History of the franchise
2. What the franchise package includes (products and services)
3. Franchisee support services (to show continuing value)
4. Corporate structure (chart)
5. Photos of corporate officers
6. Photos of corporate offices
7. Marketing tools available
8. Training schedules
9. Target market
10. Insurance programs (if available)
11. Other pertinent information

After explaining the history and operations of the franchise, the franchisor or representative generally becomes a listener rather than a talker, using this time to assess the qualifications of the franchisee. The prospective franchisee should use this time to ask questions about the franchise. We include the following lists of questions, grouped in four areas and stated from the perspective of the franchisee, to give some examples of questions you as a prospective franchisee might ask of yourself or of the franchisor's representative in the disclosure meeting.

The Franchise

1. Did your attorney meticulously study the franchising contract you are considering before approving it?

2. Does the franchise call upon you to take any steps which, according to your attorney, are unwise or illegal in your state, county, or city?

3. Does the franchisor give you an exclusive territory for the length of the franchise, or can the franchisor sell a second or third franchise in your territory?

4. Is the franchise connected in any way with another franchised company handling similar merchandise or services?

5. If the answer to the last question is yes, what is your protection against this second organization?

6. Under what circumstances can you terminate the franchising contract and at what cost to you, if you decide for any reason that you wish to cancel it?

7. If you sell your franchise, will you be compensated for your goodwill, or will the goodwill you have built into the business be lost?

The Franchisor

8. How many years has the franchisor been in operation?

9. Does the franchisor have a reputation for honesty and fair dealings among the franchisees?

10. Has the franchisor shown you any certified figures indicating net profits of franchisees, which you personally checked with the franchisees?

11. Will the franchisor assist you with:

    (a) A management training program?
    (b) An employee training program?
    (c) A public relations program?
    (d) Capital?
    (e) Credit?
    (f) Merchandising ideas?

12. Will the franchisor help you find a good location for your new business?

13. Does the franchisor have sufficient financing to carry out its stated plan of financial assistance and expansion?

14. Is the franchisor a one-person company, or a corporation with an experienced, well-trained management team (so that it would always have an experienced person at its head)?

15. Exactly what can the franchisor do for you that you cannot do for yourself?

16. Does the franchisor investigate prospective franchisees carefully enough to ensure that they will be able to successfully operate a franchise and show a profit?

17. Does your state have a law regulating the sale of franchises, and has the franchisor complied with that law?

You — The Franchisee

18. How much equity capital will you have to have to purchase and operate the franchise before your income equals your expenses? What are your sources of capital?

19. Are you prepared to give up some independence of ownership in order to secure the advantages offered by the franchise system?

20. Do you really believe you have the innate ability, training, and experience to work smoothly and profitably with the franchisor, your employees, and your customers?

21. Are you ready to spend much or all of the remainder of your business life with this franchisor, offering its product or service to your public on a continuing basis?

The Market

22. Have you undertaken any studies to determine whether the proposed product or service offering has a market in your territory at the prices you will have to charge?

23. In the next five years, will the consumer population in your territory increase, remain static, or decrease?

24. Five years from now, will the product or service offered by the franchise be in greater, similar, or less demand?

25. What competition already exists in your territory for the product or service you will be offering? Is this competition from nonfranchised firms or from other franchised firms?

It is improper and generally illegal for the franchisor to sign the franchisee to a contract at this disclosure meeting. The disclosure meeting usually must occur no less than ten days before the signing of the franchising agreement.

If earnings claims have not been made in the disclosure document then the franchisor will most likely not make any earnings claims during the disclosure meeting. Most franchisors will refer the prospective franchisee to other existing franchisees to learn about such claims. Franchisees should ask whatever questions they desire during the disclosure meeting.

The Signing

One of the most exciting moments for both the franchisor and the franchisee occurs at the signing of the franchising agreement. At this time, there may also be other agreements, including lease, location, and purchase agreements, which need to be signed.

The franchisor will usually require that the franchisee have his or her attorney witness the signing of the franchising agreement (the franchisor commonly requests the franchisee's lawyer to be present at all contract signings). This meeting may be held at either the franchisor's or the franchisee's offices. At this time all fees, payments, and royalties should be understood and agreed upon, and any major problems should be resolved. Also, training programs, site selection, architectural designs, and startup activities should be discussed and planned at this meeting.

Training/Grand Opening/Operations

Once the franchising agreement has been signed, it is time to start the franchised business. The location and site must be selected, and the franchisee must receive the training necessary to open the franchised unit.

Successful franchisors consider proper training to be one of the most critical components of a successful franchise. The training can last from five days to three months, or however long it takes the franchisor to adequately instruct the franchisee in sales, operations, management, and marketing techniques. It is important that the franchisee have a thorough grasp of all aspects of the franchised business.

Following the training program, the next major function is the grand opening or startup of the business. Often the franchisor will send representatives who will help open the franchise. For a simple operation, one representative may be sufficient to get the business ready for the grand opening. In large, complex franchises, however, 14 or 15 representatives may be sent to ensure a smooth opening for the franchise. Representatives of the franchisor will often stay from a week to a month to make sure that the operations are running efficiently. The franchisee will generally pay the salary or wages of those visiting from the franchisor's headquarters.

In addition, representatives of the franchisor often provide the initial training for new franchise employees; these representatives may even help in the hiring of all new franchise employees. This enables new franchisees to learn the hiring and training processes which they may use later in the business operations.

Just as it is a common belief of many bank loan officers that the character of the applicant is worth 50 percent of the loan application, so most franchisors believe personality and personal characteristics, or worthiness, of the franchisee to be very important factors in the determination of whether or not to grant a franchise. Therefore, all meetings, discussions, and contacts between a franchisor and a franchisee are very important for both parties in determining whether the franchising agreement would be a beneficial experience for both parties.

Chapter 15 Investigating Franchise Opportunities 427

> # SUCCESS STORY
> ## LEON "PETE" W. HARMAN
>
> Leon "Pete" W. Harman was born the son of a farmer in Granger, Utah. His mother died of pneumonia when Pete was only two days old, leaving his father alone to care for nine children. When Pete was five, his father also died, so Pete was raised by his aunt, Carrie Harman.
>
> After leaving school at age 15 to earn a living, Pete worked his way to San Francisco, where he got a job as a dishwasher. An astute observer, he learned a great deal about the restaurant business in those early years of gradually increasing responsibility.
>
> In 1941, with only $15 to his name and with a loan from his brother, Pete and his wife, Arline, purchased a 16-seat hamburger restaurant in Salt Lake City. Their first day's sales amounted to only $13.
>
> Just when business was starting to improve, Pete was drafted into the service. Arline ran the restaurant until he returned; but postwar prosperity would be a long time coming for Pete Harman.
>
> In 1951, Pete met Colonel Harlan Sanders at a National Restaurant Association convention in Chicago. A year later, he struck up a franchise deal with the Colonel and sealed it with a handshake. It was then that the 6,400-unit worldwide Kentucky Fried Chicken franchise was born.
>
> Pete Harman's management philosophy is what is unique about his success story. He feels that anyone willing to work hard can look forward to career advancement. He allows his managers to purchase up to 40 percent of the stock in their stores, because he feels ownership provides the best possible motivation for people to do their best.
>
> To encourage competition among stores, Pete initiated a "Top Ten Contest" to recognize the most successful stores in the system. This prestigious honor includes a presentation at an awards banquet. He also "names" his stores after long-time employees.
>
> Photo and information provided courtesy of Leon W. Harman, September, 1985.

SUMMARY

The success of new franchisees is often determined by their knowledge and understanding of the franchise system. With proper training, sufficient capital, and a desire to succeed, many new franchisees can become very successful and profitable. The franchisee must approach the opportunity with care and wisdom, and must use all available resources to ensure the greatest possibility of success for the new business.

The recruitment of new prospective franchisees is very important to the success of the franchise system. In a sense, the franchisees become the children of the franchisor's business family.

The prospective franchisee who properly investigates and chooses the right franchise will be very happy and more likely successful. This investigation and selection process includes the steps of self-evaluation, understanding the business arena, investigating the franchise (including the four "P's" of franchising: product, process, profitability, and people), studying disclosure documents, verifying profit/earnings claims, seeking professional advice, understanding and knowing one's legal rights, utilizing the disclosure and signing meetings, and proper development of training, grand opening, and the operations of the franchise. The successful franchisee will spend sufficient time investigating and researching the various franchises. The right selection comes only after meeting the people involved and understanding the franchising process.

CASE STUDY
SUE'S SOUTHERN KITCHEN

Sue Zimmerman wants to start her own franchised business. She loves southern-style cooking, especially southern fried chicken, and is interested in opening a restaurant in her local Colorado community. She has more than $85,000 to invest and feels that now would be a good time to start a franchised business.

The main reason Sue wishes to establish a franchised outlet is that she lacks management and marketing experience, as she has never been a manager or been in charge of any marketing or promotional activities. She knows it will take a great deal of time to develop these skills, but she believes that the correct franchisor will provide her with the necessary training and marketing tools to enable her to be a successful business owner.

Sue is particularly interested in the Popeyes Famous Fried Chicken and Biscuits franchise system. She has recently written to and received materials from Popeyes, and has learned that the system offers seven weeks of extensive training, in addition to having accounting, operations, marketing, advertising, and real estate expertise available to franchisees. The training is provided for two persons per store, and includes station training, the operation of every job in the restaurant from cashier to sanitation, management expertise, sales motivation, employee counseling techniques, personnel training, and goal setting. A "pro" crew is sent by the franchisor to get the new store off to a flying start. This team of experts will train restaurant employees and make certain that grand opening growing "pains" are turned into "gains." Evaluations are regularly made of each store with a detailed checklist, which helps keep franchised units operating at the high level of efficiency demanded by Popeyes because of its unique recipes and procedures.

The Popeyes advertising department will supply complete, professionally produced series of creative advertising for local, regional, and national campaigns. Sue has also learned that Popeyes advertising has won many awards, including the coveted Silver "Addy" Award for the South. These advertising campaigns help generate consumer activity in all market areas.

The startup costs include the following:

Estimated Cash Requirement for Five Units

Franchise License Fee	
First unit fee	$25,000
Second unit option fee	$10,000
Third unit option fee	$10,000
Fourth unit option fee	$10,000
Fifth unit option fee	$10,000
Total of Fees and Deposits	$65,000

Equipment and Fines per Unit

(Down Payment)	$15,000
Operating Capital	$15,000
Total Cash Required First Unit	$95,000
Cash Required for Each Additional Unit	
(Balance of Franchise)	$15,000
Equipment and Signs	
(Down Payment)	$15,000
Startup Operational Capital	$ 5,000
TOTAL	$160,000

For a franchise purchasing land and building, the additional costs which might be incurred include:

Building with 45 Seats and a Drive-Thru	$135,000
20,000 sq. ft. of land estimate	$100,000
TOTAL	$235,000

Sue is very excited about starting her new business, but she is unsure of how to begin, and she is still apprehensive because of her limited background in management and marketing. She is wondering what she should do to overcome these fears and inhibitions.

CASE QUESTIONS

1. What kind of management and/or marketing assistance should the franchisor provide to Sue?
2. What specific areas of management training should Sue request of the franchisor?
3. What specific marketing assistance should she expect from a franchisor?
4. What else should Sue do before opening her franchised business?

REFERENCES

1. Anderson, Evan E., "The Growth and Performance of Franchise Systems: Company Versus Franchisee Ownership," *Journal of Economics and Business*, Vol. 36 (December 1984), p. 421.
2. Bresler, Stanley, "Franchising: Road to the American Dream; It Can Give the Budding Entrepreneur Decided Advantages Starting Out," *American Banker*, Vol. 149 (March 16, 1984), p. 54.
3. Carner, William J., "An Analysis of Franchising in Retail Banking," *Journal of Retail Banking*, Vol. 8 (Winter 1986), p. 57.
4. Dailey, Michael J., "Assessing Franchises for Client Purchase," *Journal of Accountancy*, Vol. 161 (March 1986), p. 120.
5. Davis, Howard A., "Road Map to Selecting a Franchise," *Entrepreneurs Franchise Yearbook*, Vol. 2 (1987/1988), pp. 318-319.
6. "Franchise Directory," *Entrepreneurs Franchise Yearbook*, Vol. 2 (1987/1988), pp. 32-282.
7. "Franchise Evaluation Checklist," *The Franchise Handbook*, No. 3, 1986, p. ix.
8. Golden Square Services Limited, "Choosing a Franchise," *The Successful Franchise*, Aldershot, Hantz, England: Gower Publishing Company Limited, 1985.
9. James, Andrew, "Business Format Franchising: Making the Right Choice," *Accountant's Magazine*, Vol. 90 (September 1986), p. 43(2).
10. Kostecka, Andrew, *Franchise Opportunities Handbook*, U.S. Department of Commerce, International Trade Association, Washington, DC: Government Printing Office, November, 1987.
11. Kostecka, Andrew, *Franchising in the Economy, 1986-1988*, U.S. Department of Commerce, International Trade Association, Washington, DC: Government Printing Office, January, 1988.
12. Marx, Thomas G., "The Development of the Franchise Distribution System in the U.S. Automobile Industry," *Business History Review*, Vol. 59 (Autumn 1985), p. 465.

13. Mosser, Frederick W., and Connell Hotel & Restaurant, "Franchising and the Spirit of Enterprise," *Administration Quarterly*, Vol. 26, (May 1985), p. 13.
14. Weinrauch, J. Donald, "Franchising an Established Business," *Journal of Small Business Management*, Vol. 24 (July 1986), p. 1.

CHAPTER 16
FINANCING YOUR FRANCHISED BUSINESS

In studying this chapter, you will:
- Understand the financing requirements of a franchisee.
- Learn about possible funding sources for a franchisee.
- Understand the franchisor's role in providing funding for franchisees.
- Be able to distinguish among available financing methods, including franchisor, family, banks, and outside funding agencies.
- Develop an understanding of how to prepare a financial package for a loan application.

INCIDENT

Mary wants to open her own executive placement service. For the past ten years, she has been working for an executive placement agency and is very competent at matching employees with employers and vice versa. She feels there is a local need for a placement service for employers and discontented executives. To begin such a business, Mary needs a large network of employees and employers. She has decided that the best and quickest way to accomplish this is to become a franchisee of a large, national employment service franchise.

    Mary's chief concern is how she will finance the venture. Although she has some savings, she is realistic about how much capital is necessary to start a business. She must consider startup costs and business expenses, as well as all fees that must be paid to a franchisor. She is confused about the many alternatives. Which type of financing would she be most likely to qualify for? What would be the most attractive payment plan in the short and long run? Would it be possible to finance the venture with several types of loans?

INTRODUCTION

The primary goal of any company is to make a profit. In a franchise system, if franchisees are unable to make a profit, the company will not survive, and the franchisees will be forced out of business. A primary goal of the franchisee is likewise to generate a profit and thus increase personal wealth. One of the main ways for owners to increase their wealth is to increase the value of the business. Profitability is very important, as are growth, sound investment, financial stability, and good management.

FINANCIAL OBLIGATIONS OF FRANCHISEES

Before a franchisee can seriously think about making a profit, he or she obviously must choose a franchise system and open a franchised unit. The opening involves several important financial considerations, particularly startup costs. Startup costs include building expenses (land, building, equipment, fixtures, decorating, remodeling); one to three months' salaries and wages, inventory, and advertising costs; business expenses (including telephone and utilities, insurance, legal, and other professional fees, vehicles, supplies, and licenses), and living expenses (moving expenses, salary for owner or manager). These costs are crucial considerations for the franchisee.

In addition to the startup or turnkey costs associated with beginning a business, the franchisee is also required to pay the franchisor several fees including:

1. Franchising fees
2. Royalty fees
3. Advertising fees
4. Training fees
5. Other fees

The franchisee's major financial obligation is to the franchisor. This obligation includes an up-front franchising fee which usually ranges from $5,000 to $50,000. In addition to paying the franchising fee, the franchisee is expected to pay royalty fees (3 to 7 percent of gross revenues) on a weekly, biweekly, or monthly basis; advertising fees (0.5 to 3 percent of gross revenues); and sometimes leasing or rental fees, either a fixed monthly payment or from 1 to 8 percent of gross revenues. Besides these basic expenditures, the franchisee may incur the costs of initial training — travel, lodging, and meals. Also, the franchisee should be alert to the possibility of additional costs relating to on-site visitations, computer rental fees, equipment leasing fees, or travel expenses to regional or national franchisor meetings. (See the examples in Figure 16-1.)

OTHER FRANCHISEE REQUIREMENTS OR OBLIGATIONS

The franchisee is generally required to purchase specific items of equipment or inventory often carrying the logo of the franchisor. The equipment used by the franchisee must meet the specifications set by the franchisor. However, most franchisors do not require the franchisee to purchase directly from the franchisor. Rather, the franchisee has latitude to purchase supplies from various sources. Thus, it is generally held that the franchisee, while obligated to acquire the equipment and items of inventory listed in the franchising agreement, is not required to purchase these items from the franchisor. The franchisee may purchase all such items from any reputable supplier. The franchisee is not required, but has the option, of acquiring all or any of these items from the franchisor. To the best understanding of the franchisor, there are numerous sources of supply of most such items. The franchisee is initially advised to purchase a few items bearing the franchisor's trademarks and logos from the franchisor affiliate.

The franchisor is required to specify in writing, in both the disclosure document and the contract, any obligations a franchisee has which may result in profit to the franchisor. Although the franchisor may not require a franchisee to make purchases from the parent corporation, the franchisor may require that the franchisee obtain equipment, furniture,

Figure 16-1
Development Costs
Postal Instant Press (PIP)

Franchising Fee	$40,000
Inventory and Supply Package*	$ 7,200
Equipment Package*	$35,400
TOTAL	$82,600

*Equipment and inventory and supply prices subject to change every 30 days. Amount excludes sales or use tax (if applicable).

Source: Postal Instant Press, Franchisee Prospectus, 1985.

and fixtures from an approved list of suppliers who meet or exceed the prescribed standards as established by the franchisor.

The franchisor is also required in both the Uniform Franchise Offering Circular and the disclosure document to state the franchisee's initial investment. Many times, however, because of the variability of the investment obligations, the franchisor may simply state that the total cost of the project is not ascertainable. This satisfies, in essence, the requirement of the disclosure documents. Often, though, the franchisor will strive to provide some low, middle, and high estimates for the prospective franchisee. Many franchisors may also fulfill this disclosure requirement by listing estimated costs as in the following:

Franchising fee:	$ 30,000
Equipment (estimated):	$ 60,000
Starting working capital:	$ 15,000
Additional capital recommended:	$ 10,000
Total:	$115,000

Other franchisors work rather hard to establish estimates of total startup expenses. They want the franchisee to realize the total amount to be expended before the business startup. It is important for the franchisor to be honest with the franchisee. The franchisee must recognize that the figures are only estimates that will vary from one location to another. Franchisees need to know the basis of the estimates made by the franchisor and perform their own business and financial analyses (see Chapter 3) before making any final decisions. The total cost of any franchise operation will depend on a number of factors, including the location of the franchise and the local market and economic conditions. The franchisee may use any estimates provided by the franchisor, but should seek additional information from other franchisees, suppliers, and builders in order to arrive at more accurate final cost figures.

FRANCHISOR FINANCING ARRANGEMENTS

Almost every franchisee must utilize outside financial sources. And franchising, like any business opportunity, is a risk. However, because of its use of established business formats, proven products, and effective advertising techniques, franchising reduces the chance of failure of small-business entrepreneurs. The franchisee has basically four major financial resources: the franchisor; family, friends, and relatives; the bank; and venture capitalists or outside funding agencies.

Ideally, business startup or expansion would always be financed by self-generated capital. In the real world, however, most franchisees and franchisors are unable to start a franchising program on existing capital resources. Even established franchisees who wish to expand into multi-unit franchises find it very difficult to generate sufficient internal capital.

Some Arrangements by Franchisors

Most franchisors will not become involved with the financing of new franchises, although a few of the well-established franchisors, including McDonald's and Postal Instant Press (PIP), will help finance franchisees. One of the main reasons for franchising is that it enables the franchisor to use the capital of franchisees to expand and develop franchised units. Therefore, most franchisors require the franchisee to have sufficient capital to pay the initial franchising fee as well as to start and develop the franchised unit. In their disclosure documents, many franchisors simply state that "neither the franchisor, nor any of its related agents, offer either directly or indirectly any financing arrangements or opportunities to any prospective franchisees."

The two opposing schools of thought regarding financing by the franchisor are (1) that lending is not a primary business and should not be engaged in, and (2) that financing should be offered to prospective franchisees to encourage buildups and the development of multi-unit franchisees. Almost all franchisors, however, prefer that franchisees have at least part of their own capital committed to the franchised unit. There are virtually no franchisors who will provide 100 percent backing without some financial commitment on the part of the franchisee to develop the franchising business. Most franchisors also prefer the franchisee to pay all initial franchising fees out-of-pocket. For instance, the $30,000–$40,000 franchising fee for Dunkin' Donuts of America, Inc., must be paid entirely out-of-pocket. Dunkin' Donuts will help finance all of the equipment needed, with the franchisee having the option of either a straight loan or a leasing package. None of the big four rental car businesses — Hertz Corporation (New York), Avis Rent-A-Car, Inc. (Garden City, NY), National Car Rental System, Inc. (Minneapolis), and Budget Rent-A-Car (Chicago) — offer financing for franchisees. They require that the entire franchising fee be financed up front by the franchisee, but will help develop lines of credit from the major automotive companies or third-party lenders.

Some franchisors, including the Ann Arbor-based Molly Maid housekeeping franchise, will finance up to 40 percent of the initial investment capital requirement because they want to help franchisees get started. They know that the franchise system's growth comes from franchisees and from the royalties franchisees will pay to the franchisor. The 7-ELEVEN franchise division of Southland Corporation buys all locations, puts up the buildings, and leases them to the franchisees. This lessens the burden of financing on franchisees and encourages a strong relationship between the franchisor and the franchisee. Both the temporary home support service franchisor Sara Care Franchise Corp. (El Paso, Texas) and the business services Mail Boxes Etc., Inc. (Carlsbad, California) do not provide financial assistance for the first franchised unit but will help the established franchisee finance up to 50 percent of the cost of additional units.

It is important to mention, however, that franchising fees may differ even within the same franchise system, depending on the number of franchises to be opened. For instance, one system may reduce the base franchising fee of $20,000 per store to $16,000 per store if five or more stores are to be opened, and to $11,000 per store if ten stores are to be opened. Another franchise system might reduce the initial royalty fee of 4.5 percent of gross revenues for a single store to 3.3 percent if three or more stores are opened.

When a multi-unit program is started, the franchisee should work with the franchisor to develop a payment schedule. For example, if the franchisee agrees to open ten units over a five-year period, the franchising fee payments may be arranged to include one-half of the total fees payable when the original agreement is signed. This one-time, up-front fee is generally nonrefundable. The balance of each of the ten franchising fees would then be payable as each unit opens.

Once they are fully developed and staffed, some franchisors will have sufficient resources to help finance the startup costs of their franchisees. New franchisors rarely become involved with the financing of either franchising fees or startup costs simply because these franchisors do not have sufficient capital available.

One franchisor that provides financial backing to new franchisees is Postal Instant Press (PIP), which makes ten-year financing available to startup franchisees in need of assistance (see Figures 16-2 and 16-3).

Other Financing Arrangements Provided by the Franchisor

Some franchisors may make arrangements with a commercial lender to provide financing of certain franchising fees, startup costs, fixtures, equipment, and furniture to prospective franchisees who meet the lender's financial requirements. The terms and conditions are established by the lending institution for the franchisee and may be changed without the knowledge or consent of the franchisor. These loans are usually secured by a combination of real and personal property, and a portion of this financing may be guaranteed by or through the franchisor.

Certain franchisors may provide discounts on the initial franchising fee to franchisees making full cash payments prior to their attending training programs (see Figure 16-4). This kind of discount is more likely to be offered by small franchisors than by large franchise systems.

Figure 16-2
Franchising Fee and Supply Package
Postal Instant Press (PIP)

Franchising Fee			$40,000
Down Payment		$15,000	
Inventory and Supplies	$6,800		
Estimated Freight	400		
Total Supply Package		−7,200	
(Paid from Down Payment)			
Remainder of Down Payment			−7,800
Amount to be financed			$32,200*

*PIP will finance this balance over a 10-year period @ 12.5% APR.

OPTION I ——
    120 Payments @ $471.33 per month, 10 years

OPTION II ——
    36 Payments @ $275.00 per month, then
    24 Payments @ $500.00 per month, then
    24 Payments @ $600.00 per month, then
    36 Payments @ $790.00 per month

Source: Postal Instant Press, Franchisee Prospectus, 1985.

Figure 16-3
The PIP Estimated Monthly Cost Summary

Year	Franchising Fee and Supply Package (PIP-Contract Payment)	Equipment Lease (PIP Capital-Lease Rental)	Total Monthly Payment
1	$275.00	$514.00	$ 789.00
2	$275.00	$514.00	$ 789.00
3	$275.00	$514.00	$ 789.00
4	$500.00	$514.00	$1,014.00
5	$500.00	$514.00	$1,014.00
6	$600.00	$514.00	$1,114.00
7	$600.00	$514.00	$1,114.00
8	$790.00	$514.00	$1,304.00
9	$790.00	—	$ 790.00
10	$790.00	—	$ 790.00

Source: Postal Instant Press, Franchisee Prospectus, 1985.

Figure 16-4
How Much Does a Sir Speedy Printing Center Business Cost?

A Sir Speedy Franchise Package is valued at $111,000. Here is how the $111,000 amount is allocated:

The Sir Speedy Franchise Fee $17,500

The Franchise Fee includes the use of the Sir Speedy name, logos, and trademarks. Seven thousand five hundred dollars ($7,500) is paid upon applying for a franchise. The balance of ten thousand dollars ($10,000) is payable prior to the franchisee's attendance of the required Sir Speedy Training Program.

Startup Costs $22,500

This amount includes payment for training; travel and lodging during the training period; market research; site location; lease negotiation assistance; applied window and wall graphics (whenever possible); and initial fixtures; furniture and inventory not included in the equipment package. This is payable prior to the franchisee's attendance of the required Sir Speedy Training Program.

Equipment $71,000

Sir Speedy has selected and tested specific equipment to offer you a unique and first rate equipment package. This total equipment package is available through Sir Speedy; however, you are not obligated to purchase this package from them. Inasmuch as service, training, and quality control must be maintained, Sir Speedy does require you to use the recommended equipment.

Also included in the equipment package are signage, cabinets, counters, shelving and furniture — all color-coordinated to attract customers and provide pleasant working conditions.

Total Package $111,000

Sir Speedy recommends that a franchisee have a minimum of $8,000 to cover pre-opening expenses. This fund is not paid to Sir Speedy, but must be available to meet your pre-opening expenses such as leasing deposits, utility deposits, etc. Operating capital will also be needed to cover the expenses during the first few months of operation; the operating capital needed will vary depending upon needs, location of business, etc.

Source: Sir Speedy, Franchisee Prospectus, 1988.

FINANCIAL RESOURCES OF FRANCHISEES

Financing may be properly defined as the acquisition of funds to cover expenses and to allow the purchasing of assets which provide revenue for a new business. The franchise's capital structure is the makeup of its business finances — that is, how much is debt (borrowed money) and how much is equity (owner's share).

Debt Financing and Equity Financing

Every franchisee needs to understand the two primary forms of long-term financing available to a franchise: debt financing and equity financing. Equity financing is selling the ownership of the company to other investors. This includes dividing the business and its managerial responsibilities among the different partners, owners, or investors. The original owner does not have to repay these other investors in cash, but instead gives them a share of the business profits and managerial responsibilities. The investors receive money from the business through the division of profits in the form of dividends. The primary sources of equity capital include oneself, one's friends and relatives, and venture capital companies.

Debt financing may be divided into two categories — financing for working capital and financing for capital expenditures. The advantage of debt financing is that it enables one to borrow money and pay it back to the lender over time, on an appropriate, affordable repayment schedule. The major sources of debt financing include banks and other financial institutions, friends, and relatives.

Debt financing for working capital ordinarily involves short-term debt incurred to help purchase inventories or cover accounts payable. This is often necessary when inventories and payrolls must be increased in order to generate higher sales or profits for the franchise. Working capital debt is usually financed through short-term bank loans, trade credits, or credit unions. Whereas financing for working capital is normally short-term, financing for capital expenditures (land, building, equipment, and fixtures) is almost always obtained through long-term debt agreements. Capital expenditure financing is most often required for startup expansion or for remodeling of the franchise. The major sources of capital expenditure financing include commercial banks, the Small Business Administration, venture capitalists, vendors, life insurance companies, and other commercial lenders.

When borrowing money, it is important that the franchisee understand the "four C's" of debt financing, since the lender will be examining these same elements:

1. Capacity of the franchisee to repay the loan
2. Character of the franchisee
3. Capital or investment of the franchisee
4. Collateral offered by the franchisee

The franchisee should be aware that borrowing is both an art and a science. The owner's ability to obtain the money is going to be based on personal history, credit history, business track record, and ability to effectively (and legally, of course) influence the lender.

Debt Financing. The capital structure of the franchise may include short-term, intermediate-term, and long-term financing.

Short-Term Financing. Short-term financing generally involves the use of money for less than one year. These funds are often sought for short-term needs such as the purchase of inventory or specialty sales items. Short-term financing is frequently used to handle the lag period between the time when expenses are incurred (cash outlay) and the time when sales revenues are received (cash input). The franchisee may usually secure this type of financing through trade credit, commercial paper, unsecured bank loans, or inventory financing.

Trade credit, the most common form of short-term financing, is a means by which the franchisee can receive credit from suppliers and/or service companies. The supplier (seller) generally allows the franchisee (buyer) a certain number of days before the bill must be paid. The trade period may be from 30 to 120 days, usually with little or no interest charged for this period. Franchisees' ability to obtain trade credit is determined almost solely by their reputation and credit history.

Commercial paper is a short-term promissory note which the franchisee signs and sells to an investor. It is normally sold for short periods, from 30 to 270 days. Because it is very difficult for most franchisees to afford, this practice is ordinarily reserved for large corporations with strong financial backing.

Intermediate-Term Financing. The franchisee will typically use short-term financing only to handle an emergency or inventory purchases. Intermediate-term financing more often fills the one- to three-year financing requirements. This type of financing is normally quite flexible and is frequently used by franchisees undergoing rapid growth. The company may initially seek short-term financing, which the bank may extend for a one- or two-year period; but the bank is usually unwilling to give additional extensions. Many franchisees look to intermediate-term financing as a way to obtain funds for starting up or for limited expansion.

If the franchisee has a strong credit rating, the bank may provide an unsecured or signature loan. This type of bank loan may be for a certain line of credit, a revolving credit agreement, or a transaction loan. Or, a franchisee may be able to obtain an inventory loan based upon the inventory on hand. Most banks in this case require the franchisee to actually present the purchase orders and an audited account of inventory on hand. These types of loans are generally not available to franchisees, although they may be in certain cases.

Long-Term Financing. Long-term financing is most often used to provide funds for the purchase of long-term or permanent assets, which may include land, buildings, and certain types of equipment. Long-term financing ordinarily involves a period of five to 20 years. These arrangements are typically handled not by banks, but by such institutions as insurance companies, pension funds, or the Small Business Administration, or by the issuance of bonds or stocks.

There are also new companies developing in the United States which will provide sale-lease back financing for land, buildings, and equipment specifically for franchisees. Franchise Finance Corporation of America (FFCA) is a financial institution which offers private financing to franchisees primarily in the restaurant industry for the purchase of land, buildings, and equipment. FFCA provides franchisees with a financing package of fixed and affordable rates and sufficiently long lease terms for development of franchise locations. The financing offered by FFCA provides 100 percent financing for land, building, and equipment from a single source.

Types of Debt Financing. Franchisees can utilize several types of debt financing when they are in need of capital to improve or expand their businesses.

Bank Term Loans. A term loan is a formal agreement between a bank and the franchisee for the use of a specific sum of money (principal) at a given interest rate for a specific period of time (term). These loans normally require that portions of both the interest and the principal be repaid on a monthly basis. Occasionally a balloon payment may be allowed, by which only a portion of the principal is repaid during the term of the loan and a large "balloon" payment is due at maturity. These loans often require collateral — land, buildings, fixtures, equipment, or other fixed assets — that is promised to the bank if the franchisee is unable to meet the repayment requirements.

Equipment Lease Financing. An important financial program which has become more widely available in recent years is the lease financing arrangement. This arrangement enables the franchisee to obtain equipment at a lower cost, eliminate risk of ownership, and obtain service and maintenance agreements from the lessor. Many franchises which use unique equipment often seek to arrange lease arrangements for their franchisees through third parties. (See Figure 16-5.)

Equipment Financing. Certain franchisors will arrange to finance the necessary startup equipment through a leasing company. The terms and conditions of the lease financing are determined by the leasing company and the franchisee, and they may be easily changed without the knowledge or consent of the franchisor. An initial payment equal to the first and last monthly installments may be required. These types of financial arrangements are often made outside the control of the franchisor. Under certain conditions, however, the franchisor may be the lessor, in which case the franchisee is liable and responsible to the franchisor. At

Figure 16-5
Equipment Package-Lease Program
Postal Instant Press (PIP)

Equipment Cost	$33,700
Estimated Freight	$ 1,700
Total Estimated Cost (without sales tax)	$35,400

Lease Payments: 8 years @ $514.00 per month plus any applicable sales tax. Purchase option at the end of lease term.

Franchise owner has an option to purchase the leased equipment at the end of the eight-year period for the then fair market value. The franchise owner can either pay this at the end of the lease or PIP will finance over a two-year period.

Source: Postal Instant Press, Franchisee Prospectus, 1985.

the end of the leasing agreement, the franchisee typically has the option to purchase the equipment outright (at its fair market value). If the franchise is terminated for any reason, the lease becomes immediately due and payable in full.

A franchisee who has decided to purchase equipment may be able to obtain a loan using the equipment as collateral. Banks, finance companies, and equipment manufacturers often engage in this type of lending. The franchisee may decide to use a manufacturer or finance company to obtain this type of loan, leaving bank loans to be used for other asset accounts.

Federal Financing. In 1953, Congress passed the Small Business Act, by which it established the Small Business Administration (SBA) to help small businesses (including franchisees) obtain loans for startups and other activities. The SBA helps franchisees obtain capital through (1) the SBA loan guarantee program, (2) the 502 program, or (3) small business investment companies (SBICs).

The SBA guaranteed loan program was established to help small businesses in the acquisition, construction, or improvement of a building; the purchase of inventory and equipment; startup costs; and working capital. The money is lent to qualified business owners by participating banks or non-bank companies, including the Money Store Investment Corporation (Sacramento, California) and Allied Lending Corp., a subsidiary of Allied Capital Corp. (Washington, D.C.). The government generally guarantees 90 percent of the loan for amounts up to $555,000, with interest rates usually 2 to 3 percent above prime. Most working capital loans are to be repaid within seven years, equipment loans within ten years, and real estate purchases within 25 years. Most SBA-guaranteed loans require personal guarantees of the officers, directors, or stockholders.

Additionally, Minority Enterprise Small Business Investment Companies (MESBICs) provide limited investment capital. MESBICs have been established to help "disadvantaged Americans" obtain funds for business activities. MESBICs are officially SBICs. Those qualifying for MESBIC loans normally fall into three categories: (1) ethnic minorities, (2) U.S. military personnel, and (3) U.S. citizens who have been hampered by social, economic, or other, personal difficulties.

Equity Financing. There are several means by which a franchisee can obtain equity financing in order to improve or expand a business.

Stock Sales. A franchisee may obtain long-term financing by selling stock to family and friends or to the public through public offerings. The stockholders become the actual owners of the corporation or franchise, and they bear the risk of the business. If the business fails, the stockholders lose their investment. If the business succeeds, they earn a return on their investment in the form of dividends paid by the business or through the appreciation of the stock's price.

One advantage of common stock financing is that the franchisee is not obligated to pay dividends, as long as the stockholders agree to this when the stock is issued. Many franchisees who are able to sell stock do not anticipate paying dividends for ten years or more. A second advantage of common stock financing is that there is no set maturity date by which repayment has to be made.

The issuance of common stock often enables the franchisee to obtain the funds necessary to start the franchise. The franchisee needs to be careful, however, to maintain managerial control of the franchise. Owners of common stock have a right to a voice in management. As long as the franchisee is able to maintain 51 percent ownership of the business, then the franchisee will be able to run the business according to how he or she sees fit.

Partnership. A rather common method of financing any business is to include partners in the business. Partnerships may be developed based upon the desire of individuals to work together and the agreement to contribute certain initial capital for anticipated outlays. All general partners may act as agents or representatives of the franchise. In a general partnership, all partners are fully liable for all the debts of the business and may be actively involved in its management. Each partner is taxed individually on his or her share of the profits.

A second form of partnership involves limited partners. The limited partnership must include at least one general partner, usually the franchisee. The limited partners' liability is limited to the amount of capital contributed or the amount of risk they agree to bear. Limited partners are not allowed to help run or manage the franchise. When a partner does participate in management, that person automatically becomes a general partner, and so will incur the same risk and liability as that of any other general partner.

Many franchisees use limited partnerships in order to raise capital to start a franchise. Limited partners may be able to invest $10,000 to $20,000 for a 5 to 10 percent interest in the business. This means that a general partner may be able to raise $100,000 while only giving up 50 percent of the business and retaining all of the managerial responsibilities. Limited partners reduce their financial risk and liability because their maximum losses are "limited" to the amount invested and the loans which they agree to guarantee. The main advantages for the limited partner are the opportunities to share in a profitable venture and to receive personal tax benefits.

Venture Capital Companies. Venture capital companies have been formulated to provide profits for their owners by helping businesses grow and, to a limited extent, by assisting business startups. Venture capitalists are seeking entrepreneurs who are achievers and who have a positive and aggressive approach to life and business. A franchisee should have complete understanding of his or her franchise situation before approaching a venture capitalist.

Venture capitalists review and analyze a business based on a number of factors: the entrepreneur's personal investment, up-side or profit potential, down-side risk, additional funding available, and exit opportunities. Individuals who are unwilling to invest their own money usually find it very difficult to attract venture capital. Most venture capitalists seek a profit target of five times the initial investment to be returned over a five-year period. If the initial investment were to double over the five-year period, this would compute to a rate of return of only 15 percent per annum. Multiplying the initial investment by three over a five-year period would yield a compounded annual return on investment of only 25 percent. The "five times" figure yields a compounded annual return of 38 percent; the venture capitalist will be very interested in this investment. What we have given are only general guidelines, however, for each investment has a particular profit target based on the risk and profitability potential of the firm.

The final agreement which the franchisee makes with a venture capitalist firm is usually broken down into five major sections.[1] These include:

---

[1] David J. Gladstone, *Venture Capital Handbook* (Reston, VA: Reston Publishing Co., Inc., 1983).

1. Terms of investment
2. Collateral and/or security
3. Conditions of the investment
4. Presentations
5. Conditions of commitment

The terms of the investment depend on whether the venture capitalist is providing a loan or intends to purchase shares. For example, the venture capitalist company may make a loan of $300,000 for ten years at an annual interest rate of 12 percent, or it may purchase 100,000 shares of common stock in the company at $2 per share. The collateral and security of the loan or investment is often secured with second mortgages, second deeds of trust, and/or a life insurance policy on the life of the franchisee for the amount of the loan.

Conditions of the investment are requirements which must be fulfilled. Generally included are financial statements issued at weekly, biweekly, monthly, and yearly intervals. Additionally, written reports of the firm's activities are often sent out monthly. Conditions are also established and contracted so that no change in control or ownership of the company can occur without the consent of the venture capitalist firm. The conditions of the investment include how the money will be used, debt or equity position of the venture capital firm, and assurance that no lawsuits against the company are currently outstanding and that no taxes are past due. The conditions of the commitment simply state how the funds will be paid and what the closing situation will be — whether it will be a buyback or a sale by the venture capitalist firm back to the franchisee.

PREPARING A FINANCIAL PACKAGE

The franchisee needs to realize the importance of preparing and properly documenting a financial package which may be shown to prospective investors. This package should include all information required by the lending office. It is designed simply to explain the needs for the loan, the amount requested, and the specific purposes or uses of the loan amount. When properly completed, a financial package should enable the bank, loan office, or investor to understand the operations, functions, and potential profitability of the franchise.

A properly prepared financial package would include the following:

1. Executive Summary
    a. Company name and address
    b. Contact person
    c. Type of business franchise

    d. Objective of the franchise
    e. Management
    f. History of the franchisor
    g. Amount requested (including collateral)
    h. Use of funds (including financial history and financial projections for 3 to 5 years)
    i. Exit
2. Marketing
    a. Product description
    b. Target market
    c. Location (property and facilities)
    d. Price determination
    e. Marketing strategy including promotion and advertising
    f. Industry
    g. Competition
3. Management
    a. Directors and officers (names and history of individuals)
    b. Key employees
    c. Organizational structure
    d. Management strategy
    e. Labor force and employees
    f. Policies about management
    g. Risk factors
    h. Remuneration (wage and salary administration)
    i. Stock option plans
    j. Inventory control methods
4. Accounting, Finance, and Taxes
    a. Startup or turnkey costs
    b. Equity and credit references
    c. Proposed financing (loans or equity: amounts, types, and conditions)
    d. Collateral
    e. Return on investment
    f. Projected income statement
    g. Projected balance sheet
    h. Projected cash flow (first year)
    i. Working capital
    j. Break-even analysis
    k. Provisions for taxation
    l. Sale/buyback of equity
5. Legal aspects
    a. Financial agreements (conditions, guarantees)
    b. Franchise agreements, licenses, and other legal documents

c. Business structure
   d. Insurance: types and costs
6. Appendix
   Product literature, brochures, pictures, articles, graphs, charts, layouts, diagrams, résumés, other

Executive Summary

The executive summary is the most crucial part of the financial presentation because it explains the business and sparks the interest of the investor. It spells out what is intended to happen. In addition, the executive summary should include the amount requested and how it will be used — i.e., for land, buildings, fixtures, furnishings, equipment, etc.

The franchisee needs to state clearly and precisely what is going to be done and how it is going to be done. The summary should be short, no longer than three pages. The business proposal which follows is generally attached, but most bank officers or investors will not be interested in plowing through a detailed proposal until they understand the business from a summary position. The summary is designed to entice the bank officer or investor into an interest in the business proposal and the franchise. Therefore the executive summary is, in effect, an advertising document, a sales pitch for the franchisee and the franchise.

Marketing

The marketing section should indicate to the financial officer how the business is going to generate its profit. Here the franchisee must accurately and in great detail describe the product or service which will be offered by the franchise. It is also important to identify who the target market or customers will be. Facts about the location, promotion, advertising, competition, industry, supplies, and any information regarding the marketing strategy should also be included. It is important to remember that the lending officer ordinarily has a very limited knowledge of the franchise or business that is planned.

Management

In the management section, the franchisee lists the names and histories of all principal directors, officers, and owners of the franchise. This may include only the principal franchisee, or it may involve several people, including spouses. The organizational structure should also be outlined. All management policies, remunerations, wage and salary guidelines, key employees, and any management strategies should be discussed in this section. Again, the loan officer will have a very limited knowledge of the specific management requirements of the franchise. It is important that this section of the financial package accurately and thoroughly explain the management functions and operations which will occur in the franchise.

Accounting, Finance, and Taxes

One of the most important items in any financial package is the startup or turnkey analysis. The section containing this information should enumerate all expenses which are necessary before the first customer sets foot in the franchise outlet. Information about the proposed financing and its use must be presented. If the franchisee will be establishing a fast-food restaurant, then costs might include building and land; utilities and telephone; insurance, legal, and advertising expenses; fixtures, equipment, cash registers, window display fixtures, tables, chairs, lighting, outside and inside signs, and delivery equipment; inventory; permits; installation of equipment, counters, cabinets, shelves, and even plumbing and restroom facilities. All of these costs need to be itemized and a total projected.

It would also be appropriate for the franchisee to develop pro forma income statements and balance sheets. As we know from earlier discussions, these are projected income statements for the first year of operation as well as balance sheets generally for the first day of operation. An investor or loan officer may also request to see pro forma cash flow statements projected for one year of operation. Other information about working capital, break-even volume, output, sales, and provisions for taxation should even be included in this section.

Legal

The franchisee should include in the financial package the franchising agreement between the franchisor and the franchisee. This will enable the loan officer to understand all contracts, licenses, and other legal requirements of the business. Additionally, the loan officer will often want to know the business structure — proprietorship, partnership, or corporation — which the principal owner will use. It is also appropriate in this section to include information about the types and costs of insurance which the new franchise will use.

Appendix

The appendix includes any additional product literature, pictures, articles, brochures, diagrams, or layouts which may be appropriate for the business. It may also include financial accounting or marketing diagrams or charts which may relate to discussions in the rest of the package.

SUCCESS STORY
CRAIG CORMACK

Craig Cormack's start in the fast-food industry was like that of many people — a part-time summer job while going to college. But what developed from this part-time job is far different from the ordinary case.

In 1975, Burger King was opening its first restaurant in Sioux Falls, South Dakota, with a first-time franchisee. Cormack took a job as a food handler. After just four weeks, he was offered the position of Assistant Manager. Uncertain of what career he wanted to pursue, he accepted the position with the intention of returning to college at a later time.

As it turned out, that later time never came. Cormack stayed with the growing Burger King franchise system and helped develop the South Dakota area. He went from Assistant Manager to Restaurant Manager, Training Manager, and then Director of Operations for all of eastern South Dakota.

In 1980, the South Dakota franchisee and Cormack bought two existing restaurants in Lincoln, Nebraska, with Cormack as the Operating Partner. Within two years, Cormack bought out his partner and began to develop the Lincoln area on his own. His company has since grown to 16 restaurants located in Nebraska, Kansas, and South Dakota, with total annual sales of over $15 million.

The future still looks promising for Craig Cormack, and he continues to investigate opening new restaurants and acquiring existing Burger Kings. He is also becoming involved in the real estate part of the business.

He states his philosophy of running a profitable business as follows: "Our success is based upon obtaining a strong commitment from our employees to be the best. Hopefully no one feels that he/she works for me, but that we work together. As long as we can keep good people, we will continue to grow." With this spirit of teamwork, Cormack also strives to be one of the leaders in benefits that he provides to his employees.

Cormack serves on various civic organizations and feels strongly about the importance of community involvement. In addition, he sits on regional and national planning councils for Burger King Corporation that provide franchisee input to the corporation.

When he isn't working, Cormack tries to spend as much time as possible skiing down the mountains of Colorado.

Photo and information provided courtesy of Craig Cormack, August, 1987.

SUMMARY

One of the essential ingredients of the proper operation of a franchised business is the sufficient financial planning and support of that business. It is important for all involved parties to recognize the financial obligations associated with purchasing and developing a franchise operation, including franchising fees, royalty fees, advertising fees, training fees, and other associated costs. Some franchisors, typically those who have been in existence for a long time, will provide financial support to potential franchisees; however, most franchisors are unable to offer such assistance, and franchisees must seek financing on their own. A prospective franchisee must determine if financial support is available from the franchisor.

The franchisee needs to research sources of potential financial support — family, friends, relatives, and financial organizations, including banks, credit unions, and other lending institutions. The franchisee must determine if he or she will accept debt financing (generally from banks or financial institutions) or equity financing (generally from family, friends, or relatives). The franchisee must also prepare a business plan or feasibility study showing the cost and projected income from the franchising operation. This may be used to show prospective contributors the financial strength and investment potential of the franchised business.

REVIEW QUESTIONS

1. Enumerate the possible financial obligations of a franchisee relative to becoming a franchisee.
2. What general financial arrangements will most franchisors provide new franchisees in their franchised business? Why?
3. What type of financing, debt or equity, is appropriate for a franchisee?
4. Why is a business plan or feasibility study important in developing the financial package of a franchisee?
5. List the major components of a feasibility study.

CASE STUDY
ONE-HOUR MARTINIZING*

Dry cleaning is a $2 billion industry primarily because the natural fabrics popular today, like wool and linen, require professional cleaning. For more than three decades, customers have known and trusted Martinizing Dry Cleaners for service and quality in cleaning their non-washable clothing.

---

*Trademark of Martin Franchises Inc. Information provided courtesy of Martin Franchises Inc., September, 1987.

Guy and Ardis have just opened a One-Hour Martinizing franchise. To help select a suitable location, the franchisor used a computerized market evaluation system that included in-depth mapping and demographic studies as well as customer profile reports. This system provided information on the age, gender, family income, occupation, life-style, and education of the consumers in the target area. The franchisor also customized the store design and plant layout to ensure efficient work flow and provided a comprehensive training program. The advertising guidelines and programs provided by the franchisor have given Guy and Ardis a strong edge in opening their store and in developing their clientele. They're looking forward to additional promotional and advertising materials that have been designed to generate immediate traffic and build a strong image of the store in the community. They are interested in opening another store as soon as this one becomes successful and they are able to realize a profit.

The total capital required to start the franchise was approximately $190,000. This included the initial franchising fee of $20,000, the cleaning equipment cost of $85,000, and other necessities of opening the business, such as lease improvements, working capital, and miscellaneous expenditures. In addition, the franchisor's regional manager served as liaison between the franchisee and the home office, providing consultation on business plans and operations and updates on services and materials available from the franchisor.

Guy and Ardis are excited about their franchise, but they are uncertain about their legal obligations, especially with respect to the franchisor. Can they provide additional services besides those required by the franchisor? Will they have the opportunity to modify their franchising agreement? The term of their franchising agreement was a period of three years, but Guy and Ardis are concerned that the franchisor may be able to terminate the agreement after the franchise has become successful. They are also not sure what they will do with the franchise when they retire. Could they sell the franchise to their children? Additionally, they have leased the land and the building for a ten-year period. They want to find out if this would create a conflict with their three-year franchising agreement.

CASE QUESTIONS

1. What are the legal rights of a franchisee?
2. Should Guy and Ardis have their own legal counsel?
3. What legal action should Guy and Ardis take to ensure the continuation of the franchise?
4. How should a franchisee respond to a franchisor with regard to legal matters?

REFERENCES

1. Bracker, Jeffrey S., and John N. Pearson, "The Impact of Franchising on the Financial Performance of Small Firms," *Journal of the Academy of Marketing Science*, Vol. 14, No. 4 (Winter 1986), pp. 10-17.
2. Fratrik, Mark R., Ronald N. Lafferty, and Roger D. Blair, "Unanswered Questions about Franchising," *Southern Economic Journal*, Vol. 51 (January 1985), p. 927.
3. Garsson, Robert, "Franchise Program Will Turn a Profit in 1986, First Interstate Chief Says: Acknowledges That Mandatory Name Change is a Stumbling Block," *American Banker*, Vol. 149 (February 28, 1984), p. 3.
4. Gladstone, David J., *Venture Capital Handbook*, Reston, VA: Reston Publishing Company, Inc., 1983.
5. Jones, Constance, and The Philip Lief Group, *The 220 Best Franchises to Buy: The Source Book for Evaluating the Best Franchising Opportunities*, New York: Bantam Books, Inc., 1987.
6. "New Firm Plans Franchised Financial Services; Envisions Century 21-Type Operation for Small Banks and Finance Companies," *American Banker*, Vol. 152 (March 10, 1987), p. 3.
7. Pollock, Andy, "Sell the Business Format and Grow Bigger," *Accountancy*, Vol. 98 (October 1986), p. 90.

CHAPTER 17
MARKETING AND MANAGING YOUR FRANCHISED BUSINESS

In studying this chapter, you will:
- Learn about franchisees and their characteristics.
- Understand the marketing phenomena in a franchised business.
- Be able to develop a marketing plan.
- Learn about focus groups and how they may be used by franchisees.
- Develop an understanding of franchised business management.
- Understand the management process of a multi-unit franchise subsystem.

INCIDENT

Cheryl has just started her own business. Having managed someone else's beauty salon for 15 years, she felt it was time to open one of her own. After much consideration, she decided it would be best to start a franchised salon. By becoming a franchisee, Cheryl would have the help of the franchisor in setting up her salon with the necessary supplies and business guidelines.

    Cheryl has hired three full-time and two part-time hairdressers. Rather than hire a full-time receptionist, she feels the hairdressers will be able to handle the phone calls and schedule the appointments. If this arrangement does not work out, a receptionist will be hired at a later time. Cheryl thinks she may have difficulty with promotion, advertising, and marketing, because she has only limited experience in these areas. She has never been responsible for creating new advertising designs or layouts, but she hopes to have the assistance of the franchisor in this area.

Since Cheryl is not always at the shop, she has developed a rotating responsibility schedule for the three full-time hairdressers. The person in charge for the day will handle any problems that arise and will be responsible for closing up the salon at the end of the day. With this arrangement, Cheryl hopes to eliminate any potential rivalries among the three equally qualified hairdressers.

Is the rotation schedule an appropriate arrangement? What should Cheryl do about promotion and advertising? What other types of policies should she be developing for her full-time and part-time employees?

INTRODUCTION

Franchisees are people who desire to go into business for themselves. Thousands of people each year will start their own businesses, but only a few will succeed. While many organizations and individuals spend time investigating the opportunity and the requirements of starting a new business, the entrepreneur is actually opening and developing a new business. This person, who provides the desire, insight, and strong gut feeling, and who will place savings and career on the line to start a business — this is an entrepreneur.

The franchisee is technically an entrepreneur. The franchisee is the one who will make the final decision either to start or not to start a franchised business. Entrepreneurs will need a cadre of individuals to help them develop, run, and manage the business. They will need to hire people to operate the store and ensure its success. However, the franchisee will take the greatest risk by investing personal savings, leaving a secure job, mortgaging a home, and often locating in a new community to start an operation which, while often highly successful, may be undercapitalized and simply might not succeed.

The franchisee has no new, unique characteristics or traits which will ensure success. There is no stereotypically successful franchisee. Franchisees come with all sorts of personalities, characteristics, and abilities. The entrepreneur is generally hardworking, often technically competent in the endeavor chosen, innovative, creative, a controller, and a doer.

The personality characteristics often associated with successful franchisees as well as other entrepreneurs and small business owners would include ambition, strong self-motivation, ability to think on one's feet, willingness to accept personal responsibility, ability to see the big picture, responsiveness, and stick-to-itiveness. Most franchisees are the independent, self-reliant type rather than the "company-man" type. They prefer innovative rather than routine work patterns and are willing to take moderate risks rather than needing security. Contrary to what some might believe, franchisees are not gamblers. They make a point of minimizing risk before ever starting a business.

Successful franchisees are of all ages and both sexes. Ray Kroc started McDonald's Corporation at age 52 and Colonel Harlan Sanders began Kentucky Fried Chicken at the retirement age of 65, whereas J. Willard Marriott began the Marriott empire in his early twenties and Sybil Ferguson was in her early forties when she started the Diet Center franchise system. In fact, as women become a more prevalent force in the business world, they are also taking on and starting more and more successful franchised businesses.

MARKETING

Marketing affects everyone — franchisor, franchisee, and consumer. The franchisor, who faces a number of challenges in deciding how to place and sell products, must also examine a number of critical issues. The franchisee wants to offer the right mix to optimize sales, and the consumer wants, of course, a reliable product.

An Example of Marketing

The effects of marketing may be illustrated through the example that follows.

The Franchisor. Jim Herzberg is a franchisor who specializes in computer hardware and software. To be effective in his job, he must look at a number of major critical issues:

- What is the target market for computer hardware and software?
- What computer hardware do consumers want?
- What should be the pricing structure for different computers?
- What guarantees, warranties, or services should be provided to the consumer?
- What kinds of advertising, personal selling displays, and giveaways should be provided to move the products?
- What kind of design and packaging should be used?

As a franchisor, Jim faces a great number of challenges as he tries to decide how to place and sell his product in the market. The computer market is very tricky and often demanding. The franchisor must utilize the most modern marketing skills and talents available to be successful with the consumer and with the franchisee.

The Franchisee. Charlene Babcock, a computer store franchisee, is interested in offering the right mix of computer hardware and software to optimize her store's sales. Charlene sees many computer components and watches very closely the products being developed and introduced into the market. There are many questions she must answer:

- Is there a good mix of computers available to sell to the consumer?
- Are the right brand names fairly represented?
- Are the prices competitive and fair?
- Is the sales staff helpful, courteous, and honest?
- Are there sufficient guarantees and warranties on the products?
- Is there sufficient advertising and promotion of the store and its products?
- Does the franchisor provide sufficient marketing assistance for the franchised unit?
- Are there many customers with loyalty to Charlene's franchised outlet?

The Consumer. Ken Spero works in a downtown business and wants to purchase a new personal computer from Charlene's store for his home. Both he and his spouse are interested in using it for personal and business activities. They are looking for word processing and financial software. Ken is specifically interested in finding answers to the following questions:

- Is this a reliable franchised outlet?
- Will this franchisee provide sufficient service and guarantees after I purchase this product?
- Are the brand names reputable?
- Is the hardware exactly what I want, at the right price?
- Are the manufacturers making a high-quality product that I would feel secure in buying?
- Were the salespeople and service people fair and honest in dealing with me?
- Is the advertising fair and honest in its approach?

Ken is very concerned about purchasing the right product at an affordable price. He also knows he will need some initial training and help in using the computer system. He hopes that he can take some instructional courses either through the franchise or at the community college.

Marketing is a very important aspect of the franchisee's business. Most progressive and committed franchisees will need to address at least four major areas of marketing, either by themselves or with the assistance of the franchisors, which include marketing services, advertising services, field marketing, and marketing research.

Marketing Services

The franchisor generally provides marketing services to the franchisee which include essential target market analysis, sales analysis, new product development, and product improvement. Before new products and promotions are developed and introduced to consumers, they must be thoroughly researched and analyzed. Most major franchisors will provide these services to their franchisees because they encourage sales and increase profitability for the franchisees.

The marketing services area should help develop the market and sales forecasting required by the franchise. In addition, a measurement of market demand and a marketing information system will generally be developed. Market plans and market controls will be established for the franchisee. An analysis of the demographic, economic, ecological, technological, political, and cultural environments will often be performed and provided to the franchisee. Market segments will also be developed and analyzed.

Advertising Services

Advertising, one of the major activities of a franchised business, is a form of communication which often provides legitimacy to a product or service and frequently encourages buyers to purchase a product. Advertising is often persuasive, expressive, and personal as it attempts to create wants or needs in consumers (see Figure 17-1) and show how these needs may be satisfied through the use of a particular product or service. The three key words most often used in advertising are (1) "free," (2) "now," and (3)

Figure 17-1
Twelve Basic Advertising Appeals

1. **Better health.** Greater strength, vigor, endurance; possibility of longer life.
2. **More money.** For spending, saving, or giving to others.
3. **Greater popularity.** Through a more attractive personality or through personal accomplishments.
4. **Improved appearance.** Beauty, style, better physical build, cleanliness.
5. **Security in old age.** Independence; provision for age or adversity.
6. **Praise from others.** For one's intelligence, knowledge, appearance, or other evidence of superiority.
7. **More comfort.** Ease; luxury; self-indulgence; convenience.
8. **More leisure.** For travel, hobbies, rest, play, self-development.
9. **Pride of accomplishment.** Overcoming obstacles and competition; desire to "do things well."
10. **Business advancement.** Better job; success; reward for merit; be your own boss.
11. **Social advancement.** Moving in better circles; social acceptance; "keeping up with the Joneses."
12. **Increased enjoyment.** From entertainment, food, drink, and other physical contacts.

Source: Charles Piper, University of Nebraska, Advertising Department, 1987.

"new" — the latter of which may be used to describe a product up to six months after its introduction.

In making an advertising decision, a franchisor or franchisee will focus on five major areas: (1) development of objectives, (2) budget considerations, (3) message development, (4) choice of media, and (5) evaluation of feedback. The primary objectives of advertising are often either to inform, persuade, or remind. Advertising to inform encourages customers to come into the store to purchase some product or service and is generally used during the introductory or growth stages of a business product. Advertising to persuade is often utilized during the maturity stage of a product, and advertising to remind is not used until the declining stages of product sales. To deliver their message effectively, most franchisors will utilize every available advertising method and media, including television, radio, print, billboards, and point-of-purchase displays.

The franchisee should rely heavily on the franchisor's advertising materials. Often a franchisor has already developed materials and advertisements for all the different media. The franchisee needs to work with the franchisor to develop the proper advertising mix and present it to the local consumer markets.

Field Marketing

Possibly one of the greatest advantages a franchising organization provides a franchisee is an in-depth field marketing program. Franchisors may divide the country into regions to help provide on-the-spot marketing services for each franchisee. A field marketing representative will often assist the franchisee in analyzing local market situations and conditions. The representative will also recommend advertising and marketing procedures to maximize business opportunities and profits.

The field marketing representative brings to the franchisee the complete advertising and marketing resources of the franchisor. The franchisor may provide many promotional items which the franchisee can readily use in local media as well as give away or sell to customers. Corporate marketing specialists work with public relations, promotion, and advertising agencies at both national and local levels to help create and implement highly successful marketing programs. The combined power of franchisor and franchisee advertising dollars ensures greater coverage than can be achieved by independent stores.

Marketing Research

Almost every franchisee at some time will need marketing research. Marketing research is very beneficial to a franchisee, for it helps to determine target markets, advertising successes, promotional activities, repeat customer business, market position of franchise, sales forecasting, sales potential, and product acceptance.

Marketing research can easily be performed by the franchisee alone or in cooperation with the franchisor. Franchisees may develop their own marketing research questionnaires to attempt to determine consumers' preferences and buying behaviors.

A basic marketing research outline might include questionnaire development, market sample design, data collection, and analysis and forecasting. The marketing research questionnaire may be broken down into different themes, which might include:

- Where do consumers go to make purchases?
- Why do they go there?
- Is the pricing fair?
- Are the services and products valuable?

Once several major themes have been developed, three or four questions may be constructed for each theme. These might include:

- Which convenience food store do you patronize most often?
- What do you consider to be your primary fast-food restaurant — the one from which you buy mostly lunches or the one from which you buy mostly dinners?
- Why do you go to that particular restaurant?
- How does home cleaning business A compare with home cleaning businesses B and C?
- How would you compare a McDonald's advertisement with a Burger King advertisement?
- Have you ever read, seen, or heard any advertisements for restaurant A?
- Can you recall the slogan for restaurant A?

Once the questionnaire has been developed, the franchisee may collect the information in one of three ways — by mail, by telephone, or by personal interview. Once the information has been collected, the franchisee may simply add up the figures and analyze their relevance to the business.

Franchisor Support

Most franchising agreements require that the franchisee pay a percentage of gross revenues to a national advertising budget. This percentage is often approximately 1 to 5 percent of gross sales, which is placed in a headquarters marketing fund. The advertising fees are divided between national network television buys and local marketing efforts. The local funds are often spent in the local ADI (area of dominant influence) through the combined efforts of local franchisees. (An ADI is a specific television viewing audience.) In many franchising agreements, the franchise headquarters has little discretion over the funds, but most franchising organizations have established marketing franchisee councils which provide input from franchisees on marketing decisions. These councils often determine how advertising funds which have been received by the franchisor will be allocated.

Most franchisor marketing plans are developed annually (see Figure 17-2). Specific programs for regional or local areas are usually developed on a quarterly or monthly basis. In some markets where a franchisee controls the entire franchising population, the franchisee will also oversee local marketing programs. If these programs would deviate from the national campaign, the approval of corporate headquarters is generally required. Many franchisees budget an additional 2 percent for local advertising and promotions.

Focus Groups

There is another marketing practice that is very important to franchisees. It is the development and use of a "focus group," or a target market consumer group, which meets to discuss the advantages and disadvantages of the franchise's marketing and advertising ideas. The focus group consists of individuals who use or purchase the product. They meet in a group of generally eight to 16 people and are asked certain questions about the use and development of advertising relative to the product. The focus group is usually led by a moderator from the franchise who directs the discussion of the group.

The focus group often investigates the major marketing aspects of the business, including the product and its uses, the design or modification of the product, promotion and selling of the product, the advertising timetable, the advertising platform, and the preparation of advertising or ideas concerning advertising. The members of the focus group are asked to express their honest opinions and attitudes about these areas. The outline presented in Figure 17-3 may be used in guiding their discussion.

The advertising platform consists of primary and secondary objectives of the business. The members of the focus group discuss what they believe should be the primary uses of the product and how the product will interest the consumer (see Figure 17-3). In addition, the advertising platform also develops and describes the target audiences, including the primary audience (heavy users) and secondary audiences, and describes the media/selling mix which might be utilized to help promote the product. Major benefits of using the product should also be identified and discussed by the focus group. Secondary and supporting benefits should be enumerated, and the positioning of the business in the marketplace should be discussed as well as how it might be improved to sell more

Figure 17-2
Marketing Calendar
Fiscal 199—
First, Second, Third, Fourth Quarters

	JAN 1 2 3 4	FEB 1 2 3 4	MAR 1 2 3 4 5	APR 1 2 3 4	MAY 1 2 3 4 5	JUNE 1 2 3 4 5	JULY 1 2 3 4	AUG 1 2 3 4 5	SEPT 1 2 3 4	OCT 1 2 3 4	NOV 1 2 3 4 5	DEC 1 2 3 4
National Program	CHICKEN		BREAKFAST			BIG HAMBURGER			BREAKFAST			TOY
National Program		HAMBURGER		CHICKEN		CHICKEN		99¢ SALE	BIG HAMBURGER			PROMO
National Program				BIG HAMBURGER								
Regional Program					BIG HAMBURGER		BREAKFAST		FRIES		CHEESEBURGER	
Regional Program		KIDS' FOOD			CHEESEBURGER					BREAKFAST		
Local Options		KIDS' FOOD	FRIES	KITES	COMBO ORDER	CAMERA PROMO			CHICKEN	BIG HAM-BURGER	KIDS PROMO	CHEESE-BURGER
Local Options			BREAKFAST	CHEESE-BURGER				BACON BURGER				TOY PROMO

Figure 17-3
Focus Groups: Advertising/Promotion

WHO	1. Define users.
WHAT	2. Determine what users want.
	3. Discuss design or modification of product.
HOW	4. Decide how to promote and sell product.
WHEN	5. Develop advertising and marketing timetables.
HOW MUCH	6. Measure effects of advertising and modify as needed.
	7. Seek outside help.
WHAT	8. Prepare the advertising platform.
WHAT	9. Prepare the advertising.

Advertising Platform

Objectives
Target Audiences
   Primary Audience (Heavy User)
   Secondary Audience
Media/Selling Mix
Major Benefits
   12 Basic Appeals
   Secondary/Supporting Benefits
Positioning
Measurability

Source: Charles Piper, University of Nebraska, Advertising Department, 1987.

product or service. The focus group should also discuss how to measure the effectiveness of advertisements.

Throughout the discussion of the focus group, ideas are often developed and may even be used as the headline or body of advertising copy or as the slogan line, which is often the tail of the advertising copy. Most of the focus group discussions are recorded so that the ideas generated may be reviewed and used at a later time.

One franchisee asked a group of customers if they would meet one afternoon every three months to discuss the products and services provided by the franchise. The franchisee generally provided food and also a token gift for all participants. This franchisee also met for about an hour each week with the franchisor's staff to discuss promotion and advertising opportunities. The staff got heavily involved in the advertising program and created many of their own advertisements, and they reviewed advertisements from other franchisees, used those that were the best, and discarded the others. The franchise system made a twofold increase in profits during the first year that focus groups were used.

MANAGEMENT

Franchising enables an individual to become an independent business owner, reducing the risk of failure because of the franchisor's past experience and expertise. A strong franchisor is able to provide ongoing support in marketing, finances, research, and product development. The franchisee pays for these services through royalty fees and advertising fees. An added benefit to the franchisee, however, is the franchisor's time commitment, which clearly helps make the operation more cost-effective and profitable for the franchisee.

The most common type of franchisee is the single-unit operator, often found in rural areas where the limited population will not enable the franchisee to expand. This franchisee would generally not want to face the problems of "long-distance" management of stores outside a small geographic area. Most franchisees begin by performing all functions, including management, accounting, marketing, operations, sales, and development. As the business grows and profits increase, additional staff may be brought in to assist with the management function.

While franchisees are in one sense typical business owners, concerned with the basic management functions of organizing, planning, staffing, directing, and controlling, they are also unique in that they work with a franchisor or headquarters organization. The franchisee works within two specific systems: (1) a total proven business system and (2) a system of people.

Total Proven System

The new franchisee is granted the opportunity to use the proven trademarks, service marks, products, services, and operating procedures of the franchise system. The franchisee is provided an umbrella of operational expertise with the expectation that he or she will operate with strict adherence to the standards established by the franchisor.

The franchisor umbrella of operational expertise includes the basic management functions of organizing, planning, staffing, directing, and controlling, as well as help in site selection, construction, training, purchasing of supplies and equipment, advertising, marketing, market research, and day-to-day operations. The franchisor's headquarters organization helps the franchisee achieve success because it has the know-how and ability to assist others in being successful.

The franchisee should see the franchise as a package which brings a consumer into the business expecting something special. The decor and ambience of the business outlet should offer an enjoyable and worthwhile visit. The product or service should provide quality and dependability and should encourage customers to return. Offered as part of the franchising package, comprehensive training at national centers will often help to ensure friendly, courteous, and efficient management and employees.

The franchisee should also anticipate help from the franchisor through top-flight support staff and ongoing operational assistance. In general, the franchisor should provide a total blueprint for success in operating the business.

System of People

A franchise system is a system of people. There are important relationships which need to exist between these people — between franchisor and franchisee, and between franchisees and employees. As employees are properly trained to be able to perform their jobs well, they generally develop a positive attitude. A happy employee who works hard will be a successful employee, and a successful franchise system is made up of successful employees. For this reason, the franchisee needs to develop and foster a constructive franchisee-employee relationship.

From the employee's perspective, the franchisee-employee relationship revolves around sufficient training, pay, and incentives. Although many franchise employees are paid minimum wage, they often respond very favorably to incentive programs, which may be simple programs such as awards for employee-of-the-week or month, tickets to movies, sporting events, or concerts, or even trips to amusement parks or vacations. An incentive program should reward outstanding performance and achievement.

Feasibility Study or Business Plan

It is crucial that the prospective franchisee find time to develop a business plan or feasibility study before starting a franchised business. A thorough business plan should outline and correctly analyze the managerial, marketing, accounting, financial, and legal requirements of any business opportunity (see Figure 17-4). This plan should thoroughly review and examine all financial requirements and profit or earnings claims of the franchise. It is recommended that at least three to five projected revenue levels (sales levels) be used in every franchise analysis to illustrate the different strengths and weaknesses of the franchised operation.

When properly completed, the feasibility study will provide a first-year business plan for the franchisee. It will show the income and expenses the franchisee can expect during the first year of operation. In addition, the study will outline the proper managerial and organizational structures necessary to ensure success. It will also outline the target market and advertising or promotional strategies that will be beneficial to the franchise operation. This feasibility study should be reviewed by

**Figure 17-4
Franchise Feasibility Study**

I. Executive Summary
    A. General Overview
    B. Summary of Findings
    C. Uses of Funds
    D. Final Recommendations

II. Marketing
    A. Major Marketing Objective
    B. Market Plan
    C. Pricing Strategy
    D. Location Selection
    E. Grand Opening Plan
    F. Customer Advertising Plan

III. Management
    A. Operations Manual
    B. Training Manual
    C. Organizational Structure
    D. Policies
    E. Personnel (Wage, Salary, and Promotions)
    F. Development PERT Chart

IV. Financing and Accounting
    A. Startup or Turnkey Cost (itemized)
    B. Financial Position for Securing Franchise
    C. Pro Forma Income Statement
    D. Pro Forma Balance Sheet
    E. Projected Cash Flow (Operations Statement)
    F. Break-even Analysis
    G. Ration Analysis
    H. Bookkeeping Methods
    I. Provisions for Taxation

V. Legal Aspects
    A. Contracts, Licenses, Trademarks, Prospectus, Disclosure Document
    B. Business Structure
    C. Insurance: Type and Cost
    D. Provisions for Franchise and Business Termination

VI. Appendix
    A. Building Plans
    B. Layout Design
    C. Graphs
    D. Working Papers
    E. Diagrams
    F. Layouts
    G. Charts

both franchisee and franchisor, as well as by personal friends and relatives, to ensure completeness and accuracy. Local bankers or accountants may also review these documents to guarantee that they are thorough and useful.

Promotion

The promotion and advertising offered by the franchise will establish and develop the image of the business. The expenses for advertising and promotional items will generally range from 0 to 7 percent of gross sales for most franchised businesses. Often, the franchisor may require payment of a national advertising fee of 0.5 to 3 percent of gross sales. These funds collected by the franchisor will be used exclusively for advertising and promotions-related expenditures.

Most franchisors will also provide publicity ideas for write-ups which may be submitted by the franchisee to local newspapers to announce the startup and any special activities of the business. These write-ups are often selected by the local newspapers to be included in their morning or evening edition.

Legal Aspects

Every franchisee needs to know and understand the legal obligations required in a franchising agreement. There are also other legal considerations which the franchisee should be aware of, including all contracts, licenses, and liabilities that pertain to the franchise. Proper legal counsel should be sought before any contracts or agreements are signed with a franchisor, property owner, or other businessperson.

Franchisees should also understand basic antitrust laws and how they affect price fixing, tying, and territorial arrangements. Franchisees should be aware of all rules and laws pertaining to the franchising agreement signed with the franchisor, including information about the term or duration of the contract and the renewal or termination of the agreement. Many franchisees realize only at the end of the term that there is no renewal clause in the original contract and that the franchisor may terminate the contract at will.

Insurance

The franchisee should realize that often certain insurance requirements must be fulfilled before a business can be started up. The act of insuring something is simply a means of transferring a "pure risk" to another institution (the insurance company).

Insurance is generally used by the franchisee to cover three major areas: (1) property risk, (2) liability risk, and (3) personal risk. Property insurance basically covers damage or loss of tangible property due to natural disasters, including flood, fire, hail, lightning, windstorm, or other so-called acts of God. Liability insurance covers those losses of assets or future incomes resulting from bodily injury or property damage to others. Franchisees have been held legally liable for injury resulting from defective products, slipping on lettuce, or falling as a result of inadequate snow or ice removal from business properties. Personal insurance primarily covers the owner's loss of ability to produce income because of death, retirement, accident, sickness, or other disability. Most franchisees will purchase sufficient insurance to cover these "pure risks."

Multi-Unit Franchisees

A current phenomenon spreading throughout the franchising field is that of franchisees with multiple units. When franchisees purchase their first unit, many are already looking to add more units as soon as the first one is operating successfully. Second, third, and fourth stores are often developed as rapidly as possible, utilizing the profits and revenues from previous franchises to help build these units.

The key to franchisees becoming multi-unit operators quickly and successfully is for them to get the right people to staff and oversee the units. Usually the franchisee has staked almost all resources in the start-up and development of the first franchised business. It is very difficult to find people willing to make similar commitments. The key to proper expansion is never to lower one's standards or expectations of people but to find those with the proper strengths and expertise.

Some franchisors may offer franchises only to franchisees who agree to establish a specific number of units during a certain time period — e.g., five new units in four years. The number of units to be developed under a multi-unit agreement and the time period for development will vary according to market potential and available capital. The initial agreement is often referred to as an "Option Agreement." A separate "Franchise Agreement" is executed for each successive unit developed.

Multi-unit franchisees generally are located in urban areas with high population densities. This allows the franchisees greater ease in the management of locations and closer liaison with management and employees. Multi-unit franchisees, while wearing many hats, need to work very closely with the people hired to manage operations at each unit, for these are the people who will become the supervisors and directors of operations throughout the subsystem.

Concerning the management of the franchise subsystem, Craig Cormack, owner of 16 Burger King franchises in Nebraska, Kansas, and South Dakota, suggests that "the franchisee multi-unit corporate structure will vary greatly depending on the size of the company. The operation supervisor needs to be in place for each four to six restaurants (for a

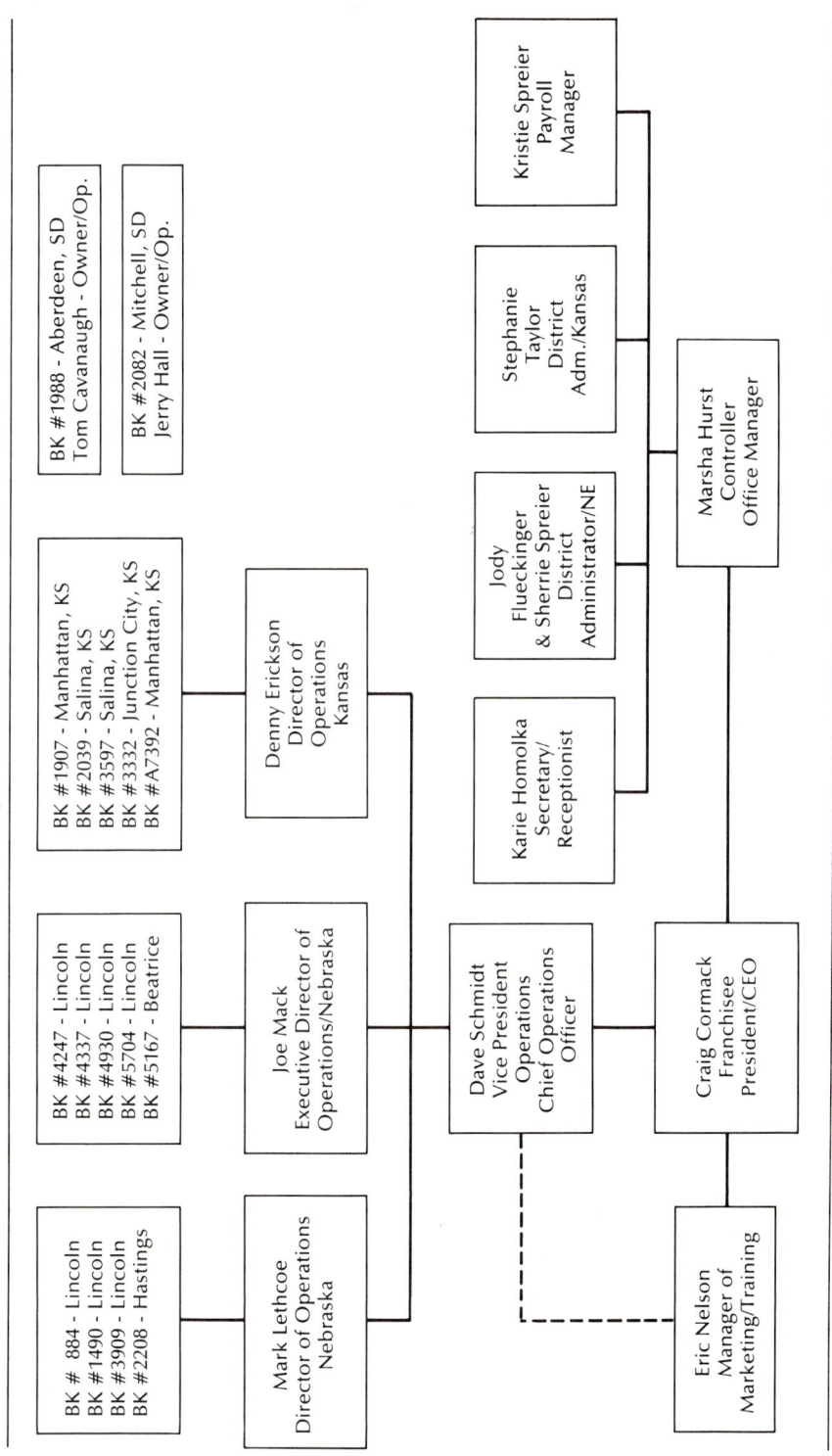

**Figure 17-5
Cormack Enterprises, Inc.
Organizational Chart**

```
┌─────────────────────────┐   ┌─────────────────────────┐   ┌─────────────────────────┐
│ BK # 884 - Lincoln      │   │ BK #4247 - Lincoln      │   │ BK #1907 - Manhattan, KS│
│ BK #1490 - Lincoln      │   │ BK #4337 - Lincoln      │   │ BK #2039 - Salina, KS   │
│ BK #3909 - Lincoln      │   │ BK #4930 - Lincoln      │   │ BK #3597 - Salina, KS   │
│ BK #2208 - Hastings     │   │ BK #5704 - Lincoln      │   │ BK #3332 - Junction City, KS│
│                         │   │ BK #5167 - Beatrice     │   │ BK #A7392 - Manhattan, KS│
└────────────┬────────────┘   └────────────┬────────────┘   └────────────┬────────────┘
             │                             │                             │
┌────────────┴────────────┐   ┌────────────┴────────────┐   ┌────────────┴────────────┐
│ Mark Lethcoe            │   │ Joe Mack                │   │ Denny Erickson          │
│ Director of Operations  │   │ Executive Director of   │   │ Director of Operations  │
│ Nebraska                │   │ Operations/Nebraska     │   │ Kansas                  │
└────────────┬────────────┘   └────────────┬────────────┘   └────────────┬────────────┘
             └─────────────────────────────┼─────────────────────────────┘
                                           │
                              ┌────────────┴────────────┐
                              │ Dave Schmidt            │
                              │ Vice President          │
                              │ Operations              │
                              │ Chief Operations Officer│
                              └────────────┬────────────┘
                                           │
                              ┌────────────┴────────────┐
                              │ Craig Cormack           │
                              │ Franchisee              │
                              │ President/CEO           │
                              └────────────┬────────────┘
```

BK #1988 - Aberdeen, SD — Tom Cavanaugh - Owner/Op.
BK #2082 - Mitchell, SD — Jerry Hall - Owner/Op.

Eric Nelson
Manager of Marketing/Training

Karie Homolka
Secretary/Receptionist

Jody Flueckinger & Sherrie Spreier
District Administrator/NE

Stephanie Taylor
District Adm./Kansas

Kristie Spreier
Payroll Manager

Marsha Hurst
Controller
Office Manager

Source: Material provided with permission from Craig Cormack, Burger King franchisee, Lincoln, Nebraska, January, 1987.

franchisee developing quickly, an operation supervisor should be in place at the second restaurant). After three operation supervisors are in place, a position needs to be created to oversee the operation personnel. This individual should oversee between three and six operation supervisors."[1] (See Figure 17-5 on p. 469.)

Cormack further states that "because of the capabilities of personal computers, accounting now can be done in-house with as few as two or three stores. About the time the franchisee develops ten to 12 restaurants, they should begin to look at having an individual to administer and coordinate marketing programs. Unless a franchisor has very aggressive expansion plans, most franchisees will be involved in their own development."[2]

Administrative costs for most multi-unit franchisees are typically 3 to 6 percent of total sales. These costs will pay salaries of both professional and clerical staff made necessary by the multi-unit corporate structure. This corporate staff becomes the liaison between the franchisor and the franchisee-managed stores.

[1] Craig Cormack, President, Cormack Enterprises. Material presented in Visiting Executive Lecturer Series at the University of Nebraska-Lincoln, April 7, 1987.
[2] Cormack.

SUCCESS STORY
E. JAMES GAYLORD

Jim Gaylord graduated from Bradley University in Peoria, Illinois, in 1953 with a bachelor of science in business administration. After college, he served two years in the army, then spent ten years developing and selling real estate properties in Peoria through a company he formed with some associates.

Gaylord initially became interested in franchising in 1965 after talking with one of his real estate customers, a Kentucky Fried Chicken (KFC) franchisee who was developing the Greater Peoria market. This initial exposure led him to inquire at the KFC headquarters company to see if the firm had any territories available. He was granted the KFC franchise for the Quad-Cities area (encompassing the towns of Davenport and Bettendorf, Iowa, and Rock Island and Moline, Illinois) that same year. In 1968, he acquired the franchise rights for Lincoln, Nebraska, and moved his family there to develop that market. His first restaurant in Lincoln was actually a remodeled filling station. He

> opened another store there six months later, then added one store each in the fall of 1968 and the summer of 1969.
>
> As of 1986, Gaylord had developed 14 Kentucky Fried Chicken restaurants — nine in the Quad-Cities area and five in the Lincoln area — an amazing feat for someone with no background in the food business and no experience in hiring people. He is currently the president of the Upper Midwest Franchisee Association, a group comprising fellow KFC franchisees in the Midwest region.
>
> Photo and information provided courtesy of E. James Gaylord, March, 1986.

SUMMARY

The franchisee is an entrepreneur who has decided to utilize the operating format of an existing organization to start a new business. Franchisees are generally independent people who enjoy the excitement of a new business opportunity.

Franchisees learn very rapidly that they must wear several different hats. One of the most important hats is that of a marketer as promoter and advertiser. The franchisee will be responsible for all local advertising and will work with the franchisor to develop major advertising programs. Because advertising is important to the success of the franchisee's plan and program, the franchisee needs to make sure that the field marketing research and franchisor support are all appropriately developed and used. The franchisee should also learn how to use focus groups to explore why consumers prefer or dislike the products or services being offered. Focus groups are an important marketing tool for the franchisee.

Franchisees are also managers. They are required to use a hands-on management style and to seek profits and improvements in the franchised business. The franchisee will be working with a proven operating system and utilizing a great number of employees to ensure the success of the business. By completing a franchise feasibility study, new franchisees will get a good idea of the potential of the franchised business.

Multi-unit franchisees are becoming more and more common in franchising. These owners of two or more stores generally located in heavily populated urban areas have become a major influence in many franchising organizations and may often be found with ten to twenty different franchised stores.

REVIEW QUESTIONS

1. What is a marketing calendar?
2. Why and when is it advisable to use focus groups?

3. What is the role of marketing to a franchisee?
4. Discuss how a franchisee uses the franchisor's marketing program.
5. What are the major management functions a franchisee must perform?
6. Why is a franchise feasibility study so important to a new franchisee?
7. Discuss multi-unit franchisees and their role in franchising today.

CASE STUDY
SNELLING AND SNELLING*

The Snelling and Snelling story began in 1951 with the husband-and-wife team of Lou and Gwen Snelling. Since then, this international, publicly held firm has grown to become the world's largest employment service. The highly trained specialists of the more than 500 individually owned offices have made Snelling and Snelling known as the "Placement People."

Today, Bob and his wife Anne Snelling preside over this very successful and innovative firm. They have continued to build the company based on close interaction with their franchisees and with the nation's finest employers. The franchisor's dedication, confidentiality, and professionalism come from the continual, in-depth training. Their franchisees are in close contact with employers and job seekers at all organizational levels. They have become the most successful in "finding people for places" all over America.

Initial training for the franchisee consists of two weeks at the home office in Sarasota, Florida, plus field training for owners and staff. Video tapes covering virtually every aspect of the profession are backed up by detailed training manuals for each position in the franchise. Initial startup costs include the following:

Startup Costs

	Snelling and Snelling	Snelling Temporaries	Bryant Bureau
Franchise Fee	$14,000	$10,000	$10,000
Setup Costs and Working Capital	$60,000 – $80,000	$70,000 – $110,000	$53,000 – $73,000
Total	$74,000 – $94,000	$80,000 – $120,000	$63,000 – $83,000

The franchise royalty and the advertising fund contribution are 7 percent and 1 percent of actual revenues received, respectively, paid by the tenth day of the following month. The setup costs and working capital can vary depending upon the individual office, location, size, furniture, and fixtures selected.

---

*Information provided courtesy of Snelling and Snelling, Inc., September, 1987.

In looking for 1,500 additional offices, the Snelling and Snelling headquarters office is very concerned about finding the "correct" franchisee. They look for individuals who are willing to help others, are dedicated to professionalism, are willing to work diligently toward goals, enjoy people, have a strong desire to be their own boss, have a knack for getting the best out of others, are willing to work hard, and have a need to seek their own "comfort level."

CASE QUESTIONS

1. What are the major criteria that Snelling and Snelling needs to use in choosing franchisees?
2. What are some negative factors that might eliminate prospective franchisees?
3. What are some of the best methods that Snelling and Snelling can use to recruit additional franchisees?

REFERENCES

1. Agmon, Tamir, and Donald R. Lessard, "Investment Recognition of Corporate International Diversification," *Journal of Finance*, September, 1977.
2. Anand, Punam, "Inducing Franchisees to Relinquish Control: An Attribution Analysis," *Journal of Marketing Research*, Vol. 24 (May 1987), p. 215.
3. Britton, Noelle, "The Right Site," *Marketing*, Vol. 29 (May 14, 1987), p. 25.
4. Errunza, Vihang R., and Lemma W. Senbet, "International Corporate Diversification, Market Valuation, and Size-Adjusted Evidence," *Journal of Finance*, Vol. 39 (May 1984), pp. 727-742.
5. "Franchising Is Management for Success," *Small Business Reporter*, Vol. 7, No. 1, 1986.
6. Gibbs, Phillip, "How Mac Made It Big," *Marketing*, Vol. 28 (March 26, 1987), p. 39.
7. Justis, Robert T., Richard J. Judd, and Stuart M. Spiro, "Franchising Organizations: Using Strategic Planning," *New Directions and New Dimensions*, San Antonio: Small Business Institute Directors Association, 1987, pp. 120-124.
8. Kim, W. S., and E. Lyn, "Excess Market Value, the Multinational Corporation, and Tobin's q-ratio," *Journal of International Business Studies*, Spring, 1986, pp. 109-125.
9. Kostecka, Andrew, *Franchising in the Economy, 1986-1988*, U.S. Department of Commerce, International Trade Association, January, 1988.

10. Lyn, Esmeralda O., "International Franchising, Excess Market Value, and Advertising Intensity," Proceeding of the Society of Franchising, September, 1986.
11. Seltz, David, "International Franchising," *The Complete Handbook of Franchising*, Reading, MA: Addison-Wesley Publishing Company, 1982, pp. 233-240.
12. Silver, R., "Marketers Move into Fastframe Franchise," *Marketing*, Vol. 16 (February 23, 1984), p. 7.
13. Stockstill, Lowell E., "Multilevel Franchise on Pyramid Scheme?" *Journal of Small Business Management*, Vol. 23 (October, 1985), p. 54.
14. Zeidman, Philip F., and H. Brett Lowell, *Franchising*, Federal Publications Inc., 1986.

CHAPTER 18
LEGAL RIGHTS
OF FRANCHISEES

In studying this chapter, you will:
- Understand the franchisee's legal rights in the franchising agreement.
- Realize the usefulness of the defense manual.
- Learn about the laws regulating franchises.
- Understand the limitation of territorial rights and obligations.
- Learn the most common legal problems of franchising.

INCIDENT

Bruce has been very successful as a Kleen Kar Wash franchisee for the last two and a half years. During the past year, he has noticed the lack of advertising for the Kleen Kar Wash business in his city. He has become increasingly concerned about the monthly national advertising fee he has been paying, since he feels he has not seen his share of national advertising in his community.

Bruce is also concerned about a recent inspection of his car wash which was performed by the field representative of the Kleen Kar Wash system. The inspection evaluation concluded that Bruce is only an average franchisee, and it pinpointed a couple of trouble spots the franchisor would like him to take care of. Bruce is becoming worried about his relationship with the franchisor's staff, since they appear to be questioning him about minimum performance in a couple of areas which seem somewhat insignificant.

Bruce wants to resolve these problems with the franchisor, but he also wants to know his legal rights as a franchisee with respect to meeting and maintaining all the requirements of the franchisor. Bruce feels he is being treated unfairly by the franchisor. He wants to know if his right to maintain the franchising agreement is being threatened by the franchisor's criticisms of his performance. What are the legal implications of these criticisms?

INTRODUCTION

The ideal franchisor-franchisee relationship is one built on mutual trust, consideration, and cooperation. It should involve shared effort and should enhance profits and maximize market share, product sales, and growth for the franchisor and the franchisee.

The franchisee should understand the legal rights attached to involvement in a franchised business. These rights fall into four major classifications: (1) franchisor-franchisee relationship, (2) franchising agreement, (3) defense manual, and (4) laws regulating franchising.

FRANCHISOR-FRANCHISEE RELATIONSHIP

Most of the activities and actions between franchisor and franchisee are guided by the rules of common sense. However, franchisees need to recognize and assert their legal rights in order to protect their own business interests. They need to know how they are protected by antitrust laws, as well as the kind of help and support these laws provide in limiting the activities of franchisors with respect to price fixing and tying agreements. The franchisee should know that the antitrust laws in general prohibit unreasonable restraint of competition.

In addition (as discussed in Chapter 4), the franchisee has the right to full disclosure of the franchise operation before signing the franchising agreement. The disclosure document, or Uniform Franchise Offering Circular, must be in the hands of the prospective franchisee at least ten days prior to the signing of the franchising agreement. This document provides a rather complete description of the business operations and practices of the franchisor. The franchisee should understand the terms of the franchising agreement (contract) and discuss them with a competent attorney. Franchisees should discuss all legal matters with legal counsel before signing any agreements or contracts.

The term "franchise" has evolved legally to include those business and commerical interactions which involve (1) distribution — the franchisee selling the trademark goods or services of the franchisor, or (2) the operation of a commercial enterprise by the franchisee under the trade name of the franchisor, wherein the franchisee is advised or required to meet the quality standards of the franchisor.[1]

The first portion of this franchise description was developed by the Federal Trade Commission. It covers all those individuals who typically refer to themselves as distributors, dealers, retailers, wholesalers, jobbers, and/or independent sales representatives. The second portion of this description includes those individuals who see themselves principally as franchisees or licensees. The term "franchise" covers many relationships at various levels within different industries. Within the liquor industry, both the liquor store owner and the distributor are considered to be franchisees, and within the petroleum industry, the gas station owner/licensee, the petroleum products jobber, and the gasoline wholesaler are all considered franchisees.

The Federal Trade Commission requires that the following three elements be satisfied in the franchising relationship: (1) distribution of goods or services by the franchisee using the franchisor trademark ("trademark" element); (2) "significant degree of control over the franchise method of operation," or significant "assistance to the franchisee in the latter's method of operation" ("control" element); and (3) payment of a fee by the franchisee to the franchisor prior to or during the first six months of the franchisee's operation ("required payment" element).[2] Almost all franchised business owners comply with these three elements and thus run bona fide franchise operations.

Franchisor Power

While the franchisor and the franchisee need to rely on each other for success, it is the franchisor who generally retains absolute power in contractual relationships with franchisees. Franchisors traditionally wish to be able to keep franchisees under their thumb. This is one reason it is vital for franchisees to be aware of the tremendous power and authority franchisors derive from the contractual relationship. The franchisee should understand the nature of the power and authority franchisors generally possess, as well as the limits of that power. The franchisee should save any information which might be used later as a defense against actions brought by the franchisor in case of coercion or termination. This information would be stored in the franchisee's defense manual, which we will discuss later in this chapter.

Most franchisees have committed their entire life savings and all their available time to the development of their franchise. Too often they do not anticipate the business problems that can arise with a particular

---

[1] 16 C.F.R. § 436.2 (a) (1) (i) (A).
[2] 16 C.F.R. § 436.2 (a) (1) (i) (B).

franchise, but foresee only great success and profits. Some of these problems can result from a lack of understanding about the power of the franchisor.

Termination

Possibly the major business problem associated with a franchised business is not failure but termination of the franchising agreement by the franchisor. Most franchising agreements make termination an easy and relatively inexpensive action for the franchisor to take against the franchisee. It may often be done without cause or justifiable reason, so the franchisee should always be aware of this possibility.

During the 1960s, the Supreme Court ruled on the coercive relationship which existed between oil companies and their franchisees, the gasoline dealers. In its final ruling, the Court specified three major factors inherent in coercive power arrangements:

1. A great difference or disparity in the economic powers of the parties;
2. Franchising agreements (or provisions) which allow for termination without cause or justifiable reasons; and
3. The franchisor's control over the products supplied to and purchased by the franchisee or dealer.[3]

The Court ruled as follows in the case of *FTC* v. *Texaco, Inc.*: "The sales commission system for marketing tires, batteries and accessories is inherently coercive. The service station dealer, whose very livelihood depends upon continuing good favor of a major oil company, is constantly aware of the oil company's desire that he stock and sell the recommended brand of tires, batteries, and accessories."[4]

The inequality of bargaining power which exists between most franchisors and franchisees is enormous. The franchisee may be replaced without any change in the operation of the franchise. Fast-food franchisees are especially dependent on the trademarks and distinctive designs of their franchises. If their agreements are not renewed, they ordinarily will not be able to retain the facilities, goodwill, or specialized equipment of the franchise.

The federal government has left it up to the states to legislate the right of termination or nonrenewal of franchises. Many state legislatures are in the process of developing laws concerning termination and nonrenewal. In most cases, the franchisor must show "good cause" or justification for either action. Both the laws and the court decisions have shown a preference for the franchisee if good cause for termination or nonrenewal has not been demonstrated by the franchisor.

---

[3] *FTC* v. *Texaco, Inc.*, 393 U.S. 223, 226-27 (1968); *Atlantic REF Company* v. *FTC*, 381 U.S. 357, 368-69 (1965).
[4] *FTC* v. *Texaco, Inc.*, 393 U.S. 223-27 (1968).

Many contracts will provide for automatic renewal as long as the franchisee is not in violation of any of the conditions or provisions of the agreement. In other cases, the franchisee may be given an option to renew as long as he or she agrees to renew under current conditions and obligations — i.e., signing a new agreement which may contain different conditions and stipulations, completing a remodeling or renovation program, paying a renewal fee, and agreeing to any new royalty, advertising, or other fees under the new franchising contract. The franchisor may also reserve the right of automatic termination in case of bankruptcy, insolvency, criminal conviction, refusal to do business, abandonment, or loss of the lease. If a default occurs, the franchisee is often given a period of time to solve the problem.

THE FRANCHISING AGREEMENT

When properly constructed, the franchising agreement takes into account the interests of both parties. However, franchising agreements are generally prepared and written by attorneys who seek to maximize the franchisor's position. Almost without exception the written agreement will place the franchisor in the dominant economic and legal position. The franchisee is often left in a position of submission and blind compliance.

The problems which arise in many franchising agreements result from the franchisor's right to terminate the arrangement without cause and the short-term nature of the agreement, in which the right to renew is controlled solely by the franchisor. The written agreement generally maximizes the franchisor's rights while minimizing the franchisee's rights which may exist under state contract law and/or the Uniform Commercial Code. A very important point to make here is that all franchising documents need not be the same. Many franchisees wield the economic and personal power to negotiate favorable franchising agreements for themselves and their franchises.

To ensure a favorable franchising agreement, the franchisee should develop a negotiating team. This team should consist of the franchisee, plus at least two other members, an attorney and an accountant. An attorney who is knowledgeable about franchising and the needs of a small business can provide great assistance in the negotiating process. An accountant experienced in franchising can point out financial obligations the franchisee will be taking on by signing the agreement. Negotiable areas would include the territory granted for operation of the franchise; right of first refusal for additional franchises near the original territory; financing for the land, building, and/or equipment; rights of termination and renewal; and method of payment for financial obligations to the franchisor. The accountant should also be able to make a basic determination of whether the prospective franchisee could live up to the financial obligations of the franchising agreement.

Contract Rights

The franchisee should realize that a number of rights are granted in the written franchising agreement. These rights include but are not exclusive to those in the following list:

1. Treatment by the franchisor in a fair and equitable manner.
2. Long-term or automatically renewable agreement.
3. Termination only upon proof of good cause.
4. Fair and equitable performance standards.
5. Fair and equitable quotas and/or allocations.
6. Written and complete statements of all alleged discrepancies or deficiencies.
7. Right to require franchisor to prove all matters of discrepancy or deficiency.
8. Right of transfer to franchisee's heirs.
9. Right to transfer or sell business.
10. Right to relocate within designated sales area.
11. Exclusive or territorial rights (when applicable).
12. Warranty reimbursement for services rendered.
13. Creation of an independent appeals board.
14. Right to develop independent franchisee trade association and advisory counsel.
15. Termination
    a. At least 90 days notice.
    b. Right to sell franchise, subject to franchisor's agreement.
    c. Adequate compensation for damages and losses on property and future profits.
    d. Right of appeal to appeals board.

The franchising agreement is often lengthy, technical, and complicated. Steps should be taken by both franchisor and franchisee to ensure that the length and complexity are minimized. Overly technical documents do not benefit either party.

Other Rights

Some other rights need to be protected in the franchising agreement. For example, franchisees in some businesses may be required to carry large inventories of parts for last year's models, potentially resulting in considerable loss due to obsolescence. Franchisors should be required to provide the right to the franchisee to return slow-moving or obsolete parts.

In addition, for protection of their franchise system, some franchisors also require that franchisees and their families not engage in similar businesses for a specified period after the franchising agreement expires. For example, this "covenant not to compete" may prohibit the franchisee from starting a similar business within 20 miles of the franchise and for two years after the termination of the agreement. Covenants not to compete are generally considered valid if their terms are reasonable with respect to time, area, and activity.

A long-term contract often helps develop goodwill between the franchisor and the franchisee. A renewal clause in the agreement also helps foster positive attitudes and a constructive relationship between the two parties.

The franchisor does not need unlimited power to terminate as protection against poor franchisee performance. Performance may be controlled through enforced quality standards and sales quotas. Competition among franchisees is beneficial, and a requirement to meet expected levels is common. Most franchisees are quick to encourage fellow franchisees to improve poor performance.

THE FRANCHISE DEFENSE MANUAL

To avoid termination or nonrenewal of the franchising agreement, the franchisee must follow proper practices and procedures of the business. As a kind of leverage against the inherent business advantages held by the franchisor, a franchisee should keep track of all the suggestions and correspondence from the franchisor's organization. This information is collectively referred to as the **franchise defense manual**. The defense manual should contain the following items:

1. Documents stating legal rights, including copy of franchising agreement and current law relative to franchising
2. Information and dated records
   a. Accounting requirements
   b. Pricing policies
   c. Quotas and/or allocation requirements
   d. Purchasing or buying requirements for all products
   e. Purchasing requirements for any accessories, supplies, or parts
   f. Advertising fee requirements
   g. Any coercion, threats, or pressure tactics employed by franchisor
   h. Favored franchisees
   i. Sales policies and positions
3. Copies of all documents received from the franchisor
4. Transcripts of conversations with attorney, accountant, and business consultant
5. Written explanations of any unfair sales quotas or new requirements
6. Names of staff members present at meetings with the franchisor and appropriate records of these meetings

7. Records of trade association and franchisee group meetings
8. Record of refusal to sign documents concerning unfair quotas, regulations, or any deficiencies
9. Written records of all promises made by the franchisor

It is important that every franchisee maintain a thorough, chronological file of all interactions with the franchisor. This file will become very important if at any future time differences arise between the franchisor and the franchisee. It is also important that the franchisee have documented proof of any allegation of wrongdoing or misconduct made by the franchisor. Generally, franchisors with proper legal consultants will not make mistakes in their relationships with the franchisee. However, their field representatives may make statements which could be helpful to a franchisee in proving wrongful acts by the franchisor.

The three main points in keeping a defense manual may be summarized as follows: (1) consult an attorney or accountant if ever anything goes amiss in the franchising relationship; (2) keep written documents of all transactions with the franchisor; and (3) make sure two or more officers of the franchisee are present at all important meetings with the franchisor. It is important for the franchisee to work constructively with the franchisor's organization. It is also important that the franchisee work well with other franchisees within the franchise system. These relationships can provide psychological as well as practical support in improving business practices and in bolstering the franchisee should any problems with the franchisor occur.

LAWS REGULATING FRANCHISING

Laws have been established in the United States to help those who may be injured by certain business practices. Franchising as a method of doing business continues to be significantly regulated by the laws and rules of the federal government. Franchising is regulated at the federal level throughout all states because of the disclosure requirements of the Federal Trade Commission Rule. Today the legal requirements for franchising are much less volatile than they were during the 1970s and early 1980s. The laws regulating franchising that are important for franchisees may be put into the following four categories: (1) what the franchisor can do, (2) what the franchisor cannot do, (3) what the franchisee can do, and (4) what the franchisee cannot do.

What the Franchisor Can Do

The franchisor legally establishes a relationship with a franchisee through the franchising agreement. The franchising agreement is a legally enforceable contract. It normally contains many provisions with respect to the day-to-day operations of the franchise, and it also calls upon the franchisee to live up to the quality standards of the business by adhering to the operations manual. The operations manual is the rulebook and encyclopedia of activities for the business.

There are several areas in which the franchisor may choose to have significant control over or establish specific requirements for franchisees: establishing a territory; determining royalty, advertising, and other fees and how they shall be paid; requiring direct participation by franchisees in the actual operations of the franchise; and placing any restrictions on goods and services offered by the franchisee. (See Appendix for illustrations of these subjects under items 5, 6, 12, 15, and 16.)

In the franchising agreement, the franchisor usually reserves the right to specify territorial restrictions and arrangements. Under the contract, the franchisee is ordinarily granted a specific, exclusive geographic area in which to operate the franchise. The location is considered exclusive in that the franchisor will not place another outlet, franchised or company-owned, within that territory. The Appendix illustration identifies a territory within a one-half-mile radius of the business site. Some franchise contracts have virtually no territorial restrictions, while others may contain a county, market area, regional area, or state-sized territory.

The franchisor may specifically ban the franchisee from operating outside the agreed-upon territory. This territorial clause may require, then, that the franchisee sell products/services only from a given location. A territorial restriction clause is illustrated in Figure 18-1 as contained in the SpeeDee Oil Change & Tune Up franchise contract. (See also Appendix, item 12.)

Laws governing territorial restrictions have become very complex and are now often judged under the "rule of reason." Since the 1977 case of *Continental T.V., Inc.* v. *GTE Sylvania*,[5] the Supreme Court has favored the rule of reason rather than stating that all territorial restrictions are *per se* illegal. A territorial restriction simply defines a geographical area outside which the franchisee is not permitted to sell products. The rule of reason allows the court to investigate all circumstances surrounding the imposition of such restrictions. Thus, franchisors must now offer commercial justifications for allocating territorial rights. These justifications may include quality control, as well as the encouragement of promotional activities, private investment, or growth opportunities for specific dealers. Certain territorial restrictions therefore may be found to be legal because they are beneficial to both the franchisor and the franchisee.

---

[5] *Continental T.V., Inc.* v. *GTE Sylvania, Inc.*, 443 U.S. 36, 46, 55-59.

**Figure 18-1
Exclusive Area or Territory**

Each Franchisee is granted the right to conduct his franchise at a specific geographic location only. The Region will not grant to any person other than the Franchisee the right to locate a SpeeDee Oil Change & Tune Up® Car Care Service Center within a one-half (1/2) mile radius of the Franchisee's approved location. The Region has the right to approve the Franchisee's site selection, and such approval will not be unreasonably withheld. There is no pattern of time which elapses between the signing of the Franchise Agreement and site selection, since the ability to obtain acceptable sites varies from area to area, but the Franchise Agreement requires the Franchisee to open the SpeeDee Oil Change & Tune Up® Car Care Service Center no later than one hundred twenty (120) days after the date of execution of the Franchise Agreement. In the event that special circumstances beyond the control of the Franchisee prevent the opening of the Car Care Service Center within such one hundred twenty (120) days, the Region will consider such special circumstances (upon written notification and request by the Franchisee to the Region prior to the expiration of such 120 day period) and the Region may (but is not legally obligated to) extend such deadline for an additional period, the length of such extension and any related conditions to be determined in the Region's sole and absolute discretion. The Region may itself, from time to time, operate SpeeDee Oil Change & Tune Up® Car Care Service Centers in this state or elsewhere. (Sections 2.6 and 4.4)

Source: SpeeDee Oil Change & Tune Up® of the Gulf Coast, L-UFOC v. 2.6, July 20, 1987. Used with permission.

The franchisor may also legally require the payment of fees in a franchising relationship. Franchisees will usually pay a one-time license fee or franchising fee which allows them to use the trademark and/or "system" of the franchisor. This fee also includes all costs of the franchisor for training and other services and for maintaining standards throughout the system.

The royalty fee is generally a fixed percentage of gross sales which is remitted to the headquarters organization. There is usually little or no room for negotiation of the royalty fee. The franchisor also may require the franchisee to use a standard record keeping system which allows for an easy method of auditing and reporting gross sales and activities of the franchisee. Royalty fees which enable franchisees to earn a respectable profit and an attractive return on investment and also provide the franchisor with income sufficient to cover expenses and profits will generally be acceptable to both parties.

The franchisor may also require an advertising fee payment. This contribution, like the royalty fee, is often a percentage of gross sales, though it may be a flat sum based on an assessment for items sold. The franchisee may also be required to make minimal payments for local advertising in addition to contributions for regional or national advertising. Franchisees should be aware of all fee payments that will be required by the franchise system.

Franchisors may also specify hours of operation and develop quality-control mechanisms to protect standards of operation. Quality controls are used to ensure that the products and services offered throughout the franchise system consistently meet the standards established by the franchisor.

Through the quality-control mechanism, the franchisor may also control the appearance of the store, as well as its interior layout and design. The franchisor may stipulate what the store may or may not carry and display, and may require that the franchisee buy only from the franchisor or authorized suppliers.

What the Franchisor Cannot Do

The franchisor is required to conduct business in a reasonable and fair manner. Franchisors may not engage in unfair business practices or violate the contract or franchising agreement, nor may they engage in price fixing, require tying arrangements, or make any representations about actual or potential sales except in the manner set forth by the Federal Trade Commission.

Price fixing occurs when the independence of the pricing decision by those who resell another's goods is hindered or diminished through coercion. The franchisor has the right to charge whatever price it wishes for the products it sells to the franchisees. However, the franchisor does not have the right to influence or determine the price at which the franchisees must sell the product to their customers. This is price fixing and the practice is illegal.

The Supreme Court, in its 1984 decision in *Monsanto Company* v. *Spray-Rite Service Corporation*, found that any conduct by the franchisor designed to influence the pricing behavior of the franchisees beyond mere suggestion of pricing is *per se* an illegal activity.[6] However, some changes are occurring with respect to price fixing. The court has on occasion dismissed resale price maintenance claims, even though in some of these cases the manufacturer has advertised special retail prices without disclaimers such as "at participating stores" and has threatened to terminate noncomplying franchisees. These cases continue to be reviewed by the courts and such actions still remain *per se* illegal.

[6] *Monsanto Company* v. *Spray-Rite Service Corp.*, 465 U.S. 752 (1984).

The practical, real-life experiences of many franchisees demonstrate that these rules, laws, and regulations are not always adequate. For example, although price fixing is illegal, if McDonald's runs a national campaign advertising breakfast for 99¢, any franchisee who does not participate may incur the ill feelings of customers. Although laws exist to protect franchisees, the franchisees may still feel intense pressure to participate in sales promotions, purchase unwanted items, or take part in other advertised activities.

Another illegal practice is the "tying" arrangement. This occurs when the franchisor offers a product the franchisee wants to buy — such as an automobile ("tying product") — and requires the franchisee to buy an additional product — tires, batteries, accessories ("tied product") — the franchisee does not want or would not otherwise buy. If the franchisor tells the franchisee that he or she will not be able to purchase the automobile without also purchasing tires, batteries, and accessories, this is a tying arrangement, and it is illegal under antitrust laws.

The franchisor must follow the Federal Trade Commission's trade regulation rule regarding the sale of franchises to prospective franchisees. The rule states that the franchisor may not make any actual or potential sales representations except in compliance with this rule. The rule further requires disclosure, but not registration, of offerings or sales of any franchises throughout the United States. If any earnings claims or sales claims are made in an oral, written, or visual representation to a prospective franchisee, the franchisor is required under the rule to present to the franchisee a formal Earnings Claim Document. Further, any earnings claims made in the media that suggest a specific level or range of potential or actual sales, income, growth, or profits also require a formal Earnings Claim Document.

An Earnings Claim Document must contain materials sufficient to substantiate the accuracy of the claim that a franchise in a specific geographic area will be able to reach a certain level of sales. In addition, any document claiming earnings or profits must also report the percentage of franchisees earning more than and/or less than what is claimed. A statement must also be presented explaining the basis and assumptions upon which the earnings claim was made.

What the Franchisee Can Do

The franchisee is often limited by the franchising agreement which is to be signed. The terms of the agreement have often already been approved by other franchisees, and it is important that it remain generally intact and not be modified to any great extent if at all. Most franchise salespersons are not permitted by the franchisor to negotiate any of the terms of the agreement. However, franchisees do have certain rights and opportunities to negotiate the terms of their specific agreement, and they of course have the final option of whether or not to purchase the franchise.

Within the structure of the franchising agreement, the prospective franchisee may often negotiate the territory granted for the operation of the franchise. The franchisee has the right to discuss territorial boundaries and limitations and to suggest possible locations. The franchisee also has the right to negotiate a right of first refusal for additional franchises that may later be opened within the territory in which the franchise has been established. This right of first refusal is important to the franchisee and should be negotiated into the contract.

Also, the franchisee may find it important to discuss and negotiate the financing of the franchise purchase price. The franchisor may propose different methods of financing the franchising fee or the purchase of equipment, land, or building associated with the franchise operation. The method of financing may be through either the franchisor, independent banks, or venture capitalist firms. All of this is subject to negotiation.

In addition, the franchisee has the right to set the price structure for all sales at the business. Price fixing is illegal, and the franchisee has the final say in determining all prices on goods and services.

Franchisees may also negotiate for themselves and their employees the amount of training to be received at the national or regional headquarters and at the franchised business outlet. They may also negotiate the amount of grand opening support and any additional service support to be provided by the franchisor.

What the Franchisee Cannot Do

The franchisee must adhere to the signed franchising agreement as well as to the operations manual of the franchise organization. The franchisee is restricted from involvement in group boycotts or horizontal territorial restrictions.

Group boycotts (two or more franchisees joining together to exclude a third or prospective franchisee) are prohibited as intrinsic violations of the Sherman Antitrust Act. The Supreme Court defined a group boycott as occurring when "businessmen concert their actions in order to deprive others of access to merchandise which the latter wishes to sell to the public."[7] Let's say a franchisor asks a group of franchisees in the state of Ohio if a prospective franchisee should be allowed to operate in the Ohio region; the group says no, whereupon the franchise is denied. A group boycott would be in effect, and the franchisor would thus be in violation of the Sherman Act.

[7] *United States* v. *General Motors Corporation,* 384 U.S. 127, 146 (1966).

Note that by statute, these kinds of business practices (price fixing, tying arrangements, etc.) are automatically presumed to be unreasonable restraints of trade. Under legal standards guided by a "rule of reason," however, the court considers the circumstances or the franchisor's motives before making a final determination.

Cases in which franchisees seek to exclude other franchisees from specified territories or activity are referred to as horizontal territorial restrictions and are still *per se* illegal. The term "horizontal" simply means it is operators or competitors selling similar products who group together to exclude a third party from competing. It is illegal for franchisees to band together to exclude a prospective franchisee from any fair business opportunity.

If a franchisee has been "injured in this business or property by reason of" an antitrust violation, the franchisee has the right to sue the franchisor in federal court. Section 4 of the Clayton Act allows that a franchisee successful in such a suit would recover "three-fold the damages" plus "cost of suit, including a reasonable attorney's fee."[8] The main cause of this business injury is often the termination of the franchising agreement by the franchisor. If this termination is the result of an activity which is an antitrust violation (price maintenance, tying, price discrimination, or territorial restriction), the franchisee has the right to sue for damages. The franchisee need only demonstrate that the illegal practice resulted in the termination of the franchise.

THE MOST COMMON LEGAL PROBLEMS OF FRANCHISEES

Franchising relationships are not always harmonious. Porter and Renforth have identified the ten most common legal problems encountered by franchisees; these are listed in Table 18-1.[9] The most frequent problems concern the sharing of advertising costs by franchisees, particularly when they believe they have not received their fair share of advertising expenditures. This usually occurs when local franchisees feel their areas have been neglected or have not received sufficient attention. Franchisees often wish to write into the contract the specific amount of advertising to be utilized in local areas. Other frequent difficulties involve evaluation of the minimum performance requirements established by franchisors. Many times franchisees see these requirements as problem areas created by the franchisor, or they feel the franchisor does not require all franchisees to adhere to the same standards. Franchisees sometimes dis-

---

[8] Clayton Act, Section 4, 15 U.S.C. § 15.
[9] James L. Porter and William Renforth, "Franchise Agreements: Spotting the Important Legal Issues," *Journal of Small Business Management* 16, No. 4 (October 1978), pp. 27-31.

Table 18-1
Ten Most Common Legal Problems of Franchisees

Frequent Problems	Rank*
Sharing Advertising Costs	1
Inspection/Evaluation by Franchisor	2
Minimum Performance Requirements	3
Occasional Problems	
Royalty Payments	4
Fees for Support Services	5
Territorial Limits	6
Rare Problems	
Penalties for Violation of Contract	7
Restrictions on Products or Prices	8
Employee Conduct/Training Requirements	9
Limits on Competitive Businesses	10

*The ranks were determined by summing the weights assigned (on a point scale of 1 to 5) to each factor by the survey respondents.

Source: James L. Porter and William Renforth, "Franchise Agreements: Spotting the Important Legal Issues," *Journal of Small Business Management* 16, No. 4 (October 1978), pp. 27-31.

agree with the inspection evaluations and request further elaboration by the franchisor, but the franchisor may be reluctant to offer additional clarification of the evaluations, often creating serious problems between franchisors and franchisees.

Occasional problems also exist because of the royalty and fee payments owed to the franchisor. These payments must be clearly understood and outlined in the contract. Special attention should be paid to the definition of gross revenues upon which almost all royalty and fee payments are based. Also, if fees are to be charged for support services, these should be spelled out at the beginning of the relationship.

Territorial limits are also an occasional source of problems between franchisors and franchisees. These kinds of difficulties are often precluded by an understanding of the definite boundaries and the conditions of first refusal for additional franchises in the territory. Other problems which have been reported but have occurred only rarely include penalties for violation of contract, restrictions on products or prices, employee conduct/training requirements, and limits on competitive businesses. One such problem occurred when a franchisee of a large, nationally known fast-food franchise began to offer Jell-O as a regular menu item. He was quickly told by the franchisor that this was inappropriate and not within the franchising agreement and was requested to stop serving Jell-O at the restaurant.

Most franchisees will never have legal difficulties with their franchisor. There are some major differences between franchisees who often have legal troubles and those who rarely have such problems. Most franchisees who avoid or experience few legal difficulties are usually successful, profitable, and willing to follow the format of the franchisor. Franchisees with legal problems are often less successful, discontented in their franchising relationship, and generally heedless of the uniform procedures and standards of the franchise.

Some identifying characteristics of franchisees with and without legal problems have been identified by Porter and Renforth. Franchisees who are able to avoid legal problems have usually had previous business experience, know their rights in the franchising agreement, conduct independent market research, and are able to negotiate the terms of their franchising agreements. These are some of the areas identified in Table 18-2.

It has been noted that franchisees with legal problems are often involved in their first business undertaking, do not receive professional legal advice, typically accept franchisor's projections without independent research, and have problems in other areas of the business. Often the success of franchisees who can avoid legal problems results from a positive attitude. The prior experience of these franchisees enables them to conduct negotiations with diplomacy and professionalism. They often utilize private attorneys, market research firms, and independent advertising agencies. Successful franchisees have a cooperative, "win-win" relationship with the franchisor. They anticipate difficulties but expect to

Table 18-2
Characteristics of Franchisees With and Without Legal Problems

Franchisees With Problems	Franchisees Without Problems
Are involved in their first business undertaking	Have previous business experience
Do not have the agreement reviewed by their own lawyer	Obtain legal counsel to review the franchising agreement
Accept standard contracts without modification to accommodate individual or local conditions	Request modification of standard agreement formats
Generally have problems in other operational areas of the business	Have generally successful, profitable businesses
Accept franchisors' estimates without verification	Conduct an independent market survey
View business as a zero-sum game	Expect to resolve occasional, routine legal disagreements in the normal course of business

resolve occasional disagreements that arise during normal business activities. To minimize potential problems it is advisable for franchisees to negotiate the original franchising agreement to accommodate local or special conditions. It is also advisable for franchisees to work to maintain a strong, productive relationship with the franchisor.

SUCCESS STORY
HERBERT KAY

At Rider College in Lawrenceville, New Jersey, Herbert Kay was an outstanding basketball player and was elected to the small-college all-American team in 1948. After graduating with a degree in business, he went on to play professional basketball with the Baltimore Bullets of the National Basketball Association.

In the mid-1950s, Kay and three close friends started a real estate development company. The company developed shopping centers, office buildings, apartment complexes, and hotels. In 1969, these same principals decided to build and operate hotels on a full-time basis. They went public with the company and the stock was traded in the over-the-counter market.

From those relatively humble beginnings emerged the present company, Prime Motor Inns, Inc. Its stock is traded on the New York Stock Exchange, and sales from hotels and restaurants alone reached $300 million in the year ending June, 1985. The four principals of the company are still involved, and the company still acquires land, obtains approvals, and constructs and operates hotels.

Prime Motor Inns can be thought of as a chain of chains, since it operates about 70 hotel and motel facilities under various franchises, including Ramada Inns, Sheraton, Hilton, Holiday Inns, Days Inns, and Howard Johnson's. The four original partners personally own, but do not operate, approximately 40 other various real estate ventures. These were all developed prior to the formation of the public company.

As Herb Kay explains: "Possibly the most important ingredient for our success is that senior management has been together for approximately 30 years and all four are capable of overseeing any segment of the company . . . that coupled with a significant emphasis on training and extremely qualified middle management personnel, will result in a smooth transition of senior management in the event of any changes."

Photo and information provided courtesy of Herbert Kay, August, 1985.

SUMMARY

It is important for both franchisor and franchisee to understand the rights and responsibilities they have in their business. Some laws and regulations favor the franchisor; others improve the position of the franchisee. Most important, though, is that both parties realize the value of a fair and equitable franchising agreement, the need for a franchisee to maintain a defense manual, an awareness of the laws governing franchising, and an understanding of the common legal problems of franchisees.

An understanding of these rights and responsibilities as they relate to franchising laws will help the franchisee to have a long and successful franchising operation. When the laws are properly followed, the participants in a franchising relationship will be more likely to enjoy a very profitable business venture.

REVIEW QUESTIONS

1. List several legal rights of a franchisee in a franchising relationship.
2. Discuss the franchisee's rights in negotiating a franchising agreement.
3. What are the advantages of keeping a franchise defense manual?
4. Discuss those laws regulating franchising activities which are favorable to franchisees.
5. What territorial rights and restrictions are attached to a franchising agreement?

CASE STUDY
LONG JOHN SILVER'S, INC. (JERRICO, INC.)*

Long John Silver's, Inc., is a food service company operating over 950 company-owned and 480 franchised restaurants. Marilyn is a licensed franchisee of Long John Silver's and has permission to use the trademarks, trade names, and other proprietary benefits of the system.

She has been operating a Long John Silver's Seafood Shoppe franchise for the last six years. The quick self-service, dine-in or carry-out restaurant seats 86 and is designed in the traditional wharf-like atmosphere. The menu includes fish, shrimp, clams, chicken, fries, hush puppies, cole slaw, seafood salads, desserts, and a variety of hot and cold beverages.

Marilyn owns the land and the building comprising the premises of the seafood shoppe, and her franchise was granted for a term of 25 years "without any right to renew the franchise upon the expiration of said term."

*Information provided courtesy of Long John Silver's, Inc., November, 1987.

Today's Startup Costs	Range
Initial Franchise Fee	$15,000
Land	$175,000-360,000
Building and Site Work	$240,000-355,000
Equipment	$130,000-170,000
Initial Inventory	$ 10,000- 15,000
Working Capital	$ 10,000- 20,000

Marilyn pays the ongoing royalty fee of 4 percent of monthly sales to Long John Silver's, Inc. She also pays an additional advertising fee of 5 percent of sales each month, which is administered by Long John Silver's designated advertising agency and field marketing staff.

Marilyn has been impressed with the help and support provided by the franchisor. The company provides resources for accounting, construction, food and beverages, equipment purchasing, marketing/advertising, operations, personnel, purchasing, real estate, security, and training. These services are provided from the national headquarters, as well as at regional offices. Marilyn successfully completed the eight-week formal training course in the field and at the Jerrico Training Center in Lexington, Kentucky.

Now Marilyn is taking a look at her legal relationships with the franchisor. She is wondering about the renewal clause and what will happen at the end of the franchise term. In addition, because of her tremendous success, she is interested in learning about opportunities for expansion into nearby locations. She knows that her own territory is rather restricted, and she wonders if she could expand into nearby neighborhoods or cities. She is also concerned about termination rights of the franchisor, and how she can develop a better relationship with the headquarters operation.

CASE QUESTIONS

1. What are Marilyn's legal rights for renewal?
2. What are the rights of the franchisor regarding termination and renewal?
3. What rights and expectations should Marilyn have with regard to help and support from the franchisor?
4. What should Marilyn do to improve the franchisor-franchisee relationship and thereby improve the possibility of renewal and expansion?

REFERENCES

1. Axelrad, Norman D., and Lewis G. Rudnick, "Overviews in Laws Affecting Franchising," *Franchising: A Planning and Sales Compliance Guide*, Chicago: Commerce Clearinghouse, Inc., 1987.
2. Braun, Ernest A., "Policy Issues and Franchising," *Franchise Law Review* (policy issues in franchising), Vol. 1 (Winter, 1986), No. 1.

3. Hammond, Alexander, *Franchise Rights — A Self Defense Manual*, Grenvale, NY: Panel Publishers, 1979.
4. Knight, Russell M., "The Independence of the Franchisee Entrepreneur," *Journal of Small Business Management*, Vol. 22 (April 1984), p. 53.
5. Moad, Jeff, "Strength in Numbers," *Datamation*, Vol. 32 (June 1, 1986), p. 44.
6. Seltz, David D., "Legal Considerations," *Complete Handbook of Franchising*, Reading, MA: Addison-Wesley Publishing Co., 1982.
7. Sheffet, Mary Jane, and Deborah L. Scammon, "Legal Issues in Dual Distribution Systems," Proceedings of the Society of Franchising, 1986.
8. Zeidman, Philip F., and H. Brett Lowell, *Franchising*, Federal Publications Inc., 1986.

PART SIX

FRANCHISOR-FRANCHISEE RELATIONSHIPS

CHAPTER 19
THE FRANCHISING RELATIONSHIP

In studying this chapter, you will:
- Learn about the four phases of the franchisor-franchisee relationship.
- Understand the advantages and disadvantages of franchise advisory councils (FACs).
- Realize the importance of communication, awareness, rapport, and expertise in a franchising relationship.
- Understand some of the principal areas of concern to franchisees in the franchising program.
- Understand the importance of advertising, pricing, and profits for the franchisee.

INCIDENT

Tom is a successful bowling alley franchisor. Tom's brother Tim wants to start one of Tom's bowling alley franchises. Tim has had relatively little business experience but has graduated from a local community college with an associate degree in accounting.

Tom wants to help his brother get started, but he has reservations about involving him in the franchise. Tom feels he must consider the other franchisees in operation and how they would feel about the franchisor's relative becoming a franchisee.

Is Tom right to be concerned? Would prospective franchisees that Tom had turned down have any legal right to take action against him if they feel Tim is no more qualified than they to operate a bowling alley? How should Tom handle this situation?

PHASES OF THE FRANCHISING RELATIONSHIP

The most critical facet of the franchised business is the relationship between the franchisor and the franchisee. This relationship often follows the basic steps of a new business or a product life cycle; that is, it goes through the following phases:

1. Introduction (built on trust, faith, and hope)
2. Growth
3. Maturity
4. Decline/Development

Introduction

The introduction of the relationship between the franchisor and the franchisee should be one of trust, mutual interdependence, and a shared desire for success and profitability. On the part of the franchisee, the relationship starts out as one of extreme optimism, often blind faith, and expectation of great success. The franchisor also puts forth its best face, since it is interested in making a very positive and friendly approach to the franchisee, but the franchisor will also be measuring the qualifications as well as selling to the franchisee during their initial encounters. It is during this initial stage that the rapport, understanding, and confidence between the franchisor's organization and the franchisee develops.

Growth Stage

When the franchisee has the grand opening, and the business commences operations, the growth stage begins. From the time the franchisee has signed the franchising agreement and begins the training program to become a qualified operator, the franchisor-franchisee relationship begins to develop. A thorough training program will build a strong and close relationship between the franchisor and the franchisee. Assistance with the grand opening, layout, and initial advertising and promotion will strengthen the relationship and help to cement a positive bond between the franchisor and the franchisee.

The support system provided by the franchisor to the franchisee for the ensuing months and years will help solidify the relationship. This relationship may be cultivated through monthly magazines or newsletters, plus local, regional, or national franchisee clubs and even birthday calls from the franchisor expressing personal regards for the franchisee.

The franchisor's field representative should provide support materials, accounting aids, marketing suggestions, and promotional and advertising support on a regular basis to maintain an active franchising relationship.

If the support systems are not properly set up, however, and if the franchisor offers only a second-rate training program or fails to provide ongoing support services, the relationship will likely become strained and unproductive. When communication with the home office breaks down, the franchisor-franchisee relationship is severely threatened.

Maturity

The third phase of the franchisor/franchisee relationship is referred to as the maturity stage. In this stage, the franchisor and franchisee know what to expect from each other. If the relationship has gone well, they have developed a mutual friendship and mutual understanding. The franchisee is able to rely on the franchisor to provide useful support services, advertisements, marketing aids, and new products. In return the franchisor can expect good sales volumes, clean stores, and quality services from the franchisee.

The maturity stage of the franchisor-franchisee relationship revolves around the communication and interaction between the two principals. Franchisees attend the annual franchisor-franchisee meeting and participate in local or regional franchisee meetings, and they carefully read company newsletters and/or magazines and participate in other local or regional activities. They utilize the new products or services being provided, implement new programs, and use the new computer software developed for the system.

The hazard of the maturity stage exists when the franchisee feels he or she is not receiving continuing value from the franchisor. The franchisee expects ongoing support and direction as well as new products and services from the franchisor. For some franchisees, just the opportunity to use the franchisor's name, logo, or products is often sufficient continuing value. Other franchisees require extra attention in the form of frequent communication, assistance with advertising and marketing, and other additional support services from the franchisor.

It is during the maturation stage that the franchisee gets an idea of the franchisor's competence and expertise and begins either to question or to value the franchisor's contributions. Many new franchisees find this a difficult period because the franchisor is continuing to try to sell new franchises to prospective franchisees and so may often ignore the needs of existing franchisees. This can cause a strain in communication and in the relationship and may bring the franchisee to question the worth of the franchisor in the operation of the franchise. The franchisor needs to make an effort to provide communication and support to all its franchisees.

Decline/Development

The final phase of a franchisor-franchisee relationship often involves the decline of the business and may lead to the franchisee seeking termination of any contractual obligations. Alternatively, in the final phase, the franchisee may develop a stronger relationship and seal the bond with the franchisor as the business continues to grow and prosper. If a franchisor is only interested in selling more and more franchises without providing support services to existing franchisees, then most of the relationships with these franchisees will decline, business will begin to fall off, and lawsuits will commence.

During the decline stage, many franchisees start to relax their compliance with the rules, regulations, and standards of the franchisor. Those who become disenchanted with the franchisor may seek to terminate the franchise. If a franchisor allows this decline to occur in relationships with many franchisees, the franchise system will eventually collapse. It is critical that the franchisor who seeks to remain a strong business entity provide continuing support services for all franchisees. Inevitably, there will be some who become disenchanted, but the franchisor must work with these franchisees to restore a positive relationship which will bring strength and prosperity to the franchising organization.

In 1986, the International Franchise Association named Postal Instant Press (PIP) as the winner of its first annual franchisee relations award. This award was presented in recognition of PIP's outstanding leadership in establishing and maintaining good relationships with its franchisees. PIP follows proper franchisor-franchisee guidelines (see Table 19-1) and encourages franchisee involvement in its system through such tools as a franchisee advisory committee and an advertising committee, both of which are made up of PIP owners elected by their peers, and through regional seminars, an international convention, and various incentive and award programs. In addition, PIP publishes two bimonthly newsletters for its franchisees, entitled "PIPline" and the "Insider," and maintains a toll-free hotline for franchisees to use when problems arise that require timely resolution.

PIP also provides a monthly package, "PIPers' Exchange," which contains new ideas, promotions, and publicity tips for fellow PIPers and gives franchisees a chance to share ideas with one another. PIP also provides a marketing encyclopedia which is designed to answer basic questions about advertising and marketing. PIP regularly holds regional seminars to inform owners and their employees of the newest marketing techniques and financial strategies and to keep them abreast of the latest advancements in printing technology. In addition, PIP holds conclaves every other year in which PIP franchisees from all over the world, including the United States, Canada, Japan, and the United Kingdom, exchange ideas and learn more about the newest developments in printing.

Table 19-1
Guidelines of the Franchisor-Franchisee Relationship

Franchisor	Franchisee
1. Develops strong training program	Participates in all training opportunities
2. Holds national and regional meetings	Attends all national and regional meetings
3. Develops franchise advisory council (FAC)	Participates in all FAC activities
4. Supports and maintains advertising committee	Gets involved in advertising and promotional committee activities
5. Develops newsletters, memos, and other means of information exchange	Provides information about franchise for newsletters and memos
6. Develops 24-hour toll-free hotline	Utilizes hotline when appropriate
7. Develops incentives for performance and sales	Participates in incentive programs
8. Develops award structure for achievers	Seeks and achieves awards
9. Develops promotional advertising packages and fliers	Obtains information and develops promotions for other franchisees
10. Provides financial and managerial reports	Uses the information in these reports to improve the franchised business

PIP treats its franchisees with great care and concern and is successful because of it.

During the decline/development stage the franchisee has to face many new problems and concerns. If solutions are not found, then the franchisee may blame and find fault with the franchisor. The franchisee may often question the royalty, advertising, and other fee requirements. The franchisor, on the other hand, may question the gratitude and loyalty of the franchisee. If franchisors fail to provide for effective communication or offer incentives and rewards, then franchisees may go elsewhere to find contentment and success. (See Table 19-2.)

There are many problems which may occur between the franchisor and the franchisee as they build their relationship. Franchisors must realize they need to extend themselves in their communication and development of the franchise system. It is important for the franchisor to meet and listen to the franchisees. In fact, many franchisors seek all of their information about new products and services from franchisees rather than through R&D departments at the corporate headquarters, as franchisees often have the best insight into the products or services customers want. Franchisors are very wise when they listen to and support franchisees in the development of their businesses.

Table 19-2
Franchisor-Franchisee Problems and Their Resolutions

Problems	Resolutions
1. Poor advertising and promotional materials	Use franchisees on advertising and promotional committee
2. Incomplete operating manuals	Use franchisees to help update and revise manuals
3. Poor training	Revamp training program and use suggestions of franchisees for how to improve training
4. Lack of proper disclosure of information	Improve newsletters, memos, and communication materials
5. Inadequate availability for advice	Set up hotlines and increase number of field representatives
6. Inadequate marketing research	Establish franchisee marketing research committees and improve headquarters marketing research programs
7. Insufficient follow-up training and information	Offer refresher courses, and publish bulletins and updates on operating procedures
8. Inadequate equipment package	Form franchisee advisory council to evaluate and improve equipment and procedures
9. Inappropriate or poor site selections	Evaluate and improve site selection criteria for both franchisor and franchisees

Franchise Advisory Councils

Franchise advisory councils, or FACs, are generally set up by the franchisor to encourage communication, creativity, ingenuity, and responsiveness from its franchisees. At the same time, FACs are a formalized method of coordinating a relationship between the individual units and the corporate headquarters. Most FACs are started at the initiative of the parent company, although some have arisen out of a need to discuss the concerns and problems of franchised unit owners. Costs of group meetings are covered by some corporations, while the costs of meetings in other systems are independently met through franchisee membership dues. Franchise advisory councils have proven very beneficial to many franchised organizations. Sometimes franchisees will use FACs to solve problems or present suggestions to the franchisor.

Merry Maids, Inc., the leader in the domestic cleaning industry, has a FAC made up of 11 geographic regions. A coordinator is appointed by the headquarters office for each region. These coordinators call for semiannual regional meetings to offer marketing and service ideas. For the franchisees, as well as for the franchisor, this council provides an opportunity to have many questions answered.

Franchisors can also benefit from franchisee organizations. They can gain valuable insights from franchisee reactions to new products and services as well as receive practical advice and marketing suggestions. Additionally, many new products developed at the franchisee level are first presented to the FAC organization before being submitted to the headquarters organization, allowing other franchisees a chance to express their opinions or offer suggestions about the product before it is brought to the attention of the franchisor.

Merry Maids also provides a system of rewarding its franchisees for different levels of sales performance. This has proven to be a very big incentive to the franchisees. The awards range from the Statesman Circle (which almost all franchisees will receive) to the exclusive President's Circle, given to only the top 1 percent in sales volume. Other honors include the Monarch Circle, Diplomat Circle, Regency Circle, and Chancellor Circle awards. The names and pictures of the recipients are included in the monthly newsletter.

Midas International Corporation's franchise advisory council came into being when franchisees joined together to represent their specific interests to the corporate headquarters. Midas subsequently started its own advisory committee and paid all franchisee expenses for travel and lodging. Later the membership decided to support the FAC entirely by franchisee dues. Midas today has an outstanding record of franchisee relations, with a very strong franchise advisory council and a supportive headquarters operation. Franchise advisory councils are very important means of providing strategic plans and pointing the way for future success and growth of the franchise system.

The development of a franchise advisory council must be carefully undertaken with the cooperation of all franchisees and the corporate headquarters. There are some major areas of concern which need to be investigated before the council is developed. These areas include creation, membership, functions/committees, meetings, role of the franchisor, expenses, officers, and legal and administrative functions. (See Figure 19-1.) It is important that all franchisees be included within the advisory council or at least have representatives on the council. The advisory council enables franchisees to discuss new products and services and promotional/advertising programs, as well as the success and failure of different operations. Franchisees must not become involved in discussing pricing or the acceptance or nonacceptance of prospective franchisees, for these two activities are illegal under antitrust legislation.

Figure 19-1
Franchise Advisory Council

1. Creation
   a. By franchisor
   b. By franchisees
   c. Jointly
2. Membership
   a. Appointed by franchisor
   b. Open to all franchisees
   c. Elected by franchisees
3. Functions/Committees
   a. Advertising/marketing
   b. Operations
   c. Services
   d. Research and development
   e. Finance
4. Meetings
   a. National (once a year)
   b. Regional (one to four times a year)
   c. Committees (two or more times per year)
5. Franchisor role
   a. Top management
   b. Limited/advisory
6. Expenses
   a. Shared (most common)
   b. Franchisees pay all
   c. Franchisor pays all
7. Officers
   a. President or chairman
   b. Secretary/Treasurer
   c. Vice-presidents
8. Legal and Administrative
   a. Do not discuss pricing
   b. Do not discuss who can or cannot be a franchisee
   c. Do not exclude anyone from FAC without good cause
   d. Do have a written set of by-laws
   e. Do use agendas and minutes
   f. Do follow-ups

C.A.R.E.

Probably the main ingredient in the franchisor-franchisee relationship is the feeling that the franchisor cares about the success and activities of the franchisee. "C.A.R.E." refers to several ingredients of the relationship — communication, awareness, rapport, and expertise.

Communication

One of the major concerns of a strong franchisor is that the franchisee always be able to communicate and feel a part of the franchisor's organization. Effective communication is a key to any successful business activities. Most franchising organizations create newsletters to help enhance communication throughout the system.

In addition, many franchisors use franchisees to form advertising committees, new product and development committees, grievance committees, and operations committees. Franchisors will often provide regional seminars, training programs, and field representatives to ensure that communications are kept strong.

Awareness

Awareness is a very important ingredient of a successful franchise system. The franchisor should make its franchisees aware that they are appreciated and are a vital component in the success of the organization. Most franchisors provide awards to show their awareness of franchisee performance levels. Some franchisors offer performance incentives, such as cash or trips, for successful franchisees. These kinds of things enhance the awareness between the franchisor and the franchisee. Franchisors should also take periodic surveys of their franchisees to learn their feelings and concerns. Also, franchisors can encourage local or regional clubs to help franchisees support each other as well as develop common advertising and marketing systems.

Rapport

The franchisor should try to develop a strong personal rapport with each franchisee. Some franchisors do this by providing birthday gifts, flowers on special days, and remembrances for services performed or goals reached. Additionally, recognition is often given at annual meetings or through the newsletters for promotional service, publicity service, performance levels, and even community service. Developing rapport will help keep the franchise system strong and unified.

Expertise

The franchisor needs to provide expertise to the franchisees. Most of the initial meetings are concerned with the nuts and bolts of the operation, but as the relationship matures, meetings should concentrate on specific areas such as finance, management, personal growth, marketing, and even special promotions. A toll-free hotline is often set up to allow the franchisee immediate access to the expertise in the central office. The headquarters may provide computer expertise and marketing and promotional expertise, as well as product or service research and development.

The franchisor-franchisee relationship will amount to nothing if the franchisor fails to demonstrate genuine care. The franchisor must deal openly and honestly, with integrity and mutual respect for the franchisee. The Golden Rule is directly applicable to the franchising relationship. When it is followed, success, prosperity, and growth will more likely occur. When it is not followed, franchisees will become disenchanted, legal problems will arise, and the franchise will generally fail.

Franchisor-Franchisee Activities: An Opinion*

Richard de Camara
Former President, Midas International Corporation

Introduction

The franchisor-franchisee relationship of today is radically different from that even in the recent past. Historically, a vertical hierarchy existed, with the franchisor presiding over the subordinate franchisee. Today the successful partnership is more horizontal — that is, peer-oriented rather than superior-subordinate-oriented.

The relationship is one of equality between franchisor and franchisee because of their mutual interdependence and desire to ensure each other's success. Franchisors have learned that franchising cannot be a success unless both are successful. Because of the interdependent nature of this relationship, the activities of the franchisor and the franchisee become very important to each other. There is a need for pragmatic, supportive, uplifting activities which will help draw out the best in both business situations.

In the midst of all franchising activity, there is a disquieting, underlying threat. That threat is the intrusion of government into the contractual relationships which exist between franchisors and franchisees. It is the opinion of bureaucrats that any form of distribution which has become as big and successful as franchising must need the intervention of federal and state governments to protect somebody from something. There are, admittedly, legitimate areas of concern to both franchisors and franchisees, and these concerns should be addressed. The big question facing us today is whether federal intervention will do for franchising what it has done for the post office, the railroads, and the public utilities. There are fraudulent practices by unscrupulous operators who want to use the franchise system for their own purposes. Governments (state and federal) now prescribe a Uniform Franchise Offering Circular which is sufficiently detailed and explicit to enable the average investor to identify the "quick-kill artists" who offer very little in exchange for a franchising fee. However, the areas of deep conflict between franchisors and franchisees need to be resolved between the principal parties, and in these matters government intervention is neither necessary nor desirable.

---

*DeCamara Auto Svc., 465 South Street, Elmhurst, IL 60126.

Concerns of Franchisees

Let's look first at the principal areas of concern to franchisees.

Profit. First and foremost is profit. Franchisees may feel that the franchisor has guaranteed a profit and so feel aggrieved when that profit does not materialize. Our experience has been that a good franchisee will make a profit in virtually any viable market. An indifferent franchisee, on the other hand, can be granted a franchise in an outstanding market and can still manage to lose money. Franchising does not eliminate the need for alert, aggressive entrepreneurs managing their own businesses with a keen eye to profit.

Termination or Renewal. John, who has devoted 20 years of his life to building a successful franchise, is appalled at the thought that, at the expiration of the contract, "his" business will revert to the company or be transferred to another franchisee. He wants renewal of the agreement (often wishing to keep the business in his family) or the right to sell the franchise as a going business. (We will discuss later on in this section how Midas International Corporation has addressed this major concern of franchisees.)

Expansion or Encroachment. By way of definition, *expansion* occurs when the franchisee opens another shop. When the franchisor or another franchisee opens another shop, that is often viewed as *encroachment*. There is no cut-and-dried solution to this problem. It cannot be satisfactorily resolved by giving the franchisee a protected radius, because markets are constantly changing and a franchisee is often unwilling or unable to exploit the market. Every established franchisor has had experience with special agreements made in the early days of franchising whereby an individual was granted an entire city or perhaps a state or group of states. This can stifle a program. Moreover, there are serious questions as to the legality of exclusive territorial concessions.

Something for Their Money. Franchisees pay a royalty fee to the franchisors, or they buy product from the franchisor, or both. Franchisees transfer money to the franchisor, and as they increase their number of franchises, the monthly check made out to the franchisor gets bigger and bigger. All too often franchisees question whether they receive sufficient value for this transfer.

Curtailment of Freedom. Most individuals who go into business for themselves have a strong desire for independence. But when they choose franchising, they forgo some of their independence. A successful franchise requires a certain amount of discipline. Stores or shops must generally look alike; certain detailed procedures must be followed; prescribed forms must be filled out; the franchisor is authorized to audit the books; the franchisor has the right to terminate the franchise, in some agreements, on 30-days' notice and without cause. Franchisees — especially as they grow more successful — understandably chafe under the conditions imposed by the franchising agreement.

Advertising. Most successful franchisors collect advertising monies from franchisees and pool it to launch an advertising program. Where and how to spend advertising dollars and the effectiveness of the creative part of advertising are subjects on which widely differing opinions can be held. It is sometimes extremely difficult to get a consensus of franchisee opinion on such an important topic.

Real Estate. Most franchising agreements require the leasing of real estate from the franchisor or a transfer of real estate control to the franchisor. Some do not permit a franchisee to own the real estate. Real estate investment is one of the attractive tax benefits of franchising and, in turbulent times such as these, can be a source of increasing financial equity.

Pricing of Product. In franchise systems in which the franchisor makes product available for sale to franchisees, the pricing of that product affects the profitability of both parties. In the case of products that are required to be purchased from the franchisor, the pricing structure can boost the franchisor's profitability at the expense of the franchisee.

Concerns of Franchisors

Having looked now at the principal areas of concern to franchisees, let's shift focus and take a look at some of the principal areas of concern to franchisors.

Profit. It should come as no surprise that franchisors and franchisees have the same chief concern. Either party can affect the profitability of the other. A franchisor that sells supplies or equipment has its profitability affected if the franchisee, for whatever reason, chooses to buy independently.

Ability to Expand As Needed. In some instances, franchisees will "sit on a market." They might recognize that the market could support additional franchises and yet resist expansion because they do not care to expand but are unwilling to share the market with anyone else.

Real Estate Control. To protect the franchise system, franchisors need to control the real estate where the business is transacted in order to prevent the goodwill associated with the franchise name and location from going to competitors.

Failure to Pay Royalties. Many franchising agreements have a provision for payment of royalties to the franchisor based on gross sales. Franchisees who want to cheat the system and understate sales can avoid royalties, sales taxes, and lower their income taxes. Franchisors have an obligation to the entire franchised body to collect all royalties due.

Non-Compete Clauses. There are many trade secrets, marketing strategies, long-term expansion plans, etc., revealed to franchisees which, if released to competitors, could be harmful to the program. For this reason, franchisors are reluctant to have their own franchisees competing with them under a different name.

This recitation of areas of concern to franchisors and franchisees would seem to imply there are insurmountable obstacles to the establishment of good relationships between the two principals. Nothing could be further from the truth. In fact, there is a mutuality of interests between franchisor and franchisee which, with a modicum of enlightenment on both sides, can result in the resolution of all differences, large and small. This mutuality of interests is based on *profit*, which we have listed as the chief concern of both franchisors and franchisees. Franchising is a shining example of synergism at work. The pooling of strengths of franchisor and franchisees produces a result which is convincing evidence that two plus two can equal five or six or seven. Midas International Corporation, with more than 1,600 franchised shops in North America, has found a formula for achieving a satisfactory resolution of major problems confronting it and its franchisees. In an attempt to be specific, I will detail how each of the major problems has been approached and how Midas has managed thus far to resolve them.

Organization

A franchisor cannot work effectively with individual franchisees, given their widely disparate personalities, capabilities, financial resources, and business acumen. If there is no franchisee association, advisory council, or some such organization, then the franchisor must take the lead in establishing one. At Midas we have gone through the normal evolutionary process of first having no franchisee organization, then having a group of regional franchisee associations, then a company-sponsored president's advisory council, and finally a completely independent, autonomous dealer association. The latter has matured to a point where its leaders now accurately represent the membership. The company can negotiate with this association, knowing that whatever is agreed upon will be sold to the membership. The existence of a functioning representative dealer body is prerequisite to resolving the areas of mutual concern referred to earlier.

With our organization in place, let me indicate how Midas has jointly handled areas of concern in the recent past.

Profit

Midas and the association have a complete understanding that unless Midas and its dealers continue to go forward together, we will all retrogress. We have agreed, for example, that Midas will not implement any programs (with the exception of price changes) which could affect dealer profitability without first discussing them with the dealer association. This has been extended to include such minutiae as forms to be filled out at the shop level. A striking example of how Midas has been able to function for the common good occurred in the negotiations leading to the announcement of a lifetime guarantee for foreign-car mufflers. With substantial dollars at stake, the issue to be decided was the proration of the cost between the two parties. After protracted negotiation, Midas and the dealer association were able to arrive at a formula which was satisfactory to both parties and which has progressed without a hitch since its implementation on October 1, 1978. This program has had a positive effect on the profitability of both parties. Each of us realized that the mutual benefits to be achieved were greater than the combined costs.

Renewal or Termination

The Midas franchise operation was born in the mid-1950s, even though Midas had been making mufflers for 25 years before that. Until 1974, all franchising agreements were subject to cancellation by either party on 30-day written notice. In 1973, Midas offered a 20-year franchising agreement which permitted termination for cause. Under this contract, the franchisee has specific rights in termination including arbitration. (Incidentally, Midas has yet to take the first case to arbitration.) Midas negotiated with the franchise association a new agreement which provides for renewal of the franchise at the end of 20 years. In the event Midas elects not to renew, it must, prior to the eighteenth year, advise the franchisee, giving the reasons for refusal to renew. The franchisee has an opportunity to correct the deficiencies cited, which could lead to renewal, or has the option of selling the franchise to a new franchisee acceptable to Midas. In exchange for granting this concession, Midas changed the wording of the new agreement in several ways, thus altering terms which had become outdated through the passage of time. One of these deleted terms was a penalty of six percent interest on unpaid accounts.

Expansion and/or Encroachment

Cumbersome as it may be, the only solution Midas has found to the myriad problems of expansion or encroachment is to deal with each case individually. We try first to reconcile differences between the franchisee and Midas at the district or regional level. If that is not successful, the franchisee can appeal to the corporate office or can elect to have the dealer association plead the case. All of the facts are considered by members of the dealer association and the corporation, and a solution is agreed upon. In every case so far, we have been able to arrive at a consensus which we have been able to sell to the affected franchisee.

Advertising

A franchisor's most valuable input comes from its franchisees, who have a direct relationship with the customer. Midas endeavors to capitalize on the talent of franchisees by working closely with committees of the dealer association. All comments and suggestions are analyzed by franchisees and company personnel, and joint recommendations for action are submitted. For example, the dealers have an opportunity to participate in determining advertising content through the dealer advertising committee.

Payment of Royalties

One of the potential problems of franchising is the underreporting of sales by franchisees in order to avoid royalty payments. The Midas dealer association believes that a franchisee who understates gross sales not only deprives Midas of its royalties, but also is cheating fellow dealers. The association is on record that it will not condone underreporting of sales and will not support a dealer or defend that dealer against actions which might be taken by the company as a result of such infractions.

In conclusion, the continuing prosperity and health of franchising as a form of distribution depends on enlightened understanding and cooperation between franchisor and franchisees. The death knell of franchising would be sounded if Congress were to enact legislation intended to protect franchisees from all forms of abuse at the hands of many different types of franchisors. If gasoline station operators have a legitimate grievance against their oil company franchisors, I suggest that these grievances should be settled amicably by the principals involved.

Franchising offers one of the last bastions of free enterprise and small business, and the government should be fostering and nurturing this type of organization. However, legislation which attempts to eliminate all potential areas of fraud and abuse from all franchises will result in a regulatory system which will cause the demise of franchising as we know it today. Franchised companies always have an option — namely, to open company stores or to franchise. If regulations were to become burdensome or if the balance in favor of franchisees should become unrealistic, then franchisors will revert to operating company stores. We are confident that the current drive in Congress to lessen regulatory controls will preclude passage of adverse legislation. This will ensure that franchising will continue to grow and prosper.

SUCCESS STORY
JAMES A. COLLINS

After graduating from UCLA in 1950 with a civil engineering degree, James A. Collins spent two years with a construction company, helping to build churches. In 1952, Collins's father-in-law convinced him to become a small business owner by opening up a restaurant on a ten-acre parcel he owned in Culver City, California. In September, 1952, he opened his first fast-food outlet and named it Hamburger Handout. By 1959 he was operating four such drive-ins.

In early 1960, Collins met Colonel Harlan Sanders and obtained a franchise for a then little-known brand of fried chicken — Kentucky Fried Chicken. In the years that followed, Collins became the exclusive franchising agent for Kentucky Fried Chicken stores in Southern California and was responsible for developing the chain from San Luis Obispo to the Mexican border. During this time, Collins also formed several wholesale companies for distributing products to his own and other stores in the area.

By 1967 he had established over 200 KFC units, 26 of which he owned and operated himself. That same year he and two associates acquired the ten-year-old Sizzler Family Steak House chain. With the sale of 300,000 shares of stock, Jim Collins took his company public in November of 1968 as Collins Food International, Inc. It has been listed on the New York Stock Exchange since 1973.

Today, Collins Food International is the largest operator of Kentucky Fried Chicken franchises, with 252 units in California, Oregon, Washington, Idaho, and Queensland, Australia. Collins Foods owns 70 percent of the stock of Sizzler Restaurants International Inc., and operates or licenses 465 units in 32 states plus Guam, Japan, Kuwait, and Saudi Arabia. Collins Food Service, a wholesale arm, provides one-stop shopping for the retail operator at seven distribution centers.

As one who picked up his management training the hard way, from managing several part-time employees at one hamburger stand to employing more than 10,000 in 1985, and with corporate revenues that year of over $468 million, Collins says his secret lies in listening to his subordinates, giving them authority and letting them make a few mistakes.

Photo and information provided courtesy of James A. Collins, September, 1985.

SUMMARY

The relationship between the franchisor and the franchisee is critical to the success of both parties. The relationship can be examined in the context of a business life cycle, since it goes through four phases as follows: first, the *Introduction* — the development of understanding between the parties, building hope for success and relying upon each other to perform their respective functions; second, *Growth* — from the grand opening onward, regular and effective support and service between the parties to achieve results for the franchised business; third, *Maturity* — mutual respect and understanding demonstrated by continued interaction between franchisor and franchisees to maintain the franchise system, making modifications as they become necessary; and fourth, *Decline/Development* — decline or termination of the relationship, often as a result of a decrease in the level of business activity, which may be due to failure by the franchisor and/or franchisees to maintain high standards, discontinuity of services by the franchisor, or disenchantment by the franchisee. These conditions may foster a rejuvenation and further development of the franchise system if the partners are able to revive respect and trust for each other.

Franchise advisory councils are a popular and proven means of addressing the differences that can develop in the franchising relationship. These councils may be established either by direct action of the franchisor or by voluntary participation of the franchisees.

Generally, a franchise advisory council, whether formally or informally established, serves as a communication vehicle for both franchisor and franchisee. A council can be used to present suggestions, solve problems, and provide information through conferences, newsletters, and sponsored training sessions. The topics addressed can be as varied as changes under consideration in the franchising agreement, promotions for the coming year, new product development efforts, new equipment, equipment modifications, performance standards, and financial reporting methods. Even sensitive matters such as store renovations, franchise termination, and fairness and compliance are often addressed by advisory councils to the satisfaction of franchisor and franchisees.

For the franchisee, the advisory council can serve as a "big brother" in dealings with the usually more powerful franchisor. For the franchisor, the council is often a vehicle for receiving new ideas for the front lines of the business, revealing problem areas that need attention, and disseminating and legitimating important information that all franchisees should be aware of.

Richard de Camara provides a fresh and compelling view of franchise advisory councils, utilizing the Midas Muffler franchise system as an illustration. He broadens the example to identify concerns often felt by franchisees in a typical franchise system. The overriding factor is that of franchisees seeking to achieve a sense of equality or balance among themselves in relation to the franchisor.

Many concerns can arise within a franchise system. The franchisees' concerns are typically in six or eight areas, including termination/renewal, expansion requirements or limitations, advertising, franchisor-recommended pricing schedules, and issues of real estate if the franchisor happens to have a real estate program as part of the franchising agreement. The franchisor, on the other hand, is often concerned with the ability to expand or contract as market opportunities and threats present themselves, control of real estate, covenants concerning clauses not to compete and activities by the franchisees, and, of course, profitability of the franchise system.

Though difficulties in areas such as these may appear insurmountable when considered in their entirety, acceptable solutions can usually be worked out. The mutual interest of the franchisor and the franchisees is profit — the chief concern of both partners in the franchising relationship or any business relationship. With combined effort, satisfactory solutions can be found to problems within a franchise system while at the same time the profitability of the participants in the system may be enhanced.

A balanced relationship can be helpful to franchisors and franchisees from an external perspective as well. If the balance of power shifts too much in favor of franchisees, franchisors may revert to operating company-owned stores, limiting opportunities for potential franchisees at a time when the economy is ripe for people seeking to enter this kind of business. Reverting to company-owned stores also decreases the impact of franchisee-owned units within a franchise system. If, on the other hand, a franchisor's power becomes too great, Congress may be pressed to establish further regulations upon the franchise industry, which almost certainly will curtail the power and managerial prerogatives of franchisors. At present there is a sense in Congress to lessen regulatory control, which can help to ensure continued growth and prosperity for firms in the franchise industry.

REVIEW QUESTIONS

1. Of what importance is it that the franchisor-franchisee relationship goes through different stages of development?
2. Are franchise advisory councils of value to either the franchisor or the franchisee? Discuss.
3. Is it important that the franchisor and the franchisee be aware of each other and develop a rapport in their interactions?
4. Discuss the relevance of Richard de Camara's report, "Franchisor-Franchisee Activities."

CASE STUDY
MR. STEAK*

Mr. Steak is a full-service family steak restaurant with seating facilities for up to 190 persons. During its store hours (generally 11 A.M. to 10 P.M.), Mr. Steak serves USDA-choice steaks as well as seafood, chicken, and sandwiches. There are currently over 145 franchises located through the United States.

Mr. Steak provides a mandatory comprehensive seven-week training program for its franchisees. Five weeks of on-the-job training at one of Mr. Steak's training restaurants is the first step, followed by two weeks of intensive course work at the international headquarters in Denver, Colorado. Management techniques, inventory control, accounting, marketing, advertising, public relations, and other topics of importance to franchisees are taught by the Mr. Steak experts in the related departments.

The franchising fee for a Mr. Steak restaurant is $16,000, due upon the signing of the franchising agreement. In addition, the franchisee is required to pay a weekly royalty fee of 3 percent of the gross receipts from the operations of the business. The franchisor also requires payment of a monthly advertising fee of 1 percent of the total gross income of the restaurant. However, this 1 percent is not currently being collected.

Startup Costs

Franchising Fee	$ 16,000
Equipment (approximate)	200,000
Land (50,000 sq. ft.)	37,000
Construction	50,000
Initial Working Capital	15,000
Additional Capital Recommended	40,000
Total	$358,000

If the franchise uses leased land and buildings, then the starting cost is reduced significantly. And if the original equipment is purchased on credit with a down payment of $40,000, the estimated total startup costs could be reduced to $111,500. Mr. Steak provides marketing and management assistance to the franchisee, in addition to providing a franchise accounting system.

All new franchising agreements are limited to 20-year terms with a ten-year option. Mr. Steak also provides its registered service marks, trademarks, site analysis and selection help, sample lease forms, building plans and construction inspections, specification books, operations manuals, volume buying, manager selection, training programs, and grand opening as-

---

*Information provided courtesy of Jamco Limited, December, 1987.

sistance. The company provides tremendous help in the marketing, advertising, promotions, and publicity areas. The accounting system is thoroughly explained and taught in the accounting segment of the franchisee training program. The franchising accounting service is optional, but the requirements of reporting certain data are outlined in the franchising agreement.

CASE QUESTIONS

1. What are the advantages and disadvantages of Mr. Steak as a franchise?
2. What additional information would you request from a franchisor before signing a franchising agreement?
3. Would Mr. Steak be a good franchise to invest in? Why or why not?
4. What else would you need to know before entering into a franchising agreement with Mr. Steak?

REFERENCES

1. Axelrad, Norman D., and Lewis G. Rudnick, "The Franchisee and the Franchise Relationship," *Franchising: A Planning and Sales Plans Guide*, Chicago: Commerce Clearinghouse, Inc., 1987, pp. 39-50.
2. Justis, Robert T., and Richard Judd, "Master Franchising: A New Look," *Journal of Small Business Management*, Vol. 24 (July 1986), p. 16.
3. Knight, Russell M., "Franchising from the Franchisor and Franchisee Points of View," *Journal of Small Business Management*, Vol. 24 (July 1986), p. 8.
4. Kostecka, Andrew, "What Is Franchising?" *Franchise Opportunities Handbook*, United States Department of Commerce, International Trade Administration, November, 1987, pp. xxix-xxxiii.
5. Luxenberg, Stan, "Growing Plains," *Roadside Empires, How the Chains Franchised America*, New York: Penguin Books, 1986, pp. 220-251.
6. Michie, Donald A., and Stanley D. Sibley, "Channel Member Satisfaction: Controversy Resolved," *Journal of the Academy of Marketing Science*, Vol. 13 (Winter 1985), pp. 188-205.
7. Nedell, Harold, "Marriage and Divorce — Franchise Style," *The Franchise Game*, Olemco Publishing, 1980, pp. 35-39.
8. Seltz, David D., "Providing Supportive Backup to Franchisees," *The Complete Book of Franchising*, Reading, MA: Addison-Wesley Publishing Co., 1982, p. 171-196.

CHAPTER 20
FAIRNESS AND COMPLIANCE

This chapter was prepared by Lewis G. Rudnick and Joseph W. Sheyka of Rudnick & Wolfe, Chicago, Illinois; and Charles J. Averbook of Schmier & Feurring Properties, Inc., Boca Raton, Florida.

In studying this chapter, you will:
- Learn about structuring a sound economic relationship between the franchisor and the franchisee.
- Understand how to structure a sound legal relationship between the franchisor and the franchisee.
- Learn about documenting and recording the franchising relationship.
- Understand disclosure regulation and compliance.
- Understand how fairness in dealing with franchisees interrelates with legal compliance in a franchising relationship.

INCIDENT

Renee has started a new drive-thru fast-food hamburger restaurant. She has been operating for two years now and has been very successful with her six company-owned stores. She has been able to realize approximately $75,000 in profit from each of her stores during the last year.

Renee started to franchise this past year. She has been very successful and currently has 23 franchised units. She has four multi-unit franchisees who are in the process of adding new units to their geographical areas. Although she is now receiving royalty payments from the franchisees, she is concerned about adequate cash flow and is worried that royalties are insufficient to meet the expansion needs of the headquarters operation.

Renee serves only hamburgers, chicken, french fries, and soft drinks. She provides no seating, so customers must "drive thru" to order and pick up the food. Her units are small — approximately 600 square feet each — but overhead is low and the potential profits are high. Her hamburgers and chicken have received rave notices and she has many regular customers.

She currently has no advertising program for the franchisees, although she does recommend that each franchisee use 3 percent of gross revenues for local advertising. She does not know what she should require, but she wants to be fair with her franchisees. Renee wants to develop a positive and helpful association with the franchisees, but she has heard rumors that it is not a good idea to provide full disclosure from the headquarters to the franchisees because the franchisees may later use this information against the franchisor.

Renee used to provide information to prospective franchisees about the financial operations of her company-owned stores. She has stopped doing this but is wondering if there is any way she can provide earnings claims or if she even should do this for prospective franchisees.

INTRODUCTION

To be successful over the long term, a franchise system must be fair to both the franchisor and the franchisee, and both sides must comply with their respective obligations. In this chapter we discuss certain mistakes franchising companies make in structuring franchising relationships, selling franchises, expanding their franchise systems, and dealing with their own and their franchisees' obligations.

As the previous chapters of this book have pointed out, there are many kinds of franchises and many kinds of industries. Correspondingly, there are just as many ways to design or formulate all of the variables in the relationship between the franchisor and the franchisee. Nevertheless, there are certain common mistakes or problems that franchisors have made over the years, and, unfortunately, continue to make. There are four general categories in which these mistakes seem to fall:

1. Financial problems arising from the failure to structure a sound economic relationship;
2. Problems arising from lack of fairness and the failure to structure a sound legal relationship;
3. Poor record keeping by the franchisor; and
4. Failure by the franchisor to carefully follow state and federal rules and regulations governing franchising relationships.

STRUCTURING A SOUND ECONOMIC RELATIONSHIP

One of the most important aspects of a sound, well-designed franchise system is the existence of a good economic relationship between the franchisor and the franchisee. The relationship can be effective only if financial problems can be averted or readily resolved. Let's look at the economic problems that sometimes arise in franchising.

Generating Sufficient Income

A carefully thought out and successful franchise system is one in which both the franchisor and the franchisee make money. After all, that is usually why both sides have entered into the relationship. Some franchise programs fail because one side or the other is not generating sufficient revenue from the relationship to make it worthwhile. Although one might think it is usually the franchisee who fails to generate a sufficient amount of income, quite often it is the franchisor who has the financial problems. This can occur when a franchisor fails to adequately anticipate the costs and expenses of providing support functions and services to its franchisees. Sometimes the failure to generate sufficient income has resulted from setting a percentage royalty, an initial franchising fee, or a required advertising contribution that is too low, or from designing a franchising program that obtains a significant portion of its revenues from sales of goods or services that franchisees are required to purchase.

The first three problems can be minimized by (1) careful planning and calculation of the franchisor's likely expenses before the franchise program is set up, (2) increasing those fees for any new franchises that are sold after the franchisor discovers the problem, or (3) asking existing franchisees to voluntarily increase their fees. (Naturally, it will be difficult to obtain consent to a voluntary increase.) The fourth problem — dependence on franchisee purchases — usually appears if franchisees discover they can purchase goods at a lower cost than from the franchisor. They then begin to complain about the problem, file antitrust suits, or simply breach their franchising agreements by not purchasing from the franchisor. This results in either declining franchisor income or, if the franchisor tries to enforce the purchase requirements, rising legal and administrative expenses. The best way, naturally, to avoid this last problem is to try to set up a franchising program that minimizes the amount of revenue the franchisor is expecting to receive from required purchases by the franchisee.

Some franchise systems suffer from just the opposite problem. That is, the franchising agreement requires the franchisees to pay so much in initial fees, royalties, advertising fees, and other charges that it is very difficult for them to make a fair return on their investment. Naturally, when the franchisees have a difficult time making a profit, there will be a high rate of franchisee failures, terminations, turnover, and litigation.

Not surprisingly, the problem of insufficient franchisee income is easier to rectify than a situation in which the franchisor is not generating sufficient income. That is because a franchisor is generally free to voluntarily reduce the fees being charged, although the franchisor cannot, under most agreements, increase them at whim. Unfortunately, some franchisors do not respond to the franchisee profitability problem by reducing fees or restructuring the requirements of the franchising relationship. Instead, they simply work harder at selling more new franchises as the existing ones go out of business. This strategy, of course, rarely works in the long run, since eventually the franchisor will be unable to find buyers for the franchises.

Providing Meaningful Services

Another aspect of a sound economic relationship, and one whose neglect sometimes leads to problems, is that the franchisor must during the entire term of the franchising relationship continue to provide services, ideas, supervision, and assistance to franchisees that the franchisees feel are important and meaningful. If at any time the franchisor stops providing services that its franchisees feel are valuable, there is a higher likelihood that an economic problem will develop. Franchisees will become reluctant to pay those fees month after month after month if they feel that they learned everything there was to learn in the first few months or years of the franchising relationship and that they are no longer getting anything of value for their royalties or advertising payments. A franchisee who feels this way might begin to think about breaking away from the franchisor. **Breaking away** occurs when a franchisee sets up a new business at another location, substantially similar to the franchised business, but under a different name, or when the franchisee simply changes the signs at the franchised location.

Services that are meaningful to established franchisees will vary from one franchise system to another. In most systems, however, an effective advertising program which continues to maintain the goodwill of the franchisor and combat the competition is a very important service. Research and product and service development programs to open up new markets are also important. A franchisor's maintenance of purchasing and supply programs that pass the benefits of volume purchasing through to the franchisee is also felt to be an important reason for staying in a franchise system.

Giving franchisees some role in planning for the evolution of the franchise system may be as important as the franchisor furnishing meaningful services. This role may be as modest as establishing a small franchise advisory council, or as expansive as permitting a regular, formal, strategic planning role for a franchisee association. Some franchisors object to giving franchisees such a role in system planning and decision making. However, franchisees may be less likely to become disenchanted with the system if they believe they have a significant role in determining the destiny of the system.

Some franchisors feel that no matter how significant they think their franchisee services are, after a certain number of years in the franchise system, it is inevitable that some franchisees will begin to feel a reluctance to continue to pay fees. As a result, they have designed their franchising agreements so that royalties actually decline over time or as a percentage of sales. They believe this is the most practical way to keep franchisees happy over the long haul.

STRUCTURING A SOUND LEGAL RELATIONSHIP

If a franchisor can overcome the financial problems in structuring a franchising program, it often next must overcome nonfinancial problems. Structuring a franchisor-franchisee relationship that is fair and sound with respect to the nonfinancial requirements can be just as important as having a sound economic base for the franchise system.

Treating the Franchisee as a Captive Market

As a result of recent changes in the antitrust laws, it appears to be less risky, from a legal standpoint, for franchisors to require their franchisees to purchase goods and services directly from the franchisor. For example, requiring the franchisee to lease the franchise location from the franchisor is a typical requirement of some franchises. Often the amount of rent due under the lease increases as the sales at the location increase. Franchisees sometimes resent this requirement since they are already paying royalty or advertising fees to their franchisor. Franchisees who can afford to purchase their own real estate (and build up equity in that real estate) are hurt the most. Naturally, those franchisees who rent a location from a third-party landlord would not have the same level of objection.

From a franchisor's standpoint, if the franchisor can afford the cost of acquiring or leasing the franchise premises, controlling real estate by subleasing to the franchisee is an excellent way to control both the nonconforming and the potential breakaway franchisee, since a franchisee who must vacate his premises in order to leave the system is likely to think twice about not complying with the franchising agreement. In addition, it can be argued that a franchisee who knowingly joins a franchise system that does not permit him to purchase his own real estate does not have much to complain about.

When it comes to requiring franchisees to purchase goods and services other than real estate, problems are likely to result if the franchisor charges his franchisees prices that are higher than what they could have paid if they were free to purchase elsewhere. A possible exception could be the sale by a franchisor of finished, trademarked products that the franchisee simply resells without further processing. Designating a single supplier (including the franchisor) for quality-control purposes or for the purpose of passing on to franchisees the price discounts of volume buying is generally appropriate. When the designation of a single source becomes a substantial profit center for the franchisor and when comparable products are available from other sources at lower prices or no supportable grounds exist for imposing such a restriction, the soundness of the purchasing restriction may be questionable. In short, a royalty and service fee based on the gross revenues of the franchised unit remains the most secure and least objectionable source of revenue for most franchisors.

Advertising Programs

Some franchisors, when first starting to sell franchises, encounter franchise applicants who are reluctant to contribute advertising monies to a franchisor-controlled ad fund because they know the franchise system in its early stages is too small to effectively take advantage of the benefits of national or regional advertising. For this reason, some franchisors eliminate the ad fund requirement for the first group of franchisees. When that happens, however, franchisees who come into the system later will point to their predecessors and argue that if the early ones don't have to pay, neither should they. Tension develops which can damage the franchise system by causing an ineffective advertising program. This problem can be minimized by providing in the franchising agreement — for all franchisees — that an advertising contribution of a specific amount will be required at such time in the future as the franchisor establishes a national or regional advertising program.

Anticipating Change

In every franchise system, the business concept will have to be changed over time in order to meet competition and take advantage of market opportunities. In establishing a franchising relationship, it is essential to try to anticipate the kinds of competitive conditions that may require modifications in the obligations of the franchisor or franchisee during the term of the relationship, and to develop a legal mechanism for implementing these changes.

Most franchisors incorporate into their franchising agreements the concept of a modifiable operations manual. Through changes in standards, specifications, and operating procedures detailed in the operations manual, franchisors retain the flexibility to adjust to some market conditions. However, some modifications in concept or format cannot be effectively implemented by modifying an operations manual. An example would be a change in concept or format requiring a substantial franchisee investment.

There are a number of things to consider in implementing a serious change of this nature. Should the franchisor have to make the change in company-owned outlets and test it for a minimum period of time before franchisees are required to make the investment? Should the change require approval by a specified minimum percentage of franchisees or by an association of franchisees? Should the change be required only if there is a minimum period of time left on the franchising agreement so that the franchisee will have time to effectively benefit from the cost of the investment?

Because there are so many issues to consider in anticipating and providing for major changes in a franchising agreement, many franchisors simply do not address the issue or do so without sufficient detail. If provisions requiring change are not clear or fair to both sides, they will be difficult and costly to enforce and will be disruptive to the system. On the other hand, a franchisor who fails to deal with the issue of major change may find himself unable to effectively react to changes in his market.

Fairness Generally

Fairness is an important element in structuring a sound legal relationship. As stated earlier, some franchisors think that a good franchising agreement is one that imposes severe restrictions on franchisees and grants broad rights to the franchisor. Unfortunately, those kinds of franchising agreements can often be counterproductive. Franchisors and their lawyers sometimes lose sight of the fact that contracts are not automatically enforceable. They must first be examined and understood by a judge, jury, or arbitrator, who, if they believe the contract has gone too far in taking advantage of one party, may simply refuse to enforce it. In short, an agreement that is fair to both parties is more likely to be enforceable by a court of law exactly as written than an agreement that is extremely one-sided. The concept of fairness has many applications in a franchising agreement. A few examples will serve to illustrate.

Franchisors typically want to be able to terminate a franchising agreement as soon as possible after giving the franchisee notice of default. Yet, it is a rare event that a franchise is terminated quickly if the franchisee resists. Most franchise terminations are accomplished over an extended period of time. This is due to a combination of courthouse delays and typical efforts by franchisors to find a solution short of termination.

This suggests that a short-notice termination clause — an irritant to franchisees — may not be an important provision of a franchising agreement. On the other hand, contract terms that permit immediate termination of a franchisee who commits fraud or is a habitual violator of the franchise agreement are not unfair and should be included in every franchising agreement.

Fairness is also important in dealing with the consequences of termination. If the franchisor is also the franchisee's landlord, termination will result in the franchisee being dispossessed of the business premises. Removing fixtures, equipment, and inventory from the location is often impractical for the franchisee. In those situations, the only method available to the franchisee to salvage any part of the investment is the sale of the business to a new franchisee. Most franchisors prefer to deal with sale of the business after termination of the franchising agreement on a case-by-case basis rather than as a contractual obligation. However, to be prepared for the case in which the termination is essentially the result of the franchisee's business failure, franchisors should consider including in the franchising agreement a procedure for permitting the franchisee to sell the business to a new franchisee so that some of the franchisee's investment can be preserved.

When the franchisor does not control the franchisee's business premises (or business premises are not used or are unimportant), franchisors typically seek to severely restrict the franchisee's business activity after termination. Not infrequently, the franchisor imposes a post-termination agreement against competition by the franchisee that is very broad in scope of prohibited activity, geographic coverage, and duration. Sometimes the rationale for this type of franchising agreement requirement is that it is a "scare tactic," to be used as a bargaining tool to negotiate a lesser restriction with which the franchisee will voluntarily comply. A similarly overbroad approach is sometimes taken toward de-identification (i.e., changing the identity of the business premises after termination). It is reasonable for a franchisor to impose a post-termination restriction against competition and require the franchisee to reasonably de-identify the business premises. However, the proper objective of these provisions is protection of the goodwill of the franchisor's system and franchise, not banishment and destitution of the franchisee. Post-termination restrictions on competition should be designed primarily to cause a break in the continued presence of the franchisee in his market, which can be accomplished with a modest restriction. De-identification obligations should be as specific as possible and require a minimal investment where feasible (for example, repainting rather than rebuilding).

Fairness should also be incorporated into restrictions on transfer of the franchise and provisions dealing with the effect of the franchisor's election not to renew a franchisee. Franchisors may fairly restrict and impose conditions on the transfer of their franchises. However, these restrictions should not be made so burdensome that transfer becomes impossible. Franchisors frequently regard transfer as an opportunity to update the franchise by requiring the purchaser to execute the current form of franchising agreement, which may require greater fees and other more burdensome obligations than the current franchising agreement. The seriousness of this requirement is not always appreciated. For example, the purchaser's obligation to pay higher royalties and advertising fees when he or she becomes the new owner will presumably reduce the price that purchaser is willing to pay for the franchisee's business. Alternatives are either to permit the purchaser to assume the franchising agreement, or to enter into a new franchising agreement which continues the former payment structure until the date of expiration of the seller's franchising agreement.

Nonrenewal of a franchising agreement is a particularly sensitive issue in franchising. Few franchisors would seriously consider giving up their right not to renew what they regard as an unsatisfactory franchising relationship. This approach is not unfair, but failure to deal reasonably with the franchisee's rights and obligations on expiration of the franchise can create an impression of unfairness. If the franchisor is also landlord, nonrenewal has the effect of appropriating to the franchisor whatever goodwill or going-concern value the franchisee's business has (which may be considerable), unless the franchisee is given an opportunity to sell the business to a successor franchisee. This approach requires the franchisor to reach a final decision regarding renewal well in advance of expiration in order that the franchisee will have a reasonable period within which to sell his business. This method of allocation of the goodwill and equity of the franchisee's business is probably fair to both parties. The franchisor retains the goodwill attributable to its name and system when it grants a new franchising agreement at its current value, and the franchisee realizes the remaining goodwill by selling the business. The franchise then represents estate-building potential for the franchisee, without regard to whether it is renewed.

DOCUMENTING AND RECORDING THE FRANCHISING RELATIONSHIP

A sound legal relationship can be undermined unless it is effectively documented and proper files and records are kept of all documents, correspondence, and other materials relating to each franchising relationship. A few examples of documentation errors that franchisors sometimes make are as follows:

- No record is made or kept of the background check on the franchisee or verification of the statements on the application.

- Individuals are permitted to execute agreements on behalf of a corporation without significant assets or without giving a personal guarantee. Alternatively, the capacity in which the parties sign the agreements is unclear or all parties to agreements do not execute them.
- Blanks to be filled in at time of execution are left blank.
- Documents requiring recordation (e.g., collateral lease assignments) are not recorded.
- Franchisees who open several units in rapid succession are inadvertently permitted to open one or more units without signing franchising agreements for those units.

Problems can also result from poor systems and procedures, such as the following:

- Failure to retain in an orderly, easily locatable manner the executed originals of the agreements,
- Failure to retain a complete chronological record of each page of the operations manuals, bulletins, newsletters, and other communications to franchisees, all of which can be important in enforcement of the franchising agreement, and
- Failure to keep signed copies of the documents franchisees sign acknowledging receipt of franchise offering circulars and other related documents.

COMPLIANCE WITH DISCLOSURE REGULATIONS

As mentioned in previous chapters in this book, the offer and sale of franchises is strictly regulated today by state and federal laws. These laws prescribe detailed rules on information which must be disclosed to prospective franchisees in connection with the offer of a franchise. Compliance with disclosure regulations is an element of the franchising relationship in which franchisors are prone to commit numerous errors. As in other areas, these errors are the result of negative attitude, poor planning, and failure of execution.

Attitude

There is nothing to be gained, and much that can be lost, from a negative attitude toward registration and disclosure regulations — scorning disclosure compliance as the franchisor's curse, to be circumvented whenever possible. This attitude will permeate a franchisor's management and sales personnel. As a result, disclosure regulation violations will become inevitable. It is more sensible to accept the current pattern of disclosure regulation as government overregulation that may be improved in the future, but must be observed in the present.

Planning for Compliance

Planning a disclosure regulation compliance program is more complex than it might appear. Failure to plan thoroughly and carefully is a cause of many of the compliance mistakes that franchisors make. The first element of compliance planning is determining the assignment of responsibility for compliance. Smaller franchisors tend to lodge that responsibility with their outside attorney, but they sometimes fail to establish an effective liaison between the outside attorney and the company personnel responsible for keeping disclosure information current and communicating with sales personnel. To do effective work, the outside attorney requires a source of timely, complete, and reliable information from the franchisor and a responsible manager to whom the attorney can communicate compliance status and procedures.

Franchisors with small law departments may divide responsibility for disclosure compliance between the law department and the outside attorney. Franchisors with larger law departments typically delegate compliance responsibility exclusively to their law departments. Both types of delegation can work effectively, provided that assignments are clear and the law department has sufficient resources and exercises independent judgment and its opinions are respected by management.

Whether compliance is made the responsibility of an outside attorney, the law department, or both, it is important for the franchisor to delegate executive responsibility to a senior manager whose perspective on the franchisor's development and performance is not limited to sales of new franchises. Sales personnel seem to have a natural antipathy toward lawyers, sometimes calling them the "sales-prevention department." Sales personnel are less likely to be uncooperative with a senior executive.

In addition to ensuring compliance with disclosure law, franchisors must also be able to prove that compliance in court. Some franchisors fail to establish any system or procedure for logging all sales prospects and all contacts with and materials furnished to them. Franchisors lacking these systems may not have adequate business records to enable their personnel to testify in court to the procedures followed and to otherwise rebut a claim made by a franchisee that he or she was given earnings claims or other information with the offering circular, or that financial projections made for the franchisee's outlet after signing the franchising agreement were in fact delivered before signing, or that the offering circular was not timely delivered and the franchisee was requested to backdate the receipt. Document and information storage and retrieval systems are frequently deficient, rendering franchisors unable to produce essential evidence. Some franchisors fail to implement a disclosure training program for sales personnel. Franchisor executives other than sales personnel may not thoroughly interview the prospective franchise purchaser after that prospect has received a "sales presentation" but before execution of documents. Those kinds of interviews are an essential element in franchisee selection and can help determine whether sales personnel are complying with company policies on disclosure regulation compliance and franchisee selection.

Perhaps the most difficult procedural problem in disclosure compliance is stopping the franchise sales program while registrations and offering circulars are renewed or amended. No other aspect of disclosure regulation seems to arouse the ire of a franchise salesman as much as the prospect of a delay in closing a sale that appears to be in the bag. The salesman is invariably convinced that delay or redisclosure will let the prospect off the hook. The delays and interruptions in franchise sales inherent in registration, and periodic amendments of registrations and offering circulars, are serious annoyances, but are an unavoidable adjunct of disclosure regulation. Franchisors who cut corners may save a few sales, but the infirmity of those sales can cause serious future problems.

Full Disclosure

For obvious reasons, negative information represents one of the most difficult disclosure compliance problems for franchisors. Certain negative information, such as deteriorating financial performance and condition or increasing development and operating costs confronted by franchisees, must ultimately be disclosed when offering circulars are updated. With respect to other information (e.g., litigation or system problems), the issue will be whether the new development is significant enough to require disclosure. With respect to timing of offering circular amendments, it is important to keep in mind the danger of continuing to grant franchises with knowledge of a material event or change that may require disclosure. The longer amendment is deferred, the greater the risk that sales made before the amendment will be challenged as having been made illegally.

When the issue is whether disclosure must be made at all, the prospect of eventual disclosure is not as clear-cut, but franchisors should be aware that later events may cast doubt on the correctness of the initial decision to omit disclosure. For example, a lawsuit may be arguably immaterial when filed. However, changes in the nature of the litigation — for example, discovery of facts not revealed initially — as it progresses may remove all doubt as to materiality, thereby raising an issue of whether disclosure was required when the lawsuit was filed.

There are no clearly defined rules to guide a franchisor to always accomplish full disclosure. However, if franchisors are guided by the general standard that they should disclose all information that is material, they will be right (and relatively safe) most of the time. Information is **material** if it would have a significant influence on the investment decision of a reasonable person who is a prospective franchise purchaser.

Under that standard, franchisors must disclose some warts and blemishes — and that disclosure may result in lost sales. The alternative is significant legal exposure and potential losses and expenses.

Earnings Claims

Many franchisors do not include projections of a typical franchisee's likely earnings in their offering circulars. This is often due to the resistance of franchising law administrators to approve these kinds of claims, or to franchisors' concern that they will be unable to satisfy the burden of substantiating the exact factual basis for every assumption that has to be made to develop earnings projections. Yet most franchisors candidly admit that it is difficult, if not impossible, to close a franchise sale without responding to questions from the prospective franchisee regarding sales and profits. Although disclosure rules are strict, after one or two years of franchising, most franchisors can make and substantiate historical data or earnings projections that will be acceptable in most states. The claims might be as limited as the gross sales of existing franchised and company-operated outlets. The alternative — the omission of earnings claims from the offering circular — can leave this element of franchise sales wide open to unauthorized statements by sales reps. Even a limited claim, coupled with a statement that it is the only authorized claim, is a check on embellishment by sales personnel and may weaken franchisees' claims in court that they relied on earnings claims made by sales personnel.

SUCCESS STORY
DAVID B. KENNEY

After 12 years of successful lodging and restaurant property ownership and management, David Kenney joined Atlanta real estate developer Cecil B. Day to develop a concept for budget luxury motels. Kenney became the president of Days Inns of America, Inc. in early 1970. Since its inception, Days Inns has become the world's largest budget motel chain, consisting of more than 300 locations with over 40,000 motel rooms in 33 states. David Kenney has appeared on the cover of numerous trade publications and has been quoted extensively in national business and news weeklies. He has also been invited to the White House four times and to testify before the U.S. Senate on the impact and effects of energy legislation on the hospital-

> ity industry. In addition to his role as chairman of the board of Kenney Management Company, Kenney is also president of Motel Ventures, Inc., a corporation established to own hotels and motels. He is an equity partner of each motel managed by Kenney Management Company.
>
> Photo and information provided courtesy of David B. Kenney, August, 1985.

SUMMARY

Franchising relationships are among the most complex in today's business world. The best way to maintain long-term, positive relationships is to develop a franchising program founded on principles of fairness, and to initiate the program and carry it out carefully and in compliance with all the rules and obligations governing it.

REVIEW QUESTIONS

1. Discuss how to develop a sound economic relationship between a franchisor and a franchisee.
2. Explain how to develop a sound legal component in a franchising program.
3. Why is it important to document the franchising relationship?
4. Discuss the advantages and disadvantages of full disclosure compliance.
5. Is it appropriate to provide earnings claims for franchisees?

CASE STUDY
THE STEAK SHOPPE

Cheryl is the founder and owner of the Steak Shoppe, located in a suburb of Dallas, Texas. She has been very successful since opening her first business in 1979, expanding with her second store in 1983 and her third and fourth in 1986. Her average monthly sales have jumped to $75,000, and she has been able to keep her costs of goods sold and wages under 60 percent of total sales.

Cheryl started the Steak Shoppe with the concept of serving steak dinners within the family budget. She provides a family atmosphere and earnestly seeks the family trade as well as a strong business trade during the lunch hour. Her decor is western in style and she has been very well received in the Texas marketplace.

Cheryl charges a $20,000 initial franchising fee with a monthly royalty fee of 4.5 percent plus a monthly advertising fee of 1.5 percent.

Estimated Initial Costs

Franchising Fee	$20,000
Land	$150,000-$250,000
Building	$250,000-$350,000
Equipment Package	$150,000
Fixtures and Incidentals	$17,000
Inventory and Paper Goods	$17,000
Pre-Opening Training	$7,000
Signage	$24,000
Working Capital and Pre-Opening Expense	$12,000

NOTE:
1. The building and land may be financed through the franchisor.
2. The equipment package may be 3/4 financed through the franchisor.

Cheryl is also thinking of a sliding franchise fee for additional stores. She anticipates a 10 percent reduction for each additional store opened by an existing franchisee, plus a reduction of 0.5 percent in the royalty fee for the second and third stores, leaving a 3.5 percent royalty fee for the franchisee in all stores after the third store has been opened.

The Steak Shoppes that have been averaging over $75,000 monthly sales have been showing profits over $5,000 each month, while those stores under $75,000 in sales have been averaging $2,400 profit each month. However, Cheryl has heard that she may not be able to tell prospective franchisees about the profit potential. Cheryl has one store that is averaging around $92,000 sales per month with profits of $13,000. She knows the potential is there, but she is a little concerned about how to convey this to prospective franchisees. She knows what steps she should take to make an effective presentation to franchisees while also maintaining good customer relations and increasing the profitability in both company-owned and franchised stores. Cheryl is very concerned about marketing her products in other communities or states. Will it be necessary to change the decor, pricing, or business structure?

CASE QUESTIONS

1. Should Cheryl go ahead and franchise?
2. What kind of market information does she need?
3. What steps should Cheryl take to franchise her business to prospective franchisees?
4. Why is Cheryl thinking of franchising rather than developing more company-owned stores?

CHAPTER 21
BREAKAWAY FRANCHISEES AND NONCOMPLIANCE

This chapter was prepared by Lewis G. Rudnick and Joseph W. Sheyka of Rudnick & Wolfe, Chicago, Illinois; and Charles J. Averbook of Schmier & Feurring Properties, Inc., Boca Raton, Florida.

In studying this chapter, you will:
- Understand the nature and causes of breakaway franchisees.
- Learn about covenants not to compete, their purpose and limitations.
- Learn about the options to acquire the franchisee's business.
- Understand how to reduce the likelihood of breakaway franchisees.
- Learn about dispute resolution, litigation, and/or arbitration.

INCIDENT

Beverly is the vice-president of franchising for a large franchisor of computer retail stores. She has been involved with franchising for the last 12 years and in that time has seen her system grow to over 600 units spread throughout the United States and Japan.

Beverly recently has grown very concerned about several franchisees who are in the process of unilaterally terminating the franchising relationship. Three franchisees in the past six months have simply stopped paying royalties and have changed their name and logo while continuing their basic operations and work.

Beverly knows that they have a covenant not to compete in the original franchising agreement. Yet they continue to operate under their own names and operations.

Beverly wants to know how to handle these franchisees — what actions she can take, whether she can buy the franchisees out, and how she can avoid such problems in the future. In the last six months she has also received 12 complaints from franchisees regarding their operation and their support from the franchisor. The number of these complaints has been increasing, and Beverly wants to know how best to handle them and what actions should be taken to solve the breakaway problem. She is concerned about her failure to maintain effective communication with the franchisees and wants to learn how to improve the relationships.

BREAKAWAY FRANCHISEES

A major problem facing many franchisors is that their franchisees will sometimes decide to break away from the franchise system once they have been set up in their franchise and have learned the ins and outs of operating in that industry. Let's take a look at this problem and discuss how a franchisor might avoid or resolve it.

The Nature and Causes of Breakaway Franchisees

The incidence of attempted termination of franchising agreements by franchisees appears to be increasing. These "unilateral terminations" — in which the franchisee wants to end the relationship but the franchisor doesn't — typically follow one of two patterns. In the first pattern, the franchisee simply stops participating in the franchisor's system and terminates the franchising relationship without consulting the franchisor. Franchisees may undertake a de-identification program, but often are very casual about taking steps necessary to eliminate their image as franchisees. This is a particularly common problem when the premises of the franchisor's system are of distinctive design and a significant expenditure is required to modify the premises sufficiently to eliminate its identity with the system. Furthermore, the former franchisee may intentionally seek whatever advantage can be gained from continued identification with the franchisor's system and advertising. This form of breakaway may also occur in the context of a franchisee's attempt to sell the business to a buyer who does not want the franchise identity, thereby taking a franchised outlet out of the system.

The second breakaway pattern involves intentional noncompliance by the franchisee in an effort to avoid restrictions of the franchise or to provoke termination by the franchisor. The noncompliance may simply be consistently late payment (or nonpayment) of royalties and advertising fund contributions, or it may extend to noncompliance with quality control and other requirements of the franchise. Noncompliance may also take the form of the franchisee's development of similar outlets under a different trademark outside the franchisor's system using confidential information acquired as a franchisee and retaining all the benefits of the franchise system and advance knowledge of its competitive strategy and marketing program. This type of franchisee expansion is frequently in violation of franchising agreement restrictions on competition and use of trade secrets or confidential information. As in the case of the franchisee who simply declares the franchise terminated, the franchisee seeking to provoke termination by the franchisor will generally claim that the franchisor has committed multiple breaches of its obligations as franchisor.

The breakaway franchisee causes multiple damage to a franchise system. In addition to a loss of revenue from royalties, advertising contributions, and sales to the franchisee, a breakaway franchisee can diminish the strength of the system by removing one or more outlets, harming the image of the franchisor, and establishing another competitor. A number of breakaway franchisees have even become successful franchisors of the same or similar business concepts.

The breakaway franchisee is typically a problem in franchising systems in which (a) the franchisor does not control the premises of its franchisees' businesses; (b) franchisees do not believe that loss of identity with the franchisor's system or loss of services available from the franchisor (e.g., advertising, training, guidance) is likely to significantly impair their businesses; and (c) franchisees do not fear a post-termination restriction against competition because the franchising agreement does not contain such a restriction or because applicable state law precludes or limits enforcement of such a restriction. In many service-business franchise systems, the franchisor cannot effectively control the franchisee's business facility because the franchisee can readily relocate the business and the specific location is of little significance. Even where location control is significant, relatively few franchisors can afford the capital investment or contingent liability associated with location control.

In franchise systems where advertising programs are focused on the local market of each franchisee or targeted at a relatively small group of identified customers, franchisees may conclude that they can advertise as effectively as the franchisor. If the industry in which the franchise system operates is characterized by successful independent operators as well as franchise systems or centrally owned chains, the franchisee will be more willing to operate as an independent retailer or service business. The breakaway franchisee may be a multiple-outlet operator or two or more franchisees operating in concert, thereby already having some of the economies of operation offered by a franchise system. Even if the breakaway franchisees are not large, multiple-unit operators, there is a danger that they will attempt to induce other franchisees to follow their example.

What type of individual is likely to become a breakaway franchisee, and what are the causes of adopting this course of action? Breakaway franchisees are generally persons of great self-confidence. They believe that they know as much or more than the franchisor about operating the business or that they know their market better than the franchisor and can exploit it more effectively outside the franchise system. For example, these franchisees may believe that the products or services they are required to offer have become less competitive in their market and that they could increase sales by adding new products or services which the franchisor does not authorize; or that franchisee contributions for national or regional advertising would be more effectively spent in the local market. Breakaway franchisees invariably find the financial obligations of the franchise to be burdensome, the more so if they have high sales and are consequently obligated to pay a larger royalty and advertising contribution. In addition to perceiving the royalty and advertising contributions to be too high, breakaway franchisees may regard maintenance of required standards, specifications and operating procedures as imposing a cost that could be greatly reduced by departure from the system. They will also tend to rationalize that the initial franchising fee and royalties previously paid to the franchisor are sufficiently generous compensation for the services and assistance that the franchisor has furnished, which they may be inclined to belittle.

The explanation for some breakaways may be as simple as the fact that some people, because of their temperament and personality, are not meant to be franchisees, but discover this fact only after becoming a franchisee; or, though reasonably suited to a franchising relationship at its inception, they change so much after five or ten years that the limitations and restrictions of the franchising relationship are unappealing. To this type of franchisee, small problems are perceived as large issues calling for a drastic solution. The large investments required by many franchises, and the legal relationships required to support the financing of those investments, may lead to franchising relationships whose terms are longer than practical in light of human nature.

In addition to the typical mind-set of the breakaway franchisee, a number of specific problems that arise in the franchising relationship can trigger the breakaway syndrome. Franchisees may want to expand the range of products or services they offer, but may find the franchisor unwilling to agree to such proposals. The franchisor may impose obligations to upgrade the business premises of its franchisees or to add new products or services, requiring substantial capital investment. The franchisor may be extending the terms of franchises or offering renewal rights to franchisees who upgrade, but such rights are of little interest to a franchisee who is opposed to the required changes and is therefore thinking of leaving the system. Unwillingness of franchisees to make the required capital investment, coupled with upgrading by many other franchised outlets, can further isolate them from the system and hasten their departure. Alternatively, the confrontation could arise out of efforts of franchisees to expand into multiple-unit operation. They may unsuccessfully attempt to obtain an additional franchise, as a result of conflicting expansion rights or territorial claims of other franchisees or because of their failure to meet financial or management criteria for an additional franchise. Finding expansion within the franchise system blocked, the breakaway franchisee begins to think of other ways to expand.

The breaking away of franchisees can also be a symptom of other franchising problems, some of which were discussed in the previous chapter. Burdensome economic relationships, overreaching, failure to develop or maintain a competitive business and franchise system, failure to provide meaningful services, failure to develop a franchised market sufficiently to properly support the franchisees operating in that market, weak trade identity, weak controls on area franchisees, failure to maintain standards and procedures, poor communication with franchisees, and excessive litigation — all are causes of breakaway franchisees.

Dealing with Breakaway Franchisees

It is difficult, at best, for a franchisor to deal with franchisee defection after the fact, other than by legal action. Though advance planning can reduce the incentive of a franchisee to disaffiliate, and planning to contain the breakaway-franchisee syndrome is important, it is difficult to initiate significant changes in the franchisor's program in response to what is initially only a few disaffected franchisees. The management of most franchisors would conclude that in addition to the difficulty of quickly implementing significant changes, to do so in response to one or a few breakaway franchisees could be more damaging to the system than the loss of those franchisees. The franchisor's problem is magnified when the breakaway franchisee is a successful and respected franchisee, since that type of franchisee has a greater likelihood of attracting the support of others to his or her cause.

How can franchisors deal with the breakaway franchisee problem? Historically, the principal efforts of franchisors have been focused on contract enforcement. Control of the franchisee's business premises, generally by means of lease-sublease arrangements, gives the franchisor effective control. Franchisees are not likely to remove their business from the system if the location of the business is a significant factor in its profitability and the franchisee cannot effectively shift the business to an alternate location. Assuming appropriate consideration of federal bankruptcy law, proper drafting of franchising agreements and subleases (or lease assignments), and observance of state law requirements for recording interests in real property, termination of the franchise will usually constitute a termination of the franchisee's sublease (or enable the franchisor to exercise a conditional lease assignment), leaving the franchisee in the unenviable position of forfeiting leasehold improvements and having the obligation to remove equipment, fixtures, furnishings, and inventory that will have little resale value, or negotiating the best deal with the franchisor or the successor franchisee.

Franchisors who have been financially unable to control the business premises of their franchisees have generally used post-termination restrictions on competition, collateral lease assignments, liquidated damages, options to buy the franchisee's business or specific assets, rights to an assignment of telephone numbers used by the franchisee's business, restrictions on use of trade secrets and confidential information, and de-identification requirements. All of these rights and obligations generally are enforceable to some extent (though not necessarily to the extent that franchisors would deem effective) when a franchisee has unilaterally terminated the franchise without good cause.

Covenants Not to Compete. Restrictions against competition by franchisees with their own franchised outlet or with outlets operated by the franchisor or other franchisees are relatively common in franchising agreements. These restrictions are generally deemed lawful under federal antitrust law, but face greater difficulties under state law. In some states, they may be enforceable only by a buyer of a business against the seller or under other limited circumstances. In a few other states, courts may enforce restrictions against competition merely by requiring limited de-identification and insignificant changes in products or services sold by the former franchisee.

Nevertheless, in most states, restrictions against competition are generally valid and enforceable under state law if the restrictions imposed are reasonable. What is deemed reasonable will vary with the facts of each situation, the applicable state law, and the nature of the claim asserted. A court being asked to enforce a non-compete restriction will typically determine first whether the franchisor is seeking to protect a legitimate interest, and second, whether the restriction is appropriately limited with respect to the scope of the business interests and activities prohibited, duration of the restriction, and geographic area of the restriction. This analysis requires a factual evaluation of the nature of the franchised business, the necessity of a ban on competition, the scope of the market in which the franchisee has operated, and what confidential information the franchisee has received. Generally, courts are willing to enforce much broader restrictions in an in-term situation — that is, during the term of the franchising agreement when the franchisee is continuing to operate the franchise — than in a post-term situation where both the franchising agreement and the franchising relationship have been terminated.

Geographic Scope. Many in-term non-competition restrictions (covenants not to compete) contain no territorial limitations whatsoever. While the rules regarding geographically unlimited covenants not to compete vary by state, there are a few states, such as Georgia, whose courts have held that a covenant not to compete is invalid if not limited as to time and geography. Other states are more willing to allow a trial court to modify a restrictive provision which is merely overbroad as to geographical scope, reducing its scope to make it reasonable. When a court makes that type of modification, it is said to have **blue-penciled** the original contract to make it reasonable.

A good example of blue penciling is found in the case of *Armstrong v. Taco Time International* (Wash. Ct. App. 1981), in which a court reduced the duration of a post-term covenant not to compete from five years to two and a half years and changed the geographic area in which it would be enforced from the continental United States to a 50-mile radius around the franchisee's location and that of other franchisees. In *Westbury Donuts, Inc. v. Dunkin' Donuts of America, Inc.* (D.C.N.Y. 1983), a federal district court upheld an in-term covenant which contained no geographical limitations. The court did note that the franchisee made no attempt to hide the existence of his competing donut shop; in fact, he advertised his "Donut Queen" shop in his franchised Dunkin' Donuts shop.

One court explicitly recognized the different purposes of in-term and post-term restrictions:

> The post-term covenant is designed to prevent direct competition and loss of goodwill; the in-term covenant is designed to guard against the unauthorized use of confidential information. Although the purposes of the post-term covenant can be fulfilled with a relatively narrow territory restriction, if there is any breach of an in-term covenant, the unauthorized use of confidential information may well injure [a franchisor] over a broader geographic area.

In a January 4, 1982, opinion, the Michigan Attorney General stated that a franchisor may terminate a franchisee's franchising agreement if the franchisee violates an in-term covenant by opening a similar business during the life of the franchise and fails to promptly cure the breach of its covenant. Despite the fact that post-term covenants not to compete were then prohibited by Michigan statute as against public policy, the Attorney General stated that in the absence of clear legislative language prohibiting an in-term covenant, there is no reason why a franchisor may not require prospective franchisees to bind themselves to devote full attention to the operation of a franchise. The opinion goes on to state that, if a franchisee finds such a covenant to be a burden, "he is free to decline entering into the franchise agreement."

To be effective in dealing with the breakaway franchisee, a covenant not to compete, whether in-term or post-term, need not be geographically expansive. If franchisees can be barred from continuing to conduct business within the same metropolitan area, or even within a smaller submarket of it, they may be effectively prevented from taking their business out of the franchisor's system. In-term covenants have other purposes, such as protecting confidential information and preventing a franchisee from using the benefits of the franchise in operating other businesses for which no fee is paid to the franchisor. Such purposes may dictate use of a geographically broader covenant. However, the applicable court decisions suggest that adoption of a geographically limited covenant is more likely to be enforceable and will therefore have greater deterrent effect. A franchisor should carefully analyze the principal purposes of in-term and post-term covenants for its system and tailor its restrictions accordingly.

Duration. By definition, an in-term covenant exists during the entire term of the franchising relationship. In most states, a post-term covenant is unlikely to be enforceable for more than two or three years after the franchising agreement expires or is terminated, unless the franchisor has purchased the franchisee's business and the purchase has included some payment for goodwill or "going-concern" value.

Scope of the Prohibited Activity. Finally, in order to be enforceable, a covenant not to compete should not be too broad in the activities it attempts to restrict. For example, a hamburger franchisor's restriction against competing in the fast-food hamburger business is more likely to be enforced than a restriction against operating any fast-food business, and a restriction against operating another fast-food restaurant generally is more likely to be enforced than a restriction against being in *any* restaurant business.

Options to Buy the Franchisee's Business. Options to buy the franchisee's business are sometimes used as a fall-back enforcement device in case a covenant not to compete is unenforceable or of little practical benefit to the franchisor. Though exercise of an option to buy the franchisee's business may be practical in some franchised businesses, it generally would be impractical if the franchisees' business is personal service, which requires regular contact with their principal customers, and it would be difficult for the franchisor itself or a new franchisee to step into the business and operate it as profitably as the former franchisee did. Thus, though generally enforceable if the purchase formula is fair, a purchase option may confront the franchisor with two unappealing choices: permit the franchisees to take their business out of the system or incur an unanticipated and possibly undesirable investment in a business the franchisor does not wish to operate and may find difficult to quickly resell.

Franchisee's Obligation to Pay to Terminate Franchise. The converse of the franchisor's option to buy the franchisee's business is a provision in the franchising agreement obligating unilaterally terminating franchisees to, in effect, buy their way out of the franchising agreements, as a tenant may pay to cancel a lease. Though an obligation to buy out of the franchise may not dissuade all disaffected franchisees from unilaterally terminating, it will constitute some deterrent and will also afford the franchisor some financial protection. Keep in mind, however, that ascribing a "value" to the franchisee and allowing a franchisee to buy his or her way out of the contract may adversely affect the franchisor's right to protect confidential information. It will usually be preferable for the franchisor to have the money than to have an unhappy franchisee who has the potential to disrupt the system and infect other franchisees with the breakaway virus. Determination of a reasonable buy-out price is extremely difficult. Since this provision will be subjected to judicial analysis as either an enforceable contract provision providing for liquidated damages (an integral part of the franchising relationship) or an unenforceable penalty, the desire of the franchisor to make the price high enough to constitute a deterrent or produce substantial revenue will inevitably conflict with the lawyer's advice to avoid making the payment so high that it clearly appears to be a penalty. (Penalties for breach of a contract are not enforceable.)

Damages and Liquidated Damages. Franchisors have other legal remedies when a franchisee unilaterally terminates the franchise. Though few (if any) franchisors have been able to convince a court to require the franchisees to maintain the business within the franchise system if they do not want to, several courts and arbitrators have required breakaway franchisees to pay substantial damages for breaching their franchising agreements. Damage theories have included loss of revenue to the franchisor and expenses for re-establishing the system in the affected market.

The uncertainties inherent in proving damages caused by a breakaway franchisee suggest that it might be a good idea for a franchisor to include in a franchising agreement a provision for liquidated damages if the franchisee unilaterally terminates. If the agreement affords the franchisees an opportunity to buy out of their obligations under the franchise, liquidated damages for unilateral termination by a franchisee might be set higher than the buy-out price in order to encourage the franchisee to comply with the prescribed method for unilateral franchise termination (that is, prescribed advance notice and refraining from conspiring with other franchisees to exercise their buy-out options). In evaluating the reasonableness of a liquidated damages provision, a court would presumably be less sympathetic to a franchisee who ignored an opportunity to buy his freedom and then challenges the reasonableness of a higher liquidated-damage obligation. As mentioned earlier, however, care must be exercised to avoid imposing an unenforceable penalty.

Planning to Avoid Breakaway Franchisees

The second approach to the breakaway franchisee problem, more evident in recent years, is advance planning to avoid the breakaway-franchisee syndrome. Recognizing franchisee perception of the burden of constantly increasing royalty and advertising contributions, the declining need by successful franchisees for franchisor support and assistance programs, and other tensions of the franchising relationship that must inevitably result in wanderlust on the part of a certain percentage of franchisees, some franchisors are experimenting with such concepts as decelerating royalty percentages, lower fees and advertising obligations for multiple-outlet franchisees, and greater flexibility in applying restrictions on outside business interests of franchisees. Franchisors are also paying greater attention to those elements of the franchise system that franchisees will perceive as a significant loss if they disaffiliate. In addition to the obvious services of effective advertising and a strong trademark, franchisors are considering such services as improved procurement programs; research and development; franchisor-sponsored warranty programs; accounting, data processing, comparative statistical information and insurance packages; and other authorized products and services.

Also significant in the view of some franchisors is involvement of franchisees in developing and implementing such programs. This is being done through franchisee associations and franchise advisory councils. Greater franchisee involvement in the evolution of the franchise system, though not without tension and pitfalls when the franchisor rejects franchisee advice, is viewed by some franchisors as a significant factor in maintaining continued motivation of franchisees. Franchisee involvement in planning and operations of a franchise system, and generally good communications with franchisees, can produce early warnings of problems that can ultimately result in the breakaway disease.

Notwithstanding all of the efforts discussed above, some franchisors recognize that there will always be breakaway franchisees. There is considerable variation, however, in deciding what to do about it. Some franchisors have adopted the position that any franchisee who wants out of the system should be allowed to leave. Some companies actually provide for that option in their franchising agreements. Others have decided that the likelihood of counterclaims and expensive and disruptive litigation makes it a mistake to enforce their franchising agreements against unilaterally terminating franchisees. Those franchisors have come to believe that they are better off removing a disenchanted franchisee from the system. Some also believe that the optimum (and most effectively enforceable) approach to resolving the problem of the breakaway franchisee is to acknowledge the possibility of unilateral termination by the franchisee and to establish a fair method for disassociation, to be agreed upon in advance.

There is no best approach to the breakaway-franchisee syndrome. Several approaches may be valid, and frequently a combination of solutions is appropriate for a given franchisor. It is clear that there is no simple or easy solution to this problem. To a large extent, the breakaway-franchisee phenomenon is a natural outgrowth of a successful franchise system, which is composed of both a successful franchisor and successful franchisees. While both are struggling against competitors, their common goals and objectives hold the system together. As the system achieves varying levels of success, the earlier bonds begin to weaken. As a result, the breakaway franchisee may be a business and legal problem for franchisors for many years.

DISPUTE RESOLUTION

We have stated that there are bound to be problems in virtually any franchise system. The wise franchisor, who is usually the successful franchisor, will attempt to alleviate problematic conditions or, when a serious difficulty arises, find a quick and relatively painless solution.

Review and Mediation

As noted in this and previous chapters, a common denominator of the problems discussed is their potential to lead to litigation. There is one additional "problem" that arises before litigation begins between franchisors and their franchisees: the failure to resolve disputes by other means. Alternative means have been suggested in this chapter, including a transfer of the franchisee's business and franchise and a plan to anticipate and resolve problems. The effectiveness of these dispute-resolution approaches may depend in part upon the manner in which a franchisor confronts and deals with disputes. If the franchisor approaches every infraction of its rules, and every franchisee objection to a policy, action, or inaction of the franchisor, as a disrespectful challenge to its authority, the franchisor may generate a great deal of litigation and will be less likely to detect fundamental problems when they are small and more easily addressed. At the opposite end of the spectrum is the franchisor that establishes internal review and "mediation" procedures and resorts to litigation only after all other avenues to resolution, including franchisor concessions, are thoroughly explored. This franchisor may detect more problems in their early stages of development and so may avoid litigation, but it may also come to be perceived as weak and indecisive and ultimately lose the respect of its franchisees and the control of its system.

A middle ground can achieve much "litigation avoidance" without loss of control. The establishment of procedures for senior management review of disputes and for mediation of certain kinds of disputes — for example, a disagreement between a franchisor's field representative and a franchisee about whether the franchisee is complying with standards and procedures — is beneficial. Review and mediation can take a variety of forms, from formal to informal. They are usually carried out in informal meetings in which senior management of both the franchisor and the franchisee review information presented by their respective field personnel. More significant than the degree of formality is the degree of fairness perceived by franchisees. If franchisees view the review and mediation program as a stacked deck, these programs will not contribute significantly to dispute resolution and litigation avoidance. If franchisees think that they can obtain a reasonably objective hearing, they are more likely to acquiesce in the result. It should be noted, however, that franchisees do not usually think that the franchisor's management can be completely objective.

Although it is rarely done, franchisors may want to seriously consider hiring persons outside their management to review or mediate disputes with their franchisees. This approach has the advantage of creating greater objectivity, and the disadvantage that it may cause disagreements between the franchisor and the independent mediator, who may have differing opinions on standards and procedures that the franchisor regards as gospel. Review and mediation procedures are by nature voluntary and nonbinding upon franchisees. If franchisees are dissatisfied with the outcome, they can seek a better one in court.

Franchisor Assistance to Noncomplying Franchisees

Another way to help resolve disputes is for the franchisor to have a program to help franchisees comply with the obligations of the franchising agreement. The franchisor's approach to dispute resolution will be judged in part by its willingness to assist franchisees whose problems are the result of competitive market conditions, poor location selection, high interest rates, general economic recession, and other causes beyond the franchisee's control. Furthermore, even where noncomplying franchisees are uncooperative, obstinate, and not achieving the potential of the franchise, and even if the franchisor's efforts to assist the franchisees in complying with their obligations are likely to be ineffective, making an effort to help can at least help to influence a judge or jury if the dispute later ends up in court.

Litigation Evaluation

At the same time that a franchisor is trying to resolve a dispute without litigation, it should carefully and thoroughly review its litigation position and undertake a cost/benefit analysis of the anticipated litigation. Review of the franchisor's litigation position should include analysis of all potential franchisee counterclaims; the state of the franchisor's file on the franchisee; the testimony that will be given by current and former franchisor employees, the franchisee, and other franchisees who may be called as witnesses by the franchisor or the franchisee; the extent to which litigation may raise issues regarding the franchisor's enforcement of its franchising agreements generally; the place where the dispute is likely to be litigated (hometown advantage or disadvantage); whether a preliminary injunction is likely to be sought by either party and the probability of its being granted; the goals of the franchisor in the litigation and the extent to which they are likely to be realized; the importance to the franchisor of demonstrating its tenacity in enforcing franchising agreement obligations; the extent to which a victory or loss is a beneficial or detrimental example that could affect other disputes; and the likely impact of the litigation on attitudes and behavior of other franchisees.

Litigation Versus Arbitration

Discussion of all the relative advantages and disadvantages of litigation and arbitration is beyond the scope of this chapter. Briefly, the proponents of arbitration assert that it is faster, cheaper, and less acrimonious than litigation; that arbitrators are more likely than judges to understand the franchising relationship; that it enables the franchisor to conduct dispute resolution in its home city; that for the franchisor, arbitration is a safer method for deciding claims of disclosure law violation or fraud; and that loss of an arbitration proceeding does not establish a harmful precedent. Advocates of litigation disagree with most of these claims and say that limited procedural techniques available to gather information and the tendency of arbitrators to make Solomon-like compromises make arbitration an uncertain process of compromising positions; that unavailability of appeal leaves the franchisor vulnerable to the decision of an incompetent or lazy arbitrator; and that arbitration eliminates the possibility of a quick and decisive reaction to the other party's breach of contract (e.g., filing a court action for a preliminary injunction against some type of franchisee behavior).

There is merit to all of the arguments on both sides of the litigation-versus-arbitration debate. Neither method of deciding disputes is clearly better than the other in all circumstances. For the small franchisor struggling to establish itself, however, arbitration may on balance be the better method. The costs of litigation are so high that the small franchisor may simply be unable to afford to use the courts to enforce its franchising agreements. If a franchisor opts for arbitration as a mandatory method of adjudication, it is taking some risk and may well experience unsatisfactory results in one or more arbitrations. However, if it chooses and pre-

Chapter 21   Breakaway Franchisees and Noncompliance   545

pares its enforcement actions carefully, the advantages of arbitration — primarily quick and relatively inexpensive disposition of the dispute in the franchisor's home city — should on balance outweigh the disadvantages.

SUCCESS STORY
IRL H. MARSHALL

Irl Marshall first joined Duraclean in 1949, and he has served in every department of the corporation. Duraclean International, headquartered in Deerfield, Illinois, is a franchise organization of professional on-location cleaning specialists throughout the world who clean homes, offices, and businesses with Duraclean's unique foam absorption cleaning system, plus ten related fabric care and damage restoration services.

From 1949 to 1961, Marshall was responsible for establishing the Duraclean Training Center, annual convention, regional dealer meetings, research and development laboratory, and monthly house organ, the *Duraclean Journal*.

In 1961, he left Duraclean to spend 16 years with Montgomery Ward in Chicago, where he held various executive positions. During this period he also found the time to earn an MBA from the University of Chicago, in 1968. After returning to Duraclean in 1977, Marshall became the motivating force behind the development of a new line of patented *Extractovator* and *Fabricrafter* cleaning machines and proprietary cleaning formulations.

A founding director of the International Franchise Association in 1960, he drafted the first IFA Code of Ethics. Since returning to Duraclean, he has again been made a director of IFA and has been president of the association. He also serves as a director of the First National Bank of Deerfield and is a member of the Chicago Crime Commission and Economics Club of Chicago.

Photo and information provided courtesy of Irl H. Marshall, August, 1985.

SUMMARY

Chapters 20 and 21 have dealt with a wide variety of problems encountered in the franchising relationship and have presented various solutions to those problems. As can be seen, there typically is not just one right approach or answer. Two common threads found in most of the problem areas are (1) failure to detect and react to problems when they first arise and are relatively easy to resolve and (2) failure to maintain effective communications with franchisees. Failure to detect and react to problems is largely a reflection of human nature and is a common phenomenon in the business world. Failure to maintain effective communications with franchisees may result from an attitude that franchisees are the enemy, or that franchisees have no meaningful contribution to make to the system, or simply from a failure to use franchisees as a resource in developing the franchise system. Experienced and successful franchisors know that franchisees are the source of much of the innovation and dynamism in a franchise system and are a source of ideas and opinions that a franchisor cannot afford to ignore. To minimize and deal effectively with problems, a franchisor must communicate with its franchisees individually, through an advisory council or franchisee association. Problem solving begins with an understanding of the franchisees' perceptions of the system. Without that knowledge, the franchisor is blind; with it, the franchisor can address the real problems and respond to the real concerns and objections of its franchisees.

REVIEW QUESTIONS

1. Discuss the main reasons and causes for breakaway franchisees.
2. How should a franchisor deal with breakaway franchisees?
3. What are the advantages and disadvantages of covenants not to compete?
4. What options are available to the franchisor in dealing with a breakaway franchisee?
5. How might a franchisor develop a dispute resolution program for franchisees?

CASE STUDY
POPEYES FAMOUS FRIED CHICKEN AND BISCUITS*

In 1972, Al Copeland, founder of Popeyes Famous Fried Chicken and Biscuits, developed his special recipe to appeal to his hometown's love of

---

*Information provided courtesy of Popeyes Famous Fried Chicken and Biscuits, December, 1987.

highly seasoned food, a happy marriage of Creole and Cajun wonders from Louisiana's winding bayous. When the spicy-chicken craze swept the fast-food industry nationwide, Popeyes was catapulted into the number-one spot as the country's largest privately held chicken chain.

Copeland's original objective was to put food on the table for his family. Just 15 years after opening the first Popeyes, A. Copeland Enterprises puts it on the table for almost 3,000 parent-company employees and 13,000 franchised operation employees worldwide. It all started with a few borrowed dollars, one small restaurant, and a man whose burning ambition was to "get out of the trap," as Al Copeland puts it.

Popeyes Famous Fried Chicken and Biscuits achieved a sales total of $400 million in 1988. Serving over two million meals per week at over 700 restaurants in operation in the United States and several foreign countries, Popeyes easily outdistances the entire chicken industry in sales per square foot of any type of restaurant.

Copeland, chairman of the board, is a strong believer in using as incentives the very things he values himself. He rewards his key management staff with opportunities to be in business for themselves. This is probably one of the biggest carrots in the climb to the top at Popeyes. He makes it possible for them to buy their own franchises.

The Popeyes organization is very concerned about recruiting and keeping the best franchisees. To maximize management, advertising, and market penetration, Popeyes operates under the "multiple-unit concept" only. The minimum number of units allowed multiple-unit franchisees is five under a predetermined time schedule within an area described in their franchising agreement. The fees required consist of an option fee of $10,000 and a franchising fee of $15,000 for the first unit opened. Each additional unit also has a $15,000 franchising fee. The estimated initial investment by franchisee per unit requires approximately $194,200 to $243,000, excluding building and land. The typical building site requires 20,000 to 30,000 square feet, with the actual building using 1,800 to 2,800 square feet. Total site development costs often range from $350,000 to $550,000.

Breakaway or noncompliant franchisees have not been a problem for Popeyes. However, the corporation is aware that this possibility does exist in an operation of its size and has investigated the causes that could precipitate problems. In its concern for continued good franchisee relations, Popeyes has developed steps and grievance procedures that will help to handle difficulties and prevent problems.

CASE QUESTIONS

1. What program should Popeyes develop to handle breakaway franchisees?

2. Should Popeyes use a covenant not to compete in its franchising agreement?
3. What grievance or dispute resolutions procedures should Popeyes use?
4. What steps might Popeyes take in the case of a breakaway franchisee?
5. Should Popeyes go to litigation or arbitration to resolve breakaway disputes?

CHAPTER 22
INTERNATIONAL FRANCHISING

In studying this chapter, you will:
- Learn about how to start franchising internationally.
- Know about the different levels of growth of franchising in foreign countries.
- Be able to understand those steps and considerations necessary to engage in international franchising and the different ways of accomplishing them.
- Understand the hindrances associated with franchising in international marketplaces.
- Get an idea of what the future will hold for franchising.

INCIDENT

Kunio Morita is interested in becoming a franchisee of an American-based franchise company in Japan. Kunio spent two years studying at the University of Southern California before returning to his homeland. During his time in the United States, Kunio became aware of the large role franchising plays in the U.S. economy. He wrote to several U.S. franchisors who he believed had product/services that would be appropriate and successful in his native country. Through the correspondence and literature supplied, he has learned that most U.S. franchisors who operate on an international basis do so by utilizing a conglomerate organizational structure within the host country. Thus, Kunio believes his best approach would be to contact a local corporation handling the franchise that he desires to open.

Kunio is interested primarily in becoming a fast-food restaurateur in Japan. There are many fast-food restaurants in Japan, and Kunio knows they are expensive to start. Through friends and relatives, however, he would be able to raise approximately $112,000. This would enable him to open a small restaurant or food-service business, because in Japan, such businesses are generally only half the size of those in the United States.

Some of the most attractive points of owning and operating a franchise in Japan are the advertising, marketing, and promotional packages that have been developed by the franchisors. The franchisor will also help him in the selection of the site and the layout of the store. In addition, two to six weeks' training would be provided. Quality control and proper franchisee performance are closely monitored in the Japanese firms. Kunio believes he would be a big success if he could just get the store open and operating properly.

INTRODUCTION

American franchisors generally consider their market to be consumers living in the United States. The domestic market is so big that most franchisors see little if any reason to export or go elsewhere to improve their profits or business. It is both simpler and safer to develop the U.S. market and advertise to the American consumer. This eliminates the need to learn a foreign language, become accustomed to foreign laws and regulations, handle foreign currency, experience legal and political uncertainties, or even adapt the product to local cultures and conditions. There are, however, two good reasons why a franchisor may become involved with international marketing. First, franchisors may be pushed into foreign markets because of the lack of expansion opportunities in the United States; they may have already exhausted all the available territories and major marketing areas. Second, the franchisor may be pulled into the foreign market by growing opportunities and demand for the product abroad. Coca-Cola and Chrysler, both major franchising companies, earn more than half their profits in foreign markets. Other companies find that foreign operations may grow faster than domestic fields.

Coca-Cola has been able to overcome the difficulties of foreign laws, trademark infringements, foreign exchange, different languages, and different cultures to become one of the largest international franchisors in the world. The company has had its share of difficulties, however. After it had entered the Chinese market in 1982, it found that one translation of its trademark, "Coca-Cola," was "backbite the wax tadpole." After some professional advice, the Chinese characters which Coca-Cola currently uses translate as "permit the mouth to rejoice."

THE INTERNATIONAL MARKETPLACE

The decision to sell in foreign markets requires that a franchisor learn many new aspects of business. The company needs to develop a thorough understanding of international commerce, trade laws, economic considerations, political environments, and markets. A 1985 survey conducted by the International Franchise Association (IFA) reported that "46 percent of responding members are currently franchising internationally, while an additional 34 percent plan to within the next five years."[1] This survey indicated a continual growth in international franchising. International sales have also increased from 25 to 250 percent over the last five years with no respondents reporting a decrease.[2]

The international trade environment has changed significantly during the past decade. Japan has emerged as the leading economic power in world markets. The international financial system has developed a strong currency exchange and has improved currency convertibility. The United States has fallen into an unfavorable balance of trade and has seen its dominant position in world markets erode. Major oil-producing countries have emerged as economic powers and important investors in international trade. New markets have gradually opened in China, the oil-rich Arab countries and, to a limited extent, the Soviet Union.

Canada, Japan, Australia, and the United Kingdom are today the most popular countries for American international franchise expansion. These are closely followed by France, West Germany, Singapore, and Malaysia as markets most often targeted by franchise developers.

The increase of franchising in international markets is due to several important economic and demographic trends in foreign countries: (1) increased disposable income, (2) rising educational levels, (3) universal cultural trends, (4) increasing number of women in the working force, (5) shorter work weeks, (6) younger generations willing to try new products, (7) demographic concentrations of people in urban areas, and (8) smaller families with two or more incomes. Kentucky Fried Chicken anticipates increased growth in international markets especially because of the growing numbers of working women and the increase in available disposable income. It seeks to expand into countries with these characteristics.

Holiday Corporation, the world's largest hotel chain, plans to triple its European holdings within the next ten years. It also plans to expand into Asia with emphasis on China, Japan, and Australia as the

---

[1] *Franchising World*, International Franchise Association, Washington, DC, Vol. 17, No. 4 (Fall 1985), p. 4.
[2] *Franchising World*, International Franchise Association, Washington, DC, Vol. 17, No. 4 (Fall 1985), p. 4.

biggest potential tourist markets. It is expected that two-thirds of the Holiday Inns will be franchised. Holiday Corporation is the parent holding company for Holiday Inns, Embassy Suite, Granada Royale, Hampton Inns, Holiday Inn Crown Plazas, Residence Inns, and Harrah's (Casino hotels).[3]

Legal and Trade Restrictions

A franchisor seeking to develop markets in foreign countries needs to be aware of the various restrictions of world trade. Tariffs — taxes levied by a government against specific imported products — are the most common restrictions in international trade. Tariffs may be based on a product's value, weight, or volume. They are generally designed to raise taxes for government (revenue tariff) or to protect domestic products or firms (protective tariff). An additional trade restriction facing exporters is the quota — a limit on the amount of goods that the importing country will allow into that company in specific business classifications. Quotas are also designed to protect domestic industry, prices, and employment, as well as to maintain a favorable trade balance. Another trade restriction, the embargo, simply bans all products in a prescribed classification.

A major problem that many franchisors will also face is an exchange control, which regulates the currency exchange between countries. An exchange control limits the amount of foreign exchange available and regulates its exchange rate against other currencies. A franchisor may find it difficult, if not impossible, to return profits to the home country. In addition, American franchisors may face nontariff barriers such as discrimination against American products or prices. Some governments even establish quality standards or standards of operation which discriminate specifically against American products.

Economic Considerations

There are three major characteristics which a franchisor must analyze before investing in a business in a foreign country. These include the country's distribution of income, its industrial structure, and its political and legal environment. The distribution of income may be categorized into six different types:

1. Variable family incomes
2. Mostly low family incomes
3. Very low or very high family incomes
4. Low, medium, and high family incomes
5. Mostly medium family incomes
6. Mostly high family incomes

---

[3] *Franchise Review*, International Franchising, South Melbourne, Victoria, Australia (January/March 1986), p. 2.

It would be difficult for General Motors or Ford Motor to sell Cadillacs or Continentals or other luxury cars in countries within income distribution type one or two. Most restaurant franchisors would primarily be interested in the income distribution types three through six.

The country's industrial structure is a very important indicator of its economic strength and growth potential. The industrial structure may be broken down into three common classifications:

1. Developed, industrialized nations
2. Developing, emerging, industrializing nations
3. Nondeveloped, nonindustrialized nations

In the nondeveloped, nonindustrialized nations, most of the population is engaged in simple agricultural production. The people consume a great deal of their own output and exchange or barter the rest for other services or goods. These nations provide little real opportunity for franchised operations. On the other hand, both the developed, industrialized nations and the developing, emerging nations provide strong opportunities for franchised outlets. Coca-Cola, Kentucky Fried Chicken, and Hertz have all sold franchises in European, South American, and Pacific Rim countries.

Political and Legal Environment

The franchisor, before beginning to invest in foreign operations, should investigate many aspects of foreign markets, among which would be political stability, monetary controls, and government regulations.

It is very important for a franchisor to gauge the political stability in the prospective host country. Many governments change hands every four to ten years. It is important to realize that one regime that allows a franchisor access to the country's market may be replaced by a government that is opposed to the franchisor's business or methods. The franchisor should also be aware of the monetary controls a country places on its currency. A fluctuating exchange rate offers monetary instability. Some countries may have very restrictive exchange controls that make it very difficult for the franchisee to remit payment to the franchisor or to send profits from the foreign country back to the home office.

Government regulations and bureaucracy are also very prevalent in foreign markets. While unacceptable by American business standards, many foreign officials expect a suitable payment (consulting fee) to be made by franchisors expanding into their countries. One common method to circumvent government restrictions for at least a limited time is to use members of the ruling party as franchisees in a particular country.

Additionally, it is important to understand how generally receptive foreign countries are to having franchised businesses operate within their countries. Many countries, Mexico included, provide investment incentives, site location services, and favorable currency exchanges to attract foreign businesses to their country. Other countries establish import quotas, currency controls, and requirements that a high percentage of the management team be citizens. These kinds of restrictions often cause franchisors to leave countries even after they have already become established.

INTERNATIONAL MARKETING DECISION

Before the final decision is made to enter foreign markets, it is important that an analysis of different countries and markets be completed. The franchisor must determine if marketing opportunities in other countries are strong enough to allow entry into the international franchising field. The decision to start international franchising should include five major steps. We discuss the steps in this section.

Appraising and Deciding to Franchise Internationally

A growing number of franchisors are making the decision to take advantage of the opportunities of expanding their systems outside the United States. While the expansion into international markets does demand extra preparation and effort by the franchisor, the rewards are often substantial, especially when the franchisor is able to gain a dominant position in the foreign market. The franchisor must consider the practical financial and profit issues before entering the foreign market. It must analyze and appraise the profitability and longevity of a foreign market. The distance required to deliver product and services may be prohibitive, or the language and cultural differences may adversely affect operations. The franchisor should seek advice about the receptivity of the foreign market to the product or service. It is best that the product or service be test-marketed in the foreign country before formal development of a franchising system in that market. Many foreign countries also have legal limitations on the form of investment and technology transfer allowable in those countries.

Before entering any foreign market, the franchisor needs to appraise the opportunity of securing trademark registration and of dealing with reputable and competent companies or individuals, and it should review and be able to understand all applicable foreign laws. The franchisor may determine that it would be impossible to enter a particular foreign market simply because the host country is unwilling to comply with international trademark laws or because competent and reliable franchisees would be too difficult to find.

Which Countries to Enter

The franchisor must determine the suitability and compatibility of any country or market into which the franchisor would expand. The country should be analyzed for economic stability, political and legal environment, stage of economic development, and target market demand. In addition, it would be appropriate to analyze and estimate (1) current market potential, (2) sales potential, (3) future market, (4) expense and cost estimates, (5) profit potential, and (6) potential return on investment.

Each country should be analyzed in terms of its economic and market potential. It may be easiest to begin with English-speaking countries, most of which have common cultures, language, and somewhat similar consumer preferences. However, it is also important to realize that even countries that share a language have unique cultures and may have different market demands for specific products. (See Table 22-1.) It would be appropriate to perform marketing research in the preferred countries to determine possible market demand and sales potential. The countries should be ranked according to their market potential, market growth, potential profit, cost of doing business, risk level, and cooperative attitude.

How to Start

Once the franchisor has decided which country to enter (and it should only enter one at a time), it must decide the best mode of starting a business in that country. There are five major starting strategies, as shown in Figure 22-1: (1) establishing a master franchisee, (2) joint venture (doing business with foreign companies or individuals), (3) licensing, (4) direct investment, and (5) exporting (producing at home and selling abroad). Each of these strategies has different costs, risks, commitments, and profits associated with it.

Master Franchisee. The master franchisee may be an individual, a small business, or a large corporation which assumes the rights and obligations of establishing franchises throughout the country. The franchisee is taught all the operations and developments in the business by the franchisor. Normally the franchisee starts one or two stores during the first year and expands to 25 to 30 stores within five or ten years. Master franchisees may choose either to engage subfranchisees or to open all stores themselves.

The master franchisee in a foreign country assumes the role of franchisor. Royalty fees are generally paid by each subfranchisee through the master franchisees; the master franchisees keep up to 50 percent of these royalty payments and submit the other 50 percent back to the headquarters operation. Almost all advertising fees are also paid

Table 22-1
International Franchising: 1985[1] — Location of Establishments

Type of Franchised Business[2]	Total	Canada	Mexico	Caribbean	Europe United Kingdom	Europe Other	Australia	Japan	Asia Other	Other[3]
TOTAL - ALL FRANCHISING	30,188	9,054	542	803	2,291	4,398	2,511	7,124	1,755	1,710
Business Aids and Services	3,905	1,279	15	15	426	547	475	936	65	147
Construction, Home Improvement, Maintenance, and Cleaning Services	1,693	695	1	23	193	227	17	471	31	35
Restaurants (All Types)	6,122	1,542	119	312	615	539	635	1,436	499	425
Hotels, Motels, and Campgrounds	515	276	31	18	28	61	13	9	40	39
Recreation, Entertainment, and Travel	177	66	0	6	5	27	30	32	0	11
Rental Services (Auto-Truck)	5,758	714	230	263	361	1,798	587	512	427	866
Laundry and Drycleaning Services	132	112	0	9	1	10	0	0	0	0
Automotive Products and Services	2,203	1,045	27	41	124	457	176	122	101	110
Retailing (Non-Food)	3,510	1,599	62	19	475	582	448	181	81	63
Educational Products and Services, Rental Services (Equipment), Convenience Stores, and Miscellaneous	4,033	767	50	8	25	115	115	2,659	288	6
Retailing (Food Other Than Convenience Stores)	2,140	959	7	89	38	35	15	766	223	8

[1] Represents 342 franchisors.
[2] Does not include automobile and truck dealers, gasoline service stations, and soft drink bottlers, for which data was not collected.
[3] Includes South America (515), Africa (626), New Zealand (402), and Central America (167).

Source: Andrew Kostecka, *Franchising in the Economy, 1985-1987*, U.S. Department of Commerce, International Trade Administration (Washington, DC: U.S. Government Printing Office, January 1987), p. 45.

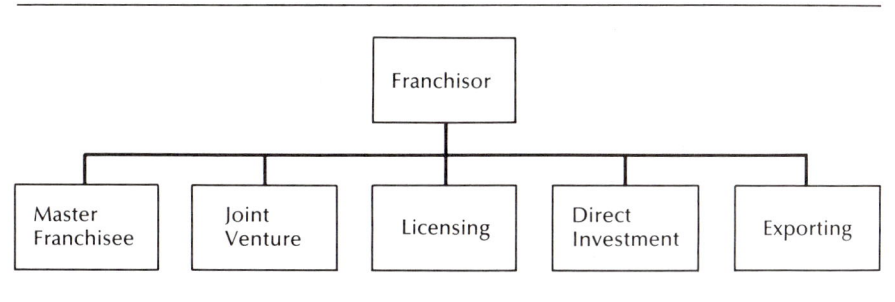

**Figure 22-1
Franchisor Starting Strategies**

Franchisor → Master Franchisee, Joint Venture, Licensing, Direct Investment, Exporting

directly to the master franchisee, who then uses them for local (or national) advertising.

Regarding the use of master franchisees, the IFA survey reports: "Master franchising is the method used by 57 percent of responding members franchising internationally.... Individual contracts (licenses) are used by 19 percent of respondents to the new survey, joint ventures by 12 percent and foreign subsidiaries (direct investment) by 6 percent. Of those responding, 66 percent have an international division in their corporate structure to oversee foreign franchise development."[4]

Joint Venturing. An often-used form of franchise investment in foreign countries is the joint venture. With this method, the franchisor joins with local citizens in setting up production and/or market locations. The advantage of joint ventures is that they lead to investment by both the franchisor and the franchisee in the foreign business operations. Joint ventures are generally established through (1) joint ownership ventures, (2) management contracting, and (3) contract manufacturing.

Many foreign countries require that the franchisor invest or buy interest in the local franchised unit before starting the business. This joint ownership venture pairs local investors with the franchisor in the creation of local businesses with shared ownership and control. McDonald's Corporation recently opened a joint venture restaurant in the popular Piazza di Spagna in Rome. Italy is the last of the large European markets McDonald's has entered, and the Rome location is a joint venture between Food Italia Spa and McDonald's. In late 1985, McDonald's also entered Mexico. In compliance with Mexican law, McDonald's owns 49 percent and a Mexican partner owns the remaining 51 percent. The

---

[4] *Franchising World*, International Franchise Association, Washington, DC, Vol. 17, No. 4 (Fall 1985), p. 4.

partner also received 12 months' training at Hamburger University at the McDonald's headquarters in suburban Chicago, Illinois.[5]

A second method of joint venturing is through management contracts by which the franchisor provides management know-how to the foreign company, which furnishes the necessary capital and obtains the necessary licenses and permits to start the business. The Hilton Hotel system uses management contracts to manage its hotels throughout the world. This method allows the franchisor a low-risk entry into foreign markets. An additional way of entering foreign markets is to contract manufacturing in the foreign countries. Most major automotive manufacturers have agreements with foreign countries and governments to allow the manufacturing and selling of their products in foreign markets.

Licensing. One of the most common methods of international franchising is for the franchisor (licensor) to enter into an agreement with a licensee (franchisee) and offer the right to use a product, good, service, trademark, trade secret, patent, or other valuable item in return for a royalty fee. The licensee gains the extra knowledge and capability of the franchisor and enables the franchisor to enter the market at little or no risk. Coca-Cola has entered most of its international markets by licensing bottlers (technically, franchising bottlers) throughout the world and providing the syrup necessary to produce the soft drink.

Direct Investment. The fourth method of entering foreign markets is direct investment, by which the franchisor simply invests in company-owned stores in foreign countries. This is a very high-risk way of entering foreign markets, however, and franchisors are well advised to avoid this method. But after several franchises have already been established, it may be appropriate for a franchisor to begin direct investment and establish company-owned stores. Direct ownership does show the country and its people the desire of the franchisor to invest in the country's growth and development. The franchisor maintains full control over the operation and management of the franchise. The major problem with this type of investment is the exposure of a large investor to many business and political risks. Currency controls, market changes, or even expropriation may cause the demise of these franchises in foreign countries.

Exporting. Many franchisors, including General Motors and Goodyear Tire and Rubber, enter foreign markets through exporting. They manufacture their products here in the United States and sell them through franchisees to customers in foreign countries. The foreign franchisee becomes the dealer or operator for the franchisor. The products may or may not be specially modified for the foreign market. This method

---

[5] *Franchise Review*, International Franchising, South Melbourne, Victoria, Australia (January/March 1986), p. 1.

of entering foreign markets is generally the least costly and requires the minimum change in the operation of the franchisor's company.

Franchise Program

Franchising organizations which operate in foreign countries must decide how much to change their franchising program, if at all, to adapt to conditions abroad. It is important when deciding how to franchise in foreign countries that the franchisor examine the product, promotion, price, and distribution system. The marketing plan must be carefully developed and adapted to local conditions.

Three major strategies may be used to sell products in a foreign market. The first strategy is **straight product utilization**, by which the franchisor offers the same product in the foreign market as in the domestic country. Before this is done, it is important that marketing research be performed to ascertain the attitudes of consumers toward the product. Generally, the Coca-Cola Company has been very successful in using this method to introduce its soft drink throughout the world; however, straight product utilization has failed for other companies, because many cultures simply do not use the same products that we do in the United States.

The second product strategy is called **product adaptation** and involves changing the product to meet local conditions and consumer demands. Many companies find it necessary to adapt their product to customer preference in order to ensure greater marketability and profitability for the franchising organization.

Harris Cooper, president, chairman, and CEO of International Dairy Queen, Inc., recalls starting a Dairy Queen franchise in Japan with a big grand opening and very favorable press coverage. Many Japanese came into the store and bought ice cream, but they were not returning to make repeat purchases. Market research indicated that nearly everyone enjoyed the ice cream, but it failed to reveal why customers were not coming back. Finally, after many visits, investigations, and transoceanic phone calls, Cooper suggested the employees look in the garbage cans, and there was the answer: The Japanese were not finishing the portions being offered. Nearly every dish had some ice cream left in it. The lesson: the Japanese eat smaller portions. The franchisee reduced the size of the serving and also cut the price proportionally. Dairy Queen is now quite successful in Japan. Many other franchised restaurants are also doing very well internationally. (See Table 22-2.)

Product invention is the third strategy, and as one might assume, it requires the creation of a new product. Many fast-food companies that enter foreign markets may add to their basic menu to include local food favorites. These foods may even become major items on the basic menu. For example, McDonald's in Hawaii serves a cup of saimin (noodle soup)

Table 22-2
International Restaurant Franchising in 1985: Location and Number of Establishments*

	Firms	Total	Canada	Mexico	Carib-bean	Europe United Kingdom	Europe Other	Australia	Asia Japan	Asia Other	South America	Africa	New Zealand	Central America
Chicken	8	1,878	11	65	144	371	62	247	540	187	13	183	45	10
Hamburgers, franks, and roast beef	13	3,251	1,146	4	98	236	462	223	754	212	52	2	21	41
Pizza	14	578	127	31	43	6	15	147	74	78	1	10	26	20
Mexican food	6	109	83	0	22	0	0	2	0	1	1	0	0	0
Seafood	3	13	6	0	0	0	0	0	0	7	0	0	0	0
Pancakes, waffles	2	15	3	0	0	0	0	0	12	0	0	0	0	0
Steak, full menu	13	271	161	19	4	2	0	16	56	13	0	0	0	0
Sandwich, other	2	7	5	0	1	0	0	0	0	1	0	0	0	0
Total	61	6,122	1,542	119	312	615	539	635	1,436	499	67	195	92	71

*Includes company-owned, franchisee-owned, and joint ventures.

Source: Andrew Kostecka, *Franchising in the Economy 1985-1987*, U.S. Department of Commerce, International Trade Administration (Washington, DC: U.S. Government Printing Office, January 1987), p. 76.

as part of the menu. Product invention is the most costly of all the basic strategies, but it may also provide the greatest appeal for the customers. Product invention is also generally adopted after a product has been used and it has been determined that the new product has increased sales and profits.

Promotion. Franchisors may continue to use their same promotional advertisements abroad or adapt them to the local market. What may be very appropriate in the home country may be offensive in the foreign country. Sometimes the advertisement can simply be translated into the foreign language, with new photographs depicting local citizens rather than Americans. Often, however, it may be best just to develop a different advertising or promotional program from the beginning, in order to be sure to reach the target audience in that country.

Price. Franchisors find it is often necessary to change pricing structure for foreign operations. The population may have lower incomes and lowering the price is necessary in order to sell the goods or services. The low price may also be required to build market share or simply to promote the product. Charging a lower price in a foreign country than that in the home country is referred to as "dumping." Some countries levy fines on companies that are dumping products (getting rid of excess production) into their country. Pricing decisions should be left with the local franchisee in accordance with the costs and profit motives of the company.

Channels of Distribution. Distribution begins at the organization headquarters, then moves to the channel between nations, and finally to the channel within a nation. All three channels are very important to ensure the successful distribution and availability of product in the foreign country. The headquarters organization is responsible for ensuring that a domestically manufactured or developed product makes it to the exporting dock in the franchisor's country. Those people involved with the channel between nations ensure that the products are shipped to overseas markets. The third link, or channel within a nation, sees to it that the product arrives at the retail outlet in a condition to be sold to consumers.

For many franchisors, the final channel, the one within a country, may be the only channel for the franchise system. This channel is activated when the product arrives in the foreign country and is distributed within that country. At this time, it is important and necessary that all people involved in delivering the product to the store are properly managed and supervised. In less developed countries, distributors and importers are very important and must be carefully sought out and enlisted. Many franchisors will be required to offer exclusive distribution rights to a local "product" distributor and the organization's ability to provide the product to the store will depend upon how well the local distributor has been chosen.

Franchise Organization. Almost every franchise system handles international franchising activities in its own peculiar way. The organizational arrangements for international franchising often depend upon the company's method of operation within those foreign countries. The franchising organization generally establishes either an export department or an international division. An export department is responsible primarily for shipments of goods or products. As activities continue to grow, this department will often become an international division. The international division will eventually become involved in a number of different international markets and business ventures. The franchisor will have to determine how it will interact with each particular country and develop its franchises within that country. Most of these activities will be done in one of the methods by which master franchisees are provided joint ownership of the franchise organizations.

HINDRANCES TO INTERNATIONAL FRANCHISING

Many American franchisors have voiced their reluctance to expand into foreign countries because of government red tape, high costs, and import restrictions.

Kentucky Fried Chicken has recently moved into Korea with four franchised stores. It is entering the Korean market very cautiously because KFC is concerned about the quality and availability of chicken in Korea. This is in sharp contrast to its experience in Japan, where 305 franchised and 168 company-owned Kentucky Fried Chicken restaurants have already been established.[6] The major difference appears to be that the government controls regarding chicken production in Korea are much more stringent than those in Japan.

Hoteliers are also interested in foreign markets, and they too have run into government red tape and have found it necessary to proceed very slowly. The rule of thumb is one hotel at a time and one property at a time. They wait to see how the government will respond to that hotel and if restrictions will be lessened.

Cookie franchisors often find it difficult to get through existing channels of distribution in foreign marketplaces. They tend to look for partners with power or "oomph" in the local marketplace. The local partner could be either a master franchisee or a joint venture partner. Standard royalty fees would be approximately 4 to 5 percent, while some

---

[6] KFC Corporation, *Annual Report 1986*.

governments estimate the value of the franchise trademark from 6 to 8 percent, payable to the host country.

FRANCHISING IN THE FUTURE

Franchising will be an even more prevalent method of doing business in the future. *Megatrends* author John Naisbitt projected for a 1985 study commissioned by the International Franchise Association (IFA) that by the year 2000, over one-half of all retail sales in the United States would be made through franchised outlets.[7]

Prior to World War II, franchising was a little-used word in the American business vocabulary. Today, franchising is an integral part of our economy, and it refers to an entire method of doing business rather than a simple distribution system relating to a single product. Franchising today refers to an ability to standardize and replicate business practices and business formats which provide quality products and services to the consumer.

Franchising will continue to grow because of the benefits it provides both franchisors and franchisees. Through franchising, new businesses are able to start up without extensive capital outlays by the headquarters organization. Even though the market demand and profit potential may exist, it is still difficult for franchisors to readily raise capital for expansion. The franchising method provides this capital through the franchisees.

The franchisees are able to act as entrepreneurs and start in proven and profitable businesses by investing their money in a complete business format. For franchisees, this means being able to adopt a proven product or service and offer it through their own private businesses. The franchising method provides the franchisee with the opportunity to realize the American dream of financial independence and success through owning their own business.

As franchising continues to grow, franchisors will continue to utilize their technical skills and knowledge to help franchisees learn daily operations, choose the best locations, establish proper marketing/promotional activities, develop appropriate procedures and policies for personnel, and improve all aspects of the marketing format. Franchising will continue to grow in the service sector, especially in professional and computerized services.

---

[7] *The Future of Franchising: Looking Twenty-Five Years Ahead to the Year 2010*, a study for the International Franchise Association by The Naisbitt Group (Washington, DC: International Franchise Association, 1986), p. 1.

Franchising markets will grow as manufacturers and distributors of high-tech equipment utilize franchised outlets to sell their products. Computers, telecommunication services, and information processing will all be expanded through franchised stores. Franchisors of food products will continue to expand, especially in specialty and/or ethnic food areas. Non-food retailing will continue to expand to accommodate demands for new products.

We will also see growth in the number of multi-unit franchisees and in the adoption and utilization of franchise advisory councils and associations. The advisory councils have shown to be strong and supportive groups for franchisors. They have often been the source for new products and innovation for companies.

Name recognition and product quality are two reasons why franchising will continue to grow into the twenty-first century. More companies will utilize the franchising method for the sale of their products and services. Franchisors will realize the importance of private ownership by the franchisees as one of the great motivating forces in a marketing system and so will use the franchising concept to expand into almost all industries in which individuals can establish private stores to sell products or services. Franchising will probably be the main method of doing business in the next century.

SUCCESS STORY
JOHN P. THOMPSON

Southland Corporation has its roots in a company formed 60 years ago by a group of ice plant and retail ice station owners in Dallas, Texas — Southland Ice Company. On the board of the company was a 26-year-old recent University of Texas graduate, Joe C. Thompson.

Over the years that followed, Southland began to expand and diversify under the leadership of Joe Thompson. In 1946, Southland developed the 7-ELEVEN stores, marking the beginning of the modern convenience store. By the end of 1960, 490 7-ELEVENS were located from Texas into Florida and the East Coast.

In 1961, John P. Thompson, the oldest of Joe's three sons, became the president of Southland Corporation. The rapid expansion of the 7-ELEVEN convenience stores continued, until there were 1,050 stores doing business in 250 cities and towns by 1963. The desire to expand operations to the West Coast prompted Southland to buy a chain of 124 franchised convenience stores called Speedee Mart. This purchase gave Southland immediate access to the West Coast and the system's expertise in franchising. The name Speedee Mart was eventually dropped and the stores were renamed 7-ELEVEN.

Franchising proved so successful for Southland that today 7-ELEVEN stores are found in 43 states, the District of Columbia, and Canada. Stores are also operated through area licensees in Japan, Australia, Taiwan, Hong Kong, Singapore, the United Kingdom, and the Philippines. Under John Thompson's guidance and insight, Southland has grown in 25 years to be the world's largest operator and franchisor of convenience stores.

Photo and information provided courtesy of John P. Thompson, August, 1985.

SUMMARY

International franchising is very important in world commerce, and it provides mutually beneficial returns for both the home and host countries. International franchising by American franchisors continues to increase and allows American businesses to gain international recognition and promote their trade names, trademarks, products, and services abroad. The American form of franchising is one of the most competitive forms of business in the world today. Successful franchised businesses are often sought by foreign countries, and they provide local entrepreneurs and businesspeople the opportunity to develop new businesses and operations.

Canada is the largest foreign market for American franchisors. Other countries are growing in their use of American franchised businesses. Japan is the second largest market, with over 4,990 units in categories including restaurants, convenience food stores, donut shops, and ice cream shops. Opportunities for growth continue to be available for franchisors in foreign markets.

Auto and truck rental services and restaurants are the businesses most frequently franchised internationally, as was shown in Table 22-1. Other major franchised businesses operating outside the United States include educational products and services, equipment rental services, convenience stores, retailing (non-food), automotive products and services, and business aids and services.

International franchising is the wave of the future, as more and more franchisors in the United States seek foreign markets. Many companies from Japan and Europe are currently looking to enter into the American marketplace through franchised units, including automotive manufacturers, electronics manufacturers, and computer hardware and software stores. International franchising is another step in making the world smaller and more livable.

REVIEW QUESTIONS

1. Discuss the importance of analyzing the international marketplace before entering a country with a foreign franchise.
2. Define the economic considerations which are important in analyzing foreign markets for franchising.
3. Discuss the international marketing decision and analyze what steps need to be taken before starting a foreign operation.
4. Review the five different methods of starting a franchise in a foreign country.
5. Discuss the advantages and disadvantages of international franchising.

CASE STUDY
TIDY CAR*

The Tidy Car Total Auto Appearance Center offers a range of services to car owners, including rustproofing, soundproofing, sunroof installation, interior drycleaning, and other automotive services. There are currently more than 1,000 Tidy Car franchises throughout the United States, Canada, and 30 other countries.

The initial franchising fee is $9,500, plus a weekly royalty fee equal to 9 percent of the gross volume. A weekly advertising and marketing fee of $200 to $600 is also required depending upon the size of the market in which the business is located. The startup costs for a Tidy Car center range from $43,900 to $61,900 for a leased premise. If the property and building are bought by the franchisee, the cost will go up according to the price of the land and the building. The franchisor provides no financial assistance to the franchisee.

Startup Costs

Initial Franchising Fee	$ 9,500
Equipment	$ 9,000-$16,000
Inventory	$ 7,000-$ 7,500
Real Estate	$ 3,500-$ 7,000
Insurance	$ 4,000-$ 6,000
Initial Advertising	$ 5,000
Vehicle	$ 900
Working Capital	$ 5,000-$10,000
Total	$43,900-$61,900

Lori wants to buy a Tidy Car franchise. She is very excited about the opportunities available but does not currently have sufficient financing to start. She has $15,000 of personal savings and would really like to start within the next six months.

*Information provided courtesy of Tidy Car, Inc., September, 1987.

CASE QUESTIONS

1. How much money must Lori have to start the franchise?
2. Where should Lori go for additional financing?
3. Should Lori talk to the franchisor for possible financial support? Why?
4. What are the best financial resources available to prospective franchisees and/or franchisors?

REFERENCES

1. Ashman, Richard T., "Born in the U.S.A.; Although Uniquely American in Method and Style, Franchising Is Making a Hit Internationally," *Nation's Business*, Vol. 74 (November 1986), p. 41.
2. Auld, Alan, "Worthiness Is the Key to Bank Finance," *Accountancy*, Vol. 98 (October 1986), p. 87.
3. Brandenberg, Mary, "Free Yourself from Servitude," *Accountancy*, Vol. 98 (October 1986), p. 82.
4. Brennan, Denise M., "International," *Restaurant Business Magazine*, Vol. 86 (March 20, 1987), p. 172.
5. Cherkasky, William B., "Foreign Markets Open for Franchisors," *Nation's Restaurant News*, Vol. 19 (August 12, 1985), p. 11.
6. Dunnigan, J. A., "Franchising in Maple Leaf Country," *Entrepreneurs Franchise Yearbook*, Vol. 2 (1987/88), pp. 308-312.
7. "Fast and Fashionable," *Economist*, Vol. 294 (January 5, 1985), p. 57.
8. Gilmour, John, "Business Expansion Through Franchising," *Accountant's Magazine*, Vol. 90 (August 1986), p. 26.
9. Justis, Robert T., and Cheryl Babcock, "Franchising: Strategies in East Asia," *Proceedings of the Pan Pacific Conference for May 1987*, pp. 588-590.
10. Justis, Robert T., and Eiji Kuriyama, "Franchising: A Growing Phenomena in Japan," *Proceedings of the Pan Pacific Conference for May 1987*, pp. 571-587.
11. Zeidman, Philip F., "Franchising 'Down Under': New Legislation Poses a Challenge to Australian Food Service Operators," *Nation's Restaurant News*, Vol. 20 (October 6, 1986), p. F51.

APPENDIX

SAMPLE FRANCHISE CONTRACT

An example of a franchising agreement is presented on the following pages. No claim is made as to the present legality of the contract provisions stated therein. The agreement is reproduced to illustrate a format used by a franchisor and to give the reader some indication of what elements are likely involved in a franchising agreement.

As you prepare your own franchising agreement, or if you are a prospective franchisee, it is imperative that you receive professional advice from competent legal counsel.

Regional Franchisor: G.C. & K.B. Investments, Inc. d.b.a.
SpeeDee Oil Change & Tune Up®
of the Gulf Coast

Date of Issuance of Disclosure Statement: July 20, 1987

INFORMATION FOR PROSPECTIVE FRANCHISEES
REQUIRED BY FEDERAL TRADE COMMISSION

To protect you, we've required your franchisor to give you this information. We haven't checked it, and don't know if it's correct. It should help you make up your mind. Study it carefully. While it includes some information about your contract, don't rely on it alone to understand your contract. Read all of your contract carefully. Buying a franchise is a complicated investment. Take your time to decide. If possible, show your contract and this information to an advisor, like a lawyer or an accountant. If you find anything you think may be wrong or anything important that's been left out, you should let us know about it. It may be against the law.

There may also be laws on franchising in your state. Ask your state agencies about them.

FEDERAL TRADE COMMISSION

Washington, D.C.

SpeeDee Oil Change & Tune Up® of the Gulf Coast
L-UFOC   v. 2.6   July 20, 1987
Reprinted with permission.

Sample Franchise Contract

SpeeDee
OIL CHANGE & TUNE-UP

**FRANCHISE OFFERING CIRCULAR
FOR PROSPECTIVE FRANCHISEES REQUIRED
BY THE FEDERAL TRADE COMMISSION AND STATE LAW**

Franchisor ("SOCS"):

SpeeDee Oil Change Systems, Inc.
6660 Riverside Drive
Suite 101
Metairie, Louisiana 70003
Phone: (504) 454-3783

Sub-Franchisor ("Region"):

G.C. & K.B. Investments, Inc. d.b.a.
SpeeDee Oil Change & Tune Up®
of the Gulf Coast
6660 Riverside Drive, Suite 101
Metairie, Louisiana 70003
Phone: (504) 454-3783

This Offering Circular describes the SpeeDee Oil Change & Tune Up® car care service subfranchise offered by G.C. & K.B. Investments, Inc. d.b.a. SpeeDee Oil Change & Tune Up® of the Gulf Coast, the "Region" listed above. This franchise offering is made solely by the Region, which will be the only entity with any obligations to, or a contractual relationship with, the Franchisee. The franchise offered by the Region covers operation of a SpeeDee Oil Change & Tune Up® Car Care Service Center using the SpeeDee Oil Change & Tune Up® name, service marks, associated logotypes and system.

The franchise fee is Twenty-Five Thousand Dollars ($25,000), and is due and payable in full upon the execution of the Franchise Agreement.

Each Franchisee is required to provide the supplies necessary for the operation of his/her business. In addition, each Franchisee will be responsible for the payment of the expenses involved in setting up and operating his business, including the expenses of securing a location, business license, telephone service, advertising, insurance, and maintenance. It is estimated that the aggregate amount required to pay such costs will range from $87,000 to $213,000. These figures assume that the Franchisee will lease the required land and building, as is usually the case.

The Franchisor has no contractual relationship with or obligations to the Franchisee, any such relationship or obligations being those of the Region only.

The effective date of this Offering Circular is July 20, 1987.

SpeeDee Oil Change & Tune Up® of the Gulf Coast
L-UFOC   v. 2.6   July 20, 1987
Reprinted with permission.

THIS OFFERING CIRCULAR IS PROVIDED FOR YOUR OWN PROTECTION AND CONTAINS A SUMMARY ONLY OF CERTAIN MATERIAL PROVISIONS OF THE FRANCHISE AGREEMENT. THIS OFFERING CIRCULAR AND ALL CONTRACTS AND AGREEMENTS SHOULD BE READ CAREFULLY IN THEIR ENTIRETY FOR AN UNDERSTANDING OF ALL RIGHTS AND OBLIGATIONS OF BOTH THE FRANCHISOR AND THE FRANCHISEE.

A FEDERAL TRADE COMMISSION RULE MAKES IT UNLAWFUL TO OFFER OR SELL ANY FRANCHISE WITHOUT FIRST PROVIDING THIS OFFERING CIRCULAR TO THE PROSPECTIVE FRANCHISEE AT THE EARLIER OF (1) THE FIRST PERSONAL MEETING; OR (2) TEN BUSINESS DAYS BEFORE THE SIGNING OF ANY FRANCHISE OR RELATED AGREEMENT; OR (3) TEN BUSINESS DAYS BEFORE ANY PAYMENT. THE PROSPECTIVE FRANCHISEE MUST ALSO RECEIVE A FRANCHISE AGREEMENT CONTAINING ALL MATERIAL TERMS AT LEAST FIVE BUSINESS DAYS PRIOR TO THE SIGNING OF THE FRANCHISE AGREEMENT.

IF THIS OFFERING CIRCULAR IS NOT DELIVERED ON TIME, OR IF IT CONTAINS A FALSE, INCOMPLETE, INACCURATE OR MISLEADING STATEMENT, A VIOLATION OF FEDERAL AND STATE LAW MAY HAVE OCCURRED AND SHOULD BE REPORTED TO THE FEDERAL TRADE COMMISSION, WASHINGTON, D.C., 20580.

It is requested that a copy of any notice, process or pleading be mailed to: David E. Holmes, Esq., 18377 Beach Blvd., Suite 214, Huntington Beach, California, 92648.

STATEMENT OF PROSPECTIVE FRANCHISEE

A. The following dates are true and correct:

1. _____, 19____   The date of my first face-to-face meeting with a Regional Franchise Marketing Representative or any other person to discuss the possible purchase of a Franchise.
   (Month Day)

2. _____, 19____   The date on which I received a Uniform Franchise Offering Circular about the SpeeDee Oil Change & Tune-Up (R) Local Franchise.
   (Month Day)

3. _____, 19____   The date when I received a fully completed copy (other than signatures) of the Franchise Agreement I later signed.
   (Month Day)

4. _____, 19____   The earliest date on which I signed the Franchise Agreement or any other binding document (not including the Letter of Receipt).
   (Month Day)

SpeeDee Oil Change & Tune Up® of the Gulf Coast
L-UFOC   v. 2.6   July 20, 1987
Reprinted with permission.

5. _____, 19_____   The earliest date on which I delivered
   (Month Day)   cash, check or consideration to the Regional Franchise Marketing Representative or any other person.

B. Representations

   1. No promises, agreements, contracts, commitments, representations, understandings, "side deals" or otherwise have been made to or with me with respect to any matter (including but not limited to any representations or promises regarding advertising (television or otherwise), marketing, site location, operational assistance or other services) nor have I relied in any way on any such except as explicitly set forth in the Franchise Agreement or a written Addendum thereto signed by me and the President of the Region except: _____
   (If none, the prospective Franchisee shall write NONE and initial)

   2. No oral, written or visual claim or representation, promise, agreement, contract, commitment, understanding or otherwise which contradicted or was inconsistent with the Offering Circular or the Franchise Agreement was made to me except: _____
   (If none, the prospective Franchisee shall write NONE and initial)

   3. No oral, written, visual or other claim or representation, which stated or suggested any sales, income, expense, profits, cash flow, tax effects, or otherwise was made to me by any person or entity, except: _____
   (If none, the prospective Franchisee shall write NONE and initial)

   4. I will attend the very next scheduled Franchisee Orientation provided that I have executed the Franchise Agreement and paid the Franchise Fee at least fourteen (14) days prior to the next Orientation, unless I have good cause for not attending.
   Date _____   Initial _____

SpeeDee Oil Change & Tune Up of _____ (the "Region") does not make or endorse nor does it allow any Franchisee or other individual to make or endorse any representations, warranties, projections or disclosures of any type of any financial information, data or results with respect to this or any other Franchise, whether with respect to sales, income, expenses, profits, cash flow, tax effects or otherwise, whether made on behalf of or for the Region, any Franchisee or other individual expressly disclaims any such financial information, data or results. If any such representations have been made to you by any person, immediately inform the attorney for the Region (Phone: 714-842-9833) and the Region's Regional Director. In addition, the Region does not permit any promises, agreements, contracts, commitments, representations, understandings, "side deals" or otherwise or variations or changes in or supplements to the Franchise Agreement except by means of a written Addendum thereto signed by the Franchisee and the President of the Region.

The Prospective Franchisee understands and agrees to all of the foregoing.

Date _____

_____

Prospective Franchisee(s)

All of the above is true, correct and complete to the best of my knowledge:

_____

Regional Franchise Marketing Director

Approved:

_____

Regional Director

_____, 198____

SpeeDee Oil Change & Tune Up of _____, Inc.

_____

_____

Re: <u>Personal Guarantee</u>

Gentlemen:

    This will set forth our agreement that we personally guarantee all obligations of _____ [Franchisee Corporation] _____ to _____ [Region] _____ and/or to SpeeDee Oil Change Systems, Inc., of whatever nature, past, present or future, whether arising under or in connection with or related in any way to the Local Franchise Agreement between _____ [Franchisee Corporation] _____ and _____ [Region] _____, or otherwise, without limitation, it being the undersigned's intention that this Guarantee be unqualifiedly general in scope and effect and without limitation of <u>any</u> type or nature.

Sincerely yours,

_____

_____

_____

© 1986 Law Offices of David E. Holmes

AUTHORIZATION FOR CREDIT AND BACKGROUND CHECK

In order to make possible full evaluation of the undersigned's suitability to become a SpeeDee Oil Change & Tune Up® Franchisee, the undersigned authorize[s] {Region's Name} to perform or have performed for it any credit and background check on the undersigned which is deemed appropriate by {Region's Name}.

_____   _____
Applicant's Name [printed]   Applicant's Name [printed]

_____   _____
Applicant's Name [signed]   Applicant's Name [signed]

_____   _____
Address   Address

_____   _____
Date of Birth   Date of Birth

_____   _____
Social Security Number   Social Security Number

© 1986 Law Offices of David E. Holmes

TABLE OF CONTENTS

ITEM 1.	THE FRANCHISOR, SUBFRANCHISOR AND ANY PREDECESSORS	578
ITEM 2.	IDENTITY AND BUSINESS EXPERIENCE OF PERSONS AFFILIATED WITH THE FRANCHISOR OR SUBFRANCHISOR; FRANCHISE BROKERS	580
ITEM 3.	LITIGATION	582
ITEM 4.	BANKRUPTCY	583
ITEM 5.	FRANCHISEE'S INITIAL FRANCHISE FEE	583
ITEM 6.	OTHER FEES	584
ITEM 7.	FRANCHISEE'S INITIAL INVESTMENT	591
ITEM 8.	OBLIGATIONS OF FRANCHISEE TO PURCHASE OR LEASE FROM DESIGNATED SOURCES	593
ITEM 9.	OBLIGATIONS OF FRANCHISEE TO PURCHASE OR LEASE IN ACCORDANCE WITH SPECIFICATIONS OR FROM APPROVED SUPPLIERS	594
ITEM 10.	FINANCING ARRANGEMENTS	599
ITEM 11.	OBLIGATIONS OF THE REGION; OTHER SUPERVISION, ASSISTANCE OR SERVICES	600
ITEM 12.	EXCLUSIVE AREA OR TERRITORY	602
ITEM 13.	TRADEMARKS, SERVICE MARKS, TRADE NAMES, LOGOTYPES AND COMMERCIAL SYMBOLS	602
ITEM 14.	PATENTS AND COPYRIGHTS	604
ITEM 15.	OBLIGATIONS OF THE FRANCHISEE TO PARTICIPATE IN THE ACTUAL OPERATION OF THE FRANCHISE	604
ITEM 16.	RESTRICTIONS ON GOODS AND SERVICES OFFERED BY FRANCHISEE	605

SpeeDee Oil Change & Tune Up® of the Gulf Coast
L-UFOC   v. 2.6   July 20, 1987
Reprinted with permission.

ITEM 17.	RENEWAL, TERMINATION, REPURCHASE, MODIFICATION AND ASSIGNMENT OF THE FRANCHISE AGREEMENT AND RELATED INFORMATION	605
ITEM 18.	ARRANGEMENTS WITH PUBLIC FIGURES	610
ITEM 19.	ACTUAL, AVERAGE, PROJECTED OR FORECASTED FRANCHISE SALES, PROFITS OR EARNINGS	611
ITEM 20.	INFORMATION REGARDING FRANCHISES OF THE SUBFRANCHISOR	611
ITEM 21.	FINANCIAL STATEMENTS	612
ITEM 22.	CONTRACTS	612

EXHIBITS:

- A. FINANCIAL STATEMENTS
- B. FRANCHISE AGREEMENT
- C. EXISTING FRANCHISES OF THE REGION
- C-1. PRE-EXISTING FRANCHISES IN THE TERRITORY CURRENTLY BEING SERVICED BY THE REGION
- C-2. UNITS OWNED BY REGION
- D. LOANED EQUIPMENT AGREEMENT
- E. LETTER OF CREDIT

SpeeDee Oil Change & Tune Up® of the Gulf Coast
L-UFOC   v. 2.6   July 20, 1987
Reprinted with permission.

ITEM 1: THE FRANCHISOR, SUBFRANCHISOR AND ANY PREDECESSORS

This Offering Circular describes the SpeeDee Oil Change & Tune Up® car care service franchise offered by G.C. & K.B. Investments, Inc. d.b.a. SpeeDee Oil Change & Tune Up® of the Gulf Coast (the "Region"), which is the Subfranchisor. This franchise offering is made solely by the Region, which will be the only entity with any obligations to, or a contractual relationship with, the Franchisee. The Region has been licensed by SpeeDee Oil Change Systems, Inc. (the "Franchisor" or "SOCS") to sell and service Franchises of the type offered herein within a specified territory. **The Franchisor has no contractual relationship with or obligations to the Franchisee, any such relationship or obligations being those of the Region only.** The franchise offered by the Region covers operation of a SpeeDee Oil Change & Tune Up® Car Care Service Center offering basic car care services to the general public.

Franchisor Information:

The name of the Franchisor is "SpeeDee Oil Change Systems, Inc.", a Louisiana corporation incorporated on November 3, 1982, and currently doing business under the name "SpeeDee Oil Change & Tune Up®". SpeeDee Oil Change Systems, Inc. is referred to in this document and its exhibits as Franchisor or SOCS. The Franchisor is located at 6660 Riverside Drive, Suite 101, Metairie, Louisiana, 70003. The Franchisor's predecessor was SpeeDee Oil Change, located at 1500 Veterans Memorial Boulevard, Kenner, Louisiana, 70063. Such predecessor operated oil change and tune-up facilities from its inception in December of 1980 until December of 1982. Oil change and tune-up franchises were not offered by such predecessor.

The Franchisor operates and sells regional and local licenses for the operation of a distinctive method of providing efficient and speedy car care service, including oil changes, tune-ups, transmission services, differential services, radiator flushes and replacement of filters.

The first "SpeeDee Oil Change" unit opened in December of 1980; the first "SpeeDee Oil Change & Tune Up®" unit opened in September of 1983. The Franchisor has conducted a business providing oil change services since 1980 and has conducted businesses providing oil change and tune-up services (substantially similar to those to be operated by the Region and its local Franchisees) since 1980. The Franchisor has franchised such businesses since December of 1982. There are currently seventeen units in operation [including five stores owned by one or more companies owned by Gary Copp and Kevin Bennett, both of whom are officers of Franchisor] and six units in construction, site selection or planning stages. [One additional store is owned by a company owned by Gary Copp and Kevin Bennett, and is currently not operational.] The above-mentioned seventeen units include two Area Franchises as follows: Baton Rouge and Lafayette, Louisiana [three units each under contract — one unit each open]. Since 1985 Franchisor has franchised ten regional

SpeeDee Oil Change & Tune Up® of the Gulf Coast
L-UFOC   v. 2.6   July 20, 1987
Reprinted with permission.

franchises that offer local franchises similar to the one offered herein, and of those ten regional franchises, as of March, 1987, eight have commenced operations.

SOCS owns the "SpeeDee Oil Change & Tune Up®" trade name and service mark, and the Regional Franchise Agreement between SOCS and the Region entitles the Region to use the trade name and service mark as more particularly described in this Offering Circular and the Franchise Agreement attached hereto as Exhibit B. SOCS currently holds federal service mark registrations for "SpeeDee Oil Change & Tune Up®" and "SpeeDee Oil Change 9 Minute Oil Service." In addition, SOCS owns the Louisiana state-registered trade name and fanciful logo which appears with the trade name. The federal service mark registrations also include the fanciful logo.

As of the date thereof, Franchisor has not offered or sold any franchises in any line of business other than the car care service business, but has sold and may continue to sell franchises directly to franchisees for the operation of car care service businesses substantially similar to those which would be sold by the Region and may operate such businesses itself.

Subfranchisor (the "Region") Information:

The name of the Region is G.C. & K.B. Investments, Inc., a Louisiana corporation. The Region is doing and intends to do business under the name SpeeDee Oil Change & Tune Up® of the Gulf Coast. The Region is located at 6660 Riverside Drive, Suite 101, Metairie, Louisiana, 70003.

The Region was incorporated in Louisiana on April 7, 1987, and has been, since July of 1987, engaged in the selling of licenses for the operation of a distinctive method of providing efficient and speedy car care service, including oil changes, tune-ups, transmission services, radiator flushes and replacement of filters. The Region may itself, from time to time, operate SpeeDee Oil Change & Tune Up® Car Care Service Centers in this state or elsewhere.

The Region's predecessor, SpeeDee Oil Change Systems, Inc., in April, 1987, granted the Region its Regional Franchise and the Region has agreed to provide services to previously existing franchisees of SpeeDee Oil Change Systems, Inc. located within the Region's territory. A list of such pre-existing franchisees is attached hereto as Exhibit "C-1".

As of the date hereof, the Region has not sold franchises in any other lines of business.

SpeeDee Oil Change & Tune Up® of the Gulf Coast
L-UFOC   v. 2.6   July 20, 1987
Reprinted with permission.

ITEM 2: IDENTITY AND BUSINESS EXPERIENCE OF PERSONS AFFILIATED WITH THE FRANCHISOR AND SUBFRANCHISOR; FRANCHISE BROKERS

Franchisor Information:

The officers, directors and management personnel of SOCS are Gary L. Copp, Kevin M. Bennett, Brian Cooney, C.B. Walker II, and Peter Gebbia III.

  Gary L. Copp   President

Mr. Copp is President of SOCS and, for two years prior to his association with SOCS, had been in sales with Lealand Mast Directory Company. Since December 1979, Mr. Copp has been exclusively employed by SOCS and its affiliates and has been responsible for the development and planning of the general business operation of SOCS and its affiliates. Mr. Copp presently has an ownership interest in a SpeeDee Oil Change & Tune Up® Region, G.C. & K.B. Investments, Inc., d.b.a. SpeeDee Oil Change & Tune Up® of the Gulf Coast.

  Kevin M. Bennett   Vice President, Franchise Director & Secretary

Mr. Bennett is Vice President and Secretary of SOCS and, for two years prior to his association with SOCS, was the owner and President of Mr. Clean Car Wash in Metairie, Louisiana, with which he continues to be associated. Since December 1979, Mr. Bennett has been employed by SOCS and its affiliates, and currently holds the position of Franchise Director. Mr. Bennett presently has an ownership interest in a SpeeDee Oil Change & Tune Up® Region, G.C. & K.B. Investments, Inc., d.b.a. SpeeDee Oil Change & Tune Up® of the Gulf Coast.

  Brian Cooney   Chief Financial Officer

Mr. Brian Cooney is Chief Financial Officer of SpeeDee Oil Change Systems, Inc. For nine and one-half years until joining the Franchisor in November of 1986, Mr. Cooney was employed by Mechanical Equipment Co., Inc. in New Orleans, Louisiana. For the four years most recent years, Mr. Cooney held the position of Chief Financial Officer, and prior to that was Controller for Mechanical Equipment Co., Inc.

  C.B. Walker II   Vice President — Franchise Sales

Mr. C.B. Walker is Vice President of Franchise Sales for SpeeDee Oil Change Systems, Inc. For twelve years prior to his association with SpeeDee Oil Change Systems, Inc. Mr. Walker had been in the real estate, franchise and shopping center business, with Sizeler Realty Co. of New Orleans, serving as Vice President. Since

SpeeDee Oil Change & Tune Up® of the Gulf Coast
L-UFOC v. 2.6 July 20, 1987
Reprinted with permission.

October of 1986, Mr. Walker has been exclusively employed by SpeeDee Oil Change Systems and its affiliates, and has responsibility mainly in the areas of guidance, support and training for the Regional owners. Mr. Walker presently has an ownership interest in two SpeeDee Oil Change & Tune Up® franchised locations located in the Gulf Coast Region.

      Peter Gebbia III   Director of Regional Store Operations

Mr. Gebbia is the Director of Regional Store Operations with SpeeDee Oil Change Systems, Inc. He has been employed by the Franchisor since mid-1984. Prior to his employment with Franchisor, he was Secretary-Treasurer of A-1 Transmission of New Orleans for 6 years.

In addition, information is provided regarding M. N. "Joe" Camp, Jr., an independent consultant advising SOCS from time to time.

      M. N. "Joe" Camp, Jr.   Consultant

Mr. Camp, doing business as "Networks," an independent consultant, provides consulting services to SOCS from time to time, including the rendering of advice regarding franchise structuring, franchise development and related areas. Neither Mr. Camp nor Networks acts as franchise sales agents for SOCS. Mr. Camp has been acting as an independent franchising consultant since June, 1983, in the areas of conceptual development, franchise structure and related marketing efforts. His particular expertise is in the area of regional franchise systems (subfranchising). Prior to that, he was the Field Marketing Director for Century 21 Real Estate Corporation (International Headquarters) and prior to that held franchise marketing positions (including Vice President of Marketing for the Southeast) in the Century 21 system since 1978. Mr. Camp presently has an ownership interest in a SpeeDee Oil Change & Tune Up® Region, Arrowhead Oil Corporation, d.b.a. SpeeDee Oil Change & Tune Up® of Southern California.

Networks acts in a consulting capacity to SOCS in providing, among other things, certain franchise marketing services and may, on occasion, assist SOCS in the presentation and sale of regional franchises.

Subfranchisor Information:

The officers, directors and management personnel of the Region are Gary Copp, Kevin Bennett, and Earl Batty.

      Gary L. Copp   President & Chief Financial Officer

SpeeDee Oil Change & Tune Up® of the Gulf Coast
L-UFOC v. 2.6 July 20, 1987
Reprinted with permission.

Mr. Copp is President and Chief Financial Officer of the Region, and, for two years prior to his association with Franchisor, had been in sales with Lealand Mast Directory Company. From December 1979 to the formation of the Region in April of 1987, Mr. Copp was exclusively employed by SOCS and its affiliates and has been responsible for the development and planning of the general business operation of SOCS and its affiliates.

        Kevin M. Bennett   Vice President, Secretary & Franchise Director

Mr. Bennett is Vice President, Secretary and Franchise Director of the Region and, for two years prior to his association with Franchisor, was the owner and President of Mr. Clean Car Wash in Metairie, Louisiana, with which he continues to be associated. From December 1979 to the formation of the Region in April of 1987, Mr. Bennett has been employed by SOCS and its affiliates.

        Earl Batty   Field Service Representative

Mr. Earl Batty is Field Service Representative for the Region, and has been since April, 1987. From January of 1985 through April of 1987, Mr. Batty was manager of several company-owned stores for SOCS. From 1982 through 1984 he was manager at Mr. Clean Car Wash in Metairie, Louisiana, and for the 15 years prior Mr. Batty was International Sales Representative for George Engine Company located in Harvey, Louisiana.

ITEM 3: LITIGATION

Neither the Franchisor, Subfranchisor nor any person identified in Item 2 above:

(a) Has any administrative, criminal or material civil action (or a significant number of civil actions irrespective of materiality) pending against it or him alleging a violation of any franchise or securities law, fraud, embezzlement, fraudulent conversion, restraint of trade, unfair or deceptive practices, misappropriation of property or comparable allegations.

(b) Has ever been convicted of a felony or pleaded nolo contendere to a felony charge or, during the ten year period immediately preceding the date of this Offering Circular, has been convicted of a misdemeanor or pleaded nolo contendere to a misdemeanor charge or been held liable in a civil action by final judgment or been the subject of a material complaint or other legal proceeding if such misdemeanor conviction or charge or civil action, complaint or other legal proceeding involved violation of any franchise or securities law, fraud, embezzlement, fraudu-

SpeeDee Oil Change & Tune Up® of the Gulf Coast
L-UFOC   v. 2.6   July 20, 1987
Reprinted with permission.

lent conversion, restraint of trade, unfair or deceptive practices, misappropriation of property or comparable allegations.

(c) Is subject to any currently effective injunctive or restrictive order or decree relating to the franchise or under any federal, state or Canadian franchise, securities, antitrust, trade regulation or trade practice law as a result of a concluded or pending action or proceeding brought by a public agency, or is subject to any currently effective order of any national securities association or national securities exchange suspending or expelling such person from membership in such association.

ITEM 4: BANKRUPTCY

Neither the Franchisor, Subfranchisor nor any predecessor or officer of either has, during the 15 year period immediately preceding the date of this Offering Circular, been adjudged a bankrupt or reorganized due to insolvency or was a principal officer of any company or a general partner in any partnership that was adjudged a bankrupt or reorganized due to insolvency during or within one year after the period that such person held such position in such company or partnership and no such bankruptcy or reorganization has been commenced, except as described below:

Peter Gebbia, Director of Regional Store Operations for Franchisor, on December 3, 1981, filed a petition for bankruptcy in the United States Bankruptcy Court for the Eastern District of Louisiana (Case No. 81-02222) and received an adjudication and discharge on April 5, 1982. Mr. Gebbia has informed the Franchisor that such proceeding was the result of, and connected with, a divorce action in which Mr. Gebbia was involved at or about such time, and that such proceeding did not occur as the result of the operations of any company of which Mr. Gebbia was a principal officer or general partner and related only to such marital dissolution.

ITEM 5: FRANCHISEE'S INITIAL FRANCHISE FEE

(a) The franchise fee is Twenty-Five Thousand Dollars [$25,000] and is due in full upon execution of the Franchise Agreement, and is not refundable under any circumstances, except where the Franchisee, in the Region's sole and absolute discretion, has failed to successfully complete training, in which case the Franchise Agreement will be terminated, the Franchisee will sign a form of release and indemnity in favor of the Region and SOCS and the Region will return to the Franchisee any Initial Franchise Fee paid by the Franchisee less the greater of (1) Five Thousand Dollars [$5,000] subject to adjustment for cost-of-living or (2) the total of any expenses incurred by the Region as a result of or in connection with the sale of such

SpeeDee Oil Change & Tune Up® of the Gulf Coast
L-UFOC   v. 2.6   July 20, 1987
Reprinted with permission.

franchise, including but not limited to amounts paid by the Region with respect to such sale and/or any associated training, home office orientation, franchise sales commissions, legal fees or otherwise. See Section 6.3 (a) (6) of the Franchise Agreement and Item 17 herein.

The Region intends to use the franchise fee for general working capital purposes and for the expenses incurred in the recruiting of Franchisees, and does not allocate any sum to any specific expense to be incurred by the Region under the Franchise Agreement, except that the Region and the Franchisee have agreed that Twenty Thousand Dollars ($20,000) of the Franchise Fee is paid with respect to services to be provided by the Region to the Franchisee, and One Thousand Five Hundred Dollars ($1,500) is allocated by the Region for payment of its expenses in relation to Franchisee's initial training at SOCS headquarters in Metairie, Louisiana.

ITEM 6: OTHER FEES

LOCAL BUSINESS DEVELOPMENT FEE

The Franchisee pays a recurring, non-refundable Local Business Development Fee of five percent [5%] of the Franchisee's gross revenues during the franchise term, payable on Wednesday of each week for gross revenues received or earned during the preceding week. Such Local Business Development Fee is subject to a minimum weekly obligation of One Hundred Twenty-Five Dollars [$125.00] per week per SpeeDee Oil Change & Tune Up® Car Care Service Center operated by the Franchisee, is subject to annual cost-of-living adjustment, must be paid even if the Franchisee's SpeeDee Oil Change & Tune Up® Car Care Service Center closes or fails to open on the date agreed between the Region and the Franchisee and is to be paid by autodraft or other means acceptable to the Region. (See Sections 4.2 and 4.3 of the Franchise Agreement)

ADVERTISING — GENERAL

With respect to the Local Franchisee's advertising contributions, in broad terms the Local Franchisee is required to pay to the Region an advertising contribution of 8% of gross revenues [10% after December 31, 1987]. **Of this amount, 30% is to be spent on a local, regional, and/or "Area of Dominant Influence" (ADI) basis for the same Region in which the Franchisee operates and 70% will be spent on a local, regional or ADI basis for the same Region in which the Franchisee operates until such time as SOCS determines, in its sole and absolute discretion, that part or all of such 70% should be spent on a national basis.** Production, administrative and related costs are paid out of Franchisee advertising contributions. National, Regional and Local co-ops may also be created (subject to 2/3 vote) and may require additional advertising contributions and a Grand Opening advertising expenditure of $3000 by

SpeeDee Oil Change & Tune Up® of the Gulf Coast
L-UFOC   v. 2.6   July 20, 1987
Reprinted with permission.

the Local Franchisee is required. Detailed information is contained below and in Sections 4.16 and 5 of the Franchise Agreement.

ADVERTISING — CONTRIBUTIONS AND REGIONAL PORTION

The Franchisee pays a recurring, non-refundable SpeeDee Oil Change & Tune Up® Advertising Fund ["SpeeDee Ad Fund"] Contribution of eight percent [8%] [ten percent (10%) for periods after December 31, 1987] of the Franchisee's gross revenues during the franchise term, payable on Wednesday of each week for gross revenues received or earned during the preceding week. Such SpeeDee Ad Fund Contribution is subject to a minimum weekly obligation of One Hundred Seventy-Five Dollars [$175.00] per week per SpeeDee Oil Change & Tune Up® Car Care Service Center operated by the Franchisee, is subject to annual cost-of-living adjustment, must be paid even if the Franchisee's SpeeDee Oil Change & Tune Up® Car Care Service Center closes or fails to open on the date agreed between the Region and the Franchisee and is to be paid by autodraft or other means acceptable to SOCS and the Region.

With respect to Ad Fund Contributions made by the Franchisee, thirty percent [30%] of such contributions [the "Regional Portion"] will be spent with respect to local, Regional and/or Area-of-Dominant-Influence ["ADI"] advertising, publicity and/or promotions covering areas served by the Region. The Franchisee should note that some ADI territories may not cover the entire Region and/or may extend beyond the Regional boundaries and therefore some ADI expenditures may not cover the entire Region and may not cover Franchisee's location and/or may cover areas outside the Region or outside the Franchisee's location. With respect to such Regional Portion, at least eighty-five percent [85%] of the Regional Portion is to be spent on local, regional and/or ADI media [and related production costs] that cover all or part of the area served by the Region, in each case less reasonable accounting, bookkeeping, auditing, reporting, administrative, legal and similar or related expenses. Up to fifteen percent [15%] of the Regional Portion may be spent on a disproportionate basis on test marketing, surveys of advertising effectiveness or other purposes deemed beneficial by SOCS [or the Region if SOCS so specifies], in its absolute discretion, to the general recognition of the SpeeDee Oil Change & Tune Up® name and/or success of the SpeeDee Oil Change & Tune Up® System within all or a portion of the Region's territory.

ADVERTISING — NATIONAL PORTION SUBJECT TO LOCAL EXPENDITURE

With respect to Ad Fund Contributions made by the Franchisee, seventy percent [70%] is known as the "National Portion" and may be spent by SOCS or the Region with respect to national advertising, publicity and/or promotions, except as detailed below. Until such time as SOCS in its sole and absolute discretion determines that all or any part of the National Portion is to be spent with respect to national advertising, publicity and/or promotions, such part shall be spent in the same

SpeeDee Oil Change & Tune Up® of the Gulf Coast
L-UFOC   v. 2.6   July 20, 1987
Reprinted with permission.

way as the Regional Portion detailed above, subject to any further restrictions delineated by SOCS and may be remitted to or retained by the Region as specified by SOCS. The portion [if any], timing and manner of the National Portion to be spent on local, Regional, Area-of-Dominant-Influence ["ADI"] or national advertising, publicity and/or promotions, is solely within the absolute discretion of SOCS which shall allocate such portions as it determines from time-to-time. Of the National Portion not spent as the Regional Portion detailed above, at least eighty-five percent [85%] is to be spent on either [1] media [and related production costs which are regarded in the advertising industry as "National Media" or [2] local, regional and/or ADI media [and related production costs] that cover all or part of the area served by the Region, in each case less reasonable accounting, bookkeeping, auditing, reporting, administrative, legal and similar or related expenses. Up to fifteen percent [15%] of the National Portion not spent as the Regional Portion detailed above may be spent on a disproportionate basis on test marketing, surveys of advertising effectiveness or other purposes deemed beneficial by SOCS in its absolute discretion to the general recognition of the SpeeDee Oil Change & Tune Up® name and/or success of the SpeeDee Oil Change & Tune Up® System.

Neither SOCS nor the Region make any promises or warranties as to when, as, if or whether any SpeeDee Advertising Fund Contribution will be spent on national media, television or otherwise. SpeeDee Advertising Fund Contributions are paid by the Franchisee directly to the Region [which may remit all or any portion thereof to the SpeeDee Ad Fund] provided that upon notice from SOCS to the Franchisee, all SpeeDee Ad Fund Contributions shall be paid directly from the Franchisee to SOCS, all without any holdback or offset. (See Section 5 of the Franchise Agreement)

ADVERTISING — GRAND OPENING

In connection with the opening for business of the Franchisee's SpeeDee Oil Change & Tune Up® Car Care Service Center, the Franchisee is required by the Local Franchise Agreement to spend, during the period from fifteen [15] days in advance of the grand opening to thirty [30] days following the grand opening, no less than Three Thousand Dollars [$3,000], subject to cost-of-living adjustment, on advertising, promotions and/or publicity in connection with such grand opening. Within thirty [30] days following the grand opening, the Franchisee must supply the Region with proof [by means of cancelled checks, paid invoices, copies of advertisements or otherwise] of the purchase and publication of the grand opening advertising, promotions or publicity. The Franchisee may utilize third-party suppliers [which have been approved by the Region] of grand opening or other advertising, promotions and/or publicity or may, at the Franchisee's option, request the Region and/or SOCS to place such advertising, promotions and/or publicity on the Franchisee's behalf and at his/her sole expense and which may involve payment by the Franchisee to the Region and/or SOCS therefor and for which the Region and/or SOCS may charge amounts in excess of the Region's and/or SOCS' costs and/or receive com-

SpeeDee Oil Change & Tune Up® of the Gulf Coast
L-UFOC   v. 2.6   July 20, 1987
Reprinted with permission.

missions from suppliers of advertising services and materials. When the Franchisee has requested the Region and/or SOCS to place grand opening or other advertising for the Franchisee, the Region and/or SOCS will require payment of such advertising costs in advance.

ADVERTISING — NATIONAL CO-OP

At any time, on thirty [30] days prior written notice from SOCS [or an entity appointed by it to manage the SpeeDee Ad Fund] to the Region, SOCS or such entity may cause the formation of an advisory committee or committees consisting of a representative from SOCS or such entity and a representative from each SpeeDee Oil Change & Tune Up® Region in good standing. Such advisory committee or committees will have such powers with respect to the SpeeDee Ad Fund as SOCS or such entity shall direct, including but not limited to the right to advise [but not direct] SOCS or such entity in the disbursement of SpeeDee Ad Fund contributions. In addition, SOCS or such entity may at any time call a meeting of SpeeDee Oil Change & Tune Up® Regions to discuss special competitive and marketing circumstances or opportunities in the oil change and tune up industry. Following such meeting, SOCS or such entity may forward to all SpeeDee Oil Change & Tune Up® Local Franchisees a proposal to increase SpeeDee Ad Fund Contributions to the national portion for a specified period by not more than an additional two percent [2%] of the Franchisee's gross revenues, to be collected and disbursed as set forth in such proposal. Such proposal shall become effective and binding on the Franchisee and the increased SpeeDee Ad Fund Contributions shall be assessed upon and begin to be paid by the Franchisee upon written approval of two-thirds [2/3] of the SpeeDee Oil Change & Tune Up® Local Franchisees (voting on the basis of one vote per open SpeeDee Oil Change & Tune Up® Car Care Service Center in good standing) responding in writing to such proposal within the time specified in such proposal but not less than thirty [30] days nor to exceed ninety [90] days from the date such proposal is sent to SpeeDee Oil Change & Tune Up® Local Franchisees for approval, such proposal to be sent to all SpeeDee Oil Change & Tune Up® Local Franchisees in good standing. (See Section 5 of the Franchise Agreement)

ADVERTISING — REGIONAL CO-OP

At any time, SOCS or such entity (which may be the Region) may cause the formation of an advisory committee or committees consisting of a representative from the Region or such entity and certain SpeeDee Oil Change & Tune Up® Local Franchisees in the Region selected by SOCS [or the Region if SOCS so specifies] or such entity, which Local Franchisees must be in good standing and current in contributions to the SpeeDee Ad Fund. Such advisory committee or committees shall have

SpeeDee Oil Change & Tune Up® of the Gulf Coast
L-UFOC   v. 2.6   July 20, 1987
Reprinted with permission.

the right to advise [but not direct] SOCS, the Region or such entity in the disbursement of SpeeDee Ad Fund contributions. In addition, by two-thirds (2/3) vote of all Franchisees (voting on the basis of one vote per open SpeeDee Oil Change & Tune Up® Car Care Service Center) in good standing in the Region, the Franchisee's required SpeeDee Ad Fund contribution may be increased by an additional one percent (1%) of the Franchisee's gross revenues. (See Section 5 of the Franchise Agreement)

ADVERTISING — LOCAL CO-OPS

At the Region's election, the Region may cause the formation of such local and/or regional co-operative advertising associations and covering such areas as the Region deems appropriate taking into account all relevant business and marketing considerations and the SpeeDee Ad Fund may disburse such funds as it believes are appropriate from the SpeeDee Ad Fund to be utilized by such local and/or regional co-operative advertising associations for local and/or regional advertising. In addition, upon the formation of such local and/or regional co-operative advertising associations, the Franchisee will be deemed to be a member of such association(s) as cover the area in which the Franchisee's Car Care Service Center is located and will be bound by any decisions made by such association(s) upon a 2/3 majority vote of all members (voting to be on the basis of one vote per open SpeeDee Oil Change and Tune Up Car Care Service Center in good standing), including but not limited to assessment and payment of additional advertising contributions by the members. (See Section 5 of the Franchise Agreement)

OTHER GENERAL ADVERTISING PROVISIONS

Beginning after the Franchisee makes SpeeDee Ad Fund contributions pursuant to Section 5.1 of the Franchise Agreement, the Franchisee will receive on a regular basis, at least annually, a report on how SpeeDee Ad Fund contributions were spent, including financial statements relating to collection and disbursement of SpeeDee Ad Fund contributions.

SpeeDee Ad Fund contributions are maintained by SOCS, the Region or such entity in a separate bank account labeled as a trust account, in order to avoid subjecting SpeeDee Ad Fund contributions to the claims of any creditor. SOCS, the Region and/or such entity may reimburse themselves from SpeeDee Ad Fund contributions for reasonable accounting, bookkeeping, auditing, reporting, administrative, legal and similar or related expenses. The Franchisee agrees that neither SOCS, the Region, any other entity nor any of their shareholders, directors, officers, employees, agents, attorneys or accountants shall be held liable for any act or omission with respect to the SpeeDee Ad Fund which is consistent with the Franchise Agreement or done in good faith. [See Section 5 of the Franchise Agreement.]

SpeeDee Oil Change & Tune Up® of the Gulf Coast
L-UFOC   v. 2.6   July 20, 1987
Reprinted with permission.

If the Franchisee's previously open SpeeDee Oil Change & Tune Up® Car Care Service Center closes or ceases operation or fails to open on the date agreed upon for any reason, the Franchisee will still pay weekly Local Business Development Fees and SpeeDee Ad Fund Contributions based on the average weekly revenues of each of the Franchisee's SpeeDee Oil Change & Tune Up® Car Care Service Centers for the previous six [6] months but in no event lower than each of the minimums set forth above. (See Sections 4 and 5 of the Franchise Agreement).

ADVERTISING — SUPPLIER CONTRIBUTIONS

In some instances, where SOCS has designated an approved brand name supplier of products or services, such supplier may make payments with respect to the sale, use or otherwise of such product(s) or service(s) by SOCS, the Region and/or the Franchisee. Such payments (with the exceptions described below) are paid by the supplier (not the Franchisee) directly to SOCS or an entity appointed by it (which may be the Region with respect to the sale, use or otherwise of such product or service by the Region and/or the Franchisee) to be spent in accordance with any restrictions or conditions imposed by such approved brand name supplier(s). Such conditions or restrictions as imposed by such supplier may include requirements of exclusive use of a particular product or service, minimum levels of use of a product or service, limited reimbursement of advertising expenditures by the Franchisee or other provisions associated with "co-operative advertising" programs. Payments made to SOCS with respect to the sale, use or otherwise of such product(s) or service(s) by SOCS owned and/or operated by officers of SOCS or Region(s) are retained by SOCS. Payments made with respect to the sale, use or otherwise of such product(s) or service(s) by SpeeDee Oil Change & Tune Up® Regions or Franchisees not operating under franchise agreements containing provisions similar to those described in this paragraph (such as "direct franchisees" of SOCS) are collected and spent in accordance with restrictions and conditions imposed by such approved brand name supplier(s). See Item 9 herein for a description of an approved brand name supplier program currently in effect.

OTHER FEES AND CERTAIN COSTS

In connection with any resale or assignment of the franchise [including but not limited to transfer in the event of death or incapacity of the Franchisee] a transfer fee of $2000 [subject to cost-of-living adjustments] will be charged.

If the Franchisee requires consultation services from the Region relating to site selection and development beyond those set forth in Section 3.5 of the Franchise Agreement, Franchisee will pay Region all expenses incurred in connection with such services including, but not limited to, travel, living expenses and a per diem fee of $300 per day [subject to cost-of-living adjustments]. (See Section 3.5 of the Franchise Agreement)

SpeeDee Oil Change & Tune Up® of the Gulf Coast
L-UFOC   v. 2.6   July 20, 1987
Reprinted with permission.

Under Section 4.6 [8] of the Franchise Agreement, the Franchisee is required to submit to the Region such reports of gross revenues together with supporting materials as are specified from time to time in the Confidential Operating Manual. The Region has the right to audit such reports and on the determination that gross revenues have been under-reported by two percent [2%] or more for any period, the Franchisee must immediately pay such deficiency plus the costs of audit and collection, including but not limited to auditor's and attorney's fees.

No fees paid by the Franchisee are refundable once the Franchisee has signed his/her Franchise Agreement, except that a portion of the Initial Franchise Fee may be refunded in certain limited circumstances. (See Item 5 and Section 6.3 (a) (6) of the Franchise Agreement) In the event the Region ceases operation or is terminated by Franchisor or otherwise no longer continues as a SpeeDee Oil Change & Tune Up® Region or a dispute arises between SOCS and the Region, SOCS may require that the Franchisee pay all sums owed or to become due directly to SOCS or its assignee and SOCS will, in such event, assume and be obligated to perform all obligations of the Region to the Franchisee.

In connection with an equipment loan program offered by an approved brand name supplier, the Franchisee can be required (if he/she elects to obtain such equipment from such supplier) to obtain an irrevocable standby letter of credit in favor of the supplier in connection with the loan of such equipment, the amount of such letter of credit to be equal to the original value of such equipment plus installation. Banking and interest charges in connection with such letter of credit are the responsibility of the Franchisee. See Item 9 for further details including a discussion of the possibility of collection on such letter of credit.

Late payments or contributions of any amounts due to be paid or contributed by the Franchisee under the Franchise Agreement or otherwise accrue interest at the lesser of twelve per cent per annum or the applicable legal maximum, interest to accrue beginning ten [10] days after the date on which such payment or contribution was originally due.

Sections 2.4, 6.2 (e) and 7.1 (e) (among others) of the Local Franchise Agreement require the Franchisee to remain in compliance with changes in the SpeeDee Oil Change & Tune Up® System as from time to time may be announced by SOCS. Such changes may include (without restriction) such items as possible building conversion, facilities upgrade, new equipment, signage, store layout, remodeling, changed products or services, operational methods, hours or computerized accounting and/or reporting and the likelihood, timing or costs (which must be borne by the Franchisee) of such future changes cannot be predicted.

There are no other recurring or foreseeable one-time fees or payments required in the form of additional franchise fees, royalties, training fees, lease payments, commissions, advertising fees or other similar payments to be made by the

SpeeDee Oil Change & Tune Up® of the Gulf Coast
L-UFOC   v. 2.6   July 20, 1987
Reprinted with permission.

Franchisee to SOCS, the Region or persons affiliated with either. At its option, the Franchisee may purchase materials and supplies from Franchisor at standard prices charged to all Franchisees.

ITEM 7: FRANCHISEE'S INITIAL INVESTMENT

Each Franchisee is required to provide the services, materials and supplies necessary for the operation of his business and the improvement or construction [as necessary] of each SpeeDee Oil Change & Tune Up® Car Care Service Center to be operated by him. The Region will provide the Franchisee with one [1] copy of the SpeeDee Oil Change & Tune Up® Confidential Operating Manual and standard plans and specifications to be utilized only in the construction of a SpeeDee Oil Change & Tune Up® Car Care Service Center.

The initial franchise fee is $25,000, and is due and payable upon execution of the Franchise Agreement.

Each Franchisee will also be required to pay for the expense involved in the operation of his/her business, including expenses of securing appropriate business licenses, telephone services, advertising, rent and liability insurance, salaries, wages and benefits, taxes, vehicle maintenance and purchase of other materials and supplies. Generally, such sums will not be refundable (except for telephone security deposits and the like) and will require an initial lump sum cash payment.

The Region does not offer financing arrangements of any kind.

The Region estimates that the Franchisee should expect to make the following initial investment (described by a high-low range) in connection with the operation of a franchise prior to the commencement of business and for a short period of time thereafter. THE FOLLOWING FIGURES ARE GERMANE ONLY WITH REFERENCE TO THE EXPLANATION CONTAINED IN THE PRECEDING PARAGRAPHS.

Typical Costs Related to Establishment of the Car Care Service Center:

NATURE OF INVESTMENT	HIGH	LOW	TO WHOM PAID	WHETHER REFUNDABLE
Franchise Fee	$25,000	$25,000	Region	No
Travel and Expenses [in connection with Training]	2,000	500	Provider of meals, lodging and transportation	No

SpeeDee Oil Change & Tune Up® of the Gulf Coast
L-UFOC v. 2.6 July 20, 1987
Reprinted with permission.

Typical Costs Related to Establishment of the Car Care Service Center

NATURE OF INVESTMENT	HIGH	LOW	TO WHOM PAID	WHETHER REFUNDABLE
Equipment				
Oil Dispensing[3]	60,000	20,000[3]	Suppliers	No
Tune Up	25,000	2,000	Suppliers	No
Tools[1]	2,000	1,000	Suppliers	No
Inventory[1]	23,000	8,000	Suppliers	No
Legal and Accounting	4,000	1,000	Attorney/Accountant	No
Misc.	5,000	2,000	Suppliers	No
Office and Lounge Supplies	5,000	2,500	Suppliers	No
Payroll	4,000	1,000	Employees	No
Signage (Outdoor)	15,000	4,000	Suppliers	No
First Month's Rent, Permits and Deposits[2]	5,000	2,000	Landlord/Utilities	No
Advertising: Grand Opening Advertising	3,000	3,000	Suppliers/Region	No
Insurance[2]	10,000	5,000	Insurers	No
Working Capital	25,000	10,000	None	No
Total:	$213,000	$87,000	**See Notes Below**	

(1) Varies

(2) Generally not refundable but portions of utility deposits and insurance premiums may be refundable in certain circumstances. Amounts depend on factors such as rental rates and land and building costs in the Franchisee's area and whether the Franchisee currently has an office. Other payments include such items as business licenses and legal and accounting fees as may be necessary in Franchisee's area.

(3) Varies depending on whether equipment is purchased, leased or is available on loan from Suppliers. See Item 9. Optional leasing arrangements may be available to the Franchisee from third parties unaffiliated with the Region or the Franchisor. In the event that oil dispensing equipment is available on loan from Castrol, a $20,000 Letter of Credit may be required by Castrol in connection with use by the Franchisee of certain of Castrol's equipment in addition to the costs reflected in the above table. Such Letter of Credit may only be available from the Franchisee's bank(s) on approved credit and/or by the Franchisee depositing compensating balances. Prospective Franchisees should note that in the event they do not

SpeeDee Oil Change & Tune Up® of the Gulf Coast
L-UFOC v. 2.6 July 20, 1987
Reprinted with permission.

obtain such equipment from Castrol and instead obtain similar equipment from other sources (approved by the Region and/or SOCS) no such Letter of Credit would be required by Castrol or the Region and the Franchisee would make independent arrangements regarding such equipment with such other supplier[s].

Although most prospective Franchisees will choose to lease the property and improvements on which the business would be conducted, it is possible that a prospective Franchisee would purchase and construct a facility himself. The above figures assume that the prospective franchisee will lease land and building. In the event that the prospective franchisee purchases and constructs the facility, the acquisition cost of a suitable location could vary widely depending on desirability of specific location, local demographics, traffic count and region of the country. Land cost could range from $75,000 to $400,000 and the cost of constructing a suitable facility could range from $95,000 to $175,000 (plus any costs of site preparation, landscaping, architect's fees, etc.) depending on desirability of specific location, local demographics, traffic count, region of the country, number of service bays in the store and local construction costs. The prospective Franchisee is strongly urged to research location availability, lease, acquisition and construction costs prior to purchasing a franchise.

THERE ARE NO OTHER DIRECT OR INDIRECT PAYMENTS IN CONJUNCTION WITH THE PURCHASE OF THE FRANCHISE.

ITEM 8: OBLIGATIONS OF FRANCHISEE TO PURCHASE OR LEASE FROM DESIGNATED SOURCES

The Franchisee is not obligated to purchase any goods, services, supplies, fixtures, equipment, inventory or real estate from Franchisor or the Region in connection with the operation of his franchise. However, each of the goods and services supplied by the Franchisee to the public are subject to the quality standards necessary to uphold the reputation and public image of the SpeeDee Oil Change & Tune Up® System and the Franchisor and Region will require that all goods, services, supplies, fixtures, equipment, inventory and real estate used to serve the public meet the standards of the SpeeDee Oil Change & Tune Up® System as set forth in the Confidential Operating Manual and other publications and as subject to change from time to time. On occasion the Franchisor, Region, or an affiliated entity offers for sale to the Region and/or its franchisees various items, including supplies, materials, products, inventory and equipment through its warehouse facility. The Region's franchisees are not required to purchase such items from the Franchisor, Region or such entity nor is the Franchisor or any such entity obligated to sell such items. To the extent that the cost of such items is less than their sale price, the Franchisor, Region, or such entity may realize a profit as a result of such sales.

SpeeDee Oil Change & Tune Up® of the Gulf Coast
L-UFOC   v. 2.6   July 20, 1987
Reprinted with permission.

ITEM 9: OBLIGATIONS OF FRANCHISEE TO PURCHASE OR LEASE IN ACCORDANCE WITH SPECIFICATIONS OR FROM APPROVED SUPPLIERS

To insure uniformity and quality in all units, whether franchised or otherwise, all Franchisees are required to purchase supplies, materials and products that are equal to or exceed the specifications of SOCS. In addition, all SpeeDee Oil Change & Tune Up® Car Care Service Centers must meet the construction and appearance as well as equipment standards set forth in the Confidential Operating Manual, however Franchisees are not required to have construction services performed by any specific entity. Specifications may include minimum standards for building size and style, sign(s), equipment types, quality, delivery, performance, warranties, logo and trademark design and compliance, appearance and other restrictions. Such specifications are part of the Confidential Operating Manual which is issued to the Franchisee on execution of the Franchise Agreement and payment of the franchise fee.

The Region and SOCS each have the right to sample, review or test all equipment, products, materials and supplies to determine compliance with SpeeDee Oil Change & Tune Up® standards and conformity (as well as other factors such as advertising contributions, marketing assistance, and equipment loan arrangements). Those items failing to meet such standards will be disapproved and it will be the responsibility of the Franchisee to replace such items with those meeting such standards. Approval of equipment, products, materials and supplies will not be unreasonably withheld, however Franchisor (SOCS) reserves the right to require that the Region and/or its local Franchisees purchase and use specific brand name items to be used in the operation of the franchise (although the Franchisee is free to purchase such items from sources identified by the Franchisee and meeting Franchisor's reasonable requirements) to obtain quality control, uniformity, and marketing and advertising contribution benefits. Where SOCS has designated an approved brand name supplier and such supplier has agreed to make payments with respect to such approved product or service conditioned on use, sales or otherwise by SOCS, the Region or the Local Franchisee, all such payments by such approved brand name supplier are made to SOCS or an entity appointed by it [which may be the Region] and shall be spent by SOCS or such entity provided that any expenditure or other handling of such payments must be consistent with any restrictions or conditions imposed by such approved brand name supplier. Franchisor reserves the right to require that all products used by the Region and/or its local Franchisees meet Franchisor's quality standards and other reasonable requirements. Except to the extent that locations owned and/or operated by the Region or the Franchisor would benefit from the advertising contribution and other programs of approved suppliers as outlined herein, neither the Region nor the Franchisor will derive any income from the purchase of materials or services from any other parties [except as disclosed herein], but will derive income from purchases from them by the Franchisee equal to the profit margin on such materials and services.

SpeeDee Oil Change & Tune Up® of the Gulf Coast
L-UFOC   v. 2.6   July 20, 1987
Reprinted with permission.

In connection with the sale by A & G Supply Company [a company owned by Gary Copp, President of SOCS, and Kevin Bennett, Vice President and Director of Franchising of SOCS and engaged in a warehouse business which may sell supplies to SpeeDee Oil Change & Tune Up® Franchisees] of certain assets of such company [including inventory and goodwill], the purchaser [Norman W., Barry M. and Brian G. Prendergast] has agreed to pay a portion of the purchase price for such business [attributable to goodwill] on the basis of one percent of the first $500,000 in future annual sales to SpeeDee Oil Change & Tune Up® Franchisees and two percent of future annual sales over $500,000 to SpeeDee Oil Change & Tune Up® Franchisees, each indefinitely. Subject to the purchasing company meeting reasonable approved supplier standards imposed by SOCS on behalf of SpeeDee Oil Change & Tune Up® Franchisees, the purchasing company is to be an approved supplier of certain items to SpeeDee Oil Change & Tune Up® Franchisees and the sellers have agreed to assist the purchasing company in maintaining business that the selling company had received in the past [or may receive in the future] from SpeeDee Oil Change & Tune Up® Franchisees in the Region 12 [Louisiana/Mississippi] area. The purchasers have agreed that the two of them will be involved in the on-going day-to-day operation of the business, that they will use their best efforts to supply SpeeDee Oil Change & Tune Up® Franchisees with products of a quality approved by SOCS, that product costs will be net of any vendor advertising rebates and that volume discounts will be available depending on the level of monthly sales volume to SpeeDee Oil Change & Tune Up® Franchisees. No SpeeDee Oil Change & Tune Up® Franchisee is required to deal with the purchasing Company although they are an approved supplier and SOCS recommends dealing with them. This arrangement may result in future receipt of income by SOCS or Messrs. Copp and Bennett [or companies owned by them] with respect to the future sale of items to SpeeDee Oil Change & Tune Up® Franchisees by such purchase of the warehouse business.

The Franchisor has designated Burmah-Castrol, Inc. ("Castrol") as the exclusive lubricant supplier at all affiliated SpeeDee Oil Change & Tune Up® locations and as the recommended primary lubricant supplier at all franchised locations. Castrol is currently the only approved supplier of lubricants to affiliated and franchised SpeeDee Oil Change & Tune Up® locations and the Franchisor has the right, under the Franchise Agreement, to require the Franchisee to only use approved brand-name items (including lubricants) although the Franchisee is free to purchase such items from any supplier meeting the Franchisor's reasonable requirements.

In connection with the appointment of Castrol as an approved supplier of lubricants, automatic transmission and brake fluids, Castol has agreed to assume or "buy-out", on behalf of SOCS and/or Messrs. Copp and Bennett [or companies owned by them], existing equipment loans for equipment placements at SpeeDee Oil Change & Tune Up® locations owned and/or operated by Messrs. Copp and Bennett [or companies owned by them]. Such agreement will operate to relieve Messrs. Copp and Bennett [or companies owned by them] from obligations other-

SpeeDee Oil Change & Tune Up® of the Gulf Coast
L-UFOC   v. 2.6   July 20, 1987
Reprinted with permission.

wise owed or to be owed to a previous approved supplier of lubricants, automatic transmission and brake fluids with respect to such equipment.

Castrol is the only entity currently meeting the Franchisor's standards (including advertising contribution and equipment arrangements) for lubricants, automatic transmission and brake fluids and is the Franchisor's only recommended lubricant supplier. The Franchisor and the Region derive no direct income from purchases or use by the Region or SpeeDee Oil Change & Tune Up® Franchisees of Castrol products (except to the extent income is realized by A & G Supply Company — see below — acting as a distributor in New Orleans area) and would derive indirect income only to the extent that affiliated stores benefited from the arrangements detailed herein and/or available to all SpeeDee Oil Change & Tune Up® Franchisees.

Castrol has agreed to appoint A & G Supply Company, a company owned by Gary Copp and Kevin Bennett, Directors and Officers of SOCS [each of which are also Directors and Officers of the Region], as a Castrol distributor for the purpose of supplying affiliated and franchised locations in the New Orleans area. Franchisees are not required to purchase Castrol lubricants from A & G Supply Company [being free to purchase such products from any source] but if they do so a profit on such sales may accrue to A & G Supply Company to the extent that the sale price of such items exceeds their cost. Sales of Castrol products by A & G Supply Company to stores owned by Officers of SOCS may be at lower prices than charged by A & G Supply Company to Franchisees in the New Orleans area. Prices charged by Castrol to A & G Supply Company as a distributor will be the same as charged by Castrol to other distributors. Franchised locations outside the New Orleans area are serviced by Castrol and/or independent distributors.

The designation of Castrol by the Franchisor has been made based on a review of the product quality, delivery and terms which such products are sold, as well as the advertising contributions, equipment arrangements and other significant marketing assistance to be provided by Castrol to affiliated SpeeDee Oil Change & Tune Up® locations and franchised locations. Equipment provided to the Franchisee by Castrol is made available under the terms and conditions set forth in Exhibit "D" attached hereto and subject to a standby letter of credit required by Castrol (Exhibit "E" attached hereto).

Under the terms and conditions required by Castrol, as set forth in Exhibit "D", the Franchisee is required to, at its expense, keep the equipment in good condition, insure the loaned equipment against all risks and not encumber or remove the equipment, which remains the property of Castrol and in which Castrol retains a security interest. Castrol requires that the loaned equipment be used only for the storage, handling, dispensing and sale of Castrol products and for no other purpose. The equipment is loaned by Castrol without any warranties by Castrol, SOCS or the Region, express or implied, including warranties or merchantability or fitness, or as

SpeeDee Oil Change & Tune Up® of the Gulf Coast
L-UFOC   v. 2.6   July 20, 1987
Reprinted with permission.

to the design, condition, capacity, performance or any other aspect of the equipment or its material or workmanship. Castrol, SOCS and the Region disclaim any liability to the Franchisee, any third parties (including but not limited to customers and members of the general public) or any employees of any of the foregoing as a result of any defects, latent or otherwise, in the equipment and the Franchisee agrees to not assert any claim against Castrol, SOCS or the Region for any loss or damages with respect to or caused in any way by the equipment. The Franchisee also agrees to indemnify Castrol, SOCS and the Region arising from use of the equipment and assumes total responsibility for any taxes levied with respect to the equipment.

The Franchisee is given the right [but is not obligated to] to purchase the entire equipment from Castrol at any time at its depreciated value, calculated on a ten-year, straight-line basis with no residual value. After 10 years, Castrol claims no rights to the equipment.

Under the terms and conditions required by Castrol, as set forth in Exhibit "D", if the Franchisee fails to purchase at the rate of 10,000 gallons [8 lbs. grease/gear oil = 1 gallon] per year of Castrol products, or if the Franchisee uses the equipment for other than Castrol products, fails to pay for purchases of Castrol products when due, or breaches the terms and conditions required by Castrol, as set forth in Exhibit "D", in any way, the Franchisee will be required by Castrol to purchase the equipment from Castrol at its then depreciated value or, at Castrol's option, return the equipment to Castrol.

Castrol has agreed to supply under the Loaned Equipment Agreement, free of charge, up to $20,000 in lubrication equipment (including installation) to new affiliated and franchised locations. This equipment is to include air and hand-operated pumps, compressors, overhead reels, grease and gear oil dispensers, oil drains and above-ground storage tanks, together with an illuminated sign and hanging metal sign (subject to compliance with local zoning and other ordinances). The equipment is required by Castrol to be used solely for storage and dispensing of Castrol products. Castrol has agreed to either pay the equipment supplier directly for the equipment or reimburse SOCS or the Franchisee based on actual original invoices from the equipment supplier.

During the first two years of the term of the Loaned Equipment Agreement, the Franchisee must provide Castrol with an irrevocable standby letter of credit equal to the original value of the equipment and installation and issued or confirmed by a major U.S. bank. All banking and/or interest charges associated with the letter of credit are the responsibility of the Franchisee. Collection by Castrol on the letter of credit would occur if the Franchisee is not using the equipment solely for the storage, handling, dispensing and sale of Castrol products or the Franchisee is past due in any monetary obligation to Castrol by sixty (60) days or more twice during any

SpeeDee Oil Change & Tune Up® of the Gulf Coast
L-UFOC   v. 2.6   July 20, 1987
Reprinted with permission.

six-month period, or is in default in any other obligation to Castrol (which could include failure to purchase required quantities of Castrol products as set forth above) for 60 days or more, and could involve payment by the Franchisee to the bank issuing the Letter of Credit in the amount of any collections against the Letter of Credit, and in connection therewith, should Castrol exercise its option of collection on the letter of credit, the issuing Bank may acquire a security interest in the equipment in the amount of its payment on the letter of credit to Castrol plus any costs of collection. Since terms and conditions of such collections may vary from bank to bank, the prospective franchisee should discuss this particular aspect with his/her bank of choice prior to the signing of any such letter of credit or related documents. At the end of the first year, Castrol will review the Franchisee's financial position and may (but is not obligated to) release the Franchisee from the letter of credit obligations for the second year. Castrol has reserved the right to review each new Franchisee's financial position and other circumstances prior to committing to the free use of equipment and may withhold such use in Castrol's sole judgment if the Franchisee is a poor financial risk or for other good faith business reasons.

Castrol has also agreed to make available to all SpeeDee Oil Change & Tune Up® Franchisees all of its merchandising and promotional allowance programs. These programs could be revised by Castrol in the future but currently include the following items:

Castrol provides free-of-charge merchandising and sign items, such as "menu boards," clocks, fender covers, litter bags, promotional literature, key rings, pennant strings, etc.

As part of their New Product Placement Program, Castrol will pay with respect to new and existing locations $1 per gallon up to a maximum of $1000 on their initial orders (first 60 days) of each Castrol product stocked.

As part of their advertising allowance program, Castrol will accrue with respect to each affiliated and franchised location 15¢ per gallon of Castrol products purchased. From that fund, Castrol will pay up to 100% of the cost (maximum 15¢ per gallon) of advertisements featuring Castrol products. Castrol will also pay an additional bonus allowance of 8¢ per gallon when certain Castrol approved advertising claims are included in advertisements.

All such advertising contributions are paid by Castrol to the SpeeDee Ad Fund or such entity or (if SOCS so designates) to the Region (not to the Franchisee) and disbursement of such contributions will be by the SpeeDee Ad Fund or such entity or the Region concerned and will generally not be paid to individual Franchisees but will be spent in accordance with any terms and conditions imposed by such brand name supplier.

SpeeDee Oil Change & Tune Up® of the Gulf Coast
L-UFOC   v. 2.6   July 20, 1987
Reprinted with permission.

Approval of any other supplier for lubricants, automatic transmission and brake fluids will depend on an evaluation of the proposed supplier's quality, terms of sale, delivery capability, national reputation, performance, warranties and proposed advertising contribution and equipment arrangements, in addition to other factors. Detailed criteria, specifications and standards are not currently issued by the Franchisor to any person for the approval of suppliers. Approval by the Franchisor of any other supplier than Castrol as the "primary supplier" of lubricant items to franchised locations could cause the loss of the benefits supplied by Castrol to all SpeeDee Oil Change & Tune Up® locations as outlined above (including Castrol collecting on the letter of credit) and is not viewed by the Franchisor as likely at this time. However, the Franchisor reserves the right to disapprove Castrol and/or approve another supplier in the future as its best business judgment determines. Approval of any additional suppliers would be announced by inclusion in SpeeDee Oil Change & Tune Up® manuals and/or separate written announcement to Regions and Franchisees.

Under Section 6.3 of the Franchise Agreement, if the Franchisee breaches any agreement between an approved supplier and the Franchisee, such breach can be cause for termination of the Franchise Agreement by the Region.

The Franchisee is required to only use advertising, promotions and/or publicity materials, items, campaigns, advertisements, concepts, programs, services and suppliers as are approved in advance by SOCS. The Franchisee may utilize third-party suppliers [which have been approved by SOCS] of advertising, promotions and/or publicity or may, at the Franchisee's option, request the Region to place such advertising, promotions and/or publicity, all of which are for the Franchisee's account and at his/her sole expense and which may involve payment by the Franchisee to the Region therefor, in which case the Region may charge amounts in excess of the Region's costs and thereby derive income [and/or reimbursement of administrative or other expenses] or on which the Region may derive income [and/or reimbursement of administrative or other expenses] as a result of advertising or other commissions paid by advertising media or otherwise. The Franchisee is required to spend $3000 (subject to cost-of-living adjustment) on Grand Opening advertising, promotions and/or publicity, the media, content and suppliers of which must be approved by the Region and/or SOCS and, at the Franchisee's option the Region and/or SOCS may be such a supplier. See Item 6 of this Offering Circular and Section 4.16 of the Franchise Agreement.

ITEM 10: FINANCING ARRANGEMENTS

The Region does not offer any financing arrangements of any kind or nature for the Franchisee's purchase or operation of a franchise. Any financing obtained by the Franchisee from third parties would be the sole responsibility of the Franchisee.

SpeeDee Oil Change & Tune Up® of the Gulf Coast
L-UFOC   v. 2.6   July 20, 1987
Reprinted with permission.

The Region has no past or present practice or intent to sell, assign or discount to a third party, in whole or in part, any note or other financing instrument executed by the Franchisee in connection with the purchase of a franchise, but is not prohibited from doing so.

Neither the Region nor SOCS receives any payments from any person for the placement of any financing with any person or entity.

ITEM 11: OBLIGATIONS OF THE REGION; OTHER SUPERVISION, ASSISTANCE OR SERVICES

The Region's obligations to the Franchisee up to the time of commencement of the Franchisee's business are as follows (references are to the Franchise Agreement):

(a) To provide a Confidential Operating Manual. (Section 3.1);

(b) To arrange for Franchisee's Initial Home Office Orientation at Franchisor's headquarters in Metairie, Louisiana. The Initial Home Office Orientation is mandatory, shall be of approximately three (3) days duration, shall commence as soon as practicable after the signing of the Franchise Agreement, and must be completed prior to Franchisee's Regional training and subsequent commencement of business. Franchisee shall be responsible for his/her transportation, meals and lodging arrangements and expenses to, from, and while at Initial Home Office Orientation. (Section 3.2)

(c) To furnish the Franchisee with Regional training in the operation of his/her franchise. The training will commence as soon as practicable after the signing of the Franchise Agreement, completion of Franchisee's Initial Home Office Orientation at Franchisor's location in Metairie, Louisiana, and payment of the franchise fee, and must be completed prior to commencement of Franchisee's conduct of business. Training will be conducted at Metairie, Louisiana, or at such other place as may be designated by the Region (which may be at the Franchisor's headquarters in Metairie, Louisiana), and will consist primarily of a comprehensive introduction to the operation of a SpeeDee Oil Change & Tune Up® Car Care Service Center, and includes training of the unit manager in the day-to-day operations of the franchised facility, familiarization with operating procedures and systems and a complete review of SpeeDee Oil Change & Tune Up® methodology. The training is conducted by Region's personnel, and is of approximately 10 working days duration. The Franchisee is responsible for his/her transportation, meals and lodging expenses while traveling to, from and while at training. The Region may [but is not required to] make available such continuing advisory assistance in the operation of the franchise,

SpeeDee Oil Change & Tune Up® of the Gulf Coast
L-UFOC   v. 2.6   July 20, 1987
Reprinted with permission.

rendered in person or by bulletins made available from time to time to all Franchisees, as Region may deem appropriate. (Section 3.3)

      (d) The Region will make available standard plans and specifications to be utilized only in the construction of a SpeeDee Oil Change & Tune Up® Car Care Service Center. No modifications or deviations from the standard plans and specifications may be made without the written consent of Region. The Franchisee will obtain, at his own expense, all further qualified architectural and engineering services to prepare surveys, site and foundation plans and adapt the standard plans and specifications to each individual site, applicable local and state laws, regulations and ordinances. The selection of a site for the franchised service center will be subject to Region's approval, which will not be unreasonably withheld. The Region will provide consultation at its home office to the Franchisee with respect to site selection and development, together with one visit to three [3] potential sites in the company of Franchisee for the purposes of joint site evaluation. In the event that the Franchisee requires consultation services beyond those expressly provided above, then Franchisee will pay Region all expenses incurred in connection with such consultation, including, but not limited to, travel, living expenses, and a per diem fee of $300 per day, subject to cost-of-living adjustments. The Franchisee will bear any cost of preparing plans containing deviations or modifications from the standard plans and all costs of site acquisition and construction, and neither the Region nor SOCS shall have any liability with respect to such deviations or modifications nor with respect to the evaluation of Franchisee's selection of site nor the acquisition nor construction and operation of the SpeeDee Oil Change & Tune Up® Car Care Service Center to be erected thereupon, whether in accordance with standard plans or otherwise, all such responsibilities being solely those of the Franchisee. (Section 3.5)

The Region's obligations to the Franchisee during the operation of the franchise are as follows:

      (a) The Region may [but is not required to] make available to Franchisee or Franchisee's employees from time to time such additional training programs as Region in its sole discretion may choose to conduct. Attendance at such training programs and any Regional conventions may be mandatory. The cost of the instruction and required materials will be borne by the Region but all other expenses during the training period, including costs of accommodations, meals, wages and travel, will be borne by the Franchisee. The Region may [but is not required to] make available such continuing advisory assistance in the operation of the franchise, rendered in person or by bulletins made available from time to time to all Franchisees, as Region may deem appropriate. (Section 3.4)

The Region is not required to provide any other supervision, assistance or service prior to the opening of the franchise business or during its operation.

Franchise locations are determined as set forth in Item 12.

SpeeDee Oil Change & Tune Up® of the Gulf Coast
L-UFOC   v. 2.6   July 20, 1987
Reprinted with permission.

The typical length of time between the signing of the Franchise Agreement or the first payment of a consideration for the franchise and the opening of the Franchisee's business is two to four months.

The Franchisor (SpeeDee Oil Change Systems, Inc.) has no obligations to the Franchisee and all obligations to the Franchisee are the sole responsibility of the Region with the exception of obligations created in Section V of the Franchise Agreement with respect to the management of the National Advertising Fund.

ITEM 12: EXCLUSIVE AREA OR TERRITORY

Each Franchisee is granted the right to conduct his franchise at a specific geographic location only. The Region will not grant to any person other than the Franchisee the right to locate a SpeeDee Oil Change & Tune Up® Car Care Service Center within a one-half (1/2) mile radius of the Franchisee's approved location. The Region has the right to approve the Franchisee's site selection, and such approval will not be unreasonably withheld. There is no pattern of time which elapses between the signing of the Franchise Agreement and site selection, since the ability to obtain acceptable sites varies from area to area, but the Franchise Agreement requires the Franchisee to open the SpeeDee Oil Change & Tune Up® Car Care Service Center no later than one hundred twenty (120) days after the date of execution of the Franchise Agreement. In the event that special circumstances beyond the control of the Franchisee prevent the opening of the Car Care Service Center within such one hundred twenty (120) days, the Region will consider such special circumstances (upon written notification and request by the Franchisee to the Region prior to the expiration of such 120 day period) and the Region may (but is not legally obligated to) extend such deadline for an additional period, the length of such extension and any related conditions to be determined in the Region's sole and absolute discretion. The Region may itself, from time to time, operate SpeeDee Oil Change & Tune Up® Car Care Service Centers in this state or elsewhere. (Sections 2.6 and 4.4)

ITEM 13: TRADEMARKS, SERVICE MARKS, TRADE NAMES, LOGOTYPES AND COMMERCIAL SYMBOLS

The service marks and commercial symbols to be licensed to the Franchisee consist of the names SpeeDee Oil Change™ and SpeeDee Oil Change & Tune Up® and the attendant logotypes represented in the upper left-hand corner of the facing page of this Offering Circular.

SpeeDee Oil Change & Tune Up® of the Gulf Coast
L-UFOC   v. 2.6   July 20, 1987
Reprinted with permission.

The following service marks were registered with the United States Patent and Trademark Office on the principal register on the dates, and receiving the registration numbers (where applicable), indicated:

Mark	Date	Number
"SpeeDee Oil Change & Tune Up®" [with oil can and funnel]	June 18, 1985	1,343,310
"SpeeDee Oil Change 9 Minute Oil Service" [with oil can and funnel]	June 4, 1985	1,339,517

The following service marks were registered with the state offices on the dates indicated:

Mark	State	Date	#
"SpeeDee Oil Change & Tune Up" [with oil can and funnel]	Florida	4/4/85	T03082
"SpeeDee Oil Change, Inc."	Louisiana	4/15/81	N/A
"SpeeDee Oil Change and Logo"	Louisiana	5/6/81	N/A
"SpeeDee Oil Change, Inc. and Logo"	Louisiana	9/13/82	N/A
"SpeeDee Oil Change & Tune Up, plus Design"	Louisiana	2/15/85	N/A
"SpeeDee Oil Change & Tune Up"	Louisiana	2/15/85	N/A
"SpeeDee Oil Change & Tune Up, plus Design"	Louisiana	4/12/85	N/A
"SpeeDee Oil Change & Tune Up, plus Design"	Oklahoma	1/29/86	20487
"SpeeDee Oil Change & Tune Up"	Louisiana	4/12/85	N/A
"SpeeDee Oil Change & Tune Up, plus Design"	Mississippi	9/10/85	N/A
"SpeeDee Oil Change & Tune Up, plus Design"	Texas	1/29/86	45930

Sections 2.1 and 4.13 of the Franchise Agreement provide that neither the Region nor Franchisor can guarantee that there is not a conflicting use of the licensed names, service marks or logotypes somewhere in the Franchisee's Territory, and that in the event the Region or the Franchisees are prevented from using such names, service marks or logotypes, the sole remedy shall be to operate under alternative

names, service marks or logotypes reasonably acceptable to Franchisor. It is SOCS's usual policy that in the event (which SOCS considers unlikely) that any restrictions on a Region's or Franchisee's use of the names, service marks or logotypes in any state were to arise, SOCS would allow the Region or Franchisee to continue to utilize its entire system with all of its operating features and details under another mutually agreeable name, and the Franchise Agreement would continue in full force and effect with respect to all other terms.

Neither the Region nor Franchisor is aware of (i) any presently effective determination of the United States Patent Office, the trademark administrator of any state or any court, any pending interference, opposition or cancellation proceeding or any pending material litigation involving Franchisor's service marks and which is relevant to the Franchisee's use of these service marks in this state, (ii) any infringing uses of a trademark which could materially affect the Franchisee's use of Franchisor's service marks in this state, or (iii) any agreement currently in effect that would significantly limit the right of Franchisor to use or license its service marks in this state. Neither the Region nor Franchisor warrant their right to use the licensed names, service marks or logotypes and have no obligation to protect the rights which the Franchisee has to use them or to defend the Franchisee against third party claims with respect to their use (Sections 2.1 and 4.13).

ITEM 14: PATENTS AND COPYRIGHTS

Neither the Region nor Franchisor own any rights to any patents or copyrights [other than the copyrighted Confidential Operating Manual] which are material to their businesses.

ITEM 15: OBLIGATIONS OF THE FRANCHISEE TO PARTICIPATE IN THE ACTUAL OPERATION OF THE FRANCHISE

The Franchisee is not obligated to participate personally in the direct operation of the Franchise so long as it fulfills its obligations pursuant to the Franchise Agreement, however the Region highly recommends personal involvement on the part of the Franchisee, as the purchase of this Franchise is not a passive investment, but rather is a business dependent upon Franchisee's independent efforts, business judgment and skills, as well as market conditions and the general economy. The Franchise owner is required to maintain personal financial control of the Franchise and to be personally responsible for all of the Franchisee's obligations to the Region. The Franchisee is required to appoint a qualified Operations Manager [who may be the Franchisee himself] who has successfully completed SpeeDee Oil Change & Tune Up® home office training. If the Franchisee operates five [5] or more units or multiples thereof, he is required to appoint a qualified supervisor for each five units.

SpeeDee Oil Change & Tune Up® of the Gulf Coast
L-UFOC   v. 2.6   July 20, 1987
Reprinted with permission.

If any franchise is owned or operated by a corporation, the obligations of such corporation to SOCS and the Region must be personally guaranteed by an individual or individuals approved by the Region.

ITEM 16: RESTRICTIONS ON GOODS AND SERVICES OFFERED BY FRANCHISEE

The Franchisee is limited to performance of the following services on motor vehicles: oil changes, tune-ups, transmission services, differential services, radiator flushes, air conditioner recharges and replacement of filters.

The Region will not grant to any person other than the Franchisee the right to locate a SpeeDee Oil Change & Tune Up® Car Care Service Center within a one-half (1/2) mile radius of the Franchisee's approved location.

During the term of the Franchise Agreement, the Franchisee may not own, maintain, engage in or have a controlling interest in a similar business to that licensed by the Franchise Agreement unless operated under a SpeeDee Oil Change & Tune Up ® Franchise Agreement.

ITEM 17: RENEWAL, TERMINATION, REPURCHASE, MODIFICATION AND ASSIGNMENT OF THE FRANCHISE AGREEMENT AND RELATED INFORMATION

TERM AND TERMINATION

The term of the Franchise Agreement is fifteen [15] years and may be renewed by the Franchisee for two subsequent five [5] year terms if at the time of such proposed renewal the Franchisee has complied with each of the following conditions: (a) the Franchisee has delivered to the Region written notice of its intention to renew not more than 180 nor less than 90 days prior to the expiration of the prior term; (b) the Franchisee executes the then-current form of Franchise Agreement [which may contain different terms including, without limitation, higher fees] including a form of release in favor of Franchisor and the Region; (c) all liabilities of the Franchisee to the Franchisor and to the Region are paid in full and all other liabilities of the Franchisee are provided for to the Region's reasonable satisfaction; (d) the Franchisee is in full compliance with all terms of the Franchise Agreement, including but not limited to all payment obligations, and is a SpeeDee Oil Change & Tune Up® Franchisee in good standing; (e) the Franchisee remodels and modernizes and otherwise brings into full compliance the SpeeDee Change & Tune Up® Car Care Service Center as the Region designates to conform to then-current standards (similar to the requirements for a sale or assignment — see below) all at the Franchisee's sole

SpeeDee Oil Change & Tune Up® of the Gulf Coast
L-UFOC   v. 2.6   July 20, 1987
Reprinted with permission.

cost and expense; and (f) the Franchisee pays the Region a renewal fee of ten percent [10%] of the then-current initial franchise fee established by the Region for new franchises.

The Region may terminate the Franchise Agreement and the Franchisee's rights thereunder effective immediately and without notice and opportunity to cure:

(1) If any information supplied to Region by the Franchisee with or in connection with the Franchisee's application for franchise is inaccurate or incomplete;

(2) If Franchisee becomes insolvent or makes a general assignment for the benefit of creditors, or if a petition in bankruptcy is filed by Franchisee, or such a petition filed against and consented to by Franchisee, or if Franchisee is adjudicated a bankrupt, or if a bill or equity or other proceeding for the appointment of a receiver of Franchisee or other custodian for Franchisee's business or assets is filed and consented to by Franchisee, or if a receiver or other custodian [permanent or temporary] of Franchisee's assets or property, or any part hereof, is appointed by any court of competent jurisdiction, or if a proceeding for a composition with creditors under any state or federal law should be instituted by or against Franchisee, or if a final judgment remains unsatisfied or of record for thirty [30] days or longer [unless supersedeas bond is filed], or if execution is levied against Franchisee's franchise or property, or a suit to foreclose any lien or mortgage against the premises or equipment is instituted against Franchisee and not dismissed within thirty [30] days, or if the real or personal property of Franchisee's franchise shall be sold after levy thereupon by any sheriff, marshal or constable;

(3) If Franchisee has received from Region two [2] or more Notices to Cure pursuant to this Franchise Agreement for the same, similar or different defaults in any twelve month period, in which event a Notice of Termination may be sent in lieu of any subsequent Notice to Cure;

(4) If Franchisee transfers any rights or obligations arising from this Franchise Agreement to any third party without Region's prior written consent, contrary to the provisions of the Franchise Agreement;

(5) If Franchisee abandons the business or ceases to actively remain open for business at the location granted in the Franchise Agreement for ten [10] consecutive days, or any shorter period after which it is reasonable under the facts and circumstances for the Region to conclude that the Franchisee does not intend to continue to operate the business as a SpeeDee Oil Change & Tune Up® Franchise, or fails within fifteen [15] days after notice to remedy any material default under any lease or sublease for the franchise premises, or equipment therein, or loses the right to possession of the premises or otherwise forfeits the right to do or

SpeeDee Oil Change & Tune Up® of the Gulf Coast
L-UFOC   v. 2.6   July 20, 1987
Reprinted with permission.

transact business in the jurisdiction where the franchise is located; provided, however, that if any such closure or loss of possession results through no fault of Franchisee, and the premises are damaged or destroyed by a disaster such as they cannot, in Region's judgment, reasonably be restored, then the Franchise Agreement shall not be terminated for that reason for sixty [60] days thereafter, provided Franchisee applies within that time for the approval of Region to relocate, for the remainder of the term hereof, to other premises, for which approval shall not be unreasonably withheld.

(6)   If, in the sole and absolute discretion of the Region, the Franchisee fails to successfully complete initial home office orientation and/or regional training, in which case the Franchise Agreement will be terminated, the Franchisee will sign a form of release and indemnity in favor of the Region and SOCS and the Region will return to the Franchisee any Initial Franchise Fee paid by the Franchisee less the greater of (1) Five Thousand Dollars [$5,000] (subject to cost-of-living adjustment) or (2) the total of any expenses incurred by the Region as a result of or in connection with the sale of such franchise, including but not limited to amounts paid by the Region with respect to such sale and/or any associated training, home office orientation, franchise sales commissions, legal fees or otherwise.

The Region may terminate the Franchise Agreement effective at the end of thirty [30] days after notice and opportunity to cure for good cause, which shall include, but not be limited to, the occurrence of any of the following:

(1)   Franchisee refuses, neglects or fails to perform any provision of the Franchise Agreement or any other agreement with SOCS and/or the Region and/or any entity associated with either or any agreement between Franchisee and any SpeeDee Oil Change & Tune Up® approved supplier or fails to remain in full compliance with each of the provisions of the then-current SpeeDee Oil Change & Tune Up® Confidential Operating Manual as revised from time to time;

(2)   Franchisee persists in default of any payment due to SOCS and/or the Region and/or any entity associated with either;

(3)   Any final judgment against Franchisee relating to his franchised business remains unsatisfied for a period of thirty [30] days.

The Region may terminate the Franchise Agreement effective thirty [30] days after notice and opportunity to cure if Franchisee's heirs or estate fail to comply with the provisions on death or disability of Franchisee set out in the Franchise Agreement.

Upon termination of or failure to renew the Franchise Agreement, the Franchisee is required to:

SpeeDee Oil Change & Tune Up® of the Gulf Coast
L-UFOC   v. 2.6   July 20, 1987
Reprinted with permission.

(a) Pay to SOCS, the Region and/or any entities associated with either, within 30 days of such termination, all monies then due;

(b) Turn over to the Region, or otherwise dispose of as the Region may direct, all records, papers, manuals, supplies, etc., in Franchisee's possession which had previously been supplied by SOCS and/or the Region;

(c) Cease conducting business under the service mark SpeeDee Oil Change & Tune Up® and not thereafter use such service mark, logotype, or any other mark or name associated therewith or confusingly similar thereto and the Franchisee shall relinquish all interest in the Franchise and execute all documents necessary to terminate any phone listing under such service mark or logotype;

(d) Be liable to SOCS and/or the Region for any damages incurred by SOCS and/or the Region as a result of any breach by Franchisee;

(e) Forfeit all fees paid;

(f) Agree that no payment shall be made to Franchisee with regard to the termination of its right to use SOCS' service marks, names, logotypes, or any goodwill established by Franchisee either prior to or during the operation of the Franchise.

The Region may, but is not required to, elect to waive any right to sue the Franchisee for Business Development Fees and/or Advertising Contributions due to be paid after the termination of this Agreement and, in such event, no inventory, equipment, goods, materials or otherwise shall be repurchased by SOCS and/or the Region. In the event of non-renewal of the Franchise Agreement, no inventory, equipment, goods, materials or otherwise will be repurchased by SOCS and/or the Region.

The Region has the right [but not the duty] exercised by mailing a Notice of Intent no later than thirty [30] days after termination or expiration, to purchase any or all real estate, improvements, advertising material, products, materials, supplies, or otherwise used or useful in the conduct of the Franchisee's business, and any items bearing Region's Proprietary Marks at fair market value. If the parties cannot agree on a fair market value within a reasonable time, an independent appraisal shall be determined by arbitration hereunder. If the Region elects to exercise any option to purchase herein provided, it has the right to set-off all amounts due from Franchisee under the Franchise Agreement and the cost of the appraisal, if any, against any payment therefor. In the event the premises on which the franchised business is conducted [land and/or improvements] are leased to Franchisee, Franchisee is required to at any time, including but not limited to in the event of termination or non-renewal and on Region's request and at no cost to Region, assign, set over and transfer unto Region, at Region's sole option and discretion, all of Franchisee's in-

SpeeDee Oil Change & Tune Up® of the Gulf Coast
L-UFOC v. 2.6 July 20, 1987
Reprinted with permission.

terest in said lease(s) and the premises demised thereby including improvements. Any such lease(s) entered into by Franchisee shall contain a clause setting forth the landlord's consent to assign such lease(s) to Region or its assignee at any time.

In the event that the Region should cease operations or be terminated as a SpeeDee Oil Change & Tune Up® region, SOCS or its assignee has the right to succeed to all of the Region's rights in and to any and all franchise agreements and other agreements between the Region and the Franchisee [including but not limited to franchise promissory notes, rights to receive development fees, advertising contributions and franchise note and/or other payments] and in such event SOCS or its assignee would be obligated to perform the Region's duties under any such agreements.

SALE OR ASSIGNMENT OF THE FRANCHISE

The Franchisee may not sell, assign, transfer, convey, pledge or encumber any interest in the franchise without the prior written consent of the Region (and review by Franchisor of all forms and procedures), which is subject to certain terms and conditions. For example, the assignee is required to (a) assume all duties, obligations and liabilities of Franchisee to Franchisor or the Region; (b) take the training described in the Franchise Agreement; (c) pay to the Region a $2000 transfer fee, subject to adjustments for changes in cost-of-living. In addition, the Region's consent may be further conditioned by requiring that all of Franchisee's ascertained and liquidated liabilities to Franchisor and/or the Region are paid in full at the time of assignment and that the Franchisee has executed an assignment in form and substance satisfactory to the Region and providing for a release and indemnity in favor of the Franchisor and the Region. The Region may also require that the operation of the franchised Car Care Service Center be brought into full and complete compliance with all requirements of the then-current SpeeDee Oil Change & Tune Up® Confidential Operating Manual or otherwise, including but not limited to possible building conversion, facilities upgrade, new equipment, signage, store layout, remodeling, changed products or services, operational methods, hours or computerized accounting and/or reporting, all at the sole cost and expense of the Franchisee. In addition, any attempted assignment, pledge or alienation will trigger a right of first refusal in the Region to match the terms of the requested assignment, pledge or alienation. The right may be exercised for a period of 14 days after receipt of notice and payment of transfer fee by the Franchisee. The Region may disapprove any proposed assignment, pledge or alienation not in the best interests of the region or other SpeeDee Oil Change & Tune Up® franchisees. The Region does not have any other option or right of first refusal to repurchase a franchise. Any attempted assignment of any interest in or to the Franchise Agreement by the Franchisee in violation of the terms of the Franchise Agreement is a violation of the Franchise Agreement and cause for termination by the Region. All or any of the foregoing requirements (as well as the right of first refusal discussed above) may be waived by

SpeeDee Oil Change & Tune Up® of the Gulf Coast
L-UFOC   v. 2.6   July 20, 1987
Reprinted with permission.

the Region as may appear appropriate in its business judgment and as the particular situation requires.

The Franchise Agreement contains no limitation on the right of the Franchisor or Region to assign their rights and obligations under the Franchise Agreement, either in whole or in part, except that in the case of an assignment by the Region (a) the Region's commitments to establish the franchise have been met or provided for, and (b) the transferee explicitly undertakes to provide required contractual services.

MODIFICATIONS

The Franchise Agreement may not be modified, altered or changed except in a writing signed by both the Franchisee and the Region and approved by the Franchisor.

DEATH OR INCAPACITY OF FRANCHISEE

Upon the death or incapacity of the Franchisee his rights under the Franchise Agreement will pass to his heirs or beneficiaries. In that event, the Franchisee's successor in interest must designate a person satisfactory to the Region who will be responsible for the performance of the Franchisee's duties under the Franchise Agreement. If such a person has not been designated and approved within 60 days after the Franchisee's death or the determination of his incapacity, the Region may terminate the Franchise Agreement. The Region may also require such a person to successfully complete training at the Franchisor's office and in the Region and pay a $2000 transfer fee, subject to adjustment for changes in cost of living.

COVENANT NOT TO COMPETE

According to the Franchise Agreement, the Franchisee may not, during the term of the Franchise Agreement and for two years thereafter, engage in any business or become associated with any business in competition with Franchisor or the Region or any other SpeeDee Oil Change & Tune Up® Region or with any of their franchisees or then-existing programs located within a 250 mile radius of such business whether as a consultant, owner, employee, stockholder or otherwise. This provision of the Franchise Agreement is subject to various federal and state laws limiting covenants not to compete, and in some states may not be enforceable in strict accordance with its terms.

ITEM 18: ARRANGEMENTS WITH PUBLIC FIGURES

Neither the Franchisor nor the Region have any arrangements of any kind to engage or compensate any public figures in connection with any endorsement or

SpeeDee Oil Change & Tune Up® of the Gulf Coast
L-UFOC   v. 2.6   July 20, 1987
Reprinted with permission.

recommendation of the franchised business, nor have any right to use the name of the Franchisor or the Region nor have any public figures made an investment in the Franchisor or the Region or in any SpeeDee Oil Change & Tune Up® franchise.

The Franchise Agreement does not prohibit the Franchisee from individually obtaining the endorsement of public figures with respect to his franchise.

ITEM 19: ACTUAL, AVERAGE, PROJECTED OR FORECASTED FRANCHISE SALES, PROFITS OR EARNINGS

Neither the Franchisor nor any Region make, authorize or endorse any representations, express or implied, regarding actual, average, projected or forecasted Local Franchise sales, profits, earnings, or expenses.

ITEM 20: INFORMATION REGARDING FRANCHISES OF THE SUBFRANCHISOR

A list of the names, addresses and telephone numbers of all existing Franchisees of the Region under Franchise Agreements similar to the one offered herein by the Region and which are located in the state where the Franchise offered hereby is to be located (or the ten most proximate such Franchises in the event fewer than ten such Franchises are located in such state) is attached hereto as Exhibits "C" through "C-2". Businesses that have commenced operations are noted. As of the date of this Offering Circular, there are a total of seventeen units in operation, including five stores owned by one or more companies owned by Gary Copp and Kevin Bennett, both of whom are officers of Franchisor. It is estimated that during the next 12 months following the date of this Offering Circular, three more units may be opened by one or more companies owned by Gary Copp and Kevin Bennett, both of whom are officers of Franchisor.

As of the date of this Offering Circular, there are a total of six units in the process of construction and/or site selection.

During the one year period following the date of this Offering Circular, the Region proposes to sell up to 10 franchises of the type offered herein in this state.

During the last three fiscal years of the Region's business, no franchises have been cancelled, terminated or reacquired by the Region. No franchises have failed to have been renewed by the Region. Franchisor's predecessor terminated two franchises.

SpeeDee Oil Change & Tune Up® of the Gulf Coast
L-UFOC   v. 2.6   July 20, 1987
Reprinted with permission.

ITEM 21: FINANCIAL STATEMENTS

Audited financial statements of Franchisor for fiscal years 1984, 1985 & 1986 and unaudited financial statements for the period January 1, 1987 through April 30, 1987, are attached as Exhibit "A". Unaudited financial statements of the Region dated April 30, 1987, are attached as Exhibit "A-1".

ITEM 22: CONTRACTS

Attached as Exhibit "B" is a copy of the form of Franchise Agreement to be executed by Region and Local Franchisee. Attached as Exhibit "D" is the form of Loaned Equipment Agreement to be executed by Franchisee and Franchisor's approved supplier of lubricants (Castrol®), and attached as Exhibit "E" is a sample form of Letter of Credit, to be executed by Franchisee's bank.

SpeeDee Oil Change & Tune Up® of the Gulf Coast
L-UFOC   v. 2.6   July 20, 1987
Reprinted with permission.

G.C. & K.B. Investments, Inc. d.b.a.
SpeeDee Oil Change & Tune Up®
  of the Gulf Coast
6660 Riverside Drive
Suite 101
Metairie, Louisiana   70003

   The undersigned acknowledges receipt of the Offering Circular dated July 20, 1987 of the Region — G.C. & K.B. Investments, Inc. d.b.a. SpeeDee Oil Change & Tune Up® of the Gulf Coast, including all Exhibits consisting of the audited financial statements of SpeeDee Oil Change Systems, Inc., for the fiscal years 1984, 1985 & 1986 and unaudited financial statements covering the period January 1, 1987 through April 30, 1987 (Exhibit A), the unaudited financial statements of the Region as of April 30, 1987 (Exhibit A-1), the Franchise Agreement (Exhibit B), a list of franchisees of the Region (Exhibit C), a list of pre-existing franchises in the territory currently being serviced by the Region (Exhibit C-1), a list of units owned by G.C. & K.B. Investments, Inc. d.b.a. SpeeDee Oil Change & Tune Up® of the Gulf Coast (Exhibit C-2), Loaned Equipment Agreement (Exhibit D), and Letter of Credit (Exhibit E).

Dated: _____   _____
                                        Signature

                                        _____
                                        Name (Please Print)

SpeeDee Oil Change & Tune Up® of the Gulf Coast
L-UFOC   v. 2.6   July 20, 1987
Reprinted with permission.

EXHIBIT A

FRANCHISEE'S

START-UP MATERIALS

CONFIDENTIAL OPERATING MANUAL

SpeeDee Oil Change & Tune Up® of the Gulf Coast
L-UFOC   v. 2.6   July 20, 1987
Reprinted with permission.

EXHIBIT B

LOCAL FRANCHISE AGREEMENT

SpeeDee Oil Change & Tune Up® of the Gulf Coast
L-UFOC   v. 2.6   July 20, 1987
Reprinted with permission.

SpeeDee Oil Change & Tune Up®
Local Franchise Agreement

This Local Franchise Agreement (the "Agreement") is entered as of this _____ day of _____, 19_____, by and between G.C. & K.B. Investments, Inc. d.b.a. SpeeDee Oil Change & Tune Up® of the Gulf Coast [the "Region"] with its principal place of business at 6660 Riverside Drive, Suite 101, Metairie, Louisiana, 70003, and _____ ["Franchisee"], who resides or has his principal place of business at _____
_____.

1. RECITALS

1.1 SpeeDee Oil Change Systems, Inc. ["SOCS"] was incorporated in Louisiana on November 3, 1982, and its business currently encompasses all aspects of providing basic car care service and the licensing of efficient specialty centers for the offering of such basic car care service.

1.2 SOCS has developed techniques, systems, procedures and know-how [some of which constitute trade secrets] in the development, location, operation and providing of efficient specialty centers for the offering of such basic car care service as well as the franchising and related servicing of others to conduct such business, including the development of a standardized franchise agreement and related documents, together with a specially designed building with interior and exterior layouts, signs, trade dress, slogans and other identification schemes, proprietary methods of rendering car care service, standards and specifications for equipment, equipment layout, products, operating procedures and management and advertising programs, all of which are subject to change from time to time and all of which constitute part of the SpeeDee Oil Change & Tune Up® System [the "System"].

1.3 SOCS has established a common law service mark in the name "SpeeDee Oil Change & Tune Up®" and other names and associated logotypes and obtained registration of certain of these names and associated logotypes with the United States Patent and Trademark Office and certain state offices.

1.4 The Region was incorporated in Louisiana on April 7, 1987, has been granted by SOCS the right to sublicense the use of certain SpeeDee Oil Change & Tune Up® service marks and certain aspects of the System in connection with the operation of car care service centers and in connection therewith to utilize the name SpeeDee Oil Change & Tune Up® and associated logotypes together with the Sys-

SpeeDee Oil Change & Tune Up® of the Gulf Coast
L-UFOC   v. 2.6   July 20, 1987
Reprinted with permission.

tem and will be actively engaged in the business of selling and servicing SpeeDee Oil Change & Tune Up® franchises.

1.5   Franchisee desires to engage in the business of car care service utilizing the SpeeDee Oil Change & Tune Up® name, associated logotypes and certain aspects of the System and to benefit from the expertise of the Region and therefore wishes to enter into this Agreement with the Region, understanding the Region is the only entity having any obligations to the Franchisee.

1.6   Franchisee understands the vital importance to SOCS, the Region and all members of the SpeeDee Oil Change & Tune Up® family of companies [including other SpeeDee Oil Change & Tune Up® Regions and Franchisees], as well as the public, of the constant maintenance of high and uniform standards of quality, appearance, cleanliness and service and the necessity of opening and continuously operating Franchisee's SpeeDee Oil Change & Tune Up® franchise in conformity with all aspects of the System as it may be modified from time to time.

IN CONSIDERATION of the above recitals and of the terms and conditions and mutual promises herein, the Region and Franchisee hereby agree as follows:

2.   GRANT OF FRANCHISE

2.1   Grant.   The Region hereby grants to the Franchisee, during the initial term and any renewals of this Agreement, subject to the conditions hereof, and Franchisee's full and complete performance of each and every of its obligations thereunder, and the Franchisee hereby accepts from the Region, the license, rights and franchise to use the SpeeDee Oil Change & Tune Up® name and associated logotypes, together with techniques, systems, procedures and know-how developed by SOCS, in connection with the operation of a single standard SpeeDee Oil Change & Tune Up® Car Care Service Center for the providing of basic car care services, as specified in the then-current SpeeDee Oil Change & Tune Up® Confidential Operating Manual as it may be revised from time to time, at the following approved location only:_____.
Neither the Region nor SOCS can guarantee that there is not a business already operating using the SpeeDee Oil Change & Tune Up® name or a substantially similar name or service marks or logotypes similar to those used by SOCS, which business may have the right to continue to use such name, service marks or logotypes if it has been using such name, service marks or logotypes for a sufficiently long period of time. Nothing in this Agreement will limit in any way the rights of the Region to do any form of business using the SpeeDee Oil Change & Tune Up® name, service marks or logotypes or to grant to others rights similar to those granted the Franchisee hereunder. Franchisee has separately initialed this section in recognition

SpeeDee Oil Change & Tune Up® of the Gulf Coast
L-UFOC   v. 2.6   July 20, 1987
Reprinted with permission.

2.2 *Use of Name and System.* Franchisee shall not be permitted to use any SpeeDee Oil Change & Tune Up® names or associated logotypes, techniques, systems, procedures or know-how or any other aspect of the System in any location other than as approved in writing in advance by the Region or for any purpose other than as permitted in Section 2.1 hereof. In the event the Franchisee wishes to operate a SpeeDee Oil Change & Tune Up® Car Care Service Center at more than one location, Franchisee shall execute a separate SpeeDee Oil Change & Tune Up® Local Franchise Agreement for each such location. Franchisee has separately initialed this section in recognition of its special significance and the fact that it has been fully read, discussed and understood._____

2.3 *Ownership.* The ownership of all right, title and interest in and to the SpeeDee Oil Change & Tune Up® names and associated logotypes, together with all techniques, systems, procedures or know-how or any other aspect of the System is and shall remain solely vested in SOCS and all material and information now and hereafter provided or revealed to Franchisee shall be maintained by Franchisee in complete confidence except as is necessary for Franchisee to fulfill its obligations under this Agreement. Any use of the SpeeDee Oil Change & Tune Up® name, service marks or associated logotypes or System shall inure to the benefit of SOCS and shall only be with SOCS's prior written consent. Franchisee has separately initialed this section in recognition of its special significance and the fact that it has been fully read, discussed and understood._____

2.4 *Changes.* The Franchisee acknowledges that the SpeeDee Oil Change & Tune Up® System must continue to evolve in order to reflect the changing car care services business and related markets and changing consumer demands and business opportunities, and that accordingly variations and additions to the SpeeDee Oil Change & Tune Up® System are anticipated to be required from time to time in order to preserve and enhance the public image of the System and business opportunities associated therewith and to ensure the continuing operational efficiency of each SpeeDee Oil Change & Tune Up® Car Care Service Center. It is, therefore, understood and agreed that from time to time SOCS may make changes in any aspect of the System, including but not limited to new, changed or additional names, service marks, associated logotypes, techniques, systems, operational aspects, facilities, furnishings, signage, remodeling, hours, computerized accounting and/or reporting, layout, equipment, procedures, services and products to be provided to the public, manuals [including but not limited to any aspect of the SpeeDee Oil Change & Tune Up® Confidential Operating Manual] and forms and/or otherwise, and that Franchisee will promptly comply with all such changes at the time directed and cause each of its employees to similarly comply, all at the Franchisee's sole cost and expense. Franchisee has separately initialed this section in recognition of its special significance and the fact that it has been fully read, discussed and understood._____

    2.5   <u>Approval of Materials.</u>   Franchisee shall submit to the Region and not use or permit the use of, without prior written approval by the Region, all contracts, manuals, forms, literature, advertisements, materials, products or equipment to be used or sold by Franchisee in connection with the operation of his SpeeDee Oil Change & Tune Up® franchise and his use of the SpeeDee Oil Change & Tune Up® name, service marks and/or associated logotypes or System. The Franchisee shall only use such advertising, promotions and/or publicity materials, items, campaigns, advertisements, concepts, programs, services and suppliers as are approved in advance by SOCS. Franchisee has separately initialed this section in recognition of its special significance and the fact that it has been fully read, discussed and understood._____

    2.6   <u>Territory.</u>   The Region will not grant to any person other than the Franchisee the right to locate a SpeeDee Oil Change & Tune Up® Car Care Service Center within a one-half [1/2] mile radius of the Franchisee's approved location.

3.   **OBLIGATIONS OF THE REGION**

    3.1   <u>Manual.</u>   The Region shall provide Franchisee with one [1] copy of the SpeeDee Oil Change & Tune Up® Confidential Operating Manual (including Confidential Price List), which shall be for the private and confidential use of the Franchisee himself only and the contents of which shall not be disclosed to employees or others. The Region may also, during the term of this Agreement, advise Franchisee of any improvements in or changes to such Manual through supplements, newsletters and annual conventions or otherwise, as applicable, with which Franchisee shall thereafter comply.

    3.2   <u>Initial Home Office Orientation.</u>   The Region will arrange for, and the Franchisee will be required to attend, subsequent to the execution of this Franchise Agreement, an initial home office orientation at SOCS' headquarters located in Metairie, Louisiana. The orientation shall be of approximately three (3) days duration, shall commence as soon as practicable after the signing of this Franchise Agreement, is mandatory, and must be successfully completed prior to Franchisee's Regional training and subsequent commencement of business. Franchisee shall be responsible for his transportation, meals and lodging arrangements and expenses to, from, and while at initial home office orientation.

    3.3   <u>Regional Training.</u>   The Region shall provide for Franchisee to be trained in the operation of a SpeeDee Oil Change & Tune Up® Car Care Service Center at Region's headquarters or such other location as may be designated by

SpeeDee Oil Change & Tune Up® of the Gulf Coast
L-UFOC   v. 2.6   July 20, 1987
Reprinted with permission.

Region and which may be at SOCS' headquarters. Such training shall commence as soon as practicable after the completion of Franchisee's initial home office orientation, is mandatory, and must be successfully completed by Franchisee prior to the commencement of Franchisee's operation. Franchisee shall be responsible for his transportation, meals and lodging arrangements and expenses to, from, and while at the training location.

3.4   <u>Subsequent Regional Training.</u>   Region may [but is not required to] make available to Franchisee or Franchisee's employees from time to time such additional training programs as Region in its sole discretion may choose to conduct. Attendance at said training programs and any Regional conventions may be mandatory. The cost of the training [instruction and required materials] shall be borne by Region. All other expenses during the training period, including costs of accommodations, meals, wages and travel, shall be borne by Franchisee. Region may [but is not required to] make available such continuing advisory assistance in the operation of the franchise, rendered in person or by bulletins made available from time to time to all Franchisees, as Region may deem appropriate.

3.5   <u>Standard Plans and Specifications — Site Evaluation.</u>   Region shall make available standard plans and specifications to be utilized only in the construction of a SpeeDee Oil Change & Tune Up® Car Care Service Center. No modifications or deviations from the standard plans and specifications may be made without the written consent of Region. Franchisee shall obtain, at his own expense, all further qualified architectural and engineering services to prepare surveys, site and foundation plans and adapt the standard plans and specifications to each individual site, applicable local and state laws, regulations and ordinances. The selection of a site for the franchised service center shall be subject to Region's approval, which will not be unreasonably withheld. Region will provide consultation at its home office to Franchisee with respect to site selection and development, together with one visit to three [3] potential sites in the company of Franchisee for the purposes of joint site evaluation. In the event that Franchisee requires consultation services beyond those expressly provided above, then Franchisee will pay Region all expenses incurred in connection with such consultation, including, but not limited to, travel, living expenses, and a per diem fee of $300 per day subject to cost-of-living adjustment as set forth in Section 4.3. Franchisee shall bear the cost of preparing plans containing deviations or modifications from the standard plans and all costs of site acquisition and construction, and neither the Region nor SOCS shall have any liability with respect to such deviations or modifications nor with respect to the evaluation of Franchisee's selection of site nor the acquisition, construction or operation of the SpeeDee Oil Change & Tune Up® Car Care Service Center to be erected thereupon, whether in accordance with standard plans or otherwise, all such responsibilities being solely those of the Franchisee. Franchisee has separately initialed this section in recognition of its special significance and the fact that it has been fully read, discussed and understood._____

SpeeDee Oil Change & Tune Up® of the Gulf Coast
L-UFOC   v. 2.6   July 20, 1987
Reprinted with permission.

4. OBLIGATIONS OF THE FRANCHISEE

4.1 <u>Initial Franchise Fee.</u> The Initial Franchise Fee is Twenty-Five Thousand Dollars ($25,000), and is due and payable upon execution of this Franchise Agreement by Franchisee. Said $25,000 Franchise Fee shall be fully earned by Region upon execution of this Franchise Agreement by Franchisee and is not refundable under any circumstances [except as set forth in Section 6.3 (a) (6) herein]. Franchisee and Region have agreed that Twenty Thousand Dollars ($20,000) of the Initial Franchise Fee is paid with respect to services (including but not limited to home office orientation, site evaluation, administrative and other services as set forth in this Agreement) to be provided by the Region to the Franchisee, and One Thousand Five Hundred Dollars ($1,500), subject to cost-of-living adjustment, of the Franchise Fee is allocated by the Region for payment of its expenses in relation to Franchisee's initial training at SOCS headquarters in Metairie, Louisiana. Franchisee has separately initialed this section in recognition of its special significance and the fact that it has been fully read, discussed and understood._____

4.2 <u>Local Business Development Fee.</u> Franchisee shall pay a recurring, non-refundable Local Business Development Fee of Five [5%] percent of gross revenues during the franchise term, payable on Wednesday of each week for gross revenues received or earned during the preceding week [or such other basis as may be set forth in the then-current SpeeDee Oil Change & Tune Up® Confidential Operating Manual as revised from time to time].

The gross revenues with respect to which such Local Business Development Fee is payable shall include all revenue [except sales tax] received or earned during the prior week with respect to products, services, materials, inventory, equipment or any other items of whatever nature provided, sold, rented or otherwise distributed at, through or in association with or with respect to, the Franchisee's SpeeDee Oil Change & Tune Up® Car Care Service Center or which are received or earned by Franchisee or on his behalf and which relate to or are of the type[s] of services, materials, inventory, equipment or any other item[s] which could be provided, sold, rented or distributed at, through or in association with a SpeeDee Oil Change & Tune Up® Car Care Service Center or are provided, sold, rented or distributed in association with any use of the SpeeDee Oil Change & Tune Up® names, service marks or associated logotypes, techniques, systems, procedures, know-how or any other aspect of the SpeeDee Oil Change & Tune Up® System.

Such Local Business Development Fee will be payable as of the first Wednesday after the week in which the SpeeDee Oil Change & Tune Up® Car Care Service Center is scheduled to open and shall in no event be less than One Hundred Twenty-Five Dollars [$125.00] per week per SpeeDee Oil Change & Tune Up® Car Care Service Center operated by the Franchisee [the "Minimum Local Business Development Fee"], subject to cost of living adjustment as set forth in Section 4.3 here-

SpeeDee Oil Change & Tune Up® of the Gulf Coast
L-UFOC   v. 2.6   July 20, 1987
Reprinted with permission.

of and shall be paid even if the Franchisee's SpeeDee Oil Change & Tune Up® Car Care Service Center closes or ceases operation or fails to open on the date agreed between Franchisee and the Region for any reason. In no event will payment by the Franchisee of any Minimum Local Business Development Fee or other sums due under this Agreement restrict the Region from terminating this Agreement and obtaining all other remedies legally available to it for any other or prior breach of this Agreement.

If for any reason Franchisee's SpeeDee Oil Change & Tune Up® Car Care Service Center franchised to the Franchisee closes or ceases operation or fails to open on the date agreed between Franchisee and the Region for any reason, the Franchisee shall continue thereafter to pay weekly Local Business Development Fees [and SpeeDee Ad Fund Contributions as outlined in Section 5] based on the average weekly revenues of each such Center for the previous six [6] months but in no event less than One Hundred Twenty-Five Dollars [$125.00] weekly Local Business Development Fees and One Hundred Seventy-Five Dollars [$175.00] weekly SpeeDee Ad Fund Contributions per Center, subject in each case to cost of living adjustment as set forth in Section 4.3.

Minimum Local Business Development Fees are to be paid by autodraft or similar arrangement satisfactory to the Region. Unless specified otherwise in the SpeeDee Oil Change & Tune Up® Confidential Operating Manual, payment of Minimum Local Business Development Fees for each week shall be received by the Region no later than the Wednesday after the close of such week. No portion of the Local Business Development Fee shall be refundable in any event.

Franchisee has separately initialed this section in recognition of its special significance and the fact that it has been fully read, discussed and understood._____

4.3   Cost of Living Adjustment.   Effective June 1 of each year, beginning June 1, 1988, the Minimum Local Business Development Fee and the Minimum SpeeDee Advertising Fund Contribution set forth in this Agreement shall each be adjusted based on the change up or down in the Metropolitan Area Consumers Price Index For All Urban Consumers — All Items [1967 = 100] as published by the U.S. Department of Labor — Bureau of Labor Statistics or successor index, in each case measured on April 1 as compared to April 1 of the previous year. Franchisee has separately initialed this section in recognition of its special significance and the fact that it has been fully read, discussed and understood._____

4.4   Car Care Service Center.   The Franchisee shall, within one hundred twenty [120] days from the date of this Agreement, establish and open for business and continuously maintain as open for business thereafter, at a location mutually approved by Region and Franchisee, a SpeeDee Oil Change & Tune Up® Car Care Service Center, such Car Care Service Center to be always operated in complete compliance with each provision of the then-current SpeeDee Oil Change & Tune

SpeeDee Oil Change & Tune Up® of the Gulf Coast
L-UFOC   v. 2.6   July 20, 1987
Reprinted with permission.

Up® Confidential Operating Manual as it may be revised from time to time. Failure to establish, open and maintain as open and to so operate such unit shall be considered a substantial failure to comply with this Agreement and shall be a default of this Agreement subjecting it to termination. In the event that special circumstances beyond the control of the Franchisee prevent the opening of the Car Care Service Center within such one hundred twenty (120) days, the Region will consider such special circumstances (upon written notification and request by the Franchisee to the Region prior to the expiration of such 120 day period) and the Region may (but is not legally obligated to) extend such deadline for an additional period, the length of such extension and any related conditions thereon to be determined in the Region's sole and absolute discretion. Any lease(s) entered into by Franchisee shall contain a clause setting forth the landlord's consent to assign such lease(s) to Region or its assignee at any time. Franchisee has separately initialed this section in recognition of its special significance and the fact that it has been fully read, discussed and understood._____

    4.5   <u>Facility Standards.</u>   The Franchisee shall at all times maintain and operate a standard SpeeDee Oil Change & Tune Up® Car Care Service Center in conformity with Region's high standards, public image and the then-current SpeeDee Oil Change & Tune Up® Confidential Operating Manual as it may be revised from time to time, and in conformance therewith to make such additions, alterations, repairs, revisions and replacements [but no others, without Region's prior written consent] as may be required by such Manual as it may be revised from time to time, including but not limited to the following specific obligations:

    1)   To keep the SpeeDee Oil Change & Tune Up® Car Care Service Center in the highest degree of cleanliness and repair, including, without limitation, such periodic repainting, repairs or replacement [as the Region shall direct] of impaired or obsolete equipment, signs, facilities or otherwise as Region may direct;

    2)   To meet and maintain the highest governmental standards and ratings applicable to the operation of the franchise and to always comply with all state, local and federal laws and regulations;

    3)   To refurbish the SpeeDee Oil Change & Tune Up® Car Care Service Center upon Region's request, but no more often than once every five [5] years, to conform with the Trade Dress to be consistent with Region's then-current public image, including, without limitation, such extensive structural changes, remodeling and redecoration, and such modifications to existing improvements, as may be necessary to do so.

    4.6   <u>Operating Standards.</u>   The Franchisee shall at all times operate the SpeeDee Oil Change & Tune Up® Car Care Service Center in conformity with such uniform methods, standards, procedures and specifications as Region may from time to time prescribe in the then-current SpeeDee Oil Change & Tune Up® Confi-

SpeeDee Oil Change & Tune Up® of the Gulf Coast
L-UFOC   v. 2.6   July 20, 1987
Reprinted with permission.

dential Operating Manual as it may be revised from time to time to insure that the highest degree of quality and service is uniformly maintained; shall, in conducting its business hereunder, observe high ethical standards of operation reasonably calculated to maintain the uniformity of image, public goodwill and reputation attached to the business of the Region and SOCS and to the SpeeDee Oil Change & Tune Up® name, service marks and associated logotypes, and shall not engage in any activity which may harm the SpeeDee Oil Change & Tune Up® name, service marks and associated logotypes or the reputation of the Region and/or SOCS and/or any of either of their franchisees; shall refrain from any deviations therefrom and from otherwise operating in any manner which reflects adversely on the SpeeDee Oil Change & Tune Up® name, marks and associated logotypes and goodwill and in connection therewith Franchisee agrees:

1) To maintain in sufficient supply, and use at all times, only such equipment, facilities, services, products, materials and supplies as those which conform with SpeeDee Oil Change & Tune Up® standards and specifications and to refrain from deviating therefrom by using nonconforming items without prior written consent;

2) To sell or offer for sale and/or use only such products and services as meet SpeeDee Oil Change & Tune Up® uniform standards of quality and quantity, as have been expressly approved in writing by SOCS and the Region, and as have been prepared in accordance with SpeeDee Oil Change & Tune Up® methods and techniques, and, where specified by SOCS and/or the Region, to use only brand name items expressly approved by SOCS and/or the Region;

3) To purchase and install, at Franchisee's expense, all equipment and improvements specified in the then-current approved standard plans and specifications, and such others as Region may reasonably direct from time to time in the then-current SpeeDee Oil Change & Tune Up® Confidential Operating Manual as it may be revised from time to time; and to refrain from installing or permitting to be installed on or about the franchise premises, without prior written consent, any equipment or improvements not previously approved as meeting SpeeDee Oil Change & Tune Up® standards and specifications;

4) To permit Region or its representative, without notice, to enter upon the franchise premises without liability for trespass or other tort, and at Region's option, to remove, replace, repair and/or remodel, at Franchisee's expense, any items which do not conform with Region's then-current standards and specifications after Franchisee's delay or refusal upon request promptly to do so; to make such other modifications or alterations as may be necessary to achieve such conformity; and to bill Franchisee for all costs and expenses reasonably incurred in doing so;

SpeeDee Oil Change & Tune Up® of the Gulf Coast
L-UFOC   v. 2.6   July 20, 1987
Reprinted with permission.

5) To purchase all products, materials, supplies and improvements required for the operation of the franchise solely from suppliers who demonstrate, to the continuing reasonable satisfaction of SOCS and the Region, the ability to meet SpeeDee Oil Change & Tune Up® standards and specifications for such items; and who possess adequate quality controls and capacity to supply Franchisee's needs promptly and reliably;

6) Except as otherwise approved in writing by Region, during the term of this Franchise Agreement, to devote, or have his designated, approved and fully trained manager devote full time, energy and best efforts to the management and operation of the franchise granted herein;

7) To require all employees, as a condition of their employment, to execute an employment agreement, as provided in the then-current SpeeDee Oil Change & Tune Up® Confidential Operating Manual [as it may be revised from time to time] or otherwise in writing, prohibiting them during the term of their employment or thereafter, from communicating, divulging or using for the benefit of any person, persons, partnership, association or corporation any confidential information, knowledge or know-how concerning the methods of operation of the business franchised hereunder which may be acquired during the term of their employment with Franchisee and prohibiting them from having any association with a competitive business;

8) Franchisee shall regularly supply to SOCS such reports of gross revenues in such form and format and with such supporting material (including but not limited to cash register receipts, invoices, bookkeeping and accounting records and reports, sales tax forms and reports and state and federal income tax filings relating to the franchised business) as SOCS shall from time to time specify in the then-current SpeeDee Oil Change & Tune Up® Confidential Operating Manual. SOCS shall at all times have the right to audit any such reports and upon determination that gross revenues have been under reported by two percent [2%] or more for any period, the Franchisee shall immediately pay such deficiency plus the costs of audit and collection, including but not limited to auditor's and attorneys' fees;

9) If Franchisee or any entity controlled by or associated with him operates five [5] or more SpeeDee Oil Change & Tune Up® Car Care Service Centers, to employ a supervisor, who shall meet such standards as may reasonably be set forth in the then-current SpeeDee Oil Change & Tune Up® Confidential Operating Manual as it may be revised from time to time, for every five [5] service centers operated by Franchisee to supervise and coordinate the operation of the units. Such supervisor shall be employed upon the commencement of operation of every fifth franchise unit or multiple thereof;

10) To submit (through the mail, return receipt requested) to Region for its approval prior to use, samples of all promotional and advertising materials to

be used by Franchisee that have not been prepared or previously approved by Region;

11) To continuously comply with all other requirements set forth in this Franchise Agreement and in the then-current SpeeDee Oil Change & Tune Up® Confidential Operating Manual as it may be revised from time to time and to refrain from any deviations from SpeeDee Oil Change & Tune Up® standards and specifications without Region's prior written consent.

Franchisee has separately initialed this section in recognition of its special significance and the fact that it has been fully read, discussed and understood._____

4.7   Costs of Operation.   Franchisee shall be responsible for payment of all costs and expenses involved in the operation of his Franchise, including but not limited to the expenses of site acquisition, construction, equipment, obtaining appropriate business licenses, telephone service, advertising, office and automobile liability, worker's compensation and all other insurance, vehicle maintenance, and obtaining materials, supplies and services of employees and others, and shall at all times provide the Region with copies of all insurance policies, in the amounts and as otherwise required by the then-current Confidential Operating Manual as revised from time to time, naming the Region and SOCS as co-insured. Franchisee has separately initialed this section in recognition of its special significance and the fact that it has been fully read, discussed and understood._____

4.8   Confidentiality Agreement.   Franchisee and its personnel shall not make known to any other person, firm or corporation, except Franchisee's personnel and then only so far as necessary to conduct normal business operations, any part of the SpeeDee Oil Change & Tune Up® System, each part of which is agreed by Franchisee to be confidential in nature and proprietary to SOCS and not known to him prior to entering into this Agreement. Franchisee has separately initialed this section in recognition of its special significance and the fact that it has been fully read, discussed and understood._____

4.9   Covenant Not To Compete.   Franchisee [including but not limited to any entities associated with, controlling, controlled by or under common control with him] shall not, during the term of this Agreement and for two years after its termination or nonrenewal, engage in any business or become associated with any business which is in competition with the Region, SOCS, any other SpeeDee Oil Change & Tune Up® Region, or any Franchisee of any of the foregoing or any of their then-existing programs, located within a 250 mile radius of such business, whether as a consultant, owner, employee, stockholder or otherwise and in no event will Franchisee during such periods engage in any aspect of the car care service business or any business related thereto or made possible thereby in any capacity except subject to the terms of this Agreement; provided that if a court of competent jurisdiction determines that such restrictions are excessive in geographic

SpeeDee Oil Change & Tune Up® of the Gulf Coast
L-UFOC   v. 2.6   July 20, 1987
Reprinted with permission.

scope, time period or otherwise, such court may reduce such restriction to the level which provides the maximum restriction allowed by law. Franchisee has separately initialed this section in recognition of its special significance and the fact that it has been fully read, discussed and understood._____

    4.10   Efforts of Franchisee. Franchisee understands that the Franchise granted hereunder is not a passive investment but rather is a business dependent upon Franchisee's independent efforts, business judgment and skills, as well as market conditions. Franchisee, through training and otherwise, will familiarize himself thoroughly with the standards and methods of operation of the Region and the SpeeDee Oil Change & Tune Up® System. Franchisee shall not commence operation of the Franchise prior to successful completion of the home office and regional training described in this Agreement. Franchisee will render assistance to and cooperate with the Region and other franchisees as may reasonably be necessary to carry out the intents and purposes of this Agreement and to maximize sales under the SpeeDee Oil Change & Tune Up® name, service marks and associated logotypes. The Region makes no representations, express or implied, regarding potential earnings of Franchisee's business or of the Region's business. The Region makes no representations regarding any activities or services to be engaged in or provided by the Region or SOCS, except as expressly provided herein. Except with respect to any obligations of SOCS regarding management of the SpeeDee Ad Fund, the Franchisee understands that he will look only to the Region and not to SOCS in connection with the performance of any obligations to the Franchisee under this Agreement or otherwise. Franchisee has separately initialed this paragraph in recognition of its special significance and the fact that it has been fully read, discussed and understood._____

    4.11   Restrictions on Employment of Others. Franchisee shall not, during the term of this Agreement, directly or indirectly, employ or seek to employ any person who is employed by the Region or SOCS or any other franchisee of the Region and/or SOCS.

    4.12   Compliance With Laws. Franchisee agrees to comply with all federal, state and local laws and regulations applicable to Franchisee and its business, including, without limitation, all laws and regulations concerning business licensing, employee and public safety and health, employee-management relations, worker's compensation and other insurance, zoning, buildings and signs, consumer protection, financing and trade practices.

    4.13   Conflicting Names. Neither the Region nor SOCS can guarantee that there is not a business operating somewhere in the state in which the Franchisee will do business or elsewhere using the SOCS® name or a substantially similar name, service marks and/or logotypes similar to those used by SOCS or the Region, which business may have the right to continue to use such name, service marks or logotypes if it has been using the name, service marks and/or logotypes for a sufficiently

SpeeDee Oil Change & Tune Up® of the Gulf Coast
L-UFOC   v. 2.6   July 20, 1987
Reprinted with permission.

long period of time. Franchisee and the Region agree that in the event that Franchisee or the Region be enjoined, restrained or otherwise prevented from operating under the SOCS® name, service marks and/or associated logotypes as a result of a binding order entered by any court of competent jurisdiction, the Region and/or Franchisee may thereafter operate under such alternate names, service marks and/or associated logotypes as are reasonably acceptable to SOCS and the Region. Such right shall be the sole remedy of the Franchisee in such event and the Franchisee shall hold SOCS and the Region harmless from any claims by Franchisee with respect thereto. Franchisee has separately initialed this section in recognition of its special significance and the fact that it has been fully read, discussed and understood._____

4.14   Notification.   In the event of any litigation involving the Franchise or the business franchised hereunder, the Franchisee shall keep the Region advised of all developments and provide the Region with copies of all pleadings and other documents generated in such litigation.

4.15   Assignment of Lease.   Any lease(s) entered into by Franchisee shall contain a clause setting forth the landlord's consent to assign such lease(s) to Region or its assignee at any time.

4.16   Franchisee's Grand Opening and Other Advertising Obligations.
In connection with the opening for business of the Franchisee's SpeeDee Oil Change & Tune Up® Car Care Service Center, the Franchisee shall spend, during the period from fifteen [15] days in advance of such grand opening to thirty [30] days following such grand opening, no less than Three Thousand Dollars [$3,000], subject to cost-of-living adjustment as set forth in Section 4.3, on advertising, promotions and/or publicity as approved by SOCS in connection with such grand opening. Within thirty [30] days following such grand opening, the Franchisee shall supply the Region with proof [by means of cancelled checks, paid invoices, copies of advertisements or otherwise] of the purchase and publication of such grand opening advertising, promotions or publicity.

The Franchisee shall, in the grand opening and all other operations and marketing of the franchised business, only use such advertising promotions and/or publicity materials, items, campaigns, advertisements, concepts, programs, services and suppliers as are approved in advance by SOCS. The Franchisee may utilize third-party suppliers [which have been approved by SOCS] of advertising, promotions and/or publicity or may, at the Franchisee's option, request the Region to place such advertising, promotions and/or publicity, all of which shall be for the Franchisee's account and at his/her sole expense and which may involve payment by the Franchisee to the Region therefor and for which the Region may charge amounts in excess of the Region's costs and/or receive commissions from suppliers.

SpeeDee Oil Change & Tune Up® of the Gulf Coast
L-UFOC   v. 2.6   July 20, 1987
Reprinted with permission.

5. SPEEDEE OIL CHANGE & TUNE UP® ADVERTISING FUND

5.1 Establishment and Contributions. There is established a SpeeDee Oil Change & Tune Up® Advertising Fund [the "SpeeDee Ad Fund"] to be managed by SOCS or an entity appointed by it, which can be the Region with respect to all or any portion of the SpeeDee Ad Fund. All SpeeDee Ad Fund contributions shall be paid directly to the Region [which may remit all or any portion of the SpeeDee Ad Fund contributions to SOCS or such entity] provided that upon notice to the Franchisee from SOCS, all SpeeDee Ad Fund contributions shall be paid directly by the Franchisee to SOCS or such entity, in each case without any holdback or offset. SOCS or such entity shall manage and disburse all SpeeDee Ad Fund contributions received and retained by it.

Beginning on the week during which the Franchisee first opens his SpeeDee Oil Change & Tune Up® Car Care Service Center, or one hundred twenty [120] days after the date of execution of this Agreement, whichever comes first, and continuously thereafter, the Franchisee shall thereafter contribute to the SpeeDee Ad Fund eight percent (8%) [ten percent (10%) for periods after December 31, 1987] of gross revenues calculated and paid on the same basis and using the same autodraft [with respect to Minimum SpeeDee Ad Fund Contributions] and other payment procedures as set forth in Section 4.2, subject to a Minimum SpeeDee Ad Fund Contribution of no less than One Hundred Seventy-Five Dollars [$175.00] per week per SpeeDee Oil Change & Tune Up® Car Care Service Center franchised to or operated by the Franchisee, subject to cost of living adjustment as set forth in Section 4.3 hereof. All SpeeDee Ad Fund contributions shall be paid even if the Franchisee's SpeeDee Oil Change & Tune Up® Car Care Service Center closes or ceases operation or fails to open on the date agreed between Franchisee and the Region for any reason. Minimum SpeeDee Ad Fund contributions shall be paid directly to the Region (except as provided above) by autodraft or similar arrangement satisfactory to SOCS and the Region. Franchisee has separately initialed this section in recognition of its special significance and the fact that it has been fully read, discussed and understood._____

5.2 Purposes and Disbursements. SpeeDee Ad Fund contributions shall be used for advertising, promotions and/or public relations services and materials intended to advertise, promote and/or publicize services offered by SpeeDee Oil Change & Tune Up® franchisees and shall not be used to advertise the sale of franchises by SOCS or the Region; provided that advertisements funded by SpeeDee Ad Fund contributions may contain a small notice or announcement to the effect that information regarding franchises may be obtained from SOCS, the Region or otherwise. With respect to Ad Fund Contributions made by the Franchisee, thirty percent [30%] of such contributions shall be known as the "Regional Portion" and shall be spent with respect to local, Regional and/or Area-of-Dominant-Influence ["ADI"] advertising, publicity and/or promotions covering areas served by the Region. With respect to such Regional Portion, at least eighty-five percent [85%] of the Regional Portion is to be spent on local, regional and/or ADI media [and related production costs] that cover all or part of the area served by the Region, in each case less reasonable accounting, bookkeeping, auditing, reporting, administrative, legal and similar or related expenses. Up to fifteen percent [15%] of the Regional Portion may be spent on a disproportionate basis on test marketing, surveys of advertising effectiveness or other purposes deemed beneficial by SOCS or such entity [or the Region if SOCS so specifies], in either's absolute discretion, to the general recognition of the SpeeDee Oil Change & Tune Up® name and or success of the SpeeDee Oil Change & Tune Up® System within all or a portion of the Region's territory.

With respect to Ad Fund Contributions made by the Franchisee, seventy percent [70%] shall be known as the "National Portion" and all or any part thereof may be spent by SOCS or such entity (or the Region if so designated by SOCS) with respect to national advertising, publicity and/or promotions except as detailed below. <u>Until such time as SOCS or such entity in its sole and absolute discretion determines that all or any part of the National Portion is to be spent with respect to national advertising, such part shall be spent in the same way as the Regional Portion detailed above, subject to any further restrictions delineated by SOCS or such entity, and may be remitted to or retained by the Region as specified by SOCS or such entity.</u> The portion [if any], timing and manner of the National Portion to be spent on local, Regional, ADI or national advertising, publicity and/or promotions, shall be solely within the absolute discretion of SOCS or such entity which shall allocate such portions as it determines from time-to-time. Of the National Portion not spent as the Regional Portion detailed above, at least eighty-five percent [85%] is to be spent on either [1] media [and related production costs which are regarded in the advertising industry as "National Media" or [2] local, regional and/or ADI media [and related production costs] covering areas served by the Region, in each case less reasonable, accounting, bookkeeping, auditing, reporting, administrative, legal and similar or related expenses. Up to fifteen percent [15%] of the National Portion not spent as the Regional Portion detailed above may be spent on a disproportionate basis on test marketing, surveys of advertising effectiveness or other purposes deemed beneficial by SOCS or such entity in its absolute discretion to the general recognition of the SpeeDee Oil Change & Tune Up® name and or success of the SpeeDee Oil Change & Tune Up® System.

Neither SOCS nor the Region make any promises or warranties as to when, as, if or whether all or any portion of any SpeeDee Advertising Fund Contribution will be spent on national or any other form of media, television or otherwise. Franchisee has separately initialed this section in recognition of its special significance and the fact that it has been fully read, discussed and understood._____

5.3   Reports.   Beginning after the Franchisee makes SpeeDee Ad Fund contributions pursuant to Section 5.1 hereof, the Franchisee shall receive on a regular basis, at least annually, a report on how SpeeDee Ad Fund contributions were

SpeeDee Oil Change & Tune Up® of the Gulf Coast
L-UFOC   v. 2.6   July 20, 1987
Reprinted with permission.

spent, including financial statements relating to collection and disbursement of SpeeDee Ad Fund contributions.

    5.4   National Committees. At any time, on thirty [30] days prior written notice from SOCS or such entity to the Region, SOCS or such entity may cause the formation of an advisory committee or committees consisting of a representative from SOCS or such entity and a representative from each SpeeDee Oil Change & Tune Up® Region in good standing. Such advisory committee or committees shall have such powers with respect to the SpeeDee Ad Fund as SOCS or such entity shall direct, including but not limited to the right to advise [but not direct] SOCS or such entity in the disbursement of SpeeDee Ad Fund contributions. In addition, SOCS or such entity may at any time call a meeting of SpeeDee Oil Change & Tune Up® Regions to discuss special competitive and marketing circumstances or opportunities in the car care services industry. Following such meeting, SOCS or such entity may forward to all SpeeDee Oil Change & Tune Up® Local Franchisees in good standing a proposal to increase SpeeDee Ad Fund Contributions to the national portion of the SpeeDee Ad Fund for a specified period by not more than an additional two percent [2%] of the Franchisee's gross revenues, to be collected and disbursed as set forth in such proposal. Such proposal shall become effective and binding on the Franchisee and the increased SpeeDee Ad Fund Contributions shall be assessed upon and begin to be paid by the Franchisee upon written approval of two-thirds [2/3] of the SpeeDee Oil Change & Tune Up® Local Franchisees (voting on the basis of one vote per open SpeeDee Oil Change & Tune Up® Car Care Service Center in good standing) responding in writing to such proposal within the time specified in such proposal but not be less than thirty [30] days nor to exceed ninety [90] days from the date such proposal is sent to SpeeDee Oil Change & Tune Up® Local Franchisees for approval. Franchisee has separately initialed this section in recognition of its special significance and the fact that it has been fully read, discussed and understood._____

    5.5   Regional Committees. At any time, SOCS or such entity (which may be the Region) may cause the formation of an advisory committee or committees consisting of a representative from the Region and certain SpeeDee Oil Change & Tune Up® Local Franchisees in the Region selected by the Region or such entity, which Local Franchisees must be in good standing and current in contributions to the SpeeDee Ad Fund. Such advisory committee or committees shall have the right to advise (but not direct) SOCS, the Region or such entity in the disbursement of the Regional portion of the SpeeDee Ad Fund.

    In addition, the Region may at any time call a meeting of SpeeDee Oil Change & Tune Up® Franchisees in its Region to discuss special competitive and marketing circumstances or opportunities in the car care services industry. Following such meeting, the Region may forward to all SpeeDee Oil Change & Tune Up® Local Franchisees in good standing in the Region a proposal to increase SpeeDee Ad Fund contributions, to be spent as a part of the Regional portion, for a specified period by

SpeeDee Oil Change & Tune Up® of the Gulf Coast
L-UFOC   v. 2.6   July 20, 1987
Reprinted with permission.

not more than an additional one percent (1%) of the Franchisee's gross revenues, to be collected and disbursed as set forth in such proposal. Such proposal shall become effective and binding on the Franchisee and the increased SpeeDee Ad Fund contributions shall be assessed upon and begin to be paid by the Franchisee upon written approval of two-thirds (2/3) of the SpeeDee Oil Change & Tune Up® Local Franchisees (voting on the basis of one vote per open SpeeDee Oil Change & Tune Up® Car Care Service Center in good standing) in the Region responding in writing to such proposal within the time specified in such proposal but such specified time will not be less than thirty (30) days nor will it exceed ninety (90) days from the date such proposal is sent to SpeeDee Oil Change & Tune Up® Local Franchisees in good standing in the Region for approval. Franchisee has separately initialed this section in recognition of its special significance and the fact that it has been fully read, discussed and understood._____

5.6   Local Advertising Co-operatives. At Region's election, the Region may cause the formation such of local and/or regional cooperative advertising associations and covering such areas as the Region deems appropriate taking into account all relevant business and marketing considerations and SOCS or such entity may disburse such funds as it believes are appropriate from the SpeeDee Ad Fund to be utilized by such local and/or regional cooperative advertising associations for local and/or regional advertising. In addition, upon the formation of such local and/or regional cooperative advertising associations, the Franchisee shall be deemed to be a member of such association(s) as cover the area(s) in which the Franchisee's Car Care Service Center is located and shall be bound by any decisions made by such association(s) upon an 2/3 majority vote of all members voting (voting on the basis of one vote per open SpeeDee Oil Change & Tune Up® Car Care Service Center in good standing), including but not limited to assessment and payment of additional advertising contributions by the members. Franchisee has separately initialed this section in recognition of its special significance and the fact that it has been fully read, discussed and understood._____

5.7   Administration. SpeeDee Ad Fund contributions shall be maintained by SOCS, the Region, or such entity in a separate bank account (or accounts) labeled as trust account(s), in order to avoid subjecting SpeeDee Ad Fund contributions to the claims of any creditor. SOCS, the Region and such entity (as the case may be) may reimburse themselves from SpeeDee Ad Fund contributions for reasonable accounting, bookkeeping, auditing, reporting, administrative, legal and similar expenses. Franchisee agrees that neither SOCS, the Region, such entity, nor any of their shareholders, directors, officers, employees, agents, attorneys or accountants shall be held liable for any act or omission with respect to the SpeeDee Ad Fund which is consistent with this Agreement or done in good faith. Franchisee has separately initialed this section in recognition of its special significance and the fact that it has been fully read, discussed and understood._____

SpeeDee Oil Change & Tune Up® of the Gulf Coast
L-UFOC   v. 2.6   July 20, 1987
Reprinted with permission.

5.8 **Supplier Advertising Contributions.** Where SOCS has designated an approved brand name supplier and such supplier has agreed to make payments with respect to such approved product or service conditioned on use, sales or otherwise by SOCS, affiliated entities, the Region or the Local Franchisee, all such payments by such approved brand name supplier shall be made to SOCS or an entity appointed by it [which may be the Region] and shall be spent by SOCS or such entity in accordance with any restrictions or conditions imposed by such approved brand name supplier.

6. TERM OF AGREEMENT, RENEWAL, TERMINATION

6.1 **Term.** The term of this Agreement shall commence on and as of the date that this Agreement is executed by both parties and shall remain in effect for fifteen [15] years provided that Franchisee continues to operate the Franchise in compliance with the terms of this Agreement.

6.2 **Renewal.** This Agreement may, subject to each of the provisions of this Agreement including the full and complete performance by the Franchisee of each of its obligations hereunder, be renewed by the Franchisee for two [2] subsequent five [5] year terms, provided that upon such proposed renewal the Franchisee has complied with each of the following conditions:

(a) The Franchisee delivers to the Region written notice of its intention to renew not more than 180 days and not less than 90 days prior to the expiration of any initial or renewal term;

(b) The Franchisee executes the then-current form of SpeeDee Oil Change & Tune Up® Franchise Agreement with the Region [which form of Agreement may contain different terms, including without limitation higher Business Development Fees and Advertising Contributions then currently exist] together with a form of release and indemnity in favor of the Region and SOCS;

(c) All ascertained and liquidated liabilities of the Franchisee to SOCS, the Region or any entity associated with either are paid in full at the time of renewal and all other liabilities of the Franchisee are provided for to the Region's reasonable satisfaction;

(d) The Franchisee is in full compliance with each of the terms of this Agreement including but not limited to all payment and other obligations, and is a SpeeDee Oil Change & Tune Up® franchisee in full good standing;

(e) Franchisee remodels and modernizes the Car Care Service Center, including without limitation, new interior and exterior design, signs, equipment,

SpeeDee Oil Change & Tune Up® of the Gulf Coast
L-UFOC v. 2.6 July 20, 1987
Reprinted with permission.

furnishing, decor and otherwise, as the Region shall designate so as to conform with the standards and specifications as contained in the then-current Local Franchise Agreement, SpeeDee Oil Change & Tune Up® Confidential Operating Manual or otherwise and otherwise brings the operation of the franchised Car Care Service Center into full and complete compliance with all requirements of the then-current SpeeDee Oil Change & Tune Up® Confidential Operating Manual or otherwise, including but not limited to possible building conversion, facilities upgrade, new equipment, signage, store layout, remodeling, changed products or services, operational methods, hours or computerized accounting and/or reporting; and

(f) The Franchisee pays a renewal fee of ten percent [10%] of the then-current initial franchise fee established by the Region for new franchises.

6.3   Termination by the Region.

(a)   <u>Immediate Termination.</u>   The Region may terminate this Agreement and all rights granted hereunder effective immediately without advance notice or opportunity to cure if:

(1) If any information supplied to Region by the Franchisee with or in connection with the Franchisee's application for franchise is inaccurate or incomplete;

(2) If Franchisee shall become insolvent or make a general assignment for the benefit of creditors, or if a petition in bankruptcy is filed by Franchisee, or such a petition filed against and consented to by Franchisee, or if Franchisee is adjudicated a bankrupt, or if a bill of equity or other proceeding for the appointment of a receiver of Franchisee or other custodian for Franchisee's business or assets is filed and consented to by Franchisee, or if a receiver or other custodian [permanent or temporary] of Franchisee's assets or property, or any part hereof, is appointed by any court of competent jurisdiction, or if proceeding for a composition with creditors under any state or federal law should be instituted by or against Franchisee, or if a final judgment remains unsatisfied or of record for thirty [30] days or longer [unless supersedeas bond is filed], or if execution is levied against Franchisee's franchise or property, or a suit to foreclose any lien or mortgage against the premises or equipment is instituted against Franchisee and not dismissed within thirty [30] days, or if the real or personal property of Franchisee's franchise shall be sold after levy thereupon by any sheriff, marshal or constable;

(3) If Franchisee has received from Region two [2] or more Notices to Cure pursuant to this Franchise Agreement for the same, similar or different defaults in any twelve-month period, in which event a Notice of Termination may be sent in lieu of any subsequent Notice to Cure;

SpeeDee Oil Change & Tune Up® of the Gulf Coast
L-UFOC   v. 2.6   July 20, 1987
Reprinted with permission.

(4) If Franchisee transfers any rights or obligations arising from this Franchise Agreement to any third party without Region's prior written consent, contrary to the provisions of this Franchise Agreement;

(5) If Franchisee abandons the business or ceases to actively remain open for business at the location granted in the Franchise Agreement for ten [10] consecutive days, or any shorter period after which it is reasonable under the facts and circumstances for the Region to conclude that Franchisee does not intend to continue to operate the business as a SpeeDee Oil Change & Tune Up® Franchise, or fails within fifteen [15] days after notice to remedy any material default under any lease or sublease for the franchise premises, or equipment therein, or loses the right to possession of the premises or otherwise forfeits the right to do or transact business in the jurisdiction where the franchise is located; provided, however, that if any such closure or loss of possession results through no fault of Franchisee, and the premises are damaged or destroyed by a disaster such as they cannot, in Region's judgment, reasonably be restored, then this Franchise Agreement shall not be terminated for that reason for sixty [60] days thereafter, provided Franchisee applies within that time for the approval of Region to relocate, for the remainder of the term hereof, to other premises, which approval shall not be unreasonably withheld; or

(6) If, in the sole and absolute discretion of the Region, the Franchisee fails to successfully complete initial home office orientation and/or regional training, in which case the Franchise Agreement will be terminated, the Franchisee will sign a form of release and indemnity in favor of the Region and SOCS and the Region will return to the Franchisee any Initial Franchise Fee paid by the Franchisee less the greater of (1) Five Thousand Dollars [$5,000] (subject to cost-of-living adjustment) or (2) the total of any expenses incurred by the Region as a result of or in connection with the sale of such franchise, including but not limited to amounts paid by the Region to SOCS or otherwise with respect to such sale and/or any associated training, home office orientation, franchise sales commissions, legal fees or otherwise.

(b) <u>Termination Effective After Notice and Opportunity to Cure.</u> The Region may terminate this Agreement effective at the end of thirty [30] days after notice and opportunity to cure for good cause, which shall include, but not be limited to, the occurrence of any of the following:

(1) Franchisee refuses, neglects or fails to perform any provision of this Agreement or any other Agreement with SOCS and/or the Region and/or any entity associated with either or any agreement between Franchisee and any SpeeDee Oil Change & Tune Up® approved supplier or fails to remain in full compliance with each of the provisions of the then-current SpeeDee Oil Change & Tune Up® Confidential Operating Manual as revised from time to time;

SpeeDee Oil Change & Tune Up® of the Gulf Coast
L-UFOC   v. 2.6   July 20, 1987
Reprinted with permission.

(2) Franchisee persists in default of any payment due to SOCS and/or the Region and/or any entity associated with either; or

(3) Any final judgment against Franchisee relating to his SOCS® business remains unsatisfied for a period of thirty [30] days.

Franchisee has separately initialed this section in recognition of its special significance and the fact that it has been fully read, discussed and understood. _____

(c) <u>Death or Incapacity.</u> The Region may terminate this Agreement effective thirty [30] days after notice and opportunity to cure if Franchisee's heirs or estate fail to comply with the provisions on death or disability of Franchisee set out in this Agreement. Franchisee has separately initialed this section in recognition of its special significance and the fact that it has been fully read, discussed and understood. _____

6.4 <u>Effect of Termination.</u> Upon termination of or failure to renew this Agreement, Franchisee shall:

(a) Pay to SOCS, the Region and/or any entities associated with either, within 30 days of such termination, all monies then due;

(b) Turn over to the Region, or otherwise dispose of as the Region may direct, all records, papers, manuals, supplies, etc., in Franchisee's possession which had previously been supplied by SOCS and/or the Region;

(c) Cease conducting business under the service mark SpeeDee Oil Change & Tune Up® and not thereafter use such service mark or any other mark or name associated therewith or confusingly similar thereto and the Franchisee shall relinquish all interest in the Franchise and execute all documents necessary to terminate any phone listing under such service mark;

(d) Be liable to SOCS and/or the Region for any damages incurred by SOCS and/or the Region as a result of any breach by Franchisee;

(e) Forfeit all fees paid;

(f) Agree that no payment shall be made to Franchisee with regard to the termination of its right to use SOCS' service marks, names or any goodwill established by Franchisee either prior to or during the operation of the Franchise.

Franchisee agrees that the Region may, but is not required to, elect to waive any right to sue the Franchisee for Business Development Fees and/or Advertising Contributions due to be paid after the termination of this Agreement and that, in such event, no inventory, equipment, goods, materials or otherwise shall be repurchased

SpeeDee Oil Change & Tune Up® of the Gulf Coast
L-UFOC   v. 2.6   July 20, 1987
Reprinted with permission.

by SOCS and/or the Region. The Franchisee further agrees that in the event of non-renewal of this Agreement, no inventory, equipment, goods, materials or otherwise shall be repurchased by SOCS and/or the Region.

Region shall have the right [but not the duty] to be exercised by mailing a Notice of Intent no later than thirty [30] days after termination or expiration, to purchase any or all real estate, improvements, advertising material, products, materials, supplies, or otherwise used or useful in the conduct of the Franchisee's business hereunder, and any items bearing Region's Proprietary Marks at fair market value. If the parties cannot agree on a fair market value within a reasonable time, an independent appraisal shall be determined by arbitration hereunder. If Region elects to exercise any option to purchase herein provided, it shall have the right to set-off all amounts due from Franchisee under this Franchise Agreement and the cost of the appraisal, if any, against any payment therefor. In the event the premises on which the franchised business is conducted [land and/or improvements] are leased to the Franchisee, Franchisee agrees to at any time, including but not limited to in the event of termination or nonrenewal and upon Region's request and at no cost to Region, assign, set over and transfer unto Region, at Region's sole option and discretion, all of Franchisee's interest in said lease(s) and the premises demised thereby including improvements. Any such lease(s) entered into by Franchisee shall contain a clause setting forth the landlord's consent to assign such lease(s) to Region or its assignee at any time.

In the event that the Region should cease operations or be terminated as a SpeeDee Oil Change & Tune Up® Region, SOCS or its assignee has the right to succeed to all of the Region's rights in and to any and all franchise agreements and other agreements between the Region and the Franchisee [including but not limited to franchise promissory notes, rights to receive development fees, advertising contributions and franchise note and/or other payments] and in such event SOCS or its assignee would be obligated to perform the Region's duties and assume all obligations under any such agreements. Franchisee has separately initialed this section in recognition of its special significance and the fact that it has been fully read, discussed and understood._____

7. ASSIGNABILITY

7.1   Assignment by Franchisee.   Franchisee shall not, during the term of this Agreement, sell, assign, transfer, pledge or convey any interest in the Franchise or the underlying business without the prior written consent of the Region and review by the Region and SOCS of all forms and procedures. Such consent shall not be unreasonably withheld provided that any consent to such action may carry with it terms and conditions prescribed by the Region, including, without limitation, the following conditions:

SpeeDee Oil Change & Tune Up® of the Gulf Coast
L-UFOC   v. 2.6   July 20, 1987
Reprinted with permission.

(a) Franchisee's assignee shall assume all the duties, obligations and liabilities of Franchisee to the Region and/or SOCS and shall have executed the then-current form of SpeeDee Oil Change & Tune Up® Local Franchise Agreement [to expire on the initial expiration date of this Agreement but subject to the renewal terms of the then-current Local Franchise Agreement] together with all other documents then typically required by the Region in connection with the sale of a new franchise, the parties acknowledging that the then-current Local Franchise Agreement may contain different terms, including without limitation higher Business Development Fees and Advertising Contributions than currently exist;

(b) Franchisee's assignee shall agree to take the training specified in Sections 3.2 and 3.3 hereof;

(c) Franchisee's assignee shall pay to the Region a transfer fee of $2,000, subject to adjustment for changes in cost-of-living as set forth in Section 4.3, to cover the Region's investigation, training, accounting and other expenses [but not including legal expenses] incurred in connection with such assignment; and

(d) All ascertained and liquidated liabilities of Franchisee to the Region and/or SOCS are paid in full at the time of the assignment and Franchisee has executed an assignment in form and substance satisfactory to the Region and SOCS and providing for a release and indemnity in favor of the Region and SOCS.

(e) The Franchisee is in compliance with all provisions of this Agreement and the then-current versions of any SpeeDee Oil Change & Tune Up® manuals and has brought the operation of the franchised Car Care Service Center into full and complete compliance with all requirements of the then-current SpeeDee Oil Change & Tune Up® Confidential Operating Manual or otherwise, including but not limited to possible building conversion, facilities upgrade, new equipment, signage, store layout, remodeling, changed products or services, operational methods, hours or computerized accounting and/or reporting, all at the sole cost and expense of the Franchisee.

Any attempted assignment, pledge or alienation of any interest in the Franchise or the underlying business shall trigger a right of first refusal by the Region to match the terms thereof, which right may be exercised for a period of 14 days after receipt of notice together with transfer fee from the Franchisee. Notwithstanding such right of first refusal the Region may disapprove any proposed assignment, pledge or alienation whenever it determines that the proposed action is not in the best interests of the Region's franchisees or other SOCS franchisees. Any attempted assignment, pledge or alienation by Franchisee of this Agreement, or any of the rights granted hereunder, in violation of the terms of this Agreement shall be an item of default under and violation of the terms of this Agreement. Franchisee has separately initialed this section in recognition of its special significance and the fact that it has been fully read, discussed and understood._____

SpeeDee Oil Change & Tune Up® of the Gulf Coast
L-UFOC   v. 2.6   July 20, 1987
Reprinted with permission.

7.2   Assignment by the Region.   Subject to any required consent of SOCS, the Region reserves the right to sell or assign any portion of its interest in this Agreement, provided that its commitments to establish the franchise have been met or arranged for, and the transferee explicitly undertakes to provide further required contractual services. In the event that the Region should for any reason cease operations or be terminated or otherwise no longer continue as a SpeeDee Oil Change & Tune Up® Region, SOCS or its assignee may make available the services for Franchisee which the Region is obligated to provide hereunder and the Franchisee shall, upon notice from SOCS or its assignee of such event having taken place, deal directly with SOCS or its assignee and pay directly to SOCS or its assignee all amounts then due or to become due under or related to this Agreement and SOCS or its assignee shall thereupon succeed to all of the Region's rights in and to any and all Franchise Agreements and other agreements with Franchisee, including but not limited to franchisee promissory notes or otherwise, between the Region and Franchisee, and including but not limited to rights to receive development fees, advertising contributions or otherwise. Franchisee has separately initialed this section in recognition of its special significance and the fact that it has been fully read, discussed and understood._____

8.   DEATH OR INCAPACITY OF FRANCHISEE

8.1   Upon the death of Franchisee or the determination of Franchisee's incapacity or the dissolution of Franchisee if the Franchisee is a corporation or partnership, Franchisee's interest in this Agreement shall pass to Franchisee's heirs or beneficiaries or other successors in interest. In such event, the Region may terminate this Agreement upon 30 days written notice to the Franchisee's last business address unless such heirs or beneficiaries or other successors in interest [a] designate a person as being responsible for the performance of the Franchise pursuant to this Agreement within 60 days after such death or determination, and [b] provide adequate assurance, satisfactory to the Region, that such person's qualifications and abilities are sufficient for the continued operation of the Franchise, the observance of all duties of Franchisee under this Agreement, and the protection of the Region's and SOCS' valuable service marks and name. Where the Region reasonably deems it appropriate for the operation of the franchise the Franchisee's heirs or beneficiaries or other successors in interest may be required to, at such individual's sole expense, successfully complete training at the Region or such other location as the Region may designate, and to pay $2,000, subject to adjustment for changes in cost-of-living as set forth in Section 4.3, to cover the Region's legal, investigative, training, accounting and other expenses in connection therewith.

SpeeDee Oil Change & Tune Up® of the Gulf Coast
L-UFOC   v. 2.6   July 20, 1987
Reprinted with permission.

9. MISCELLANEOUS

9.1 Relationship of the Parties. The relationship between the Region and the Franchisee is that of franchisor and franchisee. No other relationship is intended or created hereby. The Region is in no sense an agent of SOCS and all obligations to the Franchisee are those of the Region only, SOCS having no obligations to the Franchisee under this Agreement or otherwise except with respect to the management of SpeeDee Ad Fund funds received and held by SOCS or the SpeeDee Ad Fund. Neither Franchisee nor any person employed by him or her shall be, or shall at any time represent or hold itself out as being, an employee, partner, joint venturer subsidiary or affiliate of the Region or SOCS. Franchisee shall not incur any obligation on behalf of the Region or SOCS and shall, without limiting the generality of the foregoing, specifically refrain from promising or holding out to any of his customers any support or assistance by the Region or SOCS. Franchisee is and shall remain an independent business entity and nothing in this Agreement or otherwise shall be construed to create an agency relationship, a partnership or joint venture between Franchisee and either the Region or SOCS. Neither Franchisee, the Region nor SOCS shall act as the agent of the other, and neither Franchisee, the Region nor SOCS shall guarantee or become in any way responsible for the obligations, debts or expenses of the other. Neither the Region nor SOCS shall be entitled to share in the profits of the Franchisee nor be required to share in Franchisee's losses or liabilities, nor have any ownership or equity interest in the Franchise nor regulate the hiring or firing of Franchisee's employees or other persons performing functions on behalf of the Franchisee nor regulate working conditions or determine whom the Franchisee shall accept as customers, except to the extent necessary to protect SOCS' name, service marks and associated logotypes and goodwill associated therewith. The conduct of Franchisee's business shall be determined by its own independent reasonable business judgment and discretion, subject only to the provisions of this Agreement and the SpeeDee Oil Change & Tune Up® Operating Manual. Nothing herein or otherwise shall create the relationship of trustee and beneficiary between Region [and/or SOCS] and the Franchisee. Franchisee has separately initialed this section in recognition of its special significance and the fact that it has been fully read, discussed and understood._____

9.2 Indemnity. Franchisee agrees to indemnify and hold the Region and/or SOCS harmless, and to pay the costs of defense of the Region and/or SOCS, against any and all claims, demands, damages, causes of action, liabilities, costs or expenses arising out of any service, representation, promise, agreement or any other act or omission by Franchisee or any of his or her agents or employees. With respect to any equipment, products, services, goods or otherwise provided by approved suppliers ("supplier items"), such supplier items are provided by such suppliers without any warranties by SOCS or the Region, express or implied, including warranties of merchantability or fitness, or as to the design, condition, capacity, performance or any other aspect of the supplier items or their material or workman-

SpeeDee Oil Change & Tune Up® of the Gulf Coast
L-UFOC v. 2.6 July 20, 1987
Reprinted with permission.

ship, the Franchisee agreeing that approval by SOCS or the Region of any supplier items or of any relationship with a supplier is made by SOCS or the Region as an accommodation only and SOCS and the Region shall have no liability with respect thereto, the Franchisee agreeing to look only to the supplier and not to SOCS or the Region with respect to any claims with regard to such supplier items or their use. SOCS and the Region disclaim any (and the Franchisee agrees and warrants that there shall not be, and shall indemnify SOCS and the Region with respect to any) liability to Franchisee, any third parties, customers or members of the general public or any agents or employees of any of the foregoing as a result of any defects, latent or otherwise, in the supplier items and the Franchisee agrees to not assert any claim against SOCS or the Region for any loss or damages with respect to or caused in any way by the supplier items. The Franchisee also agrees to indemnify SOCS and the Region arising from use of the supplier items and assumes total responsibility for any taxes levied with respect to the supplier items. Franchisee has separately initialed this section in recognition of its special significance and the fact that it has been fully read, discussed and understood._____

9.3 <u>SpeeDee Ad Fund Indemnity.</u> Franchisee agrees to indemnify and hold the Region harmless for the management or expenditure of any SpeeDee Ad Fund contributions paid by Franchisee (as described in Section 5.1 herein) except for any SpeeDee Ad Fund contributions paid by Franchisee to Region for forwarding to the SpeeDee Ad Fund. In that event, Region's only responsibility is to promptly forward such funds to the SpeeDee Ad Fund without any holdback or offset. Franchisee has separately initialed this section in recognition of its special significance and the fact that it has been fully read, discussed and understood._____

9.4 <u>Notices.</u> All notices hereunder shall be deemed delivered five days after deposit in the United States mail, postage prepaid, addressed to either party at the following addresses:

Region: SpeeDee Oil Change & Tune Up® of the Gulf Coast
6660 Riverside Drive, Suite 101
Metairie, Louisiana 70003

Franchisee: _____
_____
_____

All notices of termination hereunder shall be in writing, posted by registered, certified or other receipted mail, or delivered by telegram or personally to the Franchisee. Such notices shall contain a statement of intent to terminate the Franchise together with the reasons therefore and the effective date of termination. Any cure periods required with respect to such notices shall run from the date of depositing such notices in the U.S. Mail, postage prepaid or the date of other dispatch to Fran-

SpeeDee Oil Change & Tune Up® of the Gulf Coast
L-UFOC v. 2.6 July 20, 1987
Reprinted with permission.

chisee. Franchisee has separately initialed this section in recognition of its special significance and the fact that it has been fully read, discussed and understood. _____

9.5   Captions.   Any titles or captions contained in this Agreement are for convenience of reference only and shall not be deemed as part of the context of this Agreement.

9.6   Attorneys' Fees.   In the event that any action or proceeding is filed by one party against the other party to enforce any of the covenants or conditions hereto, the party in whose favor final judgment shall be entered shall be entitled to recover from the other reasonable attorneys' fees, to be fixed by the court in which the judgment is entered.

9.7   Governing Law and Arbitration.   The legality of the offer and sale of the Franchise consummated hereby shall be governed by the applicable franchise investment law of the state in which the sale was made and, to the extent required as a condition of sale of the Franchise within such state, the rights and obligations of the Region and Franchisee hereunder shall be construed in accordance with such law. Franchisee hereby irrevocably submits any claim, dispute, suit, action or proceeding arising out of or relating to this Agreement or any of the transactions or documents contemplated by, referenced in or related to this Agreement to binding arbitration under the rules for commercial arbitration of the American Arbitration Association at its office located nearest to the office of the Region.

9.8   Severability.   If any provision of this Agreement shall be invalid or unenforceable for any reason and to any extent, the remainder of this Agreement shall not be affected thereby, but rather shall be enforced to the greatest extent permitted by law.

9.9   No Waiver.   The failure of the Region to give notice of default or to pursue any remedy for a breach of this Agreement shall not affect its right to give notice of termination upon that or subsequent defaults or to pursue any remedy upon subsequent breaches, under this or any other agreement or in the case of any other Franchisee.

9.10   Entire Agreement.   This Agreement contains the entire understanding between the parties and supersedes any prior understandings and agreements between them respecting the within subject matter. **THERE ARE NO REPRESENTATIONS, WARRANTIES, EARNINGS, REVENUE OR OTHER CLAIMS, AGREEMENTS, PROMISES, ARRANGEMENTS OR UNDERSTANDINGS, ORAL OR WRITTEN, BETWEEN OR AMONG THE PARTIES HERETO RELATING TO THE WITHIN SUBJECT MATTER WHICH ARE NOT FULLY EXPRESSED HEREIN.** Franchisee has separately initialed this paragraph in recognition of its special significance and the fact that it has been fully read, discussed and understood. _____

SpeeDee Oil Change & Tune Up® of the Gulf Coast
L-UFOC   v. 2.6   July 20, 1987
Reprinted with permission.

9.11 **Amendment and Approval.** Any modification to or change in this Agreement must be in writing and signed by each of the parties thereto, and this Agreement and any modification or change thereto must be approved in writing by SOCS before this Agreement or any modification or change can take effect or bind either party.

9.12 **Insolvency.** No corporation, firm or person other than the Franchisee shall have or acquire any right or rights sold to the Franchisee hereunder by virtue of any bankruptcy, insolvency or assignment for the benefit of creditors or reorganization proceedings, or any receivership or other legal process, either under attachment, execution or otherwise, or in any manner whatsoever growing out of any proceeding or suit in law or in equity, without the prior written consent of the Region. In the event of any such proceeding being had or taken by or against the Franchisee or any assignee or successor in interest of the Franchisee under any provisions of the law, including the various chapters of the bankruptcy act, or for the involuntary winding up of the Franchise or any assignee or successor in interest of the Franchisee, without such proceeding being dismissed or such levies released within five [5] days therefrom, the Region shall have the option of terminating this Agreement immediately. In the event of any proceeding to wind up or dissolve the Franchise or any corporate assignee or successor in interest of the Franchise, the Region shall have the option of terminating this Agreement immediately.

9.13 **Late Payments.** Late payments or contributions of any amounts due to be paid or contributed by the Franchisee under this Agreement or otherwise shall accrue interest at the lesser of twelve per cent per annum or the applicable legal maximum, interest to accrue beginning ten [10] days after the date on which such payment or contribution was originally due. Franchisee has separately initialed this section in recognition of its special significance and the fact that it has been fully read, discussed and understood._____

IN WITNESS WHEREOF, the undersigned have executed this Franchise Agreement to be effective the day and year first written above.

REGION: G.C. & K.B. Investments, Inc. d.b.a.
           SpeeDee Oil Change & Tune Up® of the Gulf Coast

           By _____
              Its President

SpeeDee Oil Change & Tune Up® of the Gulf Coast
L-UFOC v. 2.6 July 20, 1987
Reprinted with permission.

FRANCHISEE: _____
NAME (Please Print)

_____
Signature

The undersigned hereby personally guarantees each and all obligations of the above Franchisee to SOCS and/or the Region, whether past, present or future, arising out of this Franchise Agreement, any promissory note or otherwise, all without limitation of any kind or nature. Neither SOCS nor the Region need bring suit first against the Franchisee in order to enforce this guarantee.

_____

SpeeDee Oil Change & Tune Up® of the Gulf Coast
L-UFOC v. 2.6 July 20, 1987
Reprinted with permission.

EXHIBIT C

LOCAL FRANCHISES

OF

G.C. & K.B. INVESTMENTS, INC. d.b.a.

SPEEDEE OIL CHANGE & TUNE UP® OF THE GULF COAST

("REGION")

EXHIBIT C-1

PRE-EXISTING FRANCHISES IN THE TERRITORY

(CURRENTLY BEING SERVICED BY THE REGION)

Carlube, Inc. d.b.a. SpeeDee Oil Change & Tune Up®
Mr. Ed Mikkelsen
10330 Florida Blvd.
Baton Rouge, Louisiana   70815
(504)   273-3776

Accardo Enterprise d.b.a. SpeeDee Oil Change & Tune Up®
Mr. Vince Accardo, Owner/Operator
2015 E. Judge Perez
Chalmette, Louisiana   70043
(504)   271-6754

Accardo Enterprise d.b.a. SpeeDee Oil Change & Tune Up®
Mr. Vince Accardo, Owner/Operator
Claiborne Hill at Highway 190
Covington, Louisiana   70433
(504)   893-5540

TZH Oil Services d.b.a. SpeeDee Oil Change & Tune Up®
Terri & Henry Ziegler, Owner/Operator
616 Terry Pkwy.
Gretna, Louisiana   70053
(504)   362-4562

SpeeDee Oil Change & Tune Up®
Mr. Jack Jenevein
180 Pebble Beach
Slidell, Louisiana   70458
*Baton Rouge Store Under Construction/Site Selection

**The above operational units were originally franchisees of SOCS and are operating under a form of franchise agreement different in some respects to that offered by this offering circular.

SpeeDee Oil Change & Tune Up® of the Gulf Coast
L-UFOC   December 31, 1987
Reprinted with permission.

EXHIBIT C-1 Continued.

S & W Oil Services, Inc. d.b.a. SpeeDee Oil Change & Tune Up®
Mr. Sid Schilhab, Owner/Operator
Mr. C.B. Walker
1503 Moss Street
Lafayette, Louisiana   70501
(318)   233-4222

S & W Oil Services, Inc. d.b.a. SpeeDee Oil Change & Tune Up®
Mr. Sid Schilhab, Owner/Operator
Mr. C.B. Walker
3935 W. Congress St.
Lafayette, Louisiana   70506
(504)   981-8842

B & E of Louisiana d.b.a. SpeeDee Oil Change & Tune Up®
Mr. Ed Mikkelsen
647 Gause Blvd.
Slidell, Louisiana   70458
(504)   641-9186

Schwing Investments d.b.a. SpeeDee Oil Change & Tune Up®
Messrs. George & Kenny Schwing
693 N. Beal Parkway
Fort Walton, Florida   32548
(904)   863-4243

20th Century Oil d.b.a. SpeeDee Oil Change & Tune Up®
Mr. Don Ory, Owner/Operator
3214 Hardy Street
Hattiesburg, Mississippi   39401
(601)   264-5200

SpeeDee Oil Change & Tune Up®
Messrs. Don & Keith Ory, Owner/Operator
Mr. Gerard Landry
212 Highway 49 South
Hattiesburg, Mississippi   39401
(601)   583-2223

**The above operational units were originally franchisees of SOCS and are operating under a form of franchise agreement different in some respects to that offered by this offering circular.

SpeeDee Oil Change & Tune Up® of the Gulf Coast
L-UFOC   December 31, 1987
Reprinted with permission.

EXHIBIT C-1 Continued.

SpeeDee Oil Change & Tune Up®
Mr. John Montecino
P.O. Box 1365
2444 W. Thomas Street
Hammond, Louisiana   70401
*Gulfport Store Under Construction/Site Selection

North American Ship Holding d.b.a. SpeeDee Oil Change & Tune Up®
Mr. Robert Perez, Owner/Operator
6308 N. Davis Highway
Pensacola, Florida   32504
(904)   479-4772

**The above operational units were originally franchisees of SOCS and are operating under a form of franchise agreement different in some respects to that offered by this offering circular.

KneeDee, Inc. d.b.a. SpeeDee Oil Change & Tune Up®
Mr. Ed Mikkelsen
5389 Government Street
Baton Rouge, Louisiana   70815
(504)   922-9299

SpeeDee Oil Change & Tune Up®
Mr. Jack Jenevein
9225 Lake Forest Blvd.
East New Orleans, Louisiana   70127
(504)   244-9191

SpeeDee Oil Change & Tune Up®
Mr. Ed Mikkelsen
112 Highway 51
Hammond, Louisiana   70401
(504)   542-0074

SpeeDee Oil Change & Tune Up®
Mr. Denny Otillio
147 Brookside Drive
Mandeville, Louisiana   70448
*Under Construction/Site Selection

SpeeDee Oil Change & Tune Up® of the Gulf Coast
L-UFOC   December 31, 1987
Reprinted with permission.

EXHIBIT C-1 Continued.

Goldspeed, Inc. d.b.a. SpeeDee Oil Change & Tune Up®
Mr. Sanford Goldstein
1125 Cadiz Street
New Orleans, Louisiana   70115
*Under Construction/Site Selection

SpeeDee Oil Change & Tune Up®
Mr. James Hufft
111 Hufft Drive
Belle Chasse, Louisiana   70037
*Under Construction/Site Selection

J.A.G., Inc. d.b.a. SpeeDee Oil Change & Tune Up®
Messrs. Alan, John and Gary Vinturella
5413 Rebecca Blvd.
Kenner, Louisiana   70065
*Under Construction/Site Selection

SpeeDee Oil Change & Tune Up®
Mr. Ed Mikkelsen
9535 Richmond Avenue
Houston, Texas   77063
(713)   952-1180

SpeeDee Oil Change & Tune Up®
Mr. Ed Mikkelsen
4820 Elmwood Pkwy.
Metairie, Louisiana   70003
*Under Construction/Site Selection

SpeeDee Oil Change & Tune Up®
Mr. Ed Mikkelsen
4820 Elmwood Pkwy.
Metairie, Louisiana   70003
*Under Construction/Site Selection

SpeeDee Oil Change & Tune Up® of the Gulf Coast
L-UFOC   December 31, 1987
Reprinted with permission.

EXHIBIT C-2

UNITS OWNED BY G.C. & K.B. INVESTMENTS, INC. d.b.a.

SPEEDEE OIL CHANGE & TUNE UP® OF THE GULF COAST

("REGION")

SpeeDee Oil Change & Tune Up® No. 1
4942 Veterans Blvd.
Metairie, Louisiana   70002
(504)   454-1840   *Operational

SpeeDee Oil Change & Tune Up® No. 3
1901 Barataria Blvd.
Marrero, Louisiana   70072
(504)   340-5007   *Operational

SpeeDee Oil Change & Tune Up® No. 6
1714 Veterans Blvd.
Metairie, Louisiana   70005
(504)   831-8254   *Operational

SpeeDee Oil Change & Tune Up® No. 7
3211 Williams Blvd.
Kenner, Louisiana   70062
(504)   443-3489   *Operational

SpeeDee Oil Change & Tune Up® No. 8
3333 S. Carrollton Avenue
New Orleans, Louisiana   70118
(504)   482-7002   *Operational

SpeeDee Oil Change & Tune Up® No. 9
4001 Veterans Blvd.
Metairie, Louisiana   70002
*Under Construction

SpeeDee Oil Change & Tune Up®
5606 Canal Blvd.
New Orleans, Louisiana   70124   *Non-Operational

SpeeDee Oil Change & Tune Up® of the Gulf Coast
L-UFOC   December 31, 1987
Reprinted with permission.

EXHIBIT D

LOANED EQUIPMENT AGREEMENT

SpeeDee Oil Change & Tune Up® of the Gulf Coast
L-UFOC   December 31, 1987
Reprinted with permission.

LOANED EQUIPMENT AGREEMENT

TERMS AND CONDITIONS

1. Borrower acknowledges receipt of equipment in good condition and shall at its expense keep it in good condition, insure against all risks, and not sell, encumber, remove or otherwise dispose of said equipment, which shall remain the property of Burmah-Castrol Inc., who shall have a security interest in said equipment to protect its interest therein.

2. Said items are loaned at the request of Borrower to be solely, actively and continuously used by him on said premises for the storage, handling, dispensing and sale of Castrol products ONLY, and for no other purpose. BURMAH-CASTROL INC. LOANS EQUIPMENT WITHOUT ANY WARRANTY, EXPRESS OR IMPLIED, INCLUDING WARRANTIES OF MERCHANTABILITY OR FITNESS, OR AS TO THE DESIGN, CONDITION, CAPACITY, PERFORMANCE OR ANY OTHER ASPECT OF THE EQUIPMENT OR ITS MATERIAL OR WORKMANSHIP. Burmah-Castrol Inc. further disclaims any liability for loss, damage, or injury to Borrower, its employees or third parties as a result of any defects, latent or otherwise, in the equipment whether arising from Burmah-Castrol Inc.'s negligence or failure to keep the equipment in proper condition or repair or application of the laws of strict liability. Regardless of cause, Borrower will not assert any claim whatsoever against Burmah-Castrol Inc. for loss of anticipatory profits or any other indirect, special or consequential damages. Borrower shall indemnify Burmah-Castrol Inc. from any liability whatsoever arising from use of said equipment and shall assume total responsibility for all personal property or other taxes levied with respect to said equipment.

3. Borrower at its option may purchase said equipment as a whole and not in part at any time at the depreciated value, depreciation to be taken on a ten year, straight-line basis with no residual value. After 10 years, Burmah-Castrol Inc. claims no rights in said equipment.

4. Should Borrower fail to purchase at the rate of 10,000 gallons (8 lbs. grease/gear oil = 1 gallon) per year of Castrol products, or use said equipment for other than Castrol products, become past due in any monetary obligation to Castrol for 60 days or more twice during any six-month period, or breach this agreement in any other way for 60 days or more, Borrower shall be required to purchase said equipment from Burmah-Castrol Inc. at its then depreciated value, or at Burmah-Castrol Inc.'s option shall surrender and return said equipment to Burmah-Castrol Inc. and allow Burmah-Castrol Inc. to enter onto premises and remove said equipment without recourse to process of law.

5. The above agreement contains the entire contract between the parties hereto, any verbal stipulations on the part of the parties or their representatives notwithstanding.

_____   _____
Borrower   Burmah-Castrol Inc.

EXHIBIT E

LETTER OF CREDIT

SpeeDee Oil Change & Tune Up® of the Gulf Coast
L-UFOC   December 31, 1987
Reprinted with permission.

FORM OF LETTER OF CREDIT

(Bank name and address)

(Date)

Burmah-Castrol Inc.
401 Hackensack Avenue
Hackensack, New Jersey 07601

Attn: (   )

Gentlemen:

We hereby establish our irrevocable letter of credit (number) in your favor for the account of (name and address of dealer) up to the aggregate amount of US $20,000 available by your draft(s) at sight on us marked "Drawn under (Bank) credit (number)" and accompanied by the following documents:

1. A signed letter from the President, Vice President, Secretary or Treasurer of Burmah-Castrol Inc. stating that for the second time in a 6-month period, an invoice to (name of dealer) is 60 days or more past due from the due date and remains unpaid, with a copy of the unpaid invoice attached, or stating that (name of dealer) has been in default in an obligation to Burmah-Castrol Inc. for 60 days or more.

2. A copy of a letter sent by Burmah-Castrol Inc. to (name of dealer) notifying it that Burmah-Castrol Inc. intends to draw on the letter of credit.

This letter of credit covers monies owed to Burmah-Castrol Inc. by (name of dealer) which have not been paid for 60 days after said monies became due. Burmah-Castrol Inc.'s drafts shall be honored even if (name of dealer) disputes the statement referred to in (1) above.

Multiple drawings are permitted.

We hereby undertake to honor draft(s) drawn under and in compliance with the terms of this credit when accompanied by document(s) specified when presented within two years from the date hereof at our counters.

THIS CREDIT IS SUBJECT TO THE UNIFORM CUSTOMS AND PRACTICE FOR DOCUMENTARY CREDITS (1983 REVISION) INTERNATIONAL CHAMBER OF COMMERCE PUBLICATION NO. 400.

(Bank)

BY _____
AUTHORIZED SIGNATURE

INDEX

NOTE: The symbol (F) or (T) following a page number indicates that information is presented in a figure or a table, respectively.

A

A & G Supply Company, 595-596
A & W Root Beer drive-ins, 27, 39
Aamco Transmissions, Inc., 178
Abandonment, and franchisor's right of automatic termination, 479
Accounting services franchises, 36, 166, 290-292, 384
Accounting systems for franchises, 64, 541
ADIs (areas of dominant influence) (*see also* Arbitron Company), 207-210, 207(F), 212-214, 216, 224, 248, 460-461
    county/ADI size classification for New York State, 209(T)
    general advertising fee, sample franchising agreement, 584-585
Advertising, 63, 86, 106, 110, 168-170, 195, 378-379
    Anything Fast Food Company case study, 212-213, 213(T)
    budget based on percentage of sales, 214
    committees, 500, 511
    cooperative costs shared by franchisees, 44, 174, 304, 356, 488, 489(T), 501
    Dunkin' Donuts case study, 198-199
    earnings claims for potential franchisees, 422
    false and misleading, 123, 143
    fee determined by franchisor, 483
    fee requirements records kept in franchise defense manual, 481
    fees collected by master franchisee, 251
    fees increased at transfer, 525
    fees paid by franchisees to franchisor, 433, 460, 467, 475, 485, 508
    focus groups and platform, 463(F)
    franchise advisory councils, 503
    franchise choice, 419
    franchisor operational expertise, 464
    growth stage of franchising relationship, 498
    high-impact benefits to franchisee, 6, 35-36
    included in operations manual, 347(T)
    international franchise fees, 555-557
    legal relationship provision in franchising agreement, 522
    local market focus, 534
    McDonald's Corporation 1983 expenditure, 187
    mass, as tool of promotional strategy, 186-189, 193, 486
    promotion information provided in advertising manual, 355-357
    promotions, and sales programs, 36, 41, 64, 82, 173-174, 208-210, 375
    publicity campaigns, 190
    Silver "Addy" Award for the South, 429
    survey of franchisees, 256-257
    testing ideas at prototype unit, 332
    twelve basic appeals, 458-459, 458(F)
Africa, U.S. franchise expansion, 560(T)
Age characteristics, demographic data, 220, 221(T)
Alcoa Aluminum, 5
Allied Capital Corp., 443
Allied Lending Corp., SBA guaranteed loan program, 443
American Bar Association Forum Committee, 195
American Council on Education, 350
American Dairy Queen Corporation, 115-118
American Hotel and Motel Association, Educational Institute of, 235
American Hotels Corporation, 235
Annual Statement Studies, Robert Morris Associates, 292
Antitrust laws, 109, 115, 147, 152-153, 190, 503, 537

655

background and basis of laws, 140-143, 476, 486
  legal problems involving franchisees, 64-65, 99, 108, 111-112, 521
Anything Fast Food Company, hypothetical company case study, 211-213, 213(T)
Arab countries, U.S. franchise expansion, 551
Arbitron Company (see also ADIs), 207-210, 213, 248
Arby's Roast Beef Restaurants, 334
Area development agreements, 249
Area representatives. See Franchisor's representatives
Areas of dominant influence. See ADIs
Armstrong v. Taco Time International, 538
Asia, U.S. franchise expansion, 551-552, 556(T), 560(T)
Associate dealership programs, 13-14
Australia, U.S. franchise expansion, 551-552, 556(T), 560(T), 565
Automobile and truck dealerships, 8, 65, 75-76, 185, 189-190, 194-195, 220
  corporate images, 244
  elaborate site selection criteria, 361
  foreign market franchises, 550
  number of establishments and sales in 1987, 28(T)
Automobile and truck rental services, 23-25, 25(T), 29(T), 194, 263, 329, 436
  Certain-teed Rental System, case study, 369-370
  international franchising, 556(T), 565
Automobile manufacturers, 12, 190, 214, 436, 558, 565
Automobiles, distribution of, 12-13, 35, 42-43
Automobile washing businesses. See Car washing businesses
Automotive products and repair businesses (aftermarkets), 16-19, 19(T), 54, 72, 137-138, 168, 170
  auto body repair firm, media schedule, 174, 175(F)
  comparative franchises, 228
  customer satisfaction, 244
  demographic data use, 220
  development of target trade areas, 214, 217-218, 219(F)
  financial ratios useful, 289
  international franchising, 556(T), 565
  marketed under a family branding approach, 354
  mechanics repair shop, 137-138

muffler shop franchises in general, 65, 210
  number of establishments and sales in 1987, 28(T)
  repair shops' site inspection criteria, 361
sample franchising agreement, 569-654
site profiles, 226
undercoating businesses, 228
Avis Rent-A-Car, Inc., 194, 436
Avon Products, Inc., 14, 186

B

Balmer, Thomas A., 139
Banking system franchises, 26, 333
Bankruptcy, 101, 479, 536-537, 583
Barn'rds International, 334
Basement waterproofing franchises, 183
Bean, James H., 97
Beauty salons, 26, 149, 293-294, 329, 454-455
Beeder, Wayne, 398
Beer franchise systems, 195, 231-232
Bennett, Kevin, 595-596, 611
Berger, Ron, 333
Best Western motels, 23
Bethlehem Steel Company, 266
Better Business Bureau, source of information about franchises, 416-417
BIC®, coined trademark, 122
Blue-pencilling, 538
"Blue-chip" franchises, 48, 404
Blueprint development, 50, 51(T)
Bookkeeping services franchises, 149
Bottlers and distributors, soft drink, 8, 29(T), 194, 231
Bowling alley franchises, 497-498
BPIs (buying power indices), 207(F), 210-214, 216
Brand or name recognition, 186, 564
Brand or trade names, 64-65, 476-477
Breaking away, 520, 532-546
Bresler, Stanley, 55-56
Bresler Ice Cream Company, 55
Bresler Realty Company, 56
Bresler's 33 Flavor's Inc., 55-56
Brewing companies, 11
Budget Rent-A-Car, 194, 436
Budweiser, 187
Burger King Corporation, 179, 185-187, 194, 221, 450, 460
  Cormack's success story, 450, 468-470, 469(F)
Burglar and fire alarm franchises, 189

Index

Burmah-Castrol, Inc. (Castrol), 595-599, 612, 652, 654
Business aids and services franchise systems, 14, 16, 26, 166, 189, 203, 437
   international franchising, 556(T), 565
   number of establishments and sales in 1987, 28(T)
   training significant for franchise success, 327(T), 384
Business day, definition, 100n.
The Business Franchise Guide (Commerce Clearing House), 99n.
Buybacks, 446, 537, 539
Buying power index. *See* BPIs

C

California (*see also* First Interstate Bancorp), 19, 100n., 106-107
Campgrounds. *See* Hotel/motel franchises
Canada, U.S. franchise expansion, 100, 500, 551, 556(T), 565, 566
Capital, 38, 44, 50-53, 51(T), 102
   expenditure financing, 439-444
   questions asked during disclosure meeting, 424-425
   working, 282-283, 296-311, 302(F), 303(T), 305(F), 310(F), 311(T)
     cash flow "balancing act," 314(F)
     projected cash flow figures, 315
     requirements in basic disclosure documents, 413
Caribbean, U.S. franchise expansion, 556(T), 560(T)
Carpet cleaning franchises, 52, 54, 186
Carpeting businesses, 189
Car washing businesses, 189, 475-476
Cash flow. *See* Financial statements for franchises
"Catalog corner" concept, 188
Catalog stores, 228
Census, U.S. Bureau of the, 209-210, 216
   source of demographic data for franchise site selection, 220(T), 221(T), 222(T)
Center for Economic Education, Old Dominion University, 154
Central America, U.S franchise expansion, 560(T)
Century 21 Real Estate, 16, 35-36
Certificate of Registration, trademark, 125
Certified Hotel Administrator, 235
CESA Publications, Inc., 410-411

Chevrolet Motor Division, 186
Chief executive officer (CEO), role in franchise, 74
Chimney cleaning franchises, 188
China, U.S. franchise expansion, 551-552
Chrysler Corporation, 185, 550
Church, Nancy, 12
Clayton Act, 142, 147, 488
Clean water systems franchises, 186
Clothing system franchises, 14, 229, 335-336
Coca-Cola Company, 35, 48, 121, 181, 194
   international franchising, 550, 553, 558-559
Colgate Doctrine, 145
Collins, James A., 512
Collins Food International, Inc., 512
Collins Food Service, 512
Commerce, U.S. Department of, 67, 189
   franchise category handbook, 408-410
   franchise protection, seven area, 48-49, 49(T)
Commercial symbols, 104, 110
Commissioner of Patents and Trademarks, 124, 129
Commodities, sale of, 151
Common law (state), source of trade secret protection, 132
Common law rights, 121
Competition (*see also* Tying arrangements), 13, 20, 146, 152, 206, 214-215, 228
   covenant not to compete, 41, 112, 135, 481, 524, 534, 537-539
   restrictive clauses, 509, 610
   unlawful restraint, 142-143, 476
Comprehensive Accounting Corporation, 290-292
   sample financial forms for franchises, 364, 365(F), 366(F), 367(F)
Computer products franchises, 15, 34, 48, 76, 228, 290, 532-533
   computer expertise not necessary for franchisees, 328
   future expansion foreseen in international marketplace, 564
   international franchising, 565
   marketing effects, 456-457
   prototype inappropriate to copy, 333
   quality control consistent for all franchises, 330
   software package designs, Sally's case study incident, 372-373
   training program development, Sally's case study incident, 372-373
   training significant for franchise success, 384

The Conference Board survey of franchisees, 256
Confidentiality agreements, 133
Congress, legislation for franchisee protection not recommended, 511, 514
Consideration, definition, 100n.
Consignment basis agencies, 12
Construction company franchises, 16, 26, 28(T), 556(T)
Continental T.V., Inc. v. *GTE Sylvania*, 483
Control Data Corporation, 207
Convenience store franchise systems, 14-15, 17-18, 18(T), 56, 58-60, 232, 460
  competition, 217, 228-229
  international franchising, 564-565
  number of establishments and sales in 1987, 29(T)
Convenient Food Mart, Inc., 56
Cooper, Harris, 115
Copeland, A., Enterprises, 547
Copeland, Alvin C., 394-395, 546-547
Copeland's of New Orleans, 395
Copp, Gary, 595-596, 611
Copyright Office (Washington, D.C.), 126-127
Copyrights, 104, 108, 120, 126-128, 279
Cormack, Craig, 450, 468-470, 469(F)
Cormack Enterprises, Inc., 469(F)
Corporation Records, Standard & Poor's, 292
Corporations, expansion, 43-44, 46
"Corvette," product attributes, 178
Cosmetics franchises, 14, 186, 188, 228
Crest®, arbitrary trademark, 122
Criminal conviction, and franchisor's right of automatic termination, 479
Culligan franchise system, 14, 183
Curtis Mathes Corporation, 183
Customer referral network, 16

D

Dairy Queen, Inc., 115-118
Dale Carnegie Courses, 364
Data Management software system, Merry Maids, 136
Day, Cecil B., 529
Day care centers, 16, 189, 333
Days Inns of America, Inc., 186, 529
De Camara, Richard, 513
Defense manual, of the franchisee, 477, 481-482
De-identification obligations, 524, 533, 537
Dental services franchises, 36
Department stores, outlets, 12

Designated market areas. *See* DMAs
Development schedules, 249-251
Diet Center franchise system, 456
Diet centers, 189, 228
Disclosure documents (offering circular, prospectus), 15, 48-49, 49(T), 63, 82, 86, 476
  corporate consolidated financial statements, 413
  earnings claims, 413, 421
  Franchise Rule of FTC, 98-106
  provided to potential franchisees, 417, 422
  receipt noted in follow-up contact information form, 343(F)
  statement of franchisee's initial investment, 435
  statement of franchisor to not finance, 436
  Uniform Franchise Offering Circular, 100-106
Disclosure/registration requirements, adopted by some states, 15
Disclosure regulations, compliance, 526-529
Distribution, 7, 12, 173, 194-195, 194(F), 207-210, 476-477
  overhead considerations for site selection, 204-205, 204(T)
  policies included in marketing manual, 355
  prototype development, 322
DMAs (designated market areas), 249
Donut shop franchises, 39, 197-199, 228, 266-267, 338-339, 394, 403-404
  international franchising, 565
Drive-thru window, first, 27
Dry cleaning services franchises, 26
Dual distribution, 152-153
Due consideration, 63
Dun & Bradstreet, 240-241, 241(F), 416
Dunkin' Donuts of America, Inc., 197-199, 266-267, 436
  Dunkin' Donuts University, 198, 385
  Westbury Donuts, Inc. v. *Dunkin' Donuts of America, Inc.*, 538
Duraclean International, 545
Dutch Boy, 187

E

"Earnings Claim Document," 105-106, 413, 417, 421-422, 425, 485, 529
Econo Lodges of America, Inc., 153-154
Economic Census, 230
"Economic Census of Retail Trade," 229

Economic order quantity (EOQ) approach, 301
Educational products and services, 26, 29(T), 189, 556(T), 565
Electronics industry franchises, 15-16, 33-34, 48, 65, 75-76, 228, 565
  corporate images, 244
Embassy Suite, 552
Employment agency franchises, 189, 203, 432-433, 472-473
Employment characteristics, demographic data of one county, 223(T)
Entertainment services. *See* Recreation, entertainment and travel services franchises
Entrepreneur magazine, source of information on franchises, 410, 416
Entrepreneurs vs. managers, comparison of needs, 254(T)
Equipment rental agencies, 26, 29(T), 189, 565
Europe, U.S. franchise expansion, 553, 556(T), 557, 560(T), 565
European International Symposium on Franchising, 154
Exclusive Dealing, 143, 151
Exercise studios and/or diet franchises, 159-161, 166(F), 171, 189, 228, 456
Expansion, 42-44, 166-168, 167(F), 202-204, 375, 493, 550
  breakaway franchisees, 534
  capital expenditure financing, 440
  capital hard to raise, 563
  concerns of franchisees, 507
  concerns of franchisors, 510-511
  continuing training programs for franchisees, 388-389
  long-term plans secret from competition, 509
  prototype development important for loans, 331, 333
  three-step approach to identifying areas, 206-207, 207(F)
Exxon Corporation, 289-290

F

Famous Barr Stores, 46
Far East International Symposium on Franchising, 154
Federal Trade Commission (*see also* Franchise Rule), 15, 273, 413, 422, 477, 485-486
Federal Trade Commission Act, 123, 143
Federal Trade Commission Rule, disclosure requirements, 482
Ferguson, Sybil, 456

Field representatives. *See* Franchisor's representatives
Financial package, preparation of, 446-449
Financial services, 26, 384
Financial statements for franchises, 271-290, 293, 315, 364, 612
  annual statement, 274(F)
  balance sheet, 278(F)
  cash flow "balancing act," 314(F)
  cash (funds) flow statement, 281(F)
  financial primary ratios, 284(T), 289(F), 290(T), 306
  included in formal training program for franchisees, 352(T)
  income statement, 274(F)
  retained earnings statement, 283(F)
  sample forms, 365(F), 366(F), 367(F)
Financing of a franchise, 433-446, 487
First Interstate Bancorp of California, 26, 35-36
First refusal, right of, 479, 487, 489
Floor care franchises, 189
Florida, greatest concentration of franchised restaurants, 19
Focus groups, 461-463, 463(F)
Food Italia Spa, 557
Food products, specialty and/or ethnic, 564
Food-service franchises, 10
Ford, Henry, 13
Ford Motor Company, 181, 185-186, 204, 330, 553
France, U.S. franchise expansion, 551
Franchise Advisory Councils (FACs), 502-504, 504(F), 521, 541, 564
Franchise brokers, 101, 252
Franchise defense manual, 477, 481-482
Franchise Disclosure Act, 15
Franchise disclosure documents. *See* Disclosure documents
Franchisee advisory committees, 500
Franchisee associations, 541, 564
Franchisee councils, 155, 263-266
Franchisee hotline, 500
Franchisees (*see also* Advertising; Training programs), 34-42, 45-55, 102-104, 109-115, 134-135, 188, 461-465
  advertising services, 458-459, 458(F)
  breakaway, 520, 532-546
  choice of franchise system, 408-428
  concerns, principal, 507-508
  cost objectives and profit margins, 191
  defense manual development, 477, 481-482
  definition, 6-7

direct selling, 193
early imitator marketing strategy, 168-170
field support manual detailing services from franchisors, 357-358
financial reports required, 408
franchise package received from franchisor, 338-370
interview form, sample, 409(F)
key points specified by Rocky Rococo Corporation, 224, 224(T)
legal obligations, 64-65, 467, 540
legal rights, 422, 475, 480, 486-491, 489(T), 490(T)
management, 76
marketing effects, 456-457, 459-460
master, 205, 251-252, 292, 555-557, 562
membership dues, 502
multi-unit, 248-252, 436-437, 468-470, 469(F), 536, 541, 547, 564
operations and success package, 64-65
personality characteristics, 455-456, 490(T)
professional parties consulted during site selection, 222-223
recruitment package and selection, 63, 72-73, 82-86, 99n., 253-255, 257, 423-425
review and mediation procedures, voluntary and nonbinding, 543
sales report to franchisors, frequency, 263(T)
self-evaluation, 406-408, 407(F)
startup operations, 426
  financing of franchise, 432-449
support organization, 373-376, 381-382
survey by *The Conference Board*, 256-257
Franchise feasibility studies, 62, 65-87, 68(T), 74(F), 331, 465-467, 466(F)
  PERT (Project Evaluation Review Technique) chart, 84(T), 85(T)
Franchise fees. See Franchising fees
"Franchise 500," 410
Franchise Handbook, 410-411
Franchise Industry Advisory Council, University of Nebraska-Lincoln, 196
Franchise Legal Digest, 196
Franchise Opportunities Handbook, 48, 408-410, 422
Franchise opportunity, three major components, 6-7, 8(T)
Franchise package, 338-340, 344-364
  operations manual, 347(T)-348(T)
  pre-opening manual, activity checklists, 359(T), 360(T)
  reporting manual (financial statements), 365(F), 366(F), 367(F)
  sample information forms, 341(F), 342(F)-343(F)
  site inspection manual, 361(F)-362(F)
Franchise Rule (*see also* Federal Trade Commission), 82, 98-107, 417, 419, 422
Franchises (*see also* Renewal), 38-39, 47-55, 49(T), 104, 107-111, 134-135, 226-228
  business plans, 62-65, 72-73
  choice of, 404-405, 408-428, 418(F)
  definition, 476-477
  distribution channels, 194-195, 194(F), 204-205, 204(T)
  expansion matrix, 167, 167(F)
  financial process overview, 313(F)
  history, 347(T)
  marketing effects, 456-467, 458(F), 466(F)
  multi-unit, 224, 248-252
  PERT chart, 62, 82-86, 84(T), 85(T)
  real estate programs, 203
  regulation, 99
  sales director, authority and responsibilities, 251(T)
  statistics, 5, 5(F), 8, 15-16
  termination of agreements, 113-114, 135, 488, 520, 523-524, 532-546
  transfer, 524-525
Franchise Studies Advisory Council, University of Nebraska-Lincoln, 136
Franchising, 99n.
Franchising, 6-17, 8(T), 9(F), 9(T), 10(T), 30
  conversion, 16, 26
  international, 17, 549-567, 556(T), 557(F)
  laws regulating, categories, 482-488
  multi-unit, 248-252
Franchising agreements, 40-41, 63, 105-115, 253-254, 468, 479-488, 484(F)
  advertising, legal relationship, 522
  delivery to prospective franchisee, 100, 422
  development schedule, 249-251
  fees and royalties established, 46
  franchisee request for disclosure document, 82
  franchisor rights to system, 133
  liquidated damages provision, 540
  motivation programs necessary, 239
  negotiation of terms, 490

Index 661

nonrenewal, 525
overhead and distribution details, 204-205, 204(T)
receipt noted on form, 343(F)
sample contract, SpeeDee Oil Change & Tune Up of the Gulf Coast, 569-652
  amendment and approval, 643
  assignability, 637-638
  attorneys' fees, 642
  bankruptcy (insolvency), 583, 643
  captions, 642
  Confidential Operating Manual, 594, 614
  contracts, 612-613
  covenant not to compete, 610
  credit and background check, 575
  death or incapacity, 610, 639
  earnings, 611
  entire agreement, 642
  exclusive area or territory, 602
  fees in addition to franchising fee, 584-590
  financial statements, 612
  financing arrangements, 599
  franchisee's initial investment, 591-593
  franchises of the subfranchisor, 611
  franchising fee, initial, 583
  franchisor-franchisee relationship, 640
  governing law and arbitration, 642
  history of franchisor and predecessors, 578-579
  history of persons affiliated with franchisor and subfranchisor, 580-582
  indemnity, 640-641
  introduction and franchisor history, 570-572
  late payments, 643
  letter of credit, 653-654
  litigation, 582-583
  loaned equipment agreement, 597, 651-652
  local franchise agreement, 615-628
  local franchises being serviced by the Region, 645-649
  modification and assignment of franchise agreement and information, 605-610
  New Product Placement Program, 598
  notices, 641
  no waiver, 642
  obligation to participate in franchise operation, 604-605
  patents and copyrights, 604
  public figure arrangements, 610-611
  purchase or lease obligations from designated sources, 593
  purchase or lease obligations with specifications or from approved suppliers, 594-599
  Region's additional obligations, 600-602
  renewal, 605-610
  repurchase, 605-610
  restrictions on goods and services offered, 605
  severability, 642
  signing of agreement, 643-644
  SpeeDee Ad Fund, 598, 629-633
  SpeeDee Ad Fund Indemnity, 641
  statement of prospective franchisee, interview history, 572-574
  table of contents, 576-577
  termination, 605-610
  term of agreement, renewal, termination, 633-637
  trademarks, service marks, trade names, logotypes, and commercial symbols, 602-604
  units owned by the Region, 650
signing, 425-426
statistics, 15
subject to laws of a contract, 98
termination, 135, 478-479, 500, 507, 540
terms and renewal options recorded, 420, 467
territorial exclusivity provided for, 146-147, 213
time period before franchised business operating, 293
training obligations and support programs, 420
typical elements included, 53, 54(T)
violation by breakaway franchisees, 534, 541
Franchising fees, 40, 46, 51, 54(T), 102, 334
  collected by master franchisee, 251
  determination of, 208
  different within same franchise system, 437
  discussed in franchising agreement, 108
  financial obligation of franchisees, 433, 436
  franchise choice, 419, 425
  in sample franchising agreement, 583-584
  Jo-Ann's Nut House, Inc., case study, 155
  nondebt nature, 408

quality-control standards, 484
training program fees, 398
Franchising in the Economy, 1985-1987, 189
Franchising Political Action Committee, Inc., 154
Franchisor-franchisee relationship, 5, 34-47, 53-56, 55(F), 82, 87, 476-479
  accountability, areas of, 377
  C.A.R.E. (Communication, Awareness, Rapport, and Expertise), 504-505
  documentation necessary, 525-526
  federal intervention, 506
  franchise advisory councils, 263-266
  franchise choice, 417
  horizontal, 357
  information systems, 377-382
  interdependence of principals, 240-241, 241(F)
  legal documentation, 62-63, 82
  legal problems, 64-65
  marketing strategy choice, 170
  newer look diagram, 240(F)
  phases, 498-502, 501(T), 502(T)
  purchases of specified products and services, 111-112
  vertical, 239
Franchisors, 40, 103-106, 109-115, 134-135, 147-153, 186-191
  activities not permitted, 485-486
  activity reports sent to franchisees, 379
  advantages and disadvantages, 42-47
  assistance to noncomplying franchisees, 543
  concerns, principal, 508-509
  definition, 6-7
  dispute resolution, 542-545
  fees paid, 419
  financial requirements, 50-51, 51(T)
  franchise defense manual, 477, 481-482
  franchise package administration and operation, 338-370
  instruction of staff of first franchised unit, 325-326
  lease contract responsibility question, 203
  major organizational developmental tasks, 242-244, 243(F)
  management, 247-266, 249(F), 250(F), 347(T), 464-470
  marketing, 456-461, 458(F)
  method of selecting suppliers in disclosure document, 102-103
  mistakes, categories of, 518-521
  motivation programs for franchisees, 239-242, 241(F), 253, 254(T)
  new product information and services, 501
  overhead and distribution considerations, 204-205, 204(T)
  "parity" for franchisees, 210
  policies, 256
  producer/manufacturer, 194-195, 194(F)
  questions asked by franchisees, 424
  record keeping, standard system, 484
  sample interview form for franchisees, 409(F)
  site selection, 221-223
  strategic planning process, 244-247, 245(F)
  support organization for franchisees, 373-376
  support package, 64-65, 87
  timely reports of franchisee information, 263
  trademarks, 120
  training operations, development of, 384-395
  training visits for franchisees, 381
  warranty programs, 541
  written history and description of business, 326
Franchisor's representatives, 383(T), 426, 459, 475, 482, 543
  area, 252
  field, 350, 357-358, 375, 381-383, 386-389, 465
FTC v. *Texaco, Inc.*, 478
Fuller Brush franchise system, 14
Full-line forcing, 150-151
Funding programs and franchisees, 188

G

Gardening service franchises, 188, 228
Gardner, James N., 139
Gasoline service station franchises, 8, 17, 29(T), 35, 188, 477-478, 511
g-stores, combination with convenience stores, 17-18, 18(T), 397
Gaylord, E. James (Jim), 53, 470-471
G.C. & K.B. Investments, Inc. (Region). *See* SpeeDee Oil Change & Tune Up of the Gulf Coast
General Electric®, valid trademark, 122
General Foods, 5
Generally accepted accounting principles (GAAP), 273

General Motors Corporation, 12-13, 35-36, 42-43, 48, 185, 194, 204
   international franchising, economic considerations, 553, 558
Geographic areas (territories), 8, 12-13, 41, 43, 103-104, 109, 113
   antitrust laws, 467
   assignment based on population, 210
   establishment and franchise choice, 420, 483
   exclusive area statement from sample franchising contract, 484(F)
   exclusive territory rights, 139-140, 146, 151-153
   horizontal territorial restrictions, 488
   initial development fees, 251
   legality of exclusive territorial concessions, 507
   location control costs expensive, 534
   site selection, 203-220
   territorial fees, 213
   territorial limits and occasional problem, 489, 489(T)
Georgia, limited covenant not to compete, 538
Getchell, Eugene, 389-390
Glickman, Gladys, 99n.
Goodyear Tire and Rubber, 183, 187, 558
Gourmet Ice Cream franchises, 144, 147
Granada Royale, 552
Grocery franchise systems, 14, 91-93, 92(T), 93(T), 232
Group boycotts, 487

H

Hair salons. *See* Beauty salons
Hamburger Handout, 512
Hamburger Prince restaurants, case study, 31-32
Hampton Inns, 552
Hardware and paints franchises, 228
Harman, Leon "Pete" W., 427
Harrah's (Casino hotels), 552
Hawaii, U.S. franchise expansion, 100n., 106-107, 559-560
Health-care facilities, 16, 36, 361
Health club franchise systems, 119-120
Hertz Corporation, 5, 194, 436, 553
Herzberg, Jim, 456
Hilton Hotel system, 558
Holding companies, 101, 164, 176-177
Holiday Corporation, 551-552
Holiday Inn Crown Plazas, 552

Holiday Inns, Inc., 5, 22-23, 35-36, 178, 194, 235, 552
   Holiday Inn University (training center), 327, 385
   sign changes in mid-1980s, 190
   site selection and building design, 87
Home cleaning services. *See* House cleaning services
Home furnishings and accessories franchises, 16, 18, 42, 228, 231-232, 361
Home repair and improvement franchises, 16, 556(T)
Home support service franchises, 437
Honda, 168
Hong Kong, U.S. franchise expansion, 565
Hotel/motel franchises, 10, 16, 22-23, 24(T), 29(T), 52, 54
   budget motel business introduced, 153-154
   demographic data use, 220
   development of target trade areas, 214
   elegance and entry into gaming industry, 311-312
   high franchising fees, 52
   international franchising, 552-553, 556(T)
   motor lodges, 14
   ongoing training of employees, 350
   rejection of a proposed buyer, 145-146
   restaurant added on premises, 167
   site inspection criteria, 361
Hot tub sales franchises, 271-288, 274(F), 278(F), 281(F), 283(F), 304
   Bonnie's Hot Tubs Inc., case study, 295-297, 298(F), 302, 305(F), 308-311, 309(F), 310(F)
House cleaning services franchises, 26, 28(T), 136, 166, 189, 460, 502-503
   customer satisfaction, 244
   financing of initial capital requirement, 436
   international franchising, 556(T)
   Marshall's success story, 545
Howard Johnson franchise system, 14, 22-23, 194
"How to Succeed in Business" seminars, 291-292

I

Ice cream store franchises, 61-62, 115-118, 144, 147, 149, 228, 565

Illinois, franchise documents, 100n., 106-107
Illinois Franchise Advisory Board, 195
Imperial 400, 23
Income groups, demographic data, 220, 222(T)
Independent Grocers Association (IGA), 14
Indiana, franchise documents, 100n., 106-107
Industry Advisory Council, 235
Industry Surveys, Standard & Poor's, 292
Information processing, expansion in future foreseen, 564
Insurance for franchises, 36, 82, 102, 347(T), 449, 467-468
Insurance services franchises, 384, 541
Interior decorating businesses, 189, 226
Internal Revenue Service (IRS), 75, 273, 277
International Dairy Queen, Inc., 115, 559
International Franchise Association (IFA), 7, 17, 196, 384, 412, 500, 545
  Hall of Fame Award recipient Rosenberg, 267
  international franchising survey, 551, 557, 563
  past officers
    Bresler, Stanley, 56
    Marshall, Irl H., 545
    Rosenberg, William, 267
    Rudnick, Lewis, 195
    Tarbutton, Lloyd, 154
International House of Pancakes, 14
Inventory, 38, 51, 93(T), 310-311, 311(T), 348(T)
Iron industry, 12
Isbell, Marion, 311
Issue fee, patent application, 130
Italy, U.S. franchise expansion, 557

J

Jamco Limited, 515n.
James, Philip, 334
Japan, U.S. franchise expansion, 500, 549-552, 556(T), 559, 560(T), 562, 565
Jerrico, Inc., 389-390, 492-493
Jerry's Restaurants, 391(F), 392(F)
Jo-Ann's Nut House, Inc. franchises, 155-156
Johnson, Howard, 14
Journal of the Forum Committee on Franchising, 196

K

Kahler Corporation, 234-235
Kay, Herbert, 491
Kenney, David B., 529-530
Kenney Management Company, 530
Kentucky Fried Chicken Corporation, 14, 35, 53, 183, 194, 204, 327
  Collins's success story, 512
  the Colonel, 187, 456
  Gaylord's success story, 470-471
  Harman's success story and franchise's beginning, 427
  international franchising, 551, 553, 562
  Kentucky Fried Chicken Corp. v. *Diversified Packaging Corp.*, 150
Kleen Car Wash franchises, 475-476
Kodak®, coined trademark, 122
Korea, U.S. franchise expansion, 551-552, 556(T), 560(T), 562
Kostecka, Andy, 408
Kroc, Ray, 14, 26-27, 456

L

Labels, as intangible assets, 279
Lanham Act, 121, 123, 125
Laundry franchises, 14, 29(T), 556(T)
Lauzen, Leo G., 290-292
Lawn care and landscaping franchises, 14, 189, 319
Leadership Training Institute, Inc., 364
Lease contracts, 203, 419, 425, 436-437, 521, 536-537
  fees as financial obligations, 433, 508
  franchisor's right of automatic termination, 479
Legal counsel for franchisees, 421-422, 425, 467, 476, 479
Legal documents (*see also* Disclosure documents; Franchising agreements), 83-86, 97-115, 378-379
Legal services franchises, 36
Licensees, 39
Life insurance companies, source of capital expenditure financing, 440
Ligget, Louis, 13
Lily, 26-27
Liquidated damages, 537, 540
Liquor sales franchises, 477
Litigation, 46, 101, 257, 332, 419, 543-545, 582-583
Logotypes, 104, 356, 602-604
Long John Silver's, Inc., 263, 492-493

Jerrico Center for Training and Development, 385, 389-390, 391(F), 392(F), 393(F), 493

M

McClelland theory of motivation, 253, 254(T)
McCormick Harvesting Machine Company, 11
McDonald, Dick, 27
McDonald, Maurice, 27
McDonald's Corporation, 5, 14, 26-27, 35-36, 48, 72, 87
   advertisement comparisons in marketing research, 460
   "Big Mac" product attributes, 177-178
   comparative-parity approach in promotion, 185
   conversion to Chicken McNuggets product, 180
   expansion plans, 204
   franchisee financing, 436
   Hamburger University, 27, 327, 349-350, 385, 557-558
   international franchising, 557, 559-560
   McDLT massive promotional advertising, 195
   mass advertising, 186-188, 190, 486
   Ronald McDonald® as registered service mark, 121, 187
   Sidney's shop design similar in case study, 97-98
   started by Ray Kroc, 456
Macy's, 188
Mail Boxes, Etc., Inc., 437
Mail campaigns, direct, 12
Maintenance of equipment and facilities, 348(T), 352(T)
Malaysia, U.S. franchise expansion, 551-552, 556(T), 560(T)
Management by objectives (MBO), 255
Managers vs. entrepreneurs, comparison of needs, 254(T)
Manners, Big Boy, 187
Manpower, 203
Marketing calendar, 462(F), 464
Marketing franchisee councils, 461
Marketing mix, 161, 191
Marketing research, 50, 51(T), 258, 355, 388, 459-460, 490
   prototype development, 322
   recommended before international franchising, 555
Market share, 229-231
Market strategies, 45, 159-162, 352(T), 509

Marriott, J. Willard, 27, 456
Marshall, Irl H., 545
Martin Franchises Inc., 451n.
Martinizing Dry Cleaners, 451-452
Marvin, Samuel, 334
Mary Kay Cosmetics, Inc., 186
Maryland, disclosure documents, 100n., 106-107
Maslow theory of motivation, 253, 254(T)
Materiality, concept of, 106
Mather, James A., 364
May Company, 46
Media mix, advertising, 186-187, 461
Medicine Shoppe International franchises, 268-269
Megatrends, 563
Meineke Discount Muffler Shops, 210
Mergers, corporate, 142-143
Merry Maids, Inc. franchise system, 136, 390, 502-503
Metzger, William E., 12-13
Mexico, U.S. franchise expansion, 553-554, 556(T), 557, 560(T)
Michigan, disclosure documents, 100n., 106-107, 538
Midas International Corporation, 35-36, 87, 183, 186, 289, 327, 510
   expansion plans, 204, 210
   franchise advisory council, 503
   independent autonomous dealer association, 509-511, 513
   termination or renewal of franchising agreement, 507
Miller Brewing Company, 186
Minnesota, disclosure documents, 100n., 106-107
Minnesota Hotel & Motel Association, 235
Minority Enterprise Small Business Investment Companies (MESBICs), 444
Mister Donut franchises, 39
Mr. Goodwrench, 183
Mr. Steak, Inc., 364, 515-516
Mobil Corporation, 164, 289-290
Mobile Innkeepers Association, 235
Mode o'Day, 14
Molly Maid housekeeping franchises, 436
Money Store Investment Corporation, and SBA guaranteed loan program, 443
Monopolization, 141, 143
Monsanto Company v. *Spray-Rite Service Corporation*, 485
Montgomery Ward's, 289-290
Moody's, 292
Morris, Robert, Associates, 292
Motels. *See* Hotel/motel franchises

Motel Ventures, Inc., 530
Motivation, 253, 254(T), 261-262
Moto Photo, 178
Motorcycle market, 168
Motor lodges. *See* Hotel/motel franchises
Multimixers, 27

N

Naisbitt, John, 563
NAMCO Systems, Inc., 210, 379, 380(F)
National Car Rental System, Inc., 436
National Restaurant Association, 427
National Video, Inc., 331, 333
NBC television network, three-tone chime as service mark, 121
New York, disclosure documents, 100n., 106-107
The New Yorker® magazine, valid trademark, 123
New York Stock Exchange, 491, 512
New Zealand, U.S. franchise expansion, 560(T)
Nielsen, A. C., station index, 249
Non-union businesses, 44
Norrell Temporary Services franchises, 88-90
North American Securities Administrators Association, 100
    Industry Advisory Council Committee, 196
North Dakota, disclosure documents, 100n., 106-107
Nursing home franchises, elaborate site inspection criteria, 361

O

Occupations of heads of households, demographic data, 220, 221(T)
Offering circulars. *See* Disclosure documents
Official Gazette, 124-125, 130
Ohio, greatest concentration of franchised restaurants, 19
Oil company franchises, 12, 42, 185, 214, 511
Operating documents, 83-86
Operations manuals, 54, 64, 76, 82, 107-108, 110-111, 483
    adherence by franchisee, 487
    arbitration provision, 115
    directives given in narrative, 252
    in franchise package, 345-348, 347(T)
    modifiable, 523
    necessary for prototype development, 326
    promotion of operation standards, 134
    success of operation, 376
    termination of franchising agreements, 135
Optician services franchises, 36
Option agreements, 468
Orange Julius, 35, 39
Oregon, disclosure documents, 100n.
Owren, Turid L., 119

P

Pacific Rim countries, U.S. franchise expansion, 553
Packaging, 173
    Kentucky Fried Chicken Corp. v. *Diversified Packaging Corp.*, 150
Parent companies, 101, 176-177, 186, 377-378
Parking services, 18, 189
Patents, 104, 108, 120, 128-131, 558
Penalties, breach of contract, 540
Pepsi Cola Bottling Company, 121, 186, 194
Percentage-sales method, 308-309, 309(F)
Personal-contact information forms, 340-342, 341(F), 342(F), 343(F)
Personal selling, 186-187, 189-190
Personal services franchises, 327(T)
PERT chart. *See* Franchise feasibility studies, PERT chart
Peterson, Dallen, 136
Peterson, Jim, 257-263, 267
Petroleum sales franchises, 477
Pharmacies, 188-189, 228, 268-269, 324, 325(F)
Philadelphia Cream Cheese®, valid trademark, 123
Philippines, U.S. franchise expansion, 565
Phone book covers franchises, 54, 210
Photocopying franchises in general, 153
Picture framing franchises, 228
PIP. *See* Postal Instant Press
"Placement People," 472
Plate cost/sales mix (franchise), 393(F)
Plumbing repairs franchises, 186
Popcorn shop franchises, Ramona's case study incident, 403-404
Popeyes Famous Fried Chicken and Biscuits franchise system, 394-395, 428-430, 546-548

Porter, James L., 488, 490
Postal Instant Press (PIP), 414, 414(F), 434(F), 436-437, 438(F), 500
Preliminary injunctions, 544
Pricing, 139-140, 143-145, 147, 150-152, 173, 355, 508
 discounting, 40-41
 fixing, 467, 476, 485, 487-488
 included in operations manual, 347(T)
Primary service area (PSA), 70-71, 215-216, 218-223, 220(T), 221(T), 222(T)
Prime Motor Inns, Inc., 491
Principal Register, 125
Pringle's New-Fangled Potato Chips, 181
Printing franchise systems in general, 10, 14, 228
Proctor & Gamble Company, 181
Product testing and introduction, 45, 47, 266, 389, 457-458, 503, 535
 guarantees and warranties, 456-457
 managed by franchisor, 464
 review committees, 155
Professional development plan (PDP), 393(F)
Profiles
 customer, 69-71, 192, 206, 220-222, 220(T), 221(T), 222(T)
 information provided in marketing manual, 355
 franchisee, 86
 site, 226-229, 227(T), 323
Profit margin, 36, 59, 76, 79-80, 191, 285, 445
Property rights, 120-121
Prospectus. *See* Disclosure documents
Prototype development, 50-51, 51(T), 319-333, 321(T), 325(F), 327(T), 350
 analysis, 83
Public figure involvement in franchise system, 104-105, 610-611
Public relations, 44-45, 88, 357, 379
Purchase agreements, 425
Purchasing power, 44, 464

Q

Quality-control standards, 37, 40-41, 111-112, 150, 262-263, 481-482
 designation of a single supplier, 522
 evaluation forms in franchise package, 358
 franchising fee, 484-485
 included in marketing manual, 354
 included in operations manual, 347(T)
 meaning of "franchise," 476-477
 noncompliance by breakaway franchisees, 533-534
 operational consistency and early imitator marketing strategy, 168-170, 259
 profitability, 376
 prototype development, 329-330
Quality Court Motels, 22-23
"Quick-kill artists," 506

R

Ramada Inns, Inc., 22-23, 194, 311-312
Real estate, cost and site selection, 206
Real estate development companies, 491, 529-530
Real estate franchises, 10, 16, 333
Record sales franchises, Eva and Carlos' case study incident, 201-202
Recreation, entertainment and travel services franchises, 29(T), 189, 228, 263, 556(T)
Refusal to do business, and automatic termination, 479
Registration, franchising contract documents, 106-107
Registration and Licensing, Department of, 81
Renewal of franchising agreements, 104, 108, 113, 420, 479-481, 510, 525
Renforth, William, 488, 490
Repurchases, 20, 21(T), 104
Resale price maintenance claims, 190, 485
Research, industrial, 50, 51(T)
Residence Inns, 552
Restaurant franchises, 42, 244, 257-261, 375-376
 ADI concepts and profiles, 209, 213-214, 220, 226, 228-229
 breakfast added to scope of business, 167, 173
 case studies, 515-516
 competition, 216-217
 coupon booklets, 188
 elaborate site selection criteria, 361
 fast-food, 16, 394-395
  advertising and promotions, 35, 183, 185
  case studies, 97-98, 230, 238-239, 517-518, 549-550
  competition, 216, 539
  consumer awareness, 187
  dependence on trademarks and distinctive designs, 478

expenditure in state, average, 230
fiscal responsibility, 260
indoctrination training, 65
international franchising, 559
marketing strategies, 173, 195, 460
products limited by franchising agreement, 489
sales decline as competition intensifies, 179, 228
scope expanded, 166
success stories, 450, 512
timeliness of service, 263
training significant for franchise success, 384
initiator marketing strategy used, 168
inside a motel, 167
international franchising, 553, 556(T), 559, 560(T), 565
market segmenter, 170, 460
number of establishments and sales in 1987, 29(T)
quality control at prototype, 330
statistics, 10, 14-17, 19-23, 20(T), 21(T), 22(T), 23(T)
timeliness of service, 263
training of employees, ongoing, 350
Restraints, 142-145, 152
Retailing franchises, 232, 361, 564
franchise distribution channels, 194-195, 194(F)
non-food, 16, 327(T), 556(T), 565
statistics, 4-5, 4(F), 29(T), 220, 222(T), 556(T)
Return on investment (ROI), 222
Rexall drugstores, 13
Rhode Island, disclosure documents, 100n., 106-107
Robinson-Patman Act, 143, 151-152
Rocky Rococo Corporation, 213, 224, 224(T)
Roof repair franchises, 188
Rosenberg, William, 266-267
Royalties (royalty fees), 40, 46, 155, 251, 334
deceleration over time, 521, 541
different within same franchise system, 437
failure to pay, 509, 511
financial obligation of franchisees, 433
franchise choice, 419, 436
increased at transfer, 525
international franchising, 17, 555, 558, 562-563
least objectionable source of franchisor's revenue, 381, 522
no negotiation, 483-485
patent enforcement, 131
problems among franchisees, 489, 489(T), 501, 507

signing of franchising agreement, 425
total sales guesstimate, 413
Rudnick, Lewis, 195-196
Rudnick and Wolfe, law firm, 195
"Rule of reason," 483, 488

S

Sales, three critical estimating variables, 230
Sales and Marketing Management magazine, 210, 230
Sales manuals, 82, 348(T)
Sales mix sheets, 393(F)
Sales of a county vs. city SMSA, 1983-1986, 222(T)
Sales projections (forecasts), 206, 301, 307-309
Sales promotion campaigns, 186-188
Sales prospectus, 423
Sales quotas, 481
Sales restrictions, 103-104
Sanders, Colonel Harlan, 14, 427, 456, 512
Sara Care Franchise Corp., 437
Schreck, Freida, 88-90
Sears, 188
Secretary of State, Office of, listing of business name, 81
Securities, 109, 115
Securities and Exchange Commission, mandating format of financial statements, 273
Security systems franchise systems, 14
Sells, Arthur, 379
Service marks, 104, 110, 119-121, 356, 464, 602-604
7-ELEVEN Convenience Stores, 183, 210, 397-399, 436-437, 564-565
Sheraton Corporation, 235
Sherman Antitrust Act, 141-144, 147, 405, 487
Shoe store franchises, 228
Shopping center concept, 71
Siding spraying franchises, 188
Singapore, U.S. franchise expansion, 551, 565
Singer Sewing Machine Company, 11-12, 35-36
Sir Speedy Printing Center, franchise package costs, 439(F)
Site/store layouts, 82, 231-234, 234(T)
Site/store location selection, 201-236, 353-354, 420, 425-426, 464
inspection manual in franchise package, 361-363
and prototype development, 322-323, 331-332
Situation audits, 246

Sizzler Restaurants International Inc., 512
Sloan, Alfred P., 42-43
Small Business Act, 443
Small Business Administration (SBA), 440, 443-444
Small Business Committees, U.S. Senate and House of Representatives, 15
Smith, Douglas D., 97
SMSA (standard metropolitan statistical area), 210, 216, 220, 220(T), 221(T), 222(T)
Snap-On Tools, 36
Snell, Richard, 311-312
Snelling and Snelling, 203, 472-473
Soft drink industry, 8, 29(T), 194-195, 231, 550, 558
South America, U.S. franchise expansion, 553, 560(T)
South Dakota, disclosure documents, 100n., 106-107
Southland Corporation, 210, 397-399, 436-437, 564-565
Southland Ice Company, 564
Soviet Union, U.S. franchise expansion, 551
Speedee Mart, 564-565
SpeeDee Oil Change & Tune Up of the Gulf Coast, sample franchising agreement, 483, 484(F), 569-654
SpeeDee Oil Change Systems, Inc. See SpeeDee Oil Change & Tune Up of the Gulf Coast
Sporting goods franchises, 228
Sprite®, arbitrary trademark, 122
Standard & Poor's publications, 292
State contract law, and franchisee rights, 479
State departments of revenue, and personnel management, 75
Statutory filing fee, patent application, 129
Statutory filing fee, trademark registration, 124
Statutory rights, 121
Steak Shoppe, Cheryl's case study, 530-531
Steam cleaning franchises, 188
Stock placements, 273, 288
Strategic planning, 161-175, 162(F), 163(F), 166(F), 169(T), 171(F), 172(F)
   marketing mix determination, 176-196, 177(F), 179(F), 194(F)
   process useful to franchisors, 244-247, 245(F)
Subfranchisees, 39, 101, 555
Subfranchisors, 251, 611
Subleasing, 35
Supreme Court, 478, 483, 485, 487

"Survey of Buying Power," 210, 212, 229-230
Synergism, 509

T

Taco John's International, site selection guidelines, 224, 225(T)
Taco Time International, *Armstrong* v. *Taco Time International*, 538
Tailoring franchises, 14
Taiwan, U.S. franchise expansion, 565
Tarbutton, Lloyd T., 153-154
Tarbutton Associates, 153
Target trade areas, 214-217
Teflon®, coined trademark, 122
Telecommunication services, expansion in future foreseen, 564
Telephone numbers, franchisor's right to assignment upon termination, 537
Television market areas. See ADIs
Temporary employee service businesses, 88-90, 186, 203
Territorial rights. See Geographic areas
Texas
   disclosure documents, 100n., 106-107
   greatest concentration of franchised restaurants, 19
Thomas, R. David, 52
Thompson, Joe C., 564
Thompson, John P., 564-565
Tidy Car Total Auto Appearance Centers, Lori's case study, 566-567
Tire makers, 12
Tire outlets, retail, 18
Trademark Act of 1946. See Lanham Act
Trademarks, 6, 16, 64-65, 86, 119-126, 476-478
   arbitration provision, 115
   avoidance of tying claims, 149-150
   breakaway franchisees, 533-534
   description necessary in disclosure document, 104
   description required in franchising agreement, 110
   intangible assets, 279
   international franchising, 554, 558, 562-563
   management by franchisor, 464
   protection stressed in advertising manual, 356
   termination of franchising agreements, 135
   translation into foreign languages, 550
Trade or brand names, 82-83, 104, 110

Trade publications, 36, 230
Trade secrets, 112, 120, 131-133, 509, 534, 558
Training manuals, 65, 76, 82-86, 320, 326, 349-354, 387(T)
Training programs, 385-395, 398, 464-465, 498-499
   fees a financial obligation, 103, 433-434, 437
   formal and ongoing, 349-354, 352(T), 353(T)
   franchise choice, 412, 417, 419-420, 426
   in franchising agreement, 111, 134
   managed by franchisor, 464
   necessary for prototype development, 320, 326-328, 327(T), 332
   subject to negotiation, 487
Transfer rights, 41
Traveling salespeople, 12
TraveLodge, 23
Travel services. *See* Recreation, entertainment and travel services franchises
Turnkey operations, 6, 336
Tying agreements, 143, 147-150, 467, 476, 485-486, 488

U

Umbrella entity, 153
Uniform Commercial Code, 112, 479
Uniform Franchise Offering Circular (the "UFOC"), 100-106, 117, 417, 435, 476, 506
Unilateral refusal to deal, 145-147
Union Carbide, 5
United Kingdom, U.S. franchise expansion, 500, 551, 556(T), 560(T), 565
United States Patent and Trademark Office, 119-120, 122-125, 129-130
U.S. Post Office, population estimates, 216
U.S. Steel, 5
United States v. *General Motors Corporation*, 487
Unit quotas, 251
Upholstery business franchises, 189
Upper Midwest Franchisee Association, 471

V

Value Line, source of information about franchisees, 416

Value Line Investment Survey, 292
Vaughn, Charles L., 46
Vending franchise systems, 14
Vendors, 440
Venture capitalists, 440, 445-446
Venture Stores, 46
Video equipment franchises, 16, 150-151, 331
Virginia, disclosure documents, 100n., 106-107

W

Wages, 326, 347(T)
Walker, Robert V., 234-235
Wal Mart Stores, Inc., 46
Warehouses, layout, 231-232
Warranty programs, franchisor-sponsored, 541
Washington (state), disclosure documents, 100n., 106-107
Water conditioning franchises, 189
Wearever®, valid trademark, 122
Weight-reducing program franchises, 148, 151-152
Wendy's International Inc., 52, 204, 213-214, 221, 224, 327
   Wendy's Old Fashioned Hamburgers, 35-36, 52, 187, 194
Westbury Donuts, Inc. v. *Dunkin' Donuts of America, Inc.*, 538
West Coast Auto Parts franchise system, 72
Western Auto, 13-14
West Germany, U.S. franchise expansion, 551
Whataburger, Inc., 257
Wig sales franchises, 188
Wisconsin, disclosure documents, 100n., 106-107

X

XEROX®, 125

Y

Yogurt shop franchises, case studies, 139-140, 403-404
"Your Franchised Business," case study, 314-316